Policing in the Community

DEAN J. CHAMPION
Minot State University

GEORGE E. RUSH
California State University, Long Beach

Prentice Hall, Upper Saddle River, New Jersey 07458

Library of Congress Cataloging-in-Publication Data

Champion, Dean J.
   Policing in the community / Dean J. Champion, George E. Rush.
      p.   cm.
   Includes bibliographical references and index.
   ISBN 0-13-681248-1
   1. Community policing—United States.   2. Public relations—
Police—United States.   3. Police training—United States.
I. Rush, George E. (George Eugene) (date).   II. Title.
HV7936.C83C45   1997
363.2'3—dc20   96-28494
                                                                CIP

Acquisition Editor: Neil Marquardt
Editorial Assistant: Rose Mary Florio
Managing Editor: Mary Carnis
Project Manager: Linda B. Pawelchak
Manufacturing Buyer: Ed O'Dougherty
Cover Design: Miguel Ortiz
Cover Art: Garin Baker/The Stock
   Illustrated Service
Photo Research: Sherry Cohen
Marketing Manager: Frank Mortimer Jr.
Copy Editing: Susan Ball
Proofreading: Maine Proofreading Services

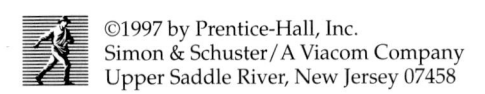

©1997 by Prentice-Hall, Inc.
Simon & Schuster/A Viacom Company
Upper Saddle River, New Jersey 07458

All rights reserved. No part of this book may
be reproduced, in any form or by any means,
without permission in writing from the publisher.

Printed in the United States of America
10 9 8 7 6 5 4 3 2 1

ISBN 0-13-681248-1

Prentice-Hall International (UK) Limited, *London*
Prentice-Hall of Australia Pty. Limited, *Sydney*
Prentice-Hall Canada Inc., *Toronto*
Prentice-Hall Hispanoamericana, S.A., *Mexico*
Prentice-Hall of India Private Limited, *New Delhi*
Prentice-Hall of Japan, Inc., *Tokyo*
Simon & Schuster Asia Pte. Ltd., *Singapore*
Editora Prentice-Hall do Brasil, Ltda., *Rio de Janeiro*

DJC: For Gerri

GER: To my children, Susan and Michael, and their children

Contents

Preface   xvii

CHAPTER 1
An Introduction to Community Policing   1

Introduction   2

Community Policing: An Overview   3

   Community policing defined   3

   Public relations and human relations   15

   Community-based policing, problem-oriented policing, and team policing   17

Why Study Community Policing?   19

   Six reasons   19

The Evolution of Community Policing   20

   From centurions to the Middle Ages   21

   The colonies in a time of change   23

   Law enforcement from 1800 to the 1990s   24

Key Terms   28

Questions for Review   29

Suggested Readings   30

CHAPTER 2
Police Organizations 31

Introduction 32

A Typology of Model Police Roles 32
- *The legalistic approach 32*
- *The service orientation 33*
- *The watchman style 33*
- *Code of ethics and policy formulation 34*

Organizational Structure 37

Police Organization and Operations 38
- *The military syndrome 40*
- *Attaboys and aw shits 42*
- *Productivity 45*
- *Changing calls-for-service 46*

Alternative Organizational Models 47
- *Total quality management 48*
- *Organizational goals, values, and mission statements 48*

Empowerment and Decision Making 50

Participatory Management 51
- *Quality circles 52*
- *Planning 52*
- *Census tracts and crime reporting 54*
- *Coordination with other city agencies and departments 54*

Political Considerations 55
- *Economics and contracting 56*
- *Budgets 58*
- *Executive selection 59*

Key Terms 62

Questions for Review 62

Suggested Readings 63

CHAPTER 3
The Mystique of Police Officer Subculture 64

Introduction 65

Policing in a Time of Change 65

Culture: Some Definitions and Examples 67

The media's impact on public perception of the police role 68

Police Subculture 70

Police Officers and the Working Personality 72

The John Wayne Syndrome 72

Socialization and Resocialization 73

Empathy training 73

On the Meaning of "Real" Police Work 77

The Code of Silence 78

Academy Training 79

Field training officers (FTOs) 79

The ideal-real dilemma 80

Alternative academy training: The United Kingdom model 80

Public Disclosure and the Media 83

Key Terms 84

Questions for Review 84

Selected Readings 84

CHAPTER 4
The Nature and Operations of Community-Oriented Policing 85

Introduction 86

From Conventional Policing to Community-Oriented Policing 87

Density and Community 87

Community Policing and Community-Based Policing 88

    The back-to-the-community movement 88
    Community-oriented policing in Detroit 91
    The Alaska Village Public Safety Officer (VPSO) program 92
    Cultural barriers to community-oriented policing 93

Sector Patrolling, Foot Patrolling, and Beats 95
    The New York City foot beat example 95
    An example of a smaller city beat 96
    Basic car plan 97

Problem-Oriented Policing (POP) 97

Team Policing 100

Mounted Patrol, Bicycles, and Golf Carts 101
    Mounted patrol 101
    The New Orleans mounted patrol 102
    Bicycles 103
    Golf carts 104

Manifest Functions of Community Policing 105

Latent Functions of Community Policing 105
    Tension 107
    Use of force 107
    Enforcement and sentencing 109

Some Sociolegal and Political Implications of Community Policing 110
    November 2, 1993, election day 110

Selective Enforcement of the Law 112
    The spirit of the law vs. the letter of the law 112
    Problems and systemic constraints 114

Fear of Crime 115

Key Terms 116

Questions for Review 116

Appendix A: Traditional vs. Community Policing: Questions and Responses 117

Suggested Readings 118

CHAPTER 5
Officer Recruitment, Training, and Professionalism 119

Introduction 120

The Recruitment Process 121

    Letters of interest 122

    Advertising 122

    Written and oral examinations 122

    Civil service examinations and physical and agility medical evaluations 123

    Psychological screenings 124

    Background interviews and investigations 124

    Polygraph tests and certification letters 126

Hiring as a Probationary Officer 127

    Academy training 127

    Selected training programs: Topeka, Kansas, and Columbus, Ohio 128

Probationary Periods and Field Training Officers 133

Stress vs. Nonstress Academy Training 134

    Nonstress training 135

    The jail experience 136

    The use of less-than-lethal weapons 137

    Verbal judo 140

POST and Standardization: Acquiring the Police Officer Role 140

The Recruitment of Women and Other Minorities 142

Gay Police Officers, Social Sensitivity, and Affirmative Action 144

    The Sergeant Mitchell Grobeson case 147

    The aftermath of the Grobeson case 150

On Professionalism, Education, and Social Skills 151

    Sexual harassment 151

Strategies to Prevent Harassment 155
> Sample agency policy and format 155

The Americans with Disabilities Act (ADA) 158

"By the Book" and the "Dirty Harry" Phenomenon 160
> Career integrity workshops 160
>
> Posttrauma information and strategies 162

Police Stress and Burnout: Sources and Implications 164
> Burnout: The patrol officer's perspective 165
>
> The burnout syndrome 167
>
> The Burntout Policeman's Association and Friends (BPA) 169
>
> "Blue humor" 169
>
> Alcoholism and substance abuse 171

Key Terms 171

Questions for Review 171

Suggested Readings 172

CHAPTER 6
Police Discretion 173

Introduction 174

The Meaning of Police Discretion: A Conceptual Tower of Babel 177
> The police mission and police discretion 177
>
> The rationale for police discretion 178

Situationally Based Discretion and Officer-Offender Relations 183

Police and the Courts 186

Selected Constitutional Issues and Police Behavior 190
> The first amendment 190
>
> The second amendment 191

The fourth amendment 192

The fourteenth amendment 192

Police Understanding of the Law: Customized Interpretations and the Abuse of Discretion   195

Police officer rationales for customized interpretations of law and its enforcement 196

The Control of Police Discretion   201

Key Terms   203

Questions for Review   203

Suggested Readings   204

CHAPTER 7
The Forms and Nature of Police Misconduct   205

Introduction   206

What Is Police Misconduct?   208

An Overview of Types of Police Misconduct   211

Forms of Nonviolent Misconduct   215

Unofficial "perks" 216

Graft 216

Perjury and "dropsy" testimony 217

Forms of Physical Misconduct   219

The spirit and letter of the law 219

Police brutality and excessive force 220

The force continuum 221

Deadly force 223

Rationalizing misconduct 224

Internal Affairs   225

Civilian Complaint Review Boards   227

Key Terms   229

Questions for Review   229

Suggested Readings   230

CHAPTER 8
Ethnicity, Race, and Law Enforcement   231

Introduction   232

From Columbus to the Present   233

Race, Ethnicity, and Crime   237

Selective Law Enforcement and Racial Inequality   244

Tourism and crime   244

Forms of Discrimination   246

Physical forms   246

Mechanisms for Controlling Discriminatory Discretion   247

Forces in the Push for Minority Hiring   247

Black police officer associations   247

The LEAA   248

Hiring and retention   248

Political Policy, the Police, and the Community   249

Conservative vs. liberal policing ideals   249

Key Terms   250

Questions for Review   251

Suggested Readings   251

CHAPTER 9
The Legally Disenfranchised: Gays, Undocumented, the Homeless, and the Mentally Ill   252

Introduction   253

Socioeconomic Status and Crime   254

Demographics of poverty   255

Gay-Bashing and Socially Approved Police Deviance   256

Demographics   257

Queer Nation   258

    ACT-UP 258

    The gay movement and traditional policing 259

    Police and the Explorer Scout controversy 260

The Homeless and Crime Control 261

    Background 261

    Police and community strategies to deal with the homeless 263

    Demographics 267

    Santa Ana, California 268

    Alternatives 269

The Mentally Ill: A Forgotten Minority 275

    Recommendations 278

Drug Users and Abusers and the Police 278

Illegal Immigrants and Police Actions 281

    Officer Jose Diaz Vargas 283

Key Terms 284

Questions for Review 284

Suggested Readings 285

CHAPTER 10
Police-Juvenile Relations 286

Introduction 288

The Juvenile Delinquent/Adult Offender Distinction 289

    Who are juvenile offenders? 289

Parens Patriae and the Police 290

Status Offenders vs. Delinquent Offenders 292

Juvenile Policies and Political Reality 293

    The deinstitutionalization of status offenses (DSO) 295

    Establishing jurisdiction and classifying youths 297

Arresting Juvenile Offenders 298

    Police discretion: Use and abuse 298

Delinquency and Juvenile Violence   299

Legal and Extralegal Factors Influencing Police-Juvenile Relations   303

   Legal factors   303

   Extralegal factors   306

Juvenile Gangs   310

Curbside and Station House Adjustments   311

Delinquency Prevention Programs and Police Interventions   314

Key Terms   318

Questions for Review   318

Suggested Readings   319

CHAPTER 11
Comparative Community Policing   320

Introduction   321

Comparative Community Policing Defined   322

Police-Community Relations in England   325

   Type of government   325

   Types of crimes   325

   Police supervision and organization   327

   Community policing in England   328

Police-Community Relations in Canada   334

   Type of government   334

   Type of crime   335

   Police supervision and organization   336

   Community policing in Canada   339

Police-Community Relations in Japan   342

   Type of government   342

   Types of crime and crime rates   343

   Police supervision and organization   344

   Community policing in Japan   346

International Policing   347

Are There Any Cultural Universals?   349

Trends in Comparative Community Policing   349

Key Terms   351

Questions for Review   352

Suggested Readings   353

CHAPTER 12
Solutions and Recommendations   354

Introduction   355

Violence and the American Way of Life   355

A Summary of Community Problems Involving the Police   360

Violence in the schools   360

Gangs   360

Victims of Crime   360

Implementing Reforms   361

Citizen involvement and police response   361

Police retirement   361

Community and senior citizen involvement   364

Elderly citizens: The graying of America   364

Explorer Scouts   365

Cadet Programs   365

Police Community Awareness Academies   366

Internships   367

Risk management   368

Police and the Redevelopment of Inner Cities: A Practical Application of Community-Oriented Policing   368

Columbia, South Carolina   369

Expanding the new program   371

The Roanoke, Virginia, experience   372

The Savannah, Georgia, Cop-on-the-Block program   373

The Albany, New York, approach 374
The Alexendria, Virginia, Residential Police Officers program 375
Washington, D.C. 378
Portland, Oregon 379
Involvement at the federal level 379

Legal Implications 380
 Hiring standards 380
 Negligent training 381
 Weapons selection 382
 Qualification with off-duty weapons 383
 Negligent retention 383

Accountability Revisited: Ideal and Real Consequences of Sanctions 383
 Patrol car video cameras 384
 Litigation 384

Summary 385
 Other recommendations and observations: Internal 388
 Other recommendations and observations: External 393

Questions for Review 395

Suggested Readings 395

APPENDIX
Christopher Commission Report 396

Glossary 409

References 422

Name Index 467

Subject Index 475

Cases Cited 485

Preface

THE ORGANIZATION OF THIS BOOK

This book is divided into four major parts. The first part, Chapters 1 to 3, examines the background of policing in society and explores the concept of police subculture. Chapter 1 is an overview of community policing and explains why students need to study this phenomenon as part of their criminal justice and criminology background. A brief history of the police in society is also furnished. Chapter 2 presents an outline of police organization and administration. It discusses political subdivisions, such as cities and counties, and distinguishes among the different policing functions of such subdivisions. Mechanisms are described that indicate how police agencies grow and change in the context of increasing urbanization. Chapter 3 discusses the police officer mystique generated by the subculture of policing. The working personality of officers is described as well as what is meant by "real" police work. Training academy experiences are used to illustrate some of the avenues whereby such subcultures are formed and perpetuated.

Chapters 4 to 6 make up the second part and cover police discretion and professionalism. Chapter 4 describes the nature of community policing and community-based policing. The "back-to-the-community" movement is discussed, including innovative patrol styles such as sector patrolling, foot patrols, beats, team policing, and golf cart patrols. Both the manifest and latent functions of community policing are described. The Kansas City Preventive Patrol Experiments are discussed, as well as some of the sociolegal and political implications of community policing. Chapter 5 examines officer recruitment, training, and professionalism. Procedures are described whereby recruits are brought into police organizations and trained. Minority recruitment is discussed, and sensitive issues such as recruiting gays are explained. A typology of police roles is provided, and a contrast is drawn between ideal and real police role performance. Police stress and burnout account for internal departmental problems as well as psychological disturbances among officers that have a negative impact on their role performance. These phenomena are defined and discussed, as are various coping programs designed to minimize burnout and stress. Chapter 6 examines police discretion. Specifically addressed are issues relating to police and the courts and the nature of police understanding of constitutional laws and the rights of citizens. Customized interpretations of the law by police are commonplace, and such innovative interpretations are described. Several forms of police indiscretion are discussed.

The third part, Chapters 7 to 9, discusses police misconduct and shows how different populations are variously affected by it. Chapter 7 discusses several important issues at length, such as the use of excessive and deadly force, as well as various implications of these forms of misconduct. Chapter 8 describes ethnicity, race, and law enforcement. Racial inequality is pervasive in American society, and it is particularly noticeable in police-citizen encounters. Forms of discrimination are described, including physical and psychological types of discriminatory practices. Chapter 9 investigates the legally disenfranchised, including the poor, the homeless, the undocumented, and the mentally ill. Gay-bashing is described. Police relations with drug users and abusers are specified, as are police actions relating to illegal immigrants.

The final three chapters examine police-juvenile relations and the extent of community policing on an international scale. Chapter 10 investigates the police-juvenile relationship and describes various programs for dealing with juveniles. The police-juvenile relation is influenced by both legal and extralegal factors, and officers often make curbside or station house adjustments without taking any formal action against juveniles they encounter on city streets. Gang violence, however, has heightened the visibility of juveniles, and different law enforcement methods are required to deal with problems such violence generates.

Chapter 11 examines comparative community policing in selected countries, including England, Canada, and France. Several cultural universals about community policing are identified and described. Chapter 12 is a summary chapter indicating major trends in police-community relations. This summary discusses law enforcement, prosecutors, and the judiciary. Because policing is increasingly politicized, several political and social implications of such politicalization are discussed.

Among the book's pedagogical features are questions for review at chapter ends. Each chapter includes several suggested readings for those interested in learning more about the subject. A glossary includes all important key terms. An extensive bibliography, which includes some of the most current research on community-oriented policing and policing generally, is also provided. It doubles as a resource and research base from which to derive other material for papers and projects.

Several boxes have been incorporated into each chapter to humanize chapter content and show how learned terms can be applied in everyday situations involving police-citizen relations. Real-life scenes are depicted in detail to show both the positive and negative dimensions of police-community relations. It is hoped that these box materials will heighten reader interest and encourage students to want to learn more about community-oriented policing. It is to this end that this book has been written.

We would like to acknowledge the following reviewers: Thomas J. Hawley III, Central Arizona College; Wayne Madole, Broward Community College; Richard H. Martin, Elgin Community College; L. W. Parks, University of Texas at Brownsville; and John Riley, University of Maine at Presque Isle.

Dean J. Champion
Minot, North Dakota

George E. Rush
Long Beach, California

CHAPTER 1

An Introduction to Community Policing

Introduction

Community Policing: An Overview
Community Policing Defined
Public Relations and Human Relations
Community-Based Policing, Problem-Oriented Policing, and Team Policing

Why Study Community Policing?
Six Reasons

The Evolution of Community Policing
From Centurions to the Middle Ages
The Colonies in a Time of Change
Law Enforcement from 1800 to the 1990s

Key Terms

Questions for Review

Suggested Readings

INTRODUCTION

Former Attorney General Edwin Meese once said of pornography, "I can't define it, but I know it when I see it." Similar comments have been made about **community policing.** We know it when we see it, but it is hard to define. Consider the following definitions from the professional literature:

1. "[Community policing is] whenever citizens and police . . . band . . . together to fight crime" (DeWitt, 1992:1).
2. "Community policing is a police-community partnership in which the police and the community work hand-in-hand to resolve what the community identifies as 'problems.' They [problems] may concern abandoned houses, overgrown lots, zoning ordinances, school issues and other urban problems that are more appropriately in the realm of other agencies" (Findley and Taylor, 1990:72).
3. "Community policing emphasizes the establishment of working partnerships between police and communities to reduce crime and enhance security" (Moore, 1992:99).
4. "Community policing [is] a working partnership between police and the law-abiding public to prevent crime, arrest offenders, find solutions to problems and enhance the quality of life" (L. Brown, 1992:45).
5. "[Community policing is] a philosophy rather than a specific tactic . . . a proactive, decentralized approach designed to reduce crime, disorder and fear of crime by intensely involving the same officer in a community for a long term so that personal links are formed with residents" (Trojanowicz and Carter, 1988:1).

Discussed by criminal justice researchers and others since the early 1970s as a viable crime control strategy (Martin, 1992), community policing has been linked with Neighborhood Watch; the Guardian Angels of New York City; golf cart police patrolling in Tampa, Florida; neighborhood foot patrols in cities such as Lansing, Michigan, and Philadelphia, Pennsylvania; the establishment of police ministations in Detroit, Michigan; the Directed Area Responsibility Team (DART); the Village Public Safety Officer program (VPSO); Operation Identification; Operation CLEAN; COPE programs; the Report Incidents Directly (RID) program; and the Community Patrol Officer Program (CPOP). Common to these and similar programs is that the community and the police work in cooperative ways to fight and prevent crime.

The consensus is that community policing is both a law enforcement and crime prevention strategy whereby some community residents work with local law enforcement agencies to manage community crime through detection and investigation, identification of possible perpetrators, and expansion of communication and dialogue with neighborhood police officers. The context in which community policing is activated and persists is police-community relations. This chapter defines community policing and police-community relations and provides an overview of these concepts as they affect different dimensions of the community. It also provides a rationale for studying community policing and a brief history of the evolution of community policing. This chapter (and all following chapters) concludes with a list of key terms, some questions for review, and suggested readings for further study of major chapter topics.

COMMUNITY POLICING: AN OVERVIEW

Community Policing Defined

Various terms are used more or less synonymously with community policing: *police-community relations, the back-to-the-community movement, problem-oriented policing, community-based policing, proactive policing, neighborhood policing, community-oriented policing, community crime and drug prevention, community-based crime prevention, citizen coproduction of community safety,* the *new blue line, team policing, order maintenance policing, ombudsman policing, community wellness, grass-roots policing,* and *crime control policing.* Many of these terms connote a cooperative or symbiotic relationship between law enforcement and the community (Das, 1986; Manning, 1984).

If we analyze these terms to find their key features, some common policing priorities emerge, including (1) the improvement of human relations between police officers and community residents; (2) heightened community safety through improved crime control strategies; (3) maximization of crime prevention techniques; (4) a general reaffirmation of the concept *community*; and (5) greater use of citizens in quasi-policing roles.

The Improvement of Relations between Police Officers and Community Residents. Some experts believe that honing human relations skills is an important means of improving police-community relations. Police Chief Joseph D. McNamara, of the San Jose (California) Police Department, started a program to improve police-community relations in 1976 (Betsalel, 1990). McNamara encouraged his officers to be "democratic police officers" who saw their duty as serving and protecting public interests rather than making the public conform to their rigid notions of law and order. McNamara visited various neighborhoods, especially those with large minority representation, to promote an "open-door" policy, reassuring citizens that their complaints against police would be handled quickly and fairly (Betsalel, 1990). Thus, he was an early advocate of using human relations strategies to establish close interpersonal ties between officers and community residents.

Trojanowicz (1988) maintains that community policing, the most radical approach to the delivery of police services since the 1960s police reform movement, strengthens interaction between the police and community residents, which builds trust and leads to greater information exchange over time. Thus, many police officer training programs now incorporate human relations training courses, and skills such as listening, interviewing, small-group communication, public speaking, and nonverbal communication are increasingly emphasized (Womack and Finley, 1986). Other human relations-oriented subject matter includes cultural, racial, and personal differences; psychological and semantic barriers; gerontology; and child psychology (Trojanowicz and Belknap, 1986; Womack and Finley, 1986).

It is especially important to emphasize greater communication skills in police training programs, because police officers are an integral part of a multilingual society in which verbal and nonverbal communication is critical in influencing police-community outcomes (Brown and Warner, 1992; Marenin and Copus, 1991; Tafoya et al., 1992; Trojanowicz and Belknap, 1986). Thus, an emphasis is given to training courses and experiences that will yield greater numbers of "thinking police officers" more psychologically suited for their work and more inclined to reason than to use force (U.S. Department of Justice, Community Relations Service, 1987). One consequence of beefing up such training is

Police officers are relying on citizens increasingly for information about neighborhood crime. *(Magnum Photos)*

the active recruitment of more minority officers with a college education who may be more professional in their relationships with community residents (U.S. Department of Justice, Community Relations Service, 1987). At the very least, enhancing officer education through accredited agency training seems to have a positive impact on an officer's performance appraisal by others (Gianakis, 1992). Relatively little is known, however, about the nature and extent of police-citizen interactions in most jurisdictions and whether modifying policing policies to stress police-community relations will work directly to enhance citizen contact and cooperation (Hoover, 1990).

The intent of community policing programs with strong human relations skills components is to improve community acceptance of and support for police officers and to promote more positive attitudes toward them (International Association of Chiefs of Police, 1988; Knoxville Police Department, 1991). Creating greater officer awareness of ethnic and racial differences among community residents is an important first step in fostering such acceptance and support. It does not necessarily follow, however, that such awareness will eliminate racism or racist practices among officers altogether (Alpert and Dunham, 1986; Dantzker, 1987; Trojanowicz and Bucqueroux, 1991). Therefore, the International Association of Chiefs of Police has expanded its philosophy to include problem solving together with image enhancement. Sound strategies are needed to enable officers and citizens to work cooperatively toward reducing crime and restoring community safety.

One **community/police educational program,** implemented by the Philadelphia Police Department in 1980, was known as **COPE.** (This version of COPE should not be confused with the Maryland Citizen Oriented Police Enforcement program [COPE] discussed elsewhere in the text.) The COPE program in Philadelphia was designed to educate citizens on the necessity of certain police actions and to reduce their criticism of police performance. Actually, COPE was more successful at fostering better police self-perceptions and work satisfactions than at heightening community receptivity to police behaviors. Nevertheless, citing police officer perceptions of reduced community disharmony and conflict, researchers maintained that more positive police-community relations were ultimately obtained (Greene and Decker, 1989).

The influence of human relations training on police officers and police-community relations is summarized by Guyot (1991), who observes that a department that promotes competence and concern for citizens among its personnel, and treats its personnel professionally, will elicit more responsible and dedicated policing from its officers. It is difficult to put police professionalism into practice, however (Agyapong, 1987). Furthermore, the impact of increased police professionalism on police-community relations is not clear (Kennedy, 1987). However, it is generally accepted that improved relations among police officers and the public tend to enhance the public's perception of safety (Peak, Bradshaw, and Glensor, 1992). In some communities, such as Newark, New Jersey, the distribution of a neighborhood newsletter focusing on positive police actions generated more positive attitudes among the public toward the police

(Pate and Skogan, 1985). Similar results were obtained in Houston, Texas, where the Houston Police Department distributed a newsletter describing their neighborhood activities to interested residents. Although the public gave Houston police officers higher marks for their community service and conduct, citizens continued to exhibit fairly high levels of fear of victimization (Brown and Wycoff, 1987). Nevertheless, the evidence is fairly convincing that if police officers demonstrate caring attitudes and make significant attempts to understand and communicate with the public they serve, they can foster improved police-community relations (Goldstein, 1987; Skolnick and Bayley, 1988a).

In addition to such communication vehicles, aggressive strategies are needed to enlist active public support for community policing methods planned for specific neighborhoods or community areas. Probably the most important persons to recruit for police-community citizen teams are community leaders and businesspeople, because they are (1) well established in their communities, (2) respected by other community residents, and (3) capable of attracting rank-and-file membership for a community network that can help establish and prioritize community policing goals and objectives. Simply running notices in local newspapers of open meetings to discuss local crime problems and what police can do about them is only partially effective. Enlisting influential community residents can create a snowball effect, building a core of citizens sufficiently motivated to work with police officers in solving common community problems.

The police are probably in the best position to define the most obvious crime problems, such as the high-crime areas in which most arrests are made. However, community residents can be extremely helpful in targeting specific houses or apartment complexes, unknown to police, that may be harboring substantial criminal activity. Armed with specifics about such hot spots of crime activity, police can maximize their efforts to engage in "sting" operations or strikes against these persons or locations.

Heightened Community Safety through Improved Crime Control Strategies. Some experts suggest that the ability of police officers to prevent or even control crime is vastly overstated (Cameron, 1990). For instance, during 1992, four white police officers were tried in a Simi Valley, California, court for their alleged involvement in beating a black motorist, Rodney King. These officers were subsequently acquitted of most state charges against them. The predominantly minority community of South Central Los Angeles rioted following these acquittals. The rioting was perhaps the worst ever experienced by Los Angeles residents. Many bystanders were singled out and beaten by rioters. News helicopters circled overhead, and live accounts of these assaults were broadcast to Los Angeles residents on several major television networks. Police presence in those areas where the most severe rioting occurred was nonexistent, at least for several hours. Police officers were either unable or unwilling to intercede.

In many cities, large geographical territories have been taken over by youth gangs and drug dealers. The public's fear of crime in these areas has risen appreciably and for good reason. Recently, task forces in various communities have devised ways in which community residents can regain control of their neighborhoods. In Dallas, Texas, for example, a seven-phase program known as **Operation CLEAN** was implemented in March 1989. The program targeted specific areas of the city and the concerted action of several municipal departments (police, fire, streets and sanitation, housing and neighborhood services, and the city attorney's office) resulted in a major clean-up effort that led to a 71 percent reduction in street crime (Hatler, 1990). Community involvement in this clean-up effort was also required. Citizens established **Crime Watch programs** and increased their cooperation with police officers. Thus, police-resident efforts helped reduce crime and fear of crime in those affected neighborhoods (Hatler, 1990).

Traditional conceptions of policing envision police officers as responding to crime reports after crimes have occurred. This approach has caused some citizens to view police work as largely passive. However, recent shifts in policing philosophy have been in the direction of proactive policing (Couper and Lobitz, 1991; Fritz, 1990). Furthermore, police officers have begun to assist communities in establishing their own **Neighborhood Watch** programs and to take more active roles in crime prevention. One relatively recent approach to policing, **community wellness** (Wadman and Olson, 1990), is a proactive collaborative effort between police departments and community residents to initiate watch and alert programs to inform police about possible criminal activities. As neighborhood residents have taken a more active role in preventing crime, there have been substantial decreases in crime observed in those neighborhoods over time (Brown, 1991a; Wadman and Olson, 1990). Interestingly, contemporary Japanese communities practice community wellness vigorously and with strong results. Japanese residents consider law enforcement within their communities to be a shared enterprise. As a consequence, crime rates and the fear of crime in most Japanese communities are quite low. (See Chapter 11 for an extended discussion of community policing in Japan.)

It is clear that effective crime control strategies include both continuous police officer presence and close, frequent contact with neighborhood citizens (Zevitz and Albritton, 1992). Experiments with citizen contact patrols in Newark, New Jersey, and Houston, Texas, neighborhoods have been modestly successful in decreasing community fear of crime and improving quality of life (Bennett, 1991). In certain areas of New York City, **Precinct Community Councils (PCCs)** function as liaisons between police officers and local residents. These face-to-face councils have done much to foster police-community cooperation and create better conditions of community crime control (Maggs, 1986). Resistance to change among police officers and administrators in various departments, however, suggests that proactive policing and long-term cooperative arrangements with community organizations may not persist (Williams and Wagoner, 1992). For some departments, at least, rigid bureaucracies and militaristic police organization hinder the incorporation of citizen participation in law enforcement.

Maximization of Crime Prevention Techniques. Programs such as Neighborhood Watch, Crime Watch, ACOP (A Community Outreach Program),

BOX 1.1 The South Seattle Crime Prevention Council and Crime Prevention

In January 1988, South Seattle, Washington, organized the South Seattle Crime Prevention Council (SSCPC), a self-perpetuating group of community organization leaders and selected police department officials. An outgrowth of an earlier organization sponsored by the Rainier Chamber of Commerce, the SSCPC endorsed the following goals:

1. Creation of a community review committee to set priorities for reducing crime
2. Achievement of greater productivity and better communication within the police department and other city departments
3. Achievement of a proactive, not reactive, police response to citizen concerns
4. Setting of standards of achievement for police, from the chief on down
5. Establishment of reporting procedures to assure citizens that the police were making progress

A primary objective of these goals was to identify and set priorities as to various crime targets and arrange for police-citizen preventive or countermeasures. Crime targets might be specific locations in high-crime neighborhoods, abandoned vehicles (often used for drug dealing), or specific criminal offenses. Organization leaders expected police officers would engage in aggressive patrols with special attention to these targets.

By the end of 1988, police officers were working on 39 targets and had successfully attained half of these through arrests. Twenty "crack houses" were closed as the result of this yearlong activity. The substantial reports that police officers issued following these successes did much to improve police-citizen interaction. Citizen representatives became increasingly involved in assisting the police in identifying drug dealers and other types of criminals in their neighborhoods. In a rather short period, the crime rate in South Seattle declined substantially.

Police officers were affected similarly. They saw the heightened interest and involvement of citizens in crime prevention and stepped up their own crime prevention efforts accordingly, through more aggressive patrolling and investigation. Simultaneously, citizens pressured landlords who rented housing to drug dealers, urging them to evict criminal tenants. Eventually, the landlords cooperated and evicted drug dealers in large numbers.

The nature of citizen intervention and police assistance was diverse. Citizen complaints of drug activity were conveyed by telephone, in person, at the station, on the beat, or through the community hotline. Citizens also authorized police officers to enter their private premises for the purpose of investigating potential loiterers, who often were conducting drug transactions. Even the telephone company became involved by changing standard pay telephones in these high-crime areas to "call-out only" telephone stations: Only outgoing calls could be placed; incoming calls could not be received. This helped prevent telephone stations from becoming drug transaction sites or mediums. The long-term effect of the SSCPC program was to strengthen the citizen-police officer partnership as a stronger proactive coalition to prevent crime. These citizens became the eyes and ears of police in various ways, such as manning hotlines to identify potential criminal activity in progress.

Source: Charles B. DeWitt, *Community Policing in Seattle: A Model Partnership between Citizens and Police.* Washington, DC: National Institute of Justice, August, 1992:3–7.

and community wellness have been somewhat successful in decreasing the fear of crime in particular neighborhoods (Bradel and Witt, 1993; Brown, 1989b; Eck and Spelman, 1987; Walker, Walker, and McDavid, 1992). Information about a direct correlation between community-oriented policing and crime reduction is scant and inconsistent, however (Trojanowicz and Carter, 1988; Trojanowicz and Moore, 1988).

Crime reduction and control are major priorities of police-community relations. An integral feature of crime control is crime prevention, which is often facilitated through greater police presence in neighborhoods (Bennett and Baxter, 1985). Many police departments have modified police patrol styles to bring officers into closer physical contact with area residents. Thus, we have seen the revival of an old policing concept known as **beat patrolling.** Beats are small geographical areas of neighborhoods or cities that are patrolled by individual officers, usually on foot. Beats were commonplace in the early 1900s, but gradually, because of greater mobility and mechanization, police cruisers replaced beats. Although police administrators viewed cruisers as a better and more rapid means of responding to crime reports, there were serious latent sociological implications. Officers in cruisers became anonymous, impersonal entities. Technological change contributed to police officers' losing touch with their area residents and, perhaps, becoming alienated from them. This sense of detachment, disenchantment, and estrangement was not one-sided. In time, police officers and community residents became antagonists and acquired a "we" and "they" orientation.

When the **Law Enforcement Assistance Administration (LEAA)** began funding large-scale experiments in policing throughout the United States in the early 1970s, some of the experiments revived the concept of beats and investigated the significance of beat patrolling in crime prevention. Although reactions to beat patrolling have been mixed and the research literature inconclusive regarding whether beats reduce crime, investigators generally acknowledge the positive human relations benefits of beats (Einstadter, 1984; Greene, 1987b; Payne and Trojanowicz, 1985; Trojanowicz and Carter, 1988; Trojanowicz and Harden,

1985; Waddington, 1984). **Foot patrols** in Flint, Michigan, and elsewhere have been moderately successful in bringing community residents into closer touch with patrolling officers (Trojanowicz and Carter, 1988). In some areas, such as Alexandria, Virginia, police officers have visited new local residents to inform them of neighborhood events and discuss the crime prevention responsibilities of each citizen (Seiffert, 1984). Many citizens in neighborhoods utilizing foot patrols have commented that the officers provide more personalized response and service to community needs (Payne and Trojanowicz, 1985).

Not all beat patrolling is conducted on foot however. In Tampa, Florida, for instance, golf carts are used by officers to move about in designated neighborhood sectors. **Golf cart patrolling,** combined with **sector patrolling,** have been instrumental in bringing police officers closer to community residents (Morrill, 1984; Smith and Taylor, 1985). The Tampa Police Department initiated an experimental Neighborhood Sector Patrol System designed to deter criminal conduct and improve interactions between police and community citizens (Smith and Taylor, 1985). Initial findings indicated greater familiarity among police officers and citizens, less reported crime, longer business operating hours, and greater police-citizen crime prevention efforts.

Neighborhood safety and security are paramount goals of a Philadelphia Police Department program to improve police-community relationships (Greene,

Increasing crime rates, especially drug-related violence and gang activities, have caused police officers to devise more effective methods of crime control. *(Corbis-Bettmann)*

1988a). In the late 1980s, more than 200 police officers in Philadelphia participated in a program to help community residents improve their informal social control within neighborhoods. Individual police officers met with area residents and shared a variety of public safety and crime prevention strategies with them. The results were largely favorable. However, simple police officer intervention in citizen crime prevention programs is insufficient to forge long-lasting community changes. Kelling and Stewart (1990) suggest that police officers must be distributed throughout communities on the basis of need rather than political clout. Further, political interference in police-community projects must be minimized, if not eliminated. Finally, police officers must actively promote community rights and minority interests. Only by creating a realistic concept of community among neighborhood residents can police officers hope to achieve long-term changes that will maintain a high level of crime control and prevention.

General Reaffirmation of the Concept of Community. In a sense, community policing is dedicated to reinstilling among citizens a **sense of community.** For many persons, the concept of community is elusive and abstract. Community may be a specific neighborhood, consisting of several blocks of homes, where neighbors know one another well and interact more than occasionally. Another meaning of community, apart from specific geographical boundaries or territory, is shared values and goals. When people in a neighborhood become aware that they share objectives with others in adjacent parts of the community, they can establish stronger links among neighborhoods. Police organizations can be highly instrumental in bringing together representatives from different neighborhoods in a given community and allowing different vested interests to express opinions and share solutions about their respective crime problems. It is probably this latter emphasis on shared values and goals that best depicts what community-oriented policing is all about. Through such shared information, citizens from diverse parts of the community can unite for common purposes. Once such a unity of purpose exists, community-oriented policing is greatly facilitated, because police officers can draw on these interested citizens for information and cooperation to combat crime and promote a greater sense of community security and safety.

Although the idea of police officers and community residents as partners in combating crime and promoting public safety is not particularly novel, increasing ethnic and racial diversity in most U.S. communities has slowed police efforts to pull citizens together for that purpose. This problem has historical antecedents (Brown and Warner, 1992).

One method of organizing diverse community elements has been to focus on the problem as a community crime problem, to be solved through police-neighborhood cooperation (Eck and Spelman, 1987; Kelling, 1987). Whereas policing procedures traditionally involved individual crime incidents and reactive police responses (Ottemeier, 1990), experts have advised that if police departments are to combat crime more effectively, they must redefine the crime problem as a community problem-solving activity (St. Clair et al., 1992) In Oakland, California, for example, where police-citizen violence had been fairly frequent, problem-oriented policing was implemented on a limited scale in the late 1980s to determine whether the incidence of police-citizen violence could be reduced. When citizens became actively involved in defining community crime problems and suggesting solutions, it was evident that many acquired a better understanding of the police role (Toch and Grant, 1991). Ultimately, several residents showed more confidence in police officers, and the rate of police-citizen violence declined dramatically.

Problem-oriented policing, sometimes regarded as a matter of social problem definition, seems to foster neighborhood unity where it is implemented (Lindsay, 1988). Usually, participating police agencies focus on a few community crime problems, such as drug abuse and assault, and attempt to involve citizens in coproductive efforts to achieve solutions (Hill, Spelman, and Eck, 1988; Nila, 1990; Nimocks, 1988). One example of a problem-oriented community policing effort is the **Community Patrol Officer Program (CPOP),** begun as a pilot project in 1984 in New York City (McElroy, Cosgrove, and Sadd, 1990; Weisburd, McElroy, and Hardyman, 1988). Community patrol officers were assigned to foot patrols for 16- to 60-block beats, with 75 precincts participating by 1989. Between 1986 and 1988, interviews were conducted with CPOP officers in order to gauge program effectiveness. The interviews indicated that the most important function of the CPOP was the prevention of street-level drug problems, although there was no evidence to show whether CPOP affected burglary or robbery rates. Generally, citizens in these precincts believed that CPOP was significant in improving relations between the police and the community (McElroy, Cosgrove, and Sadd, 1990). Interestingly, officer job satisfaction increased substantially as a result of CPOP.

Although Moore (1992) acknowledges the working relationship between police officers and community residents for the purpose of attacking specific crime problems, effective partnerships between police officers and neighborhood citizens appropriately focus on the causes of crime rather than on specific crime incidents. Farrell (1986), who investigated selected Brooklyn, New York, precincts that used CPOP, describes how in 21 precincts individual officers were given specific tasks, including becoming involved in senior citizen escort programs, conducting drug awareness workshops, and participating in youth sports leagues. These officers also met with community residents to discuss specific crime problems and possible solutions for maintaining local order. Farrell found that residents reacted favorably to officer involvement in their neighborhood activities and that one result was a significant reduction in the frequency of citizen complaints about officer conduct (Moore, 1986).

Other examples abound. The Philadelphia Police Department, which was previously described as interested in promoting citizen safety and controlling crime, in 1986 gained a new police commissioner, who immediately recommended that police officers use community-oriented problem-solving strategies, with a special emphasis on cultivating the community concept (Philadelphia Police Study Task Force, 1987). Problem-oriented policing has also been quite effective in promoting a sense of community among residents of Newport News, Virginia, especially targeting drug-related offenders (Stephens, 1990). In addition, the Aurora, Colorado, Police Department has been somewhat successful in building a united community front against crime through the use of police area representatives who interact with key neighborhood residents on a regular basis (Williams, 1990).

Greater Use of Citizens in Quasi-Policing Roles. Although it is constitutional for citizens to arrest other citizens whenever criminal conduct is observed, most police agencies advise citizens not to engage in such practices but to call the police, who are better-trained to deal with criminals when making arrests. One dimension of police-community relations, however, is to place neighborhood residents in quasi-police roles through various neighborhood watch and community patrol programs. Giving community residents greater law enforcement responsibilities and involvement is sometimes regarded as civilianizing policing activities (Galvin, 1987; Greene, 1987b; Williams and Sloan, 1990), although not everyone agrees about how much citizen involvement in policing activities is beneficial (Dunham and Alpert, 1988).

Public law enforcement agencies have been known to use private citizens as volunteer auxiliary officers in various capacities. Although this practice varies among jurisdictions, some experts are concerned about the types and amount of law enforcement activities that private citizens should shoulder at any particular time (Grabosky, 1992). In some instances, however, policing by citizens is considered more effective than policing by public agencies. For example, the Guardian Angels represent one of the most visible examples of citizen participation in law enforcement. This self-designated anti-crime organization actively assists the New York Transit Police by monitoring subways and other high-crime areas. Their crime prevention value and intervention in apprehending crime perpetrators has been extensively acknowledged. In fact, surveys of New York City residents suggest that citizens seem more supportive of Guardian Angel activities in subway patrolling than they are of New York Transit Police activity in the same areas (Ziegenhagen and Brosnan, 1991).

Another supplement to public police protection is the walled private community or fortresslike apartment complex (Neely, 1990). These increasingly popular types of communities lend themselves to private policing and volunteer police patrols. Neely (1990) contends that the public law enforcement apparatus cannot by itself protect the public adequately and that private crime prevention organizations are necessary to supplement public resources.

Some experts believe that citizen involvement in law enforcement should be limited to planning and surveillance activities because citizens often lack the professional training in firearms use or physical combat to interact effectively with disorderly persons or criminals. Nevertheless, it is believed that citizen participation enhances understanding of the role of law enforcement officers in any public encounter. Again, from a human relations standpoint, any type of citizen involvement in policing functions helps to improve police-community interactions (Fleissner et al., 1991; Grabosky, 1992).

> **BOX 1.2 Weathering the Storms and Combatting Crime in Connecticut**
>
> Can ham radio operators replace police communications systems on a temporary basis? Yes. At least that is what was concluded by Chief Thomas G. Ganley of the Newington (Connecticut) Police Department, which in January 1983, decided to conduct an experiment. The experiment involved a simulated emergency situation in which the police communication system was disrupted for a prolonged period and individual police officers were out of touch with their supervisors. The Newington Amateur Radio League, an affiliate club of the American Radio Relay League, agreed to stand in for regular police dispatching units to regulate police patrols and direct police to emergency sites. For several hours, ham radio operators directed police activities over their own radios. Comparisons between communications from these ham operators and conventional police communication frequencies showed that the ham operator communications were superior.
>
> Ham radio operators have subsequently been assigned to informal patrol duties in various communities both within and outside Connecticut. These informal ham patrols have proved effective as "eyes and ears" for police officers whose patrol activities are overextended. Police officers cannot be everywhere at once. Thus, the ham radio patrols have curbed crime activities by identifying burglary suspects as well as a wide variety of potential crime incidents. Besides being used as quasi-patrol units, ham radio operators have provided temporary communications networks whenever weather emergencies such as tornados or hurricanes occur.
>
> *Source:* Bill Clede, "Amateur Radio: Back Up for Police." *Law and Order* (September):1–15, 1988.

The term *community policing* is conceptually distinct from *police-community relations,* although some scholars use them interchangeably. *Community policing* is an umbrella term encompassing any plan or program initiated by a law enforcement agency, citizen, or group to enable police officers and community residents to work cooperatively in creative ways that will (1) reduce or control crime, fear of crime, and the incidence of victimization; (2) promote mutual understanding for the purpose of enhancing police officer/citizen coproduction of community safety and security; and (3) establish a police-citizen communications network through which mutual problems may be discussed and resolved.

This definition addresses the key features of the back-to-the-people movement, grass-roots policing, problem-oriented policing, and community-based crime prevention, as well as the spirit of community wellness, proactive policing, and crime control policing. The key common features are cooperativeness between the police and community residents, a willingness to work collaboratively toward mutual goals, and a general desire to improve community safety though more effective crime control.

Public Relations and Human Relations

Public Relations. Most of the larger police departments in the United States have versions of **public relations** divisions responsible for reporting official police actions to the press and public. If police officers visit elementary schools or high schools and discuss the dangers of drugs to enlighten students, this is "good PR" (public relations) and may be considered newsworthy. Appropriate newspaper people are contacted, and information about such police work is disseminated. Annual awards are given to police officers who have risked their lives in the line of duty to rescue others or perform other acts of heroism. Again, the public relations divisions of police departments are responsible for conveying this information to the media. The obvious intent of such information dissemination is to create a favorable public impression or image. Thus, police department public relations divisions are in the business of the organizational equivalent of impression management.

Although the benefits of such recognition to police organizations are substantial, public relations does not equate with what is meant by community policing. Yet it is fairly easy to see how such public relations activities may be interpreted as community policing. Some programs sponsored by police departments for the purpose of impression management include citizen participation. For instance, the New York City Police Department established a citizen participation program in 1985 to keep the public informed about police activities in specific neighborhoods and to find out from residents face-to-face their complaints concerning police conduct (Maggs, 1986). This citizen participation program did not function as a crime prevention mechanism but as a means to sustain or create the notion of community among neighborhood residents (Maggs, 1986). It was found, however, that these citizen participation programs were poorly attended and that citizen participation was negligible.

Other police-citizen campaigns designed to heighten citizen awareness of crime problems have been more successful and have worked reasonably well to control or reduce crime in high-crime areas. For instance, a study of community-oriented policing was conducted over a sixteen-month period in Milwaukee, Wisconsin, in a high-crime neighborhood known as Metcalf Park (Zevitz and Albritton, 1992). In this one-year study, citizen participation was solicited to make residents aware of proactive police initiatives against local crime and to obtain neighborhood cooperation. A before-after survey disclosed varying attitudes among community residents toward the activities of police officers and the relation of their activities to crime reduction in Metcalf Park. Among the 1,055 households surveyed, many residents exhibited less fear of crime and a greater sense of personal and community safety. Compared with the 1985 New York City citizen participation program, the Milwaukee study included more citizen involvement in dealing with crime problems (Zevitz and Albritton, 1992).

Previous attempts to establish community policing in various jurisdictions relied heavily on the public relations approach (Trojanowicz and Carter, 1988). These efforts were designed primarily to portray police officers as individuals with personalities and feelings rather than anonymous authority symbols to be feared but were halfhearted at best. Tokenism characterized citizen involvement in policing activities. Friedmann (1992) acknowledges this major weakness of earlier community policing programs, noting that in many jurisdictions, police agencies did not allow or support community involvement in various crime prevention efforts. Friedmann asserts that if one accepts the assumption that a community acts as a criminogenic factor, that is, that it tends to produce crime, then ways must be found to curb the criminogenic influences that a community has on crime. He suggests establishing public policy at an interagency level that will facilitate greater police agency effectiveness on the one hand and greater control and empowerment of community residents on the other (Friedmann, 1992).

By imagining a latent continuum, at one end of which community participation in proactive policing is minimal or nonexistent and at the other end of which community participation is maximal, we can more easily understand the notion of increased citizen participation in police affairs over time. There is often a fine distinction among what some persons perceive to be community policing, police-community relations, and public relations. *Police-community relations*, then, is a generic concept that includes any program designed to promote law enforcement or make law enforcement strategies aimed at crime prevention and control more visible, including varying degrees of proactive citizen involvement.

Human Relations. **Human relations** is actually one of several alternative philosophies that underlie successful interpersonal interactions. Employers involving lower-level employees in decision making affecting their work is an example of applying human relations to a social situation. Guyot (1991) correctly observes that human relations is a school of management or philosophy that directs superiors to vest subordinates with some degree of professionalism and respect. In contrast, the traditional chain of command structure of police organizations formalizes and impersonalizes relations among officers at different supervisory levels. Relying exclusively on legal-rational authority typically featured in bureaucratic operations tends to undermine one's personal qualities that may be valuable to the organization (Bennett and Hess, 1992). The human relations school of management instead encourages employers to recognize superior qualities of personnel and to reward these qualities through special assignments. In this approach, police officers are treated as thinking, intelligent beings with particularly strategic psychological skills that may enhance their effectiveness when interacting with the public (U.S. Department of Justice, Community Relations Service, 1987).

Human relations is also closely related to **participatory (or participative)**

management, a management strategy that encourages employers to provide their employees with job enrichment opportunities and greater inclusion in decision making affecting their work roles (Gray, Stohr-Gillmore, and Lovrich, 1991). The Washington State Patrol has established a program called **Traffic Enforcement and Management System (TEAMS),** which uses participative management strategies. Gray, Stohr-Gillmore, and Lovrich (1991) describe TEAMS as following a "bottom-up" management process in which lower-level employees are encouraged to generate innovative ideas to serve the needs of the public and the department. The principles espoused by TEAMS include (1) continuous training, (2) genuine employee participation throughout the organization, (3) change of the manager's or sergeant's role from "cop" to "facilitator," and (4) encouragement of risk taking. An evaluation of this program suggests it improved staff morale, work satisfaction, and job effectiveness.

Any program that includes interactions between the police and community residents involves human relations. For example, establishing ministations—small offices staffed by police officers—at strategic points in neighborhoods with high crime rates might be regarded by residents as a positive police reaction to community crime problems. The actual presence of a neighborhood ministation may have little or no deterrent value, but a substantial human relations benefit may accrue.

As we have seen earlier, police officers receive human relations training during their recruitment and initial police education. For example, they learn various ways of dealing with feuding spouses and strategies for dispersing menacing crowds (U.S. Department of Justice Community Relations Service, 1987). When they conduct investigations they apply their human relations skills to elicit the most accurate information from community residents. Many citizens are hesitant to talk with police about anything; thus, if police officers can create a favorable interpersonal climate they may be more successful in soliciting information from possible witnesses at crime scenes.

Community-Based Policing, Problem-Oriented Policing, and Team Policing

The basic concept of community policing changed in the 1980s and early 1990s (Sheppard and Wycoff, 1992). Three terms that are linked with the concept are (1) community-based policing, (2) problem-oriented policing, and (3) team policing.

Community-Based Policing. For all practical purposes, community-based policing and community policing refer to the same phenomena. All of the elements encompassed in the definition of community policing presented earlier are also included in the term *community-based policing.* The clear emphasis of community-based policing is on getting back to the people in neighborhoods or "getting back in touch" through integrated police-citizen crime prevention and control programs (Bennett, 1990; Mastrofski et al., 1990; Sherman, 1992:123).

Problem-Oriented Policing. **Problem-oriented policing** differs significantly in meaning from community-based policing (Moore, 1992). The definitive work on problem-oriented policing is by Herman Goldstein, who defines it as recognizing different crime incidents as being the result of common underlying community problems that are resolvable through effective problem-solving strategies (Goldstein, 1990:18–23). Although early criticism of problem-oriented policing equated it with a social-problems approach to crime and not necessarily new, clarification and analysis of this concept suggest that it is a viable method of crime control (Lindsay, 1988).

Eck and Spelman (1987:5–6) illustrate problem-oriented policing by describing a series of convenience store robberies in Gainesville, Florida, in 1985. The Gainesville police determined that the many robberies of convenience stores were committed by different robbers rather than by the same perpetrators, although little evidence existed as to their identity. Utilizing a problem-oriented strategy, police observed that the layouts of the different convenience stores where robberies had occurred obscured cash registers and clerk stations from window observation from the street. With the cooperation of some convenience store owners who had been robbed, police encouraged rearrangement of store facilities and the removal of window advertising so that cash registers and clerks could be visible to passersby. Following these changes, robberies in those convenience stores decreased dramatically.

Although in the Eck and Spelman example some action by community businesspersons was required, there are many instances in which problem-oriented policing may be conducted exclusively by the police. For example, the Boston Police Department received unfavorable publicity in past years concerning police misconduct. Citizen complaints against police officers prompted much adverse publicity. A problem-oriented internal investigation revealed that only a few officers were attracting most citizen complaints. After actions were taken by the police administration to deal with those officers, citizen complaints diminished (St. Clair et al., 1992).

The Police Executive Research Forum has evaluated numerous studies on the use of problem-oriented policing to stem the illegal distribution and use of drugs (Stephens, 1990) and has found that the approach has been effective in San Diego, St. Petersberg, Tulsa, Atlanta, and Philadelphia. The crime reduction potential of the strategy is apparent (Guyot, 1990). Moreover, in cities such as San Diego and Aurora, Illinois, police agencies have begun to share information relating to interjurisdictional crime, a practice that is an integral feature of problem-oriented policing (Nila, 1990). Finally, police and citizens can work cooperatively in problem-oriented policing efforts; the approach is not necessarily limited to internal police action (Hill, Spelman, and Eck, 1988).

Team Policing. **Team policing** is a term frequently misunderstood. The idea of a team connotes pairs of officers working in tandem to patrol neighborhoods and deter criminals. Citizen-police interactions are sometimes regarded as team efforts and may be referred to as **neighborhood team policing** (Mayhall, 1985:57). These conceptions of team policing are inaccurate. Team policing is a method of crime investigation limited to a specific geographical area and involving several crime specialists, including police officers, detectives, and forensics personnel.

Police officers, detectives, and other personnel are assigned to a particular community area to work as an investigative team in solving crimes that occur in that area. A landmark example of the effectiveness of team policing has been described by Rubinstein (1974) and summarized by Walker (1992:156). In 1973, the Rochester (New York) Police Department inaugurated team policing, consisting of several teams of thirty patrol officers and six detectives. Each of these teams of officers and detectives was responsible for providing the full range of police services in specific areas of Rochester on a 24-hour basis. A follow-up evaluation revealed that the team policing approach was at least three times as effective for solving robbery crimes and 50 percent more effective for solving burglary crimes as traditional police methods and investigations (Rubinstein, 1974: 121–122; Walker, 1992:156).

WHY STUDY COMMUNITY POLICING?

Community policing has emerged since the 1970s as an increasingly important strategy for controlling and preventing crime and enhancing community safety. We should study community policing in order to (1) compare and contrast traditional policing procedures with contemporary methods; (2) understand the role of community policing as a method of crime control and prevention; (3) obtain a view of modern policing to better understand current police practices; (4) determine the political, legal, and social factors that have an impact on policing; (5) prepare students for entry-level police roles; and (6) understand implications of community policing for citizens.

Six Reasons

Compare and contrast traditional policing methods with contemporary methods. A comparison of traditional policing methods with more contemporary methods emphasizing community policing enables us to highlight the deficiencies of traditional policing. Although traditional policing methods are not entirely bad, the community policing emphasis has provided numerous strengths, including reducing neighborhood fear of crime and improving a sense of personal security.

Understand the role of community policing as a method of crime control and prevention. Community policing's key priorities are crime control and prevention. It accomplishes these objectives, in part, by developing more effective liaisons between the public and community law enforcement agencies.

Involving neighborhood residents in collaborative efforts to solve or control community crime furnishes police with indirect community support for their enforcement activities.

Obtain a view of modern policing to better understand current police practices. Modern policing is clearly directed toward the development of closer relations between the public and police. Information-sharing activities alert citizens to new crime-fighting methods used by police in different jurisdictions. Taking a proactive role in working more closely with police officers in their enforcement activities enables citizens to better understand the reasons for police conduct.

Determine the political, legal, and social factors that have an impact on policing. Several political, legal, and social factors inhibit the acceptance of community policing programs in certain jurisdictions. Understanding these factors may enable police to work with different agencies in the community to facilitate changes in policing activities that will have long-term community benefits. Also, acquiring an understanding of factors involved in resistance to change can perhaps help us develop better change strategies and present community policing in more favorable contexts.

Prepare students for entry-level police roles. Many students will subsequently enter internship programs in which they will work closely with law enforcement agencies. If they have a basic understanding of community policing and how it operates in their jurisdictions, they will be more effective interns and be of greater value to police agencies when they subsequently enter the law enforcement profession. Further, they can plan their undergraduate programs in a way that will better prepare them for law enforcement training.

Understand the implications of community policing for citizens. Community policing implies several things for neighborhood residents. It implies a more understanding and caring law enforcement component dedicated to working in collaborative ways to resolve community crime problems. It may result in fewer citizen complaints leveled at police officers, if the public comes to appreciate the benefits of community policing programs. It implies more integrated communities, as citizens band together in productive ways with the police to make their neighborhoods safer for themselves and their families. The criminal deterrent effects of community policing are obvious and will be explored more extensively in later chapters.

THE EVOLUTION OF COMMUNITY POLICING

More than a few scholars have suggested that the new and modern concept of community policing is neither new nor modern (Inkster, 1992; Mayhall, 1985; Peak, 1993; Singh, 1987; Taft, 1986; Tonry and Morris, 1992). Early records indicate the existence of police forces in ancient Egypt and Mesopotamia about 1500 B.C. (Adamson, 1991). Although the functions of these forces have not been carefully documented, it is clear that some of the police officers interacted with the public they served in various, sometimes adversarial ways. Nevertheless, their presence seems to have been intended to maintain order and control crime through neighborhood patrolling and response to community interests.

More recently, the **Metropolitan Police of London,** organized in 1829 by **Sir Robert Peel,** a prominent British government official, had duties that emphasized close interaction with the public and maintenance of proper attitudes and temperament (Lee, 1901; Mayhall, 1985:425–426; Reith, 1952). American experiences with community policing can be traced from colonial times to the 1990s (Bailey, 1987; Berman, 1985; Holden, 1990; Maguire, 1990; Robinson and Scaglion, 1987; von Hoffman, 1992). In this section we will provide a brief account of policing throughout history. This coverage is superficial and is intended only to reference pivotal shifts in police organization and administration. The reader is referred to additional sources at the conclusion of this chapter for further information about the history of policing.

From Centurions to the Middle Ages

We have already seen that ancient Egypt and Mesopotamia had police forces charged with maintaining order and resolving community disputes (Adamson, 1991). These were principally civilian forces organized and administered by civilian authorities. Adamson says that these police officers sometimes had bad reputations for molesting or beating prisoners in custody, although their testimony in court was considered generally trustworthy. In early Roman times, from about 100 B.C. to A.D. 200, **centurions** were used in both military or paramilitary units for policing purposes. Centurions usually commanded units of 100 men and were used for policing and combat. There is some evidence that in about A.D. 100 the Romans established the first professional criminal investigative units in Western history, known as **frumentarii.** The frumentarii had three principal duties, which were (1) to supervise grain distribution to Rome's needy, (2) to oversee the personal delivery of messages among government officials, and (3) to detect crime and prosecute offenders (Kelly, 1987). Kelly notes that frumentarii reenacted crime scenes, conducted custodial interrogations of criminal suspects, compared statements made to different interrogators, and offered immunity to various criminal accomplices in exchange for incriminating testimony against their confederates. Little indication is given, however, of how these frumentarii interacted with the public in their police work.

Accounts of policing in different parts of the world during the period A.D. 100 to about A.D. 800 are fragmented (Bailey, 1986). Of greatest pertinence to American policing activities is what transpired in early England at or about the time of the Norman Conquest in 1066. English jurisdictions were divided into **shires,** the equivalent of present-day counties. The chief law enforcement officers in shires were called **reeves.** Thus, each shire had a reeve. (The shire-reeve subsequently yielded the term with which we are all familiar, the [county] **sheriff.**) Shire-reeves were actually agents of the king of England and collected taxes in addition to maintaining the peace. The king also utilized **chancellors** as his agents to settle disputes between neighbors, such as property boundary issues, trespass allegations, and child misconduct. An early equivalent of the chancellor, with similar duties and responsibilities, was the **justice of the peace,** dating to about A.D. 1200. Together with the chancellors or justices of the peace, reeves maintained order in their respective jurisdictions or shires.

Policing functions during this period were shared among community residents. The Norman Conquest ushered in the **frankpledge** system, which required loyalty to the king and spread law and order responsibilities among the people. The frankpledge system directed that neighbors should form small groups to assist and protect one another against criminals. These neighborhood groups were commanded by **constables** appointed by the King's favored noblemen. These constables were the forerunners of modern police officers. Over the next 200 years some degree of specialization in law enforcement duties developed. In the seventeenth century, citizens were obligated to perform **day watch** or **night watch** duties on a rotating basis. Day and night watches were comparable to modern-day shift work. These **watchmen** were expected to raise a **hue and cry** in the event they detected crimes in progress or any other community disturbance, such as a fire or other emergency situation. The position of night watchman derives from this early practice. Citizens hired less affluent persons to perform their watchman duties. As these arrangements became increasingly popular over time, salaried watchmen evolved.

The English system of administering justice and law enforcement was at best informal. Law was uncodified, emphasizing the importance of individual and interjurisdictional judicial proclamations and precedents under the principle of **stare decisis.** Left to their own devices, reeves were often corrupt, accepting bribes from the relatives of those incarcerated in makeshift jails, called **gaols.** Debtor's prisons became increasingly common. These prisons were "Catch-22" situations, in that those imprisoned for any crime could not be released unless they could make restitution or pay a fine, yet they could not work to earn money to pay their fines because they were in prison. Many prisoners died while caught in this strange system. Even in the worst of times, however, reeves were able to exploit those confined by offering their manual labor to merchants and businesspeople who sought cheap help.

Under the debtor's prison system it was only a matter of time before English prisons were glutted with inmates. In the late 1600s and early 1700s, many inmates were transported to the American colonies to perform manual labor for England under an **indentured servant system.** Indentured servants were ordinarily obligated to give free labor to their benefactors for a period of seven years, after which they would be free to pursue their own ambitions, with obviously limited resources. The benefactors were not always affiliated with the government of England. Many merchants paid small commissions to government officials to use indentured servants.

American colonists perpetuated the system of law enforcement and jurisprudence with which they were most familiar—the English system. Besides reeves, constables were used for maintaining law and order in colonial communities. The duties of constables included collecting fees for highway usage, collecting taxes, and presiding over minor legal issues. Subsequently, the position of sheriff was created, and sheriffs became the principal law enforcement officers in various counties throughout the colonies.

The Colonies in a Time of Change

Because of the great distance between England and the American colonies, differences in law enforcement and judicial practices began to appear. Colonists developed systems whereby sheriffs were elected or appointed officials who could hire deputies to assist them in law and order and other county tasks. Nevertheless, certain law enforcement practices originating in early England were perpetuated in numerous colonial jurisdictions, such as the watchman system of using citizens on a rotating basis to maintain a round-the-clock vigil over their communities.

Because most colonial communities were small and rural, informal rather than formal policing arrangements were most practical. Indeed, between 1630 and 1790 only eight communities had populations of 8,000 or more (Hageman, 1985:16). Trojanowicz and Bucqueroux (1990:46) indicate that some jurisdictions, such as the Colony of New York, used **schouts and rattles,** meaning persons who were expected to shout and shake noise-making rattles in the event they saw crimes in progress or fleeing suspects. Rattle watchmen were paid 48 cents per 24-hour shift and often were offenders sentenced to keep rattle watch as their punishment for a legal infraction (Richardson, 1970; Trojanowicz and Bucqueroux, 1990:46).

In the early 1700s, jurisdictions such as Philadelphia established finite patrol areas supervised by constables who commanded squads of volunteers, drawn largely from the citizenry. These semiformal policing methods were emulated in other colonies throughout the 1700s. During this same period in England, **Henry Fielding,** an author turned politician, developed some innovative law enforcement ideas. In 1748 he was appointed chief magistrate of Bow Street in London (Peak, 1993:9) and organized small groups of citizens to pursue criminals. These persons, known as **thief-takers,** were selected, in part, for being "fleet of foot." Victims rewarded thief-takers whenever they returned stolen merchandise recovered from captured criminals. When Henry Fielding died in 1754, **Sir John Fielding** succeeded him and transformed the thief-takers into the **Bow Street Runners,** a small group of paid police officers who were quite successful at apprehending criminals. These activities did not go unnoticed in the colonies. Eventually, the Revolutionary War effectively separated and resolved English and American political and legal policies, although English influence on subsequent policing methods has continued.

Law Enforcement from 1800 to the 1990s

The most significant law enforcement event of the early 1800s was the establishment of the Metropolitan Police of London in 1829 by Sir Robert Peel, the British Home Secretary. This organization was formed in an era of police reform. Earlier, in 1792, an influential London magistrate, **Patrick Colquhoun,** promoted and endorsed some rather novel ideas for the time concerning the functions of police. Colquhoun had many legal reformist notions about law enforcement generally, several of which are beyond the scope of this text. Noteworthy here are his beliefs that police should be used to establish and maintain order, control and prevent crime, and set an example of good conduct and moral sense for the citizenry. He also believed that existing enforcement methods, at least in London, were antiquated and improper. He believed that some degree of professionalism among officers was necessary and should be independently funded by the particular jurisdiction (Lee, 1901). Colquhoun died before he could see the fruition of the reforms he promoted, but his ideas received strong endorsement from Sir Robert Peel. Although some segments of the public resisted a formal police force, Peel succeeded in establishing the first official law enforcement organization in England through the **Metropolitan Police Act of 1829.** Some 6,000 officers, whose primary qualifications included the ability to read and write, good moral character, and physical fitness, were hired (Mayhall, 1985; Miller and Hess, 1994; Trojanowicz and Bucqueroux, 1990).

The general principles on which the Metropolitan Police of London was founded are summarized here (adapted from Lyman, 1964:141–144):

1. Prevent crime and disorder, as an alternative to their repression by military force and severity of legal punishment.
2. Recognize always that the power of the police to fulfill their functions and duties is dependent on public approval of their existence, actions, and behavior and on their ability to secure and maintain public respect.
3. Recognize always that to secure and maintain the respect and approval of the public means also to secure the willing cooperation of the public in the task of maintaining observance of the law.
4. Recognize always that the extent to which the cooperation of the public can be secured diminishes, proportionately, the necessity of using physical force and the compulsion to achieve police objectives.
5. Seek and preserve public favor, not by pandering to public opinion, but by constantly demonstrating absolutely impartial service to law, in complete independence of policy and without regard to the justice or injustice of the substance of individual laws, by offering individual service and friendship to all members of the public without regard to their wealth or social standing; by exercising courtesy and good humor; and by offering individual sacrifice in protecting and preserving life.

6. Use physical force only when the exercise of persuasion, advice, and warning is found to be insufficient to obtain public cooperation to an extent necessary to secure observance of law or to restore order; and to use only the minimal degree of physical force that is necessary on any particular occasion for achieving a police objective.
7. Maintain at all times a relationship with the public that gives reality to the historic tradition that the police are the public and that the public are the police—the police being only members of the public who are paid to give full-time attention to duties that are incumbent on every citizen in the interests of community welfare and existence.
8. Recognize always the need for strict adherence to police-executive functions, and refrain from even seeming to usurp the powers of the judiciary (i.e., to avenge individuals or the state, judge guilt, or punish the guilty).
9. Recognize always that the test of police efficiency is the absence of crime and disorder and not the visible evidence of police action in dealing with crime and disorder.

It is noteworthy that these principles emphasize several police-community cooperative actions, including securing public cooperation in observance of the law, seeking and preserving public favor, using minimal force to effect arrests of criminals, and always maintaining favorable relations with the public in the process of crime control. It is especially important to understand that law enforcement agencies in the United States during the early 1800s were increasingly influenced by this new English police organization and its policing methods. In fact, in 1844 the New York City Police Department modeled its own organization on its London counterpart. By the late 1850s many other cities, including Chicago, Boston, Baltimore, Philadelphia, New Orleans, and Newark (Fosdick, 1920), had patterned their law enforcement organizations on London's. Today, many contemporary police departments in the United States continue to emulate in a general way this early British organization.

Urbanization and industrialization did much to change the nature of law enforcement, especially in large cities, where the size of police organizations expanded considerably. These organizations became increasingly bureaucratic, proliferating with diverse specialized divisions and departments. Gradually, state and federal law enforcement agencies evolved, and new jurisdictional boundaries were established. With the growth of these organizations and expanded law enforcement interests, police work gradually became more specialized. For example, some police departments performed probation and parole chores before specific agencies were established for these other purposes (Fosdick, 1920:377; Walker, 1992:10).

A key event in U.S. policing occurred in 1908 when **August Vollmer,** the chief of police of Berkeley, California, suggested more formal professional and educational training for police officers he commanded. Relying heavily on academic specialists in various forensics areas, Vollmer started an informal academic regimen of police training, including investigative techniques, photography, fingerprinting, and anatomy, among other subject areas. By 1917 he convinced the University of California–Berkeley to experiment with a new criminology and law enforcement curriculum for the purpose of providing his new recruits with formal academic training. These academic underpinnings of police training were forerunners of the **Peace Officer Standards and Training (POST)** that are common training programs in most U.S. jurisdictions today.

Vollmer was innovative in several respects. For instance, he pioneered the first fully motorized police force for the purpose of developing more effective patrolling activities. Ironically, motorizing the police force and decreasing the incidence of beat patrolling was a first step toward the previously mentioned police officer–community citizen alienation, as face-to-face contact with neighborhood residents was replaced by impersonal mobile units. At the time, however, mobilizing the police force was viewed as a major innovation that would enhance rapid police response to reports of crime.

Vollmer was also responsible for the two-way radio in police cruisers. This innovation greatly enhanced law enforcement effectiveness and the apprehension of fleeing suspects. In addition, his police selection methods resulted in officer appointments based on emotional, educational, and physical fitness tests. He also interviewed prospective recruits as a screening tool, sometimes using psychologists for this purpose. In many respects, Vollmer is considered the father of police professionalization. Some scholars have termed this period the **professionalization movement** (Walker, 1992:12). One of Vollmer's students was **O.W. Wilson,** a former police chief in Wichita, Kansas, and Chicago, Illinois, who in 1950 became the first dean of the School of Criminology at the University of California–Berkeley. Wilson was responsible for centralizing police administration and creating command decision making in Berkeley and many other cities during the 1950s and 1960s (Wilson and McLaren, 1977).

The first study of the U.S. criminal justice system of national magnitude was conducted under the auspices of the federal government in 1931. President Herbert Hoover appointed the **National Commission on Law Observance and Enforcement,** known subsequently as the **Wickersham Commission,** in 1929. After two years of investigation, the Wickersham Commission issued a fifteen-volume report. One volume examined "police lawlessness" and police abuse of authority. The report also found little consistency in the selection, training, and administration of police recruits throughout the United States. The obvious implication was that changes in recruiting and training practices for police officers were in order, and the Wickersham Commission recommended expeditious implementation of such changes. Both Vollmer and Wilson supported the changes. Since then more sophisticated police selection and training methods have been established in many jurisdictions and have been reasonably successful in improving the quality of officers in police departments generally.

The militaristic organization of contemporary police departments is reflective of the centralization of police organization fostered by Wilson. Moreover, World War II veterans entered law enforcement in large numbers in the late 1940s and

1950s, and the crossover of military-style organizational ideas would not have been considered unusual (Hageman, 1985:18). These were also English antecedents. In the early 1800s a career military officer, Colonel Charles Rowan, was appointed to assist in the establishment and operation of the Metropolitan Police of London. Rowan incorporated many military principles and operations into London's police organization. Long before Rowan, military units functioned in policing capacities in the first few centuries A.D. Thus, the militaristic organization of contemporary police departments is not a new phenomenon, but centuries old.

The next major stage of police reform and innovations in policing occurred in 1968 with the creation of the previously mentioned Law Enforcement Assistance Administration (LEAA). The LEAA was one outgrowth of the President's Crime Commission during the period 1965–1967, a time of great social unrest and civil disobedience. Racial and political tensions were exceptionally high. Racial segregation was being challenged in various parts of the country, the Vietnam War was escalating, delinquency was increasing, and the level of criminality was unsettling. The police took on a more prominent role in controlling community events and maintaining law and order. The LEAA allocated millions of dollars to researchers and police departments over the next decade, and many experiments were conducted with these monies, some of which led to innovative patrolling strategies in different communities. It is important to recognize the influence of the LEAA in giving greater attention to policing methods nationally and to community policing in particular as a viable method of community crime control.

In 1973, the **National Advisory Commission on Criminal Justice Standards and Goals** promulgated the following important goals for police departments in order to clarify their policing functions:

1. Maintenance of order
2. Enforcement of the law
3. Prevention of criminal activity
4. Detection of criminal activity
5. Apprehension of criminals
6. Participation in court proceedings
7. Protection of constitutional guarantees
8. Assistance to those who cannot care for themselves or who are in danger of physical harm
9. Control of traffic
10. Resolution of day-to-day conflicts among family, friends, and neighbors
11. Creation and maintenance of a feeling of security in the community
12. Promotion and preservation of civil order (National Advisory Commission on Criminal Justice Standards and Goals, 1973:104–105)

Several components of community policing are evident in these goals. These include order maintenance, conflict resolution among community residents, and assurance of a sense of security through the detection and prevention of criminal behavior and the apprehension of criminals.

KEY TERMS

Back-to-the-community movement
Beat patrolling
Bow Street Runners
Centurions
Chancellors
Patrick Colquhoun
Community-based policing
Community Patrol Officer Program (CPOP)
Community-Police Educational Program (COPE)
Community policing
Community wellness
Constables
Crime Watch
Day watch
Henry Fielding
Sir John Fielding
Foot patrols
Frankpledge
Frumentarii
Gaols
Golf cart patrolling
Hue and cry
Human relations
Indentured servant system
Justice of the peace
Law Enforcement Assistance Administration (LEAA)
Metropolitan Police Act of 1829
Metropolitan Police of London
National Advisory Commission on Criminal Justice Standards and Goals
National Commission on Law Observance and Enforcement
Neighborhood team policing
Neighborhood Watch
Night watch
Operation CLEAN
O.W. Wilson
Participative management
Participatory management
Peace Officer Standards and Training (POST)
Sir Robert Peel
Police-community relations
Precinct Community Councils (PCCs)
Problem-oriented policing
Professionalization movement
Public relations
Reeves
Schouts and rattles
Sector patrolling
Sense of community
Sheriff
Shires
Stare decisis
Team policing
Thief-takers
Traffic Enforcement and Management System (TEAMS)
August Vollmer
Watchmen
Wickersham Commission

QUESTIONS FOR REVIEW

1. What is meant by community policing? Explain how it differs from problem-oriented policing and police-community relations.
2. What are the goals of community policing? Are these goals centered around police interests or public interests? Write a brief rationale for your answer.
3. Why do you think it is important to build better relations between police organizations and the community?
4. Why are communication skills given so much importance in police training programs? Give some examples from your own experience.
5. What is meant by human relations as a philosophy? How is human relations used by police administrators? How is it used by police officers in their interactions with the public? Do you think it is a successful strategy? If so, in what senses and why?
6. What types of back-to-the-community programs can you describe? Why is it that we now have back-to-the-community programs? When did the police become more isolated from the community? What policing styles were prevalent that distanced police officers from neighborhood residents?
7. What did the Law Enforcement Assistance Administration have to do with the development of community policing?
8. Why is it important to reaffirm the concept of community?
9. What are some of the programs that have used citizens in quasi-policing roles? Is vigilantism justified? Why or why not? Under what circumstances would you consider vigilantism as a viable alternative to relying on police protection?
10. Differentiate among team policing, community-based policing, and problem-oriented policing. Give an example of each. Which approach do you think is best? Why?
11. What are some of the reasons we should study community policing?
12. How were centurions used in ancient Rome? Were there police forces prior to centurions? Give some examples.
13. After the Norman Conquest, what important developments significantly altered the nature of policing in England? Discuss these major events between 1066 and 1830.
14. Why were the Metropolitan Police of London so important to police agencies in the United States?
15. Differentiate among shires, reeves, and chancellors. Discuss several significant events in the American colonies that changed policing strategies during the 1600s and 1700s.
16. Identify the general principles of the Metropolitan Police of London that seem to reflect the philosophy of community policing in the United States today.

17. Identify some of the major contributions to policing by (a) August Vollmer, (b) O.W. Wilson, and (c) the Wickersham Commission.
18. What was the significance of the National Advisory Commission on Criminal Justice Standards and Goals?

SUGGESTED READINGS

Emsley, Clive (1983). *Policing and Its Context: 1750–1870*. New York: Schocken Books.

Kelling, George L., and Mark H. Moore (1987). *From Political Reform to Community: The Evolving Strategy of Police*. Cambridge, MA: Harvard University Kennedy School of Government.

Klockars, Carl B. (1985). *The Idea of Police*. Beverly Hills, CA: Sage.

Miller, Larry S., and Michael C. Braswell (1988). *Human Relations and Police Work (2nd ed.)*. Prospect Heights, IL: Waveland Press.

Peak, Kenneth J. (1993). *Policing America: Methods, Issues, Challenges*. Englewood Cliffs, NJ: Regents/Prentice Hall.

Tonry, Michael, and Norval Morris (1992). *Modern Policing*. Chicago: The University of Chicago Press.

Trojanowicz, Robert, and Bonnie Bucqueroux (1990). *Community Policing: A Contemporary Perspective*. Cincinnati, OH: Anderson Publishing Company.

Wadman, Robert C., and Robert K. Olson (1990). *Community Wellness: A New Theory of Policing*. Washington, DC: Police Executive Research Forum.

CHAPTER 2

Police Organizations

Introduction

A Typology of Model Police Roles
The Legalistic Approach
The Service Orientation
The Watchman Style
Code of Ethics and Policy Formulation

Organizational Structure

Police Organization and Operations
The Military Syndrome
Attaboys and Aw Shits
Productivity
Changing Calls-for-Service

Alternative Organizational Models
Total Quality Management
Organizational Goals, Values, and Mission Statements

Empowerment and Decision Making

Participatory Management
Quality Circles
Planning
Census Tracts and Crime Reporting
Coordination with Other City Agencies and Departments

Political Considerations
Economics and Contracting
Budgets
Executive Selection

Key Terms

Questions for Review

Suggested Readings

INTRODUCTION

In his work *The Limits of Criminal Sanction*, the late Herbert Packer said that American policing seemed to follow two somewhat disparate models of law enforcement. One model, the **order maintenance model**, emphasizes crime control, suppression, and apprehension. The second, the **due process model**, also concerned with public safety, tends to focus on individual liberties, constitutional protections, and the delivery of quality police service.

Similarly, James Q. Wilson described three separate police delivery systems in his work *The Varieties of Police Behavior*. These delivery systems or models are (1) the **legalistic model**, (2) the **watchman model**, and (3) the **service model**. The legalistic model emphasizes the importance of written procedure and limited individual officer discretion and promotes a "Joe Friday," "strictly-by-the-book," "only-the-facts" mentality among law enforcement officers. The watchman style is oriented toward peace-keeping functions. Both the legalistic and watchman models are reactive in nature and were easily adaptive to early, traditional policing goals and objectives. In contrast with these two models, the service model is designed to meet community needs and expectations and is therefore shaped by them. The current shift toward community-oriented policing is best described as a continuing social and political movement toward the due process model outlined by Packer and the service model described by Wilson.

A TYPOLOGY OF MODEL POLICE ROLES

The Legalistic Approach

The legalistic model has been described as the easiest approach to urban policing, because it limits the discretionary power of employees and allows for greater control by supervisors. It relies heavily on accountability, promotes lockstep uniformity, gives rise to stress, and encourages the CYA (Cover Your Ass) syndrome. The model's characteristics include the following:

1. Highly specialized, with great division of labor and a centralized style of command
2. Stress on rules, policies, and procedures and obedience thereto
3. Primarily reactive in operational thrust—suppression and apprehension
4. Impersonal attitude toward public and its problems
5. Selection of personnel based solely on achievement, criteria, tests, and education

6. Emphasis on authority to accomplish tasks
7. Narrow role of employees
8. Exemplary conduct of employees based on threat, external control, and enforcement of rules
9. Evaluation by traditional methods related to narrow job descriptions
10. Training limited to interdepartmental or regional

The Service Orientation

The service model has the following distinguishing features:

1. A generalized approach with less division of labor and a decentralized style of management
2. Stress on individual discretion and trust in individual decision making
3. Primarily proactive operational thrust—prevention and deterrence
4. Personal involvement with public and its problems
5. Selection of personnel based on tests, achievement, and ascriptive criteria, with voluntary (nonmandated) recognition of need to recruit culturally diverse people. A view toward future development and potential
6. Stress on persuasion, with subtle use of authority to accomplish tasks
7. Expansion of role of employees
8. Exemplary conduct of employees based on training, self-control, individual responsibility, and peer pressure
9. Evaluation by a holistic instrument to assess the total individual and the individual's relationship to the community
10. Training at national level and use of private-sector (nontraditional) courses
11. Encouragement of networking, planning, research, and publication

The Watchman Style

The watchman model of policing can be likened to the perception of the old-fashioned, door-rattling security guard—the peace keeper who was neither proactive nor reactive but simply maintained security and attempted to keep order. Hollywood made a lot of money and entertained a lot of people with the misadventures of the Keystone Kops. Although mere characters in slapstick comedy, the Keystone Kops portrayed a policing image of the time: the ineffective and amazingly inept policeman not even capable of "watching" without mishap.

Code of Ethics and Policy Formulation

It has often been suggested that those entering the policing occupation should be taught ethics as a part of their indoctrination. This position raises more questions than it answers. One problem is that there do not appear to be any criteria or instruments that can identify or measure an individual's honesty, integrity, or ethics. All of the admitting or prescreening procedures deal with determining if candidates have committed offenses that have gone unpunished and putting them through the psychological screening (which does not measure an individual's ethical value system). There are no measurements of an individual's propensity to engage in unethical or dishonest activities later on.

A glaring example of this problem is the number of law enforcement officers who have been convicted or administratively punished for skimming drug money. Opportunity is an unknown until experienced. Applicants would be hard pressed to visualize large sums of money that could be illegally diverted into their pockets, and it would be difficult or impossible to test a person's vulnerability to such opportunity.

Another problem is that one's ethics are developed long before an individual enters the world of law enforcement, and attempting to teach ethics is somewhat futile. This is not to say that discussing ethical situations and problems is not valuable. Far from it.

One significant reason to address ethical conduct is the sheer number of law enforcement agents who resign or are forced to leave the department because of a breach of ethics. Excluding medical retirement and lateral transfer, it has been estimated that the majority of those who leave law enforcement employment prior to retirement depart as a result of behavioral and disciplinary problems. The economic impact is tremendous, but the impact of their transgressions within the service community can take a larger toll. If the philosophy of community policing is based on community trust, the violation of that trust will undermine community-oriented policing (COP).

The Executive Committee of the International Association of Chiefs of Police (IACP) adopted a code of ethics on October 17, 1989, during IACP's 96th annual conference in Louisville, Kentucky, to replace the 1957 code of ethics adopted at the 64th conference.

Some experts have suggested that one of the major obstacles to implementing COP is the police organization itself. As we have seen, the legalistic and watchman models of policing are firmly entrenched in traditional police department organizational hierarchies. Although changes in organizational and operational philosophy can occur in police organizations as they are currently structured, they are more likely to occur in less rigidly structured police department organizations.

BOX 2.1 The Law Enforcement Code of Ethics

All law enforcement officers must be fully aware of the ethical responsibilities of their position and must strive constantly to live up to the highest possible standards of professional policing. The International Association of Chiefs of Police believes it is important that police officers have clear advice and counsel available to assist them in performing their duties consistent with these standards, and has adopted the following ethical mandates as guidelines to meet these ends.

PRIMARY RESPONSIBILITIES OF A POLICE OFFICER

A police officer acts as an official representative of government who is required and trusted to work within the law. The officer's powers and duties are conferred by statute. The fundamental duties of a police officer include serving the community; safeguarding lives and property; protecting the innocent; keeping the peace; and ensuring the rights of all to liberty, equality and justice.

PERFORMANCE OF THE DUTIES OF A POLICE OFFICER

A police officer shall perform all duties impartially, without favor or affection or ill will and without regard to status, sex, race, religion, political belief or aspiration. All citizens will be treated equally with courtesy, consideration and dignity. Officers will never allow personal feelings, animosities or friendships to influence official conduct. Laws will be enforced appropriately and courteously and, in carrying out their responsibilities, officers will strive to obtain maximum cooperation from the public. They will conduct themselves in appearance and deportment in such a manner as to inspire confidence and respect for the position of public trust they hold.

DISCRETION

A police officer will use responsibly the discretion vested in the position and exercise it within the law. The principle of reasonableness will guide the officer's determinations and the officer will consider all surrounding circumstances in determining whether any legal action shall be taken. Consistent and wise use of discretion, based on professional policing competence, will do much to preserve good relationships and retain the confidence of the public. There can be difficulty in choosing between conflicting courses of action. It is important to remember that a timely word of advice rather than arrest—which may be correct in appropriate circumstances—can be a more effective means of achieving a desired end.

USE OF FORCE

A police officer will never employ unnecessary force or violence and will use only such force in the discharge of duty as is reasonable in all circumstances. Force should be used only with the greatest restraint and only after discussion, negotiation and persuasion have been found to be inappropriate or ineffective. While the use of force is occasionally unavoidable, every police officer will refrain from applying the unnecessary infliction of pain or suffering and will never engage in cruel, degrading or inhuman treatment of any person.

CONFIDENTIALITY

Whatever a police officer sees, hears or learns of, which is of a confidential nature, will be kept secret unless the performance of duty or legal provision requires otherwise. Members of the public have a right to security and privacy, and information obtained about them must not be improperly divulged.

INTEGRITY

A police officer will not engage in acts of corruption or bribery, nor will an officer condone such acts by other police officers. The public demands that the integrity of police officers be above reproach. Police officers must, therefore, avoid any conduct that might compromise integrity and thus undercut the public confidence in a law enforcement agency. Officers will refuse to accept any gifts, presents, subscriptions, favors, gratuities, or promises that could be interpreted as seeking to cause the officer to refrain from performing official responsibilities honestly and within the law. Police officers must not receive private or special advantage from their official status. Respect from the public cannot be bought; it can only be earned and cultivated.

COOPERATION WITH OTHER OFFICERS AND AGENCIES

Police officers will cooperate with all legally authorized agencies and their representatives in the pursuit of justice. An officer or agency may be one among many organizations that may provide law enforcement services to a jurisdiction. It is imperative that a police officer assist colleagues fully and completely with respect and consideration at all times.

PERSONAL/PROFESSIONAL CAPABILITIES

Police officers will be responsible for their own standard of professional performance and will take every reasonable opportunity to enhance and improve their level of knowledge and competence. Through study and experience, a police officer can acquire the high level of knowledge and competence that is essential for the efficient and effective performance of duty. The acquisition of knowledge is a never-ending process of personal and professional development that should be pursued constantly.

PRIVATE LIFE

Police officers will behave in a manner that does not bring discredit to their agencies or themselves. A police officer's character and conduct while off duty must always be exemplary, thus maintaining a position of respect in the community in which he or she lives and serves. The officer's personal behavior must be beyond reproach.

One important consideration is that this code is aspirational in nature. It is non-directed, as there are no enforcement or compliance mandates other than those provisions specified in individual departmental policy or codified in law. Another observation is that the code appears to be a standard of organizational design and directed toward departmental productivity and goals. The code is not directed toward the individual, nor does it allow for the foibles found in normal human beings. One can only speculate what occupation could live up to these standards.

Source: Adopted by the Executive Committee of the International Association of Chiefs of Police on October 17, 1989, during its 96th annual conference in Louisville, Kentucky.

ORGANIZATIONAL STRUCTURE

Most police departments are organized on the military model, although the size of the department also affects the way it is structured. For instance, small departments are less hierarchically based, and larger departments are more complex. Thus, it is not unusual for larger police departments to have special squads or task forces to combat community problems such as rising crime, delinquency, carjackings, and drive-by shootings. Because smaller departments frequently lack the resources and personnel for such specialization, officers have more generalized work assignments and perform more diverse functions compared with officers in larger departments. Traditional police organizational structure has persisted over a hundred years, and the view of many traditional law enforcement administrators is, "If it ain't broke, don't fix it." However, organizational behavior specialists have found the traditional military model to be outdated and greatly in need of either change or replacement. The military model, with its rigid organization and authoritarian management style, has increasingly been questioned as a viable model for modern policing (Tafoya, 1990:15).

Many organizational problems can be traced to the way in which different police departments are organized. It is likely that a sound organizational structure yields a more favorable work climate, which, in turn, yields more productive and satisfied workers. With respect to community-oriented policing, more satisfied and productive workers transfer their work enthusiasm and quality to those they serve, primarily community residents. Conversely, dissatisfied and less productive employees are less able to relate positively to their clients. Frequently, dissatisfaction with the work environment has negative consequences, even to the extent that the community is harmed in various ways. Organizational dysfunctions may produce greater work stresses, which can lead to abrasive police-citizen contacts, more technical infractions and disciplinary actions, larger numbers of lawsuits against officers for misconduct, adverse court decisions, and more frequent state and federal interventions. Generally, departmental productivity declines. In a sense, police employees mirror their organizations, in that job satisfaction is partially dependent on how individual officers perceive themselves within their organizations.

POLICE ORGANIZATION AND OPERATIONS

Bureaucracy is the vital ingredient that creates division of labor and coordinates human elements. Yet bureaucracy is often seen as the single greatest enemy of efficiency and organizational effectiveness. By its very nature, bureaucracy demands and emphasizes a hierarchy of authority or chain of command.

Evidence of bureaucracy is apparent in early police department organization. Turn-of-the-century police managers placed great emphasis on internal control and accountability because most early law enforcement officers were untrained, underpaid, and susceptible to corruption. Administrative efforts toward establishing accountability and control created organizational subunits and work environments that greatly inhibited personal discretion and lower-echelon decision making. As a means of achieving the organizational goals of accountability and control, the military model served traditional police organizations well. It created a disciplinary structure within which ordinary people could be hired for an exacting job and be trained, equipped, and motivated to function effectively. It also provided the means for controlling employee behavior. During social protests, this model was useful for coordinating large numbers of officers in operations such as crowd control, riot suppression, labor strike handling, and investigative searches. Some historians have suggested that bureaucracy actually enhanced the general stature of police over the years by presenting an image of discipline, skill, and service.

According to other experts, however, blind reliance on the military model indirectly downgraded the position of the primary figure in police service: the individual officer (Meese, 1993:3). One result was that most police organizations acquired certain negative images that progressive police managers are now attempting to overcome.

> **BOX 2.2 The Magnitude of Policing in the United States**
>
> In 1990 there were 16,961 agencies in the United States with policing functions, including 12,288 local police agencies, 3,093 sheriff departments, 1,531 special police agencies, and 49 state police agencies. Combined, these agencies employed 793,020 full-time employees and 76,044 part-time employees (Bureau of Justice Statistics, 1992:2). These organizations had operating expenditures for the 1990 fiscal year of more than $64 billion (actual: $64,918,198,000) (Bureau of Justice Statistics, 1993:8). These figures reflect only operating costs; they do not include capital outlays, such as equipment purchases or construction expenses.
>
> The largest U.S. police department is the New York City Police Department, which employs 33,363 full-time personnel, of whom 25,655 are sworn officers (Bureau of Justice Statistics, 1992:2). Local police departments serving jurisdictions with populations of one million or more employed about 20 percent of all local police officers. Departments serving jurisdictions with 100,000 or more residents employed half of all sworn peace officers. Most police departments in the United States are relatively small. In 1990, about 91 percent of all departments employed fewer than 50 officers, and about half of all local police agencies employed fewer than 10 officers. Most sheriff departments are also small. Nearly two-thirds employed fewer than 25 sworn deputies, and a third employed fewer than 10 deputies. Approximately half of the sheriff departments served jurisdictions with populations of less than 25,000 (Bureau of Justice Statistics, 1992:2).

Because early administrators were political appointees not necessarily qualified for their jobs, they were not totally accepted by the officers they commanded. Many early police departments were staffed by individuals whose character, integrity, and leadership credentials were suspect. Graft, corruption, and brutality were characteristic of early American policing. Over the years politicians and reformers demanded a higher level of accountability, causing police organizations to fall into a rather rigid hierarchy. This mode aggravated the superior-subordinate modes of managers at all levels who were directed to maintain control and accountability. One by-product of this superior-subordinate arrangement was the "watch your back" syndrome, which generated volumes of regulations, standard operating procedures, guidelines, and other memoranda. In the 1990s many departments are still mired in counterproductive procedures designed to produce a sense of conformity, accountability, and control.

The professionals in contemporary organizations are more likely to have extensive and continuing professional training, a shared understanding of and commitment to extensive lateral communication, and an absence of elaborate and complex hierarchies (Meese, 1993:3). "Enlightened" managers are now urged to build a more equitable environment for front-line workers. Participative management has become popular and incorporates concepts such as quality control, total quality management, and management by objectives. Police managers are advised to "manage by walking around"—see what is going on in the workplace—and to compliment workers on their efforts. Team building is the by-word of success.

But resistance to change still exists, as many police executives continue to rely on outdated and destructive methods of supervision and direction, which ultimately hurt the relationship between police and their communities. There are no quick fixes to complex organizational problems, despite the advice in "one-minute management" bestsellers. The primary change should be in construction and design, to promote greater employee and citizen participation.

The Military Syndrome

Military protocol—the trappings of quasi-military law enforcement organizations—is seen as a major obstacle to developing more productive and responsive units (Cordner and Hale, 1992; Gray, Stohr-Gillmore, and Lovrich, 1991). Police organizations are broken into divisions, bureaus, sections, watches, and squads. Territorial units, depending on size, are referred to as beats, sectors, posts, routes, districts, or areas. Almost every police department uses titles, uniforms, and regalia borrowed from the military. Pomp and circumstance fill ceremonies, and individual achievements are often recognized with Commendation Medals, Medals of Valor, Purple Hearts and the like. An assortment of militaristic patches, insignia, and chevrons are used to designate special assignments, seniority, and rank: Police chiefs wear three or four stars, designating the rank of general, on their uniforms; commanders wear one star (for brigadier general ranking); and subordinate ranks are given titles such as colonel, major, captain, lieutenant, sergeant, and two-stripe corporals. The lowest rank (without insignia) consists of police officers or deputies (the military equivalent of a private). Stations or divisions have commanding officers, who, in turn, have their adjutants.

Ironically, most police chiefs in the United States started out in patrol, completed their respective academies, and rose through the ranks to chief, whereas it would be difficult to find a single officer in the United States Air Force, Army, or Navy who initially served as an enlisted person. Since the Korean War, the military has developed two separate and distinct recruitment sources: Officers are typically selected from among university and college graduates, whereas enlisted positions are usually filled with personnel who lack higher academic degrees or who did not meet officer-level expectations or criteria. Both military personnel

The military model is used by most large police departments as a means of organizing personnel. *(Owen Franken/Stock, Boston)*

and the quasi-military police make a distinction between themselves and civilians, however, creating a "we versus they" mentality. It is not uncommon for law enforcement officers to refer to community residents as civilians and to distinguish uniform attire from "civvies" or "civilian clothing or attire." This military protocol highlights significant differences between the police and the public, often amounting to a barrier.

An important difference between public policing and the military is in the sense of mission. The military mission is to neutralize or destroy the enemy. The explicit purpose of each branch of the service, in cooperation, is offensive action, and after periods of successful combat, the military perform occupational duties. During periods of war, military personnel seldom have the luxury of returning to "safe zones" after eight-hour shifts. The Korean War, the Vietnam War, and Operation Desert Storm are examples of 24-hour-a-day involvement. Urban police, on the other hand, are not subjected to the intensity of battlefield conditions. In the normal course of duty, they are not under protracted or intermittent attack by rocket fire, artillery rounds, concentrated machine-gun bursts, or assaults by tanks, aircraft, and other modern warfare matériel.

Another difference is that the military model assumes a military ideal that most contemporary law enforcement officers know about only indirectly, because they have not performed military service. Since the mid-1970s, the United States has not participated in a war. After the Korean and Vietnam wars, many service persons entered careers in law enforcement, but in the 1990s, these officers are approaching retirement. Those who have never seen military action can only imagine what the military ideal might be, because they experienced it only briefly in police academies. They relate their perceived (and limited) military concept to the reality of their law enforcement organizations and try to adapt their behavior and attitudes to some illusive ideal. This thinking can have dire consequences, because what officers think is expected of them under the military model may not lead them to choose wise courses of action in dealing with the public on city streets.

Many urban law enforcement agencies are more "military" than are actual military forces. Furthermore, many police managers rely heavily on negative reinforcements to motivate subordinates. Professors Mark Moore (1992) and Darrel Stephens (1987) suggest that this type of police department management inhibits the broad changes police departments must make in order to fulfill community expectations (Moore and Stephens, 1991). They suggest establishing a police management approach that moves away from traditional military command and toward a structure fostering change and innovation. These experts, and others, have outlined the crucial elements of this management philosophy, for which they have drawn heavily from private-sector business strategies.

If the police and the public are to work in partnership, antiquated military labels should be replaced or softened with contemporary management terminology and causes of action. Whatever titles police use and uniforms they wear, however, if the approach and attitudes of law enforcement officers do not reflect a commitment to community values, counterproductive practices will continue. If police officers and their leadership persist in perpetuating their similarities to military organization, viewing themselves as soldiers "at war" with society, little progress will be made, and community policing will be only a dream.

Attaboys and Aw Shits

The military mentality can be seen in the rewards and disciplinary procedures found in most law enforcement agencies. Employee reinforcements generally fall into two categories: positive and negative. In your own mind, take a test. We have listed eighteen **negative reinforcements** that could be given to a law enforcement officer who has just made a single error of judgment. You determine whether the infraction is major or minor. Your test is to write in all the "good things" or **positive reinforcements** officers could receive if they performed one outstanding feat or accomplishment.

BOX 2.3 Organizational Ideals and the Reality of the "Beat"

It is one thing to endorse a particular organizational hierarchy and quite another to carry out those roles according to the rules. In 1991, in the aftermath of the Rodney King beating by Los Angeles Police Department (LAPD) officers, other LAPD officers had to go back out on the streets and perform their duties. Commanders admonished their subordinates to "go out and do your job." But many officers were apprehensive about facing the public, afraid to turn corners because they didn't know whether they would be greeted by jeering mobs, video camera monitors, or thumbs-up support. One officer said a few days after the King incident, "We feel a little picked on. Everybody's treating us like an *occupying army* [italics ours]."

"Even little kids cried at the sight of men in uniform," said another officer.

LAPD Chief Daryl F. Gates, in a public television appearance the day following the rioting in South Central Los Angeles, announced, "I'm coming back." This statement was intended to assure people of continued police presence in their neighborhoods. At the same time, it was a warning to his police officers that they would be expected to take their places on the city streets and enforce the law.

Comments from citizens reinforce police officers' impressions of public sentiment. One citizen said, "The police have a mentality that all blacks must have a jail number." Waving a bag at a police officer on horseback, he added, "This bag contains my hair and the clothes police ripped off me when I was stopped as a bank robbery suspect a few years ago." The citizen was exonerated later, but not before he had suffered physical abuse at the hands of police who had the wrong man.

In contrast, a woman and her children waved at the same officer on horseback. Such mixed messages disconcert many officers. "We like to think we're needed and respected in the neighborhood," one officer said. "I wish there was more closeness between us and them."

As community-oriented policing becomes a greater part of police operations and procedures, this closeness is expected to grow. However, ugly scenes generated by acknowledged police brutality and excessive use of force do much to counter efforts by community leaders to foster trust in police departments and their officers.

Source: Leslie Berger and Paul Lieberman, "Police on Beat—Tense Job Gets Tenser." *Los Angeles Times*, April 8, 1991:B1.

Negative	**Positive**

1. Dismissal from the department*
2. Criminal charges
3. Civil charges
4. Verbal reprimand
5. Letter of reprimand
6. Probation
7. Demotion in rank*
8. Less than satisfactory evaluation
9. Loss of promotional opportunity*
10. Bad press (media)
11. Peer judgment
12. Transfer from a preferred assignment*
13. Suspension with pay
14. Monetary fine or suspension without pay*
15. Shift or assignment change
16. Remedial training
17. Forfeiture of vacation*
18. Extra duty*

If you were unable to supply eighteen positive reinforcements, how many did you actually record? If you listed seven positive reinforcements, the agency (or your point of reference) might tend to rely on what McGregor (1955) called the Theory X authoritarian style of management instead of the Theory Y participatory models. McGregor posited that under Theory X, workers are basically unmotivated, lazy, and in need of constant supervision and goading from supervisors to perform their work satisfactorily. An authoritative supervisory style is required to motivate these workers to perform their jobs. Under Theory Y, however, workers are credited with integrity, self-motivation, and a work ethic requiring minimal supervision. Supervisors tend to involve these workers rather than order them to perform with force or coercion. Among U.S. police agencies, a pressing, frequent question is, How many "attaboys" (positive reinforcements) does it take to negate one "aw shit" (a negative reinforcement)? There seems to be no magical formula. For some rank-and-file officers, one "aw shit" jeopardizes an officer's entire career.

Many police department executives still use outdated models, theories, and principles of management to operate their organizations. Some managers still feel that "if you want size 13 work, you need a size 13 boot." Some even open and

---

*Items derived from *Local Government Police Management*, 3rd Ed., International City Management Association, 1991:265).

inspect all incoming department mail. These managers contend that blind obedience and lockstep compliance are valuable traits in new recruits.

Under a military style of management, organizational stress factors can be high and productivity low. Many patrolmen are more "stressed out" when called to the station to report to their sergeant than when responding to a 911 or a call-for-service. Unfortunately, some supervisors have an attitude that their subordinates should and will "do a good job" because "it is their job" or is expected. Of course, this expectation is unrealistic. The management literature is replete with support for the view that positive strokes must be given to every member at all levels of an organization. Everyone needs recognition. If recognition is not forthcoming, it is sometimes sought by subterfuge. For example, during the 1984 Summer Olympic Games in Los Angeles, a police officer discovered a bomb in the wheel well of a bus transporting Turkish athletes. Upon investigation, however, it was determined that he had placed the device there himself and had subsequently "discovered" it. Why would he do this? "He felt he has not been getting recognition at Metro, and he just wanted his sergeant to recognize his good work" (Gates and Shah, 1992:253–254).

Although this example is extreme, similar stories and events abound. If individuals are not afforded status or recognition, according to Abraham Maslow (1956), certain psychogenic conflicts might be manifested in unconventional ways. These events are sought by the media, which significantly shapes public opinion. Thus, how the community perceives policing is often determined by media characterizations of the police to the public. Isolated events involving the police are often equated with collective police officer actions. Positive reinforcements in police work acquire exaggerated importance because they are rare.

Productivity

No single set of criteria can be used to measure how well the police are performing their jobs. This is because it is difficult to identify the nature of the police mission and what it is the police are supposed to do. There is no product. Justice is an abstraction, and crime rates and crime indices are of little value. If crime rates or the indices of crime were to be used as the measure of the ability of urban police to control criminal conduct, we could only conclude that police officers are failing to do their jobs. Over the years the crime index and crime rate have fluctuated greatly. Some crime information sources show crime increases; other sources show decreases in crime for the same time interval. Often these sources differ in the way information about crime is compiled and counted. Close scrutiny of arrest and clearance rates causes us to view the work of police officers with suspicion, since criminal convictions are the responsibility of district attorneys. Although police *arrest* suspects, prosecutors decide whether to *prosecute* them; therefore, clearance rates are deceptive. The number of civil suits filed against the police and monetary sums awarded resulting from these suits are difficult to interpret, as settlements are often less expensive options than going through protracted litigation and trials. In this highly litigious society, almost every chief of police or sheriff has been the target of numerous lawsuits. This does not mean that they are necessarily justified.

Traditional methods of evaluating police **productivity** include response time, or how rapidly police officers can respond to a location; numbers of arrests or citations; 911 emergency calls; and the sheer numbers of other calls-for-service. Over time, the general public has expected immediate police response to calls, regardless of their gravity. The public orientation towards community-oriented policing has resulted in the reassessment of the delivery of service (Greiner, 1986; McEvoy, 1987).

Changing Calls-for-Service

In times of increasingly scarce resources, the quality of police services rendered to the public, including 911 calls, has drawn substantial criticisms from diverse segments of the community. In the early 1980s the National Institute of Justice designed and implemented a series of Differential Police Response (DPR) experiments to determine if public expectations of police service could be modified or changed. The DPR research tested public reaction to a wide range of alternative response strategies for **calls-for-service,** such as nonemergency calls, walk-in and mail-in reporting, telephone report units, officer response delays of up to half an hour, and officer response by appointment. In Garden Grove, California; Greensboro, North Carolina; and Toledo, Ohio, police dispatchers were carefully trained regarding how to prioritize their calls and, where appropriate, how to inform callers about their new response alternatives. Administrative mechanisms were developed in each department to ensure that what dispatchers promised—for example, to have an officer arrive at a particular time to respond to a complaint and make a report—was actually delivered. The results were striking. More than 90 percent of all callers in the three cities who received the alternative responses appeared satisfied with them (McEwen, 1984:17).

Increasingly, police executives are implementing call management and differential response as part of a shift to new community and problem-solving policing strategies, together with the intent of substantially reshaping patrol and patrol-related operations (Kennedy, 1993:3).

In establishing a community policing program, the Reno (Nevada) Police Department has divided its patrol force into special projects and mobile response on a day-to-day basis. Call management is handled through the dispatching center, which provides callers with a variety of service options for nonemergency calls. Because mobile response is currently handled by about half as many officers as were used before community policing department operations were implemented, dispatching cars to low-priority scenes may take up to several hours. But with careful departmental attention paid to explaining the program to the people of Reno, citizen satisfaction, tracked by formal polling, has remained relatively high (Kennedy, 1993:3). These modifications to traditional deployment policies and policing practices have enhanced police productivity in terms of time and monetary savings while maintaining a high level of customer satisfaction.

There are certain measurable internal variables that can indicate the productivity of a police organization—variables based on employee attitudes toward the organization. There is much truth in the axiom that satisfied workers tend to produce at higher levels (Steinman, 1986). In terms of productivity, the reduction of sick time, overtime, employee turnover rates, equipment abuse, disciplinary actions, and citizen complaints generally tend to reflect a healthy organization. Conversely, unfavorable marks in these areas might be sufficient to warrant concern and remedial action.

ALTERNATIVE ORGANIZATIONAL MODELS

To provide quality police service and achieve higher productivity through motivated, dedicated, and cooperative employees, the organizational setting must be conducive to achieving those goals (Finn and McGillis, 1990; Layne, 1990). Several federal law enforcement agencies have shifted their organizational operations and rank structure away from the military model (Meese, 1993:3), and many police agencies are also attempting to bring their employees into the nonmilitary organizational mainstream. Workers at all levels within community-oriented policing organizations are being encouraged to make suggestions and recommendations and be creative in their approach to tasks. In many instances the first steps progressive agencies have taken are to provide (by consensus) the following:

1. A concise statement about the mission and goals of the enforcement agency
2. An organizational value statement developed, shared, and supported by each organizational member
3. A commitment by the highest level in municipal government to support the goals and mission of the enforcement agency

One alternative organizational model that has replaced more traditional models involves reducing "tall" organizational structures to "flat" ones (with fewer supervisory levels and broader spans of control, that is, more people supervised by fewer supervisors).

Generally, alternative models emphasize enhancing communication flow, information sharing, and participative decision making. Traditional organizational models do not necessarily have to be totally discarded in favor of different models. One key to effective modification is attitude. If employees have poor work-related attitudes, it makes little difference which type of organizational structure exists. Thus, proactive police executives strive to organize their administrations and modify their actions in ways that will increase employee satisfaction and productivity. However, "making the transition from a traditional reactive, incident-driven policing style to a more contemporary proactive, problem-driven style of community-oriented policing requires a comprehensive strategy that is based on long-term institutional change (U.S. National Advisory Commission on Law Enforcement, 1990).

Total Quality Management

Long-term institutional change must be focused, committed, and supported. In exploring the reasons for the global marketing prowess of the Japanese, many American private-sector executives were surprised to find that the strategy behind Japan's market domination had American roots. In 1931 W.A. Shewhart's book *Economic Control of Quality of Manufactured Product* described the application of the concepts of **total quality management (TQM).** In 1942 the U.S. Army established a Quality Control Section, which was succeeded in 1945 by the U.S. Civil Communications Section. This section introduced quality improvement in occupied Japan, and in 1950 Dr. Romaine Deming, an American quality management expert, presented numerous lectures on this subject to Japanese businessmen. By the 1970s Japan was beginning to dominate the international marketplace. Then in the 1980s, Ford and other U.S. manufacturers, suffering from declining markets, responded to this global competition by studying and ultimately embracing the TQM concepts.

The discussion of this particular management concept in a textbook about community policing is easily explained: Community policing and TQM are nearly synonymous. Eight principal practices of TQM are:

1. Focus on the customer
2. Effective communication
3. Reliance on standards and measures
4. Commitment to training
5. Top management support and direction
6. Employee involvement
7. Reward and recognition
8. A long-term commitment

Organizational Goals, Values, and Mission Statements

Many of those seeking change at various levels of public service have eventually realized that most police agencies have operated for many years without clear statements about their organizational goals, values, or overall mission. To provide a focus and foundation for organizational change directed toward communities, the process must be clearly defined. The Hawthorne (California) Police Department (HPD), for example, has listed its department goals as follows:

1. Improve the internal structure of HPD
2. Improve communications
3. Improve reward and recognition system
4. Reduce crime
5. Establish strong community outreach
6. Get a better understanding of the use of teams
7. Get a better understanding of community
8. Improve the promotion process

The department also provided a mission statement: "The mission of the Hawthorne Police Department is to provide a safe and secure community for its citizens while at the same time promoting a high degree of professionalism and respect for human dignity."

The following organizational values statement, in the form of a memorandum, was adopted by the city of Sanger, California, under the direction of city manager Oliver "Lee" Drummond. Interestingly, Drummond had served as chief of police and played a major role in the selection of the new police chief. This statement is not an isolated document but representative of any city, subunit, or other public-oriented agency. But in the context of community policing, the implications are enormous.

Organizational Values

Integrity

The core of our public service.
Responsible for our actions.
Willing to admit mistakes.
Ensuring our behavior builds credibility.

Openness and Sensitivity

The qualities we bring to our interactions with the public.
Responsive to our customers in a caring, helpful, and understanding manner.

Professionalism and Competency

Elements in which we carry out our work.
Clear sense of commitment, perspective.
Direction in serving the community.

Accountability and Responsibility

The fabric of the organization.
Using good judgment in taking calculated risks.
Learning from our experiences.

Encouragement and Recognition

Instill self-pride in the work force.

Demonstrating independence, action, and initiative.

Recognition that our success as an organization is realized through team effort.

Vitality

Spirit behind all our efforts.

Active, intuitive, and curious.

Approaching our work with a sense of enjoyment and excitement.

The importance of organizational values statements such as the preceding cannot be overemphasized. These statements are the heart and soul of most organizations, and they are the driving spirit behind collective endeavors. The following set of values was adopted by the Los Angeles County Sheriff's Department in January 1992:

Our Core Values

We shall be service oriented and perform our duties with the highest possible degree of personal and professional integrity.

Service Oriented Policing means:

*Protecting life and property

*Preventing crime

*Apprehending criminals

*Always acting lawfully

*Being fair and impartial and treating people with dignity

*Assisting the community and its citizens in solving problems and maintaining the peace

We shall treat every member of the Department . . . both sworn and civilian, as we would expect to be treated if the positions were reversed.

We shall not knowingly break the law to enforce the law.

We shall be fully accountable for our own actions or failures and, when appropriate, for the actions or failures of our subordinates.

In considering the use of deadly force, we shall be guided by reverence for human life.

Individuals promoted or selected for special assignments shall have a history of practicing these values.

EMPOWERMENT AND DECISION MAKING

A key element in a participatory environment in which employees can make constructive contributions is **empowerment.** Empowerment is the essence of both organizational mission and values statements. Empowerment gives employees the latitude to perform at their highest levels. Police organizational structures should be revised to decrease the levels of authority, particularly at the bottom of the hierarchy. Community policing envisions the empowerment of officers to take independent action to solve problems, work with community leaders, and improve the social environment of the neighborhoods they serve. Such a vision, however, is a far cry from the experience of most officers today (McEvoy, 1987; Meese, 1993:4; Tunnell and Gaines, 1992).

Over the years, supervisors have assumed the responsibilities and tasks of making the majority of decisions throughout the organization and at all levels (Gilsinan, 1990). Herman Goldstein (1990:27) has noted that "the dominant form of policing today continues to view police officers as automatons. Despite an awareness that they exercise broad discretion, they are held to strict account in their daily work—for what they do and how they do it . . . especially in procedural matters, they are required to adhere to detailed regulations." In large police agencies, rank-and-file police officers are often treated impersonally and prevented from participating in policy matters or discussions about them. Under these conditions, many officers quickly learn that the rewards go to those who conform to expectations, that is, that unquestioned compliance is valued. Because of the CYA (cover your ass) syndrome, very few decisions are made by police officers at the street level, and those decisions are generally routine. Such decisions might include when to issue a warning or citation, when to arrest, or when to complete a field interrogation. Ordinarily, routine decisions are not subject to review by superiors (Chen, 1990).

Many police officers resist making decisions that might be second-guessed by their supervisors (Gilsinan and Valentine, 1987). Thus, the first step toward true organizational change is to allow the widest possible latitude or trust in permitting—empowering—lower-level officers to make decisions. If law enforcement agencies want to have quality personnel selection, provide initial and continuing professional training, and offer reliable equipment, then it must be assumed that officers possess the ability to make sound, good-faith decisions (Greiner, 1986; Levine, 1986; Steinman, 1986).

Although it may seem odd, many veteran police officers are threatened by this decision-making capacity; they simply don't trust the system. As employees, they believe that trust is a commodity that must be earned and distributed equally. Like organizations, trust evolves; it is not created overnight and it is not immediately accepted.

PARTICIPATORY MANAGEMENT

Since the early 1970s, proactive U.S. police executives have been strongly influenced by private-sector business and industrial firms (Gray, Stohr-Gillmore, and Lovrich, 1991). They have followed the example of participatory management offered by many for-profit organizations (Hickman, 1990; Witte, Travis, and Langworthy, 1990). For instance, the Newport News (Virginia) Police Department employed a variety of task forces and committees to implement its problem-oriented policing project. A management committee, composed of bureau leaders and unit commanders, participated in all major patrol decisions. An operations advisory committee, composed of patrol officers and detectives, met regularly with the chief of police to discuss their mutual concerns. These subgroups dealt with many issues, from policy formulation and deployment to shift scheduling and equipment purchases (Eck and Spelman, 1987).

Quality Circles

In general terms, **quality circles (QC)** are an application of TQM (Hatry and Greiner, 1984). Through incentive programs, this approach encourages similarly classified workers (e.g., dispatchers, detectives, or patrol) to interact in group settings to resolve problems common to their work specialties. Acting as a team, these personnel can often offer recommendations that lead to savings in labor and time, enhanced service, or improved working conditions. QC has been viewed as a management tool to improve efficiency, and in the long-term, QC strengthens teams working together for common interests. Citizen satisfaction is also improved by those providing specialized services at the different levels within enforcement organizations.

Planning

Many police departments, especially smaller agencies, operate in either a crisis management or day-to-day mode (Hesketh, 1992). Until the 1980s and 1990s, few future-directed departments considered forecasting and incorporating demographic trends into their long-range **planning** (Enter, 1991). Then some began to analyze census data and other sources of demographic information.

Consider the implications of the following example. An independent study released in October 1992 projected that the population of California (then at 29.8 million) would increase to 36 million by the year 2000. The study estimated that the number of adults in the 18–34 age group would decline and that the school-age population would increase by 1.5 million between 2000–2010 (a gain of 31 percent). Those figures equate to about 160,000 new or entering students a year. The number of adults age 35–47 would rise by about 41 percent, according to the study. This increase in the 35–47 age group is projected to affect the state's economy, because many of these individuals would then be at their peak earning years (assuming a reasonably stable economy) (Enter, 1991). The report further found immigration to be the primary reason for the state's rising population and projected that by the year 2000, half of the state's population would be African American, Latino, and Asian. (In 1990, about 42 percent of the California population [12.7 million] were Latino, Asian, and African American.) This growth rate was double the rate projected for the rest of the United States (*Long Beach Press Telegram*, Sept. 23, 1992).

> **BOX 2.4 Mayor Bud Clark of Portland, Oregon**
>
> When he took office in 1985, Mayor Bud Clark of Portland, Oregon, was a community policing enthusiast. One of Clark's aides, Chuck Duffy, said, "Community-oriented policing means less relying on heavy-handed law enforcement and more getting at root causes. But we recognize the fact that you can't do it well unless you have an adequate level of police officers, because you've got to do the community outreach stuff with police on top of your base of patrol officers, and we were having trouble with our base."
>
> For many police departments, community-oriented policing means taking on difficult new responsibilities, like fighting fear and solving community problems, and using fresh tactics, like foot patrols and community organizing. Foot patrols have been used increasingly in cities such as Portland and Clark is optimistic that foot patrols will continue to counter criminal activities.
>
> Under the Violent Crime Control and Law Enforcement Act of 1994, substantial sums of money have been allocated to police departments nationally to increase their experiments with various types of patrols, including foot patrols.
>
> Police give up something when they enter into partnerships with community agencies, because they see community safety as their province and theirs alone. But they actually gain more than they lose when public safety becomes a joint police, community, and municipal responsibility. For instance, in Houston citizens became involved in helping to clean up drug activity in particular neighborhoods. Hundreds of volunteers conducted deed and title searches and induced landlords and property owners to comply with city codes and ordinances. Often, this activity forced drug dealers from the premises and eventually out of the city.
>
> New approaches to solving community crime require a dialogue about police resources and their allocation. Discussions with community residents and what they want can be extremely productive. Traditional police work is giving way to innovative and fruitful police-community coalitions and actions to decrease crime and increase public safety.
>
> *Source:* David M. Kennedy, *The Strategic Management of Police Resources.* Washington, DC: U.S. Department of Justice, Office of Justice Programs, Perspectives on Policing. 1993:1, 5–7.

This report would have significant importance for city planning and, if projections prove accurate, would have an impact on all service areas of the affected municipalities, especially on the police. Some of the plans a police department might make to cope with such demographic change include:

- Organization-wide cultural awareness training
- Bilingual dispatchers
- Bicultural and bilingual recruitment and training
- Increased juvenile bureau staffing
- Additional school resource officers
- Drug awareness programs
- Delinquency prevention programs
- Participation in community youth activities and programs

Census Tracts and Crime Reporting

To ensure equity among county, state, and federal revenue sharing, most municipalities critically assess the decennial and special census reporting data. It is extremely important for cities to take account of population increases, especially when taxation revenues are apportioned to municipalities according to the population. To exploit this census data, some police departments have realigned their reporting districts (RDs) to reflect the boundaries of their census tracts (Crank, 1990; Tremblay and Rochon, 1991). In many cases the realignment is merely a token gesture to capture relevant data. It is not suggested here that beats or RDs should be altered to coincide geographically with census boundaries. Rather, the data available through censuses, coupled with local crime statistics, tend to promote crime-reduction assignments, assist in short-range planning, and provide helpful information in long-range planning regarding aggregate and juvenile populations, migration trends, and housing (Manning, 1992).

Coordination with Other City Agencies and Departments

City and county governing bodies should coordinate all planning efforts with their respective enforcement agencies (Dane, 1989). Unfortunately, this is not the case in some jurisdictions. Parks have been built without public safety input, and some have been found to lack emergency vehicle access. Shopping centers have been erected with little or no regard to traffic flow or emergency evacuation procedures. Police and sheriff buildings have been constructed without significant police input. City planning units and police planners or forecasters often do not communicate with one another, which results in a duplication of effort or an absence of research in critical areas. Cities and municipalities that support community-oriented policing and that create intergovernmental planning units are likely to include forecasters from law enforcement in their planning. Such collaborative effort can result in cost savings, liability reduction, community involvement, and better-conceived plans (Crank, 1990; Moore and Stephens, 1991).

POLITICAL CONSIDERATIONS

Several political considerations influence the viability of police-community relations, community policing, and community-oriented programs (Hunt and Magenau, 1993). Some observers argue that cities "get the kind of policing they pay for," whereas others say that policing reflects the current political climate, conservative or liberal. Few disagree, however, that policing is an expensive proposition (Hickman, 1990; Klockars, 1989; More, 1992). During times of economic belt-tightening, programs and personnel are main targets (Manning, 1992). Police programs that might be considered outreach in nature are likely to be abandoned first. Activities not directly related to crime control and the apprehension of offenders are in constant jeopardy.

As local politicians orchestrate city budgets, police unions and associations are quick to note the pro-policing sentiments of political candidates. Highly political police unions and associations play important roles in supporting candidates supportive of their causes. For example, during the 1993 Los Angeles mayoral race, the Police Protective League of the Los Angeles Police Department endorsed Richard Riordan (Newton, 1993:A15). Riordan, a relatively unknown candidate, won the mayor's race.

Overlapping jurisdictions often make it necessary for law enforcement agencies to work cooperatively in solving crimes. *(Mark Richards)*

Immediately following the election, Mayor Riordan appointed William C. Violante deputy mayor. Coincidentally, Violante was the president of the politically supportive Police Protective League (Newton, 1993:A30). Over the years, police unions and associations across the nation have contributed heavily to political candidates in quid pro quo arrangements. In the case of Los Angeles, the former police league president, who also represents labor interests, is now empowered to advise the chief of police. The new mayor also replaced the five members of the Police Commission (Newton, 1993:A30).

Subsequently, Chief of Police Willie Williams stated that the LAPD did not have the resources to add 3,000 personnel to the police department. Williams indicated the department could train 600 to 650 officers per year, which means the LAPD could hire and train about 2,300 officers in four years (the duration of the mayor's term). But since the department loses about 300 officers a year by attrition, that projected hiring and training increase would result in a force of about 8,800 by the end of Riordan's term (Newton, 1993:A15). In response to the call for 3,000 additional officers, a retired LAPD assistant chief said the costs of adding 750 new police officers per year would be staggering, citing LAPD figures that set training costs at $95,000 per recruit. Thus, additional training costs annually would be in excess of $71 million. A police officer's annual salary and benefit package totals approximately $78,000. Therefore, the first 750 officers, once in the field, would cost $58.5 million annually to maintain. Assuming all 3,000 officers reached the field, this maintenance figure would be $234 million. The initial cost of equipping the field officers would also be substantial—$12 million for motor vehicles alone—and replacement costs would be approximately $3 million annually. The price of other equipment and support services would be millions of dollars. These were formidable figures, especially as the city had experienced a $23 million budget shortfall in 1992 (Dotson, 1993:M6).

The issue of attrition was reported in a *Los Angeles Times* article (Newton, 1996:A24), which suggested that a key question was how to keep experienced officers in the LAPD in the face of low morale and disparate wages.

Political promises and the realities of governmental and financial capabilities are sometimes at odds. The community, however, is not necessarily aware of such clashes between promises and reality and may have unattainable expectations (Reiss, 1992). Theoretically, political and budget considerations should not affect community policing, but one would have to be incredibly naive to ignore these factors. The morale of officers who feel underpaid, unappreciated, and underutilized will be affected, and morale is directly connected to productivity.

Economics and Contracting

The main reason many cities explore contracting out their policing functions to other agencies (generally sheriff's departments) is economics. In recessionary periods, cities examine many economizing options, and the policing function is not

BOX 2.5   LAPD Attrition

LAPD resignations have increased markedly during the last 10 years, hampering efforts to expand the department. Officers cite a variety of reasons, including that they are underpaid and that their department lacks leadership. In evaluating results of a 1995 LAPD poll, department officials emphasized that unhappiness about pay ranked first among all reasons employees gave for considering leaving. But the mayor's office noted that officers cited various complaints about the department's overall leadership, command support, and low morale.

Year	Recruits* Leaving	Officers Leaving	Total** Leaving
1985	15	63	243
1986	12	65	282
1987	43	55	270
1988	45	86	365
1989	51	97	403
1990	45	105	402
1991	15	109	415
1992	7	92	464
1993	11	96	436
1994	44	147	479

*Regular resignations are considered to be officers who leave with less than 10 years on the job. Recruit resignations are those of recruits still in the Police Academy.

**Yearly attrition totals include retirements, which form the largest single category, as well as dismissals, disabilities, and deaths.

Reasons given for leaving (on attrition survey):

- Pay: 41%
- Lack of top command support: 18%
- Inadequate or outdated equipment: 13%
- Lack of leadership or direction: 10%
- Low morale: 8%

Note: Totals add up to more than 100% because some employees have given more than one reason for leaving.

Source: Los Angeles Police Department, *Los Angeles Times,* January 21, 1996:A24.

immune from scrutiny. Simply stated, the police are in a competitive marketing situation. If local municipal agencies cannot provide quality service, then municipalities may shop elsewhere. This alternative is called **contract law enforcement.** Many sheriff's departments are heavily involved in contracting with police departments.

It is not the purpose of this section to revive the historic arguments regarding contract policing versus cities operating their own police departments, but the major argument against contract law enforcement has to do with control and accountability. Cities that endorse home rule wish to maintain a sense of independence by funding their own police department. The latent reason is that a city government can control a municipal police department more effectively than it can a contract law enforcement agency. City councils have the power to hire and fire police chiefs but not county sheriffs. Once the city has budgeted money for the agreed-on level of services from the county sheriff's department, the sheriff's department operates at a comfortable distance from local politics. Although it is true that the sheriff's contract may not be renewed, the costs of reestablishing a city-operated police department are prohibitive.

Cities exercise considerable **control** over their police departments through such methods as (1) budget manipulation, (2) political intervention, (3) executive selection, and (4) oversight commissions or boards. Usually, under contract law enforcement, none of these control considerations exists, and only through mutual agreement are service-oriented interests addressed. Contractors, if committed to client satisfaction, however, will endeavor to address limited "outside-of-contract" tasks. *Limited* is a key word, as contracts usually specify the level of service at predetermined rates; extra services would be subject to additional charges. Therefore, in contract law enforcement situations, the long-term provisions of the contract and the style of policing should be clearly delineated. Some jurisdictions opting for contract law enforcement have absorbed their personnel into roles within the contracting agency, at higher wages and benefits. In some instances, regardless of the level of service and commitment to community-oriented policing, scarce revenues will dictate alternative policing modes. Communities in dire financial straits that opt for contract arrangements with sheriff's departments must specify their commitment to community-oriented policing in their contractual arrangement.

Budgets

A definition for **budget** is a plan for accomplishing programs related to objectives and goals within a definite time period including an estimate of resources required together with an estimate of resources available, usually compared with past periods and showing future requirements (Ortega et al., 1989; Rich and Cahn, 1984). Probably the oldest and most common device for control within a society is funding. Budgets serve to provide planning and coordination within and among subunits, although budgets are also a device used to exercise control. If a nonmandated section, unit, or branch of a publicly funded agency does not conform to the contractor's expectations or does not toe the line of those in control (e.g., elected officials), the agency's supporting funds may be withdrawn or limited to discipline the recalcitrant section or division. This reality of power affects all public safety functions (Geller, 1991; International Association of Chiefs of Police, 1985). In some cases budget cutbacks are prorated and spread across all departmental divisions, but it is also possible that entire support sections or units may be disbanded. For instance, if a community relations section is deemed a nonessential unit, not directly focused on crime control or crime prevention, it could conceivably be eliminated. Nonreimbursed outlays for training can be eliminated. The budget is the most obvious control method.

Other methods of influence, such as political manipulation, are somewhat less apparent and often less effective. With commitment to and implementation of community-oriented policing, however, budget cuts would tend to affect only the material aspects of policing, for example, manpower, vehicles, and programs. Fiscal constraints and budget control should not alter the mission and style of service delivery. In economic hard times, law enforcement budgets are often reviewed closely. Many departments are thinned by attrition. Hopefully, in the long run budget cuts will not undermine the morale or **job satisfaction** of officers dedicated to community service.

Executive Selection

Most chiefs of police serve at the pleasure of their city councils and under the direct oversight of the city manager, who also acts as the city personnel officer. Chiefs of police are not generally under contract, but rather are subject to political whim. When city government changes, in some cases so does the position of police chief. Police chiefs often develop a keen awareness of the prevailing political climate (Hoover and Mader, 1990). They know the political composition of the city council and who on the council will or won't support them (Tunnell and Gaines, 1992). It is an often delicate arrangement, with only one or two council members providing the budgetary edge. Should the political edge be lost, those police chiefs under contract are sometimes given "golden parachutes" (i.e., a substantial severance package) or a negotiated period of time to find employment elsewhere. This situation has caused many police chiefs to acquire a degree of cynicism concerning their work (Crank, 1986).

An article written in 1981 by two police chiefs is still relevant on the concerns of urban chiefs of police. The authors suggest that in the process of appointing a chief of police, elected and appointed officials should consider the following points:

1. Recruit, select, and retain a well-qualified manager as your chief of police. Don't select . . . chief[s] on the basis of seniority, or that [they are] an "in-house" candidate, but rather on a track record of proven management results. If you have such . . . person[s] in your own organization, don't lose [them]. A known quantity, all other things being equal, involves less risk.

2. Police chief[s] should report directly to the city manager or [their] equivalent, and elected officials should follow chain of command principles in dealing with the police department. "End runs" will weaken [their] position.

3. Management rights should be spelled out and contained within a signed Memorandum of Understanding between city management and police associations to

BOX 2.6 New York Police Department (NYPD)

After flirting with the community-oriented policing concept initiated by then Chief Lee P. Brown, Mayor Rudolph W. Giuliani and his new police command announced on December 24, 1995, that they had abandoned the two-year-old COP concept and had returned to a military style of policing. The city hired an additional 8,000 new officers, and reports indicated a sharp decline in crime. Between January 1, 1993, and December 31, 1994, reports of

- Murders were down 39.7%
- Robberies were down 30.7%
- Burglaries were down 24%
- Aggravated assaults were down 12.9%
- Shootings were down 39.6%

Overall, New York crime dropped 11 percent and was on track to fall another 16 percent during 1994. Even at a time when crime had dropped nationally, those statistics were far ahead of the national average and of every other major U.S. city. The reason for the decrease, according to officials, was that the NYPD was getting bigger, tougher, and smarter. The NYPD, long famous for the size of its force, wanted to project a tougher image, starting with its uniforms. The light-blue shirts, which for decades made officers look like friendly security guards, were discarded. They were replaced by dark-blue clothing to look more authoritative—and to consciously emulate the Los Angeles Police Department (LAPD).

Meanwhile, in Los Angeles, officers have been trying to shed the very image that the NYPD covets. Officers are leaving their cars, walking beats, putting on shorts, and riding bicycles, all to be closer to the public. Far from wanting to look more intimidating, they are trying to appear more approachable. Whereas the LAPD is learning to counsel and console, the NYPD is looking to confront and arrest. Under Chief Bratton, NYPD officers began hauling in more suspects, often for low-level "quality-of-life" crimes such as aggressive panhandling. Suspects arrested for petty offenses are checked for warrants, searched for guns, and grilled about criminals active in their areas. Those are rough tactics. In fact, they remind some observers of the sweeps that former LAPD Chief Daryl F. Gates began during the late 1980s. In short, community policing in 1996 is the watchword in Los Angeles but is given only lip service in New York, which has returned to a more militaristic approach to suppress urban blight and crime.

Source: Newton, Jim, "NYPD: Bigger, Bolder—Better?" *Los Angeles Times*, December 24, 1995:A1, A24.

> **BOX 2.7 Philadelphia Police Department**
>
> On August 20, 1992, Richard Neal, age 52, succeeded Willie Williams as police commissioner of Philadelphia. Neal, who began his career as a patrolman in 1962, worked over the years in community relations, as commander of the 19th police district, as the head of Internal Affairs, and as the interim chief of the city housing police. Neal, who is black, was endorsed by the 1,500-member Guardian Civic League, an association of black police officers. When accepting the position of commissioner, Neal said, "Philadelphia is a great police department that has continually been on the cutting edge [of] fighting crime and servicing the community. . . . We're going to improve on community policing." His predecessor, Williams, who was Philadelphia's first black police commissioner, had instituted the community policing approach. Subsequently, Williams was appointed chief of police of Los Angeles in June 1992 (*Long Beach Press Telegram*, 1992:A9). One of the major reasons Williams was appointed was his willingness to implement COP and attempt to change the attitude and direction of an organization often described as reactive, traditional, and legalistically oriented.

help avoid future controversy, such as "what are the working conditions?" In those areas where labor has a legitimate interest/right, the police administrator must be willing to sit down with them and try to resolve any differences.

4. [P]olice chief[s] should be afforded basic "due process" rights regarding any personnel actions to be taken against [them]. These procedures, however, should not insulate them from removal for cause.

5. Employment contracts similar to that of a superintendent of schools, renewable on the basis of merit, perhaps should be considered for police chiefs.

6. Support the efforts of police chiefs to formulate strong, professional associations which can speak out as a group regarding critical issues which may impact the welfare of the community.

7. If the police chief[s] [are] doing a good job, tell [them] and show it by supporting [them] when they are subjected to the many pressures inherent with the job. If [they are] under attack for doing the job, defend [them]. Speak out against [their] accusers. [They] shouldn't have to stand alone if [they are] under attack for doing [their] job[s].

8. Share this article (concerns) with others. Surprisingly enough, we don't believe many people recognize the difficulties of being a police chief today. (Brown and Peart, 1981; brackets ours.)

Regardless of the political situations in which some police executives find themselves, the trend is to select chiefs qualified in contemporary policing styles, such as community-oriented policing (Greiner, 1986; Levine, 1986). This trend was evidenced in the 1990s in the appointment of several chiefs of police in Oregon, a state that has experimented with various techniques for law enforcement and administration (Levine, 1986; Websdale, 1991). When the police chief in Portland, Oregon, announced his retirement plans in 1993, the police association acknowledged in their newsletter, *The Rap Sheet* (1993), that "community policing in one form or another is here to stay." However, they noted that "maybe the new police chief will return to what we were told was the basic concept of community policing—that the neighborhood officer should be out of the car working with the people in the officer's assigned area." It appears that a provision of employment for a prospective chief of Portland is the continuation of community--oriented policing (COP).

KEY TERMS

Budget
Bureaucracy
Calls-for-service
Contract law enforcement
Due process model
Empowerment
Executive selection
Job satisfaction
Legalistic model
Military syndrome
Mission statements

Negative reinforcements
Order maintenance model
Organizational values
Planning
Positive reinforcements
Productivity
Quality circles (QC)
Service model
Total quality management (TQM)
Value statements

QUESTIONS FOR REVIEW

1. How does the concept *healthy worker attitudes* correlate with *satisfied customers?* Who are the satisfied customers? Explain.
2. Is bureaucracy necessary in organizations? Discuss why or why not.
3. Review the composition and organization of urban police departments you know about relative to their size. Do you think that the relation of size to organization is realistic? Explain why or why not.
4. What are negative and positive reinforcements? How do they influence police officer work performance and attitudes?
5. How is productivity related to management styles? How important is supervision to how officers perform their jobs? Explain.
6. What are the similarities and differences between TQM and COP? What is the significance of the differences you have noted?

7. What are some positive statements you can make about employee empowerment? What do you think the long-range goals of employee empowerment are? Discuss.
8. What is participatory management? How might it influence officer productivity and work performance?
9. How could the use of quality circles affect an employee's sense of organizational involvement?
10. Discuss how an organization's budget can be used as a controlling device.

SUGGESTED READINGS

Bouza, Tony (1992). *Bronx Beat: Reflections of a Police Commander.* Chicago: Office of International Criminal Justice, the University of Illinois at Chicago.

Couper, David C. (1991). *Quality Policing: The Madison Experience.* Chicago: Office of International Criminal Justice, the University of Illinois at Chicago.

Greenberg, Sheldon F. (1992). *On the Dotted Line: Police Executive Contracts.* Chicago: Office of International Criminal Justice, the University of Illinois at Chicago.

Scott, Michael (1992). *Managing for Success: A Police Chief's Survival Guide.* Office of International Criminal Justice, the University of Illinois at Chicago.

Stamper, Norman H. (1991). *Removing Managerial Barriers to Effective Police Leadership.* Chicago: Office of International Criminal Justice, the University of Illinois at Chicago.

CHAPTER 3

The Mystique of Police Officer Subculture

Introduction

Policing in a Time of Change

Culture: Some Definitions and Examples
The Media's Impact on Public
   Perception of the Police Role

Police Subculture

Police Officers and the Working Personality

The John Wayne Syndrome

Socialization and Resocialization
Empathy Training

On the Meaning of "Real" Police Work

The Code of Silence

Academy Training
Field Training Officers (FTOs)
The Ideal-Real Dilemma
Alternative Academy Training:
   The United Kingdom Model

Public Disclosure and the Media

Key Terms

Questions for Review

Selected Readings

INTRODUCTION

This chapter is about the police officer subculture. Some people believe that police officers have their own culture, known only to them. Because of the unusual working hours, the stressors associated with police work, and the public antagonism toward police, many law enforcement officers have turned inward to develop and perpetuate an officer code different from mainstream culture. This subculture has been described extensively in various media. The first part of this chapter examines the subculture and the media's impact on the definition of the police role. The media encompasses newspapers, television, motion pictures, radio, and published accounts in fictional and nonfictional works.

Police officer conduct is formally transmitted during an officer's training at a police academy, but much socialization also occurs among police officers through on-the-job training. Thus, the second part of this chapter examines various sources of socialization and resocialization, as police officers must learn new behaviors and thought patterns and presumably must discard old patterns and ways of thinking. There exists a dilemma between what police are expected to do and what actually occurs. Police officers encounter all types of persons on the street during their patrols, and descriptions of different types of encounters are included here. The chapter concludes with an investigation of ways officers cope with their roles and the different coping strategies employed by training academies in the United States and elsewhere.

POLICING IN A TIME OF CHANGE

American policing has undergone significant changes in philosophy. Many suggest that municipal law enforcement in the 1990s is embarking on a course toward additional change. Some scholars of policing in America have theorized about how the focus of policing has evolved. Some suggest that up until the early 1900s policing was highly political, that the period 1930–1970 was directed toward reform, and that policing shifted toward a community orientation beginning in the 1970s. But attempts to label eras of policing fall short of the mark on several fronts, mainly because not all police departments are the same. As a group they share certain similarities, but organizationally they differ in attitude, professionalism, style, and direction, and their client base (i.e., the community) also differs.

Early policing was characterized as urban policemen walking beats and interacting daily with merchants and other members of the community. The police officer was a friend in some neighborhoods and feared in others. Some officers served as the "eyes and ears" of the department, while others served as representatives and spokespersons of the community. There was also a significant group who simply took home paychecks. They performed their duties in a manner that did not break department rules and that avoided an inordinate number of citizen complaints. Policing methods were as different as were the regional jurisdictions and makeup of communities, but regardless of the style of policing or the type of community served, a few elements remained constant: One was the universal reliance on the quasi-military organizational structure and another was a formal or informal police subculture.

The existence of a police **subculture** is highly debated. Attempts to change the police organization from traditional policing modes to approaches such as community-oriented policing without taking the police culture into consideration would be a grave error.

Although city governments across the nation have increasingly been advertising for police executives with the commitment, vision, and ability to implement community-oriented policing, the selection of chiefs is only one step in a much larger scheme to promote organizational change. It is imperative that the new executives understand the desire of the system to remain stable, the need for a supporting system, the need to gauge and pace change, the need to obtain true participation, and the need to understand the nature of resistance to change (Williams and Sloan, 1990).

The occupation of policing has had a long and rich history. Policing has historically been dedicated to maintaining civil order, crushing crime, and arresting offenders. The means to combat crime has been a thorny issue over the years. The singular issue of crime control has consistently cost politicians elections. For a political aspirant to be classified as a "liberal," one who is "soft on crime," is political suicide. Conservative traditionalists argue that the end justifies the means and that legal roadblocks should be removed to allow the police greater latitude in the pursuit, capture, prosecution, and conviction of law violators. Capturing criminals has always been the focal point of law enforcement agents. Accordingly, American policing has evolved into a reactive crime-control model designed to stamp out crime. Toward that end, the police have been rigorously trained in detection and arrest techniques and organized into centralized paramilitary structures.

Advances in technology, such as the radio and patrol car, have enabled the police to respond quicker to crimes that have already been committed. Many departments have been deemed efficient based on their ability to reach the scene of a crime in the shortest time. This reactive model was supported for decades by police executives who collectively rejected any challenges to their methods as professional crime fighters. As time passed and crime rates continued to climb, many observers began to question the practical efficiency of the police in actually controlling crime. The police were beginning to be seen as simply arriving at the scene of a crime quickly and taking a report but not as preventing crime from occurring. Social critics of the police combined with adverse court decisions led the police to band closer together and seek solace from one another, like a group under siege.

Meanwhile, society, through the media, has portrayed the police as forming the thin blue line—the civil force—that separates order from anarchy. "Law and order" and "tough on crime" advocates bemoaned legal inroads restricting police practices and policy, giving further credence to the idea that the police were our salvation from the criminal menace. It is understandable that this somewhat skewed perception has been welcomed and reinforced by the police themselves.

> **BOX 3.1 Scripting Police Work:
> Mutt and Jeff**
>
> Few people know that police work is often "scripted," that is, carefully instilled in a police officer's code of conduct. When interrogating criminal suspects, for instance, police officers are taught that the key to a successful interrogation is being alone with suspects during questioning. U.S. Supreme Court Chief Justice Earl Warren wrote that officers are told that the principal psychological factor contributing to a successful interrogation is privacy. The interrogation should occur in the investigator's office. If suspects are interrogated in their own homes or offices, they are more inclined to be recalcitrant, confident, or indignant. Family and friends may be nearby as support systems. However, when suspects are isolated in unfamiliar surroundings, they are more inclined to manifest guilt, and their confidence is significantly undermined.
>
> Some officers use the "Mutt and Jeff" technique for suspect interrogations. Two agents are used: One—Mutt—appears to "know" the suspect is guilty and drives this point home by incessant questioning and belittling. Mutt soon leaves the room and is replaced by Jeff, who is sympathetic toward the suspect and appears to abhor the treatment the suspect suffered at the hands of Mutt. Mutt is the senior officer, however, and can't be kept away from the suspect for very long. Therefore, the suspect tends to confess in Jeff's presence so that he won't have to face Mutt anymore. This type of carefully scripted interrogation often works.
>
> *Sources:* Charles O'Hara, *Fundamentals of Criminal Investigation.* Springfield, IL: Charles C Thomas, 1956:99; Thomas Barker and David L. Carter, *Police Deviance.* Cincinnati, OH: Anderson, 1986:133–134.

CULTURE: SOME DEFINITIONS AND EXAMPLES

Culture is the sum of all beliefs, values, sentiments, definitions, and norms shared by members of a society. A late nineteenth-century idea, it developed out of two critical earlier sets of observations. The first, dating from the Renaissance, recognized that the customs, beliefs, social forms, and languages of Europe's past were different from those of the present. Thus, cultural, social, and linguistic change had to be explained. The second set arose during the period of exploration from A.D. 1300–1600, when it was discovered that people in different regions of the world varied widely in the languages they spoke, the rituals they practiced, and the kinds of societies they lived in. The key ingredients in forming culture are customs and traditions, together with a set of norms (*Encyclopedic Dictionary of Sociology*, 1991:74–76).

Organizations, made up of interactive components, are guided by rules and regulations (formal and informal power structures) and exhibit norms and cultures that have been passed down over time. Police organizations are influenced by internal perceptions, values, and attitudes and are also influenced by external forces. According to the police themselves, their role within the criminal justice process is a major source of anxiety. At times the police are in conflict with the district attorney, the courts, social services, and probation, parole, and community corrections at large.

The Media's Impact on Public Perception of the Police Role

Factual Police Portrayals in the Media. Television has significantly influenced the public regarding policing in America. The American public in the early days of television watched such programs as *Dragnet*, with Sergeant Joe Friday and his sidekick asking for "just the facts." Their approach to criminals and the public alike was sterile, cut and dried; they displayed little emotion. They were caustic, suspicious, and had the uncanny ability to discern fraud and deception in 30-minute time frames. This program, modeled on the Los Angeles Police Department's method of enforcement of the era, had a tremendous impact on how the public perceived policing.

The Police as Comedians. In contrast to *Dragnet*, the long-running *Mayberry RFD*, with Andy Griffith, was an astute, affectionate satire of small-town life and a homespun, common-sense approach to policing. Similar police shows of the period included *Car 54, Where Are You?* and *Barney Miller*. But *Dragnet* ran longer and held wider appeal for larger audiences.

The Police on TV. But later the public was deluged with police programs liberally laced with excitement, chases, suspense, sex, glory, and gore. Some of the more popular included *Highway Patrol, FBI, Kojak, Barreta, Starsky and Hutch, Cagney and Lacey, Hill Street Blues, Streets of San Francisco, The Mod Squad, The Untouchables, Silk Stalkings, McMillan and Wife, Jake and the Fatman, The Commish, Police Story, Hawaii Five-O, 21 Jump Street, In the Heat of the Night, Columbo, Mrs. Columbo, America's Most Wanted, Unsolved Mysteries, CHIPS, Real Stories of the Highway Patrol, Hunter,* and *Prime Suspect*. Three newcomers were *Bakersfield PD* and the steamy and controversial *NYPD Blue* (1993) and *LAPD* (1995).

The Sensationalizing of Policing. Programs such as *Inside Edition, Hard Copy,* and *A Current Affair* have jumped on the bandwagon to provide TV audiences with an "inside" look at the more colorful aspects of law enforcement. Shows with private investigators interacting with police were also popular: *Rockford Files, Magnum P.I., Barnaby Jones, Murder She Wrote, Moonlighting, Charlie's Angels* and many, many more.

Motion Picture Portrayals of Police. As if the public wasn't saturated enough with "cops and robbers" on television, the motion picture industry has added similar material. Movies such as *Police Academy* (1 through 6) caused members of police departments and a large segment of the public to wonder about actual police work as well as police mentality. The Clint Eastwood movies, featuring a fictitious San Francisco detective, "Dirty Harry, make-my-day" Callahan, projected the character into the public eye and into the hearts of police officers. Clint Eastwood posters were soon found adorning many police lockers and association/union meeting rooms. Actors Bruce Willis, Chuck Norris, and Steven Seagal could single-handedly wipe out criminal enterprises and criminal organizations operating in the United States and even in other countries. The *Death Wish* series of movies had audiences cheering as Charles Bronson, playing the role of an avenging vigilante citizen, wiped out numerous predatory street hoodlums. The gratuitous violence associated with these films had its intended effect on the viewing public.

More Television Policing. During a one-week period in November 1993, police movies shown on TV included *Blue Steel, A Case of Deadly Force, The China Lake Murders, COP and a Half, Delta Heat, Die Hard I* and *II, Eyewitness to Murder, Foster and Laurie, Full Eclipse, Madigan, Magnum Force, Man against the Mob, Police Academy 5, Assignment Miami Beach,* and *Relentless* (*TV Times*, 1993). After the *Lethal Weapon I, II,* and *III* series, which featured a lunatic police officer, came techofantasy characters such as Robocop (and sequels) who entered the fray to exterminate evildoers. On camera, major discrepancies in the application of the law became routine, and due process was a term seldom heard in illegal no-knock searches. Contraband was seized at will, and the "beat-them-until-they-confess" methods of past decades resurfaced as commonplace police occurrences. The police were characterized as heavyhanded and unrestrained by social, civil, or legal codes of behavior—all elements holding widespread public appeal in the surreal attempts to eliminate evil.

The Police in Fiction. When we add the impact of law enforcement–oriented novelists, such as ex-police officer Joseph Wambaugh, the public has to be affected. Wambaugh published several bestselling fictional novels, including *The New Centurions, The Blue Knight, The Glitter Dome, The Black Marble, The Delta Star, The Secrets of Harry Bright, The Golden Orange,* and the two police-related nonfiction books, *The Onion Field* and *Lines and Shadows*. Along with novelists, playwrights add their share to the stew of police fantasy, fiction, and fact.

Crime-Fighters on the Radio in Pre-TV Times. Before and during the development of television, when crime was on the rise and little was being accomplished at the "human" level to stem the tide, the public was saturated by "superhuman" crime-fighters on radio, created to fill the void. The American public was treated to such patriotic heroes as *Jack Armstrong, The Shadow, Spider-man, Sam Spade, Captain Marvel, Captain Midnight, Sky King, The Green Hornet,* and

Batman and Robin. Actual crime rates continued to rise, but the public took some solace in the antics of radio superheroes.

All in all, it is understandable that the American viewing public might have a distorted and glorified perception of what policing is all about. They might question much of what they read or see in theaters or on television, and wonder how much of it can be attributed to Hollywood make-believe. As a society, we have been given a glorified and unrealistic picture of policing in urban America. When the public interacts with police officers, we can only speculate about what perceptions they hold and how they were formed.

POLICE SUBCULTURE

One of the first attempts to examine the police subculture was the Gary, Indiana, police study conducted by William Westley in 1950. This study was designed to find out why the police act the way they do. Westley found that a high degree of group cohesion, secrecy, and violence existed among police (Westley, 1970). Since this early study, other investigators have attempted to define and resolve some of the mysteries surrounding the culture of police work. However, the primary literature tends to avoid this issue. Several criminologists and criminal justice authors addressed police subculture phenomena during the late 1960s and early 1970s (Neiderhoffer and Blumberg, 1976; Goldstein, 1977; Skolinck, 1966; Wilson, 1968). However, 1990s works tend to avoid the topic or, if it is discussed, give it only cursory treatment. (Two exceptions are Ken Peak's *Policing America* [1993] and Anthony Bouza's *The Police Mystique: An Insider's Look at Cops, Crime, and the Criminal Justice System* [1993].)

The police subculture is directly related to how the individual officer perceives his or her role within the organization. This perception of role is formulated within and supported by the dominant police culture that has been nurtured and developed over a period of decades and includes the formal and informal values of the department. Many officers (at all ranks) have developed a bunker mentality, based on loyalty to one another, a loyalty factor that is operative in a host of police departments. "The culture is insular and self-protective," said former Minneapolis Police Chief Anthony Bouza (Witkin and Tharp, 1992:41). It is not unusual to hear differing descriptors, but the acronym *TCOO*, meaning Take Care of Our Own, seems to sum up the situation.

The foundations of the police subculture are said to have been laid down in the past during entry-level police training or police academy exposure. This subculture probably still exists, because far too many departments attempting to move toward a different police model are experiencing norms consistent with the traditional police subculture. This is not to say that a police subculture is wrong; there are simply too many negative factors at work. The **code of silence**—the misplaced loyalty—that discourages whistle-blowing regarding misconduct of fellow officers is potentially self-destructive. A reliance on an authoritarian mode of enforcement to control conduct and compliance is also negative.

> **BOX 3.2   Playing Dumb**
>
> *Loyalty, solidarity, and secrecy*: These are some of the major characteristics among police officers. If some officers deviate or engage in misconduct, others may look the other way or furnish false accounts that support their colleagues. The following situation illustrates the problem.
>
> A young patrol officer came into the room and slumped into one of the chairs near the back. He was swinging the keys to a cruiser, and he looked upset about something. He said, "I don't know a thing about it. Nothing. Nothing at all. I wasn't there when it happened." He was the partner of an officer who had failed to report an accident. He did not want to get involved in his partner's trouble. Holt (a retired patrol officer who still visits the station regularly) gave the officer some advice. "Look, don't lie for him. If he wants to fool around, that's his business. He was stupid anyway. Don't stick your neck out. If the chief finds out, there will be hell to pay. You weren't there. You don't know a thing about it. Right?" The young officer nodded agreement, but not very enthusiastically. He was caught in the middle and did not want to get further involved.
>
> In this case, the young officer really did know all about it. His partner had witnessed a traffic accident in which a friend was at fault. He told the two teenage girls in the other car that no accident report was necessary and sent them on their way. There was extensive damage to their car. The two girls had thought the matter over, and now they had come to the station to complain. The officer was in the position that properly reporting the accident would get his partner in trouble. He finally decided to follow the advice of the old-timer and keep quiet. His solution was to say that he did not know anything, when in fact he did. For the retired officer, this was "not lying." The young officer was not so sure.
>
> *Source:* John J. Broderick, *Police in a Time of Change* (2nd ed.). Prospect Heights, IL: Waveland Press, Inc., 1987:136–137.

In fairness, the police are not solely responsible for creating an insular environment. External forces, such as the media, constantly cast the police in the role of "saviors of society" and the "last bastion of civilization." In evaluating the rise in crime during the 1960s former U.S. Attorney General Ramsey Clark said that the police officer is the most important individual in America today (Berkley, 1969:213). The community, political leadership, media, police executives, initial academy training, field training officers, peers, and the police union contribute to the formulation of a police subculture. Individual officers often assimilate the prevailing subculture. The first step in an attempt to change the traditional policing subculture is a vision. Then the subculture must be changed to match the vision (Weber, 1992:26).

The operational values of a community policing organization, in contrast to those of elite law enforcers isolated from citizens and neighborhood, are inclusive and supportive, based on respect and interdependence between the police and the community (Barnett and Bowers, 1992:5). It is important to note that older officers are more likely than young officers to accept community-oriented programs and community policing as an operating style. Maturity appears to play a significant role in older officers' greater willingness to adopt the community policing style (Brown, 1989a).

POLICE OFFICERS AND THE WORKING PERSONALITY

The mounting pressure from peers, supervisors, media, the community, and politicians to stamp out crime has prompted police officers to develop a certain fatalistic attitude in their job expectations. Dedicated older professional police officers have long understood that they really do not have the power or resources to have an impact on the incidence of crime. They can attempt to reduce the probability of crime by crime prevention and "hardening-the-target" approaches that deflect criminal opportunity, but the offenses of murder, rape, assaults, arson, theft, and robbery are not controllable or preventable by police intervention.

Law enforcement personnel can collect and analyze data and inform the community of crime trends and "who and what" to watch out for. In many cases they can take proactive steps to apprehend serial offenders. Although they can respond quickly to scenes of crimes in reactive modes, they may be unable in many cases to locate a suspect. When they do, the processing of paperwork is often more involved than are the investigation and arrest. This apparent inability to have an impact on crime rates can cause frustration at many levels. Even with expanded manpower and budget allocations, most police departments could only respond to more reports and calls-for-service. Arrest rates would not necessarily rise, convictions would not increase, and jail terms would not lengthen. This state of affairs does not satisfy younger officers who visualize themselves as being able to make a difference.

It is generally agreed that crime is rooted in social causes and fueled by opportunity. The police may influence the opportunity factor through prevention tactics but they hold little sway over other causal factors. Contemporary organizational vision, mission, and value statements can serve to clarify the role of police in modern society and reduce the anxieties felt by many officers.

THE JOHN WAYNE SYNDROME

During police academy training, the idea of a command presence is instilled to ensure prompt compliance with orders. If an officer commands an individual or a group to do a certain thing, and the individual or group believes the officer has the physical power to enforce the command, compliance generally results. Similarly, it is not uncommon in some of our major cities for citizens to observe police

Is there such a thing as a "police personality"? *(John Running/Stock, Boston)*

officers wearing dark sunglasses (even at night), a large emblem of the American flag on one shoulder of a leather jacket, and leather (jack) boots, creating the image of an intimidating storm trooper.

The problems with confrontational stances and intimidating appearances are readily apparent. To take an immediate position that could be construed as confrontational, coercive, noncommunicative, or bullying may more easily lead to physical altercations. But some officers appear to love it. If they arrive at a scene and nothing is going on, there soon will be. These officers' reports are replete with "contempt of cop" terms such as *resisting arrest, interference,* and *failure to disperse*. The attitude of the officer at the scene, therefore, is often crucial to the outcome of the situation. This John Wayne syndrome cannot coexist with community policing. Officers must either conform to the articulated mission and values or leave. Peer pressure and concerned supervisors can help to weed out or influence those individuals.

SOCIALIZATION AND RESOCIALIZATION

Empathy Training

Empathy has both Latin and Greek roots. *Em,* from the Latin, means "to see through," and *pathy,* from the Greek, means "the eye of the other" (Thompson,

1993:63). *Webster's New Riverside Dictionary* (1984:229) defines the term as "identification with and understanding of the thoughts or feelings of another."

Over the years the supporters of American policing have employed various strategies to inform the public about crime suppression, crime control, citizen apathy, lack of support, and the need for funding and resources. The focus of these efforts is to alter the way the community perceives the police and their role in society.

Operation Empathy. The discussion of crime control and the conditions that cause crime has been largely a monologue rather than a dialogue. Very little has been done to raise the police's awareness of public or social issues. One innovative police executive, R. Fred Ferguson, while chief of police in Covina, and later, Riverside, California, embarked on several methods in both locales to help his officers to experience "the other side of the coin." The specific objectives of Ferguson's "Operation Empathy" were to

1. Obtain knowledge about the traditional Judaic-Christian democratic view of man generally held in the United States, and the application of the view to police-community relations;
2. Acquire skills in interpersonal and intergroup relations; and
3. Gain information from the behavioral sources about the human individual, interpersonal and group relationships, complex organizations and the community as an environment (Price and Lloyd, 1967:28).

"Operation Empathy" was praised by some and damned by others as foolish, nonproductive, and "that Communist-type sensitivity training." Others felt "that the policemen who participate would be emasculated, would not want to make arrests, and would be overly sympathetic with their clientele (Whisenand and Ferguson, 1978:405). [Note: None of the stated negatives ever came true. Arrests went up, assaults on officers were reduced to near nonexistence, and complaints against officers were greatly reduced.]

In spite of the "heat" from his colleagues, Ferguson, together with two behavioral scientists, Drs. Kent Lloyd and Kendall Price, developed many scenarios with the goal of instilling a sense of empathy in their officers. Ferguson had the support of the city manager and city council for his innovations. The first "empathy experiences" were formulated during a two-day departmentwide team-building exercise.

Upon completing their training, all "Operation Empathy" participants spent two days and one night in the nearby Riverside County Jail. With the exception of Sheriff Ben Clark, his correctional chief, and the under-sheriff, no one was aware that these were pseudoprisoners. Teams of four and five were "booked" on phony burglary and forgery charges, "to be held in transit"—not an uncommon practice. The "prisoners" were fingerprinted, photographed, deloused, issued jail clothing, and placed in large one-hundred-inmate tanks (cells). The degradation of the booking process had its effect, as did finding oneself in a cell with 100 bunks and 110 prisoners, especially when the only available floor space was the bathroom. Much was learned about the jail subculture, in which the prisoners themselves exercise certain control over one another. (For example, a prisoner never calls to a correctional officer for help, regardless of the circumstances.)

During the participants' debriefing, many experiences and anecdotes—some serious and some humorous—emerged. Cell participants agreed that although they wouldn't want to return to jail, none would have missed the experience. Even officers who had previously served as jailers in a large county jail before their Covina employment stated that they had gained a new insight into the prisoners' point of view. At the completion of the exercise, and at the express request of the sheriff, participants met with jail personnel in what began as an uncomfortable setting. The atmosphere improved as the meeting progressed, and the jailers themselves agreed that the exercise was productive. In addition to understanding more about who goes to jail, who remains there and for what reason, and who really runs the jail, the experience caused a decline in "contempt of cop" bookings (Whisenand and Ferguson, 1973:403–404).

In the second field exercise, "Operation Empathy—Skid Row," pairs of officers actually became bums and had to live in the skid row area of downtown Los Angeles. Volunteering officers were given some pocket change and three dollars to purchase clothing from used-clothing stores, were admonished not to reveal their identity, and were placed on the streets for two to three nights and days. For additional realism, they did not bathe or shave for two days before their visit. Once the ordeal (training session) was completed, the officers were debriefed. Most reported a newfound appreciation for people living on the street. The pseudobums spoke of being treated shabbily by many citizens, especially shopkeepers, who assumed they were dishonest, bad for business, and had no feelings. The "bums" were ordered to leave middle-class cafes and were followed by clerks in retail stores. They were ordered to "move on" when they stopped to observe a sick woman lying on the sidewalk, although other onlookers were permitted to remain. They began to feel powerless. They also found that rumors abound and that most denizens of skid row fear the police. Street people, they learned, regale each other with tales of police brutality, misconduct, and mistreatment, although not one skid row habitué could remember being personally abused by the police or having ever observed such abuse. Nevertheless, all of them were certain that "police look for chances to abuse, arrest, even shoot bums" (Whisenand and Ferguson, 1973:404).

Role-playing officers discovered that members of the ever-changing street population are a class of victims: They victimize each other; some have been seduced and ravaged by drugs and alcohol; others are victims of inadequate mental health programs geared to assist in community policing with mental illness; a few are hungry; many need shelter; and most lack the opportunity to alter or escape their circumstances.

Having police officers experience how street people live might not change how street dwellers perceive the police, or provide an instant remedy, but the skid row sessions certainly gave a few police officers new insights into nonmainstream attitudes. Officers assigned to these areas likely reassessed how they would approach and deal with street people and street problems. Regardless of the critics, there was a new and lasting awareness developed through this empathy training experience.

Other empathy exercises and dimensions were added, such as placing policemen in picket lines, operating outside of so-called lewd movie houses in a large neighboring city, and attending hippie "love-ins" (a 1960s subculture gathering). From these experiences a new understanding of police officer body language has emerged. As responding policemen arrived to monitor the picket lines, they got out of their patrol vehicles and then reached back inside to get batons (nightsticks), which they then holstered in baton rings. The pseudopicketers had done the same thing innumerable times, and yet when questioned later each had the same perception: "I thought I was going to get hit with that thing." They knew better, but still felt threatened as the policemen secured their batons.

At "love-ins," police "hippies" observed working police officers from a different viewpoint and became aware of the tremendously volatile mixture when hippies, motorcycle gangs, and police come together. Innumerable lessons were gained, including a bruised set of ribs incurred by one "hippie-captain." (The exercises involved all ranks.) A short time later a "love-in" was scheduled for the conservative city of Covina, and 3,500 hippies and others came. As with most such events, there was advance publicity, and the Covina Police Department had sufficient time to plan. In addition to the police, hippie leaders and members of the "Hell's Angels," a motorcycle gang, were involved in the planning. One hundred hippies became policemen for the day, while regular policemen melted into the crowd undercover as hippies, for felony-type work. The hippie monitors put down one problem after another throughout the day, including one that could have exploded if uniformed policemen had been in the crowd. As a consequence, the police were less busy than usual (Whisenand and Ferguson, 1978:406).

Casablanca. When Ferguson left Covina to become the chief of police of Riverside, California, he confronted another set of circumstances. The city of Riverside had a very large population of Hispanics. Most of them lived within the geographical confines of a mile-square barrio called Casablanca. In an attempt to develop an awareness of the Mexican-American culture, in 1974 the Riverside Police Department, in cooperation with Loma Linda University and Professors Vern Andress (psychologist), Monte Andress (social anthropologist), and Charles Teel (sociologist), developed a course titled "The Police Officer as an Agent of Change." The course included lectures; group participation sessions; films; guest presentations; total immersion (live-in experiences); experiences with the food, music, art, and dance of Mexico; readings; and examinations. The course consisted of ten four-hour class sessions. The first week's session was (1) an orientation, followed by sessions on (2) culture, race, and myth; (3) sensorium;

(4) Mexican national character and the Chicanos; (5) perceived deprivation and violence; (6) Chicano history, politics, and expectations; (7) life opportunities and ethnicity; (8) cultural experience of food, art, music, and dance; and (9) total immersion, live-in experience. The tenth and final week was devoted to debriefing, conclusions, and a final examination.

Although the academic side of the course was probably not unusual, the sidebar experiences were. For example, the policemen participants toured the barrio in a small bus, with an officer participant as a tour guide. His tour was obviously influenced by his perspective of police experiences and reports. The bus left the barrio, picked up a second guide, a native of the barrio, and returned for a second tour. The new guide pointed out areas of interest from his point of view, which was quite different, educational, and enlightening. He focused on the true culture of the community, its nature and makeup. The "graduation exercise" had the participants, on a volunteer basis, spend two nights and three days living in the barrio. They actually became a part of a Mexican-American family, sharing its food, problems, pleasures, and frustrations. Forty-six officers completed the program, and an additional 21 officers participated in a "Total Immersion Spanish Language Program," which was offered by the University of California at Davis and held in Ensenada, Mexico (Whisenand and Ferguson, 1978:530–538).

The results of programs such as this are difficult to assess, but surely with knowledge comes understanding and appreciation. In this case a large portion of the Riverside Police Department's force had the opportunity to study and interact with a significant portion of the service population. They were challenged and they responded in a positive mode that laid more than a few stereotypes to rest. It follows that true community policing must entail the knowledge, understanding, and appreciation of the various neighborhoods that make up our cities.

Two decades ago, the Riverside Police Department's experience in "Operation Empathy" attempted to bring the police into closer (empathic) contact with the public and set the stage for continuing programs. Today, however, with the exception of preservice academy training, there are few such programs across the nation designed to present law enforcement officers with viewpoints that differ from their own. With all occupations there is a tendency to succumb to "vocational myopia," and the police are certainly not immune. This work-related perspective tends to narrow the focus of individual perspectives, which can alter attitudes and behavioral patterns. This is especially likely if a small cohort (e.g., gang bangers and taggers) becomes representative of a larger population. Without opportunities for police officers to study, interact with, and understand minority differences, police perceptions will be unfairly tainted, and certain segments of the community will be unfairly labeled.

ON THE MEANING OF "REAL" POLICE WORK

In past years, being considered "soft," "liberal," or having a "social worker" mentality could easily ruin the career aspirations of young police officers.

Being left-wing or displaying social awareness and concern could cast doubt on one's ability to perform "real" police work. Peers would begin to question whether the officer under suspicion was "reliable" or could be counted on as a "stand-up" guy. In many cases, old-timers regaled newcomers with "war stories" that could rival Joseph Wambaugh novels. Police were traditionally "kick-ass" types that occasionally did not even take names. Myths and traditions were born, and officers strove to become legends in their own time—or in their own mind. Only those macho officers who appeared to be the most heartless, toughest, most brazen, and most callous and who could wreak havoc with superiors (and citizens) could serve as role models or seek fame. Those not fitting the mold were ignored and isolated, a practice often sanctioned by managers. To be labeled as such by peers was usually ended only after one's resignation. Requested backup would either not arrive when summoned or arrive after the need diminished. Outcasts were simply ignored by their peers and socially isolated.

THE CODE OF SILENCE

Throughout the history of law enforcement, peer loyalty and silence have been highly prized characteristics of police officers. The **code of silence,** considered *de rigueur,* has been a major obstacle in attempts to root out corruption, brutality, and ineptness. To inform on fellow officers was and continues to be tantamount to religious heresy. It is interesting that those officers who adhere rigidly to such an outdated and potentially job-threatening practice share some of the same char-

"Real" police work is not always related to catching criminals.
(Greg Smith/Gamma-Liaison)

acteristics as many institutionalized prisoners. The mainstay of the universal "prisoner code" is not to "rat" on another prisoner, for example.

Ardent supporters of the police establishment and of any police action, regardless of its questionable nature, continue to try to justify this outdated code of silence. They point to other occupations and cite lawyers helping other lawyers and doctors assisting other doctors. What they fail to understand is that the practice of nondisclosure or covering up illegal, immoral, and unethical behavior by peer groups makes them accessories, willingly or unwittingly compromised. Should disciplinary sanctions subsequently be brought against those who aid and abet other violators, they become liable. The outcomes of a code of silence are corruption in its many forms, public distrust, and personnel actions that take their toll in personal loss and economic forfeiture. Far too many unsuspecting, otherwise good officers who "help a buddy" through the production of manufactured evidence, tainted testimony, or "creative" reports have lost their jobs.

ACADEMY TRAINING

Field Training Officers (FTOs)

The use of field training officers (FTOs) to augment formal academy training has been in place in most law enforcement agencies for several decades. FTOs are experienced police officers who are chosen from the ranks to train newer officers. FTOs serve many functions, but their primary role is to instill organizational values, reinforce sound policing tactics and techniques, ensure compliance with departmental policy guidelines, evaluate the probationers' progress, make on-the-spot corrections, and provide encouragement.

One problem with many FTO programs is the lack of consistency in the training methods employed. In early 1989, the High Point (North Carolina) Police Department, recognizing that its program needed to be improved, formed a centralized field training team, which consolidated all FTO training into one approach to improve its management (Rankin, 1990). The traditional model required new recruits to complete 694 hours of basic law enforcement training from in-house, state-certified instructors. They were then required to complete a 12-week FTO program, but they could have three separate FTOs during their period of supervision, which sometimes led to training inconsistencies. Under reorganization the field training team consisted of one commander, two supervisors, and nine FTOs. If additional slots were needed, they were filled by off-duty volunteers from other teams. The redirection of the FTO program has benefited all concerned, with closer liaison between the FTO team and the training division, uniform standards, and exposure to all areas of the city. An important side issue concerned the minimizing of departmental liability (failure to train).

Although evaluations after the first year demonstrated the new program was successful, one negative aspect became apparent. After training recruits for two straight sessions, some FTOs approached burnout, and many veteran officers were reluctant to volunteer because they felt that "once an FTO, always an FTO." Once an officer has accepted an assignment or volunteered to be an FTO, it is difficult for him or her to return to active police work and be "accepted" as before. As incentives, the High Point Police Department provided a 5 percent pay increase for FTOs while training new recruits, special days off after each assignment, and a special FTO ribbon to be worn on their uniform in recognition for their efforts (Rankin, 1990). The role of FTOs cannot be overemphasized; they create the initial impressions and organizational value system that will affect new hires for the remainder of their careers.

The Ideal-Real Dilemma

What They Train You to Do at the Academy and What We Really Do Here on the Street. In the transition from traditional policing to alternative delivery systems such as community-oriented policing, the realities of police work must correspond with preemployment training and FTOs' supervision during the probationary period. Police academy training must emphasize community service as opposed to the traditional "crime-crushing" approach. If they are to be accepted as true representatives of the varying communities they serve, the police community must direct their energies toward conflict resolution, crisis intervention, and humane enforcement policies.

In an effort to instill more ethical behavior in police trainees, many academies have created scenarios that place the trainees in awkward positions. They are required to halt or attempt to prevent what they perceive to be illegal or unjust uses of force by their fellow officers. These training exercises are staged to elicit a predetermined "politically correct" response. The students are not ignorant of these orchestrated expectations and respond accordingly. Those who fail to respond to the situation correctly might be seen as incapable of adapting to new situations. Situational training aims to accomplish a planned response to a variety of situations.

If these newly appointed law enforcement officers "hit the street" and are told by their peers to "forget that crap you were taught at the academy," an instant conflict is created. It is further complicated if their soon-to-be peers proceed to explain the realities of police work to them. The instruction provided by FTOs may not be able overcome peer pressure.

Alternative Academy Training: The United Kingdom Model

As an alternative to sterile training that offers only the situational approach to gauge student responses, the highly acclaimed **United Kingdom Model** of academy training might be explored. Although this approach is somewhat more costly and time consuming, the long-term results may well parallel the aims and goals of community policing. This model certainly provides a greater range of evaluative material on which to judge new hires. Although training differences exist, as constables are not given lengthy firearms training, the underlying premise of training the constables in classrooms and in the community has considerable merit. The following overview of the United Kingdom Model was extracted from an article written by Dr. Edward E. Peoples, Santa Rosa Junior College, who spent the spring semester of 1992 studying Britain's criminal justice system.

Recruit Testing and Selection

Applicants who are qualified are invited to a force headquarters to compete in a testing process that is usually conducted over a three-day period. First, applicants complete a written examination that tests their grammar and writing skills, their logical reasoning, math, and ability to observe and recall. Next, they complete a series of physical fitness tests that include: an estimation of percentage body fat, a measure of grip strength, flexibility, a standing long jump, the number of pushups in one minute, the number of situps in one minute, and a 20-meter progressive run. Candidates spend the next two nights and days in rooms at force headquarters with meals being provided in the force dining hall. After the evening meal, they socialize and get acquainted; force staff assessors are there observing their social conduct. The second morning session includes a medical examination and an individual interview, followed by a group exercise. The afternoon session includes another group exercise and/or group discussion, a written exercise, an autobiographical presentation to the group and assessors, followed by dinner and more observed socializing in the force's bar and lounge. The third day's testing includes additional exercises, both individual and group. By mid-afternoon the process is concluded and the candidates return home to await the results. The selection process and the decisions to hire are made by force personnel after a complete evaluation of how well the candidates tested and presented themselves. Outside experts are not consulted.

Recruit Training in England and Wales

The job of a patrol constable has been divided into 39 tasks which have been related to 36 skills and abilities that one must possess to perform the job. Probationary recruit training is a two-year developmental process and is designed to assure that the constable acquires the skills and abilities to perform the job of constable.

Training begins with a foundation course that is 31 weeks long and is divided into seven integrated modules, each with a specific purpose, and each linked to the next in a developmental training model. Module 1 is approximately three weeks in duration and is conducted at the local force training unit. First, the probationer is issued a full uniform, completes the bureaucratic paperwork, and is acquainted with the force policies and regulations. Next, the aspirant is given a thorough orientation to the department and community and accompanies an experienced officer on patrol to observe as much day-to-day policing activity as possible. He or she also will be sent out into the community to contact related agencies, such as probation, parole, or welfare, to enhance the recruit's systems perspective. These patrol and related agency experiences are shared among the new recruits during debriefing sessions back at force headquarters.

Module II is a ten-week live-in training experience given at a regional training center. The integrated curriculum includes training in public order control, first aid, marching and drill, swimming, physical education, law, evidence and arrest procedures. Case studies and practicum activities are used whenever possible, with a focus on student-generated learning in a participatory mode rather than a lecture-testing approach. Probationer constables are continually assessed by trained evaluators and they engage in self-assessments during this period to identify their strengths and weaknesses. They also participate in development exercises to identify individual training needs for Module III.

In Module III, the individual training needs of each recruit form the basis of a five-week session back at the force training unit. The recruit is assigned a Tutor Constable who is trained in the same developmental approach. Together they participate in increasingly complex experiences of real police work in the community during which the learning from Module II is translated into street police work at a level relevant to the individual recruit's needs. Adequate time is allowed at the end of each day for debriefing, a concept thought crucial to the recruit's understanding, development and growth. Module IV is a five-week live-in session conducted back at the regional training center. There, the recruits share their experiences and problems and learn from each other as well as study new and more advanced content. Once again, they take part in skill development exercises, and individual need profiles are prepared that identify their strengths and weaknesses. Action plans are then formulated to address individual training needs during Module VI.

Module V is a one-week leave, a vacation from the rigors of their intense training. In Module VI, recruits return to their force areas to implement their Action Plans during five weeks of street patrol experience. Each recruit is again assigned to a tutor constable. This time, however, the probationer initiates the responses to calls for service and conducts the primary policing responsibilities. Also, during this period, he or she may complete short periods of independent patrol if the tutor constable recommends it and the supervising inspector approves. All supervision and patrol activities during this period are derived from the recruit's Action Plan so as to correct weaknesses and strengthen assets. Module VII is the final training stage, a one-week period of consultations and assessments, and the final decision as to the recruit's suitability for independent patrol. Then, the recruit is either granted the status of independent constable on patrol, has his training extended if it is agreed that further specific training will correct any deficiencies, or is terminated from the force. Three years from the date the probationer recruit is hired he or she is given permanent status.

The U.K. police take their training responsibilities seriously, and strive to develop the best constables possible. It is a two-year commitment by the force and the recruit to prepare for a lifetime of service to the community. After the constable completes the two-year probation period successfully, he or she may request a posting to some special operations unit, such as traffic or CID (Criminal Investigation Division).

Recruit Training in Scotland

The nature and scope of recruitment and training in Scotland are similar to that in England and Wales. However, several important differences do exist. First, there are only eight police forces in Scotland and only one police training center, the Scottish Police College at Tulliallan Castle, a remodeled 19th century castle located on a beautifully landscaped 90-acre estate.

The period of recruit training and probation covers a two-year period and is divided into 10 areas of instruction: week one is an orientation to the force and to policing conducted at the individual departments. Weeks two to nine are the basic training course at Tulliallan covering police powers, crime, laws, evidence, traffic, firearms licensing regulations, police holds and physical education. Weeks 10 and 11 are specialized training periods at the individual force training departments. Weeks 12 to 14 are for driving instruction and weeks 15 to 49 are devoted to on-the-job training on patrol under the supervision of a tutor constable. This sequence is repeated, with the exception of driving instruction, and concludes with weeks 92 to 104 on patrol under supervision. Thereafter, the decision to either grant permanent constable status or to terminate is made. This two-year training period alternates the classroom teaching with practical patrol experiences in a developmental process just as is done in England and Wales. In the classroom, however, the lecture-testing method is used rather than the case study, student-generated learning style. Also, instructors at the Police College include both sworn and civilian staff, thus broadening the instructional perspective and the student exposure. (Peoples, 1993:229–233).

PUBLIC DISCLOSURE AND THE MEDIA

Most medium- to large-sized police agencies have a Public Information Office (PIO), which serves as the principal mouthpiece for the department or simply disseminates information. In smaller departments, in which the chief is aware of all day-to-day operations, a PIO is not necessary (Nehrbass, 1988:40). Historically, the media and the police have not always enjoyed a cooperative relationship.

The relationship between the law enforcement community and the news media has altered over the years, from one in which reporters carried police badges identifying them as "police reporters" to one in which reporters and their editors are skeptical of police actions and inactions. Some in the media claim there should be an adversarial relationship between the press and the police. Some police officials believe the press is harmful to their police agency, their officers, and law enforcement in general (Bernsen, 1988:35). The average police-media relationship probably lies midway between these positions. In interacting with the media, most police authors agree, two elements are absolutely vital: truthfulness and cooperation (Garner, 1988; Bernsen, 1988; Nehrbass, 1988). Those agencies striving to implement community policing cannot hope to succeed without the cooperation of the media. Of primary concern is the mutual establishment of guidelines and policies by the police and media.

One rather sensitive area is the disclosure of internal police actions. **Public disclosure** of internal police disciplinary decisions is generally discouraged by department heads. Some of the reasons are that it makes the department look bad, it puts the city or jurisdiction in a bad light, it airs dirty laundry in public, it taints the entire department when only one or two officers are involved, it puts the spotlight on administrative or disciplinary hearings, and it makes disciplinary actions seem tacit admissions of a failure of supervision. On the other hand, the positive results of such public disclosures include public trust, openness, and admission that sometimes discipline is necessary and that police officers are human and fallible. Public disclosures can also ensure tribunal or administrative fairness and convey the message that the police department is a public agency accountable to the public.

The degree of public airing of internal police disciplinary practices varies from state to state and in many cases is subject to state public information law. Some agencies have an ongoing agreement with their local newspapers to print the results of all disciplinary actions, whereas others attempt to shield discovery. The natural assumption when information is withheld is that something is amiss. Some newspapers routinely print the license plates and names of clients of street prostitutes, and others publish the names of citizens convicted in court for driving under the influence of alcohol, or similar driving violations. This publicity is intended to discourage and censure the actions cited. Publishing the results of police reviews, personnel investigations, and disciplinary actions has the same effect.

KEY TERMS

Code of silence
Empathy
Public disclosure

Subculture
United Kingdom Model

QUESTIONS FOR REVIEW

1. Discuss the factors leading to the development of a police subculture.
2. How does the United Kingdom Model of recruit selection and training differ from pre-entry processes in the United States?
3. Why is it important to understand the impact of media on the public's perception of police work?
4. Explain the pros and the cons of disclosing police disciplinary actions to the public.
5. What are some methods to alter the traditional police subculture?

SUGGESTED READINGS

Bittner, Egon (1970). *The Functions of Police in a Modern Society.* Washington, DC: U.S. Government Printing Office.
Bouza, Anthony V. (1993). *The Police Mystique: An Insider's Look at Community Policing, Crime and the Criminal Justice System.* New York: Plenum Press.
Neiderhoffer, Arthur, and Abraham S. Blumberg (1976). *The Ambivalent Force: Perspectives on the Police, 2nd ed.* Hinsdale, IL: The Dryden Press.
Peak, Ken J. (1993). *Policing America: Methods, Issues, Challenges.* Englewood Cliffs, NJ: Prentice Hall.
Skolnick, Jerome H. (1966). *Justice without Trial.* New York: John Wiley and Sons.

CHAPTER 4

The Nature and Operations of Community-Oriented Policing

Introduction

From Conventional Policing to Community-Oriented Policing

Density and Community

Community Policing and Community-Based Policing
The Back-to-the-Community Movement
Community-Oriented Policing in Detroit
The Alaska Village Public Safety Officer (VPSO) Program
Cultural Barriers to Community-Oriented Policing

Sector Patrolling, Foot Patrolling, and Beats
The New York City Foot Beat Example

An Example of a Smaller City Beat
Basic Car Plan

Problem-Oriented Policing (POP)

Team Policing

Mounted Patrol, Bicycles, and Golf Carts
Mounted Patrol
The New Orleans Mounted Patrol
Bicycles
Golf Carts

Manifest Functions of Community Policing

Latent Functions of Community Policing
Tension
Use of Force
Enforcement and Sentencing

CHAPTER 4

Some Sociolegal and Political Implications of Community Policing
November 2, 1993, Election Day

Selective Enforcement of the Law
The Spirit of the Law vs. the Letter of the Law
Problems and Systemic Constraints

Fear of Crime

Key Terms

Questions for Review

Appendix: Traditional vs. Community Policing: Questions and Responses

Suggested Readings

INTRODUCTION

This chapter is about the development of community policing and some of its variations. Actually, community-oriented policing has its antecedents in the early 1900s. Before the advent of automobiles and other motorized vehicles, police officers either rode horses or walked through neighborhoods on *beats*. These beats were the cornerstone of early American policing, as police officers became familiar with community residents and developed a rapport with them. When patrol automobiles began to appear and became the primary means of conveying officers through neighborhoods, many residents lost touch with particular officers who knew them on a first-name basis. Patrol cars isolated officers from those they were sworn to protect. In time, this physical separation led to a degree of alienation between the police and the community. Since the 1960s, however, community policing has been rediscovered, packaged, and marketed as "new." Community policing is *not* new.

The first part of this chapter examines city density and various problems accompanying urbanization. Several examples are provided of large cities reverting to earlier police patrol methods. Various experiments have been conducted with different patrol styles. Some cities have used golf carts, dirt bikes, speedboats, and foot patrols. The alternatives to squad cars in specific areas have been classified as "back-to-the-community" police patrolling methods. Geographical territories have been used to promote sector patrolling, whereby designated neighborhoods or city blocks have been assigned to particular officers. One case described here in some detail, the Kansas City Preventive Patrol Experiment, is especially interesting but disappointing in several respects. The chapter concludes by investigating some of the manifest and latent functions of community-oriented policing. Presumably, fear of crime will decline through greater and more personalized contacts between police officers and community residents. Some of the sociolegal implications of community policing are also examined.

FROM CONVENTIONAL POLICING TO COMMUNITY-ORIENTED POLICING

Since the St. Louis Metropolitan Police Department established the nation's first formal police-community relations division in 1957, almost every major city has initiated some form of police-community relations (PCR) program (Brown, 1971:16). The majority of programs are geared toward crime prevention and a reduction in the community's fear of crime. Special staff and organizational units address problems as they periodically arise in the community. Some observers compare this approach to a firefighting unit putting out small brush fires that occasionally erupt. However, the importance and impact of the various PCR programs should not be minimized, because they created a host of programs that benefited many segments of society.

The singular outcome of educating the public on crime prevention has been to deter many would-be burglars and thieves from bothering protected neighborhoods. Police youth programs such as the Explorer Scouts and Police Athletic League (PAL) provide outlets for community youth and channel their energy into more productive activities. These programs fostered the public's appreciation of the problems faced by police officers and policing in general. However, most of these programs have been superficial, in that they do not reflect a holistic, systemic commitment by the enforcement organization. Consequently, months or years of hard work by some PCR units have been wasted because a few officers had antagonistic attitudes and the general sentiment was that such activity did not constitute "real police work."

The shift in policing philosophy during the 1990s toward a new paradigm has been accompanied by a new awareness of and association with the public served. American policing has assumed new dimensions and roles. Over the past decade, American policing has investigated, experimented with, or implemented new policing methods and approaches. Some law enforcement agencies have established problem-oriented policing (POP), community-oriented policing (COP), or other changes signaling a dramatic shift in focus. These changes are welcomed by some experts and treated with cautious optimism or outright suspicion by others. Ideally, community-oriented policing embraces a new proposition and social contract that will serve to represent all points of view within an ethnically diverse society.

DENSITY AND COMMUNITY

In assessing communities, several demographical changes that have occurred over the past several years should be examined. A significant change in **demographics** has been the gradual but dramatic increase in population **density.**

According to the 1990 census, the United States had 396 urban areas, defined by the Census Bureau as areas with a population of at least 50,000 and a density of 1,000 or more inhabitants per square mile. These urbanized areas almost always consist of central cities and their surrounding suburbs.

Urbanized areas are not the same as metropolitan areas or large cities. Cities typically lie within urban areas, and urban areas are typically part of larger metropolitan areas. Metropolitan areas are less dense than urban centers, and urban areas are less dense than cities. These differences affect city density rankings. For example, Los Angeles is the densest urban area, but New York is the densest city. Approximately two-thirds (64 percent) of all U.S. residents live in urban areas, which comprise only 1.7 percent of the land area. In contrast, 97.5 percent of U.S. land is classified as rural. Only 25 percent of the entire U.S. population lives in rural areas, of which the average density is only 18 people per square mile.

California epitomizes the U.S. pattern of wide-open spaces interspersed with densely populated cities. Los Angeles, the densest urban area in the United States, has a population of 11.4 million and a density of 5,801 people per square mile. Altogether, 19 of the top 50 densest urban areas are located in California (Larson, 1993:39–40). Crime indices and population density have a high correlation, and certain demographic aggregates have higher victimization rates than others. For instance, those living in households in the lowest income category are more likely to be victims of violent crime than those in households in the highest income brackets (Bureau of Justice Statistics, 1993:11). Urban areas also undergo continual shifts in the ethnic and cultural makeup of their neighborhoods.

Density—the sheer number of people in geographically confined areas—places special demands on the police. The volume of "call-for-service" and 911 emergency calls in high-density areas is overwhelming. Businesses, residents, and special interest groups want and demand efficient, immediate services from the police. To bring policing closer to dense urban areas and to be more responsive to community demands, law enforcement agencies have begun a movement toward foot patrolling and other contact policing methods. These methods include problem-oriented policing, community-based policing, community-oriented policing, basic car plans, team policing, and foot patrol.

COMMUNITY POLICING AND COMMUNITY-BASED POLICING

The Back-to-the-Community Movement

The introduction of the first patrol car, a 1909 Model T Ford, in Detroit, Michigan, was one of the first technological steps in a succession of events that altered the way police conducted patrols (Rush, 1991:226). One unfortunate byproduct was the subsequent decline of foot patrols and beats, which had been the eyes and ears of urban police departments. Through the beat officers, police departments knew what was happening in their communities. They could gauge social tensions, civil unrest, dissatisfaction, and through a one-on-one contact with merchants and residents, they could keep track of most criminal conduct. Through this community interaction and networking, they were often able to thwart crime.

Motorized patrols made it impractical for citizens to approach and talk with police officers. Few citizens flag down passing police cars to discuss a community problem.

One of the basic elements of community policing is the return to the walking beat patrol officer, because walking assigned beats is the most direct way to reconnect local policing with the community. Both large and small police agencies are reviving this form of urban policing, although for some departments, beat patrolling is not particularly economical.

Three other components of community policing include (1) the decentralization of urban police departments into smaller geographical zones of patrol responsibility, (2) the establishment of community watch programs, and (3) efforts to gain public trust and acceptance. One of the most widely publicized attempts to change a police department into a public service delivery system based on customer satisfaction was the creation of the experimental police district in Madison, Wisconsin, described in Box 4.1.

Foot patrols are a part of the back-to-the-community movement to bring officers closer to the citizens they serve. *(Ellis Hewig/Stock, Boston)*

BOX 4.1 Madison, Wisconsin

During the late 1960s and early 1970s, violent antiwar demonstrations turned Madison, Wisconsin, particularly the University of Wisconsin campus, into a battleground. At one point, the governor mobilized the Wisconsin National Guard to secure the university campus. The harsh tactics used to quell these demonstrations left the community with a high level of distrust of the police and their conduct. Conversely, the officers themselves believed they were battle scarred and alienated from the community they were hired to protect. In 1972, the new chief of police, former Marine David Couper, introduced some new ideas about conflict management and citizen-directed service to the Madison Police Department. At the outset, he was deluged with grievances and lawsuits from veteran police officers. Because of this widespread internal resistance, he was unable to change the philosophy of that traditionally rooted department. The chief of police took a sabbatical leave, revised his management approach, and became familiar with the fundamentals of Romaine Deming's *total quality management* (Deming and Janeksela, 1976). After some reflection, he decided "to run the department for the 95 percent who did their jobs well rather than write the rules for the 5 percent who were difficult." He identified those progressive officers interested in transforming the department and rebuilding community confidence and established them into a team.

Working as a team, these officers created an elected employee policy-making council, a committee to assess the department's future, and developed a police mission statement that promoted the task of peacekeeping as the department's primary role. The team placed the law enforcement function into a secondary role. This was a risky move, particularly in view of the possible reaction if people thought the police were neglecting detection and apprehension. However, the new strategy had broader implications. It meant the department could deploy resources to work on the underlying causes of crime, interact with schools and neighborhood organizations, develop relationships with minority and student leaders, and put a higher priority on outreach programs. Most important, the new emphasis created a *constancy of purpose*.

In 1986, the chief of police and 50 police volunteers decided to test the new mission statement. Together they believed that decentralized police districts headquartered in different neighborhoods would yield more effective peacekeeping by providing better service to residents and encouraging officers to develop closer ties with targeted neighborhoods. Police precincts were an old idea, but this model was a radical departure: Officers in the district would elect their own captains and lieutenants, determine their own staffing and work schedules as a team, and network with neighborhood associations to set law-enforcement priorities. Having worked with the chief of police for fourteen years, the police union trusted Couper and accepted the idea.

Several months of surveys and data analyses resulted in the Madison Experimental Police District on the city's South Side. Its station house was slated to be located in the aldermanic district of a relatively junior member of the city council. Because the officers had done their homework, they were able to derail efforts by the council president to locate this political plum in another ward. They showed that their proposed location would provide the best service to priority areas and populations, including the elderly, as well as provide instant access to all parts of the district.

Soon, South Side residents were seeing their police officers on the streets, at neighborhood meetings, and on their front doorsteps to interview them about their concerns. Home burglaries decreased by 28 percent between 1986 and 1989, while the rest of the city experienced a 15 percent increase in these crimes. Other statistics were equally impressive. Dollar savings included the reduced overtime and over 200 hours of patrol time saved for the entire experimental district in 1988 compared with 980 hours for an equivalent number of officers from the central office. This saving was achieved after officers in the district conducted a study of the kinds of calls that kept police on duty beyond their regular shifts. They discovered that a high percentage of such calls were not urgent, and so they arranged with dispatchers to put those calls on a "B" (waiting) list if they were received less than 45 minutes before the end of a shift. When the new shift of officers came on duty, they would respond to those calls first.

Although this procedure meant some delay in police response for some area residents, there were few recorded complaints. Tax dollars were saved, and surveys showed that citizens were satisfied with the level of police services. Furthermore, 85 percent of the officers in the special district had higher levels of job satisfaction than they had exhibited in their previous assignments (Harvard Law Review, 1991).

Community-Oriented Policing in Detroit

Since the mid-1980s, the Detroit Police Department (DPD) has employed a two-pronged approach to community policing. Predictably, the first phase involved crime prevention. The police initiated the establishment of citizen watch groups, which included local businesses, in neighborhoods. In addition, the DPD provided transportation services for the elderly and developed address lists of senior citizens living alone so that officers could check on them periodically. The police have also developed and implemented programs for local schools on topics such as drugs, crime, and police service.

"Beat" cops develop a familiarity with businesspersons and other area residents and seek to ensure their safety. *(Christopher Morrow/Photo Researchers)*

The second phase of Detroit's community policing involved dividing the city into subregions and establishing more than fifty ministations throughout the metropolitan area (Skolnick, 1988a) for the purpose of increasing the officers' knowledge of the community and encouraging the public to report problems and incidents directly and quickly. Emphasis was also placed on the utilization of unmarked police vehicles and surveillance activities to prevent crime. To clarify the ministation concept, the Detroit chief of police said that the "precincts are to enforce, mini-stations are to prevent" (Skolnick, 1986).

The Alaska Village Public Safety Officer (VPSO) Program

In 1981 rural Alaska police officials established the Village Public Safety Officer Program (VPSO) (Marenin, 1990, 1991; Marenin and Copus, 1991) with the intent of providing public safety services in various multicultural and politically and legally pluralistic settings of rural Alaska. At the outset the program focused on family problems and the social-emotional adjustment of youth. Officers selected for VPSO were given training in social work skills; for example, their patrolling emphasis was on crime prevention through family and individual intervention. Those with some counseling experience were sought for the program, but it became apparent that persons qualified to perform social work-type tasks were in short supply. Fairly quickly, residents of various rural communities came to view public safety officers more as social workers than crime-fighters.

The VPSO was found to have various shortcomings, some of which were attributable to the remoteness of communities in need of policing services. First, qualified personnel were difficult to find and, once they were found, it was difficult to keep them long enough for them to gain the experience necessary to improve their overall policing effectiveness. Second, the VPSO program was geared toward law enforcement or crime control, but crime prevention and social work chores dominated much of the safety officers' activities. Third, the VPSO program lacked the legal authority to enforce criminal laws, which led to a drop in support from community residents. Thus, it became difficult for safety officers to enlist the public's help in identifying social problems and their causes. Finally, an absence of organizational structure, evidenced by unclear lines of authority and control, created an accountability problem (Marenin and Copus, 1991). Thus, although community-oriented policing as exemplified by this VPSO program was implemented with good intentions, the results were not as beneficial as its planners anticipated. One recommendation was to improve public safety officer training, coordinate interagency activities better, and heighten officer accountability. In view of the rural dimension and the sparsely populated areas in need of policing, however, it is uncertain whether these remedies would improve the situation significantly (Marenin, 1990, 1991).

Cultural Barriers to Community-Oriented Policing

There is sometimes a strong undercurrent of cultural identity that may cause public resistance to community-oriented policing plans. Sometimes it is best to work with representatives of various ethnic neighborhoods in order to determine which policing strategy is best. Some examples from other countries where cultural diversity exists might be instructive here.

In Northern Ireland, for instance, the Irish Republican Army (IRA) has actively opposed any British control or policing. Where state-controlled police agencies have attempted to deal with crime and social disorder in traditional ways and with good intentions, their efforts have been met with terroristic attacks, including bombings and ambushes of police stations and officers. Some of this resistance to outside policing efforts has been defused by involving community residents to a greater degree in policing their own communities. However, it is difficult for state-controlled police agencies to relinquish some of their control over neighborhoods or entire communities without feeling that their authority to act in dealing with criminals has been compromised (Murphy, 1994; Zureik, 1990).

Northern Ireland contains other complex elements that fuel social instability and hinder any aggressive efforts toward establishing effective community-oriented policing. The country is sharply divided between Protestants and Catholics. The different religious tenets reflect basically different ways of defining how the power of the state should be viewed and exercised (Mapstone, 1992). Counterinsurgency policies have dictated how community-oriented policing has been designed and implemented. These policies emphasize maintaining public order, protecting the state against subversive and violent elements, and combatting violence among communities (Weitzer, 1995). From one perspective, police discretionary powers in Northern Ireland have been greatly abused and misused. Suggestions have included replacing top police managers who tolerate abuses; reconstituting the police subculture so that training and police station norms reinforce civility and the use of minimum force in police-citizen contacts; redefining neighborhoods that have been traditionally labeled as "enemy territory" so that residents no longer feel stereotyped and indiscriminately targeted as foes; and providing stricter punishment for misconduct and granting meaningful rewards for good behavior (Weitzer, 1995).

One response has been the creation of police liaison committees (PLCs), intended to promote positive relations between the public and the police, to facilitate constructive dialogue regarding police matters, and to foster solutions to local problems (Weitzer, 1992). A major problem with these PLCs has been their secrecy and elitist, restricted membership (Weitzer, 1992). On the positive side, however, some interviewees in a 17-committee survey said they believed that PLCs provided open forums for demonstrating support for the police (Weitzer, 1992).

Palestinians in Israeli-controlled areas are likewise militant in countering efforts by Israeli police to deal with crime in these communities. One suggested strategy is to incorporate community residents into a community-oriented policing enterprise to operate together with legal police authority in combatting crime. However, this is much easier said than done. Policing in divided societies is much more complex than it appears, often because of an oversimplified view of the nature of the conflict in these societies by persons who are responsible for implementing change (Brewer, 1991). In both the Northern Ireland and Israeli situations, mistrust of police is common among community residents. Police are not only mistrusted, but they are rejected as having legitimate authority to investigate crimes and apprehend criminals, especially if the suspects are of an ethnic minority. In some respects, there are parallels in the United States, where racial factors create a similar milieu of mistrust and resentment. Black suspects may often possess feelings about white police officers that are similar in nature to residents of Northern Ireland toward British officers or Palestinians in Israeli-controlled areas toward Israeli police. Thus, the cultural factor is persistent and pervasive, particularly in racially or ethnically diverse or divided jurisdictions.

SECTOR PATROLLING, FOOT PATROLLING, AND BEATS

According to the 1990 National Assessment Program sponsored by the National Institute of Justice, 38 percent of the 2,000 agencies surveyed were interested in reestablishing traditional foot patrols, a 12 percent increase from 26 percent reported in 1986 (National Institute of Justice, 1992:5).

The New York City Foot Beat Example

In the aftermath of the late-1970s budget and manpower cuts, the New York Police Department (NYPD) found that in 1984, the bulk of the patrol force was responding to 911 calls. In July 1984, the NYPD implemented a pilot community-policing program in Brooklyn's 72nd Precinct. Dubbed the Community Patrol Officer Program (CPOP), the pilot project sought to determine the feasibility of permanently assigning police officers to foot patrol in fairly large neighborhood beat areas. Further, it required officers to perform a variety of nontraditional tasks in addition to their normal law enforcement duties. **Community Patrol Officers** (CPOs) were expected to be full-service police officers and to serve as community resources. Some additional tasks included helping residents to organize community groups, attending community meetings, making service referrals, and helping to devise strategies to deal not only with local crime and order-maintenance problems, but also with social needs.

The CPOP differed in significant ways from traditional patrol deployment strategies. First, all participating officers were volunteers, which permitted the department to exercise considerable flexibility during patrol hours. Second, CPOs were recruited from the patrol force based on their agreement to work hours that would permit them to focus on the problems specific to their beat and to change their hours on a daily basis if necessary. Third, the officers were encouraged to solicit input from residents and merchants on their beats by setting patrol priorities rather than by reacting solely to crime events. Fourth, officers were encouraged to involve the community in formulating solutions to neighborhood problems. Finally, the most significant way CPOP differed from conventional patrol was that the CPOs were given the responsibility to work on problems over time and to follow up (Farrell, 1986:1–5).

The pilot CPOP program was considered successful, both by department officials and by local community representatives. The CPOs demonstrated their ability to perform a wider range of duties, and they expressed satisfaction with their new roles. The residents and merchants of Sunset Park (the 72nd District) voiced overwhelming support of the program, and other communities began to lobby for its implementation in their own areas.

NYPD attempted to expand the program in January 1985, by implementing CPOP in six additional precincts. Usually, a precinct CPOP unit requires nine police officers assigned to individual beats, one officer assigned as unit coordinator, a supervisory sergeant, and a police administrative aide. Because CPOP represented a substantial investment of personnel, the pace of program expansion was limited by the department's authority to recruit and hire additional police officers. As budgetary increases allowed the hiring of new officers, new CPOP units were created. By September 1988, CPOP had been established in each of New York City's 75 patrol precincts. The program involved more than 800 police officers (including trained alternates), 75 sergeants, and 75 administrative aides (Vera Institute of Justice, 1988:2).

An Example of a Smaller City Beat

In Garden Grove, California, 800 residents squeezed into apartments in a cul-de-sac. The residents were continually subjected to disruptions: noise, street fights, car thefts, and police officers trying to make arrests. In January 1993, under the direction of Chief Stan Knee, two police officers were assigned the neighborhood as their beat. The officers became a constant presence on the cul-de-sac and worked their beat on foot and on bicycles, trying to become acquainted with residents and preventing problems (Young, 1993:B1).

Although the impact two officers could make on a neighborhood plagued with a history of crime was problematic, their methods were proactive and innovative and involved the resources of the community. The approach of these two officers was multifaceted. They held meetings with apartment owners, surveyed residents about crime problems, and organized outings for the neighborhood's kids. They also were somewhat creative in prescribing sanctions. When two female graffiti "artists" were caught with magic markers, the officers didn't arrest them; they assigned the girls to spend ten hours on a Saturday painting over the graffiti. They nudged apartment owners to maintain outdoor lighting in an attempt to discourage public drinking and car thefts. They also encouraged the removal of trash and other debris from around buildings.

They contacted the Boy and Girl Scouts to establish troops in the neighborhood, which the organizations did. Acting as surrogate parents, the officers took children from the neighborhood to the circus when it came through town. They called on the city's Parks and Recreation Department to design a recreation area. On a different level, they called in the city's code enforcement officers to help them inspect some of the more than two dozen two-story apartment buildings that lined the avenue. Slowly, the cul-de-sac began a transformation, and the local residents began to point to their neighborhood with pride (Young, 1993:B12).

The result: After seven months, reported crimes, including car thefts, burglary and petty theft, decreased by 50 percent. The program was so successful that in August 1993, the prototype beat system was adopted citywide, increasing the number of patrol officers on the streets. The officers were dispatched to a reworked beat system with smaller patrol areas (Young, 1993:B1). Not unexpectedly, several surrounding cities, after reviewing the experiment, expressed an interest in starting a similar program.

Despite these successes with community policing, there are some drawbacks. Because police departments often do not have adequate resources to place beat officers in each area requiring their presence, police departments must prioritize those areas most in need. It has been suggested that this determination should be left to the police rather than to local politicians, who tend to curry favor and generate votes. On a positive note, Garden Grove was selected in 1984 as one of the first departments in the nation to receive additional police officers under the new federal program.

Basic Car Plan

In 1970 the Los Angeles Police Department (LAPD), under the direction of Chief Edward Davis, initiated the **basic car plan** as a method of preventing and controlling crime. A basic car team consisted of nine officers: a lead officer; five senior officers with two to three years experience, and three probationary officers. The basic car plan operated on workload analysis factors that produced a minimum radio car plan (basic car plan) for all watches. Radio cars were designated as "A" units and assigned to their own basic car districts. Three officers were assigned to a basic car district during each of the three watches. Additional radio cars, designated as "X" units, were available during periods of increased workload. The basic cars were given dispatch priority to calls within their area. In the event the basic car was not available, the "X" car responded.

Although designed to help the police prevent the commission of crime, this approach achieved many collateral benefits. Over time the community became actively involved through monthly community meetings that focused on police-related subjects and how officers and citizens could assist each other. This newly created communication link between community members and members of the LAPD was a major contribution to understanding both the problems of the police and the community. Community residents were able to meet and converse with the team members responsible for patrolling their area. The police officers were no longer nameless faces in black-and-white cruisers. The community welcomed this opportunity to interact with their "protectors" and did so with enthusiasm—79,123 citizens attended basic car plan meetings during 1970 (Felkenes and Whisenand, 1972).

PROBLEM-ORIENTED POLICING (POP)

Problem-oriented policing (POP) has also been termed *incident-driven policing*, because policing agents identify a community problem and then develop remedial strategies to solve the problem. According to Spelman and Eck (1987), POP is the outgrowth of 20 years of research into police operations that converged on the following three main themes:

> **BOX 4.2   Santa Ana, California**
>
> One of the early attempts to implement community policing was undertaken by Santa Ana, California. Under the leadership of Chief of Police Ray Davis, the city was divided into four geographical zones. Each zone had an area commander and was patrolled by officers and teams permanently assigned, to facilitate closer police-community resident contact and make it possible for members of the community and police officers to become better acquainted. Another step was to enlist community participation by adding non-sworn Police Service Officers (PSOs) to the police department staff. PSOs are civilians who wear uniforms but do not carry weapons or batons. The use of PSOs was eventually accepted by the sworn personnel, especially since the PSOs handled the bulk of minor traffic investigations. These activities effectively released sworn officers to pursue more serious law enforcement functions (Skolnick, 1986:35). In addition, the police organized Community Watch groups throughout the city and provided ongoing assistance and advice to block captains and the community watch groups as a whole. In a way, the community was brought into the process of crime prevention and detection.
>
> Another aspect of the Santa Ana experience was the establishment of police substations in each of the four zones. These substations proved quite beneficial from various points of view. For instance, the police no longer had to transport suspects to the main station; they could instead drop off suspects at the substation and continue their patrolling. Furthermore, citizens enjoyed the convenience of the substation, since they could bring minor complaints directly to officers near their neighborhoods rather than go to the main station several miles away.

1. Increased effectiveness, achieved by attacking underlying problems that give rise to incidents that consume patrol and detective time
2. Reliance on the expertise and creativity of line officers to study problems carefully and develop innovative solutions
3. Closer involvement with the public to make sure that the police are addressing the needs of citizens

Spelman and Eck include four parts in the strategy:

1. *Scanning.* Instead of relying on broad, law-related concepts—robbery or burglary, for example—officers are encouraged to group related incidents that come to their attention as "problems," which they define in precise and therefore more useful terms. For example, an incident that typically would

be classified simply as a robbery might be seen as part of a pattern of prostitution-related robberies committed by transvestites in inner-city hotels.
2. *Analysis.* Officers working on a well-defined problem collect information from a variety of public and private sources, not just police data. They use the information to illuminate the underlying nature of the problem, suggesting its causes and a variety of options for its resolution.
3. *Response.* Working with citizens, businesses, and public and private agencies, officers tailor a program of action suitable to the characteristics of the problem. Solutions to community problems may go beyond the traditional criminal justice system; the remedies must include other community agencies or organizations.
4. *Assessment.* The officers evaluate the impact of these efforts to see if the problems were actually solved or alleviated (Spelman and Eck, 1987:2).

This sequential approach to crime problems was modified and adopted by the Oxnard (California) Police Department (OPD), which carried the process one step further. OPD developed a unique Problem Identification Form to facilitate the process and provide an overview and assessment of the resolution. The OPD form is divided into the following self-explanatory sections:

1. Problem location
2. Problem(s) identified
3. Action recommended
4. Expected results
5. Problem update

A significant difference exists between problem-oriented policing and community-oriented policing. In problem-oriented policing, the police—with or without community cooperation—attempt to identify and solve problems, and the problems need not be police related. In his book *Problem-oriented Policing,* Herman Goldstein (1990) gives a range of community problems that could be addressed by the police. He defines the term *problem* as "a cluster of similar, related, or recurring incidents rather than a single incident," "a substantive community concern," and "the unit of police business" (Goldstein, 1990:66).

Sparrow (1993) cites four principles regarding information necessary for problem solving. First, because the cluster of incidents that form a problem might occur in any of several dimensions—geographic, temporal, offender class, victim class, behavior type, weapon type, and so on—analyzing the incidents that comprise a problem requires the ability to aggregate and separate incident data along one, or any combination, of these dimensions. This process requires flexible database structures with versatile access and analytic capabilities. Probably it also will require expert system management. Second, informational and analytic support for problem solving might be required at many different levels within the department, ranging from support for quickly investigated street-level problems to major and protracted investigations or programs. Third, the department's information and analytic support must be available for problems whether or not they are crime related. Fourth, information and analytic support will have to be provided for problems (a) that might not previously have been identified, (b) that might not appear to be like any previous police business, (c) that might not have any data readily available, and (d) that might be unique. Provision of the appropriate information support will require unprecedented creativity, improvisation, and innovation (Sparrow, 1993:4). It is important for the police to be open with the public regarding data that would not jeopardize or impede ongoing investigations. The purpose of COP is not intelligence gathering, although it might well be a byproduct.

TEAM POLICING

Team policing, like many other American policing methods and traditions, had its roots in England. One of the earlier experiments with team policing was the Aberdeen Plan, which gave foot patrolmen a team identity and provided for expanded field mobility. Another British team approach, called the Salford Plan, increased the flexibility of police coverage and made use of sergeants' vehicles as mobile field stations. Under this plan dependency on hand-held radio transceivers unified communications and control. A "unit beat-patrolling" function was introduced under this concept, which incorporated one mobile patrol element, two foot patrol officers, and a Criminal Investigation Division (CID) officer responsible for follow-up criminal investigations. This cooperative effort was essentially a unit assigned to a particular geographical location (Zunno, 1969).

The concept and actual practice of team policing in the United States evolved from the selected enforcement method, which has been described as a "police effort applied in relation to time, place, location, and type of violation" (Zunno, 1969). Initial efforts employing selected enforcement techniques for combating crime generally consisted of supplementing existing patrol forces. Squads of specially trained officers were deployed in high-crime areas. Tactics included patrol in unmarked cars, frequent field interviews of suspicious persons and known offenders, and, generally, relief from routine assignments or calls-for-service.

In 1964 Tucson, Arizona, implemented a "fluid patrol" system, which appears to be a precursor of the wider application of sector team policing. This application had supervisors assigned to certain sections of the city based on anticipated needs. Although severe personnel attrition coupled with dramatic workload increases caused the "fluid patrol" to be modified, during the period of full staffing, reported crime decreased and traffic enforcement rose. Most important, the patrol force gained a degree of flexibility, efficiency, and solidarity that had not been realized previously (Zunno, 1969). The tactics and application of "fluid patrol" did not incorporate the philosophical and organizational changes that characterize community policing, however.

Four years later, in June 1968, then Chief of Police Robert B. Murphy of Richmond, California, inaugurated the Team Patrol System (TPS), which had similarities to Tucson's method of patrol organization and field deployment. The TPS was a shift from one individual officer responsible for one beat to the concept of group responsibility for a large area. As in the basic car plan, workload analysis based on demographic need of coverage determined the number of police officers assigned to a patrol team. The team included one sergeant and from eight to fifteen team members. To provide increased citizen contact, this innovative approach assigned one team member to attend neighborhood meetings and city council meetings. In postevaluations, the program suffered from conflicts in training schedules and lack of cooperative involvement of middle management (Phelps and Murphy, 1969). In 1993 TPS was incorporated into the newly adopted community policing plan (Roybal, 1993).

Team policing is an interesting concept that allows a self-sufficient team of officers to police selected crimes in designated geographical areas. This approach was a major shift from centralized policing, and from a supervisorial point of view, it relied heavily on functional authority as opposed to traditional vested authority. Each member of the policing team had responsibilities in his or her special areas of expertise. One major difference between team policing and community-oriented policing is the incorporation of values, intensive community involvement, and planning. More time is taken by the police and other participating groups to prepare for the implementation of COP. Community policing strategies also use the technology available—computerized databases, mobile data terminals, crime mapping, and more—to meet its objectives (Austin and Marshall, 1992:33).

MOUNTED PATROL, BICYCLES, AND GOLF CARTS

The types of patrol are only limited by custom and technology. Geese comprised one of the earliest known detection and alarm systems. The types of patrol used today are (1) animal, (2) human, (3) mechanical, and (4) electronic. These applications include patrolling by foot, automobile, aircraft, motorcycle, horse, dog, boat, bicycle, videocamera, and television (Whisenand and Cline, 1971:18). The application and type of enforcement patrol greatly influence the ability of the officer(s) to communicate with the public—the vital link in COP. Quite obviously, electronic television monitoring or similar surveillance methods are not designed for public interaction.

Mounted Patrol

The urban police horseback patrol is perhaps a throwback to the days of the Western frontier. Visions of mounted posses chasing outlaws, stopping runaway stagecoaches, capturing criminals by leaping from horse to horse, and rescuing damsels in distress are the stuff of which late night movies are made. Modern-day policing on horseback does not involve any of this Hollywood glamor.

Certain policing and control situations require alternative forms of transportation, especially in urban areas. Mounted patrol is popular in New York; Baltimore; Los Angeles; San Francisco; Columbia, South Carolina; Lexington, Kentucky; Orlando, Florida; Detroit; New Orleans; and Nassau County, New York, to mention a few places. These patrols have been lauded as a very community-oriented enforcement method. Although horses do pose a threat to unsuspecting pedestrians and cause a few sanitation problems, they are quite effective in crowd control. They also may have a calming affect on potentially unruly crowds. The New Orleans Police Department has used horse patrols extensively during the annual Mardi Gras festivals. Horse patrols add a dimension of control that simply could not be accomplished otherwise without platoons or barriers of police officers.

The New Orleans Mounted Patrol

The New Orleans Police Department (NOPD) has employed mounted patrols in some form since the department's inception but, with the advent of the "horseless carriage," saw the use of horses decline in the early twentieth century. The first formal and separate mounted patrol unit was established in 1925, with a cadre of 24 police officers and one captain. Over the years the unit was scaled down until in 1950 it consisted of twelve officers and one sergeant.

Since 1950, the focus and organization of the mounted unit has changed many times; currently, the patrol is used in a variety of ways. The City of New Orleans, and in particular the Vieux Carré (French Quarter), is a major tourist attraction with special enforcement requirements. The mounted unit is ideally suited for the Vieux Carré sector because it is a relatively small area with a large concentration of people. During Mardi Gras the mounted unit utilizes all its horses, with two-thirds taking part in daily parades and the remainder augmenting the Vieux Carré's uniform patrol force.

In 1994 the NOPD boarded thirty-five horses in its stable located in the city park. The barn was constructed in 1972 and enlarged in 1988. A large lighted and fenced training ring and a grazing corral are also located on the grounds. With the addition of new transport vehicles in 1991, the mounted patrol became capable of transporting as many as twenty-six horses to any location.

Members of the mounted patrol must satisfactorily complete an intensive two-week training program, during which trainees are in the saddle an average of six hours per day. The training course includes the basic care of the animals and progresses to riding drills in which officers ride courses with and without a saddle and are expected to run and jump their mounts without using their hands or stirrups. The agitation training portion of the course covers the handling of horses in situations involving a crowd, noise, sirens, and fireworks, as well as firing weapons from horseback. Upon completion of training the new rider is paired with an experienced unit member for street work. As a unit they train in tactical formation riding, for deployment in demonstrations and to move and control large crowds (Smegal, 1994).

Mounted patrol is also a vital asset to the security and safety of Central Park in New York City. Patrolling on horseback provides rider visibility, and such patrols function very well in congested traffic areas and parks and to complement regular patrol forces during special events. In addition to the control factor, most people are attracted to animals, so that it is not unusual for people to stop, pet the horses, and converse with the riders. This opportunity to interact with the public through a mutual interest is conducive to orderly conduct and to reduction of tension and hostility. It is in this context that the mounted patrol is viewed as an important aspect of COP.

Bicycles

The use of the bicycle as a patrol vehicle has been as traditionally British as "bangers and mash." Constabularies in England have used this mode of transportation since the invention (or at least the popular use) of the device. It remains a common mode of police transportation that lends itself to rider mobility and accessibility.

Many police and sheriff departments across the United States have investigated and opted for the use of bicycles. Today police bicycle patrols are a positive tool in urban law enforcement. Probably the two most prominent programs are in Seattle, Washington, and Las Vegas. Seattle started its program in 1987 and fields teams on a permanent daily basis regardless of sun, rain, or snow. Bicycles are used to patrol Seattle's downtown business district, outlying business areas, and various parks. The Seattle police field up to 80 officers per night (Fleissner et al., 1991). Other cities, such as Oakland, Sacramento, Long Beach, San Jose, and Los Angeles, California, and Boston, have also formed bicycle units.

As with other enforcement tactics, the use of bicycles has supporters and critics. Critics point to the limited use of bicycles in inclement weather and at night, the inability to transport prisoners, the risk of officer injury, and the length of time to respond to emergencies. Supporters cite cost savings, the ability to access places regular patrol vehicles cannot reach, community support, the advantage of stealth, and greater visibility. The Oakland (California) Police Department described the value of bicycle patrol in the downtown area in its "Uniformed Bicycle Proposal":

> Problems, such as locked auto burglaries, public drinking, panhandling, and drug dealing, so common in the downtown area, could be satisfactorily addressed. Bicycle-mounted officers would be able to observe suspects from a reasonable distance and then proceed to their location quicker than officers on foot patrol. Bicycle patrol officers would be less visible to the suspects than an approaching marked police vehicle. Bicycles would not be hampered by traffic congestion while responding to calls. Because of their versatility, bicycles could patrol areas inaccessible to motor-

ized vehicles, such as court yards and multi-storied parking garages. (Morgan, 1990:21–22)

The Oakland proposal further stated:

In addition to decreasing the response time of officers, visibility would also be enhanced. Highly mobile officers, unrestricted by police vehicles, would come in contact with more citizens during the course of their duties. In regards to public relations, the bicycles are an excellent tool. Other municipal police departments that have adopted a bicycle patrol have discovered that their public relations image has been enhanced. Civilians are more likely to approach an officer on a bicycle patrol than they are one in a police car. Use of a bicycle patrol is a new and innovative concept in modern police work, and as such, would generate a good deal of interest from the community. (Morgan, 1990:24–25)

The Seattle Police Department's bicycle proposal, echoing Oakland's rationale, stated:

We feel this (bicycle patrol) would be a very positive program for our department. It would afford more positive contacts with the public which would be very beneficial in this time with complaints of police being over officious. It could also very easily blend into our future direction of Community Oriented or Problem Oriented Policing. (Fleissner et al., 1991:111)

The success of bicycle patrols is subject to evaluation from a variety of sources. The police officers involved in these programs must be satisfied that they are performing a vital service; The city must appreciate the efforts of the police to ensure a safer community, the city merchants should enjoy comfortable marketing zones, and the community at large must support the concept. In an interdepartmental memorandum Brea's bicycle patrol teams provided a summary of activity during the 1992 holiday season, including the following comment:

One of the biggest benefits we believe that occurred this year compared to the last several years that we have worked was the community relations aspect. Every day we worked we had several citizens and merchants contact our officers and say how happy they were to see us on the bicycles and patrolling the area. We did not hear a negative comment about the officers throughout the holiday season. We were able to stop and talk to shoppers and merchants much easier than in the past while driving patrol cars. We had several female shoppers ask "how long are you going to be here tonight? I feel much safer knowing you are around." One afternoon we assisted a child who had a flat tire on his bicycle. With the equipment we carry on our bicycles we were able to repair his tire so he could continue on. (Fleissner et al., 1991:114)

Golf Carts

Open or covered and heated golf carts have been used successfully to patrol downtown urban areas, congested areas, and shopping malls. They are especially effective in parking enforcement. These motorized units provide the benefits of both mobile and foot patrol, allowing officers to move rapidly from one place to another or to leisurely travel from one storefront to the next. Golf carts are relatively inexpensive to purchase, economical to operate, and quite easy to maintain (Geller, 1991:413). Non-sworn, reserve, or community service officers are easily assigned golf cart patrol, as they are not required to transport prisoners or leave a certain area of patrol. Golf cart patrol also presents the enforcement agency with another COP tool, because officers in golf carts are able to stop and interact with the public more readily than officers assigned patrol cars. Tampa, Florida, is one of several U.S. cities that have utilized golf cart patrols with some success.

MANIFEST FUNCTIONS OF COMMUNITY POLICING

In a National Institute of Justice report, Sparrow (1993) makes several interesting points about police and their community roles. He says that community policing, insofar as it points toward the power of partnerships, demands a reevaluation of a department's policies regarding data and information sharing with the community and other governmental agencies. He further predicts that notions of police as the "eyes and ears" of urban government, as a motivator of and partner with the community, and as a coordinator of the delivery of government services will have profound ramifications for the types of information a department keeps, as well as the way information flows, is analyzed, and is disseminated (Sparrow, 1993:4). As the delivery of police services undergoes change to implement community policing, there must be concern about the use of such information. If the public suspects that the underlying motive for a shift toward community policing is police intelligence gathering, public trust and organizational goals will fail. Police need information to facilitate crime prevention, crime suppression, and the arrest of offenders, but not at the expense of the community partnership.

LATENT FUNCTIONS OF COMMUNITY POLICING

The results of community policing are difficult to quantify, because although many benefits are present, some of them may not be obvious. When city government decides to bring citizens into the policy and review process, it is generally for two reasons. One is the pressure by certain citizen groups to become more involved because of vested interests. The second is the political mileage governing officials can gain by showing that citizens are participating in community policing efforts.

When vested interest groups ask to become involved or are invited to join in oversight or review functions regarding their police agencies, city officials must be extremely careful to examine their true intent and seek out hidden agendas. Wholesome cooperation and involvement for the community good reflect

> **BOX 4.3   Houston, Texas**
>
> An approach different from the one used in Santa Ana, California (see Box 4.2), was the Houston Police Department (HPD) program, in which increased community involvement was emphasized. The Houston Police Department formed smaller police teams that were assigned to specific areas of the city. These teams assisted community residents in organizing community watch programs, called Houstonians on Watch (Skolnick, 1986:105).
>
> These police teams went to extraordinary lengths to provide the community with crime information, even putting crime warning fliers in shopping bags at local grocery stores. In an effort to decentralize, HPD established community stations to encourage residents to interact actively with their law enforcement officers (Friedmann, 1992:156). As community problems were reported, the officers often walked from these substations into their neighborhood to attempt to resolve the problem. Officers also knocked on doors to determine if the quality of policing was adequate. They followed up by advising crime victims in their vicinity of their progress in investigating incidents or crime reports. These actions were fruitful and established a strong sense of unity between the HPD and the community. HPD's mission statement reflects this sentiment: "The mission of the Houston Police Department is to enhance the quality of life in the city of Houston by working cooperatively with the public and within the framework of the United States Constitution to enforce the laws, preserve peace, reduce fear, and provide for a safe environment" (Greene, 1988b:121).

the true spirit of **community**. However, if citizen groups are out to grind axes or if they have political aspirations and seek to use their involvement as platforms, city officials must exercise discretion.

Similarly, when concerned citizens are invited to serve on boards and commissions that review police procedure, policy, and other matters, they should be given minicourses in those specific areas under review. The concept of community-oriented policing ideally brings with it citizen involvement, but uninformed citizen involvement, particularly in the area of the law enforcement function, is tantamount to a "kiss of death." Many individuals outside the formal police organization have little or no knowledge of the various laws, codes, and directives that guide the administration of policing. More time, energy, and money should be expended in bringing these groups up to speed. They should understand city/police contracts, memorandums of understanding, police unions, employee rights, internal and external grievance procedures, and the legal provisions and restrictions regarding information and related personnel matters.

The city of Walnut Creek, California, has established a citizen Budget Review Committee that, in an advisory capacity, reviews the annual police budget. For many police agencies across the United States, however, the thought of citizen interference in police matters, especially the budget, the very heartbeat of the department, strikes terror into the hearts of more than a few executives and managers. If these groups do have vested interests, the terror is well justified. It is incumbent on city government to balance the interests of the police and outside groups. The operation of police departments should involve members of the communities they serve. An informed citizenry can do nothing but benefit the operation and practice of American policing.

Tension

Another latent effect of community-oriented policing is the reduction of tension in communities caused by hostilities between the police and the citizens. Although incidents are recorded and figures of assaults on peace officers are available, the magnitude of community tension is difficult to quantify. In referring to community tension, one officer commented, "We know it's there—we can feel it, we sort of experience it—and we also know when it is not there." Tension is a more or less invisible force.

Use of Force

Jurisdictions that have subscribed to community-oriented policing seem to be more receptive to taking a less confrontational collective approach to crime control and the apprehension of offenders. Many agencies are experimenting with or have adopted nonlethal-force options. Whereas at one time in American policing, the mere notion of nonlethal force would cause heated debate, today more and more agencies are researching and experimenting with alternative force options. Although communities have varying standards regarding the use of force, the emphasis on less-than-lethal options has been clearly articulated by the U.S. Supreme Court.

Tennessee v. Garner (1985). In March 1985, the U.S. Supreme Court declared that more than half the states' laws and many law enforcement agency policies pertaining to the use of deadly force were unconstitutionally excessive. In *Tennessee v. Garner* (1985), police in Memphis, Tennessee, responded to a call from neighbors that someone was in a vacant house nearby. Not knowing who might be prowling at 3:00 A.M., Memphis police approached. They observed someone running away from the home and yelled at the person to stop. The person continued running away, and police officers fired at the runner to prevent his or her escape. A bullet from one of the officer's revolvers struck a 15-year-old boy, Garner, in the back of his head, killing him instantly. It turned out that Garner and some friends were simply "hanging out" and had found the vacant house attractive for this purpose. Even if Garner *had* been burglarizing the house, which he had not, the police officers exacted a far greater punishment for Garner than any court might impose. He was killed because he ran away when ordered to stop. An arrested burglar might suffer one or two years in jail, not the loss of life. Inasmuch as Garner was not harming anyone by his actions and did not appear to pose a threat to pursuing officers, the U.S. Supreme Court declared their use of force in this instance to be unjustified.

The Demise of the "Fleeing Felon" Rule. The U.S. Supreme Court decision in *Garner* imposed a national minimum standard regarding the use of deadly force. This decision invalidated "fleeing felon" laws that allowed deadly force to be used to prevent suspected felons from escaping. However, the court limited its ruling by providing that if the suspect is armed and poses "a significant threat of death or physical injury to the officer or others," the use of deadly force may be applied. The court held that "the use of deadly force to apprehend an apparently unarmed, non-violent fleeing felon is an unreasonable seizure under the Fourth Amendment." This ruling sharply restricts police officer behaviors in situations in which lethal force could be used and added significantly to law enforcement interest in developing less-than-lethal weaponry.

Two years after *Tennessee v. Garner* (1985), the National Institute of Justice began to examine operational requirements for innovative less-than-lethal devices and examined several new technologies that might be developed for law enforcement use. Of interest were electrical and electromagnetic technologies, alternative impact devices, drug-delivering dart guns, and knockout gases. Guided by an advisory Medical Operations Committee, the institute in 1989 began to develop a prototype chemical device for state and local law enforcement application(s).

In 1991 and 1992 the National Institute of Justice convened two meetings of law enforcement officials, public interest groups, and criminal justice researchers and scholars in Washington, D.C., for the purpose of exploring the development and uses of less-than-lethal devices. The NIJ project focused on five scenarios in which the use of less-than-deadly force might reduce the probability of injury or death to a suspect, an innocent bystander, or a law enforcement officer. These situations included the following (Hayeslip and Preszler, 1993):

- Fleeing felon/patrol applications
- Domestic disturbances
- Barricade/tactical assault
- Search warrant/raid
- Prison/jail disturbance

There is considerable evidence that law enforcement agencies throughout the United States are exploring and examining new nonlethal compliance methods that will be more consistent with the principles underscored in community-oriented policing.

Enforcement and Sentencing

In the criminal justice system context, when law enforcement agencies fully embrace the concepts of community policing, it is not done in a vacuum. The policies of the police have an impact on the entire juvenile and adult process of criminal justice: probation, district attorneys, courts, and corrections. There appears to be a shift toward a more concerted cooperative effort within the local criminal justice system with regard to maintaining public peace and dealing with nonsocial behavior.

Santa Ana, California, one of the cities experimenting with community-oriented policing, responded to increased vandalism and graffiti with a cooperative venture. In late 1992, increased vandalism cost the city approximately $10 million per year and prompted the formation of the Tagging Enforcement Program, involving the police department, schools, neighborhood associations, and the city. Whereas previous enforcement strategies resulted in approximately 10 arrests per month, the new program produced 240 graffiti arrests in a three-month period (January–March 1993). The crackdown had three phases:

1. Prevention
2. Removal
3. Prosecution

To help prevent graffiti, the school district introduced a course on the subject. In addition, officers reminded merchants that it is illegal to sell spray paint and markers to minors. The second phase sought to have graffiti removed quickly. One result was that local merchants and large chain stores in Southern California, such as K-Mart, Target, Home Depot, and Wal-Mart, placed all spray paint cans under lock and key; customers had to ask clerks for access to the products and had to be 21 years of age or older to purchase spray paint. Warning signs similar to those on cigarette machines were posted near the paint displays.

Another result was that whereas in November 1992 public works employees worked seven days a week, the new enforcement policy allowed them to return to a five-day work week. Further, the prosecutorial phase provided some interesting sentencing sanctions. Parents were also held responsible for their children's tagging. Parents who could not afford fines could share their children's community service hours. Those who could afford the fines but refused to pay could be sued in civil court for up to $3,000. Misdemeanor vandalism carried a fine of up to $250, a mandatory probation of three years, and the loss of a driver's license for a year. Tagging offenders not of driving age had to wait an extra year to get their driver's license. First-time offenders could be assigned to complete up to 64 hours of graffiti removal, and repeat offenders could be required to do as much as 200 hours. Taggers responsible for damage of more than $5,000 could be charged with a felony (Ferrell, 1995). This proactive joint and cooperative approach to the problem of vandalism is a demonstration of community partnerships. In days past, the sentencing laws might have been stiffened, but the brunt of the problem still would have fallen directly and solely on the police.

SOME SOCIOLEGAL AND POLITICAL IMPLICATIONS OF COMMUNITY POLICING

November 2, 1993, Election Day

Crime and crime prevention have been at the forefront of political agendas and an integral part of political platforms since before the creation of national crime statistics. National elections have been fought over issues of crime and violence. On the seamier side of politics, observers suggest that the Willie Horton incident severely damaged Michael S. Dukakis's 1988 presidential bid. Horton, a dangerous criminal, was placed in a Massachusetts furlough program for nondangerous offenders. Furlough programs entitle offenders to have some freedom to move about in their communities. While on a furlough, Horton committed several crimes, including a vicious assault of a female. This was not supposed to happen, and law enforcement at various levels was blamed. As governor of Massachusetts at that time, Michael Dukakis was also blamed.

At all political levels, the absence of a strong "law and order" platform indicates to some that the political aspirant is "soft" on crime and crime issues. Gubernatorial candidates have pandered to public fears by emphasizing strong support for capital punishment, longer prison terms, more prisons, and the curtailment of prisoner "privileges." Mayoral campaigns have often exposed a "crime problem" that before the elections was not thought of as a major concern. It seems that during election campaigns across the United States, crime and the fear of crime draw strong interest from politicians. Citizens are deluged with political rhetoric and lopsided statistics.

Minneapolis is a good example. Over the years, the city of 370,000 has experienced a rise in the crime rate, although the 1992 rate of violent crime was 478 incidents per 100,000 people, nearly half of the national average for urban areas. Both mayoral candidates staked out the issue of crime and battled each other. Each wished to be seen by the voters as the stronger supporter of police protection and community safety. John Derus, one of the candidates, citing gang violence and homeowners desperate to sell their houses and move out of the city, proposed a 20 percent increase in the number of police officers (Hillbery, 1993:A5). But Council President Sharon Sayles Belton, who also ran on a "tough on crime" platform, became the city's first black mayor (Brownstein, 1993:A18).

The issue also played well in Virginia and New Jersey. In Virginia, Republican George F. Allen, a former state legislator and U.S. representative, scored a commanding victory over Attorney General Mary Sue Terry, a Democrat. Allen's campaign stressed the elimination of parole for violent criminals and bucked a national trend toward support of tougher gun control laws (the Brady Bill) by opposing his opponent's call for a five-day waiting period for handgun purchases. In New Jersey, Republican Christine Todd Whitman, vowing to cut taxes and be tough on crime, narrowly defeated incumbent Democrat James J. Florio to become New Jersey's first woman governor (Brownstein, 1993:A18).

In New York, crime and race relations were key campaign issues in the race between a former federal prosecutor, Republican Rudolph W. Giuliani, and Mayor David N. Dinkins, a Democrat. The tough-talking Giuliani, stressing crime, competence, and a better business climate, became New York City's first Republican chief executive in more than a quarter of a century. Dinkins became the first African American mayor of a major city not to win a second term. Giuliani advocated sharply curtailing benefits for the homeless, dramatically cutting the city's work force, and privatizing at least four municipal hospitals (Goldman, 1993:A18).

Elsewhere, in Washington state voters passed a "three strikes, you're out" measure mandating life terms without parole for three-time felons. Texas voters approved a $1 billion bond issue for the construction of additional prisons (*Los Angeles Times,* 1993a:A24).

On the heels of the November 2, 1993, election and continuing the tough stance on crime at the federal level, the U.S. Senate on November 8, 1993, approved mandatory life prison terms for anyone convicted in federal court of a third violent felony (known as the three-time-loser amendment) and refused to bar states from executing criminals younger than 18 years of age. In a change of stance, liberal Democrats joined conservative Republicans in voting for these measures, which would have divided the Senate in 1992. Some senators indicated the change in attitude was long overdue, but other observers have suggested that the change in attitude may have stemmed from the November 1993 election results in Virginia, New Jersey, and New York City (Eaton, 1993a:A3).

Interestingly, however, on November 9, 1993, the U.S. Senate voted (99–1) to outlaw handgun possession for virtually everyone under 18. It also demonstrated surprising support for Senator Dianne Feinstein's proposed ban on the sale and manufacture of assault weapons (Eaton, 1993c:A3). Such bans are not generally supported by tough-on-crime factions.

The initial reaction to the problem of crime control is to call for more police officers on the streets, violent offenders to be kept behind bars, and more prison cells. The day after the election, the U.S. House of Representatives rushed through a stripped-down crime bill that authorized nearly $3.5 billion to help President Bill Clinton put 50,000 more police officers on community patrol. The following day, the Senate sharply upped the ante to $22.2 billion that would pay for 100,000 more police officers over a five-year period, new jails, military-style boot camps, regional prisons, and drug treatment (Walsh, 1993:26). California voted to make permanent an existing tax to provide $1.5 billion for public safety, that is, more police and firefighters. (The crime of arson has made fire a facet of California's anxiety about crime [Will, 1993:94].)

The interesting point regarding the sometimes frenetic crime-fighting mood and hyperpolitical interest in crime control at the federal level is that only 5 percent of all codified criminal acts fall under federal jurisdiction, whereas 95 percent fall under state and city jurisdiction. For 40 years Congress has passed a crime bill in every two-year session, except in 1994. The criminal class has not been impressed, and crime rates have not decreased (Will, 1993:94).

Crime and quality-of-life issues appear to generate more conservative idealism and foster a broader base of voter appeal than do liberal democratic lines that approach the same problems from a somewhat different perspective. A more liberal approach includes targeting health and social services, such as redirecting federal housing, health, education, and labor programs to reduce public disorder and create job opportunities.

If the conservative trend continues and more politicians clamor to open more prisons, increase the size of police forces, enact tougher sentencing mandates, and eliminate parole and other "after-care" programs, the criminal justice system will become the largest employer in the United States. As with many other government-sponsored programs, these well-intended initiatives are not without strings attached. Local agencies, for instance, in the case of the projected 100,000 additional police officers, will be required to match the federal police-hiring funds, and in many communities across the nation the matching money is not available. Also of concern is how to come up with the local funds needed to continue to support the additional police manpower in terms of wages, benefits, resources, physical plants, and equipment.

As a result of the 1993–1994 trend toward conservatism, the very nature and style of policing might well change to reflect the popular political climate, a climate that gives no quarter to the accused and more power to the enforcers. This conservative justice philosophy would reflect a style of policing that could be seen as the antithesis of community-oriented policing.

SELECTIVE ENFORCEMENT OF THE LAW

The Spirit of the Law vs. the Letter of the Law

Police officers operating under the auspices of community-oriented policing ideally have a wider range of discretionary options available to them. The concept of community policing could easily have a modifying effect on the behavior and enforcement practices of participating officers. A modified and softened approach in enforcement practices will generally lead to reflective patterns.

If, however, officers are continually second-guessed and given discretion in decision making, they justifiably have a tendency to enforce the letter of the law somewhat equally, impartially, and impersonally. All violations, infractions, and offenses result in some form of intervention, and no slack is given. If officers are just "doing their job," observing the **letter of the law,** their supervisors are hard-pressed to find fault. Minor infractions or violations are often treated in the same manner as more serious offenses. Much to the consternation of the public, many police officers enforce all of the provisions of law to alleviate supervisorial review. Communities under this type of law enforcement can generally expect to be cited, knowing that no excuse will be accepted. In most cases, none will be offered. The relationship between the community and the police is adversarial.

In agencies that have adopted the community-oriented policing philosophy, there appears to be more emphasis on the intent or **spirit of the law** rather than on the strict and legalistic interpretation of the law. Officers have more leeway to invoke sanctions and often utilize alternatives as opposed to the traditional recourse of detention or arrest. A shift from a hard-line approach to optional strategies can result in three distinct benefits. The first is the humane and dignified treatment of clients that can foster community comity and wider acceptance of the police enforcement role. A second benefit is cost savings resulting from not invoking the criminal justice process. Third, officers feel that they are more a part of the system and not merely enforcers, since their roles have been expanded to include the functions of counseling, training, deflecting, and preventing—tasks already assumed by many professional officers.

Regardless of the shift in policing philosophy, there probably will always be controversy regarding the enforcement of unpopular laws. Those offenses categorized as victimless crimes are special areas of concern that appear to receive selective enforcement. Prostitution has, over the centuries, in a variety of cultures, been outlawed and suppressed, but the different enforcement approaches have never, over time, abated the practice of prostitution.

A cursory examination of U.S. statistics from 1972 to 1992 regarding prostitution arrests reveals an escalating pattern.

1972	**1982**	**1992**
33,153 women	40,111 women	47,526 women
11,591 men	22,587 men	24,401 men

These statistics show that the numbers of arrests have increased. What is important is what these statistics do *not* show. They do not explain why there was such a dramatic increase in arrests of males for prostitution. Could it be a result of the AIDS epidemic? Are there really that many more male prostitutes? Or has there been a shift in focus?

The increase in arrests of males for prostitution might be accompanied by a drop in the rate of female arrests, but that does not seem to be the case. Have urban police departments shifted their enforcement priorities in the area of vice? Are there regional differences in arrest patterns that might be attributable to religious influences? How many of these arrests actually resulted in a conviction? There are endless questions, but speculation aside, there were 44,744 arrests for prostitution in 1972; twenty years later, there were 71,927 arrests for the same violation. The only progress we seem to have made is to arrest more people—and prostitution continues.

Estimates of the number of prostitutes in the United States range from 500,000 to 2 million, with 14 as the average age of entry into prostitution. One survey found that 17 percent of American men have solicited prostitutes and 40 percent of the American public think prostitution should be legalized and regulated to reduce the spread of AIDS (*Database*, 1993).

Many Americans believe that certain types of drugs should be decriminalized and the distribution regulated by the government to eliminate illegal profits and to provide a funding base for greatly expanded drug treatment and education programs. Several states have decriminalized or reduced criminal sanctions for the possession of small amounts (less than one ounce) of marijuana from a felony or misdemeanor to an infraction (Rush, 1991:93). The sheer amount of time, money, and energy expended by local law enforcement to curb gambling, prostitution, vice, and narcotics is astronomical. The interesting point is that all these illegal activities are not limited to the geographical boundaries of municipalities, but the funds and enforcement strategies are generally local. Perhaps local police unions and other political action committees should lobby for these crimes to be the enforcement responsibility of state or county policing systems. This shift in enforcement emphasis would certainly lift a tremendous burden from local agencies and perhaps free up resources for expanded community policing. Community-oriented policing could prove useful at the local level to stem those crimes and ease the task at county and state levels.

Problems and Systemic Constraints

When community members perceive themselves at risk, unprotected from harm or inadequately served by understaffed local law enforcement agencies, they have a tendency to react. One reaction in the 1980s and 1990s has been the proliferation of private security firms.

Security guards in America were watching factories and ships at port in the 1700s, more than a century before the nation's first police department was established. Firms like Pinkerton's thrived in the 1800s, providing security for railroads, banks, and companies with violent labor disputes. In the 1990s there are approximately 1.6 million individuals working in the nation's security field—including guards, armored-car drivers, private detectives, alarm company workers, and employees of security equipment manufacturers—which is about three times as many people as in official law enforcement agencies. In 1993 there were more than 700 security firms in Los Angeles County alone, with more than 50,000 guards on foot and car patrol. These guards, who work neighborhoods from South-Central to Bel-Air, provide the city's "community-based" policing. Private security is now a $64 billion industry, with more than 10,000 firms nationwide, employing approximately 600,000 individuals (Corwin, 1993a). Because of the industry's growth and communities' fear of crime, local police receive secondary calls after private security officers have been notified.

The resurgence of private security companies and private security guards brings with it some serious problems for our municipal police, and, in a roundabout fashion, for communities as well. Although it is generally agreed that the private sector offers sorely needed protection and serves to relieve the strained resources of local policing, there are still perceptual problems that cloud the enforcement function. Many community members simply do not know (or do not care to know) the difference between private and public enforcement. A response or action from individuals in uniform, a symbol of authority, is often accepted as legitimate intervention. Unfortunately private security companies are not held to the same level of employee competence as are public police agencies. Private companies operate on a profit margin, and with high insurance rates and other overhead costs, they pay unarmed security guards minimum or just above minimum wages. Want ads in local newspapers under "Security Guards" attest to the market and demand.

The admission standards for private guards are practically nonexistent: Initial training is a short course on how to wear the uniform and how to call in. They are simply not trained, equipped, or supervised to be effective; more important, they are not representative of public policing. Security companies seem to care little about proactive management, empowerment, mission statements, or citizen involvement. There are many occasions when they become a part of the problem, not a part of the solution. When private guards commit errors in judgment or take inappropriate actions, the public has a tendency to lump them into a law enforcement category, not making a distinction between "real" police officers and rent-a-cops. Each enforcement agency generally has distinctive uniforms: Local police, state police, marshals, and sheriffs all wear different color uniforms. Private police also wear distinctive uniforms, and only the most observant citizens are able to tell the difference.

With local police agencies striving to become more customer- and service-oriented, the actions of rent-a-cops can seriously derail the most ambitious community undertakings. There are no easy solutions to complex problems. Some states are beginning to monitor private policing more closely, but, generally, the distinctions between private and public protection are murky. It is not really useful for public policing to issue disclaimers for the actions of private police. Perhaps more stringent hiring guidelines and formal training might bring a better qualified individual into the private sector of policing. But higher standards also demand higher wages, and in this highly competitive market, the profit margin is more important.

FEAR OF CRIME

When communities feel threatened and think they have exhausted all other alternatives, they often resort to the age-old tradition of self-help. In response to citizen fear of crime, legislatures have acted to allow citizens to arm themselves. In thirteen states citizens who wish to carry arms may do so, if they meet certain regulatory requirements. One state example is Florida, which enacted a concealed-carry law in 1987 guaranteeing a gun permit to any resident who is at least 21, has no record of crime, mental illness or drug or alcohol abuse, and has completed a firearms safety course. Florida's homicide rate fell following the enactment of this law, as did the rate in Oregon after the enactment of a similar law. Through June 1993, 160,823 permits had been issued in Florida. Only 530, or 0.33 percent, of the applicants have been denied permits. This indicates that the law is serving law-abiding citizens. Only 16 permits, less than 1/100th of 1 percent, have been rescinded after issuance because of the commission of a crime involving a firearm.

The solution to safe neighborhoods is elusive. Among the alternatives: give local police sufficient resources to implement community-oriented policing, which may resolve some causal factors leading to crime; bring private security under the auspices and authority of public law enforcement in relation to standards, training, and review; return to the Wild West and expand the Florida law to allow qualified citizens to carry concealed weapons; enact tougher laws and build more prisons; direct more time, energy, and funds toward the curing of social ills and shortfalls; or try a combination of governmental intervention strategies.

KEY TERMS

Basic car plan
Community
Community Patrol Officers
Density

Demographics
Letter of the law
Spirit of the law
Urbanization

QUESTIONS FOR REVIEW

1. What is the relationship between density and crime?
2. Discuss New York City's Community Patrol Officer Program.
3. Explain the application of the basic car plan.
4. Why is problem-oriented policing often referred to as incident-driven policing?
5. What is the origin of team policing?
6. List the benefits and limitations of mounted patrol.
7. Discuss the latent functions of community-oriented policing.
8. What were the findings regarding the Kansas City Experiment?
9. Explain the difference between the "letter" and the "spirit" of the law.
10. How can local politics affect community policing?
11. Explain the conflict that can be caused by the enforcement of unpopular laws.

Appendix A

Traditional vs. Community Policing: Questions and Responses
(A revised version from Sparrow, 1988)

Question	Traditional	Community-Oriented Policing
Who are the police?	A government agency principally responsible for law enforcement.	The police act as fiduciary agents of the public they serve.
What is the relationship of the police force to other public service departments?	Priorities often conflict.	One of several agencies dedicated to intragovernmental liaison and cooperation to answer public needs.
What is the role of the police?	Focusing on solving crimes.	Responding to the changing needs of the community.
How is police efficiency measured?	By detection and arrest rates.	By reducing levels of criminal conduct and community fear of crime; by police-community involvement.
What are the highest priorities?	Crimes that are high value (e.g., bank robberies) and those involving violence.	Addressing changing community needs and enforcement problems.
What, specifically, do police deal with?	Incidents.	Short-term emergency situations and long-term community public safety concerns.
What determines the effectiveness of police?	Response times.	Quality service and public satisfaction.
What view do police take of service calls?	Deal with them only if there is no other real police work to do.	An integral part of the police mission and community obligation.

Question	Traditional	Community-Oriented Policing
What is police professionalism?	Swift, effective response to serious crime.	Upgrading individual abilities and attributes; organizational standards and delivery of service.
What kind of intelligence is most important?	Crime intelligence (study of particular crimes or series of crimes).	Combinations of reliable information or data; strategic planning; considered implementation.
What is the essential nature of police accountability?	Highly centralized; governed by rules, regulations, and policy directives; accountable to the law.	External review by independent agency(s) with a consensual internal complaint process.
What is the role of headquarters?	To provide the necessary rules and policy directives.	To empower and support the patrol and auxiliary functions. To ensure ethical and quality performance.
What is the role of the press liaison department?	To keep the "heat" off operational officers so they can get on with the job.	To provide open and honest communications with the public and media representatives.
How do police regard prosecutions?	As an important goal.	As a measure of quality case preparation based on factual evidence.

SUGGESTED READINGS

Brea Police Department (1992). *Bicycle Patrol Team.* Brea, CA: Brea Police Department, Crime Suppression Team.

McElroy, Jerome E., Colleen A. Cosgrove, and Susan Sadd (1992). *Community Policing: The CPOP in New York.* Beverly Hills, CA: Sage.

Police Executive Research Forum (1992). *Problem Solving Quarterly,* Washington, DC: Bureau of Justice Assistance.

CHAPTER 5

Officer Recruitment, Training, and Professionalism

Introduction

The Recruitment Process
Letters of Interest
Advertising
Written and Oral Examinations
Civil Service Examinations
  and Physical and Agility
  Medical Evaluations
Psychological Screenings
Background Interviews
  and Investigations
Polygraph Tests and Certification
  Letters

Hiring as a Probationary Officer
Academy Training
Selected Training Programs:
  Topeka, Kansas, and Columbus,
  Ohio

Probationary Periods and Field Training Officers

Stress vs. Nonstress Academy Training
Nonstress Training
The Jail Experience
The Use of Less-than-Lethal
  Weapons
Verbal Judo

POST and Standardization: Acquiring the Police Officer Role

The Recruitment of Women and Other Minorities

Gay Police Officers, Social Sensitivity, and Affirmative Action

119

The Sergeant Mitchell Grobeson
  Case
The Aftermath of the Grobeson
  Case

On Professionalism, Education, and Social Skills
Sexual Harassment

Strategies to Prevent Harassment
Sample Agency Policy and Format

The Americans with Disabilities Act (ADA)

"By the Book" and the "Dirty Harry" Phenomenon
Career Integrity Workshops
Posttrauma Information
  and Strategies

Police Stress and Burnout: Sources and Implications
Burnout: The Patrol Officer's
  Perspective
The Burnout Syndrome
Burntout Policeman's Association
  and Friends (BPA)
"Blue Humor"
Alcoholism and Substance Abuse

Key Terms

Questions for Review

Suggested Readings

INTRODUCTION

Over the years, policing as an occupation has not been held in high regard or given the respect it deserves by the public. In fact, because of numerous and blatant instances of corruption laid at the precinct doorstep, police officers and general policing have come to be viewed with suspicion. For example, in 1947 a national survey was conducted by the National Opinion and Research Center to measure the prestige ranking of ninety occupations. The position of policeman ranked fifty-fourth, equal in status to railroad conductors and playground directors and lower than undertakers and traveling salesmen (Reiss, 1967). Unfortunately, this was reflective of the mood of that era toward police work. During the intervening decades, the task of municipal law enforcement has gradually acquired higher social status and prestige and is currently rated in the top 25 percent of occupations.

This chapter describes the recruitment process whereby police officers are chosen and trained. Police work has become increasingly routinized through training mechanisms that are fairly standardized in most jurisdictions. An officer's standards and definitions of how to perform the police role are initially learned at training academies. These academies vary in sophistication, although they generally provide similar skills and education that all officers must have to do their jobs effectively. Increasingly, officers are expected to have college degrees as one qualification for being selected for training. Their backgrounds are thoroughly investigated. Those with previous criminal convictions, even minor ones, may be excluded.

Police officers learn much more about their particular work roles after they have left training academies. On-the-job, hands-on experiences with the public under many different circumstances give officers a much better understanding of the seriousness of their work than do the lectures they received while in training. Thus, one important feature of this chapter is a comparison of what officers learn during their formal training period and how they actually go about the business of policing subsequently.

No two police officers are alike, although they have been criticized collectively as having a distinctive "police personality." That allegation has never been substantiated in the professional literature. Police officers do, however, become somewhat defensive toward the public they are sworn to protect and serve. Thus, this chapter also explores different orientations police officers develop toward their work as well as toward the people in their communities. During the last few decades, the term *professionalism* has entered the law enforcement literature. Interestingly, we have only vague notions about what professionalism means or how we might go about acquiring it. Police professionalism is frequently equated with academic achievement, although we would be hard-pressed to draw parallels between police professionalism and the type of professionalism exhibited by organizations of criminal justice professionals or criminologists, for example. Despite the lack of clarity about police professionalism, we will examine what it means to officers and explore its implications for police officer-citizen interactions.

Police work is stressful. This chapter examines police stress, including one of its products: burnout. When police officers become disenchanted with their work or become cynical, they lose some of their effectiveness. Alcoholism and substance abuse are increasingly affecting police officers who often find themselves in life-threatening situations. Police departments throughout the United States have developed several types of coping programs and forms of assistance to help officers with these and other problems.

THE RECRUITMENT PROCESS

Regarding job expectations and defining the police role in society, four formative factors come into play. These include (1) external advertisements, (2) the police selection process, (3) entry-level training, and (4) the probationary period. Police officer selection and recruitment vary among cities and other types of jurisdictions, depending on the availability and nature of jobs advertised. Job announcements for police positions often give a glamorous version of police work quite different from what new officers will actually do following their training. Generally, in an effort to create a labor pool from which the most qualified candidates can be selected, appealing media advertisements are circulated showing concerned and dedicated police professionals dealing with a myriad of urban problems. Posters and other media portrayals depict a humane and sensitive public service tinged with excitement and adventure. This approach, along with competitive starting wages and fringe benefits, make for a very attractive job opportunity for potential rookies.

The recruitment process for police applicants outlined here is a compilation of several steps and processes from a variety of police agencies across the United States. Because there are no definitive or ironclad procedures that have universal applicability, we have taken some liberty in mixing and matching several models to generate interesting contrasts. However, two requirements remain somewhat uniform and constant: possession of a general equivalency diploma (GED), high school diploma, or equivalent, and U.S. citizenship.

Letters of Interest

Letters of interest are generally provided by cities or counties to applicants for police employment when no positions are currently available. These applicants are notified as soon as the need to hire new police personnel has been determined and approved. At times there are long intervals between filing interest letters and sending notifications about position openings. This delay is generally the result of infrequent hiring and sluggish processing. Many otherwise qualified police applicants simply cannot afford to wait up to a year for the opportunity for employment and decide to seek employment elsewhere. Unless they are extremely motivated toward police work, they usually will not reapply.

Advertising

Announcements of police positions are generally placed in local newspapers and posted on community-outreach bulletin boards. Some departments have established a "recruit incentive plan" for their members. If a department member brings in an applicant who successfully completes the academy and is subsequently hired, that member is given a cash bonus for the referral. Many local radio and television stations offer free advertising for police service positions as a public service, and owners of billboards sometimes allow similar public service announcements to fill unrented space. Some law enforcement agencies have recruiting teams that regularly visit local community colleges and universities (especially those with a definite emphasis on criminal justice programs).

Written and Oral Examinations

Applicants take written examinations that include objective questions. In some cases, short essays are included designed to assess applicants' grammar, verbal expression, comprehension, and observation-description skills (Peoples, 1993:77). Some written examinations ask job-specific questions to gauge their knowledge of the law (e.g., search-and-seizure procedures), police procedure, use-of-force issues and the like.

An oral examination is scheduled one week to ten days following satisfactory completion of the written examination. Although oral examination panels vary, generally they consist of three or four individuals representing the hiring agency, the city/county personnel division, the civil service, and the community. It is not unusual to have someone from the local college or university participate in oral board interviews. Prior to the examination some applicants are required to prepare a biographical sketch and, based on the personal information, panel members ask questions regarding the application form. The oral panel members may also present the applicant with hypothetical situations. They may ask the applicant to react to a situation. For example: "You discover an apartment complex on fire at 2:00 A.M. How are you going to alert people in the building and what are you going to do?" Another example: "You are off duty, carrying your gun, accompanied by your girlfriend or spouse, and you see several gang members severely beating a 12-year-old male; what are you going to do?" A third example: "You are with your field training officer. You pull a car over, and you are told by your FTO, 'This is a known drug dealer.' Without probable cause (PC), your FTO finds drugs. He instructs you to write a false report stating that you pulled the car over for a traffic violation. What would you do? Who would you tell?"

Most of these questions and scenarios are based on common sense. Others deal with integrity and ethical behavior. Some of these hypothetical situations place police aspirants in questionable and uncomfortable positions that they could easily perceive as intended to measure their (as yet unproven) loyalty to fellow officers. Oral examinations usually last 15–30 minutes, with the board interviewing eight or more candidates per day. At the end of the day the board members rank applicants on their perceived strengths and weaknesses. It is not reasonable that the best-qualified candidates can be identified after so brief an interview (Peoples, 1993:77), which is why the oral examination has been cited as probably the weakest link in the recruitment and selection process.

Civil Service Examinations and Physical and Agility Medical Evaluations

In some jurisdictions separate civil service written and oral examinations are given in addition to in-house police examinations.

Medical evaluations are thorough. Blood and urine samples are provided prior to the evaluation. Police officer applicants in California are given a complete physical examination that includes a full set of back X-rays and a stress EKG. The general physical also includes assessing weight in proportion to height, amount of body fat, visual acuity, and audio ability.

Three to six weeks after the medical evaluation, applicants are scheduled to complete the physical agility test. This usually consists of a twelve-minute timed run; a body (dummy) 150-pound drag; the unassisted scaling of a six-foot wall (solid wood); and a grip-strength test, which consists of an overhand grip on a pull-up bar held for sixty seconds. This portion of the testing usually lasts two to three hours.

Psychological Screenings

Prior to the oral psychological screening, each applicant generally is given the Minnesota Multiphasic Personality Inventory (MMPI) evaluation, which takes approximately one hour. The results of this test are used by the screening psychologist in the evaluative process. Many different factors motivate people to seek law enforcement positions. A **psychological screening** examination may reveal certain individual traits and propensities that could result in future liabilities. These liabilities might emerge in costly lawsuits; destructive behavior that negatively affects the community; organizational disharmony; disciplinary actions; the discharge of the officer; or loss of selection and training investment.

To minimize these problems, some law enforcement agencies use qualified mental health professionals to conduct preemployment psychological screenings. Although not a precise measurement, these screenings are capable of assessing a propensity toward risk factors often correlated with hyperaggressive, violent behavior and the impairment of a prospective peace officer's ability to maintain "control of temper" (Trompetter, 1993:16).

Background Interviews and Investigations

Background interviews require the prospective officer to review the background information that was part of the initial application and meet with the background investigator, who may ask several questions to clarify points on the application. This portion of the process can last approximately three hours. That same day the applicants are photographed and fingerprinted.

The final step in the selection process is the background investigation. This investigation is also the most expensive to conduct. Internal investigators perform thorough background checks by contacting an applicant's previous employers, neighbors, friends, teachers, professors, and anyone else who can verify the applicant's employment record, performance, and selected character traits. In many cases this procedure can be a tedious task. Records and documents must be verified (for example, military discharges and high school and college transcripts). References are routinely asked to provide other references (not listed on the original application) to expand the investigative process, because, as in most job applications, applicants tend to provide references only from people they expect to give them good evaluations.

BOX 5.1 Psychological Screenings of Police Officers

Professional literature researched by Trompetter (1993) indicates that the following variables correlate with adult violent behavior:

1. The following behaviors in childhood and adolescence:
   a. Fire-setting
   b. Runaway
   c. School suspensions
   d. Vandalism
   e. Cruelty to animals
   f. Attention Deficit Hyperactivity Disorder
   g. Multiple foster home placements
2. Gang affiliation—group associations in which aggressive violence is applied and condoned.
3. A childhood or adolescent history of assuming a self-defined role in which violence is used for enforcement of norms or to protect others.
4. A history of overcompensatory behavior ("little-man syndrome") whereby violence is used to combat low self-esteem and to dramatize self-worth.
5. A history of paranoid persecutory beliefs or behavior wherein other people are incorrectly perceived as sources of threat or danger.
6. A history of aggressive behaviors in response to stressful situations (temper tantrums, verbal or physical destructiveness, and the like).
7. Bullying behavior in which pleasure seems to be obtained from the exercise of violence and terror.
8. A history of exploitation and manipulation of other people.
9. Excessive self-indulgence, self-centeredness, and narcissism with a presumption that other people exist to satisfy one's own needs and violence as the penalty for noncompliance.
10. A history of arrests for aggressive or assaultive behavior.
11. Multiple physical fights since mid-adolescence.
12. Multiple moving (Vehicle Code) violations with "Failures to Appear."
13. Multiple detentions by peace officers for investigation without arrest other than traffic stops.
14. A family history of antisocial conduct, especially crimes of violence.
15. A history of drug and/or alcohol abuse or dependence.
16. Excessive fearfulness and anxiety.
17. A history of interpersonal irresponsibility (failing to meet financial, marital, or employment obligations).
18. A history of callousness displayed by insensitivity, lack of empathy, or wide-ranging deficits in compassion and remorse.

19. A history of rebellious and defiant attitudes toward authority or social conventions.
20. A history of authoritarianism including dogmatism, closed-mindedness, social intolerance, and prejudice.
21. A history of isolating emotions or feelings in which people are viewed as objects or symbols devoid of human sensibilities.
22. A history of major mental disorder, especially paranoid, anxiety, manic, or depressive disorders.
23. A clinical presentation exhibiting quarrelsome, irritable, abrasive attitudes in addition to a demeanor that is humorless, cold, and rude.
24. A history of involuntary psychiatric hospitalizations as a danger to others.
25. A history of aggressive sexuality.
26. (If application is for a lateral transfer or elevation from reserve to regular status) a history of multiple citizen complaints alleging excessive force (both sustained and unsubstantiated but not unfounded), officious bearing, behavior unbecoming a peace officer, multiple courtesy releases for moving vehicle violations, and the like.
27. A work history involving multiple reprimands, suspensions, terminations, resignations in lieu of terminations, or altercations with customers, colleagues, supervisors, or employers.
28. Psychological test findings suggesting impulsivity, heightened aggressive/destructive/hostile impulses, excessive anxiety, poor judgment, low frustration tolerance, hyperirritability, hypersensitivity to criticism, and signs of antisocial behavior or psychopathy.
29. A history of bias, prejudice, poor verbal and interpersonal skills, and pronounced ethnocentricity.

Considering these factors in the preemployment psychological screening of prospective peace officers may help identify individuals who present unacceptable risk factors for unnecessary or excessive force. Although a determination of how many of these factors meet the threshold for disqualification is unclear, it may be worthwhile for all prescreening personnel to address the same variables uniformly until further research establishes those factors with demonstrably high predictive validity (Trompetter, 1993:19).

Polygraph Tests and Certification Letters

Many police departments use polygraph tests or lie detectors. Generally, the polygraph test is used if there are unresolved issues about the applicant's background report that need clarification or further investigation. If applicants pass all of these steps to this point, they may be sent a certification letter, which must

Police training academies attempt to simulate actual arrest situations so that officers can be better prepared when subduing suspects. *(John Gaps III, AP/Wide World Photos)*

be returned to the agency, reaffirming their employment interest. Some applicants decline to continue the process. On receipt of these letters, applicants may be assigned to an academy class with a specified starting date.

HIRING AS A PROBATIONARY OFFICER

Academy Training

Police academy courses and subject matter vary among the states. In those states where minimum training standards have been set, there is a higher degree of standardization. Over the years police training has evolved from a purely physical orientation to contemporary training that combines an educational process. Early academy training focused heavily on restraint techniques, weapon training, and "crime crushing." Today, many police training academies' curriculums are laced with academic topics such as sociology, criminology, psychology, communication skills, and computer science, emphasizing the service and community aspects of policing. Although the practice and application of enforcement techniques and the tools of enforcement are absolutely necessary, the topics of prevention and community awareness are also vital.

According to Jesse Brewer, police commission president, the Los Angeles Police Department and training procedures changed significantly in the aftermath of the Rodney King incident (Corwin, 1993b:A32). Some changes were made in accordance with the Christopher Commission report and others were made by Chief Willie L. Williams. Subsequently, more time has been devoted to studying human relations, cultural diversity, and community-based policing. The chief has emphasized the need for a less confrontational attitude toward the public and critics of the department. Following the King upheaval, one Los Angeles Police Department graduate stated, "It was instilled in us daily that they did things one way in the past and another way now. There was a lot of emphasis on dealing with people the right way . . . not acting superior, not yelling, not saying, 'Do it my way because I'm a police officer.' We learned to relate to people on a more human level" (Corwin, 1993:33).

A review of the course content of two separate police academies is instructive. These academies were in Topeka, Kansas, and Columbus, Ohio. The entire course from Topeka is presented here because it typifies formal preservice training for police officers nationally. Compared with programs in other states, one unusual element in the Topeka curriculum might be the "Tornado Spotters Course."

Selected Training Programs: Topeka, Kansas, and Columbus, Ohio

The Topeka, Kansas, Training Program. The basic mandated course for police training in Kansas comprises a total of 343 hours, but the 1993 Basic Law Enforcement Training Curriculum for the Topeka Police Department involves 438 hours. A review of the March 22–June 4, 1993, curriculum lists courses and topics by required and actual hours.

Subject	Required Hours	Actual Hours
1. Law	47	55
(2) U.S. Constitution & Bill of Rights		
(10) Kansas Criminal Code & Procedure		
(8) Law of Arrest, Search & Seizure		
(3) Kansas Juvenile Code & Procedure		
(2) Kansas Alcohol Beverage Control Laws		
(4) Kansas Traffic Code		
(3) Law of Evidence		

- (2) Civil & Criminal Liabilities
- (2) Kansas Fish & Game Laws
- (3) Abuse of Force
- (2) Overview of Kansas Criminal Justice System
- (2) Testifying in Court
- (8) Legal Guideline in Interrogations
- (4) Civil Process

55

2. Police Patrol Procedures   40   51
- (3) Introduction to Patrol
- (4) Crowd Control
- (2) Chemical Agents
- (4) Officer Survival
- (3) Mechanics of Arrest
- (5) Introduction to EVOC
- (2) Occupant Protection & Usage

Criminal Justice Information Systems

- (1) National Crime Information Center (N.C.I.C.) & Telecommunications
- (1) Police Radio Procedures
- (1) Police Records—Security & Privacy
- (8) Driving Under the Influence (D.U.I.) Recognition & Apprehension
- (4) Vehicle Stops (classroom)
- (2) Building Searches (classroom)
- (2) Crimes in Progress Calls
- (2) Principles of Doppler Radar (classroom)
- (4) OSHA Haz-Mat (hazardous material) Awareness Level Training
- (3) Tornado Spotters Course

51

3. Police Investigation Procedures   72   81
- (6) Collecting, Recording & Protecting Evidence
- (3) Lab Services
- (6) Narcotics & Dangerous Drugs
- (1) Officer's Duties at Crime Scene
- (1) Polygraph

(5) Techniques of Interviews, Admissions & Statements
(32) Accident Investigations (classroom)
(3) Arson Investigation
(2) Developing Informants
(3) Bomb Calls, Threats & Investigations

Crimes against Persons

(11) (a) Assault Investigations
     (b) Robbery Investigations
     (c) Sex Crimes Investigations
     (d) Death Investigations
     (e) Hate Bias Crimes
     (f) Hostage Situations

Crimes against Property

(1) (a) Counterfeiting & Credit Card Fraud
(1) (b) Fraudulent Checks & Handwriting
(1) (c) Burglary Investigations
(1) (d) Larceny Investigations
(2) (e) Auto Theft
(2) (f) Fingerprint Lecture

81

4. Human Relations   35   59

Interpersonal Communications

(2)   (a) Communication Process (Verbal & Nonverbal)
(2)   (b) Sensitivity Experience
(2)   (c) A Victim's Perspective
        (d) Police Professionalism
(1)   (1) Code of Ethics
(1)   (2) Officer Appearance & Demeanor
(1)   (3) Police Discretion
(2)   (e) Dealing with the Hearing Impaired
(4)   (f) Cultural Diversity

Crisis Situations

- (3) (a) Battered Women
- (2) (b) Sexual Assault Groups
- (2) (c) Child Abuse (Physical & Sexual)
- (3) (d) Family Crisis Intervention—Lecture
- (2) (e) Disputes
  - (1) Violence—Individuals & Groups
- (f) Abnormal Behavior
- (2)   (1) Depression & Suicide
- (2)   (2) Personality Disorder—Problem Group
- (2)   (3) Alcohol & Drug Abuse
- (g) Stress
- (2)   (1) Officer Stress
- (2)   (2) Morale Curve—Coping with Change
- (2)   (3) Postincident Trauma
- (2) (h) Family Violence—Crisis Intervention

Psychological Perspectives

- (2) (a) Psychiatric Introduction & Historical Perspectives
- (2) (b) Personality Growth & Development
- (4) (c) Patient's Rights—Legal Aspects & Mental Health

Police-Community Relations

- (3) (a) Crime Prevention
- (2) (b) Police-News Media Relations
- (1) (c) *Community-Oriented Policing* (emphasis added)
- (1) (d) D. A. R. E.
- (2) (e) Prejudice & Civil Rights
- (1) (f) *Problem Solving & Problem-Oriented Policing* (emphasis added)

59

5. Demonstrable Proficiency   124   163
   - (16) E. V. O. C. (field exercises)
   - (8) Vehicle Stops (field exercises & review)
   - (8) Officer Survival Exercises
     Building Searches (field exercises)
   - (2) Principles of Doppler Radar (field exercises)

Criminal Investigations Exercises
- (4) Collecting, Recording, & Protecting Evidence (field exercises)
- (2) Fingerprinting Exercise
- (8) Accident Investigation
- (4) Family Crisis Intervention (role playing)
- (10) Report Writing
- (40) Defense Tactics, Handcuffing, & Search Techniques
- (40) Firearms
- (6) Case Preparation & Mock Court & Review
- (15) Physical Training

163

6. Emergency Care   17   18
   - (8) Standard First Aid/BLS for Professional Rescuers
   - (8) Cardiopulmonary Resuscitation
   - (2) Blood-Borne Pathogens

18

7. Course Administration   8   11
   - (1) Orientation
   - (1) Notebooks and Notetaking
   - (5) Examinations
   - (4) Graduation

11

The Columbus, Ohio, Training Program. In January 1966, after meeting the standards of the Ohio Peace Officer Training Council, the Columbus Police Training Academy was authorized to conduct a continuing training and education program for peace officers. The Columbus Police Academy course consists of 840 hours of preservice instruction. This course of instruction is conducted from a "stress" orientation.

To Wit, Chain of Command:

1. The Division of Police, being a semi-military organization, utilizes a military "chain-of-command." This means that normal communications will be directed through an individual sequence of supervisors.

2. The Recruit Training Section has a Sergeant of Police in charge. This Section is directly responsible for the administration and control of recruit training. The training program is designed to develop efficient, respected, and dedicated police officers.
3. Your route of communication through the chain-of-command is as follows,
   - Recruit Class Commander
   - Recruit Training Officer
   - Recruit Training Sergeant
   - Academy Lieutenant
   - Training Bureau Commander
4. Each recruit will observe the chain-of-command. This is not to prevent recruits from seeking information from other Academy personnel or instructors, but indicates the path of normal communications.
5. Should extenuating circumstances arise, permission may be granted to see a specific member of your chain-of-command.
6. The Training Staff is available for consultation and counseling. It is the responsibility of each recruit to seek assistance regarding personal or job-related concerns.
7. The Division of Police will not discriminate in employment practices on the basis of race, color, sex (including pregnancy or sexual harassment), religion, national origin, age, or condition of handicap.
   - Each recruit has access to all levels of command in addressing concerns about fair and equitable treatment.

The training curriculum includes topics such as self-defense, patrol operations, law and legal procedures, human relations, applied behavioral science, criminal investigation, and firearms training. Upon the successful completion of academy training, each recruit is certified by the Ohio Peace Officer Training Council. Following the academy training, each recruit is assigned to more than 360 hours of field training under the close supervision of field training officers. Each recruit remains a probationary officer for a period of one year from the date of appointment (Fagan, 1985).

PROBATIONARY PERIODS AND FIELD TRAINING OFFICERS

Probation periods vary from state to state and from agency to agency. It also is not unusual to find probationary periods vary up to one year within the same state. The typical length of time in this stage of preemployment, however, is eighteen months. The probationary period is the hands-on training segment and is a key part of the new hire's socializing process into the culture of policing.

The agency field training officer (FTO) plays an indispensable role in helping individuals who have recently completed the police academy to make the transition into the "real world" of policing. FTOs take over where the academy training ends. They fine-tune new hires, and as their trainers, they hold the future of these individuals and the goals of the department in their hands. In most organizations, FTOs are selected for their ability to train, educate, supervise, and lead. FTOs must be exceptional people, because as trainers, they must serve as role models and facilitators, inculcating departmental mission, values, process, rules, and regulations (Hymas, 1989). The ideal is to enhance occupational expertise and give meaning to academy training; they must not discount previous training.

The misconception that the street is the "real world" and that academy training just provided information "good to know" has undermined police training across the United States, eroded police advancements, and seriously impeded professionalism. If new officers find that the values they learned in the academy are discounted by their superiors under actual working conditions, or that their own participation consists of mindlessly obeying orders and regulations, the idealism and initiative fostered during the training period will be neutralized, if not destroyed (Meese, 1993:7). The instructional efforts of the agency FTO are absolutely essential if a department is committed to community-oriented policing. As Goldstein noted, "However strongly the head of an agency may elicit a different style of policing, the quality of an officer's daily life is heavily dependent on how well the officer satisfies the expectations and demands of his or her immediate supervisor (Goldstein, 1990:157).

STRESS VS. NONSTRESS ACADEMY TRAINING

Effectively training officers to perform certain jobs means that the job itself must be clearly explained. In policing, opinions vary about what the job entails, which causes debate over what method of training should be used. The topics of entry-level police training are basically the same, but the delivery method can be different, depending on which school of thought prevails. Some view policing as similar to military service and emphasize militaristic **stress training.** Others suggest that policing can be imparted through an academic setting. Still others support a blend of these two methods.

Stress training is based on the theory that the individual psyche must be torn down in order to be reshaped into a mold fitting the organizational ideal. The military has relied on this particular model to achieve mass obedience and unhesitating response to orders. The similarities between the tasks of the military and of the American police have often been emphasized, but major differences do exist in mission, deployment, and individual action. Military tactics are generally highly coordinated actions involving large groups of forces with a wide variety of specialized objectives and differing firepower and delivery systems. It is imperative that members of these mission-oriented forces be regimented into a unified action to reduce their losses and inflict the greatest damage on hostile elements.

The goals and objectives of military operations and those of urban and rural American policing are strikingly different, but those differences are not reflected in the training of police officers. All too often new hires are called recruits, are taught close-order drill, and in general go through Marine Corps-style academy training. In the quest for community-oriented policing, this type of obedience-dominated training can be detrimental. It is understood that a degree of stress should be placed on aspiring officers to measure and evaluate their resolve, courage, approach, tactics, restraint, ethics, and common sense. This aspect of their training should not, however, permeate the entire training process. Military titles, marching, and adherence to military protocol create a mind-set that carries over into our communities. After receiving stress-oriented training, these new officers must go into the community under the supervision of a field training officer to exercise independent action and demonstrate the ability to deal with a myriad of problems. Prompt and reasonable assessment of situations is critical, and the ability to decide whether to intervene is paramount. Such flexibility seems incompatible with the directed action so prevalent in stress training.

Nonstress Training

If independent decision making in a largely unsupervised environment is the mode of operation for most urban police officers, then the initial training should be encouraging and supportive of that mode. Clearly, the overemphasis on lockstep obedience found in many police academies will not serve to provide new hires with a productive and independent frame of reference for performing their jobs. This is not to suggest that stress or the handling of stressful situations should not be part of law enforcement training. Clearly, police officers may well find themselves in very stressful positions while performing their duties, and it would be only prudent to evaluate their abilities to function under simulated stressful conditions. But a heavy reliance on close-order drill and other group exercises does not promote individuality and proves to be of little value in the actual performance of police duties. Moreover, stress does not belong in the classroom, as it impedes the learning process. It would be difficult to try to teach a student a concept while the student is wondering whether his or her bed has passed inspection.

If law enforcement agencies are attempting to implement community-oriented policing, the obedience-oriented mentality can cause many internal and external problems. There must be a balance between courses taught in officer safety and courses that emphasize consideration of constitutional rights and community values.

Training courses cannot ignore the violence directed against police officers. Assaults on police officers occur with regularity and have been a major problem since at least 1977, when the FBI began compiling statistics on assaults on peace officers. Approximately one million (903,111) assaults, or an average of 60,207 per year, occurred between 1977 and 1991.

1977	49,156
1978	56,253
1979	59,031
1980	57,847
1981	57,174
1982	55,775
1983	62,324
1984	60,153
1985	61,724
1986	64,259
1987	63,842
1988	58,752
1989	62,172
1990	71,794
1991	62,852

These statistics attest that assaults on peace officers have increased, but when the increase in the general population and the increase in police personnel are correlated, the proportion of assaults has remained stable.

Several schools offer postacademy training in officer safety. Although these schools are commendable in their quest to equip officers both mentally and physically to face the threat of assault or repulse actual assaults, officer safety schools that produce paranoid officers do not serve a useful purpose. Some chiefs of police have refused to send officers to certain schools because when their officers return, they walk their beats in apprehension.

The Jail Experience

Community-oriented policing requires that individual police officers have the interpersonal skills that will facilitate their dealings with community members. In some sheriff jurisdictions, new hires are assigned jail duty for three to four years after completing a rather stringent training academy. The rationale is that "it will take the shine off the badge," expose them to "the language of the street," and allow deputies to get to know the people they will be dealing with in the future. If the criminal element is indeed a small cohort of the general U.S. population, these deputies may be receiving mixed and somewhat skewed messages. Some agencies reassign deputies from jail assignments directly into the field without refresher ("defanging") courses, whereas others, realizing the rather hard and forceful nature of jail duties, require postjail or prepatrol training. The purpose of this reentry training is twofold. One, it allows breathing room between assignments to facilitate a change in job direction and focus. Two, it also allows officers to review and be tested on past training and to catch up on new laws, policies, standards, and practices.

The Use of Less-than-Lethal Weapons

In the aftermath of police actions that have involved shootings of suspects (or shootings that were suspect) there has been a public demand for restraint methods or intervention options other than use of lethal force. American policing is guided by its own policies regarding choice of weaponry and munitions. Some agencies opt for pistol loads that, under the Geneva Convention provisions on warfare, might be banned as dumdum ammunition. But with public pressure on the rise police agencies are looking closely at newly developed less-than-lethal weapons. Such weapons could have been useful in the standoff with Branch Davidian cult members near Waco, Texas, in April 1992 (Pine, 1993:A27), for example. After the abortive American attempt to rescue the hostages held in Teheran, reports circulated that part of the American tactical strategy was to employ a nonlethal agent that could render the captives' Iranian guards incapable of action (Geis and Binder, 1990:2).

Firearms training is an important component of police training. Also important is knowing when and when not to shoot. (*Rob Nelson/Black Star*)

The use of nonlethal force elements and tactics in America has been sporadic historically. The earliest method (other than physical force) was the billy club or nightstick, which gave the police only two widely disparate options of force, one lethal and one nonlethal (if correctly applied). A singular advancement was the introduction of chemical weaponry (tear gas) synthesized by a German chemist in 1869. By 1912 the idea had developed of using chemical weapons in riots or to subdue criminals (Peak, 1990:11).

The 1960s marked major technological advances in the development of police nonlethal weaponry. During a period of urban upheavals, protests, and rioting, mace-squirting nightsticks were issued in the District of Columbia, and thousands of law enforcement agencies adopted them in some form (Peak, 1990:13). In 1967 a wooden bullet, an alternative to the traditional lead bullet, was first used in Hong Kong but was soon replaced by a British rubber round. British riot police were also employing water cannons, designed to fire large jets of water at demonstrations, on the streets of Derry in 1968 and later in Northern Ireland. In some instances, dye was added to the water to facilitate suspect identification. Another unique riot-oriented weapon was unveiled in America in 1968, the "Sound Curdler," consisting of amplified speakers that produced loud, shrill, shrieking noises at irregular intervals. Attached to vehicles or helicopters, it was first used at campus demonstrations (Peak, 1990:15). In the aftermath of the killing of four Kent State University protesters in Ohio, a gun that shot beanbags rather than bullets was developed. A California metallurgist invented what resembled a large billy club with spiral grooves in the barrel, which fired a pellet-loaded bag that unfurled into a spinning pancake capable of knocking down a 200-pound person at up to 300 feet.

Several inventions were added to the nonlethal police arsenal in the early 1970s. The "Photic Driver," first used by police in South Africa, produced a strobe effect, its light causing giddiness, fainting, and nausea. A similar device—a strobe gun known as a Valkyrie—was developed by a British firm. Other inventions of the 1970s included the injector dart gun, adapted from veterinarians' tranquilizer guns, which when fired injected its drug load; an electrified water jet and an electrified baton, which carried a 6,000-volt shock; shotgun shells filled with plastic pellets; plastic bubbles to immobilize rioters; a chemical that created slippery street surfaces; and an "instant cocoon" consisting of an adhesive that, when sprayed over crowds, made people adhere to each other (Peak, 1990:16). The old standby, the baton, was retrofitted with a handle to enhance its versatility. Two other significant "tools" developed were the TASER (an acronym for "Tom Swift and his Electric Rifle") and the stun gun. The TASER shot two darts into its victim. Attached to the darts were fine wires through which a transformer sent a 50,000-volt shock that could knock a person down at a distance of fifteen feet. The stun gun, also introduced in the mid-1970s, initially rivaled the TASER as the nonlethal weapon of choice. During the 1980s came several new chemical delivery systems and the creation of "entanglement nets" and "action chain control devices" that required four officers to throw the contraptions over unwilling suspects (Peak, 1990:19).

The search for exotic incapacitating weapons has been a major focus for several decades. Early science fiction writings abound with prototypes of formidable and efficient nonlethal weaponry. Over the years we have been exposed to depictions of ray guns and similar futuristic implements that numbed or otherwise dazed a person (Geis and Binder, 1990:2). The U.S. Army is working with the U.S. Coast Guard and the National Institute of Justice to promote sting-nets and other such futuristic weapons as cutting-edge technology that could be made available to SWAT teams and other law enforcement units (Pine, 1993:A27).

Less-than-lethal devices developed for army use are designed to stun or disrupt "an enemy's troops or communications and equipment, with a minimum amount of casualties." Some examples of the kinds of technology being used in nonlethal weapons development by the Pentagon include the following:

- Low-energy lasers: multicolored beams that can damage the optical systems of conventional weapons and impair the human eye. The laser beams can be delivered by guns, ships, or aircraft.
- Polymers: super adhesives that can be applied to weapons, equipment, vehicles, or facilities to cripple them—by choking air-breathing engines or cooling systems.
- Metal-embrittling liquids: chemical agents that can weaken metals or alloys by altering their molecular structure. Easy to apply with a brush or spray gun.
- High-powered microwave: rapidly pulsing beam that can penetrate unshielded electronics systems and melt down their components by heating them rapidly and fusing their circuits.
- Isotrophic radiators: shells that use superheated gaseous plasma to burst with laserlike intensity to damage optics or human eyes. Isotrophic radiators can be dropped from the air, fired from artillery pieces, or used by hand.
- Electromagnetic pulse: created by special generators to knock out unshielded electronic devices, including communications, navigation, data processing, and computer systems.
- Infrasound: ultra-low-frequency sound waves that can disorient and sometimes nauseate individuals, making them unable to function. These sound waves can penetrate most buildings and are recommended as being "useful for crowd control."
- Antitraction technology: wide range of super lubricants that make a surface so slippery that it is practically useless. Possible targets include runways, streets, railroads, ramps, and stairs.
- Combustion alteration technology: chemical additives that can contaminate or alter the composition of fuel to choke off engines—including almost instant engine failure in helicopters.

- Calmative agents: sedatives or sleep-inducing drugs that, when mixed with dimethyl sulfoxide, penetrate human skin to sedate an opponent quickly. The substance can be sprayed through air vents.
- Visual stimulus and illusion: a grab bag of techniques, such as using high-intensity strobe lights that flash at or near the same frequency as the human brain to cause vertigo and disorientation (Pine, 1993:A27).

Although much of this technology may sound a little like a James Bond novel, most of it is already in the modern-day U.S. Army's arsenal, and law enforcement is in the wings.

Verbal Judo

The Orange County Sheriff's Academy incorporated sixteen hours of communicative skills into their training program in the early 1990s. This program, popularly known as "verbal judo," was created by George J. Thompson. Verbal judo is "the art of gentle persuasion" as opposed to physical confrontation. Thompson was in the process of teaching verbal judo to the members of the Los Angeles Police Department during 1991. Interestingly, the four officers involved in the Rodney King incident were scheduled to attend the class on verbal judo the week following the notorious confrontation. Proponents of verbal judo claim that had these officers attended the course the King incident might not have occurred or escalated.

Over the last two decades Thompson, a former English professor, martial arts master, and police officer, has taught verbal judo to almost 70,000 police officers in nearly 700 police departments across the United States (Thompson, 1993:95). Verbal judo is the development and consolidation of many skills in combination to avoid unnecessary physical confrontation. The course teaches self-awareness, self-control, motivation, empathy, and verbal courses of action to defuse events that could easily turn into physically threatening situations. Chapter 5 of Thompson's text, for instance, is entitled, "Taking Crap with Dignity . . . and Style," and Chapter 10 is entitled, "The Only Way to Interrupt People and Still Have Them Love You" (Thompson, 1993:7).

POST AND STANDARDIZATION: ACQUIRING THE POLICE OFFICER ROLE

The creation of the California Commission on Peace Officers Standards and Training (POST) was the result of a protracted and dedicated effort by rank-and-file police officers and management. Basically, POST was envisioned as a commission appointed by the governor to set standards for peace officer training in

California. The initial legislation was defeated by the California League of Cities, which opposed the mandatory provisions as being in violation of the concept of home rule. In 1959 POST came into existence after "mandated participation" was excised, basically putting municipal involvement on a volunteer footing. Former Chief of Police Edward Davis devised a funding scheme, which was deceptively simple. He suggested that "penalty assessments" be added to traffic and court fines to provide ongoing funds earmarked for statewide peace officer training. This was met with enthusiasm: Individuals cited and fined for infractions or court judgments would shoulder the financial burden, and there would be no increase in taxes. Ironically, the "bad guys" were paying for the training of the "good guys." Colleges and universities as well as private and commercial enterprises sought to have training courses certified for state reimbursement. Almost overnight, training opportunities for police agencies exploded into a wide array of choices. Now peace officers could attend courses offered in different locations throughout the state. The multitude of subjects included management, information systems, crime specifics (e.g., burglary), field technician, hostage negotiation, internal affairs, legal education, legal updates, officer safety and survival, planning and research, school resource officers, civil liability, and many other courses. The spin-off benefit of statewide training was the statewide networking of individuals performing relatively the same tasks, who were now able to communicate with each other. POST training opened new modes of inquiry and information sharing. Colleagues were now working with colleagues providing each other with technologies, methods, techniques, and information previously undisclosed or unknown.

The initial concept of the California POST legislation encouraged other states (with pressure from local law enforcement) to establish similar legislation and training mechanisms. Today, the majority of states have mandated requirements for police standards and training. This arrangement is not without drawbacks, however. When the state, for all practical purposes, controls the purse strings of reimbursable police training funds, the specter of absolute control looms. It would seem that some of the early legislative concerns of the California League of Cities come into play. The axiom of the "greatest good for the majority" is definitely an operative concept, but in reality, only the medium- and small-sized departments benefit from the POST type of reimbursement scheme. Larger departments normally can afford to provide their own training, and many do without (perceived) state interference. However, it would not be financially prudent to turn their backs on reimbursable training monies. Consequently, larger departments reconfigure and retitle courses so that they will be reimbursable. In essence, state programs to promote peace officer standards and training are really a boon to police professionalism in smaller jurisdictions, and this is exactly where the emphasis on advanced training should be. The funding of police training from fines is a viable source of revenue to upgrade police service and to provide our communities with a more professional level of service.

THE RECRUITMENT OF WOMEN AND OTHER MINORITIES

According to Census Bureau statistics, there has been a dramatic increase of women in the workplace since 1970. Women in the ranks of executive, administrative, and managerial positions rose by about 95 percent between 1970 and 1990. Among African Americans there are in fact more women than men in top positions. The percentage of women in selected occupations is illustrated in these comparisons of 1970 and 1990:

	1970	1990
Aerospace engineers	1.8%	8.1%
Athletes	11.2%	26.7%
Butchers	11.4%	19.6%
Clergy	2.9%	10.4%
Firefighters	1.5%	2.7%
Lawyers	4.9%	24.4%
Nurses	97.3%	94.3%
Physicians	9.7%	20.7%
Police officers	5.1%	14.6%
Truckdrivers	1.5%	6.0%
Veterinarians	5.3%	26.6%

These statistics illustrate that from 1970 to 1990 law enforcement agencies increased sworn women police officers by 9 percent to a total of 14.6 percent. The inroads that women have made into a male-dominated occupation represent a long and exceedingly difficult journey.

The first women employees to enter the system of criminal justice were hired in New York City in 1845 to perform duties as prison matrons. A full half-century later, in 1910, the Los Angeles Police Department, under public pressure, appointed the first sworn policewoman, Alice Wells (Horne, 1988:18). This initial appointment caused other women to seek law enforcement employment and caused agencies to reassess and in some cases alter their recruitment and hiring stances. In 1916 policewomen were found in 25 cities and in 20 of the 48 states. Their collective duties, however, were routinely confined to clerical functions and working with juveniles and women offenders. It was not until another half-century, in 1968, that the first uniformed policewoman was assigned general patrol duty in a squad car, in Indianapolis, Indiana (Horne, 1988:18). In 1972 women comprised only 2 percent of uniformed law enforcement in those cities having populations of 250,000 or more, and by 1978 women made up only 4.2 percent of sworn personnel in municipal departments serving populations of more than 50,000 (Peak, 1993:99).

The 1990 statistics demonstrate that women in sworn peace officer positions have increased approximately threefold since 1970. A 1991 Police Foundation study based on 1986 police department data of six large urban police departments revealed that women represented approximately 15.6 percent of the combined sworn strength.

Detroit	20.8%
Philadelphia	16.5%
Chicago	16.5%
New York	15.5%
Los Angeles	14.0%
Houston	10.2%

On a national scale, however, women comprise approximately 10 percent of the total sworn police population (Nazario, 1993:A1). This gender underrepresentation is slowly beginning to change, at least in Los Angeles, as a result, in part, of the 1981 Franchon Blake consent decree, which required that 25 percent of all recruits be women until one-fifth of the force was female. Los Angeles has also been thrust into the vanguard as the first U.S. city to embrace the notion of having as many women as men patrolling the streets. In 1992 a Los Angeles City Council resolution, backed by Chief Willie L. Williams, set the requirement to raise the number of sworn female officers from 14 percent (1,076) to 44 percent (Nazario, 1993:A18). This goal of full integration will be difficult to achieve because of budget constraints affecting hiring. If the gender hiring shift were based solely on normal attrition rates, it would take more than a decade to complete the process. As in the case of most departments, the forecast for hiring additional officers is bleak in Los Angeles. The growth of local law enforcement populations nationwide has risen dramatically during the past twenty years, but hiring may have leveled off in the 1990s.

The increase in women officers in the Los Angeles department was directly attributed to the lowering of the height requirement in 1981, from 5 foot 8 inches to 5 feet. Almost half the women brought into the academy between 1985 and 1991 were given preferential treatment; many received entrance test scores in the 70th percentile, whereas white males needed to score in the 90s to qualify. With pretesting coaching and encouragement, almost all female candidates now graduate from the academy, compared with only 50 percent in 1981. Accordingly, in 1993, the LAPD academy began grading its final physical test on a curve adjusted for gender and age (Nazario, 1993:A18). Pointedly in this particular instance, court-imposed hiring mandates, public pressure, and a sense of female-oriented equality have had an impact on the gender distribution of the LAPD graduating class. This trend is being experienced in urban police departments across the United States.

Even in times of economic downturn, law enforcement as a whole has enjoyed tremendous growth as a service industry. The 1990 Census also listed certain occupations that were on the rise:

	1970	1990
Computer analysts	107,580	471,290
Dietitians	43,275	90,223
Finance managers	220,483	635,911
Food service	3.3 million	5.7 million
Lawyers	288,478	779,471
Physicians	296,988	586,715
Police officers	427,607	822,283
Prison officers	47,716	184,667
Psychologists	29,575	191,962
Public relations	80,302	167,568

Clearly, the criminal justice system has experienced unparalleled growth over these two decades: The number of lawyers has multiplied (in 1970 there were 4.5 farmers per lawyer; by 1990 there were 1.4 farmers per lawyer), prisons have had phenomenal increases in staff, and the number of police officers practically doubled (*U.S. News & World Report,* 1993c:16). With the addition of federal and state correctional facilities and the emphasis on mandated sentencing, the raw numbers of prison officers at the federal, state, and local levels will undoubtedly rise at a greater rate than police officers.

The addition of expanded representation of women in the field of law enforcement has been viewed as a boon to consumer relations. Experts indicate that the verbal skills women possess often have a calming effect that defuses potentially explosive situations. This is a style of policing that has significant impact on domestic violence calls. In 1985 a study of the handling of spousal abuse cases demonstrated that female officers showed more empathy and commitment to resolving such situations (McDowell, 1992:71). The ability to communicate and to resolve situations that could easily escalate into physical confrontations is the cornerstone of COP. It would follow that greater female peace officer representation will enhance the operational concept of COP.

GAY POLICE OFFICERS, SOCIAL SENSITIVITY, AND AFFIRMATIVE ACTION

In 1979 several Northern California law enforcement officers formed a loose-knit association to discuss and address the prejudicial treatment they were receiving. They were homosexual. It appeared that still, in a more socially relaxed environment, homosexuals were being covertly and overtly castigated in the workplace.

BOX 5.2   The New York Police Department

The New York Police Department's Police Cadet Corps is an innovative program designed to bring officers with higher levels of education into the ranks of the nation's largest police department. Although it is a modest program, it focuses on the recruitment of college students while addressing racial imbalances frequently found in the sworn ranks. This emphasis should have a positive impact on the attempts by the NYPD to implement community policing (Williams, 1992).

In 1985 New York City created the Police Cadet Corps, designed to attract college students to careers as police officers. The program provided that full-time sophomores in colleges and universities in New York City who were residents of New York City or Nassau and Westchester counties could, if they met other qualifications, receive a total package of $17,490 toward their future college tuition. Some monies would be in payment for work, and the rest in an interest-free loan that would be forgiven if the cadet served two years as a police officer. They were to be given full-time jobs during the summer at $8.14 an hour and part-time employment during the school year, amounting to three days per month. A three-year recruitment effort brought into the program 133 cadets in 1986, 241 in 1987 (two classes), and 131 in 1988, for a total of 505 participants. The NYPD had the following five major objectives for the program:

1. **To increase the educational level of the department.** When the Cadet Corps was created, 12.5 percent of police officers and 17.8 percent of all personnel had a bachelor's degree or higher.

    Finding: A total of 217 cadets graduated and became police officers by early 1991, far fewer than the goal and representing less than 1 percent of NYPD's sworn personnel.

2. **To test a more rigorous selection process for recruits.** Under the usual selection process, recruits are screened by physical and psychological examinations, a background investigation, and academy training. The new program added a selection interview and in-the-field training before cadets entered the academy. The in-field training provided another opportunity to screen out those deemed not qualified to serve as police officers.

    Finding: The program altered the selection process by inaugurating an oral interview and two years of in-the-field training for cadets. While African American males and Hispanic females performed somewhat poorly on the oral interview, ethnic and gender differences on the interview were smaller than on the background investigation and psychological examination.

3. **To increase the representativeness of the uniformed force.** The requirement for cadets to reside in New York City or Nassau and Westchester counties was expected to make cadets more demographically representative.

   Finding: The percentage of African American and Hispanic cadets was consistently higher than the percentage for sworn officers or other recruit classes. White females were more representative in two classes, but less representative in the other two classes.

4. **To increase the orientation toward community policing.** As part of its commitment to community policing, NYPD initiated a Community Patrol Officer Program, whereby individual officers were assigned to a permanent beat of about 15 square blocks and worked with the community to control crime. By assigning cadets to serve as aides to these beat officers, the department expected to expose them to actual community policing practices before their academy training.

   Finding: All cohorts placed strong emphasis on both a community orientation and a helping orientation as criteria for evaluating police officer performance. Some cadets' belief in the importance of community policing was strengthened after two years in the program. *But it remains to be seen if this orientation survives after cadets become police officers and are exposed to the prevailing police culture.*

5. **To improve the leadership skills of new officers.** NYPD expected the Cadet Corps to produce a disproportionate number of its future leaders because of their college education, the higher entrance standards, and their more extensive training and experience.

   Finding: It is too early to determine to what extent such leaders have been created.

The subsequent Police Foundation study of the Police Cadet Corps, funded by the National Institute of Justice, revealed that the program brought 217 college graduates onto the force; 16.1 percent were African American and 21.7 percent were Hispanic. These percentages were significantly higher than those found in (1) other groups of recruits, (2) all NYPD sworn personnel, and (3) the New York City population. The program has shown that it is possible to increase minority representation and raise educational standards simultaneously. Given the importance of representativeness to the practice of community policing, this stands as a significant finding. Only time and continued evaluation will tell if the program succeeds in meeting its stated goals.

Source: Police Foundation Reports, 1992.

As this particular group had the legal obligation and responsibility to protect others from constitutional and civil rights violations, it was indeed a bitter pill for them to swallow. Their collective concerns of discrimination in the police workplace gave birth to the Golden State Peace Officers Association.

Over a period of years the police—the perceived last occupational bastion of male dominance—were having their exclusive turf invaded by minorities. First came the ethnic minorities and then women joined the ranks. After these battles were reasonably laid to rest, gays and lesbians began following a well-beaten path to job opportunities and workplaces free of harassment. The path, however, was and still is strewn with more obstacles than their predecessors encountered.

States with statutes against sodomy cite the statutes as a legal barrier to disallow gay applicants into police service. The scientific definition of the term *sodomy* applies "only to insertion of the penis into the rectum of a person of either sex." The laws of a number of states, however, include "oral-genital acts and bestiality" (Rush, 1991:286). Opponents of gay rights rest their arguments on religious dogma and regional legal sanctions. Given the scientific and legal definitions of the term, however, it has been observed that many heterosexual applicants might well be disqualified for police service. In most sectors of employment, private acts between consenting adults cannot serve as occupational disqualifications. Pedophilia is a mala in se crime and is not consummated between "consenting" individuals. It has been suggested that sodomy statutes should not serve as prima facie evidence that all gays engage in the narrow definition of sodomy (anal intercourse).

The roots and indicators of wider social change often are found in local municipalities, but unfortunately, change in its many forms needs the impetus of financial (economic) loss, political pressure, and court mandates. The question and issue of gay police officers is no exception.

In New York City, where openly gay officers serve throughout the department, homosexual cops have formed their own Gay Officers Action League. "We've gotten nearly every demand we've made," said Sam Ciccone, the group's executive director. Across the country, in San Diego, the chief of police was questioned about the number of gays in the department. "How many gay cops are there in San Diego? I don't know, and it doesn't matter," said Chief of Police Bob Burgreen. The San Diego police built their reputation for good relations with gays by initiating a few simple reforms. Gay leaders are guest lecturers at the police academy, and police recruits are required to do volunteer work at social service agencies, including the AIDS Foundation and the Gay and Lesbian Center. Two SDPD officers "have come out of the closet" without being taunted by colleagues (Baker et al., 1991). But 100 miles north, there is a different story.

The Sergeant Mitchell Grobeson Case

In 1975 Assistant Chief Robert Vernon, who is a police chaplain and lay elder in the Grace Community Church in Sun Valley, California, argued against hiring gay officers in an LAPD memo. Excerpts of the memo included: "Religious denunciation of homosexual conduct goes back at least several thousand years" and "The hiring of homosexual police officers is repulsive to nearly all persons." The memo further maintained that homosexuals are "emotionally ill" and pose a risk as police officers. "Homosexual acts are inherently immoral, abnormal, and criminal—usually felonies," the memo stated. The memo concluded that the department must disqualify police applicants based on confirmed homosexual conduct "to retain the current trust of the community and the high level of efficiency enjoyed by the LAPD" (Pope, 1991a). In a 1980 meeting called to improve relations between the LAPD and the gay community, Vernon told gay-rights advocates that the Bible regarded homosexuality as blasphemous (Pope, 1991b).

In the summer of 1985, police officer Mitchell Grobeson responded to a silent alarm at a jewelry store on Sunset Boulevard. Normal procedure for a robbery in progress would bring backup units from the distant corners of the Rampart division. But despite the dispatcher's repeated pleas, no backup appeared. Because of this and other alleged similar incidents, Grobeson, by all objective criteria one of the best officers on the force, resigned from the police department on June 13, 1988. On September 28, 1988, he filed a twenty-two-claim lawsuit against the city of Los Angeles, Police Chief Daryl Gates, the Los Angeles Police Commission, fifteen named police officers, and 100 John Doe officers, charging that they effectively forced him to resign from the force because he was suspected of being homosexual (Sipchen, 1989). The $5 million civil lawsuit was filed in Los Angeles Superior Court and joined by the National Gay Rights Advocates, a law firm (Holland, 1988:A11), specifically alleging violations of state and Los Angeles laws prohibiting sexual harassment and discrimination, violations of privacy, free speech, equal protection, due process, and unlawful conspiracy (Mitchell, 1988:A9).

At age 15 Grobeson joined the Explorer Scout law enforcement unit in his hometown of Culver City, California. He was elected twice to serve as class president at Culver City High School. He earned a degree in criminal justice from Chapman College and on September 9, 1981, arrived for his first day at the LAPD Police Academy. He graduated as the "honor cadet" and received awards from Chief Gates in academics, physical fitness, self-defense, and shooting. He completed his probationary year in Central division, which covers some of the city's meanest streets, from Skid Row to the garment district to the corridors of City Hall. In 1984 his outstanding performance led to his promotion to training officer and he was transferred to the Rampart division. Just before his transfer, he was stopped in West Hollywood by a Los Angeles County Sheriff's sergeant. Because he was with another male in a predominantly gay area, the sergeant assumed they were gay. Discovering a police ID, the sergeant called the LAPD with the message, "Send a supervisor, your man's a fruit" (Sipchen, 1989). According to Grobeson, "Once he (the deputy) found out I was a cop he wanted to find out if I was gay. He went through my wallet, and then he took my personal phone book and went through each page" (Stewart, 1988).

In the next few days, according to the suit, an officer at Central division called officers at Rampart and told them "a faggot" was transferring in. A sergeant then announced this to the entire Rampart watch. When directly asked by a supervisor if he was gay, Grobeson stated he was not. But incidents continued to occur. Someone glued his locker shut. Someone taped a picture of Rock Hudson to it, with the inscription "To Mitch—Love, Rock Baby." He received a package marked "AIDS Survival Kit," and someone wrote "Beware" in the dust on his squad car. Grobeson contended that several supervisors encouraged the harassment.

His problems intensified in the summer of 1985 when he decided to break the legendary police "code of silence" after a confrontation between police and a group of revelers at an outdoor fair. An officer had clubbed unconscious a man involved in a fight, and a near-riot resulted. Grobeson chose to testify to internal affairs investigators about the case because he felt the repeated "head shots" could have killed the suspect. He also felt the officer's actions put other police officers in jeopardy.

In 1986 Grobeson transferred back to Pacific division, where he was put in charge of a controversial effort to address the Venice Beach homeless problem. As the situation improved, Grobeson received national attention. In 1987 a habitué of the Venice Beach drug scene filed a complaint against him. The charges were denied and at the trial board his accuser testified that eight officers had told him Grobeson was "a faggot" and that he was granted preferential treatment for filing the complaint. Although an investigation into these officers' conduct was requested, the investigation never materialized, and evidence was destroyed (Sipchen, 1989).

On June 13, 1988, Grobeson turned in his resignation and a complaint demanding that the lieutenant be punished for allegedly asking officers to solicit complaints against him and for repeatedly taking him into an interrogation room and grilling him about his sexuality. Although Grobeson went to the Police Commission, Chief Gates, and the mayor, he could not get anyone to investigate his charges that his civil rights had been violated by three and a half years of harassment. Thus, in September 1988, he filed his lawsuit and began speaking out about his case (Sipchen, 1989).

Since his resignation from LAPD Grobeson has been invited to talk at a number of gatherings to "tell his story" and give his thoughts on police and community relations. His appearance at One Institute of Homophile Studies on March 5, 1989, concluded his speaking tour. He applied for a police officer position in Long Beach, California, but accepted a position as police officer in the city of San Francisco.

It was reported that in 1990, at Chief Daryl F. Gates's urging, the Los Angeles City Council rejected Mitchell Grobeson's offer to drop his $5 million discrimination lawsuit because it would have required the LAPD to recruit openly gay and lesbian officers. The settlement would have cost the city no money beyond paying Grobeson's legal fees—fees that had reached $300,000. The city's legal fees were expected to reach $75,000–$100,000. The City of Los Angeles assigned three staff attorneys and hired two private attorneys to defend the gay discrimination lawsuit, and the LAPD assigned a unit to investigate (Pope, 1991b).

The Aftermath of the Grobeson Case

In April 1991 Mayor Tom Bradley stated, "Over the years the LAPD has shared a dismal relationship with Los Angeles's gay and lesbian community. At present, not one openly gay man or woman is serving among LAPD's 8,300 officers. Former LAPD Sergeant Mitch Grobeson is challenging the department to change its hiring practices through a lawsuit that seeks to enforce a 1979 city ordinance prohibiting discrimination based on sexual orientation." Bradley further stated, "There have been active efforts to block the inclusion of gay and lesbian people on the police force. Chief Gates has lobbied the city council against actively recruiting new officers within the gay and lesbian community. A hostile environment in the police department prevents gay and lesbian officers from being open about their sexual orientation. In addition, questions have arisen about the treatment of gay persons by police" (*The Advocate*, 1991:106).

On June 14, 1991, for the first time in the history of the LAPD, an active duty police officer "came out of the closet." Officer Sue Herold acknowledged being lesbian, or gay, in an interview with a *Vanguard* reporter on June 5, 1991. In November 1989, Herold was one of two LAPD officers still on the force who, using a pseudonym, joined in the discrimination lawsuit brought against the LAPD by gay ex-officer Mitch Grobeson (Dwyer, 1991).

On June 19, 1991, the LAPD announced it would, for the first time, give gay and lesbian officers permission to wear their uniforms and staff a recruitment booth during the 22nd Annual Los Angeles Gay and Lesbian Pride Festival at West Hollywood Park. The decision to open a police recruiting booth at the festival grew out of a December 20, 1990, meeting between then Chief Gates and the LAPD's Gay and Lesbian Police Advisory Task Force. Chief Gates had been quoted as saying he "would never send department recruiting personnel to anything that had gay or lesbian in the title." But he also said that he "would provide the Advisory Task Force with all the recruitment material they could possibly want and would not stand in the way of off-duty officers giving their own time" (Pope, 1991a). Paul Butler, one of several gay and lesbian officers who staffed the booth, said, "I think it's going to build a better relationship between the community and the Police Department; you never really know if your partner is gay, if he has a gay child, if he has a gay partner. Maybe people will become more sensitive" (Pope, 1991b). Butler was joined at the booth by officers Kelly Shea, Karen Kos, John Smith, and Sue Herold (Larsen, 1991). San Francisco's Grobeson stated that he would join his colleagues to show his support (Orlov, 1991; Pope, 1991b).

On February 10, 1993, the Los Angeles City Council agreed to far-reaching changes in hiring and personnel practices to ensure that gay and lesbian police officers and other city workers would not be harassed or discriminated against.

The settlement also called for the reinstatement of former Los Angeles Police Sergeant Mitchell Grobeson and the payment of $770,000 in damages to Grobeson and two other officers, one of whom was Sue Herold, who joined him in filing the suit against the city. The city's blueprint for change included the following:

- Police Department recruitment at gay community events and through the placement of advertisements in gay-oriented publications.
- Expanded training of police recruits and officers regarding the city's antidiscrimination and harassment policies, appropriate ways of dealing with the gay and lesbian community, hate crime reports, people with HIV or AIDS, and proper behavior with gay co-workers.
- Prohibition of slurs, intimidation, or comments that would create a hostile working environment for gay men and lesbians or people with HIV.
- Statements that violation of the city's antidiscrimination policy amounts to serious misconduct that will be swiftly investigated and disciplined, including possible suspension or discharge.
- Elimination of any recruitment questions or tests that would reveal a person's sexual orientation.
- Screening of anti-gay applicants so that they are dropped from the recruitment pool or required to participate in special sensitivity training (Boxall and Tores, 1993).

ON PROFESSIONALISM, EDUCATION, AND SOCIAL SKILLS

Sexual Harassment

There are more working women in the workplace than any other time in history. Since 1974 the number of women in the workplace has jumped by 57 percent: In 1974 there were approximately 36 million and in 1991 there were approximately 57 million. Some researchers suggest that there may be a correlation between the higher numbers of women in the workplace and the number of **sexual harassment** and discrimination cases. In the last five years more than three million women have been added to the work force, and 91 percent more sexual harassment cases have been filed. Harassment complaints increased 3,618 in 1992, the year after the Clarence Thomas Supreme Court confirmation hearings—in which law school professor Anita Hill accused him of sexually harassing her ten years earlier. American women filed nearly 15 percent more sex discrimination claims in 1992 than in 1991 (Michaud, 1993:9). But the Thomas-Hill allegation was only one in a string of scandals, involving William Kennedy Smith, Mike Tyson, Sol Wachtler, Bob Packwood, and of course the U.S. Navy's Tailhook affair (Gage, 1993:49). The number of *harassment* cases filed nationally, 1988–1993, is listed here (Michaud, 1993:9):

1988	5,499
1989	5,623
1990	6,127
1991	6,883
1992	10,501
1993	12,537

Moreover, even though the U.S. Supreme Court outlawed *sexual discrimination* in 1971, nearly 150,000 cases have been filed nationally, 1988–1992:

1988	29,210
1989	28,325
1990	28,380
1991	29,747
1992	34,226

Although there have been increases in representation, many occupations are still white male-dominated. Proponents of gender equality argue that white males make up just 39.2 percent of the population yet account for 82.5 percent of the Forbes 400 (individuals worth at least $265 million), 77 percent of Congress, 92 percent of state governors, 70 percent of tenured college faculty, almost 90 percent of daily newspaper editors, and 77 percent of TV news directors (Gage, 1993:49).

The increased number of women in the workplace has been reflected in an increase of women officers in the once male-dominated field of criminal justice. A survey conducted by The National Law Journal, a New York-based legal trade publication, found that more than half of the female lawyers at the nation's top firms said they had been sexually harassed, one of six within the past three years. The study found that although most women do not report incidents of sexual harassment, the number of women reporting such events has nearly doubled in four years to 15 percent (*Los Angeles Times*, 1993b:D2).

Although the increase of women into the enforcement field has not been spectacular, the change toward gender balance has presented some difficulties. Some of these women, along with their counterparts in other occupations, have experienced harassment and sexual discrimination, and many have sought legal remedies. Sexual harassment suits and allegations of discrimination are filed daily. The monetary damages that have been awarded could be calamitous to both public entities and private business. This is reflected in the fact that insurance companies will now cover firms against sexual harassment suits; one Boston-area company with approximately 100 employees had a close brush with such a suit in 1992 and now pays a $25,000 annual premium for $1 million worth of coverage (Gage, 1993:49).

Sexual harassment allegations in public service, especially within the law enforcement area, have implications that transcend individual claims. When allegations of sexual harassment within police and sheriff agencies are reported, the public confidence in these agencies can be seriously eroded. Crime control issues and other concerns quickly take a second place. Public- and service-oriented departments are seen as a mirror of society and of their communities. Along with sullying the community, allegations cause even wider problems. Such misconduct brings the integrity of all law enforcement into question. The adverse actions of one state, county, or city police agency can easily affect the entire service area. The public has a tendency to stereotype. If one police department is accused of conduct amounting to sexual harassment, it could be surmised that other police departments engage in similar activities.

Chiefs of police have been fired based solely on accusations of sexual harassment, that is, mere allegations of sexual harassment are enough to remove a person who serves "at the pleasure" of city management. Thus, complaints, founded or unfounded, are career threatening at the outset and potentially destructive, not only to the community and to each individual involved in the settlement, but to the occupation of law enforcement as a whole.

The courts, in finding for the defendants in cases of sexual harassment, have often awarded extraordinarily large financial settlements. For instance, of the 6,706 sexual harassment complaints resolved by federal and state agencies in 1991, the monetary awards amounted to $7.1 million. In 1993, of the 9,965 cases resolved, monetary awards totalled $25.7 million (Gage, 1993:11). In one of the largest monetary settlements ever of a sex discrimination lawsuit, Lucky Stores agreed to pay close to $108 million to end a class action suit, ruled on in August 1992, brought by a group of female employees who worked in the grocery chain's Northern California stores. The consent decree obligated Lucky to provide some monetary benefit to about 14,000 of 20,000 women initially included in the action, finding that Lucky Stores placed women in poorly paying jobs and denied them advancement opportunities (Tassy, 1993:D1).

Two women officers, Lindsay Allison and Melissa Clerkin, from the Long Beach (California) Police Department, were awarded $3.1 million in 1991, sustaining their allegations of years of sexual harassment by male colleagues. This particular case received national attention, as the incident was portrayed in the 1993 TV docudrama "With Hostile Intent," aired on May 11, 1993. Officer Allison, who joined the department in 1981 and was the first woman on Long Beach's K–9 squad, said she was forced to look at pornographic pictures, was subjected to sexist jokes and remarks, and was placed in physical danger by fellow officers who allowed their dogs to attack her. Clerkin, who had been with the department since 1982, said that intimate details of her private life were circulated, that she was "maligned and vilified," and that she was refused crucial backup help. Both women claimed a hostility so severe that they were forced into a stress-related leave in 1988 (Mendoza, 1993:F1).

As a direct result of increasing complaints, legal actions, and large monetary settlements, law enforcement executives and supervisors at all governmental levels are implementing intensive training in employee relations, conflict management, and especially in sexual harassment. There are few departments that have not published guidelines and policies governing the provisions of Title VII of the Civil Rights Act of 1964.

BOX 5.3 Definitions of Sexual Harassment

Sexual harassment may range from sexual innuendoes made at inappropriate times, sometimes under the guise of humor, to coerced sexual relations. Harassment at its extreme occurs when a male in a position to control, influence or affect a woman's job, career, or grades, uses his authority and power to coerce the woman into sexual relations or to punish her refusal.

Harassment may include

verbal harassment or abuse

subtle pressure for sexual activity

sexist remarks about a woman's clothing, body or sexual activities

unnecessary touching, patting, or pinching

leering or ogling of a woman's body

demanding sexual favors accompanied by implied or overt threats concerning one's job, grades, letters of recommendation

physical assault

Equal Employment Opportunity Commission Guidelines on Sexual Harassment

Section 1604.11 Sexual Harassment.

a) HARASSMENT on the basis of sex is a violation of Sec. 703 of Title VII. Unwelcome sexual advances, requests for sexual favors, and other verbal or physical conduct of a sexual nature constitute sexual harassment when

- submission to such conduct is made either explicitly or implicitly *a term or condition of* an individual's employment,
- submission to or rejection of such conduct by an individual is used as the *basis for employment decisions* affecting such individual, or
- such conduct has the *purpose or effect of substantially interfering* with an individual's *work performance or creating an intimidating, hostile, or offensive* working environment.

1. In determining whether alleged conduct constitutes sexual harassment, the EEOC will look at the *record as a whole.*
2. The agency is responsible for its acts and those of its supervisors and employees *whether* behavior was *forbidden* by employer policy or not.
3. An employer is responsible for acts of sexual harassment in the workplace *unless* it can be shown it took immediate and appropriate corrective action.
4. An employer may be responsible for sexually harassing acts of *non-employees* if it fails to take immediate and appropriate corrective action.

5. When employment opportunities or benefits are granted because of submission to sexual advances or requests of sexual favors, the employer may be liable for unlawful sex discrimination against other persons qualified for but denied the opportunity or benefit.
6. Prevention is the best tool for the elimination of sexual harassment. An employer should take all steps necessary to prevent sexual harassment from occurring, such as affirmatively raising the subject, expressing strong disapproval, developing appropriate sanctions, informing employees of their right(s), and developing methods to sensitize all concerned.

Source: Equal Employment Opportunity Commission. (1984). *Guidelines in Sexual Harassment.* Washington, D.C.: U.S. Government Printing Office. (Emphasis added.)

STRATEGIES TO PREVENT HARASSMENT

The Supreme Court case of *Harris v. Forklift Systems Inc.* (1993) was an attempt to establish standards in harassment cases quickly. The court, however, did not provide a clear definition of what actually constitutes a "hostile environment." Another thorny (but sidestepped) issue is the First Amendment right of free speech—that is, whether offensive words may or may not be protected.

The success of sexual harassment claims involving high monetary remuneration and high media visibility might well cause a flood of new claims. The relatively new and somewhat ambiguous issues that surround sexual harassment may cause claims of harassment to be addressed early and settled out of court. Pessimistic jurisdictions not willing to enter into protracted and costly litigations might opt to seek early relief through settlement. One can only wonder if this will be a boon to those actually suffering harassment or encourage the filing of unreasonable actions.

Whether or not there is an increase in claims, the only sensible and prudent option for organizations is to establish policy and educate employees. It is imperative that each policing agency have a written sexual harassment policy that will allow employees unfettered opportunity to do their jobs and fairly compete in the workplace.

Sample Agency Policy and Format

The San Bernardino Sheriff's Department has suggested the following sexual harassment policy for its employees.

Purpose. To provide an approved (agency) policy informing employees of their rights and management and supervisors of their responsibilities. Further, adoption of this policy will demonstrate the (agency's) good faith effort to eliminate sexual harassment.

Policy Statement. It is the policy of the (agency) to provide a work environment free from unwelcome sexual overtures, advances and coercion. Employees are expected to adhere to a standard of conduct that is respectful to all persons within the work environment. The (agency) will not tolerate any form of sexual harassment or reprisal.

Policy Amplification. Sexual harassment is a violation of Section 703 of Title VII of the Civil Rights Act of 1964, as amended. Sexual harassment can cause physical and economical problems for its victims. In addition to the anxiety these demands may cause, there may be an underlying message that noncompliance will lead to reprisals. These reprisals can include escalation of the harassment, poor work assignments, sabotaging work, unsatisfactory evaluations, threatened demotions, transfers, poor job references, slander, gossip, blackmail, and other forms of retribution. Sexual harassment undermines the integrity of the employment relations. Sexual harassment can result in economic loss to both the (agency) and employee, excessive absenteeism and turnover, loss of morale, polarization of staff and a decrease in management credibility, and a decrease in productivity.

Definitions of Sexual Harassment:

Sexual harassment is unsolicited and unwelcome sexual advances, requests for sexual favors and other verbal, physical or visual conduct of a sexual nature which occurs under any one of the three circumstances,

1. Submission is made either explicitly or implicitly as a term or condition of employment.
2. Submission or rejection by an employee is used as a basis for employment decisions affecting the employee.
3. Such conduct has the potential to affect an employee's work performance negatively and/or create an intimidating, hostile or otherwise offensive working environment.

For the purpose of further clarification, sexual harassment includes, but is not limited to,

1. Making unsolicited written, verbal, physical and/or visual contact with sexual overtones. (Written examples, suggestive or obscene letters, notes, invitations. Verbal examples, derogatory comments, slurs, jokes and epithets. Physical examples, assault touching, impeding or blocking movements.

Visual examples, leering, gestures or display of sexually suggestive objects or pictures, cartoons, or posters.)
2. Continuing to express sexual interest after being informed that the interest is unwelcome. (Reciprocal attraction is not considered sexual harassment.)
3. Making reprisals, threats of reprisal, or implied threats of reprisal following a negative response. For example, either implying or actually withholding support for an appointment, promotion, or change of assignment; suggesting a poor work performance evaluation will be prepared, or suggesting a probationary period will be failed.
4. Engaging in implicit or explicit coercive sexual behavior which is used to control, influence, or affect the career, salary, and/or work environment of another employee.
5. Offering favors of employment benefits, such as promotions, favorable work performance evaluations, favorable assigned duties or shifts, recommendations, reclassifications, etc., in exchange for sexual favors.

Responsibilities and Procedures (Agency Responsibilities). The (agency) believes that prompt appropriate action should be taken to avoid or minimize the incidence of sexual harassment and (agency) liability. The (agency) will pursue every possible preventive measure to ensure employees are not subject to sexual harassment. The (agency) will take appropriate disciplinary action against anyone found to be in violation of this policy.

The (agency) by disseminating this policy, will inform employees of their rights and the appropriate means by which to file a complaint. This information will also be included in all orientation packages for new employees.

Employees' Rights and Responsibilities. Any employee who believes he or she has been sexually harassed has the right to file a complaint of discrimination in employment with the Affirmative Action Unit (or similar unit) following the Complaint Resolution Procedure as established by (higher authority). Employees also have the right to file with the State Department of Fair Employment and Housing and/or the Federal Equal Employment Opportunity Commission without seeking resolution through the (agency) and are assured that retaliation will not occur if such action is taken.

If the employee wishes to seek resolution with the (agency), the incident should be reported immediately to his/her supervisor. If the employee does not feel that the situation was adequately resolved or if the harasser is the employee's supervisor, he/she should report the incident to the next level supervisor. The employee may also contact the Affirmative Action Unit (or similar unit) and file a formal complaint. Additionally, the (agency) welcomes intervention by the appropriate State or Federal Agency. (Revision of San Bernardino County Sheriff's Department Standard Procedure No. 60-5-1 dated January 18, 1987).

THE AMERICANS WITH DISABILITIES ACT (ADA)

The U.S. Supreme Court decision *Plessy v. Ferguson* (1896) allowed the continuation of nonintegration and practices not only based on issues of race, but also based on age and disability. The court modified that case and declared educational segregation to be inherently unequal in *Brown v. Board of Education* (1954). *Brown* coupled with the Civil Rights Act of 1964 and advocacy groups brought about the passage of the Rehabilitation Act of 1973. This act only applied to the federal government. The passage of the Air Carrier Access Act (1986) and the Fair Housing Amendments Act (1988) expanded the range and legal obligation of private sector firms. The ADA was signed into law on July 26, 1990.

In 1991 Schneid and Gaines warned that

> The ADA may very well be the most significant piece of legislation affecting law enforcement since the Civil Rights Act. It will cause police agencies throughout the United States, as well as other employers, to adjust and, in some cases, completely overhaul their recruitment and selection procedures. Furthermore, if departments do not immediately develop changes in their personnel policies by the time the Act becomes applicable, they will expose themselves to substantial liability.

In many cases the warnings of these two scholars went unheeded because many police administrators thought that people with disabilities could not function as peace officers. The major point being made, however, was that employment could not be denied to those individuals who could perform the rigors of job-related tasks. This simply meant that the requirements for hiring must actually be job-related and consistent with necessity. Persons with disabilities who meet the specified job requirements are not considered qualified unless they can also perform the essential functions of the job with or without a reasonable accommodation (Rubin, 1993:4). As part of the urban police function, the requirement of a valid driver's permit, for instance, is not an unreasonable job-related standard.

Title I of the ADA makes it illegal to discriminate against persons with disabilities. These individuals are entitled to equal access to employment, including the processes of recruitment, hiring, promotion, and any other benefits and privileges of employment. To be "protected" (covered by Title I), the individual must have a disability and be qualified for the job. To be qualified, the individual must satisfy the job requirements, such as education, experience, and skills, and must be able to perform the essential functions of the job, with or without a reasonable accommodation.

Provision of Reasonable Accommodation. This can include modifying existing facilities to make them accessible, job restructuring, setting part-time or modified work schedules, acquiring or modifying equipment, and changing policies. However, reasonable accommodations will not be required when providing them causes an undue hardship for the agency. Undue hardship means significant expense or difficulty. More than just money may be involved; it can also mean disruption or fundamental alteration of the nature or operation of the agency. Direct threat of serious harm is defined by the law as "a significant risk of substantial harm to the health and safety of others that cannot be eliminated by reasonable accommodations." Direct threat is not a defense to an employer's obligation to provide a reasonable accommodation. A reasonable accommodation is required if it will eliminate the direct threat.

Accessibility to Facilities. In addition, Title II of the ADA requires government entities to achieve accessibility to their facilities as well as in the delivery of services and programs. Accessibility encompasses new construction and the alteration of existing facilities. It can mean anything from adding curb ramps to creating parking spaces reserved for persons with disabilities (Rubin, 1993:2):

> **"Covered Entity" Under Title 1,** An employer, employment agency, labor organization, or joint labor-management committee.
>
> **Employers,** Those businesses engaged in an industry affecting commerce who have 15 or more employees for each working day in each of 20 or more calendar weeks in the current or preceding calendar year.
>   As of July 26, 1992, only employers with 25 or more employees were affected by the provisions of ADA. On July 26, 1994, employers with 15 or more employees fell under ADA provisions. It is important to note that the term *employer* does not include the United States, a wholly owned government corporation, an Indian tribe, or a bona fide private membership club that is exempt from taxation under section 501(c) of the Internal Revenue Code of 1986.
>
> **Individual with a Disability,** An individual must satisfy at least one of the following, 1) Have a physical or mental impairment that substantially limits one or more major life activities; or 2) Have a record of such an impairment; or 3) Be regarded as having such an impairment.
>
> **Physical or Mental Impairment,** Any physiological disorder or condition; cosmetic disfigurement; anatomical loss that affects one or more of several body systems; mental illness or retardation; hearing, speech, and visual impairments; cancer or infection with HIV. An impairment does not include, Eye or hair color; Pregnancy; Obesity that is not the result of a physiological disorder or impairment that is covered under the Act; Environmental, cultural or economic disadvantages; Nicotine addiction; Psychoactive substance disorders resulting from current use of illegal drugs; Temporary, non-chronic impairments, such as the flu or a broken limb; Transvestism, and other sexual behavior disorders; Compulsive gambling; Kleptomania; Pyromania; Homosexuality; Bisexuality; and Advanced age, in and of itself.
>
> **Major Life Activity,** Those basic activities that the average person in the general population can perform with little or no difficulty, e.g., caring for oneself, performing manual tasks, walking, seeing, hearing, speaking, breathing, learning and working.

When the ADA was enacted on July 26, 1990, it was intended to augment the earlier provisions of the Rehabilitation Act of 1973. In this respect ADA expanded coverage to include employers neither receiving federal funds nor working under federal contract. Attempts to exempt law enforcement personnel failed, and their (law enforcement) delivery of public services falls under the guidelines of ADA. Criminal justice agencies have begun to apply the ADA requirements, and these requirements affect virtually every facet of the application, screening, and selection processes for law enforcement personnel (Rubin, 1993:8).

U.S. Attorney General Janet Reno has made enforcement of the act a priority and has authorized assignment of twelve more employees to the Justice Department's civil rights division. On December 28, 1993, the Justice Department filed its first lawsuit to enforce job provisions of the ADA. It asked a federal court to strike down sections of an Illinois law that denied pension benefits to disabled police offices and firefighters. The suit, filed in Chicago, accused the state of Illinois and the Chicago suburb of Aurora of excluding otherwise qualified employees who are disabled from participating in a state-established retirement fund.

The case began with a complaint filed by an eight-year veteran officer who had been hired even though he was known to have diabetes. He was later barred from making contributions to or getting benefits from the police pension fund because he failed to pass a second physical examination required by the fund's board of trustees. If the officer should be injured or wounded—even while on duty—he would be ineligible for pension benefits (Eaton, 1993b:A16).

"BY THE BOOK" AND THE "DIRTY HARRY" PHENOMENON

Career Integrity Workshops

One evening, four deputy sheriffs patrolling in an unmarked police car had a suspicion that drugs were being dealt from a particular house. After calling in their location, one officer called in an "anonymous tip" that drugs were being sold from that residence. As they were the nearest unit in the area, they were dispatched to check out the report. Differing testimony was given but the final outcome was that they forcibly entered the home, and one officer shot the resident, a nine-month pregnant African American woman, killing the fetus. One officer was convicted of 2nd degree murder and was sentenced to prison.

This "police action" and a host of similar cases across our nation raise several knotty and somewhat unnerving questions. One question is what kind of pressure is being placed on enforcement officers to engage in such obviously illegal conduct? Do they feel the end justifies the means? Do they feel so frustrated in their (law enforcement as a whole) inability to "crush crime" that they manufacture incidents? Do they feel exempt from the rules of due process and constituted procedure? Are they so in need of a "bust" for recognition (or a perceived quota) that they will resort to illegal tactics to provide one? Do they feel their supervisors, administrators, and executives approve of such actions?

In the wake of such incidents, the Los Angeles County Sheriff's Department initiated an in-service training program called **Career Integrity Workshops.** In-house instructors were trained in methods of leading small groups of deputies in creating "questionable conduct" scenarios and facilitating group discussions that delved into possible causes of actions or inactions and possible results. The student (deputy)-generated incidents were seen to be more closely in tune with reality than "canned" situations brought into the training environment. The deputies were able to create and critique situations that raised concerns about ethical conduct and officer career survival. Through the use of these workshops, deputies were slowly and sometimes painfully made aware of the consequences of unethical verbal, physical, and written conduct. One scenario was the following:

> A deputy on patrol spots a driver who appears to be under the influence and makes an unassisted stop. This incident occurs within the view of a supervising sergeant in another vehicle. Upon exiting the vehicle, the driver spits in the deputy's face. The deputy takes the driver to the ground, handcuffs him, spits into his face, places him in the rear of the patrol car and calls for the tow truck. The deputy, knowing the supervisor was watching, gives him a "wink." Three days later the driver files a complaint against the deputy for spitting on him. The deputy's report does not include any mention of this action, other than the fact the driver had spit on him. In fact, when questioned, the deputy denies the allegation. The supervisor was requested to make a report and the supervisor's account did not support the driver's claim . . . stating in essence that the sergeant did not see the deputy spit in the driver's face. The next day a telecast showing the whole incident, as filmed by a neighbor with a cam recorder, hits the six o'clock news.

Although spitting in someone's face is probably one of the most crass and disgusting acts imaginable, the action by the deputy was inexcusable. The class can ponder the consequences of this situation. One deputy lied and another covered up. What will happen to the deputy who filed a false report? What will happen to the supervisor who covered it up? What would have happened if the deputy admitted to the act? What would have happened if the supervisor had not suppressed the incident? The supervisor, simply stated, put his career in jeopardy to cover the illegal act of a "colleague." This poses several questions: Can or should this type of loyalty be expected? Would you put your career on the line for another officer who has committed an act that could result in disciplinary actions?

Career integrity workshops clearly allow enforcement personnel to examine the motives for the choices they sometimes make. If those choices are perceived to weigh heavily against continuing a career in law enforcement, then individual survival instincts might prevail. Unfortunately, the chances of being caught appear to be a prime mover in motivating ethical behavior rather than reliance on instinctive ethical standards. In terms of monetary loss, losing enforcement personnel because of unethical conduct is a very costly proposition; in terms of community trust and COP, it is a disaster.

Posttrauma Information and Strategies

Within the concept and operationalization of community-oriented policing lies the ideal of mutual support. Communities and police managers must fully and compassionately provide care and assistance to those officers involved in trauma-induced events. In the aftermath of incidents resulting in shootings, some departments mandate psychological counseling for involved officers. Other departments provide counseling and recommend that employees seek psychological assistance. Many departments simply do not have counseling available and may or may not suggest assistance. Because of long-established masculine traits that trivialize trauma as not being "manly" or regard shooting incidents as "only incidental to the job," a stigma has been placed on seeking psychological counseling. Peer pressure has prevented many seriously posttraumatized officers from seeking counseling. The mandating of psychological counseling following a shooting incident eliminates the possibility of stigma, because everyone has to abide by the same rule. The training division of the San Bernardino County Sheriff's Department published an information sheet describing the three parts of posttrauma—process, feelings, and survival:

Process

Being involved in a trauma situation, regardless of whether or not it was a shooting or a traffic collision, produces feelings equal in intensity and similar reactions to those which an actual death of a loved one can cause.
These reactions are

> *Initial Denial*—that the trauma incident took place, "this couldn't have happened to me," and produces at first a retreat into a fantasy life where it never happened. Many feel that the event happened in slow motion. After the trauma incident it took them quite a few moments to realize what happened.
>
> *Hostility and Anger*—which can be non-directed (just mad that it happened), or directed toward the person who caused you to be involved in the trauma incident. This hostility is short-lived, but returns several times during the adaptation process.
>
> *Feelings of Guilt or Bargaining*—internalized or projected, over things you did or didn't do (wishing the traffic accident didn't occur), or things you might have done differently to prevent the trauma incident or the outcome of it. Fear of loss of job is also common.
>
> *Withdrawal or Depression*—from those happenings too painful to cope with. The depression lasts the longest and may go on for weeks or months in degrees. The length of time depends on your basic personality, the amount of trauma you suffered, how the department deals with the inci-

dent, the availability and use of psychological intervention services, and the handling of the incident by the media.

Gradual Testing and Retesting Reality—to feel out the possibility of being able to cope with future situations that are similar. This leads to final *Acceptance*, acknowledging that this incident happened and that you have survived it. The pattern ends with an eventual letting go from the influence of the past experience so that a new part of your life can begin.

Note: Not all of these reactions are experienced by everyone, and not necessarily in this order, although this is the most common form of reaction to a trauma. Some feelings may return, usually anger and resentment, but not to a debilitating degree after the final acceptance.

Feelings

The feelings involved after a trauma incident consist of seven basic reactions:

Emotional Numbing—The officers distance themselves from the incident and make an effort not to feel anything. They almost deny having an emotional component, and therefore give the appearance that they are in a state of shock. They usually say, however, that they are in control and are having no problems dealing with the situation.

Isolation—They experience the feeling of being alone and that no one else knows what they are going through. They may experience irritability and agitation, and may again deny that anything is wrong.

Intrusive Thoughts/Flashbacks—They will relive the event in their minds, over and over again. If it continues, they begin to wonder or question whether they have complete control of their thoughts. This can change their final outlook, for better or worse.

Sleep Disturbances—Disturbances which can result from a trauma incident include inability to sleep, nightmares, and waking in a cold sweat. In the nightmares, the theme is fear or guilt. Guilt is common in 95 percent of trauma incidents to varying degrees. This guilt can be translated into anger or depression.

Anxiety and Fear—The fear most commonly felt is that of returning to the exact job duties as before, i.e., driving in a car or night duty.

Loss of Interest/Burnout—Loss of interest in work is difficulty in returning to it. Mundane activities suddenly become boring. The officers usually want the department to expedite the trauma incident investigation.

Reconsideration—Re-evaluation of each person's value system, goals and status is often the final step which determines the person's abilities to cope and how the person will continue with future activities. Some consider giving up law enforcement as a career. They may also re-evaluate their marital situation. Some make a stronger commitment and others get divorced.

How to Psychologically Survive

Available Psychological Services—Have available psychological services immediately, before the individual goes home. On-call counselors are ideal. This allows officers to verbalize their feelings and concerns while they are still fresh, and in an atmosphere that is "safe."

Critical Incident Group—Officers relate to a group of their peers, who have been involved in similar trauma incidents, and with whom they can share their experience. Group sessions are arranged and conducted by the counselor.

Ability to Vent Fears—The opportunity and ability to talk to their peers and/or family members about their feelings is very important. It prevents hiding negative feelings.

Tell Department Your Needs—Let the department know what you would like to do. You may wish to take a few days off, work light duty for a short time, take a sick leave or vacation.

Be Aware of Performance—While an officer is on the job or doing light duty after a trauma incident, it is important to be aware of the officer's performance and feelings about it. These officers should examine their feelings, identify those parts of the job which cause anxiety and then work on alleviating that anxiety.

Department Policy—Depending upon the nature of the incident, officers may have their weapon removed or be put on administrative leave or suspension. Often if this happens, the officer feels betrayed by the department and distrustful of it.

Ride-Alongs—The ride-along concept can be adopted as a means to gradually ease the officer back into duty after the trauma incident. The officer may feel more confident with a partner and can adjust more slowly to returning to full duty.

Re-referral if Problems Continue—If the initial counseling session(s) do not completely ease the tension and help the officer to return to productive duty, re-referral to the same source, or to another source may be necessary. Counseling may also be needed for the spouse of the officer, so they can work through their feelings together.

POLICE STRESS AND BURNOUT: SOURCES AND IMPLICATIONS

Police work has often been characterized as one of the most dangerous while at the same time most exciting jobs available outside of Special Forces military units. The glamour and excitement of law enforcement has been heightened by the media, especially television, where highway patrolmen break international drug cartels and rookie cops conquer organized crime. The danger of loss of life and limb, a given ingredient of law enforcement employment, is the main thrust of many movies and television plots.

How much of this danger is real and how much is fiction geared to sell products and promote TV ratings? In 1992, of the 136 officers who died across the United States, 82 were killed by felonious assault (64 by firearms), and 54 died from accidental causes while on duty, such as aircraft or automobile crashes, being struck by a vehicle, or drowning. The law enforcement officers killed in 1992 included 122 fatalities from 34 states, seven from U. S. federal agencies, and five from the U.S. territory of Puerto Rico. For the fifth straight year, Texas had more officers killed than any other state—thirteen—followed by Florida with eleven, California with ten, South Carolina with nine, and New York with eight. On average, the officers who died during 1992 were 36 years old and had served for nine years. Three officers were females. According to records kept by the National Law Enforcement Officers Memorial Fund, a total of 1,685 law enforcement officers have died in the line of duty during the ten-year period from 1983 through 1992. Nearly 13,000 officers have died in the line of duty since the first recorded death in 1794 (*Star & Shield*, 1993:1). Although the occupation of policing is dangerous, it doesn't compare with coal miners, firefighters, construction workers, or urban taxi drivers.

Burnout: The Patrol Officer's Perspective

It has been suggested by organizational experts that police stressors can be both external and internal. External causal factors include the other components of the criminal justice system that, at times, are perceived by the police as functioning at cross purposes. That an accused person can be arrested and be back on the street before the officer can complete all the paper work is frustrating. Some law officers see the court system as a revolving door allowing offenders to either be released or become repeat offenders while disallowing "good police work" due to court decisions. They see probation officers making recommendations for reduced sentences and permitting convicted individuals to remain in the community. The objectives of the police function and those of probation are seen as not mutually supportive. In a general sense, the police want the offender locked up, whereas probation officers want the offender placed under their jurisdiction and supervision. This situation can easily be troubling to concerned officers who believe they have made "good arrests" and want offenders jailed.

Another factor that plays a role in external stressors is the media. The negative or distorted media accounts of police activities have taken a toll. The police view the constant criticism and hindsight appraisals of police actions by the media as detrimental to their physical and mental health. In this regard, the media also influence the community and collective perceptions regarding certain police actions. There is no doubt that sensationalism sells newspapers and advertising spots on television, but when the police perceive an imbalance in coverage, it is only normal to feel slighted and unappreciated. Heroic police actions or coverage of law enforcement personnel who have been wounded, assaulted, or killed while performing their duties have not, at times, been afforded equal treatment.

Yet another source of stress can be laid at the politician's doorstep. When municipalities fail to fund the police budget fully, or when bond issues or initiatives favorable to the police are defeated at the polls, many officers take it as a personal affront, and frustration and stress levels are apt to rise. When bond issues fail, many police wonder if the community really appreciates the job they are doing and tend to question why they have elected to serve the community. Many communities, over the years, have failed to fund and maintain basic police equipment adequately. The price the community pays when police-related equipment is not properly maintained or periodically replaced is an increased attitude of the police that their lives are unnecessarily put in jeopardy. When station houses fall into disrepair as a result of benign financial neglect, it can cause police officers to question community and political support.

A 1993 report stated that the Los Angeles Police Department (LAPD) was beset by decay, its 7,600 officers handicapped by dilapidated police stations and broken-down cars—a sentiment echoed up and down the department ranks, from new patrol officers to Chief Willie L. Williams. The state of the LAPD's equipment has contributed to dismal morale in the ranks and has sent many officers packing in search of more modern police forces. The decline, according to observers, has become particularly acute during the past few years, but its roots reach back to the 1970s. In 1973, the department's share of the city budget was about 35 percent, compared to just over 25 percent in 1993. Although the size of the department has increased over the same period, politicians have made ends meet by putting off scheduled improvements in LAPD equipment and station houses. Two police stations, at 77th Street and Newton, are so dilapidated that within the ranks they have come to symbolize the department's decline. Newton and 77th Street are located in the city's urban center and are two of the busiest stations in the city. Both stations were built in the mid-1920s, and at 77th, 300 male and female officers share a single bathroom, roll calls are delivered in a trailer, and employees have to eat lunch at their desks or outside the station because it has no lunchroom. The most striking aspect of 77th Street Station is the second floor. It no longer exists. After inspectors determined a few years ago that it was about to collapse, it was condemned and lopped off the top of the building. At one end of the station, a staircase, dubbed the "stairway to nowhere," still leads upward, ending in a wall. Its only use these days is as a gag. When new arrivals ask senior officers where to look for supplies, veterans occasionally send them hunting for the second floor. Voters approved a bond issue in 1989 intended to improve the two stations, but setbacks and delays have held up improvements (Newton, 1993).

Internal stressors, or organizational causal factors, are probably more in evidence than external factors. In general, poor training, inadequate supervision, irregular working hours and conditions, little upward mobility or career development opportunities, lack of empowerment and involvement in departmental policy, buck passing, and an administrative eagerness to discipline officers for the most petty of infractions are definite factors.

It has been observed that what officers feel they must do to maintain public order often conflicts with administrators' edicts and public demands. The collateral tasks assumed by the police have also expanded to include community-based disputes, including landlord vs. tenant, customer vs. business, neighbor vs. neighbor, business vs. business, family member vs. family member, and citizens in the community vs. law enforcement (Meeks, 1993:98). These newly acquired dispute-resolution chores coupled with the ever present possibility of injury or potential danger can cause stress. But possibly most telling are the close and personal involvements in the tragedies of people in trouble that take their toll.

Another important issue, of course, is personal stressors. Although there are many such stressors, a few are the most powerful. They include self-doubt or feelings of incompetence, the continual state of apprehension regarding the danger of the job (fear), the need to conform to peer expectations, racial issues, and the full range of personal problems that affect all members of society (Eisenberg, 1993).

The Burnout Syndrome

The relationship between an occupation and stress whether it be external or internal is commonly referred to as job burnout. This has been defined as . . . a syndrome of emotional exhaustion and cynicism that occurs frequently among individuals who do "people work" of some kind. A key aspect of the burnout syndrome is increased feelings of emotional exhaustion. Another aspect is the development of negative, cynical attitudes and feelings about one's clients. . . . A third aspect of the burnout syndrome is the tendency to evaluate oneself negatively, particularly with regard to one's work with clients. Workers feel unhappy about themselves and dissatisfied with their accomplishments on the job. (Maslach, 1979:99)

The signs of burnout are divided into two general categories, which are (1) psychological and emotional and (2) physical (Fishkin, 1987:170–171):

Psychological and Emotional

- Psychological exhaustion, including mental fatigue and loss of motivation
- Inability to perceive or generate alternative solutions—loss of positive attitude
- Despair and feeling that it takes everything to just get through the day
- Social withdrawal
- Thoughts related to death and suicide

Physical

- Exhaustion—loss of energy, drive
- Physical illness
- Sleeping disorders
- Muscular tension

Occupational or Vocational Signs of Burnout
- Increased absenteeism
- Low level of job satisfaction (morale)
- Significant loss of productivity
- Overly personalizing with the job

Family-Related Signs of Occupational Burnout
- Feeling distant from loved ones
- Refusing to participate in family social events
- Verbal or physical abuse of family
- Lack of interest or desire for sexual sharing

Many organizations, recognizing that a host of internal and external stress factors can have a negative impact on enforcement officers, have initiated psychological referral programs. The trend has been slow, however. *Police Magazine* reported in 1982 that less than 5 percent of the more than 16,000 departments across the nation had started programs to address personnel stress problems. More recently, more law enforcement agencies have instituted programs that address burnout. For example, departments have initiated stress-reduction seminars or yearly job-related stress classes in their in-service training programs. In addition, supplementary peer groups and employee assistance programs have been established to help police personnel in their individual battles against stress and job burnout.

Although progress has been slow in this area, it is being made. But until police officers are made active participants in the organization and made a part of the larger community, they will feel excluded and frustrated, and will seek solace and comfort within their very closed ranks. The literature clearly suggests that Maslow's "Hierarchy of Needs" is indeed operative and that the organization has the capability to at least meet all of the basic needs. Unfortunately, the general thrust of concern regarding stress and burnout is how they affect the *organization*. The effects that burned-out police officers have on their organizations are indeed significant. Lost productivity, sickness, injuries on duty, disciplinary problems, equipment abuse, absenteeism, early retirements, and lawsuits are some very costly by-products. The singular and most neglected factor in police literature is the impact that officers suffering from burnout can have on their clients, members of the community. Without early identification and intervention to assist officers suffering from this burnout syndrome the ultimate loser will be the community. Customer service will certainly suffer at the hands of officers in the grips of stressors. Departments should train everyone in the agency regarding the symptoms of stressors and their effects. Stress has the ability to strike anywhere in the organization.

Agencies attempting to implement COP or related changes in organizational philosophy must first deal with those internal organizational factors that breed dissatisfaction, low productivity, and low morale. Ultimately, those factors affect client orientation, and without client-oriented officers, COP will never get off the drawing board.

The Burntout Policeman's Association and Friends (BPA)

The Burntout Policeman's Association and Friends (BPA) was established in 1983 to reduce stress by using job-related humor as the common denominator among police officers everywhere. BPA boasts a membership of more than 7,500 police officers across the country and in twelve other nations and has established three major steps toward their goal:

> Our first step is to encourage our brothers and sisters in blue to laugh at the problems of their profession . . . which has been proven to be a highly successful method of fighting job-related stress. . . .
>   Secondly, getting everyone in our occupation to think positive about themselves and to help each other.
>   Thirdly, to help officers realize that the personal problems they may be presently dealing with are not unique, nor are they insurmountable. We attempt to fortify the officer's self-esteem, his or her strength and positiveness, and we encourage them to become the very best that they can be.

"Blue Humor"

People often don't really understand why laughter and humor give them so much pleasure. As W. C. Fields put it, "The funniest thing about comedy is that you never know why people laugh. I know what makes them laugh, but trying to get your hands on the *why* of it is like trying to pick an eel out of a tub of water" (Pettijohn, 1991:135).

The field of law enforcement is rife with both personal tragedy and humorous situations. Humor helps officers ease stress and cope with situations. Yet this stress-reducing ploy is probably one of the most misunderstood and misinterpreted coping mechanisms. Joseph Wambaugh in his writings *(Blue Knight, New Centurions, Black Marble, The Glitter Dome, The Onion Field, Finnegan's Week,* and *Choirboys)* has given the American public insight into the dark humor law enforcement officers occasionally employ. The use of humor to blunt the reality of life and to assuage tragic situations could be termed **emotional numbing.** Officers are, from time to time, exposed to incidents that might cause "less hardened" individuals to faint, vomit, or otherwise be rendered occupationally useless.

We do not expect our law enforcement officers to show emotions that would detract from their immediate tasks. If, for instance, a busload of children is involved in a major accident, responding officers must take control of the scene; they cannot give in to the normal responses of shock, revulsion, or denial because that could impede emergency actions. Personal feelings must be set aside and dealt with later. In times of crisis individuals who can stand apart from the danger and make light of their own foibles may be reacting in a "healthy" way. The ability to laugh at oneself is reflective of a mature ego. A common saying is, "The person who can laugh at himself will never run out of material." The use of caustic humor can expose sham and deceit, but humor and comedy can also serve to mask deep-seated, unarticulated feelings.

Police association newspapers invariably have a section dedicated to humor. *The Thin Blue Line,* published by the Los Angeles Police Department's Police Protective League, features "Cops, Quips and Quirks," compilations of adventurous reports taken from other police newspapers. Some of the incidents are funny. For example, Gary Blantz, age 29, was arrested for kidnapping a bar owner near Lancaster, Pennsylvania, in February 1993. Police reported later that Blantz shot himself in the foot with his .45-caliber revolver to show the victim what would happen to him if he were disobedient. Then there was the report on a 30-year-old man in Kenmore, New York, who took a suicide leap from a building's fourth-floor window. Instead of hitting the pavement, he landed on top of a parked car. Dazed and stunned but alive, the determined would-be suicide limped into the lobby, took the elevator back to the fourth floor, jumped out the same window again—and landed on the same parked car. This time he just didn't have enough energy left to try it again. He was hospitalized (*PORAC News,* 1993:26). Another incident involved Thomas Jefferson Cobb, 38, who robbed a bank and ran, but should have made sure he hadn't left any personal belongings behind. Cobb fled leaving a ring of keys on the bank counter. Responding F.B.I. and police units simply checked parked cars for a few blocks around the bank, found a "match," staked it out, and waited for Cobb to come back with his spare key—which, of course, he did (*The Thin Blue Line,* 1991:26).

Humor is an emotional release when dealing with the bizarre, and laughter is beneficial regardless of the impetus. Finding humor in things that are stressful is an effective management tool. Relevant humor can bring about a catharsis that adds to mental relief. A police writer made this observation about humor: "But there are pitfalls in verbal and written humor. Saying the right thing at the wrong time, or the wrong thing at any time, can be hazardous. A negative or off-color remark, or a dark joke about death overheard by a family member of the recently dear departed, can generate a citizen's complaint, and justifiably so. Gallows or black humor is not bad. In fact it may be the most effective because it's so relevant to the source of stress. It just requires some discretion" (Davis, 1993b:23).

Gallows humor, the dark side of police humor, even though it might be therapeutic, can be offensive and, if not checked, can seriously damage public relations. After the Rodney King beating, for example, some police agencies sported T-shirts that said, "Come to (city) . . . we will treat you like a King." These shirts were discouraged as being in bad taste and offensive to an already sensitive public. After the choke hold was banned, a few officers in Portland, Oregon, sold T-shirts with the inscription, "Don't Choke 'em—Smoke 'em." The officers involved were fired, but in a subsequent 1985 lawsuit were reinstated with a six-month disciplinary suspension.

It would be hard to work in an environment that discouraged a reasonable degree of levity. The key word here is *reasonable*. It is reasonable to employ wit, humor, gags, and, to a certain extent, practical jokes to entertain, to relieve tension, and to put situations into proper perspective. It is, however, incumbent that individuals know the limits and impact of well-intended but misplaced attempts at humor.

Alcoholism and Substance Abuse

Contemporary and enlightened police executives realize that their employees are subject to the same ailments that affect other human beings. Police officers are subject to ingrown toenails and dandruff; they may also abuse alcohol and other legal and illegal substances. The private sector has long understood the workplace problems of substance abuse, and company-sponsored programs help those employees in need. Companies have found that the time, energy, and money spent to reclaim an otherwise productive worker is far less expensive than dismissal. The hiring and training of a replacement is costly. In addition, the organization takes on a more nurturing and caring image, and this change is not lost on employees. If police departments, attempting to implement COP, do not show that they care about the community, the program will fail. COP will just as surely fail if the organization does not care about its employees. Thus, enforcement agencies should have an active liaison with Alcoholics Anonymous and other community outreach support groups.

KEY TERMS

Americans with Disabilities Act (ADA)
Career Integrity Workshops
Emotional numbing
Ethics

Posttrauma strategies
Psychological screening
Sexual harassment
Stress vs. nonstress training

QUESTIONS FOR REVIEW

1. Discuss the process of police recruitment. Why has the oral interview portion been seen as a weak link?
2. What are the arguments for and against the use of stress-oriented training?
3. Describe the functions of field training officers.
4. How can jail experiences influence an officer's working personality?
5. Discuss types of less-than-lethal weapons and their possible functions.
6. What does the acronym *TASER* represent?

7. Explain why verbal judo courses have been included in police training at entry and in-service levels.
8. Explain the funding mechanisms for many state-level police training programs.
9. Discuss the advancements made by women in law enforcement.
10. What was the purpose of the New York Police Department's Cadet Program?
11. Outline the problem of sexual harassment in the workplace. Briefly discuss the landmark case *Harris v. Forklift Systems, Inc.*
12. How does the Americans with Disabilities Act (ADA) affect law enforcement?
13. Discuss some of the symptoms of burnout. What happens when burnout occurs? How do officers cope with burnout and stress on their jobs? Describe some of the programs used by police agencies to combat stress and burnout.
14. Distinguish between internal and external stressors.
15. Briefly explain the process involved in addressing posttrauma incidents.

SUGGESTED READINGS

Broderick, John J. (1987). *Police in a Time of Change (2nd ed.).* Chicago: Waveland Press.
Robinette, Hillary M. (1987). *Burnout in Blue.* New York: Praeger.
Thompson, George J. (1993). *Verbal Judo.* New York: William Morrow.

CHAPTER 6

Police Discretion

Introduction

The Meaning of Police Discretion: A Conceptual Tower of Babel
The Police Mission and Police Discretion
The Rationale for Police Discretion

Situationally Based Discretion and Officer-Offender Relations

Police and the Courts

Selected Constitutional Issues and Police Behavior
The First Amendment
The Second Amendment
The Fourth Amendment
The Fourteenth Amendment

Police Understanding of the Law: Customized Interpretations and the Abuse of Discretion
Police Officer Rationales for Customized Interpretations of Law and Its Enforcement

The Control of Police Discretion

Key Terms

Questions for Review

Suggested Readings

173

INTRODUCTION

Scene 1: Two police officers are cruising city streets in a patrol car at 2:00 A.M. They observe two men walking rapidly down the street toward two parked vehicles. A bar is nearby. The street is well-lit. No recent reports have been made of criminal activity in the area. It is cold, about 33 degrees. The officers stop their cruiser and observe the two men. The two men stop at the two parked cars and appear to have a conversation. Shortly, the men enter the two vehicles and drive off. One of the vehicles performs a legal U-turn on the street and passes the stopped police cruiser. The driver is not speeding. The police officers begin to follow the vehicle. The vehicle ahead of them is proceeding steadily down the street, observing the speed limit and not weaving. The officers decide to stop the vehicle and flash their lights and sound their siren. The driver immediately pulls to the curb. Both officers exit their vehicle and approach the driver from two sides. The driver immediately exits his vehicle and produces his driver's license for the nearest officer. The officer shines his flashlight in the driver's eyes, takes the license and examines it, and asks the driver if he has been drinking. The driver says that he and a friend just got off work on a late shift, stopped briefly at the bar, and consumed two beers. The two officers proceed to make the driver walk a white line and perform other manual dexterity skills. The driver responds normally to each of the police commands. One officer says to the other, "I believe this guy's drunk. Let's run him in." The driver protests but succeeds only in making both officers angry. "Do you want us to charge you with resisting arrest?" they ask.

"No," says the driver. "What did I do and why did you stop me?"

"We saw you come out of that bar for one thing, and we believe you are driving while intoxicated, for another thing," says the other officer.

The driver is arrested, placed in the police cruiser, and taken to the police station, where he is booked, fingerprinted, photographed, and given a breathalyzer test. In the meantime, the officers have ordered the person's automobile towed to the motor vehicle impound lot near the police station. The breathalyzer test registers a .03 BAC (blood alcohol level), well below the .10 BAC required to sustain a drunk-driving conviction against this driver. Already he has been detained at the police station in a drunk tank for four hours. The police officers express surprise at the low BAC reading for this driver and leave the jail. Shortly thereafter, the man is released from the jail and told that he can pay $60 to get his car from the impound lot. Daylight is dawning, and an innocent citizen has just become a victim of police discretion.

Scene 2: Two police officers respond to a report of a domestic violence incident in a lower-class neighborhood. When they arrive, they observe a man being chased about the yard by a woman swinging a baseball bat. The man appears to be bleeding about the face and arms. The woman appears to be unharmed but angry. When the woman sees the officers, she throws the bat to the ground, points at the man, and says, "Arrest that son-of-a-bitch. He pushed me." The man begins to explain things to the officers, but by this time, they have cuffed him and shoved him toward their cruiser. "Bond is gonna be $15,000 for you, buddy," says one officer. "You got somebody you can call to make that bond?"

"Fifteen-thousand dollars?" asks the man in cuffs. "For what?"

"Felony assault," answers one officer. "Your wife says you pushed her."

Later that night, a bonding company accepts some collateral from one of the man's relatives to obtain his release. The relatives have had to sign a paper indicating that they are using their home as collateral to ensure that the man will subsequently appear in court to face felony spouse abuse charges. In the meantime, a nonrefundable 10 percent of the bond, or $1,500, has been paid in cash to the bonding company. The man is released the next morning.

The wife later changes her story and refuses to press charges. Eventually, the paperwork is filed and the felony case against the man is dismissed. The relatives obtain their papers back from the bonding company, but the bonding company keeps the $1,500 as their fee for obtaining the man's jail release.

In this case, the police officers were reacting to a new "mandatory arrest" police department policy requiring them to arrest either one spouse or the other. "Most often we arrest the guy," says one of the officers. "It may not always be the best decision, but we don't like to arrest women, you know."

These two scenes say much about police discretion. In each case, the officers have some latitude as to whether they will make an arrest. They may or may not have probable cause to support their arrests, but little or no provocation is required in each case. Officers observing someone leaving a bar late at night might assume the person to be drunk or at least to have been drinking. Although this is not always true, officers' suspicions are often correct. In the investigation of the domestic violence complaint, the officers had a choice—they could arrest the man or the woman. Their own observations at the scene suggested that the man, for whatever reason, was being chased and beaten by a woman swinging a baseball bat. The man was obviously injured, whereas the woman was not. Nevertheless, they decided to arrest the man instead of the woman.

In both cases, in a sense, the persons arrested were victims of police discretion. The dollar cost to the alleged drunk driver was about $60 to remove his automobile from the police impound lot. In the case of the domestic disturbance, the cost to the man and his relatives was far greater, more than $1,500. Both cases were similar in that they became noncases; charges were either dropped or dismissed or never filed. The financially costly outcomes for both victims were the direct result of **police discretion.** This chapter examines closely the concept of police discretion, how it is defined, and some of the implications of exercising it.

The first part of the chapter describes several definitions of police discretion and how it is viewed from different levels of the police department organization. Most police discretion applies to police-citizen encounters. Thus, we will examine what is known as "situationally based" police discretion and how different police officers' actions or nonactions influence their encounters with citizens. Some implications for citizens resulting from police discretion are also described.

We also explore the role of police officers in the courts. Officers are almost always involved with courts in various ways. Whenever traffic citations are issued to drivers, or arrests made for alleged crimes, arresting officers must be present to testify. Officer testimony attempts to justify the original arrest by providing the reasons for it. Minor traffic offenses are often disputed in court by motorists who think they were driving slower or more safely than the officers allege. In cases of serious crimes, officer testimony often becomes pivotal regarding one's guilt or innocence. Did the officer have probable cause to make an arrest, detain and question a pedestrian, or stop and search a vehicle? If one's home premises are searched by police and incriminating evidence is subsequently discovered, confiscated, and used as evidence against a criminal defendant, then officer testimony discloses whether the search action was justified. Judgment calls by police officers are not always perfect; thus, court testimony is intended to reconstruct the situation preceding an arrest and arrive at the truth.

Not all police departments have a comprehensive set of policies to govern police conduct under each and every situation in which discretion must be exercised. Police training academies attempt to educate officers so that they will make prudent decisions and exercise the best discretion. But no amount of education or field training can equip officers with clear-cut behavioral guidelines to use for every police-citizen encounter. Further, the guidelines promulgated by different police departments are not uniform among all police agencies. Thus, this chapter examines existing police department policies and explores some of the alternative patterns used by departments to guide officers in their decision making.

Another section of this chapter looks at selected constitutional issues as they relate to police conduct and the exercise of discretion. Particularly relevant for police officers are the provisions of the Fourth Amendment of the Constitution. These provisions specify general conditions under which persons and their property may be searched and certain items may be seized. The U.S. Supreme Court hears many cases each year pertaining to search-and-seizure questions. Various rulings from the court provide guidelines for police officers to follow when they intend to search a person or a person's home, automobile, or other property. It is widely assumed that police officers have a clear understanding of their right to search and seize. However, we will see that police officers' understanding of the Fourth Amendment and its many exceptions and provisions varies greatly among officers and police department jurisdictions. Many police officers cultivate their own impressions of the law and how it pertains to them. Customized interpretations of the Fourth Amendment by police officers are commonplace. When police officers either knowingly or unwittingly act in ways that are contrary to Fourth Amendment decisions by the U.S. Supreme Court, this is labeled as an abuse of discretion. We will describe both proper and improper exercises of police discretion relative to the Fourth Amendment and other issues.

An increasingly important issue related to police officer discretion is when to use deadly force or engage in high-speed pursuits. Hot pursuit of traffic violators or fleeing felons creates a high level of danger to innocent citizens in the chase's path. Officers are increasingly admonished by their police departments to use common sense in deciding whether to follow someone on a high-speed chase through crowded city streets or thoroughfares. Also, if someone is suspected of committing a crime and is fleeing from pursuing officers, under what circumstances should they use deadly force to effect an arrest? These issues are considered here in some detail.

This chapter concludes by describing various strategies police departments have employed to control police officer discretion. Mandates from city councils, citizen complaint review boards, chiefs of police, and other interested parties are delivered to individual police officers in various forms. Administrative policy changes occur that are intended to define or redefine those circumstances under which certain types of police officer decision making should be modified.

THE MEANING OF POLICE DISCRETION: A CONCEPTUAL TOWER OF BABEL

Police discretion seems easy enough to define. Stenning and Shearing (1991) say, for instance, that police discretion is autonomy in decision making. Skolnick (1994) suggests that police discretion is how the police enforce the law. Other authors say that police discretion depends on the nature of decision-making activity, such as "street" decision making, "paper" decision making in police department offices, and "administrative" decision making. Another view is that police discretion depends on the role assigned it, such as discretion as the absence of law, as antithetical to law, as a relief from excessive legal regulation, as a supplement to law, or as a form of law (Doyle, 1985). Last but not least, Cohen (1985) says that police discretion is the balancing mechanism between justice that is deserved by an individual and justice as equal treatment.

The Police Mission and Police Discretion

What is the **police mission?** A persistent problem that hampers the development of a clear-cut definition of police discretion is that many police departments are still unclear about their mission (Hoover, 1993). What are the true functions of modern police departments and the officers who must interact with citizens in diverse communities throughout the United States? What roles are expected of these police departments and personnel as an integral part of our social fabric? If police departments cannot agree on their general mission and objectives, it is difficult for them to impart to their police officers what they should do and how they should do it. Furthermore, many police officers indicate they often experience conflicts between what they ideally ought to do and what they actually do when performing their jobs (Burton, Frank, Langworthy and Barker, 1993; Miller and Braswell, 1992).

Burton, Frank, Langworthy and Barker (1993), for instance, investigated the legal codes of all 50 states and identified three major categories of legislatively mandated police functions: law enforcement functions, peacekeeping functions, and service functions. Most states had codes mandating law enforcement and peacekeeping functions, but few states had service-mandated codes. Little agreement could be found about which tasks were most important. Thus, police officers must adjust their own role expectations to what is prescribed and what is preferred. Their actual roles are a blend of legislatively prescribed and preferred role expectations. Police officers are plagued by role conflict, as neighborhood residents' expectations of the police and what laws they should enforce often conflict with state-mandated police roles. The absence of service-mandated police roles causes local governments to step into the breach by establishing service priorities for police officers to follow in many jurisdictions. These service functions, however, are often diffuse and unclear, exacerbating police officers' role conflict.

The Rationale for Police Discretion

Why is there a need for police discretion, inasmuch as all criminal laws are codified in every U.S. jurisdiction anyway? These laws set forth prohibited acts and obligate law enforcement officers at city, county, state, and federal levels to enforce them. Isn't that sufficiently clear-cut? Miller and Hess (1994:71–72) identify several important reasons that police discretion is necessary:

1. Statute books are filled with archaic and ambiguous laws.
2. Some laws are never enforced, and no one expects them to be enforced.
3. Insufficient numbers of police are around to enforce every law violation; thus, there is a need for police to set priorities on the laws they will and won't enforce.
4. Discretion is important for maintaining good community relations.
5. Diverse community standards exist that influence how police officers enforce laws.

Some ambiguity associated with police discretion seems attributable to the public's expectations of officers. Although citizen input is vital to community-oriented policing, this input may lead to citizen expectations that are inconsistent with how police officers should act relative to various types of crimes.

Police officers observe numerous law violations daily. Persons may jaywalk, sleep on park benches, or loiter and beg in subway terminals undisturbed. Automobiles partially parked in red "No Parking" zones are not always ticketed. Persons in bars get into fights and commit aggravated assault, sustaining serious physical injuries, but are only warned and dismissed from the premises by police. Inattentive motorists may run red lights, and police officers in cruisers may choose to ignore the violation. An infinite number of situations exist daily in which police discretion is required. Much of this discretion is unregulated, but other forms of police discretion are governed closely by specific department policies.

Traditional, "By-the-Book" Police Discretion. Cordner and Hale (1992) describe at length the notion of *traditional police discretion.* We may glean from their use of this term in several different contexts that traditional police discretion is the exercise of decision making resulting from the confluence of factors that impinge on officers from their formal police training, education, common sense, and split-second interpretation and assessment of circumstances. The definition of police discretion that we prefer is the professional individual and/or collective judgments that preserve and promote community and citizen safety, respect for the law, and citizen rights to due process and equal treatment under the law. This definition recognizes citizen rights to privacy and equal treatment as set forth by the Fourteenth Amendment as well as the right of communities to ensure that their safety and security are not compromised. The word *professional* in this definition recognizes the formal training officers receive through police training academies and other educational experiences.

Mandatory Arrest Policies vs. Officer Autonomy. Sometimes police department policy gives officers no latitude to determine on their own whether an arrest should be made in particular areas of law enforcement. For instance, in the early 1990s many police departments implemented mandatory arrest policies related to incidents involving spousal abuse to the effect that if police were called to a scene of domestic violence, they were obligated to make an arrest of one or the other spouse (Cordner and Hale, 1992). Their department policy directed them to make an arrest if they responded to a domestic violence call, which might be regarded as a discretionless situation, in that their behavior was compulsory, regardless of their individual feelings or judgments about the seriousness of the incident.

There are mandatory policies to follow in other areas as well. For instance, the hotly debated use of sobriety checkpoints in various cities reflects policies that direct officers to take specific action against offenders who are drunk or under the influence of drugs or other substances (Allen, 1991). In many cities, police departments direct officers to establish checkpoints on major city thoroughfares, usually during late evening hours, as a means of deterring or apprehending those driving under the influence of alcohol or drugs. When these checkpoints are operated, officers usually ask to see one's driver's license and registration to verify that they are in order. When drivers respond to such officer requests, the odor of alcohol or their slow-moving, awkward responses may cause officers to suspect drivers of driving under the influence of something. This definition of the situation or **situationally based discretion** often leads to arrests and DWI charges. Many citizens object to these checkpoints generally as being unwanted barriers to driving city streets at will, but legal challenges of such checkpoints have been unsuccessful (Allen, 1991; Vaughn, 1990).

For most police-citizen encounters, however, street-level decision making is required of officers. If officers see a crime being committed, they must decide whether the crime is serious enough to make an arrest. In almost every U.S. city, relatively harmless acts are defined as criminal. It may be a misdemeanor, for

Suspicious persons may be stopped by police officers for investigative purposes; sometimes, searches of vehicles and seizures of contraband follow such stops. *(Mark Richards)*

instance, to spit on the sidewalk, litter, or jaywalk, yet officers who see citizens spitting on the street, littering, or jaywalking may decide to "look the other way" and act only if something more serious is observed. Thus, officers often set priorities on different minor and major crimes. They use their judgment about whether to go out of their way to stop and arrest a citizen for relatively minor offending behavior. Officers who use radar to detect speeders on local highways must decide whether to stop someone who is traveling 67 miles per hour in a 65 mile-per-hour zone. Often, informal standards are established, and different tolerance factors are created. Thus, police officers in certain areas may pursue speeders only if those speeders exceed the speed limit by ten miles an hour or more. These informal standards vary among jurisdictions. Some police departments instruct their officers to have zero tolerance for speeders, so that persons traveling 31 miles per hour in a 30 mile-per-hour zone are stopped and cited. One obvious benefit accruing from such zero-tolerance situations involving speeders is that more revenue is generated for city, county, or state coffers. The downside effects of such zero tolerance are poor public relations and an adverse image.

In another instance, a Wyoming state trooper stopped a late model vehicle late at night on Highway I–80. The motorist was advised that he was exceeding the posted speed limit by 20 mph. The motorist said the automobile was new and that the speedometer indicated he was traveling within the speed limit. The officer checked the vehicle mileage and determined that it was, indeed, a new vehicle. He suggested a "test" to the motorist, whereby the motorist would follow the trooper a designated distance at a particular speed. They agreed to stop shortly thereafter, and the officer would determine the speed registered on the speedometer. It turned out that the speedometer was really registering a lower speed than the automobile was actually traveling. Rather than issue a traffic citation to the motorist, the trooper advised that he should have the speedometer repaired as soon as possible. Under other circumstances, a ticket might have been issued for speeding.

The American Bar Foundation Survey. In the early 1950s a survey was conducted by the American Bar Foundation (ABF) to examine criminal justice decision making from arrests through parole supervision (American Bar Foundation, 1957). This survey sought to replicate, in part, an earlier survey of criminal justice and police officer performance conducted in the 1930s and referred to as the Wickersham Report. The ambitious and comprehensive project undertaken by the ABF was extended to include examinations of prosecutorial and judicial decision making and discretion as well as police conduct relative to arrests and other police-related matters. Parole board decision making was also examined.

Lloyd Ohlin, the ABF survey's chief consultant, has described how

> field teams of observers were sent into. . . . cities and rural areas of three states. . . . They rode in police cars on all shifts with all units. . . . They observed station house behavior. . . . They watched prosecutors review cases and charge defendants. . . . They sat in courtrooms, talked to judges, and watched arraignments and sentencing. . . . They spent time with probation officers, read presentence investigation reports, and observed supervision; they sat with parole boards and came to understand the release and revocation decisions. (Ohlin and Remington, 1993:7)

One of the survey's field representatives and research associates was Herman Goldstein. Subsequently, Goldstein (1993) summarized some of the major survey findings relative to police discretion. Some of his findings are outlined below:

1. The police do many things besides investigate crime and arrest offenders.
2. Even within conduct labeled criminal, the incidents the police are called on to handle are infinite and unpredictable, requiring flexibility in responding to them.
3. The police use their authority to arrest to achieve many objectives other than the initiation of a criminal prosecution.
4. The police—and especially individual police officers—exercise enormous discretion.
5. Although evidence of a crime may be present, the police often decide not to arrest.
6. The police are a part of the criminal justice system; their actions heavily influence other agencies in the system, whose actions, in turn, strongly influence the police.

Goldstein's observations highlight the diffuseness of police officer discretion as well as how exercises of discretion can have an impact on other important criminal justice system components. Among the police officers' actions described by ABF field observers: They were taking intoxicated persons into protective custody, clearing the streets of prostitutes, responding to a wide range of disputes, directing traffic and enforcing parking limits, checking alleged trespassers, investigating accidents, censoring movies and books, finding missing persons, checking suspicious circumstances, handling stray animals, providing first aid, and collecting overdue library books and the assessed fines (Goldstein, 1993:31).

Perhaps the most important ABF survey finding was documentation of the complexity of police officer discretion and day-to-day decision making. This finding led to (1) the establishing of police training programs that stress decision making and discretion and (2) the professionalizing of police officers in various ways. More extensive education has been added to police officer selection requirements, with a bachelor's degree preferred. Computer-simulated crime situations to teach prospective police recruits have become commonplace, and various personality and aptitude tests have also become widespread as police departments throughout the United States attempt to improve officer selection requirements and performance effectiveness. However, higher education or IQ does not necessarily translate directly into better officer effectiveness. Time in the field is one of the best teachers, and such knowledge is acquired by on-the-job, real-world experiences.

Besides practical, hands-on experience to prepare police officers, some studies have shown an inverse relation between police officer education and the number of citizen complaints. Manning (1977) examined samples of police officers from different cities and correlated their formal educational training with numbers of complaints. Those with more extensive education had fewer citizen complaints. One inference from these findings is that more education for officers enables them to acquire a better understanding of the nature and importance of social encounters. Their formal educational training has enabled them to deal with citizens in more tactful and socially acceptable ways, perhaps, compared with less-educated officers, who may choose force rather than reason.

The findings of surveys generally are not appreciated uniformly throughout the criminal justice system. Where such survey findings uncover inequities or disparities, defenders of the status quo are quick to identify survey weaknesses and faults. However, Marenin (1989) says that the community needs surveys that seek to determine the goals, strategies, and political benefits of community-oriented policing. He describes at least four types of benefits accruing from surveys of community-oriented policing, including that (1) they can alert officers to problem areas and discontent simmering beneath their attention, (2) they can help to clarify the array of choices faced by the police, even if they cannot determine what is to be chosen, (3) surveys can act as a democratizing influence on both the police and the public, particularly showing the public that police are attempting to be responsive to the public's opinions; and (4) surveys justify police discretion and autonomy.

SITUATIONALLY BASED DISCRETION AND OFFICER-OFFENDER RELATIONS

Because most of police officers' discretionary actions are known only to the officers and their targets (citizens), it is impossible to scrutinize all police actions at all times for purposes of monitoring, supervision, evaluation, or accountability. Motorists stopped on highways or pedestrians detained briefly by curious police officers in high-crime areas are usually the only witnesses to police-citizen encounters, other than the police officers themselves. Two quite different versions of events may be reported, one given by the arresting officer and the other by the person arrested. In court, judges are inclined to give greater weight to the testimony of arresting officers than to those arrested for alleged violations. One reason is the generally held belief that police officers are held to higher standards relative to traditional law enforcement. Sometimes, however, situationally based discretion is preserved on videotape. But even videotaped incidents do not enable us to determine in any absolute sense whether the officer(s) acted properly or whether the allegations of arrested persons are to be believed.

The incident involving Rodney King encountering police officers on Los Angeles streets in 1990 is often cited as a notorious example of situationally based police discretion. The motorist, King, was speeding and pursued by police officers. The subsequent stopping of King and his passengers resulted in an apparent assault on King, who was alleged by police officers to have resisted arrest. More than 20 officers surrounded King, and he was beaten with night sticks and shot several times with a stun gun before police were able to "subdue" him. An attentive apartment dweller across from the scene recorded several minutes of the incident on videotape, particularly the portion in which officers were hitting King with their sticks. Two trials were subsequently held on claims of assorted violations of King's rights as a citizen and certain criminal claims. A California jury acquitted three of the four officers charged with criminally assaulting King, but a federal court tried the officers on a different set of criminal charges, and two officers were found guilty by the federal jury. In the meantime, King sued the City of Los Angeles for damages he sustained when arrested. Although police officers had been videotaped and appeared to be beating King unmercifully, attorneys convinced the state jury that the four accused officers had acted appropriately and in response to King's resisting arrest. We all saw a recorded event, and a wide variety of interpretations were made of it. It did not resolve the matter of whether the officers had acted properly.

In the aftermath, many police cruisers have been equipped with videotaping equipment to bolster their subsequent court cases when drunk drivers and others are stopped for assorted traffic violations or suspicious behavior. The Georgia Highway Patrol, for instance, installed the In-Car Video System in many of its vehicles. Such equipment has been used to provide visual evidence of DWI stops and subsequent substantiation of court testimony against defendants (Johnson, 1992). However, the units have also made officers more conscious of their own conduct relative to citizens stopped on Georgia highways. In some respects, more extensive videotaping of police discretion on the streets has heightened police officers' consciousness of their own behavior toward citizens. But as the King incident illustrated, recording the event itself on videotape is not sufficiently convincing of wrongful police conduct.

Also in the aftermath of the King incident, many law enforcement agencies have reevaluated their arrest procedures and exposed their officers to all sorts of training geared to improve their discretion on the streets with citizens. One problem resulting from the federal convictions of Stacy Koon and Lawrence Powell, two of the four officers accused of criminal civil rights violations against King, was that some police agencies overreacted. All police officers are responsible for maintaining order and taking action against those who violate the law. Since the King incident, increasing numbers of citizens stopped or arrested by officers are alleging violations similar to those committed by Koon and Powell. Police officers have had to handle their interactions with citizens with greater finesse, in order to avoid the appearance of wrongdoing or misconduct. (Police misconduct, which often stems from abuses of police discretion, is discussed at length in Chapter 7.)

Some jurisdictions report little, if any, change from operating procedures among police officers following the King incident. For instance, paying little attention to how officers would be viewed by the public, Texas enacted a Public Intoxication Law (PIL) that provided for incarceration, release on one's own recognizance, release to another responsible adult, or release to a voluntary treatment program for chemical dependency (Olivero, Hansen, and Clark, 1993). The PIL placed Texas law enforcement officers in the position of determining whether those arrested "appeared dangerous to themselves or to others." In some of the smaller Texas communities, police officers used the new PIL to incarcerate large numbers of persons who would not otherwise be incarcerated. In short, some were arrested even if their behaviors or postures related only weakly to the "dangerousness to self or others" element of the probable cause to arrest for public intoxication. Passengers in vehicles in which the driver was or appeared to be intoxicated, for example, stood a good chance of being arrested and incarcerated themselves, simply because of their in-car postures or general appearance. Many cases resulted in $150 fines on only overnight jail stays. Thus, the PIL "widened the net" and drew in large numbers of revenue-generating suspects whose only offense was that they happened to be passengers in vehicles driven by suspected DUI drivers (Olivero, Hansen, and Clark, 1993). In this case police discretion was truly situationally based and, by inference, discriminatory.

More than a little evidence exists to suggest that police discretion is influenced by factors such as race, gender, or socioeconomic status. Powell (1990) reports, for instance, that in a survey of 4,097 officers from three large-city and two small-city police departments in two Southern states, race appeared to influence strongly the decision-making process at various stages, commencing with arrests. Interestingly, large-city officers exhibited greater arrest disparity compared with smaller-city police officers. In these larger cities, police officers were more consistently discriminatory toward black arrestees compared with white arrestees under similar arrest circumstances (Powell, 1990). Walker (1993), however, indicates that considering the history of criminal justice during the period 1960–1990, the record indicates that there has been some success at controlling discretion throughout the criminal justice system. Disparities among those arrested for various offenses on the basis of race, gender, or socioeconomic status have gradually been reduced (Walker, 1993), although many experts agree that much more needs to be done to remedy disparities observed throughout the system.

Racial, ethnic, gender, and socioeconomic minorities may not be the only ones subject to discretionary abuses by police. It has been reported, for example, that in selected cities such as Chicago, mentally ill offenders are arrested at higher rates than offenders who do not show signs of any mental illness. However, the somewhat deviant or peculiar conduct of some mentally ill persons may attract more attention compared with the population of nonmentally ill persons. A more detailed analysis of Chicago's mentally ill arrestee population suggests that only those who exhibit multiple psychological problems or severe mental illness are taken into custody, and often, the disposition of such arrests is diversion to treatment alternatives in the community (Kalinich and Sense, 1987).

Research by Teplin (1986) on the role of police in the postdeinstitutionalization community management of the mentally ill investigated 79 police encounters with 85 mentally disordered persons. Although it was clear that the mentally ill stood a greater chance of being arrested than did the nonmentally ill, certain bureaucratic and legal restrictions caused officers to divert many of these persons to hospitals rather than to jail. Teplin concludes her analysis by suggesting that (1) police officers must be trained to recognize and handle the mentally disordered offender; (2) police officers should use the least restrictive alternative, and wherever possible, they should consign such persons charged with misdemeanors to a mental health treatment facility; and (3) modes of care other than hospitals should be provided for police referrals of mentally disordered offenders (Teplin, 1986).

Situationally based police discretion is most often covert. The television show *Top Cop,* for instance, provides nightly examples of violations of constitutional law, particularly violations of the Fourth Amendment search-and-seizure provisions as interpreted by the U.S. Supreme Court. Viewers are *not* privy to the background investigations and details that preface police encounters with citizens on *Top Cop* and other "on-the-spot" police shows depicting citizen-police encounters. What we see, however, are police officers routinely cruising the streets, apparently stopping persons at random, going through their pockets, having citizens take off their shoes and socks and turn out their jacket or shirt pockets, and making them undress in other ways in front of television cameras. If illegal contraband is accidentally discovered or "falls out" during these strips, citizens watching the show are delighted that justice has been served. The police have found illegal drugs—their searches are justified by what they have found. Unfortunately, we are also not advised of the case outcomes, in which such illegal contraband has been rejected as evidence and ruled inadmissible because it was illegally seized and the searches were constitutionally unreasonable.

POLICE AND THE COURTS

The actions and decisions made by police officers in their day-to-day interactions with citizens often have an impact on other critical points in the criminal justice system. On the basis of evidence that police collect at crime scenes or reports officers file against arrestees, prosecutors may or may not be able to follow through with criminal prosecutions. The quality of evidence collected and the manner in which arrests were made and rights of suspects were observed often contaminate a prosecution. One important feature of an arrest pertains to the *Miranda* warning, including verbal advice to arrestees that anything they say may be used against them later in court; that they have a right to an attorney; that they have a right to have an attorney appointed for them if they are indigent; that they have a right to remain silent, to refrain from self-incrimination, and to halt questioning at any time; and that they have a right to have an attorney present during any interrogation (*Miranda v. Arizona*, 1966). Failure to "Mirandize" arrestees fatally flaws any arrest and subsequent information obtained from interviewing suspects. Even very incriminating information may be excluded from court testimony if the conditions under which it was obtained vary from approved police procedure and if the *Miranda* warning is not observed. Even under conditions in which suspects are Mirandized numerous times while being questioned, cases may be lost because of technical violations of interrogation rules by police officers.

There have been numerous incidents in which police discretion in Mirandizing criminal suspects has been successfully challenged by skilled defense attorneys, even where clear evidence exists of a defendant's guilt, including a voluntary confession. For instance, on December 24, 1968, a ten-year-old girl, Pamela Powers, was with her family at the YMCA in Des Moines, Iowa, watching a wrestling tournament. (*Brewer v. Williams*, 1977). She went to the restroom but was never seen again. Living at the same YMCA was a mental patient and escapee from the Iowa State Mental Hospital, Robert Williams. He was observed carrying a large bundle (with two legs sticking from it) through the YMCA lobby during the tournament. A young boy helped Williams load the bundle into Williams's car and was a critical eyewitness, because he observed the protruding legs. A subsequent investigation led to the discovery of Williams's abandoned car 160 miles from the YMCA in Davenport. No direct proof existed that Williams had abducted Powers, but a day later, Williams surrendered to police in Davenport through an attorney.

Des Moines police officers were dispatched to Davenport to transfer Williams back. Williams was Mirandized by these officers. The two officers advised Williams that he didn't have to say anything on the return trip, but the officers also said they would be conversing with one another. As the officers drove Williams back to Des Moines they began to talk about the weather. By then it was raining and sleeting, and visibility was poor. The officers, calculating that Williams probably disposed of Powers's body somewhere between Des Moines and Davenport, began to talk to one another about it. At no time did they invite

Williams (handcuffed in the back seat) to join in their conversation. They knew, however, that Williams considered himself a religious man. At one point, one officer said to the other, "You know, they're predicting snow for tonight. I think we're going to be going right past where that body is, and if we should stop and find out where it is on the way in, her parents are going to be able to have a good Christian burial for their daughter . . . [otherwise] it's very possible that with snow on the ground, you might not be able to find it." A reference to another town, Mitchellville, was made by one of the officers as probably being near where Pamela's body might be located. Williams asked, "How do you know that would be at Mitchellville?" The officer replied, "Well, I'm an investigator. This is my job, and I just figured it out." At that point, Williams declared, "You're right, and I'm going to show you where it is."

The police officers were led by Williams to where Pamela Powers's body had been placed. She had been raped and murdered. On the basis of Williams's confession, he was convicted of murder. However, the U.S. Supreme Court reversed Williams's conviction, because they reasoned that the officers' "Christian burial" speech had been nothing more than a ruse to overcome the multiple *Miranda* warnings. Williams was subsequently convicted in a new trial on other evidence. However, this case underscores how police *in*discretion can unravel an otherwise solid prosecution, with or without the recovery of the victim's body (*Brewer v. Williams*, 1977).

Dantzker (1995:39–48) cites various points within the criminal justice system at which police officer discretion is crucial to successful investigations, prosecutions, and convictions. These include (1) police officer-prosecutor relationships and communications, (2) police officer-court relationships and communications, and (3) police officer-corrections relationships and communications. We shall discuss the points one by one.

Police Officer-Prosecutor Relationships and Communications.

When police officers arrest criminal suspects, several procedural activities are obligatory. In our previous discussion we noted the standard *Miranda* warning that must be given before interrogations of suspects can proceed. Even repeated *Miranda* warnings may be insufficient under certain circumstances. Dantzker says that although the relationship between police officers and prosecutors should be one of the closest, it is often the worst (Dantzker, 1995:39). Dantzker suggests that one problem inherent in the police officer-prosecutor relationship may be the less-than-adequate training and education police officers receive concerning the finer points of the law. In short, if police officers are not continually updated concerning legal issues relating to their conduct and interactions with citizens, they may unwittingly contaminate an arrest so that a subsequent successful prosecution of a suspect is undermined. Case dismissals because of legal technicalities are common, and the source of these legal technicalities is police officer discretion when arresting suspects, collecting incriminating evidence, and otherwise carrying out duties and responsibilities relevant to the case.

An example of a questionable mix of police discretion and case contamination occurred during the double-murder trial of O.J. Simpson, a sports figure and newscaster, in early 1995. Briefly, Simpson's ex-wife, Nicole, and a friend, Ron Goldman, were found stabbed to death during the early hours of June 13, 1994, in Beverly Hills, California. Simpson became a suspect when police officers found incriminating physical evidence while attempting to notify him of his ex-wife's death and the fact that his children had been taken into protective custody. Simpson's attorneys argued that detectives who investigated this murder scene mishandled various types of evidence, such as blood and bloody clothing. Allegations of police misconduct, including planting evidence at Simpson's home to incriminate him, were also made by Simpson's attorneys. During subsequent court testimony given by the various detectives and officers involved, several irregularities in police handling of evidence were highlighted. Videotapes of police officers at the murder scene reveal that they "trampled" around the murder scene in such a way that possible exculpatory evidence (the killer's footprints in grassy areas) might have been obliterated. Also one detective took a sample of Simpson's blood home overnight before delivering the blood to the Los Angeles Police Department criminalist labs. One of the first police officers who arrived at the murder scene used the telephone in the victim's home to place one or more telephone calls. Potential fingerprint evidence on the telephone may have been obliterated by this act. Numerous other discretionary actions of investigating officers were attacked by Simpson's attorneys.

Dantzker (1995:41) has provided some insight regarding this gap between what police officers and detectives do "in the field" and the adequacy of this behavior under closer scrutiny later in court. He says that "in the world of the prosecutor, crime is represented by facts on a piece of paper that must meet strict written guidelines . . . [while] crime to police is applied—a function of the street; the requisite, neat guidelines of the courtroom do not always fit." These mismatches between police officers and prosecutors regarding how searches and seizures are or should be handled may jeopardize seriously any criminal investigation and prosecution.

Police Officer-Court Relationships and Communications. When police officers give testimony in court, any flaws in their investigations of defendants are placed under a critical microscope. Did they obtain a warrant to conduct a proper search of the defendant's premises? Did they have probable cause to justify obtaining the warrant? Did they collect evidence carefully? Did they limit the scope of their search to the specifications of the warrant? If the search was warrantless, did they have proper grounds to conduct it? If they subsequently collected evidence, did they observe the proper "chain of custody" so that the evidence would not be contaminated? Did any of their actions contaminate the crime scene or collateral evidence at the scene? Did they properly advise defendants of their rights? All of these questions and more are asked of police officers who give testimony in court.

Many officers have been accused, rightly or wrongly, of finding incriminating evidence first and then constructing a rationale to justify an otherwise illegal search. In more than a few cases, police officers, detectives, and federal agents have perjured themselves in court to enhance the likelihood of a conviction. This is police misconduct and will be discussed at length in Chapter 7. In any case, procedural irregularities in law enforcement are given little tolerance by the court and the opposing counsel. For instance, in a 1994 prosecution, a New York City detective testified that he entered the premises of a known drug dealer who was suspected of committing a homicide. One of the drug dealer's lower-level distributors was killed because of a dispute over money. New York detectives had a suspect in mind, a known drug dealer with whom the victim had a close connection. When officers entered the suspect's apartment, they had only a reasonable suspicion, not probable cause, that the drug dealer was involved. At this point, their case was in the investigatory stage. They soon found the pistol that subsequently was linked to the homicide. This incriminating evidence was sufficient for prosecutors to proceed against the drug dealer. Later in court, however, it was established that the search of the suspect's apartment was warrantless. Further, although one detective testified that he saw the pistol in **plain view** after entering the apartment at the invitation of the suspect, another assisting detective testified that he had to raise a bed mattress in order for the other detective to see the pistol, which was otherwise concealed. When cross-examined on this matter, the detective who "saw" the pistol under the suspect's mattress said that he saw the pistol "protruding" from between the mattresses. Thus, he reasoned, he had a right to seize the pistol as inculpatory evidence. Subsequently, the judge ruled the pistol inadmissible because the detectives failed to show that it had been in plain view or that it was acquired in a "search incident to an arrest." Without the incriminating pistol, the prosecutors lost their case, and the drug dealer-defendant was acquitted.

Dantzker (1995:43) observes that the educational level of police officers is often that of a high school graduate. Also, police officers' understanding of the law is often inadequate. Police officers have been known to make up their own law and operate according to some unwritten street code when conducting their patrols. Thus, street justice is often dispensed without formal court action. However, when certain cases result in prosecutions and court action, informal police codes and law interpretations are no longer relevant. In fact, they may impair prosecutorial efforts to convict criminal defendants. Dantzker cites police-prosecutor teams as a concerted effort to generate better communication and understanding among law enforcement officers at all levels and their prosecutorial counterparts (1995:43–44).

Police Officer-Corrections Relationships and Communications.
Police officer-corrections relationships arise through police investigations involving probationers and parolees. Dantzker (1995:46) says that sometimes, probation and parole officers (POs) are protective of their probationer/parolee clients. If a case of child sexual abuse occurs in a given neighborhood, for instance, and if a

local halfway house in that neighborhood currently houses a convicted child sexual abuser, that client becomes a logical suspect. Former convictions for that offense do not mean that the convicted offender is definitely the current perpetrator, but the prior record factor creates unusually high police officer interest in the client. Halfway house authorities may think otherwise, however, and thus they may not be fully cooperative with police.

POs, for example, may be asked by police officers to assist in an investigation. A parolee may be a suspect, and police officers may want to question her. The PO may furnish officers with the parolee's address, but subsequently, it may be found that the parolee has moved without giving the PO a change-of-address. Police officers may believe that the PO is derelict in his responsibility for supervising the parolee. Even when parolees are taken in for questioning by police officers, police officers may blame POs for not doing their jobs properly. They reason that if POs did better jobs supervising their clients, they (the clients) would not get into trouble and commit new crimes. Such assignments of blame to POs are not conducive to good police officer-PO relations.

SELECTED CONSTITUTIONAL ISSUES AND POLICE BEHAVIOR

The U.S. Constitution contains numerous provisions that set forth a variety of citizen rights, particularly those in the first ten amendments, known as the Bill of Rights. Police officers exercise discretion daily that may or may not infringe on one or more rights. Often, these infringements are not clear-cut or made a matter of public record, but lawsuits are sometimes filed involving allegations of law enforcement conduct that resulted in rights infringements. This section examines such potential infringements relating to the First, Second, and Fourth amendments. The Fourteenth Amendment also contains an "equal protection" clause that encompasses treatment of citizens by police officers during investigations and arrests.

The First Amendment

The First Amendment language relevant for police officers is that "Congress shall make no law . . . prohibiting the free exercise [of religion] . . . or abridging the freedom of speech, or of the press; or the right of the people peaceably to assemble. . . ." Thus, freedoms of speech, religion, press, and peaceful assembly are outlined clearly. Law enforcement officers must decide whenever citizen conduct goes beyond what is contemplated in the First Amendment.

For instance, an Alabama Highway Patrol officer observed a large truck traveling on a major highway. On the truck's bumper were several stickers, some displaying profanity. Other stickers depicted persons defecating and urinating. The officer stopped the truck and cited the driver for a violation of Alabama's obscenity ordinance, which, among other things, prohibited the display of such stickers. Subsequently, a U.S. district court in Alabama determined that Alabama's obscenity statute could not be upheld (*Baker v. Glover*, 1991). In this particular situation, a highway patrol officer was offended by the displayed stickers on the truck and exercised discretion to stop the truck and cite the driver for violating a seldom-enforced ordinance.

Another incident involving a bumper sticker occurred in a California city when a police officer stopped a female motorist for allegedly speeding. Instead of citing her for speeding, however, he criticized her political bumper sticker favoring a particular legislative bill and gave her a ticket, claiming that she had "waved a political sign at oncoming motorists and continually pressed a 'Walk' button at a crosswalk to hold up traffic." Witnesses to the incident did not support the officer's version of what she did. Instead, they indicated that the "pattern of the officer's conduct effectively inhibited the woman's political activity" (*Sloman v. Tadlock*, 1994). The court ruled the officer's conduct to be unwarranted. Further, the court said the officer's conduct "chilled" the free speech of the female motorist and was a substantial or motivating factor making the officer liable for violating her rights.

A key reason that police officers are often drawn into disputes about Constitutional rights infringements is that many of the laws police officers are sworn to uphold are unconstitutionally vague and overbroad (*Kreimer v. Bureau of Police for Town of Morristown*, 1992; *Pestrack v. Ohio Elections Commission*, 1987; *State v. Jones*, 1993). When a statute lacks precision as to what conduct is prohibited, police officer discretion becomes increasingly important. It is not up to police officers, however, to determine what is unconstitutionally vague and what isn't—courts make these decisions. Nevertheless, whenever police officers are confronted by incidents or depictions that are subject to various interpretations, their discretionary abilities come into play, and they make decisions to arrest or not to arrest.

Many city ordinances are not unconstitutionally vague, although some citizens might make this claim. For instance, a city enacted an ordinance prohibiting homeless persons from sleeping overnight in public parks on benches. A homeless person was arrested after he had expressed his views on television concerning the mayor's homeless policy making it a misdemeanor to lodge in any public place without the owner's permission. The homeless arrestee, who had indeed spent the evening sleeping in a park plaza, claimed his arrest was in response to his televised interview and thus was a violation of the "free speech" provision of the First Amendment. The court declared that police officers were simply enforcing a city ordinance prohibiting lodging overnight in a public park (*Stone v. Agnos*, 1992).

The Second Amendment

The Second Amendment provides for a "well-regulated Militia, being necessary to the security of a free State . . . [and] the right of the people to keep and bear

Arms." This particular amendment has generated considerable controversy. Many citizens believe that, because of this amendment, they are entitled to carry concealed firearms whenever they choose. However, the U.S. Supreme Court has declared that the right to bear arms is not absolute; further, the right to bear arms is subject to reasonable regulation by the state under its police powers (*Cody v. United States*, 1972; *State v. Spencer*, 1994).

The Fourth Amendment

The Fourth Amendment provides that people have the right "to be secure in their persons, houses, papers, and effects, against unreasonable searches and seizures . . . and no warrants shall issue, but upon probable cause, supported by oath or affirmation, and particularly describing the place to be searched and the persons or things to be seized." Because police officers are constantly being placed in the position of investigating, questioning, and arresting suspicious persons or crime suspects, they have various rights to search those to be arrested as well as various places within their control (e.g., automobiles, rooms in homes).

This amendment has continually been modified by changing circumstances and exceptions. Even the wording of the Fourth Amendment has been given different "spins" by the U.S. Supreme Court. First, it has been determined that not every search and seizure made without a warrant is necessarily prohibited (*Commonwealth v. Bosurgi*, 1963), nor does the Fourth Amendment forbid searches without warrants—only unreasonable ones (*Weaver v. Williams*, 1975). Thus, police officers who intend to conduct a search of a citizen or a citizen's vehicle or home must determine whether their search is reasonable or unreasonable. Various circumstances change the reasonableness interpretation made by officers.

Police officers are not always informed of updated Fourth Amendment exceptions that materially affect their work. At the other end of the spectrum are officers who know a great deal about the law and its versatility within the "totality of circumstances" context. Further, many police officers know that even if they secure a defective search warrant, they may act in "good faith," as though the warrant were without flaw, and conduct their searches anyway. Thus, the **totality of circumstances** and **good faith exceptions** to **warrantless searches** or defective-warrant searches may be used in tandem to condone almost any officer action relative to searches of persons or their possessions. Many courtroom tests of the motives that prompted police officers to conduct searches and seizures involve tests of their discretion in each situation. Considerable latitude exists when deciding the legal bases of their conduct.

The Fourteenth Amendment

Among other things, the Fourth Amendment assures U.S. citizens the right to due process and to equal protection under the law. The "equal protection" clause of the Fourteenth Amendment is most often cited by citizens when complaining about police officer excesses, misconduct, or the exercise of questionable discre-

> **BOX 6.1   Cases of Probable Cause**
>
> THE CASES OF ROMERO AND BEMIS
>
> In 1973 in a New Mexico community at 11:30 one evening, a man and five companions entered a bar and began drinking. A deputy sheriff, noticing that one of the men was wearing a firearm, approached. After an initial inquiry, the deputy seized the gun, which turned out to be an unregistered sawed-off shotgun, and arrested the man carrying it. The fact that the man was "surly" and generally uncooperative with the deputy while being questioned probably contributed to the arrest. The man was convicted of carrying an unregistered, illegal weapon. He appealed, alleging that he had a right to bear arms as set forth in the Second Amendment. His appeal failed, as the higher court ruled that in view of departmental policy, the deputy had a right to seize the weapon under the conditions (*U.S. v. Romero*, 1973).
>
> In a later case, a Massachusetts man who possessed a permit to carry a firearm was the subject of an arson investigation and was under arrest on two felony charges. Police officers sought revocation of his license to carry firearms, which was subsequently revoked. In a case appealing this revocation, the court declared that the defendant's Second Amendment right was not violated and that police officers had acted properly and within departmental policy by recommending the license revocation (*Bemis v. Kelley*, 1987).
>
> Police officers frequently stop motorists for assorted traffic violations. In the course of these stops it may be determined that certain motorists are driving under the influence of drugs or alcohol. When police officers arrest these suspects, they frequently move the suspect's vehicle to a secure location where it can be reclaimed by the motorist later, as a matter of routine departmental policy. In the course of moving the vehicle, police sometimes discover weapons under front or rear seats, in glove boxes, in purses, or in trunks. This puts officers in the position of seizing the discovered firearms or leaving them where found. Officer discretion governs these situations, and in many cases motorists are not cited for firearms infractions. In these instances, motorists consider themselves fortunate that nothing was made of the firearms discovery. Thus, police officer discretion does not always work to the detriment of the citizen.

tion. One of the most frequent allegations under the Fourteenth Amendment has to do with the relationship of stops, questioning, and arrests to one's minority status. Thus, if white police officers stop African American or Hispanic citizens for any reason, these encounters are often labeled as discriminatory (Cashmore and McLaughlin, 1991). During the 1970s, for example, the Philadelphia Police

BOX 6.2 Searches without Warrant

When persons on the street are searched by police and the primary intent of the search is for officer protection and to determine if those questioned are carrying concealed weapons, the officers are limited to making "pat downs and frisks" (*Terry v. Ohio*, 1968). There is no per se rule as to when police questioning amounts to detention; each case must be decided by examining the totality of circumstances surrounding the encounter (*Peterson v. State*, 1993). Absent a showing of probable cause that a crime has been committed by those being interviewed, police "pat downs and frisks" do not include thrusting their hands into the pockets of interviewees in an attempt to discover something illegal (*Sibron v. New York*, 1968). Even if illegal contraband or drugs are discovered during such pocket searches, these searches are often declared unconstitutional and in violation of one's Fourth Amendment rights. There are several exceptions, however. These include situations in which citizens consent to such searches. Also, police officers may search suspects they arrest as well as the premises directly within the arrestee's control. In addition, officers may observe unlawful contraband or items in **"plain view,"** such as might be on passenger seats of automobiles stopped for traffic violations. "A policeman has [a] right to observe anything that is in plain view" (*United States v. Leal*, 1972). **Exigent circumstances** may justify warrantless searches and seizures, particularly where illegal contraband exists that can be destroyed easily. The "totality of circumstances" may also condone warrantless searches (*United States v. Clark*, 1994). Warrantless searches may be deemed unconstitutional if police officers have time to obtain a warrant but do not take the time to do so.

Sometimes searches conducted even with a warrant may be questioned. In some cases police officers extend their searches beyond the scope of the warrant. A silly but effective example involves police officers searching for a stolen elephant. In the course of their search they enter a suspect's premises and look in drawers in a nightstand in the suspect's bedroom. They discover cocaine in one of the drawers and arrest the suspect for cocaine possession. The cocaine charge is later dismissed in court, because a bedroom nightstand is an *unreasonable* place to look for an elephant. The mere discovery of cocaine does not justify the search, even if the substance is illegal. The nightstand search was unreasonable within the scope of the warrant (i.e., searching for a missing elephant in places where elephants might be housed), which rendered *inadmissible* anything discovered in the nightstand, even cocaine.

Department was the subject of numerous suits brought by minority citizens alleging their rights had been infringed by Philadelphia police officers (Anechiarico, 1984). Although most of these suits were subsequently dismissed as "lacking merit," some suits were successful. Other police departments have been targets of similar suits (Crocker, 1981).

Law enforcement officers are obligated to enforce the law equitably. Race, ethnicity, socioeconomic status, and gender should not cloud one's objective application of discretion. Some experts have noted that in past years police officers have acted in discriminatory ways toward citizens, in ways that would suggest an undue influence of race or ethnicity. For instance, Sherman (1980) described numerous homicides of suspects by police associated with the now-obsolete "fleeing felon" rule that was prevalent among the states. Many of these fleeing felons who were killed by pursuing police officers were African Americans. Thus, the implication drawn by Sherman was that a disproportionate number of African Americans were being killed by police to the extent that this minority was not benefiting from the "equal protection" clause of the Fourteenth Amendment. Also, Avins (1970) has described various forms of police brutality against minority suspects in violation of their Fourteenth Amendment rights.

In recent years most police departments have adopted procedures geared to minimize violations of Constitutional rights against citizens who may become suspects and defendants. A relatively new standard exists for the application of deadly force (*Tennessee v. Garner*, 1985). This is the "defense-of-life" standard, in which police officers may use deadly force against fleeing suspects only if their own lives are in danger or the lives of other innocent citizens are in jeopardy. This deadly force standard has not substantially diminished the application of deadly force in police-suspect encounters, however. Some deadly force continues to suggest racial or ethnic disparities and influence. A more extended treatment of the deadly force issue is provided in Chapter 7.

POLICE UNDERSTANDING OF THE LAW: CUSTOMIZED INTERPRETATIONS AND THE ABUSE OF DISCRETION

An extensive analysis of police discretion from a moral perspective and grounded in social contract theory has been provided by Cohen and Feldberg (1991). These authors define officer responsibilities that are assumed by police whenever they accept the authority from the state to enforce the law. Police behaviors are theoretically regulated by a system of ethical standards by which responsible police behavior can be measured. The important thing, suggest Cohen and Feldberg, is that police officers attempt to balance individual rights with keeping the peace and weigh loyalty to colleagues versus telling the truth under oath about possible wrongdoing.

Although Rhoades (1991) is generally supportive of Cohen and Feldberg, he characterizes police ethics as an objective enterprise, under a theory of political obligation. Rhoades suggests that the police role, when conceived as that of a public agent, places obligations on police agencies and officials to behave in ways that bring basic democratic values to life. Some degree of citizen participation is required to ensure police officer adherence to these democratic values. Police officers as public agents must accept offenders as clients in a professional-client relation. A similar theme is explored by Fair and Pilcher (1991), who see morality as an important part of the police officer's decision-making process. Over time, police officers construct their own definitions of appropriate conduct with different groups of citizens in their communities. These customized interpretations of police-citizen encounters may vary from by-the-book regulations furnished by their own police agencies.

Sherman (1986b) indicates that communities vary widely in the exercise of police discretion and in problems requiring policing. In most instances, police patrols are largely unfocused, responding only to calls-for-service. Sherman believes that each community offers something unique for police officers. Primarily through close police officer-citizen contacts, police departments can establish better, more relevant patrolling procedures that will most effectively meet community needs. This is the general intent of community-oriented policing. Through greater public participation in policing, more structured discretion in police decision making is made possible (McKenzie, 1990).

Police Officer Rationales for Customized Interpretations of Law and Its Enforcement

Mayhall, Barker, and Hunter (1995:150–151) have identified at least five different rationales employed by law enforcement officers for selective enforcement decisions or discretionary actions that may appear unjust to citizens. These include the following:

1. The legislature did not intend for some laws to be applied literally; the law was intended to apply only to the situation where wrong occurs.
2. The statute in question is out of date; to apply it to a contemporary situation would work an injustice.
3. Sure, the behavior violates the law, but if I arrest the perpetrator, the official system will not handle the matter justly.
4. If an arrest is made, the official system will not treat the offense seriously enough.
5. The community does not support enforcement of the law in some cases.

If we study each of these rationales, they do much to explain some types of police officer conduct we might know of. Rationale 2 is interesting. Police officers often decide which laws to enforce on the basis of their relevance to ongoing activities in the community and whether such laws are pertinent. Whereas we know that updating the law is a legislative function, police officers make such decisions on the street daily. They observe numerous petty infractions that may, indeed, be outdated. Thus, they prioritize their arrests according to offense seriousness and community relevance. One outcome of community-oriented policing is that police officers have a clearer picture of neighborhood enforcement priorities (i.e., rationale 5). These priorities may or may not conflict with officer-defined ones.

Rationales 3 and 4 are commentaries about the present state of the criminal justice system and its treatment of arrested offenders. Many of these offenders, when apprehended, presented risks to arresting officers. Thus, it is somewhat discouraging to see these same offenders back out on the streets within a few months of their arrest for serious crimes. Police officers are justified in thinking this way about their arrests of suspects and what will likely happen to these arrested persons.

Unfortunately for both citizens and police officers, customized or individualized interpretations of the law by either party often lead to botched cases or lawsuits. But police officers in almost every jurisdiction have greater skills and expertise, as departments are upgrading their selection criteria for new recruits. Accordingly, there is a greater sense of professionalism among police officers today, and they are increasingly relied on to make good judgments and exercise sound discretion.

It might seem that strict adherence to the law by law enforcement officers is the solution to abuses of discretion, but this is not always so. Mayhall, Barker, and Hunter (1995:155) provide an interesting example: A Georgia police officer encountered a heavily intoxicated person in an open parking lot. The person could neither walk nor stand without the officer's assistance and was so intoxicated that he could not talk. Yet he was some distance from the nearest roadway, and he was not boisterous, loud, or profane. No city ordinance covered this situation so that the intoxicated person could be arrested for public drunkenness. The officer decided to leave the situation "as is." The intoxicated person was subsequently killed accidentally when an automobile ran over him, and the officer was sued in civil court in a wrongful death action.

Another example of a poor use of discretion by police officers involved one of the victims of Wisconsin serial murderer Jeffrey Dahmer. One evening in Milwaukee, Wisconsin, some months before Dahmer was discovered and arrested for multiple deaths, a scantily clad teenage male ran from Dahmer's apartment house screaming. Police officers intercepted the youth, but Dahmer approached and told them his "friend" was having problems and that he (Dahmer) would take him back inside his apartment and "help him." The police officers unwittingly released the youth into Dahmer's custody for eventual execution and dismemberment. Interviews with these officers later disclosed that "that sort of thing was common in that area," and that "those sorts of things" were expected of "those kinds of persons." In short, they determined the incident to be a "lovers' quarrel" and let the "lovers" alone.

It is often difficult for police departments in the United States to enforce consistently high standards of accountability for police in their diverse public encounters (Butler, 1985; Klockars, 1985). In short, police officers make on-the-spot decisions about whether to move beyond simple verbal warnings or reprimands to more formal actions against those stopped and questioned because of suspicion. Depending on the circumstances, law enforcement officers may be more or less aggressive.

One important implication of community policing is that in many neighborhoods, greater discretionary power over juveniles may be tacitly given, whether officers are patrolling on foot or in cruisers. Stopping and detaining juveniles is not a particularly popular activity for many police officers (Mixdorf, 1989:106), because both the juvenile and criminal courts are inclined to do little or nothing to juvenile first offenders or minor offenders (*Criminal Justice Newsletter*, 1988:4). Besides the leniency of courts, considerable paperwork is involved in processing juveniles after taking them into custody. Many police officers are reluctant to involve themselves in trivial juvenile affairs that may take as much or more time to process as the time it would take to process adult criminals following arrest.

The general public is not cognizant of the "pat down and frisk" implications of *Terry v. Ohio* and *Sibron v. New York* or justifiable searches with warrants in cases such as *Mapp v. Ohio*, where officers must have *more* than just a reasonable suspicion that youths might possess illegal substances (see Box 6.3).

Most discretionary actions by police officers do not result in violence, but there are enough instances of such officer conduct to attract citizen attention to sometimes questionable discretionary behaviors. Exercising discretion is a part of being a police officer. Not every law is clear-cut. As an officer's experience increases, so does his or her ability as an officer to make on-the-spot decisions in tough situations. It should be noted that a police officer's exercise of discretion is not bad. There are several positive aspects of police discretion. Police officers are trained to uphold the law and to make decisions about social events and persons

Arrestees are advised of their
rights, taken to jail, and booked.
(John Running/Stock, Boston)

BOX 6.3 The Exclusionary Rule and *Mapp*, *Terry*, and *Sibron*

The exclusionary rule means that if police officers obtain incriminating evidence against a criminal suspect and that evidence was obtained illegally, it is not admissible as evidence against the suspect. What was the rule intended to protect? It was meant to protect citizens against police misconduct relative to searches of persons and their effects, their homes, and their automobiles. How was the exclusionary rule created?

1. Mapp v. Ohio (1961). In May 1957, police officers in Cleveland, Ohio, sought information about someone wanted in connection with a recent bombing. Rumors of the whereabouts of the bombing suspect led them to the home of Ms. Dollree Mapp. They knocked on her door, demanding admission to her home to search for the suspect, and she asked if they had a warrant. They left, promising to return with one. Immediately she called her attorney, who arrived at her front door as more Cleveland police officers converged on her dwelling. The police forced their way into her home, waving a piece of paper that they claimed was a search warrant. Ms. Mapp and her attorney protested and demanded to see the warrant. Instead, the officers handcuffed Ms. Mapp and ordered the attorney to leave. They searched her entire home, including the attic and basement. In the bottom of an old trunk in her basement were simple pencil sketches interpreted by the searching police officers to be pornography. They arrested her for possession of pornography, and she was subsequently convicted on the basis of some obscure obscenity ordinance. She and her attorney appealed the conviction. The U.S. Supreme Court heard her case in 1961 and found that a warrant had never been issued. No one knew what the piece of paper was that was waved in the air by police prior to the search of her residence. It was never produced in court. Her conviction was overturned on the basis that (1) the search of her premises was unreasonable as set forth by the Fourth Amendment, and (2) the justification for the search was insufficient, lacking a showing of probable cause. Let us not forget what the police officers were looking for—a bombing suspect and bomb materials. The exclusionary rule doctrine was largely established by this case. It means simply that if police officers lack probable cause or fail to secure a valid search warrant for one's premises, the subsequent discovery of contraband or illegal material will be suppressed as evidence against the suspect in court. In subsequent years, the U.S. Supreme Court has amended this rule with various exceptions.

2. Terry v. Ohio (1968). Again in Cleveland, Ohio, in October 1963, an off-duty police detective, Martin McFadden, is observing two men standing on a street corner, talking. While McFadden observes these men, one of them walks up the street, looks in various store windows, and returns to continue conversing with the other man. Soon they are joined by a third man. They continue to take turns walking up the street looking in store windows, returning to the street corner, and conversing. McFadden decides to find out what is going on. In McFadden's mind, these men seem to be canvassing the area for a store to rob. At this point, these men have done nothing illegal. McFadden approaches the three men, produces a badge, and asks them for identification. So far, so good. McFadden observes what he thinks is suspicious behavior, and he anticipates that this suspicious behavior is the preamble to robbery or some other criminal activity. He is within his police rights to make inquiries of these men and their identities in his role as a Cleveland detective. The men were somewhat uncooperative, and McFadden spun one of them (John W. Terry) around and patted him down. He felt a hard object in the man's jacket, reached in, and retrieved a loaded pistol. Terry was arrested by McFadden for "carrying a concealed weapon" and was subsequently convicted. He appealed, arguing that McFadden had no right to search him for a weapon because Terry had been doing nothing illegal. However, the U.S. Supreme Court disagreed, saying that given McFadden's 35 years' experience with the Cleveland Police Department, his sense of what was occurring was valid, and he had a right to search the men in a pat down and frisk in order to protect himself against the possibility they might be armed. Thus, his experience, his reasonable suspicions of their behavior, and his fear for his own safety justified the pat down and frisk of Terry. The search of Terry and the seizure of his weapon without warrant were both justified.

Now, what about *Top Cop?*

3. Sibron v. New York (1968). In Brooklyn, New York, a convicted drug user, Nelson Sibron, was enjoying conversations with various friends in a restaurant. A Brooklyn patrolman, Anthony Martin, knew Sibron and had knowledge of his former police record. We might think this fact alone might entitle Officer Martin to search Sibron subsequently. Not so! As the evening progressed, Sibron met with other friends, some of whom Officer Martin recognized as known drug users. Officer Martin observed nothing exchanged among those with whom Sibron conversed. After a few hours, Sibron left the restaurant alone. He was immediately confronted by Officer Martin, who demanded, "OK, Sibron, you know what I want!" At that point Sibron began to reach into his jacket pocket. Officer Martin immediately thrust his own hands into Sibron's pockets and recovered several glassine envelopes containing heroin. This heroin was used against Sibron later in court, and he was convicted of possession of heroin. Was this right? Did the fact that heroin was discovered by Officer Martin justify Martin's search of

Sibron? The U.S. Supreme Court said no, the ends do not justify the means. In Sibron's case, Officer Martin had no probable cause to search Sibron. Further, his search of Sibron should have been limited to a pat down and frisk similar to Terry.

How did the U.S. Supreme Court differentiate between *Terry* and *Sibron*? In Terry's case, Officer McFadden engaged Terry in a pat down and frisk to determine whether Terry possessed a weapon that might pose a danger to McFadden. In Sibron's case, however, Officer Martin extended his search of Sibron beyond a simple pat down and frisk by inserting his hands into Sibron's pockets. It is unlikely that a pat down and frisk of Sibron would have detected several small envelopes of heroin. Certainly, these envelopes would not feel like a .38 caliber revolver such as that carried by Terry. Because Martin had absolutely no cause to search Sibron more extensively for a dangerous weapon, Sibron's conviction for heroin possession was thrown out by the U.S. Supreme Court.

It is a common misconception that if police officers discover illegal contraband as the result of a warrantless search, this somehow justifies their conduct. The U.S. Supreme Court says that it doesn't. Although several exceptions exist to cover the actions of police officers and condone warrantless searches of persons, their personal effects, homes, and automobiles, in general police are *not* authorized in routinely stopping citizens at random and forcing them to disrobe to the extent that illegal contraband is subsequently discovered. Thus, these cases should clarify why television shows like *Top Cop* may be misrepresenting to citizens what police officers may do out there on the street.

---

encountered that are consistent with this general purpose. Officer discretion is not intended to harm citizens but to help them. Accordingly, Pollock-Byrne (1989:83) notes that although officer discretion is a good thing, it is critical that an officer's moral and ethical standards be high and that one's police powers not be abused to the extent that community security and confidence in the police department are jeopardized.

THE CONTROL OF POLICE DISCRETION

Controlling police discretion does not mean stifling or repressing it. In this instance, *controlling* means to regulate conduct in ways that mutually benefit police officers and citizens. One important point of community-oriented policing is that police officers should acquire a better understanding of community interests and priorities. This understanding is enhanced by interacting with various community residents more closely and fairly regularly.

Controlling police discretion may also refer to internal and external strategies, such as Internal Affairs divisions in police departments and citizen complaint review boards. Internal Affairs investigates citizens' complaints against police officers. It also investigates information or evidence about possible officer corruption or dishonesty. However, communities are not always convinced that police departments are capable of evaluating their own personnel objectively. Many communities have established citizen or civilian complaint review boards consisting of various community leaders and police department representatives (Fyfe, 1985; Virginia State Crime Commission, 1994). These external mechanisms are intended to ignore police personalities and affiliations when investigating allegations of police misconduct or indiscretion.

More extensive coverage of citizen complaint review boards will be provided in Chapter 7. It is sufficient here to note that these boards have received mixed reviews. Police officers are wary of these boards, contending that boards do not "understand" the stresses of police work and the different factors that impinge on officers when resolving problems. High levels of police stress may adversely affect an officer's self-confidence when dealing with an emotionally charged situation. Effective police officer training programs are designed to assist officers in reducing job stressors and aid them in more intelligent decision making. In addition, a layperson's knowledge of the law is not as well-defined as a police officer's legal knowledge. Thus, what might appear as police brutality to outside observers may be standard operating procedures according to police department guidelines. Misunderstandings may arise because of what might appear to be the use of excessive force when making arrests.

In a small community-college town, for example, police officers were regularly called on to visit a home near the campus where students gathered frequently and made considerable noise at night. The primary interest of police when conducting these visits was to reduce the noise so that neighbors would not be disturbed. On one occasion, however, one of the students was upset with the police visit and an unpleasant verbal exchange followed. One of the officers then advised the student that he was being placed under arrest. The student turned, made a vulgar remark to the officer, and began to walk away from him. The officer approached the student from behind and used his baton against the student's throat to subdue him. The student was forced to the ground, handcuffed, and taken to jail, where he was charged with disorderly conduct, disturbing the peace, and resisting arrest. Subsequently his lawyer alleged that the officer had used excessive force when making the arrest, and the district attorney allowed the student to "plea out" the charge to simple disorderly conduct. A second suit contemplated against the arresting officer was dropped.

Outsiders might regard this situation in different ways, depending on the seriousness of the original disturbance reported by neighbors, the past history of complaints about this particular residence, and whether the student involved had a prior record. The officer's use of the baton was perceived by the officer as warranted. The student was larger than the officer and refused to submit to a lawful arrest. Wishing to avoid any physical harm, the officer did what he needed to do at the time to maintain his own safety and secure the arrest. The student had a different view. He later indicated he didn't think the officer "meant business" and that was why he began to walk away. But this is hindsight. Under conditions of split-second decision making, officers do not have the advantage of deciding among various behavioral options or seeing the situation from various perspectives. The officer did his duty, in his view. He was convinced that he did the right thing.

In light of the current popularity of community-oriented policing and its likelihood of continuing, it makes sense to give more credence to civilian complaint review boards as useful and integrative mediums whereby errant police officers can be sanctioned. If the student in the preceding example believed honestly that he was the victim of excessive force, this incident might likely be investigated by a review board rather than result in formal civil court action as an alleged tort committed by the arresting officer. Unfortunately, there are more than a few police officers as well as police department administrators who view civilian complaint review boards as unable to grasp the police perspective and to resolve disputes and settle allegations fairly.

KEY TERMS

Exigent circumstances
"Good faith" exception
Plain view
Police discretion

Police mission
Situationally based discretion
Totality of circumstances
Warrantless searches and seizures

QUESTIONS FOR REVIEW

1. What is police officer discretion? What factors make it difficult to define this term?
2. What is meant by police officers' "customized interpretations of the law?" Give two examples.
3. What were the interests of the American Bar Foundation Survey of Criminal Justice? How did this survey influence police professionalism and discretion?
4. What is the police mission? How does it relate to police discretion?
5. When officers are in a situation in which they must make an arrest decision, how do mandatory arrest policies guide their conduct? Give an example. In what situations do they have choices about whether to arrest law violators?
6. What are some examples of police agencies' *overreacting* to the Rodney King incident?

7. Characterize the relations between police officers and (a) prosecutors, (b) the courts, (c) corrections. In each case, give an example.
8. How can police officer conduct jeopardize a criminal prosecution?
9. How may police officers possibly violate the First and Second amendments when arresting suspects?
10. What provisions of the Fourth Amendment are especially pertinent to police officers? What are some "reasonable" searches of persons by police officers? What exceptions can you cite to justify warrantless searches of persons and their effects?
11. What rationales do police officers give for deciding which laws should be enforced and which ones shouldn't?
12. Generally, what two types of mechanisms function to control police officer discretion?

SUGGESTED READINGS

Cohen, Howard S., and Michael Feldberg (1991). *Power and Restraint: The Moral Dimension of Police Work.* New York: Praeger.

Newell, Charldeen, Janay Pollock, and Jerry Tweedy (1992). *Financial Aspects of Police Liability.* Washington, DC: International City/County Management Association.

Perez, Douglas W. (1994). *Common Sense about Police Review.* Philadelphia, PA: Temple University Press.

CHAPTER 7

The Forms and Nature of Police Misconduct

Introduction

What Is Police Misconduct?

An Overview of Types of Police Misconduct

Forms of Nonviolent Misconduct
Unofficial "Perks"
Graft
Perjury and "Dropsy" Testimony

Forms of Physical Misconduct
The Spirit and Letter of the Law
Police Brutality and Excessive Force
The Force Continuum
Deadly Force
Rationalizing Misconduct

Internal Affairs

Civilian Complaint Review Boards

Key Terms

Questions for Review

Suggested Readings

205

INTRODUCTION

Hollywood movies have done much to define **police misconduct** for us. Some examples include the following:

- In *Serpico,* a movie about Frank Serpico, portrayed by Al Pacino, Serpico is a rookie police officer on a lunch break with the "Patrolman of the Month" at Charlie's Diner. In uniform, the Patrolman of the Month and Serpico enter the diner.

    "What's the lunch special today, Charlie?" says the Patrolman of the Month.

    "Chicken sandwiches," says Charlie.

    "Let me have one of those," says the Patrolman of the Month.

    "I think I'll have turkey on rye," says Frank Serpico. Charlie eyes Serpico strangely and says, "Sure, go have a seat and I'll bring it over to you."

    Later, when Serpico sees his chicken sandwich, he says to the Patrolman of the Month, "He gave me chicken. I ordered turkey on rye." As he rises to make the sandwich exchange, the Patrolman of the Month says to Serpico, "Hey, easy, Frank. Look, take what Charlie gives you. After all, it's free, for Christ's sake."

    "What if I want to pay for what I want to eat?" asks Serpico innocently.

    "Look, Frank," says the Patrolman of the Month, "we give Charlie a break on double-parking out front for deliveries, and he lets us eat for nothin'. You know, just take what he gives you and don't cause no problems." Immediately disenchanted with this "other" side of police work, Serpico downs his chicken sandwich in silence.

- In *Dirty Harry,* a movie about a rogue cop named Harry "Dirty Harry" Callahan, played by Clint Eastwood, a San Francisco police detective does things his own way. Dirty Harry is investigating a case in which a sniper has killed several persons and has demanded $200,000 in return for the safety of a kidnapped female. Dirty Harry learns the identity of the sniper-kidnapper and goes to a sports stadium where the suspect lives as a groundskeeper. It is night, and the stadium is closed, but Dirty Harry climbs over the stadium fence anyway, while his partner enters the stadium from a different location. Without waiting to obtain proper arrest and search warrants, Dirty Harry kicks in the door of the suspect's living quarters and discovers the rifle used in the deadly snipings. Then, following a lengthy chase after the suspect throughout the stadium, Dirty Harry confronts him on the baseball field. Suddenly, the stadium lights come on, as Dirty Harry's partner has located the main stadium light switches. Dirty Harry shoots and wounds the suspected sniper-kidnapper in the leg as he attempts to flee. Dirty Harry approaches the wounded suspect and asks the whereabouts of the kidnap victim. The suspect, writhing in pain, begins to protest, citing his right to an attorney, his right to medical treatment. Dirty Harry places his foot on the suspect's painful leg wound and bears down. "Where is the girl?" persists

Dirty Harry. The scene fades out to a remote location near the San Francisco Bay Bridge, where the nude woman's body is extracted from a drainage culvert. The woman has been dead for several days. Some of her teeth have been ripped from her mouth by metal pliers to convince authorities of the seriousness of the extortionist's demand. Subsequently, Dirty Harry is berated by higher-ups for using unorthodox and illegal methods for getting the suspect's confession. The weapon and other incriminating evidence, including the confession, are thrown out as illegally seized under the Fourth Amendment, and the suspect is freed. Later, the suspect kills again, and he kidnaps a busload of schoolchildren. This time, Dirty Harry locates and frees the kidnapped children, chases and kills the suspect with his .44 magnum pistol in a suspenseful finale, and throws his detective badge away in disgust with the "system."

- In *The New Centurions,* starring George C. Scott and Stacy Keach, the personal and professional lives of new officers (such as Keach) and old ones about to retire (Scott) are depicted. These officers are partners who are assigned night patrol in downtown Hollywood. They are driving a large van designed to hold arrestees for transportation to jail. While cruising the Hollywood streets, Scott and Keach make numerous arrests of prostitutes. Scott pulls the van up to a liquor store, in which he purchases some milk, a bottle of scotch, and many plastic cups. He distributes the liquor among the prostitutes and drives them around for a few hours. Eventually, he stops at a remote location and allows all the prostitutes to leave. By this time they are thoroughly intoxicated and cannot work effectively as hookers for the remainder of the evening. "Let 'em know we're out on the streets with the meat wagon," he tells the rookie, Keach. "No harm done. We've put ten hookers out of commission for the evening. They got the point. That's all." Laughing, Scott and Keach drive away from the staggering group of hookers and back to the station to check in.

Whatever the merits of these movie vignettes, each has some basis in truth. In the case of Frank Serpico, it was subsequently discovered by the New York Police Department that widespread graft and corruption existed, from the lowliest patrolman to the top administrators in most precincts. Police officers and detectives were "on the take," and large sums of money were being skimmed from drug pushers and others and diverted to police officers' pockets in exchange for certain types of protection. Ultimately, the Knapp Commission was established to investigate allegations of corruption within the New York Police Department, and Serpico's observations were confirmed. Many police officers were reprimanded or fired after a finding of their culpability and illegal financial arrangements with crime figures.

Joseph Wambaugh, a former Los Angeles police officer, wrote extensively about his own experiences and observations about police work. His book, *The New Centurions,* was the basis for the film. The different kinds of police misconduct he described involved more serious or less serious violations of police officer ethics and protocol in dealing with civilian problems.

The case of "Dirty Harry" is fiction; but although all police departments have been compelled to follow a new deadly force standard since 1985 (*Tennessee v. Garner,* 1985) and the use of firepower to bring down fleeing felons happens less frequently every year, many police officers continue to neglect, intentionally or unintentionally, some of the legal rights of suspects they arrest. Criminal investigations, especially those involving homicides in which victims have been brutally beaten and killed, prey on officers' emotions to the extent that often the lost rights of innocent victims are given primacy, and the rights of murderers or murder suspects are observed casually.

This chapter is about police misconduct, also known as police corruption, police deviance, and excessive force. Police misconduct includes a broad array of behaviors by law enforcement officers that are more or less serious and possibly unlawful digressions from their formal responsibilities and duties. Such misconduct may include male officers obtaining sexual favors from attractive female motorists in exchange for overlooking traffic violations; officers accepting money from criminals as graft, or being "on the take" in exchange for protection or lenient treatment; officers using excessive force or unjustified deadly force when making arrests; officers deliberately lying on the witness stand when offering testimony against criminal suspects; and officers engaging in deception through entrapment, that is, enticing persons to commit crimes they are not ordinarily inclined to commit.

The first part of this chapter defines and lists various types of police officer misconduct. Types of misconduct are described, including nonviolent corruption and physical force. Different types of nonviolent corruption are indicated, such as graft, unofficial "perks," perjury, and "dropsy" testimony. Forms of physical misconduct include police brutality and excessive force. A force continuum is presented. Various types of liability result from police officers' professional work and its community application. Thus, this chapter also identifies police liability, its sources, and its consequences. The chapter concludes by examining certain internal and external control mechanisms ideally created to monitor and control all forms of police misconduct, especially corruption and excessive force. These mechanisms are Internal Affairs divisions of police departments and civilian complaint review boards.

WHAT IS POLICE MISCONDUCT?

Police misconduct is committing a crime and/or not following police department policy guidelines and regulations in the course of one's duties as an officer. Herman Goldstein (1967) was one of the first of the modern-day law enforcement experts to note the complex nature of the police function. He called for police departments to outline all forms of police misconduct as well as to identify the factors contributing to such misconduct. He was among the first to promote the use of officer training programs for the purpose of instilling officers with a commitment to their professional responsibilities that would minimize and eventually eliminate misconduct. Further, he called for the integration of both internal and external review mechanisms as means of controlling and guiding officer discretion that may involve misconduct. Radelet and Carter (1994:236–237) provide an array of behaviors that are more or less serious examples of police misconduct:

1. Accessing police records for personal use
2. Abusing sick leave
3. Lying to supervisors and managers
4. Committing perjury on reports and in court
5. Committing a crime
6. Falsifying overtime records
7. Using excessive force
8. Drinking on duty
9. Being involved in off-duty firearms incidents
10. Failing to complete police reports
11. Accepting gratuities
12. Providing recommendations for an attorney, towing service, or bail bond service
13. Failing to report misconduct of a fellow officer
14. Failing to inventory recovered property or evidence
15. Sleeping on duty
16. Cheating on a promotional examination
17. Engaging in sexual harassment or improprieties

Although all of these forms of police misconduct are serious in their own right, some of these behaviors are more important to citizens than others. For instance, citizens are perhaps more concerned about the possible use of excessive force when police officers make arrests. Also, perjury in court and sexual harassment are considered serious police misconduct. Acts such as lying to superiors about overtime records and other matters, cheating on promotional exams, sleeping on duty, and failing to inventory recovered evidence may be deemed less important because they are further removed from events that directly affect citizens. This chapter examines actions that most directly affect citizens, such as using excessive force, committing perjury, committing crimes, and accepting gratuities.

Why Is It Important to Study Police Misconduct? A survey of 1,151 law enforcement agencies in October 1990 was conducted by Newell, Pollock, and Tweedy (1992). The authors obtained a fairly representative sample of agencies from U.S. cities and counties with populations of 10,000 or above. Study results showed the existence of widespread police misconduct and numerous public allegations of it. Monetary settlements arising from tort actions by citizens against police officers were often in excess of $2 million, depending on the jurisdiction and misconduct alleged. Local government budgets were becoming overburdened with these suits, which were often traceable to nonactions by police agencies in the form of failure to train. These experts suggest that police agencies can take the following steps:

1. Train law enforcement personnel in the policies and procedures they are expected to observe
2. Ensure that all officers have copies of these policies
3. Provide regular training of supervisors
4. Create an atmosphere in which disciplinary action is the norm if policies and procedures are violated

Establishing policies and placing them in the hands of police officers, providing a chain of command for officer supervision, and creating an atmosphere in which disciplinary action will be forthcoming if the policies are violated are critical steps toward ensuring that various forms of police misconduct will be minimized or eliminated. A spirited cooperation among police officers in each agency is an equally critical requirement. One major internal impediment in the quest to remedy incidents of police misconduct is a set of unwritten rules tacitly supported by many police officers. These unwritten rules suggest strongly that fellow officers shall not betray other officers' behaviors that may or may not constitute misconduct.

Unwritten Codes of Conduct. These unwritten rules are similar to the codes of conduct generally endorsed by prison inmates: Do not rat on friends; don't be a snitch. Prison inmates insulate themselves from administrators and the correctional officers who directly supervise them (Vrij, 1989). A "we" and "they" mentality exists. In many respects, more than a few police officers envision themselves as a force of influence apart from mainstream society. In some respects, citizens are potential enemies to be tolerated. Citizens initiate lawsuits against police officers for various forms of misconduct. Many police officers believe that citizens do not understand and cannot empathize with officers who put their lives on the line daily. In this antagonistic context, it is easy to see why police develop these attitudinal stances and why certain forms of misconduct arise (Friedman, 1988). Civil liability cases against police officers in which misconduct is alleged, for instance, account for about 40 percent of all case filings against officers (Kappeler, 1993:3–4). Police officers are aware of their vulnerability to such litigation and seek to protect themselves from it in various ways.

There are several reasons that it is important to study police misconduct. These are:

1. Police officers are expected to adhere to and abide by standards higher than those expected of the general public.
2. Public confidence in police departments is based, in part, on continued good conduct of the police officers who enforce the law.

3. Police misconduct arises when certain conditions are present; it is important that these conditions are understood to the extent that something can be done to change them.
4. Police-community relations can minimize the incidence of certain forms of police misconduct.
5. Community-oriented policing promotes a cooperative atmosphere within which certain forms of police conduct are discouraged.

AN OVERVIEW OF TYPES OF POLICE MISCONDUCT

Criminologists and others have attempted to establish typologies of police misconduct. For instance, David Carter (1986:150–152) established a typology of police misconduct including (1) physical abuse/excessive force, (2) verbal/psychological abuse, (3) legal abuse/violations of civil rights, and (4) police sexual violence toward women.

1. *Physical abuse/excessive force.* Physical abuse/excessive force includes applying considerably more force than is necessary to effect an arrest. When officers injure suspects they arrest, especially when there is little or no need for the use of such force, such behavior is labeled physical abuse or **excessive force.** The ultimate excessive force is deadly force. The "fleeing felon" rule, invalidated by *Tennessee v. Garner* in 1985, permitted police officers to apprehend fleeing felons with any means available, including deadly force. (The fleeing felon rule is discussed in detail later in this chapter.) Thus, if a burglar was fleeing a crime scene and police officers pursued, they legally could use their weapons to prevent the burglar's escape. Carter's typology, however, confines physical abuse and excessive force to situations in which a life is not taken. Thus, **deadly force** might be considered in a class by itself. Officers' apprehension of criminal suspects deemed physical abuse/excessive force would include all forms of physical abuse that might or might not produce bodily injuries.

It is difficult to define clearly what is and is not excessive. Excessiveness is a characteristic that varies by degree as on a continuum. Each arrest situation, particularly one in which the suspect resists, suggests a different application of physical force to effect the arrest. How much force is needed depends on each situation, and two opinions are involved in interpreting whether too much force has been applied—the officer's opinion and the arrestee's. If arrested suspects believe they have been physically abused, they might bring a lawsuit against the arresting officers. If we see officers slam an arrestee's head down on the hood of a car and twist his arm to handcuff him, it may appear to be excessive force, but may actually be "standard" force prescribed by the officer's training when making arrests of suspects who resist. What we do *not* see is the degree of resistance by arrestees. Usually, only the officers making the arrest know how much resistance is being used to avoid arrest and how much more force is required to offset the resistance.

A clear example of excessive force involved Robert, a motorist who was driving home with his wife in New Orleans, Louisiana, on October 24, 1987 (*Garrett v. Fleetwood,* 1994). Robert was driving a pickup truck in heavy early evening traffic when an emergency vehicle driven by Fleetwood, a Mississippi River Bridge Authority (MRBA) officer, came up behind him with emergency lights flashing. Apparently, Robert could not move to another lane because of excessive traffic on the multilane highway. The MRBA officer was impatient and struck Robert's pickup with his vehicle. Eventually, Robert pulled over. Fleetwood, the MRBA officer, stopped behind Robert and proceeded to assault him repeatedly. Garrett, a juvenile passenger in the Robert vehicle, joined the fight to protect Robert and was also assaulted by Fleetwood. Other officers eventually joined Fleetwood in his attack on Robert and Garrett. After a lengthy and abusive arrest and detention at a New Orleans police station, Robert was released, and no charges were ever filed against him. Alleging various constitutional rights violations and negligence on the part of the MRBA, the Garretts filed suit against Fleetwood and various agencies. Subsequently, the court determined that Fleetwood had used excessive force in assaulting both Robert and Garrett.

2. *Verbal/psychological abuse.* Verbal/psychological abuse takes the form of taunting or ridicule. When police officers are arresting someone, they may make insulting remarks or taunt the suspect. When police officers interrogate suspects or transport prisoners from one site to another, they may engage in verbal abuse, often in settings where the actual events cannot be corroborated. In one-on-one interactions between officers and citizens, however, the courts clearly side with the testimony of officers, whether it is true or false.

3. *Legal abuse/violations of civil rights.* Title 42, Section 1983 of the U.S. Code contains provisions protecting one's civil rights, so that if police officers act in ways that may seem to infringe on those rights, affected citizens may file **Section 1983 actions.** Between 1982 and 1991 the number of civil rights cases filed in federal courts rose from 105 to 145 (Kappeler, 1993:4), and citizen-plaintiffs prevailed during those years between 35 percent and 64 percent of the time. The issues involved in the cases covered various forms of police misconduct and abuses of authority. This trend in civil litigation is consistent with figures reported from previous decades. For instance, between 1967 and 1976, the number of police misconduct suits brought in federal courts increased twelvefold and reached approximately 25,000 suits annually nationwide (Schmidt, 1985). Allegations under Section 1983 during this period included false arrest and false imprisonment, **police brutality,** illegal entry, and illegal searches.

Civil rights violations and legal abuses are frequently alleged by criminal suspects and others. For instance, more than a few police officers have been accused of creating their own grounds for searches of persons or their property. In the case of *State v. Jones* (1994), two Hackensack, New Jersey, police officers were conducting surveillance of an apartment building. They saw two men, Jones and Collier, drive into the parking lot. Although the men were not the objects of the surveillance, one of the officers recognized Collier as a person for whom an arrest warrant had been prepared. The officer did not know the nature of the warrant, which had been issued for failure to pay parking fines. The officers approached Jones and Collier, who fled into a nearby apartment and locked the door. The officers kicked in the door and placed Jones and Collier under arrest. At about the same time, the officers found some drugs and drug paraphernalia and a stolen wallet in dresser drawers in the apartment. Both were charged with burglary of an automobile from which the wallet had been taken a day earlier. The drug materials and wallet were introduced as evidence against these men, and they were convicted. They appealed, alleging that the search of their apartment without warrant was illegal. Ultimately, the appellate court declared the search unlawful, because police could not forcibly enter a home without a warrant to arrest a suspect for a minor offense. Although the officers contended that their arrest was based on "hot pursuit," this did not, by itself, justify the forced entry of the apartment. Also, the officers did not know that there was illegal contraband or evidence of a crime that could be easily destroyed. The convictions were overturned.

In the case of *Garrett v. Fleetwood* already cited, certain civil rights violations were also alleged. Garrett claimed he had been wrongfully arrested and detained by New Orleans officers. Further, he alleged that officers had beat him under the cloak of their authority. In some respects, the claims made by Garrett parallel some of the civil rights allegations in the case of Rodney King in Los Angeles.

One of the seemingly most flagrant civil rights violations occurred against Tilson, in Forest City, Arkansas (*Tilson v. Forest City Police Department*, 1994). Tilson was arrested in connection with a recent murder and for violating his parole. He was placed in a county jail. No further action, either a murder charge or a parole revocation action, was taken against Tilson, who remained uncharged. For *fourteen months,* Tilson remained in the county jail. Eventually, he sought release from jail through a petition and was released. He sued various agencies and the prosecutor alleging civil rights violations. Surprisingly, no agencies or personnel were blamed for Tilson's unlawful confinement. The court found no evidence of civil rights violations alleged by Tilson.

In another case in November 1980, Scott Sabey was stopped by military police in Waikiki, Hawaii, for having beer cans in his automobile. The police officers involved, DeCoito and Tagalicod, placed Sabey in handcuffs and ordered him to a drainage ditch nearby. After beating Sabey, the officers urinated on him and made him "bob" for toads at gunpoint in the muddy waters of the ditch. Subsequently, Sabey sued these officers and the City of Honolulu. After protracted Section 1983 litigation, Honolulu was ordered to pay Sabey $100,000 in damages for the officers' misconduct. The judge was incensed by the officers' behaviors and hoped that the settlement would send a message to other officers in that and other jurisdictions (*Crime Control Digest*, 1989:9–10).

These examples of legal abuse and civil rights abuse only partially depict the broad array of cases that arise. In each case, allegations of officer misconduct are made based on the unreasonableness of officer conduct. The intent of lawsuits

Situationally based discretion means that officers may make on-the-spot judgments to arrest or not arrest suspects, depending on the circumstances. *(Patricia Hollander Gross/Stock, Boston)*

against police is both to compensate victims and to deter future police wrongdoing (McCoy, 1984). McCoy notes that it is difficult to assess the actual impact of such civil litigation on police misconduct. Indirect gauges are available, however, such as higher insurance rates, larger compensation settlements, and increased media coverage of police misconduct issues. These cases are becoming increasingly important to police administrators. Further, administrative actions are likely to be taken within police departments in a stronger effort to deter police misconduct.

4. *Police Sexual Violence toward Women.* One of the more appalling aspects of police misconduct is police sexual violence toward women. Female motorists are regarded as fair game and preyed upon by certain police officers in various jurisdictions. It is unknown how prevalent police sexual violence toward women is. However, many laypersons and others believe that any occurrence is too much, especially when perpetrated against women by a relatively elite corps of officers sworn to uphold the law. Police sexual violence (PSV) toward women includes those situations in which a female citizen experiences a sexually degrading, humiliating, violating, damaging, or threatening act committed by a police officer through the use of force or police authority (Kraska and Kappeler, 1995:93).

In one case of PSV, two female motorists were made to strip and allow themselves to be searched in the back seat of a police cruiser. They were ordered to place themselves in the cruiser back seat on their hands and knees, with their legs spread. In this position and in plain view of onlooking male officers, female officers searched these women's vaginas with their fingers, probing for drug contraband. Their justification for this body-cavity search was that one of the women's relatives was suspected of dealing in drugs. Thus, in order to get to the relative, the police resorted to PSV. These two women were threatened with future "searches" if they did not give police incriminating evidence about the relative (*Timberlake v. Benton*, 1992).

In another case, a woman suspected of being a drug courier was roused from her sleep one evening while in bed with her husband. She was taken to a hospital where she was given a body-cavity search by several police women, who probed her vagina with both gloved and ungloved hands and fingers (*Rodriguez v. Fuetado*, 1991). In North Little Rock, Arkansas, another case involved an officer, Lukie, who regularly picked up female motorists accused of driving while intoxicated. Lukie would drive these females to remote locations where he would forget about the DWI charges in exchange for their performing oral sex on him (*Parrish v. Lukie*, 1992). In most such cases, juries were generally supportive of police officers and believed their version of events despite overwhelming evidence to the contrary.

Much of this police misconduct is attributed to the extreme power differential between policemen and female citizens (Kraska and Kappeler, 1995:106–107). Because there is often a code of silence among police officers in jurisdictions where such behavior occurs, victims of PSV are relatively powerless to cause such behaviors to be rooted out and terminated. Kraska and Kappeler (1995:107) surmise that a critical element throughout the vast PSV behavioral continuum is the sexist nature of conventional police culture.

FORMS OF NONVIOLENT MISCONDUCT

Nonviolent misconduct by police officers is most often associated with graft or corruption. Officers who accept gratuities in exchange for special favors to citizens exhibit one type of misconduct. They profit through illicit social exchanges. Some officers give false testimony in court against suspects in order to enhance the case against them and heighten the chances of a conviction. Thus, officers may receive unofficial perquisites ("perks")—graft—in the course of performing their police role, or they may offer incriminating but false information against citizens charged with crimes. These types of misconduct are described next.

Unofficial "Perks"

Incidents of corruption among police officers include everything from minor favors, such as courtesies to waive tickets for speeding or DWI for fellow officers, to bribery and extortion (Dombrink, 1991; Kleinig and Gorman, 1992). Barker (1986:12–13) says that police work is ideal for engaging in patterns of deviance and corruption, because many officers are socialized to engage in corruption and condone it over time. Barker studied police corruption in one department and identified ten types of corrupt behavior. He asked officers the extent to which each would not report to other police officers the following actions:

1. Corruption of authority (free meals, services or discounts, liquor)
2. Kickbacks (money, goods and services)
3. Opportunistic threats (victims, burglary or unlocked buildings)
4. Shakedowns (criminals)
5. Protection of illegal activities (vice operators, businessmen)
6. Traffic fixes
7. Misdemeanor fixes
8. Felony fixes
9. Direct criminal activities (burglary, robbery)
10. Internal payoffs (off-days, work assignments)

In every case, a substantial number of officers questioned said that they would rarely or never report these types of conduct to other officers. Based on this and other studies, Barker concluded that police deviance is not an unusual form of deviant conduct. Further, the police peer group indoctrinates and socializes rookies into patterns of acceptable corrupt activities, sanctions deviations outside these boundaries, and sanctions officers who do not engage in any corrupt acts (Barker, 1986:19).

Graft

Police corruption is a serious problem extending far beyond the corrupt officer, and it flourishes largely because of a police culture that promotes loyalty over integrity. Honest officers often remain silent because they fear reprisals from other fellow officers for "ratting" on them. Supervisors are often at fault, because they tacitly condone such behaviors and function as role models to many of their subordinates (New York Commission to Investigate Allegations of Police Corruption, 1994).

The Knapp Report. In the late 1960s, Frank Serpico (mentioned earlier in this chapter) and another detective from the New York Police Department testified before the Knapp Commission. This commission was convened to investigate allegations of police corruption among NYPD members. Subsequent disclosures revealed extensive corruption, which the commission made various recommendations to isolate and eliminate. Of relevance here is the commission's description of various types of officers and the nature of the corruption they exemplified.

The commission divided corrupt officers into two general categories: grass-eaters and meat-eaters. Grass-eaters are those officers who accept simple gratuities and payoffs that come their way. In contrast, meat-eaters aggressively misuse their powers for personal gain. The commission noted that while the grass-eaters may not engage in the large-scale corruption of meat-eaters, they pose a serious problem. Basically, they are rookies who come into the NYPD and are faced with a situation in which it is easier to be corrupt than to remain honest. Because of their large numbers, they make corruption respectable. Further, they perpetuate a code of silence on officer wrongdoing. It is difficult for outsiders to detect graft and corruption and to suppress it once it has been detected.

One factor defined by the commission as fostering and perpetuating this form of police misconduct is the distinction made by officers between "dirty money" and "clean money." Thus, officers may more easily accept money from gamblers than from drug pushers. A second factor is the branch of the NYPD to which one is assigned. Plainclothes work heightens one's opportunities for corruption. A third factor is the location to which officers are assigned. Certain parts of New York are more conducive to corruption than others. A fourth factor is the officer's assignment. Patrol car assignments created opportunities for officers to profit from local graft. A fifth factor is rank. The higher one's rank, the greater the monetary rewards from graft.

Perjury and "Dropsy" Testimony

Officer Perjury. More than a few convicted offenders know that their convictions are based in large part on the perjury (lying under oath) of police officers who seized illegal contraband contrary to Fourth Amendment search-and-seizure standards. **Perjury** by anyone is not condoned, but when police officers commit perjury, it is regarded as especially serious because they are committed to abiding by a higher moral standard than the general public. Under what circumstances do police officers and other law enforcement officers (e.g., DEA agents, FBI agents) commit perjury? What does perjured testimony accomplish? In general, perjury by police officers is designed to (1) justify illegal conduct or (2) strengthen weak cases against criminal defendants. In some instances, perjury by police officers occurs because of the pressures of agency policies to make more arrests for vice offenses (drugs, prostitution, and gambling) and to get convictions. This pressure encourages officers to engage in shortcuts that involve illegal practices (Greenberg, 1990). Perjury may also be committed to protect informants.

Line police officers are not the only people in law enforcement who engage in perjury, however; all law enforcement agencies have been tainted by perjury disclosures. An FBI agent committed perjury in a New Jersey federal court in a case involving interstate transportation of stolen property and copyright infringement. The FBI agent posed as a customer to obtain incriminating information against the defendant. Some allegedly stolen contraband came into the agent's possession through the defendant as a third party. Later in court, the prosecution sought to make a case against the defendant on exclusively circumstantial evidence. One element of the prosecution's case was to show a "profit" or "financial gain" motive. As part of a scenario to show that the defendant had profited considerably from the contraband, the FBI agent testified that the defendant picked him up one day in a late-model Buick, "the newer model." In fact, the defendant drove a four-year-old Buick, one of the cheaper models. The FBI agent testified further that he had paid the defendant $6,000 for the contraband, when in fact he had given only $3,500 to the defendant. Government funds were used for "buy money," and it is evident that the FBI agent pocketed the other $2,500. The agent added that an inspection of the defendant's checking account showed monthly deposits averaging $10,000, well above the defendant's take-home pay from his job. Although these points seem insignificant on their face, they were among several factors, also developed through perjured testimony, that resulted in the defendant's wrongful conviction for a federal misdemeanor. The appearance of wealth was like the smoking gun—surely, with all of that money, something illegal must have transpired. A gullible jury may believe almost any testimony given by an FBI agent. In reality, the New Jersey defendant was innocent of any wrongdoing.

The case of *Mapp v. Ohio* (1961), described previously, defined the exclusionary rule, which prohibits the admission in court of evidence that has been obtained illegally. The exclusionary rule was meant to deter and prevent police misconduct in searches of persons, automobiles, and homes. Since the *Mapp* decision, police testimony has been subjected to more intensive scrutiny to determine whether officers obtained evidence through illegal means. Ironically, however, the effect of *Mapp* has been to make some officers more cunning regarding the recovery of evidence.

Dropsy Testimony. A commentary published in the *Columbia Journal of Law and Social Problems* in 1968 reported research on the New York Police Department and police officers' accounts of how they discovered narcotics evidence. The research covered the six months prior to the *Mapp* decision and the six months following *Mapp*. The Narcotics Bureau, uniformed officers, and plainclothes detectives were questioned about how they discovered illegal drugs in the possession of drug suspects. It is fairly common for suspects carrying illegal contraband to throw it away if running from police or to conceal the illegal drugs on their person. Thus, police officers can discover these drugs either by finding contraband that was dropped somewhere or by frisks of the suspect's clothing. Before the *Mapp* decision, two-thirds of all evidence was obtained by searches of suspects' clothing. Following *Mapp*, between 80 percent and 90 percent of all contraband was "discovered" because suspects had "dropped" the contraband. Thus, **dropsy testimony** has become more prevalent in various courts, because police officers have increasingly alleged that their suspects "dropped" the incriminating evidence. It is both unusual and unlikely that suspects would suddenly begin to drop incriminating evidence for police to discover, in New York or any other jurisdiction.

Police perjury is only one example of the wide gap between the formal rules and the actual operation of police agencies (Cohen, 1972). Many attorneys believe that police perjury, especially in drug and victimless crime cases, is particularly widespread (*Georgetown Law Journal*, 1971). The U.S. Supreme Court notes that, ideally, police officers conform their conduct to the dictates of the court relative to searches of drug suspects. It is strongly indicated, however, that where police officers testify that their suspects dropped the narcotics in their presence, they have been able to avoid the Fourth Amendment prohibition against unreasonable searches and seizures—by committing perjury. Courts have found it necessary to establish safeguards to minimize such perjury, such as closely scrutinizing dropsy testimony and requiring the government to prove the legality of warrantless arrests, searches, and seizures by a preponderance of the evidence (*Georgetown Law Journal*, 1971).

FORMS OF PHYSICAL MISCONDUCT

The Spirit and Letter of the Law

The line between the spirit and letter of the law is diffuse. Police agencies are continually establishing and implementing policies seeking to clarify what officers *must* or *may* do under different sets of circumstances. Citizen reactions to police behaviors that relate to excessive force suggest that certain socioeconomic variables are influential. For instance, in a study that investigated public attitudes toward police use of excessive force (Arthur and Case, 1994), citizens in a random sample were asked whether they approved of police officers striking adult males under various circumstances. About 70 percent of the white respondents and 43 percent of the black respondents approved of officers' use of force. It was subsequently found that those respondents with greater power, status, and advantages (particularly white, more highly educated males and wealthier individuals) were more likely to favor police use of force than were less privileged groups (especially ethnic minorities, who are more frequently subjected to excessive police force).

It is generally accepted, however, that a workable framework for the development of police ethics is found in the theory of political obligation. The police role obligates officers to behave so as to bring basic democratic values to life. It requires the development of representative, democratic forms of organization to encourage citizen participation in democratic processes (Fair and Pilcher, 1991; Rhoades, 1991).

Police Brutality and Excessive Force

The Etiology of Excessive Force Behaviors among Officers. No definitive criteria exist to suggest which officers will always use excessive force. There is no consensus regarding which variables are important in excessive force situations or how these variables might interact (Kavanagh, 1994). An examination of officers who have been cited for excessive use of force suggests that in an actuarial sense, they tend to have personality disorders; previous job-related incidents, such as justifiable shootings; a heavy-handed patrol style sensitive to challenge; and other personal problems (Scrivner, 1994). Attempts to involve psychiatrists and psychologists in the training and monitoring of police behaviors have been only partially successful. Psychologists and other professionals are more likely to involve themselves in postexcessive force counseling situations. Such after-the-fact remedies do little to prevent the occurrence of excessive force applied by officers.

Even in departments and under conditions in which excessive force has been highlighted through media reports, little evidence exists that suggests police departments move aggressively to deter misconduct within their ranks (American Civil Liberties Union of Southern California, 1992). One reason for the continuing laxity of police departments to act aggressively to curtail excessive force by officers is that excessive force charges are difficult to sustain. Griswold (1994) has identified three factors operating against citizens who make complaints of excessive force against police officers:

1. Citizens making excessive force charges are often perceived as marginal individuals with little credibility.
2. Complainants have often been arrested for a legitimate offense or on a cover charge, again undermining their credibility.
3. Nonnegotiable uses of force represent the core of the police role, and high evidentiary requirements are necessary to sustain citizen complaints.

Hot Pursuit. In Knoxville, Tennessee, one afternoon, a police officer was cruising near a shopping mall. He heard a report that someone had robbed a jewelry store located in the mall and was fleeing in his direction. (At the time, the defense-of-life standard was not in effect but the fleeing felon rule was operative.) The officer observed a suspect exit the mall to a waiting vehicle. He proceeded to follow the vehicle from the mall at high speed. A chase ensued, covering several miles through the city. Both the officer's cruiser and the fleeing vehicle collided with numerous cars during the chase. Eventually, the fleeing vehicle crashed into a median while attempting to enter an interstate highway. The officer's cruiser was traveling at such a high speed that it also crashed, landing on the suspect's vehicle. Although no one died as a result of the chase, the city was billed for more than $500,000 in damages to assorted vehicles hit during the chase. The robbery suspect had netted about $200 from the jewelry store. Was it worth it?

Most police departments have "hot pursuit" policies today, some more permissive than others, that govern conditions under which fast pursuit of suspects should be undertaken. There is no question that police department hot pursuit policies influence the actual behavior of patrol officers. One study of 614 officers in 11 different police agencies found that in jurisdictions with liberal pursuit policies, the number of pursuits was twice as large as found in jurisdictions with more restrictive pursuit policies (Homant and Kennedy, 1994). However, policy guidelines regulating pursuit situations may not always be clear-cut (Britz and Payne, 1994). Further, officers may make their own interpretations of department pursuit policies (Falcone, 1994).

The Force Continuum

A **force continuum** has been described by Graves and Connor (1992). This force continuum is depicted in Figure 7.1.

The Federal Law Enforcement Training Center (FLETC) model depicts gradated or escalating amounts of force, applied in accordance with the nature of suspect cooperation or resistance. Suspects who are cooperative are given verbal orders by officers. Those who are designated "resistant" may not hear the officer's verbal orders and may need some contact control. Suspects who are actively "resistant" may need to be physically restrained through arm grips. If suspects elevate their resistance to assaultive levels and cause bodily injury to officers, officers use more aggressive defensive tactics, including disabling moves with their batons. When the aggression level rises to serious bodily injury, deadly force is a consideration, to minimize the threat posed by dangerous suspects.

Force continuums such as the FLETC model are useful in that they guide new police officers to adjust their level of force in making arrests to the level appropriate for particular suspects. These continuums serve as force guidelines rather than clear-cut indications of what officers should do under every circumstance they encounter. It is impossible to dictate precisely what each officer should do under all conditions. Developing such continuums is a good indication

Level of Resistance	Level of Enforcement	Response
Assaultive (serious bodily injury)	5	Deadly force
Assaultive (bodily injury)	4	Defensive tactics
Resistant (active)	3	Compliant techniques
Resistant (passive)	2	Contact controls
Compliant (cooperative)	1	Verbal commands

Figure 7.1. The Federal Law Enforcement Training Center (FLETC) Force Continuum. (*Source*: F.R. Graves and G. Connor, "The FLETC Use-of-Force Model." *The Police Chief*, 59:56–58.)

BOX 7.1   Excessive Force

THE CASES OF JONELIS AND ROWLAND

Jonelis was a passenger in a truck driven by a friend. At some point, his friend drove faster than the posted speed limit and was subsequently pursued at high speed by officers of the Norwalk (Connecticut) Police Department (NPD). NPD officers eventually stopped the truck, and Jonelis and his friend were ordered out of it. Both Jonelis and his friend were made to lie on the ground. One officer threatened to shoot, and shortly thereafter one officer shot and killed Jonelis's friend on the ground. Jonelis was handcuffed, beaten, and dragged in a roundabout way to the police department. He believed that he was going to be killed by these officers as well. After the incident, Jonelis brought suit against the officers for violating his constitutional rights. He alleged excessive force, negligent arrest, intentional infliction of emotional distress, and negligence. Although the City of Norwalk asked the court for a summary judgment, arguing that the city was not responsible for the officers' actions because the officers were not acting under an official city policy, the court denied their motion and the case went to trial. Jonelis was subsequently successful in his suit against the police and the City of Norwalk.

In Raleigh, North Carolina, Rowland, a mildly retarded man, was at a bus station. He was near a woman who dropped a $5 bill. He picked up the bill, claiming later that he didn't know the woman had dropped it. An officer saw the woman drop the money and saw Rowland pick it up. He approached Rowland and told him to return the money to the woman. Rowland approached the woman and waved the $5 bill in her face. The woman was also mentally retarded and rejected the money. When Rowland left the bus station, the officer followed him. The officer alleged that Rowland was running away, although Rowland claimed he was "standing still." The officer tackled Rowland, threw him to the ground, punched him several times, and eventually recovered the $5 bill, which he returned to the woman. The woman did not press charges, and the officer released Rowland shortly thereafter without making an arrest. Rowland's leg was broken and a subsequent operation left him with an ugly scar and permanent partial disability. Rowland sued the officer, alleging excessive force was used to arrest him and that the officer failed to give him proper medical treatment. He also alleged that he was detained unlawfully and that his due process rights were violated.

At a trial later, Rowland's suit was upheld to the extent that there was little evidence that Rowland posed a threat to the officer. Further, the actions by the police officer were excessive because Rowland's offense was

> a minor one. The court found for the police officer on the negligence claim regarding Rowland's leg injury, however. There was no evidence that the officer owed a duty to Rowland to provide him with medical care. He was obligated to help Rowland only to the extent that he detained Rowland so that he could not care for himself. Rowland was detained only about 15 minutes and was able to leave the scene on his own.
>
> Source: *Jonelis v. Russo*, 863 F.Supp. 84 (1994); *Rowland v. Perry*, 41 F.3d 167 (1994).

that police departments recognize the need to provide its officers with the best training so that they can anticipate in general ways what force might be needed.

Deadly Force

Deadly force is any effort to apprehend or subdue suspects that results in their death. Prior to 1985 police officers in virtually every police department in the United States followed the fleeing felon rule, a legislatively sanctioned provision that permitted police officers to prevent the escape of any fleeing felon by means of any force, including deadly force. Thus, pre-1985 fleeing felons such as burglars, rapists, robbers, car thieves, and drug dealers could be prevented from escaping from police by means of potentially deadly force. In short, police officers were entitled to shoot at, and possibly kill, fleeing felons attempting to avoid arrest.

Tennessee v. Garner *(1985).* In 1985 the U.S. Supreme Court heard the case of *Tennessee v. Garner.* In this case, which originated in Memphis, Tennessee, in the late 1970s, police had originally been advised that someone was in a vacant house in a Memphis suburb at about 2:00 A.M. Police officers arrived at the scene in time to see some boys running away. They shouted at the boys to stop, but their warnings were to no avail. Subsequently, one of the officers drew his revolver and fired at the fleeing boys, striking one in the back of the head, killing him instantly. The dead boy, Garner, was 15 years old. He and a friend had been exploring a vacant house at the time. If he had been apprehended, Garner's crime would have been simple trespass, or possibly burglary, although there was nothing in the home to steal. His punishment would have been a possible fine and probation. Instead, an officer shot and killed Garner as he fled.

The U.S. Supreme Court concluded in *Garner* that a much greater penalty had been exacted than would have been imposed under other circumstances. Accordingly, the Court set forth new "deadly force" standards and deemed the "fleeing felon" rule unconstitutional. The provisions guiding the application of deadly force by police are that deadly force will be used only when the lives of officers or innocent bystanders are jeopardized by fleeing suspects. Thus, a new

defense-of-life standard was created for all deadly force applications. Police officers must now justify their application of deadly force by showing that their own lives or the lives of innocent citizens were definitely in jeopardy by the actions of certain suspects who were subsequently killed by police.

Graham v. Connor (1989). In 1989 the U.S. Supreme Court further clarified the defense-of-life standard set forth in *Garner*. Actually, the case did not pertain to deadly force but to excessive force, regardless of whether it was lethal or nonlethal. The facts of the case are that Graham was a diabetic and was taking insulin on a regular basis. One evening at a Charlotte, North Carolina, convenience store, Graham tried to buy some orange juice to avoid a negative insulin reaction. The line in the store was too long, and Graham decided to drive elsewhere for the juice. When he left the store hurriedly and drove away to a friend's house, police officers pursued him after observing his allegedly "furtive" movements. The officers stopped Graham, who got out of his vehicle and passed out at curbside. Graham, who was propped up against the hood of his car, pleaded with officers to examine his diabetic ID card in his wallet, but he was told to "shut up" by one of the officers. He was then wrestled into a police car, where he suffered assorted injuries, including a broken foot, wrist cuts, bruised shoulders, and ear damage. Graham was subsequently released without charge.

Graham brought suit against the arresting officers. Lower courts affirmed the officers' conduct, but the U.S. Supreme Court ruled in favor of Graham, declaring that "objective reasonableness" under the Fourth Amendment should be used to assess the appropriateness of officer conduct. The U.S. Supreme Court declared the following standards should govern excessive force cases:

1. Any claim of excessive force against police officers should be analyzed using Fourth Amendment standards.
2. The proper legal standard in such matters is the objective reasonableness standard.
3. Four factors or circumstances should be considered when applying force of any kind:
   (a) Is there an immediate threat to officers posed by the suspect?
   (b) How severe is the crime(s) alleged?
   (c) Is the suspect actively resisting arrest?
   (d) Is the suspect attempting to escape custody?

It is in this context that excessive force standards are currently applied by police officers. The FLETC model we examined previously derives from *Graham*.

Rationalizing Misconduct

Over time, police officers have cultivated various explanations for their misconduct. Their rationales have become routinized and generally accepted, despite the absence of a legal basis for them. Gresham Sykes and David Matza (1957) and Ditton (1977) have described police officer actions and rationales that attempt to justify or explain away different types of misconduct. Generally, police officers tend to deny responsibility for potential or real citizen injuries. They attempt to neutralize deviance they may exhibit. For instance, if officers use excessive force on citizens who attempt to resist or who otherwise challenge police authority, they may say later, "I didn't mean it," or they may deny injury. They may say, "We didn't hurt anybody" when they commit perjury to justify illegal searches. Another neutralization technique is denial of a victim. For example, although police officers may fail to find illegal contraband when searching the premises of a known drug dealer, they may physically abuse and injure the suspect and later claim, "He had it coming. He just didn't have drugs *this time.*" A fourth neutralization technique is to condemn the condemners. Police department administrative orders and policies may seek to control officer misconduct. Nevertheless, those engaging in misconduct persist, claiming, "Everybody is picking on me." Another type of neutralization is to appeal to higher loyalties. Sometimes police officers commit perjury to protect other officers or to justify destruction of evidence. They claim, "I didn't do it for myself. I did it for the good of the department and for justice" (Kappeler, Sluder, and Alpert, 1994:127–130).

Whether we agree or disagree with these rationales, the fact is that many police officers use them, and frequently. This is because these techniques of neutralization have become internalized. Internalization is a social-psychological process of adopting and incorporating various behavioral standards and attitudes into one's personality system and regarding such standards and attitudes as fundamental and valid. If more than a few officers in any given police agency internalize these techniques of neutralization, peer justification for misconduct is established and intensified.

Detecting and Preventing Misconduct. How can police misconduct be detected or prevented? A study of the review systems used by various U.S. police agencies discloses three general types of systems, (1) internal, (2) external (civilian), and (3) hybrid (a combination of civilians and officers) (Perez, 1994). We examine internal affairs and civilian complaint review boards next.

INTERNAL AFFAIRS

A primary goal of police accountability is to attain a balance between competing public interests, and mechanisms on the one hand and responsiveness and legality on the other (Shadmi, 1994). **Internal affairs** divisions of police departments are investigative mechanisms staffed by senior police officials whose function it is to determine whether officers are guilty of any type of misconduct. Every large police agency has an internal affairs division. These divisions are viewed with some disdain by most line officers. Investigations by internal affairs personnel are often clandestine, and frequently, police officer–snitches are used for obtaining evidence against fellow officers (Heck, 1992). Some persons question whether police agencies can effectively police themselves through internal affairs. They believe that outside sanctioning mechanisms should be established, such as civilian complaint review boards.

How much force is too much when making arrests? Complaints of excessive force against individual police officers are often investigated by citizen complaint review boards or internal affairs departments. *(UPI/Corbis-Bettmann)*

CIVILIAN COMPLAINT REVIEW BOARDS

Many citizens believe that it is difficult, probably impossible, for police agencies to act as their own monitors of police misconduct. Thus, when police agencies investigate their own, the very language used in such investigations is telling (Littlejohn, 1981). There is great reluctance among police officials to punish one of their own when a citizen complains. This well-established phenomenon has been labeled the **blue curtain,** and it has been resistant to change from outside sources (Littlejohn, 1981). Why do police agencies consider the investigation of potentially corrupt officers such a personal enterprise? One would think that those most in favor of ridding their ranks of wrongdoers would be police agencies, but this is not the case. We have seen that the police culture creates its own mystique and informal ground rules for perpetuation. It is sometimes more difficult for police officers to be honest than dishonest, and too many instances of police misconduct and corruption have wearied the public to the extent that outside monitoring is regarded as essential. Increasingly, citizens want to play greater roles in monitoring the sanctioning process against bad officers.

Civilian complaint review boards consist largely of citizens independent of police agencies. Such boards investigate allegations of police misconduct and exert considerable control over police agency policies, disciplinary practices, and other internal matters related to police misconduct (Littlejohn, 1981). Littlejohn says that civilian review boards were advocated heavily in the 1960s but did not work well. One major factor hindering their effectiveness was that they weren't given enough power to handle police misconduct matters and sanctioning. In recent years, however, civilian complaint review boards have been vested with considerable sanctioning power. A survey found that between 1990 and 1992, nineteen of the thirty-four surveyed police departments developed civilian review boards, a trend that seemed indicative of national patterns, with no discernible geographical bias (Walker and Bumphus, 1992).

Proponents of civilian complaint review boards make these arguments:

1. Police agencies cannot be objective when investigating and sanctioning their own officers in response to allegations of misconduct; police agencies are biased in favor of their own officers whenever allegations of misconduct are raised.
2. Independent citizen boards *are* objective in this regard and can impose necessary sanctions if warranted and needed.
3. Public trust in police generally is enhanced through establishing independent civilian boards without police agency vested interests.
4. Citizens are more responsive to community-oriented policing when police officers are subject to independent accountability mechanisms.
5. Civilian boards can clear officers of excessive force or misconduct charges just as easily as they can find compelling evidence against them.

Opponents of civilian complaint review boards make the following points:

1. Civilians cannot empathize with police officers and the high level of risk associated with their work.
2. Civilians do not understand the necessity for police to use force in subduing suspects.
3. The authority of police agencies to sanction their own officers is terribly undermined by a parallel civilian sanctioning mechanism.
4. Civilians are biased against police officers whenever police misconduct is alleged.
5. Civilians are simply not qualified to judge the performance and behaviors of police officers; thus, civilian review boards are meaningless.

There is probably some truth to support all these views of civilian complaint review boards, pro and con. Civilian review boards are not perfect. Nevertheless, they offer an objective alternative to police agencies that are internally hobbled in their ability to investigate their own officers. Some boards have attempted to bridge the civilian-officer gap by including police administrators as board members. These situations seem productive in view of the member exchanges and discussions that occur.

Decertification. One immediate remedy for police misconduct is decertification, a process whereby a police agency revokes the certificates or licenses of police officers. In at least thirty-one states, peace officer standards and training boards implement decertification proceedings against officers who have been found guilty of misconduct, including abuse and unconstitutionally obtaining evidence against citizen suspects. Officers who have been decertified by these boards cannot work as police officers again until they are recertified (Goldman and Puro, 1987).

"Front-End" Solutions to Police Misconduct. Schmidt (1985) describes some of the more common methods used by police departments to minimize or prevent the hiring of officers who are unfit for police work and who are likely to engage in misconduct. These methods include the following:

1. Administering psychological tests to ferret out sadists, depressives, and other unqualified police applicants.
2. Use of training programs that go well beyond state-mandated levels.
3. Upgrading firearms training and awareness.
4. Hiring police legal advisers.

KEY TERMS

Blue curtain
Civilian complaint review boards
Deadly force
Defense-of-life standard
Dropsy testimony
Excessive force
FLETC model
Force continuum

Graft
Internal affairs
Police brutality
Police misconduct
Perjury
Section 1983 actions
Tennessee v. Garner (1985)

QUESTIONS FOR REVIEW

1. What is police misconduct? What are some other terms that have been used for police misconduct?
2. Give some examples of police misconduct. In your view, which forms of police misconduct are most serious?
3. Why is it important to study police misconduct?
4. What is meant by "unwritten codes of conduct"? What is meant by the "blue curtain"?
5. What are the four types of police officer misconduct established by David Carter?
6. What is the significance of the Knapp Commission and the report it delivered?
7. What is meant by "dropsy testimony"? Why is this phenomenon important to particular criminal defendants? How and why did it originate?
8. What are the conditions giving rise to the use of excessive force by police officers?
9. What is meant by hot pursuit? How is hot pursuit considered excessive or even deadly force?
10. What is a force continuum? Briefly describe FLETC.
11. What is the fleeing felon rule? Is it used today? Why or why not? What is the leading case involving the rule? What was the significance of this case?
12. How do police officers rationalize their misconduct? Indicate several mechanisms that police use for this purpose.
13. What are internal affairs and civilian complaint review boards? What are their respective functions?
14. What are some pros and cons regarding citizen complaint review boards?

SUGGESTED READINGS

del Carmen, Rolando V. (1991). *Civil Liabilities in American Policing: A Text for Law Enforcement Personnel.* Englewood Cliffs, NJ: Prentice Hall.

Geller, William A., and Michael Scott (1992). *Deadly Force: What We Know—A Practitioner's Desk Reference on Police-involved Shootings.* Washington, DC: Police Executive Research Forum.

Kappeler, Victor E., Richard D. Sluder, and Geoffrey P. Alpert (1992). *Forces of Deviance: Understanding the Dark Side of Policing.* Prospect Heights, IL: Waveland Press.

Scrivner, Ellen M. (1994). *The Role of Police Psychology in Controlling Excessive Force.* Washington, DC: National Institute of Justice.

CHAPTER 8

Ethnicity, Race, and Law Enforcement

Introduction

From Columbus to the Present

Race, Ethnicity, and Crime

Selective Law Enforcement and Racial Inequality
Tourism and Crime

Forms of Discrimination
Physical Forms

Mechanisms for Controlling Discriminatory Discretion

Forces in the Push for Minority Hiring
Black Police Officer Associations
The LEAA
Hiring and Retention

Political Policy, the Police, and the Community
Conservative vs. Liberal Policing Ideals

Key Terms

Questions for Review

Suggested Readings

Appendix

INTRODUCTION

The ideals of community-oriented policing dictate that the police should not only interact with the community but, as a service group, should understand the cultural dynamics of the communities they serve. For police departments to fully represent and be responsive to the multitude of cultures in our communities, they must learn multiethnics. Multiethnics is simply the study and appreciation of cultures (i.e., mores, traditions, and customs) other than our own.

Many police officers cannot tell the difference among persons of Vietnamese, Cambodian, Chinese, Korean, and Japanese heritage. Similarly, few know the difference between Armenians and Iranians. This ignorance, however, is not the sole province of policing agencies. Americans have over the years, through education, institutions, and socialization, distanced themselves from ethnic groups other than their own. This distancing has been compounded by ethnic groups banding together in certain regions and neighborhoods. Ethnologists offer a host of valid reasons why they cluster. But regardless of the causal factors, cultural isolation causes suspicion, misunderstanding, myths, and ignorance. Education is the key to societal change but multicultural education in our elementary and secondary schools has its opponents. Even though classes in multicultural education could help abate hate crimes, destroy myths, and overcome blatant racism, there are powerful and organized detractors.

Enforcement agencies cannot support or give preferential treatment to one culture at the expense of another. Cultural awareness is one step toward knowledgeable and sensitive police-community interactions. Most Americans have been taught and believe that they live in a pluralistic society—a "gorgeous mosaic," in the words of former New York City Mayor David Dinkins. But U.S. Bureau of Census data suggest that the demographic surface of life in the United States is a lot smoother than the term "mosaic" might infer.

For most of its history the United States has been receptive to European immigrants. This willingness brought countless nineteenth-century voyagers from the Old World pursuing the uniquely egalitarian shelter of a New World so different from Europe's rigidly structured nation-states. But in 1798 Congress raised the residency requirement for citizenship from five to fourteen years, largely to exclude political refugees from Europe who raised nationalistic fears that they might foment revolution. Later, some states imposed taxes on alien ship passengers they thought might become public charges and burdens. Such nativist sentiments were given new intensity after the Civil War as the economic depression of the time raised fears that cheap foreign labor might take American jobs. There was also the openly racist argument that some newcomers, especially Asians, because of their culture and language differences, simply could not be assimilated. Accordingly, in 1882 Congress passed the **Chinese Exclusion Act,** imposing a head tax and excluding whole categories of people—convicts and the mentally ill, for example. For the first time there were real limits on immigration. Twelve years later, a group called the Immigration Restriction League adopted the pseudoscience of eugenics to contend that breeding from "inferior stock" would fatally weaken America.

After World War I there were fears that millions of displaced Europeans, newly influenced by Bolshevism, would infect America with an alien ideology. As a result, a series of racism-tainted national-origins laws passed during the 1920s established an annual immigration quota of 150,000 that favored established groups like the Germans and the Irish. Some nationalities, notably the Japanese, were excluded entirely. The national-origins system used to establish quotas was preserved in the 1952 McCarran-Walter Act, although that notorious law did establish minuscule quotas—100 or so a year—for such previously barred groups as Indians and Filipinos.

Underlying these laws was the belief that preserving America's ethnic mix as it existed in 1920 was politically and culturally desirable. After World War II the quotas were relaxed only to allow in politically favored groups, such as the 38,000 Hungarians who fled the 1956 Soviet crackdown. Inspired by former President Lyndon Johnson's Civil Rights Act, Congress in 1965 at last ended the national-origins system and opened America's door to the Third World. The **1980 Refugee Act** radically expanded the definition of those eligible for political asylum, but because it has been poorly enforced and easily abused, it helped bring on today's growing demand for new limits on aliens. Still, for the first time in history, the United States has an immigration policy that, for better or worse, is truly democratic (Elson, 1993).

FROM COLUMBUS TO THE PRESENT

From a somewhat different approach, consider that a total of eight nationalities were represented on Columbus's first voyage to a continent that eventually received its name from a German mapmaker. Fifty-eight million Americans, out of a total population of 248 million, claim German ancestry. In second place are 38 million who say they are wholly or partly Irish. Those of English ancestry come in third, at 32 million, followed by African Americans, at 23 million. Hispanics are the seventh largest ancestry group, at 11 million. The largest ethnic group—nearly one-quarter of the U.S. population—is the least visible, a template of assimilation (Brookhiser, 1993:72). However, others who do not place a premium on assimilation at the expense of cultural heritage and identify suggest that those of German ancestry are much more able to blend into a "mosaic" that is predominately white. Hispanics and African Americans bring a different hue to the pattern, quite distinguishable, and are often subjected to less than equal status by the majority. In our society's institutions, and especially its criminal justice system, there seem to be some striking inequities.

During the 1980s the nation absorbed more than 8.6 million newcomers, mostly from Asia, Latin American, and the Caribbean. This was the largest influx since the last great wave of American immigration in the 1920s, when the nation's economy was booming. The increase in immigrants between 1980 and 1990 represents a 63 percent increase over the decade before. Although two-thirds of the immigrants went to just five states—California, New York, Texas, Florida,

BOX 8.1 Immigrants and the Law

A brief historical overview of eleven immigrant groups may help to put **cultural diversity** into perspective.

Africa. One-fifth of the population of the United States at the time of George Washington's inauguration in 1789 was African American.

British Isles. The English, Welsh, Scots, and Scotch-Irish formed a steady influx from Colonial times. More familiar with the language and customs than others, they assimilated easily and dominated America's industrial and political leadership.

Eastern Europe. The terrible pogroms of czarist Russia inspired more than 2 million Jews to seek asylum in the United States between 1881 and 1914. In 1900 fully one-third of these newcomers were employed by the garment trades.

Sweden. Nearly 1.2 million Swedes immigrated to the United States between 1851 and 1930. In 1900 Chicago had more Swedes (145,000) than any city but Stockholm. Today about 400 place names in Minnesota are of Scandinavian origin.

India. The vast majority of immigrants from India and its neighbors came after 1965, when national quotas were lifted. The largest number live in California or near New York City, where many have flourished in the field of medicine.

Mexico. Known by more labels than any other ethnic or national group, Mexican Americans are variously called Tejano, Latino, Hispano, Chicano, and Mexicano, depending on where they live and from whence they came.

Ireland. Ireland has produced the second largest immigrant group. Some 210,000 Irish fought during the Civil War, with 170,000 of them on the Union side. The Irish have deeply influenced U.S. big-city politics and the Roman Catholic Church, and they now rank among the most affluent Americans. As a group, the Irish dominated and influenced East Coast policing for more than 100 years (1840–1950).

Germany. Historically, Germans were the single largest additive to the melting pot, so that by 1990 nearly one-quarter of Americans identified themselves as being at least part German.

Greece. The New World's farm life differed so much from their own that most Greek immigrants became city dwellers, often peddling from pushcarts or running cafes. In Florida, many used to dive for sponges.

Italy. With their strong family ties, Italian immigrants early formed their own neighborhoods, many of which still flourish. Today, "Italian" is synonymous with good food, high fashion, and design.

China. By the 1870s Chinese immigrants made up three-quarters of San Francisco's woolen-mill workers and 90 percent of its cigar makers. They also worked gold mines, although ownership of the mines was limited by law (Elson, 1993). From the time Chinese Forty-Niners joined the California Gold Rush, Asians have tended to see America in terms of the old Cantonese name for San Francisco: Gao Gam Saan (Old Gold Mountain). Harassment of the newcomers, coupled with openly racist citizenship and immigration laws, encouraged the impulse to get ahead financially without bothering about assimilation into the mainstream society. Politics was something to be avoided, perhaps following the old Far Eastern maxim, "The nail that sticks out gets hammered down" (Walsh, 1993:29).

Middle East. Most of the immigrants from the Arab world were Christians rather than Muslims, until recent years. Culturally diverse, many began as peddlers strung across the United States, whereas others opened family businesses in dry goods and groceries.

Source: James Walsh, "The Perils of Success," *Time,* September 14, 1993:29; John Elson, "The Great Migration," *Time,* June 6, 1993:41.

and New Jersey—their sheer numbers have had an impact everywhere, even in remote communities. Thirty-four states saw their foreign-born populations increase during the last ten years (Loeb et al., 1993:47). In a *U.S. News & World Report* study conducted to develop a profile of immigrants who arrived between 1980 and 1990, findings regarding the top 30 countries of origin were the following (Loeb et al., 1993:49):

- Contrary to popular opinion, immigrants do not rob citizens of jobs but either expand employment niches or take jobs few Americans want.
- Most newcomers do not rely on welfare. Though public assistance increased much faster for a few immigrant groups than for citizens, overall only about 4 percent of new immigrants received welfare aid.
- Although only 20 percent of recent immigrants boast incomes higher than an average U.S. citizen's, they catch up. After a decade in this county, immi-

Tourism in Florida has been adversely affected by carjackings and violence; some citizens have reacted by wearing weapons for self-protection. *(Raul Demolina, AP/Wide World Photos)*

grants on average took home salaries comparable to those of nonimmigrant Americans.
- There is no significant difference in political opinions between immigrants and American-born citizens. Although immigrants are more likely to register as independents, immigrants and native-born citizens hold nearly identical beliefs on issues such as crime and welfare, as a comparison of polling data from the University of Chicago shows.

Certainly some communities are more burdened by immigrants than others. California, for instance, expected to pay nearly $300 million during 1993 just in welfare payments for children of illegal aliens. The picture some Americans get of immigration can be summed up in one word: Mexicans. They constitute a quarter of the newcomers, and their numbers in the United States doubled in the 1980s to 4.3 million. Any examination of immigration trends is necessarily skewed by the predominately low educational and income levels of Mexican immigrants.

The Mexican factor masks the true effect of immigration nationwide, however. Except for California, Texas, New Mexico, Arizona, and Illinois, most states have more immigrants of other nationalities (Loeb et al., 1993:51). Detroit is home to some 200,000 Arabs. The top destination choice for Puerto Ricans, who are U.S. citizens, is Hartford, Connecticut. Forty years ago, a poor economy at home brought Puerto Rican laborers to Connecticut's tobacco farms. In the 1980s, another economic downturn on the island added nearly 10,000 Puerto Ricans to Hartford. Nearly 6,000 Hmong refugees live in the Milwaukee area. They are descendants of a primitive tribe from Laos, and many Hmong fought for the United States during the Vietnam War. Of the 90,000 Hmong counted in the 1990 Census, one in five had settled in Wisconsin (Glastris, 1993:49). Émigrés from the former Soviet Union, mostly Jewish refugees entitled to special preference under U.S. immigration laws, total 40,000 in the Hollywood, California, area. They are joined by Hispanics, who make up 36 percent of Hollywood's population (Guttman, 1993:52). The East Flatbush neighborhood in New York City was the choice of immigrants from Trinidad, Jamaica, and other Caribbean countries. In 1993 more than half the neighborhood's 140,000 blacks were Caribbean immigrants (Loeb, 1993:53). The state of Florida has accepted 176,000 Cuban and Haitian refugees since 1975 (Loeb et al., 1993:53). In Fairfax County, Virginia, the school system distributes information in five languages, including Farsi. In one elementary school, students were asked how many spoke a foreign language at home. Educators counted 80 different languages (Loeb et al., 1993:54).

RACE, ETHNICITY, AND CRIME

> Xenophobia: An unreasonable fear or hatred of foreigners or strangers or of that which is foreign or strange. (*Random House Webster's College Dictionary*, 1991:1541)

It is difficult to discuss "black" crime or "Hispanic" crime without being accused of being a racist. One thing holds true: Crime is an equal opportunity employer, and racism is color blind.

The following article, "We Must Acknowledge Racism Is Color Blind," was written by Walter Williams, an African American syndicated columnist and an economics professor at George Mason University in Fairfax, Virginia. It appeared in the *Orange County Register* opinion section on December 15, 1993, page 9:

> Colin A. Ferguson's rampage, killing five New York commuter passengers and wounding 20 others, proves whites don't have a monopoly on racism. If civil-rights ministers are to keep whatever remaining modicum of rapidly diminishing credibility they still have, they must roundly condemn both Ferguson's racist behavior and his apologists. So far, I have not heard civil-rights organizations calling a press conference to do that. You can bet the rent money that, had a white person committed similar mayhem in Harlem, it would be show time for the likes of Al Sharpton, Jesse Jackson, and Benjamin Chavis.
>
> The liberal news media couldn't hide this act of racism as they've hidden other acts of barbaric black racism, such as: In July 1988, Danny Gilmore was driving his pickup truck through a black neighborhood in Cleveland. He had a minor accident

BOX 8.2 Countries of Origin for U.S. Immigrants

A 1990 U.S. immigrant census profile identified immigrants by country of origin (COA) and most popular area (MPA) to settle in (*U.S. News & World Report*, 1993:51). They were:

COA	MPA
Mexico	Santa Ana, CA
Philippines	National City, CA
Puerto Rico	Hartford, CT
El Salvador	Koreatown, Los Angeles, CA
Vietnam	Monterey Park, CA
China	Chinatown, New York City
Korea	Koreatown, Los Angeles, CA
India	Fairfax City, VA
Cuba	Hialeah, FL
Dominican Republic	Washington Heights, New York City
Taiwan	Arcadia, CA
Jamaica	East Flatbush, New York City
Japan	Torrance, CA
Guatemala	Hollywood, CA
Colombia	Kendall, FL
Laos	Fresno, CA
Haiti	North Miami, FL
Former U.S.S.R.	Hollywood, CA
Nicaragua	South Miami, FL
Canada	Pinellas County, FL
Poland	Chicago, IL
Iran	Glendale, CA
Cambodia	Long Beach, CA
England	Fairfax County, VA
Peru	Kendall, FL
Guyana	East Flatbush, New York City
Honduras	South Miami, FL
Hong Kong	Monterey Park, CA
Ecuador	Fresno, CA
Thailand	Jackson Heights, New York City

It is difficult for most citizens to distinguish between illegal and legal immigrants, as there are more similarities than differences (religion, language, and culture) and there exists a tendency for all people to stereotype. This tendency to cluster brings with it several distasteful consequences, from a law enforcement perspective. Among the most glaring are the Immigration and Naturalization Service "sweeps" of individuals who *only* because of their physical attributes are suspect. The "illegal" or "undocumented" problem, often not fully addressed by the various levels of government, is passed off to the public enforcement sector. Thus, the situation becomes a "police problem," and the police have no remedies or solutions other than to try to stem the tide. Some departments, dedicated to providing equal protection, publish bilingual community crime prevention newspapers and bulletins.

An informal 1993 survey of Orange County, California, by the *Los Angeles Times* revealed that of that county's 2.4 million residents, 564,828 were Latinos and 240,756 were Asians. According to census data, Asian residents more than doubled from 1980 to 1990, while the Latino population nearly doubled. These census figures also showed that of the 2.2 million Orange County residents over five years old, nearly one in three spoke a language other than English at home. Of those, more than half said they spoke English poorly. In 1993 comparatively few police officers in Orange County said they spoke Spanish, Vietnamese, or other languages reflective of the population.

Department	Spanish Speakers	Vietnamese Speakers	Total Officers	Note
Anaheim	40	0	351	1 German
Brea	3	0	83	
Buena Park	11	0	86	
Costa Mesa	6	0	138	
Cypress	6	0	53	1 Chinese
Fountain Valley	5	0	62	
Fullerton	14	0	160	
Garden Grove	10	3	166	1 Korean
Huntington Beach	17	1	229	3 sign
Irvine	6	0	120	
Laguna Beach	7	0	46	
La Habra	7	0	62	
La Palma	1	0	24	1 Danish
Los Alamitos	2	0	24	
Newport Beach	12	0	150	
Orange	21	1	139	
Placentia	5	0	52	

San Clemente*	8	0	49	
Santa Ana	91	2	400	3 Korean; 1 Samoan
Seal Beach	2	0	35	
Tustin	10	0	89	
Westminster	6	2	96	1 German
Orange County Sheriff	102	4	1,264	4 German, 2 Japanese, 2 French, 1 Farsi, 1 Korean, 1 Slavic, 1 Arabic, 2 sign
	392	13	3,878	

*Since this survey the San Clemente Police Department has been disbanded (in 1993). The city currently contracts for law enforcement with the Orange County Sheriff's Department. San Clemente's law enforcement personnel were absorbed into the Sheriff's Department.

Source: David Reyes, "Language a Barrier to Rescuers." *Los Angeles Times,* January 17, 1993:B16.

with a moped rider and was set upon and beaten by a group of roughly 40 blacks. When he collapsed on the street, one of them drove Gilmore's truck over him, fatally crushing his skull, to the cheers of the mob. In January 1991, Robert Herbert and three other blacks agreed that they would kill the first white person they saw. Mark Belmore, a white student at Northwestern University, had the bad luck. He was stabbed to death. In February, 1991, Christopher Peterson was arrested for murdering seven white people with a shotgun. He explained his actions by saying "he had a deep-rooted hatred for white people."

According to Department of Justice statistics, when whites commit violent crimes, blacks are their victims 2.4 percent of the time; however, blacks choose white victims more than 50 percent of the time. Blacks murder whites twice as often as whites murder blacks. Black-on-white gang robberies are 52 times greater than white-on-black. Black men rape white women 30 times more than white men rape black women.

Blacks are the primary victims of violent crime. Pick up a newspaper in cities like New York, Philadelphia, Detroit, and Los Angeles. You won't see a day pass without one black being murdered—and that's on a good day. But the interracial aspect of crime is especially socially devastating. It not only destroys racial good will, but it contributes to a rising pile of racial kindling awaiting a racial arsonist to set it ablaze.

There's a world of evidence that multi-ethnic societies are inherently unstable. We need only to witness the recent history of Bosnia, Nigeria, Sri Lanka, Lebanon, and others to see that. We risk similar conflict unless we quickly summon the courage to speak openly and honestly about our racial problems. We must condemn a president, and other politicians, who see the Ferguson carnage as a gun-control problem. When the Ku Klux Klan was murdering blacks, I don't recall our treating it as a gun-and-rope problem. We rightly saw it as racism. Those grossly ignorant academics, media people, and politicians who announce that blacks cannot be racists because they have no power must be condemned. All racial double standards must be eliminated immediately.

The primary burden for racial openness and honesty lies with blacks. But whites bear a major burden as well. As Senator Bill Bradley, D.–N.J., said in a 1991 letter to President Bush, "We will never come to grips with the problems of our cities . . . until a white person can talk about the epidemic of minority illegitimacy, drug addiction, and homicide without being called a racist."

Many Americans regard crime in terms of **ethnocentricity.** Although not many people speak of "white crime," criminal offenses such as counterfeiting, embezzlement, fraud, and swindles have been characterized as nonviolent "white-collar crime," with a not-too-subtle racial connotation. A mention of the Mafia or Costa Nostra immediately implies "Italian crime" just as the words *Tong Wars* connote a Chinese connection. Today, the mention of cocaine importation and associated drug-related crime brings Colombian nationals under scrutiny and automatic suspicion. The practice of stereotyping and placing labels on categories of persons with common traits is often erroneous, divisive, and destructive.

What many Americans have come to regard as "black crime" has compounded the overall fear of crime and has polarized urban communities. National census figures from 1990 reveal that African Americans constitute approximately 12.4 percent of our population. For U.S. Bureau of the Census indices of our criminal justice system—victims, offenders, prisoners, and arrests by the police—the rates for African Americans are disproportionate to their share of the population. African American men and women accounted for 47 percent of the individuals awaiting trial in local jails or serving short terms in 1990 (Hacker, 1992:180). They also comprised 39.28 percent of the prisoners under sentence of death and 38.69 percent of those executed (Hacker, 1992). African Americans comprised 32.5 percent of the federal prison population in 1990 (Hacker, 1992). When combined with state prison populations, they made up 45.3 percent of prisoners. Overall, in 1990 more than a million African Americans were behind bars or could be returned there for violating probation or parole (Hacker, 1992:180). In 1990 the **Sentencing Project,** a Washington-based nonprofit group, reported that 23 percent of African American men between the ages of 18 to 25 were in jail, on probation, or on parole on any given day. For whites, the figure was 6.2 percent; for Hispanics, 10.4 percent. Those figures reflected, in part, the effects of newly toughened drug laws that have caused a fivefold increase in state and federal prison populations since 1973. The drug laws affected African Americans disproportionately. Though African Americans made up 15 percent of all monthly drug users, they accounted for 37 percent of

Recruitment policies in most police departments have changed so that increasing numbers of minorities are performing officer roles. *(Phyllis Graber Jensen/Stock, Boston)*

drug-possession arrests; once caught, they were more likely than whites to do time (Cose, 1993:30).

Other studies also have found disproportionate representation. The *Dallas Times Herald* discovered that murder or rape of whites in Dallas County, Texas, was punished more severely than similar assaults on African Americans. The *San Jose Mercury News* found that whites in California received better plea bargains than did African Americans and Hispanics accused of comparable crimes. A number of scholars have concluded that African Americans who murder whites are much more likely to receive the death penalty than those who murder African Americans. Charles Ogletree of Harvard Law School cites statistics showing that African Americans are ten times more likely than whites to be shot at by police, and he argues that police in urban areas target minorities for searches. Such assertions have been challenged, but they coincide with the prevailing view in many neighborhoods (Cose, 1993:30).

The following statistics indicate the percentage of arrests of African Americans during a one-year period in relation to their share of the general population.

Selected Offense Arrest Rates by Race (1990)

Crimes	African American (% of all arrests)	Disproportion Rate (based on share of population)
Robbery	61.2	5.1
Murder and Manslaughter	54.7	4.5
Gambling	47.5	3.9
Rape	43.2	3.6
Receiving Stolen Property	41.2	3.4
Vagrancy	40.8	3.4
Drug Violations	40.7	3.4
Weapons Possession	39.8	3.3
Prostitution	38.9	3.2
Motor Vehicle Theft	38.4	3.2
Aggravated Assault	38.4	3.2
Forgery and Counterfeiting	34.0	2.8
Disorderly Conduct	32.4	2.7
Embezzlement	32.1	2.7
Domestic Violence	30.3	2.5
Burglary	30.1	2.5
Vandalism	22.6	1.9
Curfew and Loitering	17.7	1.5
Driving While Intoxicated	8.7	0.9

Source: Federal Bureau of Investigation, *Uniform Crime Reports, 1990*. Washington, DC: U.S. Government Printing Office.

The phrase *black crime* does not conjure up offenses of tax evasion or "white-collar" crime. "Black crime" is associated more closely with crimes of violence. As the table shows, although African Americans comprise approximately 12 percent of the population, they account for 61.2 percent of all robbery arrests, and they include over half of the suspects arrested for wrongful deaths. In aggregate, African American arrest rates are disproportionate for every offense except drunken driving. Moreover, what has come to be described as "black crime" also has African Americans as victims, especially in cases of wrongful death.

Research has suggested that most violent crimes are intraracial. An article in *Ebony* magazine once said that more African Americans were killed by other African Americans in the single year of 1977 in urban America than were killed altogether during the Vietnam War, which spanned a nine-year period. A total of 5,711 African Americans died in that conflict, whereas 5,734 were killed by other

African Americans at home (Kirk, 1982). FBI statistics of 1992 underscore the intraracial nature of murder (Cose, 1994:23):

Homicide Victims

Black	11,175
White	10,645
All races	23,760
Blacks slain by blacks	94%
Whites slain by whites	83%

SELECTIVE LAW ENFORCEMENT AND RACIAL INEQUALITY

There exists an enforcement and protection dichotomy that resists easy solutions. We have extremely high rates of victimization involving African American citizens coupled with high rates of criminal activity within predominately African American communities. It would appear that the criminal cohort is larger in the African American population than in the general population. Even this analysis smacks of separatism by placing African Americans in a class or social category. But carrying the argument further, if the police are seeking an African American perpetrator, all African Americans who approximate the general description immediately become suspect. This practice does not, with the same intensity, hold for any other race, especially Caucasians. On another level, in certain geographical regions African Americans victimizing other African Americans is not considered a pressing problem worthy of being addressed by local protective agencies.

Tourism and Crime

The tourist angle—not the mayhem itself—has triggered international media interest at times. Surprisingly, only one-tenth of 1 percent of the 41 million visitors to the state of Florida in 1992 were crime victims (Duffy, 1993:41), but when foreign visitors became crime victims the events became **cause celebre.** Such events, although somewhat isolated, allowed Europeans and Japanese to note once again that Americans live in a weird, gun-crazy culture. These events also allowed journalists to turn random crime into an economic story. Since Florida's $30 billion tourist trade was perhaps at stake, there was speculation that pressure from Walt Disney World and Universal Studios might be brought to bear to increase safety measures on the state's highways (Leo, 1993:18).

Unfortunately, on the heels of the murders in Florida came the killing of two foreign students in California, causing even more international furor. The shooting deaths of Takuma Ito and Go Matsuura, both nineteen years old, caused President Bill Clinton to express his condolences to Japanese Prime Minister Morihiro Hosokawa. On March 25, 1994, two Japanese students studying at Marymount University were shot in the back of the head and killed during a robbery and carjacking in San Pedro, a Los Angeles suburb. Immediately after the incident U.S. dignitaries rushed to reassure frantic parents and to counter charges that Southern California is a gun-infested danger zone. Headlines in the Japanese press decried America's fascination with guns, and Japanese exchange students throughout Southern California suddenly became more cautious and fearful about this foreign land (Moffat and Cekola, 1994:A1). Los Angeles Mayor Richard Riordan called a news conference with the Japanese consul general, hoping to assuage the alarm of tourism officials in Japan. More than 3 million Japanese tourists and students were said to visit the United States each year, about one in six of them bound for Los Angeles County. The number of Japanese students in the United States jumped from 17,000 in 1983 to a peak of nearly 58,000 in 1990, aided by the strong yen, but slipped to approximately 40,000 during 1993. Los Angeles area tourism officials expressed concerns about the impact the slayings would have on the flow of nearly 500,000 Japanese who reportedly visited Los Angeles County annually. The killings in Los Angeles, which sparked renewed outrage locally and abroad and which were widely covered by the Japanese news media, fed a longstanding Japanese perception that the United States is a dangerous place.

The shooting deaths of Japanese students in Baton Rouge, Louisiana, in 1992 (Moffat and Cekola, 1994:A26) and the case of two Japanese who were shot to death at a commuter train station in Concord (in Northern California) in August 1993 (Johnson, 1994:B11) also raised international alarm. These tragic events were covered by the Japanese press as continuing evidence of the ruthlessness of America's "Gun Society" (Moffat and Cekola, 1994:A26).

Foreign speculation that Los Angeles is not a safe haven certainly seems to have merit. According to the Los Angeles County Sheriff's Department Cargo Criminal Apprehension Team, or "Cargo cats," thieves steal $1 million worth of cargo every day from trucks and truck terminals in Southern California. An average of five financial institutions were robbed in Southern California each business day of 1993. Southern California is still known as the bank robbery capital of the nation (Lee, 1994:D1). During 1993 Los Angeles Police Department statistics revealed that 1,100 homicides, 1,855 rapes, 39,227 robberies, and 65,541 car thefts were reported (Wallace, 1994:A8), and there is no way to accurately measure *unreported* crime.

In the aftermath of the Japanese student killings, California Governor Pete Wilson urged the state legislature to reconsider a law calling for the death penalty for those who commit murder during a carjacking (Martinez, 1994:A25). On March 30, 1994, only six days after the Matsuura and Ito killings, Chief of Police Willie Williams of the Los Angeles Police Department announced the arrest of two prime suspects (Hubler, 1994:A1). The slayings of the Japanese students were only two of twenty-five homicides during that weekend in Los Angeles County (Hubler, 1994:A12), but the intense diplomatic pressure and international media coverage apparently aided in causing prompt police action and quick arrests. Less than a month later, on April 15, 1994, Kouichi Takemoto, a Japanese college student attending National College in Denver, Colorado, was shot in the chest and seriously wounded in a carjacking. The car was found abandoned in suburban Aurora later in the day (Associated Press, 1994:A31).

Some activists suggest that economic sanctions against the United States in the form of travel advisories might bring pressure to bear to stem crime. Threatening the $70 billion foreign tourism industry has a way of concentrating the mind (Alter, 1993:42) and bringing about change. Apparently it is not until random violence causes a perceived loss in revenue (tourist dollars) that attention is given and meaningful investigations are started. Similarly, without economic loss, the urban intraracial slaughter apparently will not raise much concern. There are not significant economic losses when lives are taken in our urban areas—only the loss of human life. The toll can be measured in the degree of human misery, loss of dignity, lack of protection, family disruption, social and community disorganization, and psychological depression manifested in hostility and outrage. The ominous specter of inequality is once again underscored. Tourists may become a "protected class" and receive preferential treatment while local residents wonder about the value and quality of *their* lives. If public safety for all people within our borders is not high on the political agenda, and if "money talks," then perhaps as a concerned society we should examine and consider other viable forms of pressure.

For years Florida has suffered the highest overall crime rate of any state in the union and the highest rate of violent crime. In 1992 more than eight of every 100 residents were crime victims. About one-seventh of the victims suffered horribly; they were murdered, raped, robbed, or assaulted (Duffy, 1993:41). During the 1980s Miami ghettos had their share of urban racial disturbances. In 1980 Miami's Liberty City erupted after a white jury acquitted four white policemen in the beating death of an African American businessman. The toll came to eighteen dead and $100 million in damage. In 1982 two died and many were injured in Miami's Overtown when a Cuban police officer killed a young African American man. In 1989 riots broke out after a Hispanic officer killed a fleeing black suspect (Duffy, 1993:42). In each case the catalyst was police action perceived to be unequal and racist.

FORMS OF DISCRIMINATION

Physical Forms

A 1993 FBI study based on information supplied by law enforcement agencies in thirty-two states examined 4,558 hate-crime incidents reported in 1991. The study found that racial bias motivated six of ten offenses reported, religious bias two of ten, and both ethnic and sexual-orientation biases one of ten. According to the FBI's classifications, African Americans were the targets of most bias attacks (36 percent), followed by whites (19 percent) and Jews (17 percent). The bureau's report is far from definitive, as only about 3,000 of the 16,000 plus law enforcement agencies elected to participate. That may be the survey's most telling statistic, because it suggests that local law enforcement officials need to develop greater sensitivity toward bias offenses (*Time*, 1993:22).

One example: Joe Morgan, Hall of Famer and former second baseman for the Cincinnati Reds, filed an excessive force lawsuit against the Los Angeles

Police Department in 1988. In November 1993 the Los Angeles City Council agreed to pay Morgan $796,000 to settle the claim. During a campaign against drug trafficking at the Los Angeles airport, police had arrested a suspected drug courier and were looking for an accomplice. Morgan argued that, in the course of that investigation, the police roughed him up because he was black (*U.S. News & World Report,* 1993a:18).

MECHANISMS FOR CONTROLLING DISCRIMINATORY DISCRETION

To empower police officers to accomplish their tasks under community-oriented policing (COP) they must be given wider latitude in discretionary matters. Traditionalists who oppose this idea want to return to or maintain the quasi-military "professional" model in which hard-nosed leaders limit individual officers' discretion.

Under COP, discretion must be applied and distributed evenly. Training, education, and trust help to promote equity and alleviate discriminatory practices. Regardless of the style of leadership, police officers do exercise discretion in that they can opt to invoke or not invoke the process of justice. Such discretionary decisions are not generally documented, however, because to document every discretionary action would render enforcement officers helplessly mired in reams of paper. It is hoped that discretionary decisions are based on nonjudgmental factors such as intent, harm, prevention, and learning and not on race, religion, gender, or sexual orientation. Should peers or supervisors detect patterns of uneven exercise of discretion, they have a responsibility to bring those unjust actions forward for accountability. Ideally, abuses of discretion should be handled internally before external pressures are brought to bear through the complaint process.

FORCES IN THE PUSH FOR MINORITY HIRING

Black Police Officer Associations

In 1968, shortly after the riots that followed the assassination of Martin Luther King and after Chicago Mayor Richard Daley's famous "shoot to kill" order, the Chicago Afro-American Patrolman's League (AAPL) was formed. During the 1980s the AAPL successfully challenged the Chicago Police Department's hiring and promotional practices and won a federal court order mandating the hiring of one black or Hispanic officer for each white officer added to the force. AAPL also keeps its own watch on police-community relations, turning in more than 1,000 citizen complaints of police brutality or abuse to the department's internal affairs division each year (Cory, 1979:5).

The **National Black Police Officers Association** was formed in 1971 and the National Organization of Black Law Enforcement Executives (NOBLE) was formed in 1976. Another such group, the Guardians, New York City's African American fraternal police association, supported former Mayor John Lindsay's short-lived police civilian review board. The move was denounced by the city's Patrolmen's Benevolent Association as evidence that black officers "have put their color ahead of their duty as police officers" (Cory, 1979:6). Several other police departments across the nation have chartered organizations that address the problems of black police officers. For example, there is an all-black Dallas chapter of the Texas Peace Officers Association.

The LEAA

Probably the most significant impetus for the recruitment of minorities in law enforcement during the 1970s was the availability of federal money. In order for municipalities to receive federal grants, the requesting agencies must qualify as "equal opportunity employers." This seemingly innocuous phrase sent recruiters scouring to bring minorities on board so that cities and counties could qualify for monies under federal guidelines. Through the **Law Enforcement Assistance Administration (LEAA),** Congress earmarked millions of dollars for upgrading American law enforcement. Notably, an amendment to the 1976 appropriations bill for the federal LEAA ordered a streamlining of the LEAA's civil rights investigations. If an agency chose to reject LEAA funds rather than be investigated, LEAA's jurisdiction ended, but so did the funding.

Hiring and Retention

The rapidly changing demographic composition of American cities has brought with it new challenges for urban policing. The city of Westminster, California, for instance, serves a population that is one-quarter Vietnamese, yet only one member of the 101-officer department spoke that language in 1993. This not only hindered police work, but also led to mistrust and distance between the Asian population and the largely white police force. The city undertook a program in the early 1990s to add two Vietnamese police officers within a year. Vietnamese business leaders in the city of 70,000 believed they would profit from a more bilingual police force because officers could better understand the Vietnamese culture, and would-be criminals would face a police force with stronger investigative capabilities. But hiring Vietnamese officers was not as easy as it might have seemed. A number of Vietnamese Americans attempted to become police officers during the past several years, but they never made it through the twenty-week police academy or the six-month probation period. Much like the police force itself, unsuccessful Vietnamese candidates were hamstrung by the language barrier; they couldn't write detailed police reports, for example. Two other obstacles also faced the city in its attempt to recruit Vietnamese Americans. The first problem, according to one police representative, was that some Vietnamese had to learn to act contrary to certain cultural norms that teach them not to be overly aggressive.

The more serious obstacle was the difference in tradition between Vietnam and this country: Families of would-be officers saw police work as a violent and not particularly rewarding or prestigious profession (Heiman, 1993:3).

In an effort to bring national attention to the civil rights and legal needs of Asians, the nation's fastest growing minority, the first national civil rights group representing them was established in Washington, D.C., on May 13, 1993. The consortium embodied the nation's three oldest and largest Asian American legal groups: the Los Angeles-based Asian Pacific American Legal Center, the Asian Law Caucus in San Francisco, and the Asian American Legal Defense and Education Fund in New York. The two priority issues the consortium planned to address first were voting rights and the growing tide of anti-Asian violence. An ongoing aim of the group is to ensure that Asian legal and civil rights perspectives are considered in the development of national public policy (Kang, 1993:A34).

Along the same lines, Asian Americans in Orange County, California (representing 7.4 percent of the county population), angered by incidents of what they term discrimination and harassment, have formed a new countywide organization to battle for civil rights. The newly formed group is called AWARE, which stands for Alliance Working for Asian Rights and Empowerment. AWARE is an outgrowth of a dispute over a Fountain Valley police practice of taking photos of suspected gang members and has the stated goals of serving as a police watchdog committee. Interestingly, the goals of AWARE are not too far removed from the goals of COP (Billiter, 1993:B4):

- Seeking a state law to ban police from taking photos of people who are stopped but not arrested
- Encouraging cities in Orange County to have citizens, including Asian Americans, review and comment on police procedures
- Conducting youth outreach programs, such as summer job programs for Asian American young people
- Pushing for more ethnic diversity, including the hiring of more Asian Americans in city police departments

POLITICAL POLICY, THE POLICE, AND THE COMMUNITY

Conservative vs. Liberal Policing Ideals

As previously stated, the police are somewhat political animals and, accordingly, respond to political pressure. The mood and philosophy of city councils or other local governing bodies have the tendency to alter the direction and philosophy of local policing. These elected individuals come into public office ostensibly reflecting the current concerns of the community at large. In many cases they also play to the community's fear about crime.

Conservative Policing Ideals. Conservatives are concerned with maintaining the status quo and believe that change should be gradual. From a conservative criminal justice perspective, crime and criminal conduct are basically viewed as a result of moral failure, not lack of opportunity, absence of societal deterrents, or the failure of political factors. There is strong emphasis on reactive punishment modes of general and specific deterrence. A conservative's position generally supports more prisons, elimination of all creature comforts in confinement facilities, increased penalties, a dramatically shortened appeal process, fewer social programs, a reduction in welfare, less governmental intervention at the federal level, and the imposition and increased use of capital punishment. In relation to the function of policing, conservatives tend to support the position that the police and the criminal justice system should possess more power and latitude in dealing with criminal elements. The police and the court system should be streamlined to process cases in a speedy fashion, because "swift and sure punishment" is a cornerstone of conservative deterrence philosophy. Conservatives tend to believe that the police will be fair, just, and act in good faith in upholding and enforcing the law.

Liberal Policing Ideals. The "political left" includes those elements in the political spectrum that seek radical, innovative, and somewhat rapid change in society. The concept of socialism is a dominant "left" position. The term itself derives from the seating arrangements in European legislatures, in which the radical members sat on the presiding officer's left.

Liberalism is an ideology, a political philosophy, and a constellation of related policies aimed at social reform to increase equality and democratic participation in governance. Liberals advocate the use of state power to aid disadvantaged individuals and groups. From a criminal justice perspective, they support the position that much criminal activity has its roots in the social fabric. Liberals emphasize alternative sentencing, environmental issues, education, due process, and individual rights. Liberals generally oppose the death penalty as a legal sanction. The term *liberal* in a slightly different sense also encompasses being proactive, academic, and open-minded.

KEY TERMS

Arrest rates by race
Cause celebre
Chinese Exclusion Act
Civil Rights Institute
Civil rights movement
Conservative policing ideals
Cultural diversity
Ethnocentricity

Law Enforcement Assistance Administration (LEAA)
Liberal policing ideals
National Black Police Officers Association
1980 Refugee Act
Selective Enforcement
Sentencing Project

QUESTIONS FOR REVIEW

1. Explain the term *cultural diversity*.
2. Discuss the role of the government in regulating the flow of immigrants into the United States, including the 1980 Refugee Act.
3. What are some of the problems related to assimilation?
4. Develop an argument for the implementation of COP in a city with ethnic populations.
5. Explain the differences between the conservative and liberal ideals toward the practice of policing.
6. Discuss the impact of the international press on American policing.
7. How did the creation of LEAA help minorities to enter the field of law enforcement?

SUGGESTED READINGS

Brian C. Cryderman (1986). *Police, Race and Ethnicity: A Guide for Law Enforcement Officers.* Toronto: Butterworth and Company.

Andrew Hacker (1992). *Two Nations Black and White, Separate, Hostile, Unequal.* New York: Ballantine Books.

CHAPTER 9

The Legally Disenfranchised: Gays, Undocumented, the Homeless, and the Mentally Ill

Introduction

Socioeconomic Status and Crime
Demographics of Poverty

Gay-Bashing and Socially Approved Police Deviance
Demographics
Queer Nation
ACT-UP
The Gay Movement
 and Traditional Policing
Police and the Explorer Scout
 Controversy

The Homeless and Crime Control
Background
Police and Community Strategies
 to Deal with the Homeless
City Strategies and the Homeless
 Problem

Demographics
Santa Ana, California
Alternatives

The Mentally Ill: A Forgotten Minority
Recommendations

Drug Users and Abusers and the Police

Illegal Immigrants and Police Actions
Officer Jose Diaz Vargas

Key Terms

Questions for Review

Suggested Readings

INTRODUCTION

Long ago, a document proclaimed that "all men are created equal." Sometime thereafter, someone added, "But some are more equal than others." There are many minority groups in the United States, and the numbers are growing rapidly. Minorities are typically defined according to racial or ethnic attributes. Historically, minorities have experienced differential treatment at the hands of law enforcement. The criminal justice system is replete with disparities: selective arrests, selective prosecutions, prejudicial trials, inconsistent sentencing procedures and patterns, and early-release decision making and parole. Disparities of all kinds exist, attributable to many factors. Some factors are related to race and ethnicity, whereas others concern socioeconomic status and gender. Considerations of socioeconomic status are often closely related to race and ethnicity.

Other segments of the population also exist as minorities. These other minorities cut across racial and ethnic lines to encompass persons from all walks of life and all ages. These are the legally disenfranchised: the gays, the undocumented, the homeless, and the mentally ill. Some police misconduct is directed toward persons in these groups. Most of this misconduct is socially approved.

This chapter is about these disenfranchised persons, how they are treated by police officers, and how policy decisions of law enforcement organizations affect them. The first part of the chapter provides a socioeconomic backdrop against which each of these minorities can be viewed. This socioeconomic context is important to understand, since being poor means that vital resources are not immediately available to afford members of these minorities protection from the law, especially when it is selectively applied. Persons in the lower socioeconomic strata are not only less able to defend themselves when charged with unlawful conduct or subjected to excessive police powers; they are also in positions that alienate them from the general public and its support or empathy.

The gay rights movement is described, including societal reactions, from outright opposition and disapproval to gradual and reluctant acceptance. The exercise of police powers in this milieu are also examined. A more visible minority consists of the homeless. These persons crowd city streets at all times, begging from strangers and attempting to survive from one meal to the next. Their housing consists of alleys, front doorsteps of businesses, and abandoned or condemned buildings in slum areas. Several cities have been selected to highlight policies to deal with the homeless in various ways.

Another poorly treated minority consists of the mentally ill. Although no accurate figures exist to specify how many mentally ill persons are on city streets or in local jails, police officers and jail officials believe there are substantial numbers of mentally ill persons who are brought into the criminal justice system annually and who remain untreated. One major problem accompanying mental illness is that mentally ill persons become targets of exploitation by others. Mentally ill persons are mugged, raped, and subjected to many other forms of abuse. Police jargon currently includes *mercy bookings* of the mentally ill, because these officers reason that jail rather than city streets is a safer place for the mentally ill;

at least they will be fed and have access to minimum maintenance. The chapter concludes by investigating police interactions with the chemically dependent, drug abusers, and illegal immigrants.

SOCIOECONOMIC STATUS AND CRIME

There are several enclaves within the accepted legal community that have become targets of social neglect and public scrutiny. Many large segments of our population have not received equal protection under the law or any significant social services. Although the Fourteenth Amendment vests all persons with equal protection under the law as well as due process, certain segments of our society have not benefited from these provisions. These unprotected enclaves include the homeless, undocumented workers, and others without political or economic power. Historically, the mantle of public protection has been sparingly afforded to those not classified as in mainstream America. Although the American Dream has been equated with economic success and achievement, the dream does not exist for the less fortunate, who have not had the same opportunities to ascend the ladder of social success.

Many social and political problems have landed on police precinct doorsteps for processing. But police agencies have little or no power to alleviate the problems of social or economic inequality. Whenever urban problems arise, the police are told simply to "deal with it." Then the police, reacting to political interests and lacking guidance or direction, often "deal" with these problems in heavy-handed ways. Regardless of whether it be Tonkin Park in New York City or Union Square in San Francisco, when the police are ordered to remove homeless tents and vacate occupied premises, their tactics and the results are textbook and predictable. The media, capturing these controversial actions, seek to chronicle the events for the evening news. The police are consistently cast in the role of bad guys when they are simply enforcing local political dictates. These police actions are observed by the public who, by and large, do not understand their mandated motives. Many viewers condemn the police for their actions without comprehending the political forces that trigger them.

It is not surprising that in lower-income areas or in depressed or underclass neighborhoods and slums, the incidence of crime is high. This situation is axiomatic concerning the urban centers of the United States. Many studies have suggested that poverty and depressed neighborhoods do not automatically breed criminal conduct, but that opportunity, excitement, and avarice are the major players in promoting illegal behavior. Although criminology has identified numerous variables to explain crime, there is sufficient data to suggest that the incidence of crime (reported and nonreported) is highest in these locations. Many explanations have been offered, but one logical supposition is simply that a larger cohort of persons residing in depressed areas is prone to criminal conduct. Not all persons belong to gangs, and the majority of neighborhood residents are not engaged in illegal activities, but a relatively high percentage of persons in lower-income neighborhoods are involved in criminal activity compared with more affluent neighborhoods. A major problem for urban policing is to identify those prone to criminality and provide the remaining and overwhelming majority of law-abiding residents with police protection.

Poverty plays an important role in forming and shaping the attitudes and character of youths. If poverty precipitates criminal conduct among youths, then poverty itself must be closely scrutinized. In the United States, poverty is determined by an arbitrary measure of income level below which a family is deemed to be unable to achieve a satisfactory standard of living. Poverty data based on the official government definition were first tabulated in 1959.

Demographics of Poverty

National statistics suggest that between 1978 and 1983, the number of poor people increased by 44 percent, from 24.5 million to 35.3 million. During that same period, the poverty rate rose from 11.4 percent to 15.2 percent. From 1983 to 1988, the number of poor and the poverty rate declined slightly, although both aggregates remain well above the 1978 levels. Over half of the nation's poor in 1987 consisted of children (40 percent) and the elderly (10.7 percent). Historically, the poverty rate for persons sixty-five years and over has been higher than that for the total population. But in 1983, this relationship was reversed, and the poverty rate for the elderly remained at a record low of about 12 percent between 1983 and 1987. Although minorities are overrepresented proportionately among the poor, two out of every three poor people are white. In 1987, poverty rates were 10.5 percent for whites, 33.1 percent for African Americans, 28.2 percent for Hispanics, and 18.3 percent for others. In 1988, 61 percent of poor families were headed by a female (Cole, 1991:191).

In 1992 the number of Americans living below the federal poverty level rose 1.2 million to a three-decade high of 36.9 million. Putting these figures in perspective, 14.5 percent of Americans were classified as poor. Although the rate was only slightly higher than the 14.2 percent of 1991, it marked the highest level since the postrecession year of 1983, when it was 15.2 percent. The estimated 37 million poor represent the largest number of poor since 1963, when the total U.S. population was three-fourths of its present size. The government adjusts its poverty standard each year according to prevailing prices and inflation. In 1992, the poor were defined as individuals with incomes of $7,143 or less and a family of four with earnings of $14,335 or less. The median household income has remained steady during 1991–1992 at $30,786, which is $2,000 below the 1989 level. But sharp contrasts exist among persons by region, gender, race, and ethnic background. The typical household income for white Americans was $32,368 in 1992, compared to $22,848 for persons of Latino origin and $18,660 for African Americans. In central cities of one million or more population, household income fell by 3 percent to $26,872, while the same figure for suburban households dropped by only 1.8 percent to $40,460. A sizable gender gap on earnings was evident in 1992. Men over twenty-five years of age who held year-round full-time jobs typically had incomes of $26,766 for high school graduates and $40,381 for those with college degrees. Women with the same characteristics typically had far lower average incomes of $18,648 for high school graduates and $29,284 for college graduates (Eaton, 1993d:A19).

On December 3, 1993, the federal government offered $25 million as an incentive for cities to move ahead with initiatives to house the homeless for the winter months. The money was earmarked for "innovative programs which will be available on a nationwide basis to provide services . . . to get us through the next few months." The money was a part of $100 million in special homeless assistance approved by Congress earlier in 1993. This announcement came after the discovery November 29 of the body of a homeless woman across from **Department of Housing and Urban Development (HUD)** headquarters in Washington, D.C. HUD Secretary Henry G. Cisneros called the death of 43-year-old Yetta M. Adams an event that should shock Americans and policymakers into doing more to end homelessness nationwide (*Los Angeles Times*, 1993d:A28).

In order to be a viable philosophy, the national movement of American policing toward community-oriented policing (COP) should involve all members of our communities. Police training should include education regarding the economics and dynamics of poverty. Poverty is not a crime, and people below a certain income level should not be classified as being "more prone" to criminal conduct. There are simply large numbers of individuals and families not only attempting to compete for the American Dream but also attempting to survive on a day-to-day basis. As Abraham Lincoln once said, "God must of liked poor people, because He made so many of us."

GAY-BASHING AND SOCIALLY APPROVED POLICE DEVIANCE

With the passage of many state-mandated **hate crime** statutes and the federal hate crime reporting system, gay bashing and other discriminatory practices have created greater public awareness, understanding, and, in many cases, sympathy. It was somewhat ironic that the Federal Bureau of Investigation (FBI), the agency charged with enforcing the federal hate crime statutes, had itself discriminated for many decades against FBI agents who were also gay. The public disclosure of unequal treatment came to light in December 1993, when Attorney General Janet Reno ordered the FBI to eliminate its policy of making it difficult (if not impossible) for homosexuals to be hired. She also insisted the bureau discontinue its policy of discrimination against agents based on sexual orientation.

Until 1979 an FBI policy prohibited the hiring of known homosexuals. After that the policy was changed so that homosexual behavior made it "significantly more difficult to be hired." This policy change occurred as the result of a San Francisco federal class action suit brought by a former FBI agent, Frank Buttino, 48. Mr. Buttino was a decorated twenty-year FBI veteran who was fired from his job in 1990. In 1988 his supervisors in San Diego received an anonymous note alleging that he was gay. Special Agent Buttino denied this allegation initially, explaining later that he knew he would be fired if he told the truth. After subsequently acknowledging his homosexuality, his security clearance was cancelled. Then he was fired. The FBI claimed Buttino was fired because he lied and not because he was homosexual (*Los Angeles Times*, 1993b:A28).

On December 10, 1993, the FBI reversed its policy barring openly gay men and lesbians from its ranks. This policy change was part of an agreement to settle Buttino's class action suit. Although not admitting any wrongdoing, the FBI agreed to adopt guidelines barring future discrimination against homosexuals and to hire a lesbian applicant who was rejected for a job in 1987, again because of her alleged sexual orientation (Warren, 1993:1). The end of federal sexual discrimination in hiring may prove to be the catalyst to promote more equitable hiring statutes at state, regional, and local levels. It will also provide support to agencies interested in combating hate crimes.

Gay communities throughout the United States have figured prominently in disclosing discriminatory practices against gays and lesbians and heightening public scrutiny. As a matter of interest, every large U.S. urban area has a gay community that exerts, or is capable of exerting, a considerable amount of economic and political influence. In those cities with large gay populations, such as San Francisco, police departments and gay community representatives have commenced working together collaboratively to resolve common problems. In those cities without politically significant gay populations, gays are perceived to be at greater risk. This lack of political power in certain jurisdictions might explain why gay communities have evolved.

Demographics

We don't know the exact numbers of gay and lesbian community members, but conservative estimates are that the gay population is about 3 percent of the general population. Thus, the gay population is likely larger than the Asian-American population in the United States. For instance, a survey entitled "Overlooked Opinions" (McLeod, 1991:5) found the following:

- Gay male household incomes average $51,325, and lesbian households average $45,927. The average U.S. household income is $36,520. The total gay market is estimated at nearly $400 million.
- The largest gay and lesbian markets are in Manhattan, San Francisco, Boston, Seattle, and the Oakland/Berkeley area.
- Top industries for gays and lesbians include education, publishing, social services, finance, insurance, and medicine.
- About 60 percent of adult gays and lesbians have college diplomas, whereas only 20 percent of adult Americans have college degrees.
- More than four in ten gays and lesbians hold professional or managerial jobs.

In 1993, *The Advocate,* a gay-oriented magazine, had more than 75,000 paid subscribers. Furthermore, the latest Los Angeles edition of the Community Yellow Pages—a directory of businesses that encourage gay and lesbian clientele—is more than 200 pages thick. One marketing firm (New York-based Strub Media Group) has more than 500,000 gay and lesbian households in its database (Horovitz, 1993).

Interestingly, gay and lesbian groups have not always shared issues other than discrimination and harassment. In previous decades, radical lesbians formed an organization called the Lesbian Nation and sought to build their own communities. However, the AIDS epidemic created a cohesive bond that caused lesbians and gays to work collaboratively toward common political interests (Boxall, 1993:A26). In recent years, members of gay and lesbian communities across the United States have joined together into a highly visible economic, political, and social force. As a group they have been motivated by a denial of representation, repressive groups, and outright physical abuse. In an attempt to raise their sense of community and self-esteem, many organizations have joined in celebrating Gay Pride Day across the nation. In 1991 in New York, writer Sarah Schulman and five other women founded the group Lesbian Avengers, and more than twenty chapters have been formed subsequently in cities such as Austin, Texas, and Durham, North Carolina. In 1992 the group Lesbians in Film and TV (LIFT) was formed, with the New York branch having over 650 women on their mailing list (Boxall, 1993:A26). Gays and lesbians have collectively formed vested interest activist associations and organizations such as **ACT-UP** and **Queer Nation.** These two groups, by purpose and design, have frequently come into direct conflict with law enforcement during their collective demonstrations and acts of civil disobedience.

Queer Nation

The organization known as Queer Nation was formed in May 1990 in New York City after M–80 bombs were exploded in trash cans adjacent to a gay nightclub. A group of individuals marched down the street to protest the incident and subsequently formed a looseknit organization. Queer Nation considers itself "militant and uncompromising in the fight against homophobia in all its manifestations."

ACT-UP

ACT-UP (an acronym for AIDS Coalition to Unleash Power) is an aggressive organization expressly formed to protest the lack of governmental funding for AIDS research. ACT-UP has used disruptive tactics and occasionally has resorted to civil disobedience as a means of promoting its cause. In *U.S. News & World Report,* Larry Kramer, founder of ACT-UP, said he believes in anger and dreams of a gay movement based on the Israeli guerrilla group Irgun. Kramer said,

"They started fires. They threw bombs. They kidnapped. They assassinated. They won" (*U.S. News & World Report,* 1991:26). The tactics of this group have gained national attention and media coverage. For example, on September 1, 1991, while then President George Bush was vacationing in Kennebunkport, Maine, some 1,500 ACT-UP demonstrators marched nearby noisily but peacefully. They blew whistles and carried banners within a half mile of the President's seaside compound, where police erected barricades and massed in force to stop them. National gay-oriented publications such as *The Advocate* provide the networking to share information and generate support for a variety of causes and issues.

The Gay Movement and Traditional Policing

Many traditional police departments with traditional value systems find it particularly difficult to accept the fact that there is a large population of gay and lesbian citizens with special law enforcement needs and concerns. At different times and places, the exchanges between police departments and gay and lesbian community members have been described as vindictive, harsh, volatile, and uneven. Generally behaving as the representatives of elected officials and often reflecting popular mainstream societal norms, the police have a long record of unfriendly interaction with homosexuals as individuals and with the homosexual community generally.

The Stonewall Riots. It is somewhat ironic that police hostility toward gays and lesbians has given birth, life, and veneration to the gay movement, a movement that is directed toward achieving greater public awareness and promoting the acceptance of gay rights and lifestyles. One early morning in June 1969, the New York Police Department conducted a raid of a gay bar in Greenwich Village. A warrant stated that liquor was being sold in violation of the existing premises permit. The patrons of the bar resisted. In the ensuing melee, which became known as the **Stonewall riots,** four police officers were seriously injured, and thirteen patrons were arrested. Two more riots erupted that same week; one, the next day, involved hundreds of protesters. The Stonewall riots are regarded as the birth of the gay revolution, and the anniversary of these riots is celebrated annually by gay rights activists and civil libertarians (Rush, 1994:325).

The Police and Homophobia. Not all police departments or law enforcement personnel are homophobic. The attitudes of most professional and proactive law enforcement executives and officers have reflected considerable change toward gays and lesbians and the problems they face. A strong advocate of human rights, Chief Tom Potter of the Portland (Oregon) Police Department was the first Portland chief of police to march in uniform in the Gay Pride Parade in Portland. Also, Chief Potter has been widely praised for his work in moving the Portland Police Bureau forward with community-oriented policing (*The Rap*

Sheet, 1993). But favorable contacts between the police and the gay community have been undermined from unexpected quarters. For example, the Christian fundamentalists decry homosexuality on religious grounds and protest any open celebrations of gay and lesbian alternative lifestyles. They adamantly oppose the interaction among the gay community and governmental service agencies. Also, because of their position to deny membership to homosexuals, the Boy Scouts of America demonstrates the impact of longtime beliefs and age-old dogma contrary to gay and lesbian interests.

Police and the Explorer Scout Controversy

Many police departments have joined the international organization of Boy Scouts of America in establishing Explorer Scout chapters. The Explorer Scout program has served as a training ground for young men and women between the ages of fourteen and twenty-one seeking careers in law enforcement. **Explorer Scouts** are used in supportive positions in nonsworn and nonthreatening activities. They do not enforce the law, but they serve as auxiliaries and perform community services, freeing officers for other duties.

In 1992 the Boy Scouts of America terminated the El Cajon Police Department's Explorer program after the coordination police officer disclosed that he was gay. In response, then San Diego Police Chief Bob Burgreen severed the department's ties with the Boy Scouts of America because of its policy regarding homosexuals. Similarly, in September 1993, the Laguna Beach (California) Police Department ended its twenty-year Explorer Scout program because of the Boy Scouts policy. Chief of Police Neil J. Purcell Jr. stated, "I think it's a clear-cut case of discrimination," and added, "I took a sworn oath to protect all people's rights and I know of nothing in this state that makes it illegal to be homosexual." The police department notified the Boy Scouts that it would not comply with the policy barring homosexuals from the Explorer program. Interestingly, Laguna Beach, with a large homosexual population, is the only city in Orange County with a law prohibiting discrimination based on sexual orientation (Earnest, 1993).

Some police executives in cities and counties with large gay populations are combining their efforts with local human relations commissions to train police officers in the use of sensitivity in dealing with lesbians and gays. In 1993 the Orange County (California) Human Relations Commission presented a sixteen-minute film regarding gay assaults and other hate crimes. In the film, the Placentia, California, police chief, Manuel Ortega, said that officers need to learn about gay and lesbian issues because "the simple matter is we have a responsibility to serve all of the people." The film also included interviews with two openly gay officers from the Los Angeles Police Department. Laguna Beach's Chief Purcell stated that "the Laguna Beach department prohibits officers from using derogatory language describing gays" because "if they're allowed to say it here, they will say it in the field" (Maharaj, 1993:B5). There appears to be a conscious movement in those areas having large homosexual populations to more fully accept and involve them in the process of government and to offer them all the rites of passage. It is understandable that gays form communities, because as a group they are protected, whereas as individuals within the straight society, they are isolated, ineffective, and vulnerable.

On a larger scale, gays and lesbians might take lessons from other minority groups on how to participate in the long-term freedom struggle. "Coming out" is the first step, but learning how to contribute regularly time, energy, thought, and money—how to be part of a movement—also is crucial. Gay and lesbian communities must develop ideas and strategies regarding their mutual goals. Prejudice can be effectively combatted through public information (Dawidoff, 1993:9). Currently, the gay movement consists of several fragmented organizations, some with conflicting purposes. Until the time that a national front is established to ensure a solid political and economic base with specific purposes and goals, the gay movement's struggle for equality will not achieve that goal.

THE HOMELESS AND CRIME CONTROL

Background

The Uneven History of Homelessness. Homelessness in the United States is not a new phenomenon. The topic and concern of what to do with "tramps and hobos" was discussed at police executive meetings during the late 1890s and early 1990s (Dilworth, 1976). When President Franklin D. Roosevelt took office in the throes of the Great Depression, the issues of homelessness and the lack of gainful employment opportunities provided the focal point for his party's platform. Government programs were established to improve the quality of life and provide affordable housing. The creation of the Tennessee Valley Authority, WPA, and the Conservation Corps brought tens of thousands into the work force and enhanced their quality of life.

World War II brought the United States out of the depression through new employment in defense organizations. The redirection of resources into war production brought with it a building boom, which allowed affordable housing for a new and growing industry. After World War II many businesses redirected their production and relocated in the suburbs, leaving many city buildings vacant. The emergence of the aerospace industry and other labor-intensive industries generated new demands for affordable housing, which was eventually constructed. But when these industries either relocated, shut down, or redirected their manufacturing focus, much urban housing formerly occupied by workers became available and remained vacant, for the most part.

Urban renewal and construction, together with governmental policy, proved disastrous for many citizens who wanted or needed **affordable housing.** The price of land determined most new construction projects, and thousands of houses and apartment buildings were destroyed to make way for expensive highrises. Other housing was abolished to allow for the widespread construction of freeways and thoroughfares. This approach to urban renewal was devastating for residents of many cities, including New York City.

In his work *The Assassination of New York,* Fitch (1992) said that of New York City's 7.3 million people in 1985, one million were on welfare and three-quarters of a million were officially unemployed. At least one million more were employed on a part-time basis. He further asserted that over a single generation, America's most prominent free marketeers, such as Nelson and David Rockerfeller, Felix Rohatyn, and Citibank executives, have imposed their marketing will on New York residents. Their collective goals have been simple and monolithic: to make the land they own worth more by displacing low-rent workers and factories and replacing them with high-rent professionals and speculative office buildings. The value of real estate in New York increased from $20 billion to over $400 billion in a single generation (Fitch, 1992). Clearly the availability of low-rent housing was all but eliminated. But it would be unfair to blame private business exclusively for these problems.

Government Intervention for the Homeless. The Reagan presidency saw dramatic cuts in government-assisted funding for low-income housing, and the Bush Administration only perpetuated this policy. The demolition of low-income housing and the absence of new construction left another large void in affordable housing. Businesspeople moved into the market and bought up the

Homeless and undocumented persons pose unusual problems for police officers. "Mercy bookings" are often conducted in order to provide shelter for them. *(George Malave/Stock, Boston)*

remaining affordable houses, converting them into rentals. The profit margin was so slight on low-income housing that private contractors moved toward a more profitable market, constructing middle- and higher-income real estate. The government has employed metaphors in mounting "wars" on crime, drugs, and many other social ills, but there has yet to be a war on behalf of the homeless—largely because there's no money in it.

When government agencies do select sites for low-income housing, the opposition from local homeowners, because of their fear of lowered property values, often results in political impasses. The NIMBY (Not in My Back Yard) factor has terminated more than one real estate venture and is a substantial barrier to low-income housing in many other landlocked, economically depressed areas. The unavailability of affordable or low-income properties for purchase has left a large void in the housing market, and it has obliged many families to become a part of the renter market. Many individuals classified as first-time buyers are unable to afford high down payments, insurance, and property taxes. In times of economic depression, the lack of low-income and affordable accommodations tends to drive the numbers of homeless upward.

Police and Community Strategies to Deal with the Homeless

Community Policing and the Homeless. The relation of community-oriented policing to the homeless segment of the population is not difficult to understand. The homeless play an important role in defining the concept of community and are the cause for much political posturing regarding their exact position in the mainstream, more affluent society. Although some social researchers exclude street people from their definition of a legal community, it is difficult to ignore the homeless as an increasingly visible aggregate in need of police protection. These persons come under public scrutiny, as many homeless communities or congregations are located in urban mercantile areas. Merchants and others regard their presence as detrimental to marketing and sales. Regardless of sale or giveaway store prices, few customers want to step over or around inebriates to do their shopping. With justification, store owners are concerned with their bottom line. Whereas customers feel that shopping should be free of unwanted intrusions, street people seek to beg, panhandle, or perform menial tasks, such as wiping windows, for gratuities. As Finn (1988:2) suggests, "Even the most docile street people generate repulsion and fear among many residents, shoppers and commuters. The prospect of being accosted by a drunken, disoriented, or hostile panhandler can be as frightening for many people as the prospect of meeting an actual robber." Generally, the police become involved whenever merchants request their assistance. Depending on the urban area, the police, with their predisposition toward street people, will often tell offending individuals or groups to "move along." In some cases, street people may be forcibly removed and relocated, possibly even arrested.

City Strategies and the Homeless Problem. Different cities use different strategies to deal with the homeless problem, and they monitor closely the activities and efforts of police departments in other cities. In San Francisco, more than 3,000 citations have been given under the city's "Matrix Quality of Life" program. In Southern California, eight municipalities passed anti-public sleeping ordinances within a fifteen-month period. Cincinnati city officials have removed city benches from downtown parks to prevent homeless people from congregating in significant numbers. Many observers believe that criminalizing the actions of the homeless fosters divisiveness and possibly opens the door to constitutional challenges. These policies are also seen as a wasteful use of scarce resources. In Atlanta, for instance, a local group estimates that the city spends between $300,000 and $500,000 per year incarcerating homeless people for sleeping and begging in public. San Francisco police agencies spent 450 hours and $11,000 to arrest fifteen people for begging in 1992 (Foscarinis and Scheibel, 1993:7).

Finn (1988) has observed that the two main strategies of policing are strict enforcement and benign neglect. A third strategy appears to be emerging, referral service. In this model the police act as community service agents and either deliver individuals or arrange for individuals to be taken to appropriate helping facilities. Some experts maintain that homeless street people, as citizens, are an undeniable part of our society and therefore should be included in civil protection. This means that they should also be deserving recipients of community-oriented policing. Because these people have little political strength, few resources, and little or no power, however, they are not regarded as part of legal, law-abiding, productive, tax-paying, organized society. Their numbers are simply not represented in a political agenda.

Apart from the referral service model, it would appear that police contacts with street people are primarily negative. In a general enforcement sense, this is true, but on a more personal level, individual officers have attempted to assist these persons in certain situations. Many police officers working with street people are compassionate and caring. They have taken the time to help the less fortunate find shelter and obtain menial work. On an organizational level, it is not uncommon to read about efforts to raise money for victims of tragedies or to collect funds (or toys) for needy families. Religious organizations have taken a lead in providing meals and bed space, political rallies are held, and from time to time actors and comedians perform to raise funds. Unfortunately, the major urban tragedy of large homeless populations is not being addressed adequately, nor are these persons the focus of concerted government intervention. As a group the homeless are not the recipients of sustained organized efforts to alleviate some of the major factors that cause their plight. Merely putting food on one's plate and offering an occasional bed do not constitute long-lasting solutions. Chronic unemployment, underemployment, lack of marketable skills, substance abuse, and physical and mental health problems must also be addressed effectively.

The Hazards of Handling the Homeless. The lack of health services has a ripple effect, especially on law enforcement personnel. Urban police officers, who are required to interact closely with the homeless, are faced with the hazard of increased susceptibility to communicable diseases. They often come into contact with people with body lice and highly contagious diseases, such as tuberculosis, jaundice, and hepatitis. Some urban police departments have followed the path set for prison staffs by requiring mandatory annual tuberculosis (TB) screenings and optional vaccinations for Hepatitis B for at-risk officers. In most cases, the TB test is the skin test (PPD). Together with such testing, officers receive training on health risks, symptoms, and the means of transmission and prevention of tuberculosis. In cooperation with city or county health departments, police departments share a responsibility to protect employees from exposure and the effect of exposure to bloodborne pathogens, mainly human immunodeficiency virus (HIV) and Hepatitis B (HBV). Although there is no vaccination for HIV, a safe and effective HBV vaccine has been developed and marketed (*Correction News*, 1993:1).

AIDS and the Homeless. The health problem of the homeless was intensified when the Centers for Disease Control reported that the AIDS virus had infected the nation's homeless at rates two to forty times as high as those of the general population. Culled from medical data for some 8,000 homeless people who were treated for various ailments in thirteen cities, the report indicated that 1 percent to 20 percent of the subjects were HIV-infected, depending on the city surveyed, compared to a less than 0.5 percent rate of infection nationwide. The highest rates of infection were found in New York, Atlanta, Miami, and Washington, D.C. (Washington had a rate of 14 percent). Denver, Houston, and Memphis had the lowest rates (Dahl, 1991:4).

It is with health-conscious concern that officers interact with people whose problems with merchants are compounded by their health problems. Many officers, given their preference, would eschew contact. When officers respond to calls they should be informed of health hazards, and, indeed, some Computer-Aided Dispatch (CAD) systems include HIV-positive information along with gun registration and prior police contacts. According to one legal expert, the reporting of someone who is HIV-positive at the location should not be misreported as someone with AIDS. In many states singling out HIV is a violation of health and safety codes (Mayer, 1993:7).

No Restrooms. The problems of disease transmission are compounded by a lack of public toilet facilities for the urban homeless. Street people do not have access to toilets or running water for their most basic human needs. It is quite common to see individuals relieve themselves in public without a modicum of modesty. In some urban areas public workers spray areas that are habitually used for this purpose on a daily or weekly basis, using high-pressure water hoses, to abate the spread of disease.

As the number of homeless people rises, more streets and alleys reek of human waste. Many public restrooms have been closed or declared unusable because of vandalism, drug dealing, and other criminal conduct. A plan to place thirty-three non-flush portables—the relatively primitive chemical toilets used at construction sites—around Los Angeles's Skid Row was squashed in 1992 by then Mayor Tom Bradley. Bradley responded to complaints by business owners who claimed that the units would attract drug dealing and prostitution. For a two-month period in 1992, the city funded supervised twenty-four-hour restrooms inside a shelter and a Skid Row hotel. Today, the fifty-block Skid Row district has no such restrooms (Gordon, 1993). It would seem that making public toilets available to those in need would be more constructive than making urination in public a crime.

In 1993 San Francisco negotiated with the French company JCDecaux to bring twenty-seven sleek restrooms to the pedestrian-intensive city. For four months in 1992 New York City successfully tested six Decaux units—computerized affairs with some very special features. Only fifty-five seconds after a user leaves, the Decaux model retracts and disinfects the seat as a high-pressure spray cleans the floor. To prevent camping and partying, the doors pop open after twenty minutes; if someone lingers five minutes longer, detectors trigger a siren. In addition, there is an emergency button to a 911 telephone line. With permanent installation uncertain in New York, San Francisco is expected to be the first U.S. city to give the new lavatories a practical test.

San Diego, a city that has a national reputation for helping the homeless, constructed street-level bathrooms in its civic center in 1988. On-site attendants limited breakage and minimized disorderly conduct. In an effort to save $55,000 per year, the supervision of the facilities was suspended temporarily. Supervision was restored after a two-week absence that resulted in a high incidence of vandalism, breakage, drug use, prostitution, and camping (Gordon, 1993).

Protests and Rallies. On a national scale and in a different context, the police are called into play when social activists hold rallies. Rallies in which advocates speak about the issue of homelessness in the United States frequently require police officer presence. For instance, on October 7, 1989, thousands of homeless persons and their supporters marched down the streets of Washington, D.C., to demand affordable housing for everyone.

In a Los Angeles protest, a group of Roman Catholic nuns laced up sneakers in preparation for the third annual "Run for the Homeless." The event earned thousands of dollars for area charities (*Los Angeles Times,* 1989:B1). With good reason, the police are often called to these scenes of protest to maintain order and ensure the safety of both the protesters and the public. Public protest is about as American as baseball and apple pie, but when a police presence is required to keep protests orderly and prevent violence, attending police officers are often labeled *antiprotest.* Although crowd control is seen by the public as nonsupportive of the demonstrations, many police officers share the sentiments of the protesters. They are required, however, to perform their duties and maintain public order.

Demographics

We don't know how many homeless there are. Official estimates do not accurately gauge their numbers for several reasons. Estimates range from 250,000 to 3 million. A 1988 study by the National Bureau of Economic Research indicated that between 250,000 and 400,000 Americans had no home (*Business Week,* 1988). On the other hand, in 1994 the National Coalition for the Homeless claimed their data showed 3 million persons as homeless over the course of a year, with the term *homeless* meaning temporary, episodic, or long-term homelessness.

Homeless teenagers are a population at risk in many ways other than simply lacking shelter. Officials have estimated that 10 percent to 20 percent of homeless street youths in New York have AIDS. In early 1993 one Los Angeles shelter gave HIV tests to 12 homeless youths—six of these tests were positive. Such children pose potential medical and economic time bombs. Their HIV symptoms may remain hidden for years, during which undiagnosed youths can transmit the virus to many partners. Young women living on the streets have a high rate of pregnancy. If infected with the virus they risk transmission of HIV to their babies. Homeless youths are at high risk for HIV for many reasons: intravenous drug use; sex with multiple partners, including HIV drug users; drug and alcohol abuse, which makes it less likely that condoms will be used; and a high rate of sexually transmitted diseases, which increases the chance of HIV transmission through genital sores (Roan, 1994:E2). Many of the youths on the urban streets of America are runaways. Thus, they do not readily seek public assistance, even though it is often a free service to them.

One reason an accurate count of all homeless individuals eludes compilation is that homeless persons have no permanent address. Although homeless individuals tend to congregate in certain locales, others are highly mobile. Another important reason is that many homeless individuals and families are temporarily sheltered by friends and sympathetic acquaintances for short periods. These "couch people" complicate official attempts to obtain an accurate picture of how many homeless there are at any given time in urban America.

The Composition of Homelessness.

Several different kinds of persons make up the adult homeless population. There are (1) those who are homeless only by circumstance (e.g., unemployed and poverty-stricken), (2) those who are alcoholic, (3) those who are drug dependent, (4) those who are mentally ill, and (5) those who live on the streets by free choice. The homeless population has been described as a community of thirds: One-third are alcoholic and drug dependent, one-third mentally ill, and one-third homeless by circumstance. A profile of the homeless conducted in Long Beach, California, found that the majority of the homeless population in that city were single male high school graduates, with a median age of thirty-four and blue-collar skills and background. It was found that 33 percent were veterans who had little contact with their families. In 1993 the U.S. Conference of Mayors released a report that surveyed 26 cities. The report stated that families made up an increasingly large part of the urban homeless population and that almost one-third of those families seeking emergency shelter in 1993 were turned away (Shogren, 1993:A1). Cities in which families constitute a large percentage of the homeless population are New York City, with 75 percent; Kansas City, Missouri, with 73 percent; and Trenton, New Jersey, with 77 percent (Shogren, 1993:A16).

Many intact families and women with children are homeless as the result of economic dislocation or eviction (Finn, 1988). Although single men make up the largest segment of the nation's homeless population, families, primarily mothers with small children, are the fastest growing segment, representing 36 percent of the homeless. This reflects a 2 percent increase from 1988, and some experts see no reason to believe the growth rate will taper off or decline over time (*Los Angeles Times*, 1989:B6).

It should be pointed out that the persons on streets who create problems and are disorderly are not those who must live on the streets because of unavoidable poverty. The homeless persons who attract police attention are primarily single males, often with drinking or drug problems, who appear to prefer living on the streets and who survive by begging or committing petty theft (Finn, 1988).

When free shelter is made available to homeless persons, many choose to remain on the streets, some because they dislike the regimentation of any structured living arrangement (e.g., rules against drinking, curfews, and fixed meal schedules). This preference may also reflect dislike of the severe crowding that exists in group shelters, the isolation of single-occupancy hotels, and the frequent uncleanliness of both types of living arrangements. In some cases, adequate housing is simply not available. In Chicago, for instance, there were an estimated 30,000 homeless in 1988, and only 3,000 available beds (*New York Times*, 1988). Some street people shy away from living in places like detoxification centers and psychiatric facilities that require treatment as a condition of lodging. In addition, many shelters and welfare hotels are dangerous, with frequent thefts and fighting (Finn, 1988). In other areas where limited shelter is offered, it is often refused because of high crime and drug use. According to one report in 1988, in the Fort Washington Armory in Manhattan, crack use pervaded the entire shelter. Homeless men participating in shelter work programs said they spent their weekly earnings of $12.50 on drugs. This shelter was also described as housing nothing but hardened criminals as residents (*New York Times*, 1988). Also, many facilities shut down during the day, forcing the homeless to commute back and forth between the shelter and the streets (Finn, 1988).

Santa Ana, California

On August 15, 1990, a police sweep in Santa Ana, California resulted in 64 people being arrested and taken to the Santa Ana Stadium. Then, police officers marked their arms with booking numbers and chained them to benches for six hours. The arrested people were subsequently cited with misdemeanors and released (*Los Angeles Times*, 1990:B2). In 1993 Santa Ana passed an "anti-camping" ordinance (upheld by a Superior Court) to deal with the city's 3,000 homeless. According to one observer, the homeless of Santa Ana "have survived the wettest winter in ten years, are racked with discomfort and undiagnosed illness, suffer public disapproval and the hostile attention of Santa Ana police. With considerable assurance, patrolmen may now wake them, move them, flash Polaroids at them, ticket them, arrest them and seize their toiletries as 'camping paraphernalia'" (Witter, 1993:B11).

In November 1993, the Santa Ana Police Department was selected from among sixty-five entries to receive the Herman Goldstein Excellence in Problem-Solving Award. The national contest was conducted by the Police Executive Research Forum (PERF), a forum that encourages improving the delivery of police services and studies policing techniques. Contest judges awarded the prize to the department's Westend neighborhood policing district for the way officers designed and implemented a plan to reduce crime at a shopping center. The department took action between April and June 1993, after shoppers at the plaza complained that growing numbers of panhandlers were approaching them for money. Reports of increasing numbers of burglaries and other crimes led to declining business. Combing the neighborhood near the plaza, seven police officers discovered that homeless people who were seeking shelter on the riverbed were often the same ones who used the shopping center as a place to ask for money and sometimes break into cars. The police warned the homeless to leave the riverbed, cleared their belongings from the riverbed, and began patrolling the center on bicycles, golf carts, and in police cars. They made no arrests. The police department also suggested structural changes at the shopping center, such as moving water fountains and locking bathrooms, to discourage transients from loitering there. One result was that crime declined substantially and business improved when police concentrated their patrolling efforts at the center. Twelve cars were reported burglarized at the shopping center in April but only one automobile burglary was reported in June (Di Rado, 1993:B2).

Alternatives

In 1988 Miami city commissioners unanimously rejected a proposal to jail homeless people for sleeping, bathing, or urinating on city property. Speaking for the commissioners, Vice Mayor Kennedy stated, "It was a horrendous thing . . . violators would have faced a $100 fine or 10 days in jail." He recommended more halfway houses (*USA Today*, 1988:3A).

Apart from the occasional exposé or in-depth report of homelessness by mainstream newspapers, the topic of homelessness is generally dealt with cursorily. Usually stories focus on the outward signs of poverty and decay—graffiti, drugs, alcohol, and crime rates—rather than on causal factors. Two newspapers have focused on street people, however. In New York City, a monthly called *Street News* covers celebrities, music, and homeless issues, and its editor has indicated plans to expand to Los Angeles, Denver, and other major urban centers. The *Ten-*

derloin Times, a San Francisco-based newspaper, has included features on such topics as efforts to obtain clean needles for drug addicts. An annual article includes a tally of the number of homeless people who died on the streets of San Francisco (e.g., 110 homeless persons died in 1989). Another small San Francisco community paper, *The Homeless Times,* covers local neighborhood and area concerns (Iwata, 1990).

Private Sector. In the private sector, businesspeople have formed coalitions to help alleviate some of the problems of the homeless in finding employment. A person living on the streets does not present a favorable image to prospective employers. Many business establishments offer services to enhance the impression homeless job seekers make when they apply for jobs. These services include laundry and dry cleaning, shampoos and haircuts, beauty treatments, and resumé preparation. A Phoenix-based business, Frugal Flush, provides jobs and medical and legal help for homeless people anxious for a second chance. Frugal Flush hired a reputable social service agency to interview and screen applicants (Applegate, 1993).

Individual citizens also have stepped forward. Many examples exist of individuals providing sandwiches, hot beverages, and other foodstuffs to homeless people, but one individual's effort resulted in the distribution of more than 250,000 blankets to the homeless of Orange County, California. Then, with the help of other concerned people, 73-year-old Mr. Fico developed the project, called Covering Wings, into a nationwide system for distributing inexpensive blankets and unused clothing to the disadvantaged. The space-age survival blanket the project distributes is as versatile as it is cost efficient. Mr. Fico got the idea from the blankets the astronauts took into space. The shiny silver polyurethane tarpaulin has a hood and snaps so that it can double as a poncho. With eyelets that also allow it to be used as a tent, the blanket is perfect for street survival. Made by a company in Taiwan using Fico's design, the blankets cost $2.50 each to produce. With more than 100 distribution programs, the survival tarps reach the homeless in more than a dozen states (Boucher, 1993:B7).

Homelessness is a social malaise that needs immediate government attention—homelessness is the foe, not the homeless (Foscarinis and Scheibel, 1993:7). But the government spends billions of dollars more on tax breaks and other payments to corporations than it does in welfare for the poor. Based on his analysis of the federal budget for 1994, Ralph Nader says that the value to corporations of federal tax benefits and direct payments was placed at $104.3 billion, whereas spending for social welfare programs was estimated at $75.1 billion. One of the largest federal payments was $18.3 billion in 1994 to pay for the bailout of failed savings and loan associations. About $29.2 billion went for payments and obligations for agriculture and commodity purchases and $53.3 billion for tax breaks (*Orange County Register,* 1994:5). Until the federal government takes steps to alleviate the human misery found on our streets, municipal policing will continue to act as society's enforcer of inequality and regulator of status.

BOX 9.1   A Tale of Selected Cities

Los Angeles, California.   The "wake-up call," as street people call it, shakes Skid Row to life without fail shortly after dawn every day. Los Angeles police officers cruise the streets, rousing anyone asleep on the sidewalks and telling them to move along. The police have been doing this for a number of years on orders from City Hall. The objective is to prevent the homeless from reestablishing the sidewalk encampments that lined Skid Row in 1987. The shelter problem has not improved, and so the police action serves primarily to make the homeless less visible. "No one is able or willing to provide enough shelter," said the commanding officer of the Central Patrol Division. "It's not a law enforcement problem. It's part of a much larger problem. Until someone solves it, we're stuck" (*Los Angeles Times,* 1989:36). Immediately following the police "wake-up call," city sanitation engineers arrive to clear off the sidewalks. The makeshift shelters fashioned out of cardboard boxes and small blankets are either moved by their owners to other locations or destroyed by city workers. One "home" constructed from boxes from nearby businesses is a thirty-square-foot dwelling, with a roof, windows, curtains, and a door. This structure is moved daily by its inhabitant to prevent it from being removed to the city dump (Regalado, 1993:A26).

Santa Barbara, California.   Many jurisdictions have opted for a very conservative, hard-line approach to the plight of the homeless. The city of Santa Barbara, California, became a national focal point when Gary Trudeau, author of the comic strip *Doonesbury,* published a series of political cartoons depicting the treatment of the homeless at the hands of local police. It is apparent that the police were not acting as the sole agents to stamp out the Highway 101 eyesore. Merchants, homeowners, and other vested interest groups pressured city hall to "get rid of those people." The city image was at stake, and the easiest solution was to call out the police to take care of the problem. In his Department of Justice report, *Street People,* Finn (1988) observed that the police routinely arrest street people for assault and drug dealing, cite them for being drunk or drinking in public, and in general maintain strong pressure on them to "keep moving." This approach has made it possible for merchants in a previously rundown section of lower State Street to reopen or revitalize their businesses (Finn, 1988). Through harassment, jailing, and constant police observation and interaction, the city managed to get rid of all but forty hardcore street people.

Portland, Oregon.   Over the years, a close relationship developed between the Portland Police Department and the Hooper Memorial Detoxification Center, which is funded by Multnomah County. When police personnel were cut, jails became crowded and public inebriates increasingly congregated in the downtown area. The county expanded the center's responsibilities to include accepting combative (but not violent) inebriates in 1983 and violent inebriates in 1986. Funds were provided for additional facility staff to patrol the downtown areas from 8:00 A.M. to midnight in a specially equipped van and to transport inebriates to the center. Later, the sheriff deputized the entire Hooper staff, enabling van operators to detain inebriates involuntarily. This is a case in which the criminal justice system was used to deal with actual criminal conduct only, and patrol officers were freed up to perform other duties related to maintaining order.

Boston, Massachusetts. Police in a downtown Boston police precinct may take homeless people to the Pine Street Inn at any hour of the night. The precinct captain keeps his officers informed about the small number of individuals (particularly the violent and those with serious medical problems) that the inn will not accept. The captain also instructs officers to wait a few minutes at the inn until staff members admit the homeless, rather than dropping them at the door and driving away, as in past years. The Massachusetts State Department of Public Welfare provides an off-duty officer at the inn during each shift. The special-duty officers often show other officers how to handle homeless people without inciting trouble, and they try to make sure that on-duty officers bring in only appropriate referrals. The police presence helps to maintain a calm atmosphere at Pine Street.

Santa Monica, California. Extensive deliberations about the functions of the police, the wishes of the public, and appointed officials' social policies toward the homeless have had a dramatic effect on Santa Monica. In past years, because of liberal outreach programs and nonenforcement policies, the city experienced an influx of homeless people (Melekian, 1990). The city has historically prided itself on tolerance, compassion, and rent control.

In an attempt during the 1980s to assist the homeless population of Santa Monica, an Outreach Team Coalition was created to coordinate assistance efforts. Two of these teams visited the city's parks and other areas with high concentrations of homeless persons. The coalition offered food and clothing and referred homeless people to shelters and treatment services. The task force, which included law enforcement representatives, trained police about how to respond to the homeless (Finn, 1988).

During the early 1990s, however, the city was torn between opposing philosophies. The City Attorney held that the issue of the homeless was a social problem that could not and should not be passed on to other jurisdictions. The City Attorney's Office viewed the homeless issue as a fundamentally moral one because of the larger-scale national failures that caused the problem initially. The City Attorney's Office also held that local government, including the police department, must provide a solution, albeit temporary and incomplete, until effective long-range national and state public policies could be put into effect. Prosecutorial policies excluded filings for "economic" offenses, such as sleeping in public parks, possession of shopping carts, and other misdemeanors and infractions—infractions that for the homeless are necessary for their survival. The office also held that alcoholism is a disease to be treated and that jailing alcoholics is not a suitable answer or alternative to a detoxification center.

The opposing philosophy was that although the problems of the homeless are unfortunate, a city of 8.2 square miles cannot and should not be expected to deal with a social issue of this magnitude. Not unexpectedly, this view was held by both business groups and citizens who found themselves deluged with street people.

Again, the police department was placed in the middle of these two widely differing philosophies. The dilemma generated three distinct policing problems: conflict regarding the use of public facilities, public demands for enforcement, and the need to provide police service to an economically disenfranchised class of people (Melekian, 1990).

In 1993, citing the growing homeless population, attendant problems, and differing approaches and philosophies, the City Council voted to fire the City Attorney. The City Attorney maintained throughout the hearing that the problem of the homeless was a moral problem and that he was morally and ethically bound to represent the homeless as well as the interests of others in the community.

San Diego, California. The San Diego County Alcohol Program contracts with the Volunteers of America to provide a special room, known as the Inebriate Reception Center, in which as many as eighty drunk people can sober up in a single session. One of the center's major goals is to reduce the visibility of public inebriates in downtown San Diego. The center must accept all legitimate referrals from the police and, in turn, the San Diego Police Department (SDPD) requires that its 1,576 officers bring all public inebriates to the center for treatment. Officers conclude their center business in less than five minutes, compared with about an hour of their time that is required to book inebriates into jails. The SDPD brings nearly 25,000 inebriates a year to the center; other law enforcement agencies in the county bring in over 1,000 of them (Finn, 1988). This approach temporarily removes from public view the city's inebriates and probably benefits the downtown business owners. It would be interesting to assess the recidivism rate of these alcoholics: How many times per year are the *same* people processed through the center?

New York/Jersey City. A 1987 report revealed that in a 200-yard tunnel under Manhattan, used by thousands of commuters switching from New

Jersey's rapid-transit PATH trains to New York City subways, lies Path Hotel. This "hotel" is the home of approximately fifty homeless people, who have been described as "drunks, addicts, and crazies." They are roused by the police at 7 A.M. each day, and many of them spend the rush hour panhandling. According to informed sources, the drug *crack* is smoked in "no man's land"—the middle section of the tunnel, which is unpatrolled by either the New York or the New Jersey transit police. Social workers who attempt to redirect some of the underground residents into a more productive lifestyle have met with little success (Whitman, 1987:69).

In addressing the same problem, according to another report (Finn, 1988), the 1,200 police of the Port Authority of New York and New Jersey are responsible for dealing with hundreds of homeless individuals who "live" in public transportation facilities in New York City and Jersey City. In New York City, the Port Authority and the Department of Mental Health jointly fund the Volunteers of America to "sweep" the midtown bus terminal and the downtown train terminal every day at 5:30 A.M. and 1:30 A.M. to invite the homeless to go to the organization's shelter. Vans wait outside to transport them, or just to feed them. At these shelters, referrals to mental health and detoxification services are made for those who need such services. In Jersey City, the authority teamed with the Mayor's Task Force on the Homeless to develop facilities for the homeless. The Jersey City Housing Authority and the Port Authority agreed to fund the establishment of a shelter and drop-in center. The city's Department of Housing and Economic Development arranged for in-kind services to the facilities. The drop-in center provides counseling and referrals (Finn, 1988).

On July 13, 1990, however, New York's beleaguered Transit Authority announced a new campaign to rid the subway system of derelicts, drifters, and displaced persons. The Transit Authority announced that on July 15, 1990, police officers would force all passengers to leave the A subway train when it arrived at the 207th Street station, the northern end of a 30-mile route that begins in southeastern Queens and passes through Brooklyn and the entire length of Manhattan. The trip takes approximately one and a half hours, making it especially attractive to homeless people who use the trains as a sleeping place between midnight and dawn. Workers from two outreach programs would be posted at the 207th Street station to assist any homeless persons who wanted to go to shelters. A Transit Authority spokesman explained that the behavior of some homeless people was a problem when they were awakened at 207th Street, where the subway cars are cleaned and made ready for the return trip. Another Transit Authority official said, "We did a count and found that about 135 people were just riding up and down. They carry their belongings and there are occasionally some problems with sanitation" (*Los Angeles Times*, 1990a:23). Considering the paucity of shelters in New York City and the funds expended by the police, the Transit Authority, and outreach workers in dealing with overnight sleepers, the Big Apple might find it more cost effective to run one train just for the homeless. Of course, this might be considered a radical approach.

Dade County, Florida. A 1 percent restaurant tax aimed at funding shelter and rehabilitation for the homeless was approved July 28, 1993, by the Dade County commissioners. Advocacy groups called the tax a model for the rest of the country. The National League of Cities and homeless-rights groups said they believed the tax was the first in the nation passed specifically to help the homeless. Miami-area authorities have estimated that at least 6,000 people live on its streets. The new tax, levied on meals and drinks at restaurants doing more than $400,000 annual business, is expected to bring in $7.5 million a year, and federal and foundation money should at least double that amount (*Los Angeles Times*, 1993:A24).

THE MENTALLY ILL: A FORGOTTEN MINORITY

Jails and the Mentally Ill. Our nation's jails and prisons are quickly and not too quietly becoming the largest repository for the nation's **mentally ill**. Although the exact number of mentally ill jail inmates is unknown, research on the nation's 3,338 jails indicates a serious problem. Officials at the Cook County (Chicago) Jail told the *Chicago Tribune* that on any given day, 500 to 700 of the 4,600 inmates need some type of mental health care. Officials at the Dade County Jail told the *Miami Herald* that about 30 percent of the 1,400 inmates receive psychotropic medication—drugs used to calm the severely disturbed. Mental health workers at the San Luis Obispo County Jail in California reported that 6 percent to 15 percent of the inmates on any given day are obviously psychotic—out of touch with reality and possibly hallucinating (Wax, 1987:26).

The Los Angeles County jail system is now the largest "mental institution" in the country, with more than 5,000 mentally ill inmates. The criminalization of the seriously mentally ill is a disgrace and a mockery of our pretense of being a civilized society (Liberman, Lamb, and Davis, 1993:B11). These unfortunates are victims in many senses of the word. They are victims of nonexistent or failed mental health programs, they are victims of neglect, and many roam the city streets to become victims of physical abuse. They are routinely mugged, raped, and subjected to the most degrading indignities one could imagine. Individually and as a group, they are treated as social lepers and avoided by "decent citizens." They are also the unwilling victims of criminalization. If a mentally disturbed person becomes overly loud, unruly, or obnoxious, the police are called and arrests are made. For merchants to have raving lunatics on or around their business premises is the "kiss of death." In downtown areas, it is not unusual to observe and hear the ranting of an obviously delusional person. Many mentally ill people are "self-medicating," and many simply have their medication stolen from them. Others sell their medications. Some mental patients are involved in aftercare outreach programs that bear the brunt of budget cuts; other patients have been "dumped by state hospitals" (Robison, 1988:9).

Police Policy and the Mentally Ill. In the absence of federal, state, and county treatment programs and facilities, the burden of taking care of seriously mentally handicapped people has fallen on local and county police agencies. The justification for police involvement in a mental health system is a general policy that states that (1) in accordance with the philosophy of community mental health, many mentally ill persons live in the community; (2) the lack of adequate mental health resources makes police officers front-line mental health providers; (3) police are available every hour of the day at no cost to the caller; and (4) the police are involved because they have an obligation to serve the public and its perceived needs. The official mandate of the police in dealing with the mentally ill encompasses three areas: law enforcement (e.g., response to law-breaking or disturbance), civil concerns (e.g., initiation of civil commitment), and service provision (e.g., referral to mental health resources) (Geller, 1991:70). But another model is that the police should continue in policing functions and that *health* officials should assume health-related tasks and functions. It is a sad commentary that the police must be brought in to bolster the inactivity, inability, or failure of other services.

From a law enforcement perspective, mentally ill persons must be imminently dangerous to themselves or others to receive attention under today's restrictive commitment laws. There are great numbers of people on the street who cannot take care of themselves but who also cannot be involuntarily treated (Wax, 1987:27). When individuals demonstrate that they are a danger to themselves or others, metropolitan police departments are saddled with the added responsibility of locating, detaining, and transporting these persons to an outreach program, a hospital ward, or a jail cell. The amount of time that police spend dealing with mentally ill people is staggering. It has been estimated that the average time it takes for police officers to resolve one mental health related incident is about four hours (Finn and De Cujir, 1988:1).

To shorten the amount of time spent dealing with the mentally ill, and to reduce the load at the overworked mental health unit at the Los Angeles County Jail, the Los Angeles Police Department created a twenty-four-hour Mental Evaluation Unit (MEU). The unit prescreens cases and suggests various methods for reporting officers to calm these persons. MEU officers either go to the scene to take over the case or, more often, they tell patrol officers to bring the person to the unit's downtown office. The MEU officer assesses the person's condition and may tell the patrol officers to take the person to a hospital. There an emergency ward psychiatrist quickly evaluates the person, confident that if a MEU officer referred the patient, the person probably needs to be hospitalized. If necessary, the facility then admits the patient or finds a bed at another facility. The patrol officer might have spent thirty minutes on the case and the MEU officer, about fifteen minutes.

The MEU emerged from two tragic incidents. The LAPD first came under criticism in 1984 when a mentally ill person killed two children and injured thirteen others. Shortly thereafter, when a police officer was killed by a mentally ill person, a police board of inquiry warned that unless all agencies responsible for the emergency care of the mentally ill began to cooperate, more tragedies would occur. As a result, the chief of police invited top-level officials of ten criminal justice and social service agencies to form a **Psychiatric Emergency Coordinating Committee** (PECC), which formulated a comprehensive memorandum of agreement that took effect on April 1, 1985. The administrator of each participating agency agreed in writing to a list of specific actions designed to divert mentally ill persons involved in minor criminal behavior from the criminal justice system into the health care system, where they could receive more appropriate care.

Police and the Mentally Ill. The two principals of the agreement included the chief of the LAPD and the director of the Los Angeles County Department of Mental Health. The core of the agreement is as follows:

> The police department will establish a mental health emergency command post staffed by specially trained law enforcement officers. The police department will require all officers to call the unit for assistance in screening mentally ill people before either transporting them to an emergency facility or booking them for a crime.
>
> The Department of Mental Health will maintain a high-level administrator accessible to the police 24 hours a day with responsibility for immediately resolving special situations of an urgent nature, conduct training programs for police and other network agencies concerning appropriate methods for handling psychiatric emergencies, and develop pilot programs with the police to meet the psychiatric emergency needs of mentally ill persons requiring police attention. (Finn and De Cujir, 1988:2)

At least seven other jurisdictions across the country have established cooperative agreements between agencies. For example, the Birmingham (Alabama) Police Department uses specially trained civilian social workers to relieve police officers of the responsibility of dealing with mental illness cases. Six rotating social workers are available twenty-four hours a day to go to the scene, take over the case, and transport the individual to a hospital emergency room. Once at the hospital, the social worker arranges for an evaluation. In most cases, police officers return to their patrol once the mentally ill person has been delivered to the facility, leaving the social worker as the police department's representative. The chief of police of Birmingham estimated that in 1975, the police force handled 900 disturbance calls, most of which involved a mentally ill person; in 1985, the social workers handled 1,000 similar calls—an average of almost three calls per day.

In Erie, Pennsylvania, a collaborative arrangement was initiated after the murder of a hostage by a mentally ill patient. In a memorandum of agreement between the chief of police and the Family Crisis Intervention service, the police department agreed to staff a cruiser around the clock with officers who would relieve the department's 200 other sworn personnel of difficult cases involving the mentally ill. Family Crisis Intervention staff trained the special officers to screen arrestees for mental illness, take them to appropriate facilities for treatment, and adhere to the applicable state civil statutes governing involuntary detention. In-service training included periodic updating (Finn and De Cujir, 1988:5).

A National Institute of Justice (NIJ) report contrasted twelve cities that had heavy loads of cases involving the mentally ill (Finn and Sullivan, 1988:5). All of the cities relied on networking strategies to relieve patrol officers from the time-consuming task of dealing with large numbers of mentally ill arrestees. When the police are placed in socially and politically delicate positions, they must rely on their situational discretion to cope with problems outside of their scope of skills. Police intervention is not the primary solution to the issue of mental health.

Recommendations

Several recommendations have been made about the care of the mentally ill. These recommendations include the following:

1. Establish state hospitals that will provide ongoing care for the thousands of severely mentally ill persons who have been discharged from state and county mental treatment and confinement facilities during recent years.
2. Create integrated state and local mental health programs; this partnership would result in a single system of care that would monitor the clinical status of patients wherever they reside. Redesign services to provide adequate community resources for the seriously mentally ill still residing in state hospitals.
3. Continue the support of clinical and applied research that has been advancing new treatments and better understanding of the brain and behavior mechanisms that cause mental illness or impede its effective treatment.
4. Reassume the responsibility for the most seriously mentally ill citizens by sheltering and treating them in state hospitals, not correctional facilities or prison settings (Liberman, Lamb, and Davis, 1993:B11).

DRUG USERS AND ABUSERS AND THE POLICE

Over the years, there has been fluctuating support for increasingly harsh drug laws. In 1956 Congress cracked down on drug trafficking with the Narcotic Control Act, which specified a series of lengthy and mandatory prison terms for drug crimes. In the 1960s society began to question whether long prison terms for drug crimes were justified or effective. In 1970 Congress repealed virtually all of the mandatory penalties associated with drug trafficking, but as illegal drug use increased dramatically in the 1970s, individual states began to enact their own mandatory sentencing laws.

A critical point came in June 1986, when basketball star Len Bias died in suburban Washington from an overdose of crack cocaine. Within months Congress, supported by the Reagan administration, enacted the Anti-Drug Abuse Act of 1986, which set automatic penalties for various drug crimes, including life-without-parole terms for drug traffickers. Although sponsors of the act intended attacking drug kingpins, the penalties also applied to low-level participants in the illegal drug business (Savage, 1993:A5). Caught up in the early 1980s frenzy of the War on Drugs, Congress enacted dozens of tough federal drug laws, each carrying heavy sentences. The result is that the 649 federal district judges are now inundated with drug cases that often should be tried in state courts (Edwards, 1993:F13).

The War on Drugs cost $23.7 billion in 1991. Of these funds, state and local governments spent $15.9 billion, of which almost four-fifths was devoted to criminal justice activities such as incarcerating prisoners and funding police services. The largest single cost to state and local governments was $6.8 billion for corrections—jails and prisons, followed by the police at $4.2 billion, health and hospitals at $2.8 billion, and judicial and legal services at $1.5 billion (Associated Press, 1993:A11).

It is not difficult to understand why corrections was the largest expenditure, as drug crimes are often punished more harshly than assaults and robberies. A 20-year-old female student from Mobile, Alabama, was sentenced to ten years in prison for helping her boyfriend arrange a deal to sell LSD. A 44-year-old carpenter from Portland, Oregon, is serving 12 years because he accepted an offer to unload a boat carrying a shipment of hashish. And a 20-year-old New Yorker was sentenced to 10 years because he sold an informer two ounces of crack cocaine. Under current laws, it does not matter that an arrested person had no criminal record, possessed no weapon, did not engage in violence, or was only a minor player in an illegal drug transaction. For example, the mandatory punishment for possessing or selling five grams of crack cocaine, about one-fifth of an ounce, is five years in federal prison. If the amount is two ounces of crack or more, the sentence is ten years. There are no acceptable excuses and no parole. In some states, such as Florida, wardens have had to release some of their violent criminals early to accommodate growing numbers of drug offenders (Savage, 1993b:A5).

From 1982 to 1992 criminal drug cases in the federal courts increased 197 percent, from 4,218 to 12,512. That represents 8,294 additional drug trials. In 1992 drug cases represented more than 26 percent of the criminal cases in federal courts. Over the same ten-year period, the civil caseload increased by only 10 percent. The federal prisons are bulging at 143 percent of capacity resulting from these prosecutions (Edwards, 1993:F13). The War on Drugs has been a most dismal failure and probably one of the most expensive of home-front "wars." The fate of the Drug Enforcement Administration (DEA) is illustrative. When the War on Drugs began in the late 1960s, there were two federal agencies enforcing the drug laws with a total budget of less than $10 million. In 1993 there were fifty-four agencies involved, including every branch of the armed forces, and the overall budget was $13 billion, with more than $8 billion slated for the DEA alone (Cockburn, 1993:B7).

From a political perspective, the American public was advised that developing closer ties and cooperation with neighboring countries might ease the flow of drugs from them. The passage of the **North American Free Trade Agreement (NAFTA),** according to the Commissioner of U.S. Customs, would make the interception of narcotics arriving from Mexico into the United States easier. With increased international commerce, however, would also come more opportunities for drug traffickers to camouflage their illegal drug shipments and other contraband. Besides relying on mutual cooperation, the U.S. Customs, under a congressional mandate, increased the number of its agents in the border region by about 20 percent, from approximately 1,400 to 1,700 (Gerstenzang and Ostrow, 1993:A10). It is questionable whether the concept of mutual cooperation is really a viable strategy to interdict illegal drugs, especially when in October 1993, newspaper headlines announced that the Drug Enforcement Administration was sharing information about drug shipments with the Haitian military, even though it is well known that this same military regime controls the drug trade through Haiti (Cockburn, 1993:B7).

The former Clinton administration drug czar, Lee Brown (former commissioner of the police departments in New York and Houston), has stated that rehabilitation and education are the keys to curbing the menace of drug abuse. He added that "to break the cycle of drug use, we must look at the drug problem not only as a problem for the criminal justice system but also as a public health problem." Although Brown signaled a change from the War on Drugs, he noted that the Clinton administration "is, without any reservations, opposed to legalization of illegal drugs." In an appearance before a Senate committee on October 20, 1993, Brown articulated the administration's focus on education and treatment, but he provided no estimates of costs. Senators called into question the President's commitment to fighting drugs in view of the fact that the office Brown heads has been slashed from 146 positions to 25. They also noted that the administration had consented to a reduction of nearly $200 million for drug treatment and education during 1993 (Feldman and Berger, 1993:A38). Conspicuously absent from Brown's testimony was a discussion of mandatory prison terms and a continued push for tougher laws.

One by-product of the War on Drugs has been the gradual corruption of some police forces and the involvement of certain U.S. government agencies in drug smuggling. The cost in local areas has been extremely high. In the inner cities, the drug war has been used as an excuse for search-and-destroy missions against the poor.

ILLEGAL IMMIGRANTS AND POLICE ACTIONS

The community policing concept of a partnership between the police and the community is difficult to understand, particularly in those communities with large numbers of illegal immigrants. Urban centers in border states such as California, Arizona, and Texas have large populations of undocumented workers (illegal aliens). According to reports, the influx of undocumented workers from Mexico and Central and South America has continued unabated for years. The Immigration and Naturalization Service (INS) or *La Migra* has tried to stem the flood of aliens seeking political or economic refuge, but hundreds of thousands of Spanish-speaking people illegally cross the border annually and take up residence in predominately Spanish-speaking U.S. neighborhoods. For years the *lancheros,* the smuggler-boatmen of Ciudad Juarez, and the *coyotes,* who escort illegal aliens into the United States overland from Mexico, have more or less accommodated each other. The INS cannot stop all illegal crossings. One result is that an informal code of conduct regulating the behavior and tactics of both parties has evolved. Even within an adversarial system, informal rules and arrangements have been observed—and occasionally violations of these rules have had tragic results.

Operation Blockade. The INS **Operation Blockade**—an experiment launched with $250,000 in extra overtime funds and agents shifted from inland posts—abruptly changed the rules of the game in El Paso, Texas. In the past, the Border Patrol seemed to acquiesce to the hundreds of daily illegal crossings in broad daylight. But that ended in September 1993, when about 450 agents spread along 20 miles, from southeast El Paso to mountainous Sunland Park, New Mexico, to intercept illegal aliens. Although the extensive deployment of every available vehicle gave the sense of a military mission, the results were markedly peaceful, according to both U.S. officials and the Mexican consulate, which received no abuse complaints.

In El Paso, a city that had clashed with the INS in the past, the new approach won fervent support. "We don't want the blockade lifted because we don't want it to go back to chaos," said Fred Morales, an activist in the historic riverfront barrio of Chihuahuita. Previously, Chihuahuita had been overrun by immigrants eluding capture and a tough street gang from Ciudad Juarez known as Puente Negro (Black Bridge). "We're proud of our Mexican culture, but we're Americans first. We're poor here. This country should serve the poor here first."

With this move, however, the Border Patrol set an abrupt, potentially explosive precedent. The repercussions could well reverberate across two nations confronting the issues of illegal immigration and free trade. San Diego politicians have called for a similar crackdown on the California-Mexico border, where Border Patrol officials have said they could greatly impede the flow of illegal immigration with additional resources. But the Mexican foreign relations secretary denounced Operation Blockade, as did business and political leaders in Ciudad Juarez. Economic desperation and the potential for an international incident have mounted. In a tense but nonviolent demonstration on an international bridge on September 21, 1993, Mexican protesters burned a U.S. flag in front of a phalanx of riot-equipped Border Patrol agents.

The person responsible for this new strategy, El Paso Chief Agent Silvestre Reyes, says that Operation Blockade is successful and will continue indefinitely. Reyes, an immigrant's grandson, an El Paso native, and a twenty-five-year Border Patrol veteran known for his community relations skills, took command in July 1993. He found conflicting currents of discontent with the Border Patrol in a city with deep economic and cultural ties to Ciudad Juarez. El Paso business owners and residents blamed illegal border crossers for crime and pervasive "quality-of-life" problems: panhandlers, transvestite prostitutes, and window washers at intersections. At the same time, immigrant activists spurred the creation of two community panels to monitor the Border Patrol after a series of misconduct allegations. A federal judge ruled in 1993 that agents had systematically harassed and mistreated Latinos at a high school near the Rio Grande.

Since the new strategy, arrests for illegal crossings have declined from a high of 1,000 a day to a low of 93 on September 30, 1993. In 1992 El Paso agents made about 250,000 arrests in the busiest sector outside San Diego. Unlike San Diego, where most illegal immigrants are heading to job centers in Los Angeles or other urban centers farther north, about half the immigrants from Ciudad Juarez only go to El Paso to work and shop. The rest are destined for Dallas, Denver, Chicago, and other interior cities (Rotella, 1993:25).

El Paso police believe the crackdown reduced the number of border panhandlers and others involved in petty infractions, according to one police sergeant. But other than a decrease in auto theft, which police attribute to heightened border security, the sergeant said that "it is difficult to make a connection between illegal immigration and crime rates." Statistics were inconclusive during the period of the blockade, officials said. Some property crimes declined, but other offenses remained steady or increased. Critics say illegal immigrants are scapegoats for crime and every other ill of American society.

While the INS tries to stem the flow of illegal immigration and identify those who escaped detection at the border, some local police agencies have afforded these persons equal police protection and services. They have included these persons as a protected class together with other "legal" members of the community. At one time, the California cities of Santa Ana and San Jose had declined to cooperate with the INS because of the negative public relations impact on their respective cities.

Although the heated debate over immigration reflects a complex national issue that ultimately must be addressed by Washington, the impact of the continued influx of foreigners falls most heavily on a single state, California. The Immigration and Naturalization Service released statistics about the magnitude of legal immigration to the United States and where new immigrants choose to settle. Not surprisingly, California attracted the greatest numbers. With 810,635 foreigners officially admitted to this country in 1992 (the largest one-year increase in legal immigration since the turn of the century), 41 percent settled in Califor-

Illegal aliens from Mexico and other countries attempt to cross the border into California and Arizona.
(Gerald Schumann, UPI/Corbis-Bettmann)

nia. In Orange County, California, U.S. Border Patrol agents have been boarding public transit buses randomly searching for illegal immigrants. If the INS were to be relieved of this overwhelming law enforcement responsibility, it could probably devote more time to other more important tasks, such as helping longtime illegal residents to assimilate into American life and become citizens.

Officer Jose Diaz Vargas

In Santa Ana, California, Officer Jose Diaz Vargas is the Hispanic Affairs Officer. Officer Vargas, age 57, entered the United States illegally in 1953, became a legal resident in 1959, and obtained his citizenship in 1968. He joined a small police department in 1969, transferred to the Santa Ana Police Department in 1975, and was named Hispanic Affairs Officer in 1979. During his career, Vargas has received many honors, including being named one of the top ten police officers in the United States.

His accomplishments are amazing when one considers that young Vargas was arrested and deported more than fifteen times. The last time, he was jailed at the Federal Detention Center on Terminal Island for two days. While working at his first job (as an illegal) as a garbage collector, he earned his high school diploma. He attended Fullerton College and studied criminal justice. After three years of college, at age thirty-three, he became the first former illegal immigrant to enter the Los Angeles County Sheriff's Academy. At graduation, he was immediately hired by the Stanton Police Department (Hernandez, 1993:7). Today Vargas's job as Hispanic Affairs Officer is to help the city's more than 50,000 immigrants understand their rights and responsibilities and the laws of their new country (Hernandez, 1993:1). In his speeches and through a weekly column he writes for the Spanish-language newspaper *El Rumores,* Vargas often uses his own experiences to inspire other immigrants to make the most of their lives (Hernandez, 1993:7).

KEY TERMS

ACT-UP
Affordable housing
Department of Housing and Urban Development (HUD)
Explorer Scouts
Hate crimes
Hepatitis (A, B, and C)
Mentally ill

North American Free Trade Agreement
Operation Blockade
Psychiatric Emergency Coordinating Committee
Queer Nation
Socioeconomic status
Stonewall riots
Urban renewal

QUESTIONS FOR REVIEW

1. Explain the difficulty in assessing the size of the homeless population in America.
2. Discuss the medical threat that may confront law enforcement personnel who deal with street people.
3. What are some of the approaches private businesses are using to assist those homeless persons seeking employment?
4. Why do the elderly rank high as victims?
5. What events have given rise to the gay movement?
6. Explain the purpose of ACT-UP and Queer Nation.
7. Explain the policy of police toward the mentally ill.
8. According to supporters, how will the passage of the North American Free Trade Agreement affect drug smuggling?
9. Discuss the community conflict that can be caused by INS enforcement in areas that are trying to implement COP.

SUGGESTED READINGS

Cruikshank, Margaret (1988). *The Gay and Lesbian Liberation Movement.* New York: Routledge.
Journal of Gay and Lesbian Services (1990). New York: The Haworth Press.
Journal of Homosexuality (n.d.). New York: The Haworth Press.
Hodgins, Sheilagh (1993). *Mental Disorder and Crime.* Beverly Hills, CA: Sage.

CHAPTER 10

Police-Juvenile Relations

Introduction

The Juvenile Delinquent/Adult Offender Distinction
Who Are Juvenile Offenders?

Parens Patriae and the Police

Status Offenders vs. Delinquent Offenders

Juvenile Policies and Political Reality
The Deinstitutionalization of Status Offenses (DSO)
Establishing Jurisdiction and Classifying Youths

Arresting Juvenile Offenders
Police Discretion: Use and Abuse

Delinquency and Juvenile Violence

Legal and Extralegal Factors Influencing Police-Juvenile Relations
Legal Factors
Extralegal Factors

Juvenile Gangs

Curbside and Station House Adjustments

Delinquency Prevention Programs and Police Interventions

Key Terms

Questions for Review

Suggested Readings

Scenario 1:

It is 4:30 in the morning in Omaha, Nebraska. Two officers are patrolling in their automobile in a quiet neighborhood recently experiencing considerable vandalism. They see movement in an alleyway and shine their spotlight in the darkened area. Two persons are running down the alley appearing to elude them. The officers chase them in their cruiser, eventually reaching a dead-end in the alley. The officers continue their pursuit on foot. The youths run between two houses toward another street and seem to "disappear." The officers decide to knock on doors of the two adjacent homes. Houselights come on and an elderly woman answers the door. The officers want to know if there are any youths on the premises. The woman replies, "My two grandsons live here." "Can we see them?" asks one of the officers. "Yes. Come in. I'll awaken them," she replies. A few minutes later, two barefoot youths dressed in pants and sweatshirts appear before the officers. "Were you running down the alleyway a few minutes ago?" asks one of the officers. Both youths say, "No. It wasn't us." The police officers ask if they can look in the boys' rooms. They are given permission to do so. When they enter the rooms, they find wet dirty clothes in clothes hampers. Two sets of tennis shoes are found, both with fresh mud on them. Confronted with this evidence, the boys are asked again if they were in the alley. "Yeah, we woke up early and decided to go for a walk. We didn't do nothing, though," says the older of the two boys. About that point, one of the officers receives a dispatch indicating that a home in another nearby block has been vandalized. Rocks have been thrown through windows and considerable damage has been done. Both boys' hands are dirty, as if they have been handling dirty objects or playing in the dirt. Should the officers take the boys into custody on suspicion of vandalism?

Scenario 2:

In Long Beach, California, it is 11:30 p.m. Police officers have erected temporary barriers at the ends of three city streets in neighborhoods known for gang activity. In recent weeks, several innocent pedestrians have been gunned down and others shot by youths in passing cars. All adults who approach these barricades are waved through by police. However, one car approaches with three youths. The youths are well-dressed, as if they had been to a dance or other social event. The automobile is a late-model sports car. When police approach the youths, one youth steps out of the car and shows the officer his California driver's license. His license says he is Manuel Ortega and that he lives at 3131 Miramar Dr. in Long Beach, perhaps five blocks from where the barricade has been erected. The officers ask if they can look in the trunk. The driver gives the officer the key to the trunk. When the officers open the trunk, they find an unloaded .38 special in a holster, with additional ammunition. "What's this?" an officer asks. "That is my cousin's. He's staying at our place and we went target shooting at a shooting range the other day. I guess he didn't get it out of the trunk." The police decide to take the three youths into custody because a .38 was used in the deaths of pedestrians in that same neighborhood in recent weeks.

Scenario 3:

It is 7:45 p.m. in North Miami, Florida. Four Hispanic youths have just smashed their car into the rear of a large Lincoln sedan driven by an elderly couple in a poorly lit neighborhood. A passing patrol car sees the incident happen and immediately moves in to investigate. The youths are just getting out of their car when the police arrive. The youths jump back into their car and attempt to flee. The police cruiser blocks their path, however, and two officers jump from their vehicle with drawn weapons. The four youths emerge from their car with hands raised. Each is cuffed and made to sit on the ground. The couple is examined by officers to determine the extent of their injuries. The driver, a man in his 80s, says to police that he became lost and stopped abruptly in mid-block to turn on the overhead light in the automobile to check the roadmap. One of the youths yells to police, "That guy! He stopped in the middle of the goddamned block. We couldn't do nothin'. We hit him. We didn't mean to. The son of a bitch just stopped, like, and we couldn't do nothin', man. We just run into him. We done nothin.' What you handcuffin' us for?" The police officers search the youths' automobile and discover a loaded 12-gauge shotgun on the floor under the back seat and several loose shells. Since Miami is notorious for carjackings in that same general area, and since one tactic used by carjackers is to ram victims from behind, the police arrest the four youths as carjacking suspects.

Did the police officers in any of these three scenarios do anything wrong? Did they lack probable cause in any of their actions? Which of the three scenarios above involves youths who are most likely innocent of anything?

There are no textbook answers for these questions. Each scenario differs from the others and confronts police officers with different types of problems. In each case, officer decision making will depend, in part, on the demeanor of the youths. Some of their discretion will depend on the totality of circumstances in each situation. The fact is that every police officer in every city or county law enforcement agency in the United States who has ever engaged in neighborhood patrol work has been confronted by at least one of these situations. No clear-cut guidelines exist in most jurisdictions that obligate police officers to behave in specific ways. Police officer discretion often determines the outcome of such events. Officers can act in different ways under each set of circumstances, with profoundly different outcomes depending on the nature of their intervention or lack of it.

INTRODUCTION

This chapter is about police discretion and how it pertains to a wide array of juvenile conduct. What actions should be taken by police officers who confront youths on city streets at different times? What are the circumstances? When is formal action necessary or strongly suggested? Are there statutory provisions that exist for handling certain types of police-juvenile interactions? Should *all* suspicious juveniles be arrested and taken into custody to local jails or lockups? These and similar questions will be examined in this chapter.

Since there have been several significant changes in state and federal laws during the last few decades concerning how juvenile offenders are defined and should be processed, police procedures involving juveniles have been modified greatly. Certain classes of juvenile offenders have been reclassified by law. Most notably, a clear distinction exists between **status offenders** and **juvenile delinquents** in every jurisdiction. Police officers are those who interface most often with juveniles on the streets. Particularly in inner-city settings, many youths are victims rather than perpetrators of delinquency. Police officers cannot always distinguish in a clear-cut fashion who should be investigated and who shouldn't (Sheley, McGee, and Wright, 1992:679–680). Because in many of these police officer/juvenile encounters it is unclear whether any criminal laws have been violated, police officers must use their discretion when interpreting each situation and the events observed. What is the nature of police response to changing procedures about how certain types of juveniles should be processed? Do police officers generally follow procedure and make the same distinctions between juveniles as the law requires? The implications of deinstitutionalization of status offenders (DSO) for influencing police discretion and conduct will be examined.

THE JUVENILE DELINQUENT/ADULT OFFENDER DISTINCTION

Who Are Juvenile Offenders?

Depending upon the jurisdiction, juvenile offenders are classified and defined according to several different criteria. According to the 1899 Illinois Act that created juvenile courts, the jurisdiction of such courts would extend to all juveniles under the age of sixteen who were found in violation of any state or local law or ordinance. About a fifth of all states, including Illinois, place the upper age limit for juveniles at either fifteen or sixteen. The remaining states define the upper limit for juveniles as seventeen (except for Wyoming, where the upper age limit is eighteen). In most states, the jurisdiction of juvenile courts includes all children between the ages of seven and eighteen (Black, 1990:867). Federal law defines juveniles as persons who have not attained their eighteenth birthday (18 U.S.C., Sec. 5031, 1995).

Age Jurisdiction for Juvenile Offenders. Juvenile courts define juveniles and delinquency in diverse ways. For many jurisdictions, a delinquent act is whatever these courts say it is. Such ambiguity disturbs many critics of the juvenile justice system, who believe that the authority of juvenile court judges is too broad and ought to be restricted. For instance, incorrigibility most often arises in everyday disputes between parents and their children. Thus far, the courts have mediated these disputes largely in favor of adults. At least some critics contend that juvenile courts should not intervene in less-than-life-threatening events that arise from normal parent-child relations (Guggenheim, 1985). Yet the vast bulk of incorrigibility charges that result in court-imposed sanctions on juveniles involve ordinary parent-child disputes. For some critics, these disputes are not appropriately a part of the business of American courts (Guggenheim, 1985a), but other experts contend that society has thrust on children a degree of pseudomaturity that, when coupled with the emerging rights of children, presents a compelling reason why there should be greater state involvement in parent-child disputes (Leddy, 1985).

Despite rather uniform upper age limits for juveniles that have been established in all juvenile court jurisdictions, no uniformity exists concerning lower age limits. English common law has frequently been used to define the minimum age of accountability. For instance, those persons under age seven are presumed to be incapable of formulating criminal intent, and thus these persons are beyond the reach of the criminal justice system. But many juvenile courts in the United States have not specified lower age limits for juveniles, although it is highly unlikely that a juvenile court will present a four-year-old before a judge for some type of delinquency adjudication.

Juvenile courts have almost absolute control over all children in their respective jurisdictions. Such control may involve foster home placement or community service agency control over children in need of supervision. Abused, neglected, or otherwise dependent children in need of supervision are placed in the custody of these various agencies. Generally, juvenile courts exercise broad discretionary powers over most persons under the age of eighteen. The idea that youths must be delinquent or must have committed criminal acts in order for the juvenile court to have authority over them is misleading. Also, children who are physically, psychologically, or sexually abused by parents or other adults in their homes are brought within the scope of juvenile court authority.

Most youthful offenders who appear before juvenile courts are those who have violated state or local laws or ordinances. These youths are most frequently termed **juvenile delinquents.** Federal law says that juvenile delinquency is the violation of any law of the United States by a person prior to his eighteenth birthday, which would have been a crime if committed by an adult (18 U.S.C., Sec. 5031, 1995). In law, juveniles are referred to as infants. A legal definition of a juvenile delinquent is any infant of not more than a specified age who has violated criminal laws or engages in disobedient, indecent, or immoral conduct, and is in need of treatment, rehabilitation, or supervision (Black, 1990:428). In the general case, juvenile delinquents are any minors who commit offenses that would be crimes if committed by adults. Such crimes committed by juveniles might include murder, rape, robbery, larceny, and vehicular theft. In contrast, **status offenders** are minors who commit acts that would not be crimes if committed by adults. Typical status offenses include runaway behavior, truancy, and curfew violation.

PARENS PATRIAE AND THE POLICE

Police officers encounter juveniles frequently during their routine patrolling activity. Whenever there are police-juvenile encounters, the police have broad discretionary powers about how these encounters will be interpreted. Before we examine these discretionary powers of police, it is important to place juvenile

> **BOX 11.1 12-Year-Old Killer Sentenced to Nine Years for Murder**
>
> In August 1994, two Wenatchee, Washington, twelve-year-old brothers stole three pistols and went to a nearby isolated ravine to shoot them at tin cans. An itinerant migrant worker, Emilio Pruneda, was camping near the Columbia River in a spot adjacent to the ravine. When he heard gunfire, he investigated. According to the boys' account of the incident, Pruneda, 50, began to throw rocks at the boys to make them stop shooting their pistols. The boys said they fired at Pruneda in self-defense. Subsequent investigation revealed that Pruneda was shot eighteen times near his camp with his meager possessions—a blanket, a couple of cans of food, and a blue tarp.
>
> On January 27, 1995, Duncan Sanchez, one of the brothers, was sentenced by a juvenile court judge to a long-term juvenile detention facility until the age of his majority, twenty-one. On February 10, 1995, Manuel Sanchez, the other brother, received the same sentence. Pruneda's brother, Simon Pruneda, said he understood that these sentences were the maximum the judge could impose in juvenile court, but he also said that such sentences "weren't enough." The defense lawyer for the two boys, Tom Cabrallero, indicated that he would appeal the sentences. It is unlikely that the appeals will be successful, especially in view of the fact that these were delinquency adjudications and clearly within the purview of the juvenile court.
>
> *Source:* Associated Press, "Judge Sentences 12-Year-Old Killer to Detention until He Turns 21." *Minot (N.D.) Daily News,* February 11, 1995:A2.

conduct in the historical context of the *parens patriae* doctrine. *Parens patriae* is a concept that originated with the king of England during the twelfth century and means literally, "the father of the country." When applied to juveniles, it meant that the king was in charge of, made decisions about, or had responsibility for all matters involving juvenile conduct. Chancery courts of twelfth- and thirteenth-century England and later performed many tasks, including the management of children and their affairs, as well as the management of the affairs of the mentally ill and incompetent. Thus, an early division of labor was created, involving a three-way relationship among the child, the parent, and the state (Blustein, 1983). The underlying thesis of *parens patriae* is that the parents are merely the agents of society in the area of child rearing and that the state has a primary and legitimate interest in the upbringing of its children.

The *parens patriae* doctrine is considered by many experts to be the foundation of the traditional treatment of juveniles who enter the juvenile justice system. It is manifest in a wide range of dispositional options exercised by juvenile court judges and other juvenile justice system agents involved in the earlier stages of offender processing. Most of these dispositional options are either nominal or conditional, meaning that the actual confinement of any juvenile for most offenses is regarded as the last resort. However, the strong treatment or rehabilitative orientation inherent in *parens patriae* is not acceptable to some juvenile justice experts (Springer, 1987). Many juvenile court judges stress individual accountability for a youth's actions. A growing trend in the criminal justice system toward "just deserts" and justice is being echoed in the juvenile justice system (Champion and Mays, 1991). This "get tough" movement is geared toward meting out swifter, harsher, and more certain justice and punishment to law violators, both juvenile and adult, than was previously the case under the rehabilitative philosophy.

The changing rights of juveniles are also affecting how police officers interact with and process them. Since the mid-1960s, juveniles have acquired greater constitutional rights commensurate with those enjoyed by adults in criminal courts. In fact, some experts have referred to these "rights acquisitions" as the beginning of the criminalization of juvenile courts. For instance, until the early 1970s, police officers took many suspicious youths into custody and put them in city or county jails for brief periods until their identity could be determined and their actions explained. Many of these youths were released into the custody of their parents or guardians, and many others were detained pending some formal juvenile court disposition. In 1974, however, the Juvenile Justice and Delinquency Prevention Act brought about several important changes in how subsequent police-juvenile encounters would transpire and how police officers would treat youths. A general distinction was formally acknowledged between status and delinquent offenders, and status offenders were targeted for removal from city and county jails and diverted to community shelters and treatment agencies. This general action stimulated the nationwide jail removal initiative, a general initiative to rid city and county jails of all juveniles, for whatever reason, and to relocate them in less threatening quarters in community corrections agencies or facilities.

STATUS OFFENDERS VS. DELINQUENT OFFENDERS

Status offenders are of interest to both the juvenile justice system and the criminal justice system. Although status offenses such as runaway behavior, truancy, and curfew violations are not dangerous per se, many experts believe that there are several adverse concomitants of status offenses. For example, studies of runaways indicate that many boys and girls have psychological problems and have been physically and sexually abused by their families (Janus, et al., 1987; Loeb, Burke, and Boglarsky, 1986; McCormack, Janus, and Burgess, 1986; Shaffer and Caton, 1984). Evidence suggests that many runaways engage in theft or prostitution to support their independence away from home (Garbarino, Wilson, and Garbarino, 1986). Some runaways join delinquent gangs to cope with the hostile environment. Although all runaways are not alike (Kufeldt and Perry, 1989), there have been attempts to profile them (Kaplan et al., 1989; Shane, 1989). Runaway behavior is complex and difficult to explain (Schulman and Kende, 1988), although most researchers agree that runaways generally have severe mental health needs. Runaways and missing children are given high priority by law enforcement agencies nationwide because of their greater likelihood of being victimized by others, according to the National Study of Law Enforcement Policies and Practices Regarding Missing Children and Homeless Youth conducted during 1987–1989. The research included more than 790 law enforcement agencies, 960 parents and caretakers, and 378 interviews with children (Collins et al., 1993).

Depending on how authorities and parents deal with children who have been apprehended after running away, there may be positive or adverse consequences. Empathy for runaways and their problems is important for instilling in them positive feelings (Grieco, 1984). Various runaway shelters have been established to offer runaways a nonthreatening residence and social support system in various jurisdictions. Covenant House, which originated in New York City during the 1960s, provides services to runaway youths (Ritter, 1987). Similar homes have been established in Houston, Fort Lauderdale, Toronto, and Guatemala. These shelters often locate particular services for runaways that will help meet their needs. Because many children accommodated by these shelters report they have been physically and sexually abused by family members (Janus et al., 1987), these homes sometimes cooperate with various law enforcement agencies to investigate allegations and help parents remedy the home situations (Janus et al., 1987; Ritter, 1987).

Truants and curfew and liquor law violators are also status offenders, but they tend to differ from runaways in that they are more serious offenders (Shelden, Horvath, and Tracy, 1989). Truants and liquor law violators may be more inclined to become *chronic offenders* and to engage in more serious, possibly criminal, behaviors (Shelden, Horvath, and Tracy, 1989). Violating curfew and truancy are examples of "undisciplined offenses," according to some experts. A study of 863 youths referred to the Clarke County Juvenile Court in Las Vegas, Nevada, in 1980 was conducted to determine whether runaways, truants, and curfew violators differed in their inclination to progress to more serious delinquent acts (Shelden, Horvath, and Tracy, 1989). Findings showed that compared with females, male status offenders tended to go on to more serious delinquent offenses. Furthermore, runaways were not as likely as truants or curfew violators to escalate to more serious acts after their initial court referrals. However, panels of boys in another study showed a pattern of stable or constant juvenile misbehaviors rather than a progression to more serious juvenile offenses (Rankin and Wells, 1985).

JUVENILE POLICIES AND POLITICAL REALITY

Juvenile courts seem most interested in chronic or persistent offenders and violent offenders, those who habitually appear before juvenile judges. Repeated juvenile court involvement may eventually be followed by adult criminality (Benda, 1987). It is widely assumed by experts in juvenile justice that status offenders will exhibit low rates of recidivism. However, 932 juveniles were studied in Wisconsin correctional facilities during the period 1965–1967. Of these juveniles, 166 were status offenders. These offenders were studied as long as they remained in the juvenile justice system, and they were also observed for a ten-year period as adults. It was found that 33 percent of the status offenders were returned to training schools after their first releases, largely because of new delinquent acts. Furthermore, 38 percent were subsequently convicted as adults for more serious felonies (Benda, 1987). The Benda research has received support from independent investigations of juvenile recidivism (Greenwood, 1986; Tonry and Morris, 1986).

Offender chronicity and persistence leading to multiple direct contacts with juvenile courts are considered characteristics of hard-core offenders. Frequent court contacts are believed by some researchers to stigmatize youths and cause them either to be labeled or to acquire self-concepts as delinquents (Davidson et al., 1987; DeAngelo, 1988), which has led to the diversion of certain types of juvenile offenders from the juvenile justice system to minimize these potentially adverse consequences of systemic contact (Osgood, 1983; Polk, 1984). Not everyone agrees that diversion functions to reduce personal stigmatization or labeling, however (Anderson and Schoen, 1985; Binder and Geis, 1984; Wilderman, 1984). Despite the controversy concerning diverting youths away from the juvenile justice system for informal processing, diversion programs of various kinds increased substantially in most jurisdictions during the 1970s and 1980s (DeAngelo, 1988; Schwartz, 1989).

Status offenders in many jurisdictions may be dealt with through **alternative dispute resolution (ADR)** (Hughes and Schneider, 1989). ADR for juveniles is a court-approved mediation program in which civilians selected from the community help resolve minor delinquency, status offense, and abuse/neglect cases without formal judicial hearings (National College of Juvenile and Family Law, 1989). These proceedings are helpful interventions that assist youths to avoid formal encounters with the juvenile justice system (Fine, 1984). Besides assisting youths, ADR is helpful in a purely functional respect, as it can greatly reduce caseloads and juvenile court dockets. Less serious offenders, particularly young children and status offenders, can and should be screened out of the system at early stages of processing, and informal dispositions made (McCarthy, 1987; Sametz, 1984).

Sometimes peer juries are used as alternatives to formal juvenile court proceedings (Seyfrit, Reichel, and Stutts, 1987). Peer juries consist of youths under age seventeen who make informal disposition recommendations about young offenders. These peer juries have been used in various jurisdictions. In 1980 peer juries were established by juvenile courts in Columbia County and Liberty County, Georgia. In both counties, lists of jurors were compiled by juvenile court staff. Prospective teen jurors were trained and advised of their juror responsibilities by court personnel. Over 100 juveniles had their cases adjudicated by these peer juries during several months. Whenever adjudicatory proceedings were scheduled, five teenage jurors were selected from a list of eligible youths (Seyfrit, Reichel, and Stutts, 1987). Although the investigators urge cautious interpretation of their findings because of the small sample of youths involved, evidence suggests that these peer juries were effective and quite capable of handling serious and nonserious offenders as well as juvenile recidivists, compared with the traditional juvenile court proceedings.

Many of the measures that have been devised to minimize juvenile contact with the police and juvenile courts are geared to preserving the discretionary authority of these courts over affected juveniles within the scope of *parens patriae.* Another measure that has received much attention in recent years as a major reform throughout the juvenile justice process is the removal of certain types of offenses from the jurisdiction of juvenile judges (Blackmore, Brown, and Krisberg, 1988). Because status offenses are categorically less serious than criminal offenses committed by juveniles, these have been targeted by legislatures in various states for removal from the scope of juvenile court authority. The removal of status offenses from the discretionary power of juvenile courts is called the **deinstitutionalization of status offenses** or **DSO.**

The Deinstitutionalization of Status Offenses (DSO)

The **deinstitutionalization of status offenses (DSO)** means the removal of status offenders from the authority or jurisdiction of juvenile courts, and it has been considered one of the most sweeping reforms of the juvenile justice system in many decades (Schneider, 1984a). Schneider (1984a:410) further defines the concept of DSO as "the removal from secure institutions and detention facilities of youths whose only infractions are status offenses such as running away from home, incorrigibility, truancy, and curfew violations." Schneider (1984:410–411) describes three types of deinstitutionalization that may occur, depending on the jurisdiction.

1. Decarceration. The first is **decarceration,** whereby juveniles charged with status offenses are still under court jurisdiction and subject to the filing of petitions in juvenile court. Although detention of these youths is prohibited, they may be removed involuntarily from their homes and placed in nonsecure facilities, put on probation, required to attend treatment or service programs, and subjected to other behavioral restraints.

2. CHINS. The second type of deinstitutionalization pertains to dependent and neglected children or **children in need of supervision (CHINS)** (Schneider, 1984a:411). Although the juvenile court continues to exercise jurisdiction over certain of these youths, diversion programs are established to receive status offenders directly from law enforcement officers, schools, parents, or even self-referrals.

These diversion programs provide crisis intervention services for youths, and their aim is to return juveniles eventually to their homes. However, more serious offenders may need more elaborate services provided by shelter homes, group homes, or even foster homes. However, a nationwide study of runaway youth found that over one-third had been in foster care programs during the year prior to their running away (*Corrections Compendium,* 1992b). Many of these children came from homes where they were sexually abused and/or where one or both parents had alcohol or drug problems.

3. Divestiture of Jurisdiction. The third type of deinstitutionalization is **divestiture of jurisdiction.** Under full divestiture, juvenile courts cannot detain, petition, adjudicate, or place youths on probation for any status offense. Most jurisdictions have enacted divestiture statutes (Colley and Culbertson, 1988). Early proponents of DSO believed that custodial confinement of status offenders would cause them to become delinquents, thus increasing their likelihood of committing future offenses (U.S. Senate Judiciary Committee, 1984). This belief has not received widespread support in the research literature (Datesman and Aickin, 1985; Logan and Rausch, 1985; Rankin and Wells, 1985). Some observers have thought that DSO would greatly reduce the numbers of juveniles brought into juvenile courts and/or detained in jails or lockups pending some disposition of them (Schneider, 1984a). These beliefs have been seriously challenged in most jurisdictions.

Criticisms of DSO. One of the more thorough analyses of DSO is a literature review and report by Schneider (1984a). She found the following:

1. DSO has failed to reduce the number of status offenders in secure confinement, especially in local detention.
2. Net-widening, or pulling youths into the juvenile justice system who would not have been involved before, has increased as one result of DSO.
3. Relabeling (e.g., adjudicating youths as delinquent or as emotionally disturbed who, in the past, would have been defined and handled as status offenders) has occurred extensively after DSO (Schneider, 1984a:411).
4. DSO has had little, if any, impact on recidivism rates among status offenders (Schneider, 1984a:411).
5. DSO has generated numerous service delivery problems, including inadequate services, nonexistent services or facilities, or the general inability to provide services within a voluntary system (Schneider, 1984a:411).

However DSO is viewed by experts, there is little doubt that it is widespread nationally and has become the prevailing juvenile justice policy. DSO has initiated numerous programs in all jurisdictions to better serve the needs of a growing constituency of status offenders (Blackmore, Brown, and Krisberg, 1988). This necessarily obligates growing numbers of agencies and organizations to contemplate new and innovative strategies, rehabilitative, therapeutic, and/or educational, to cope with these youths with diverse needs (Fuller and Norton, 1993; Krause and McShane, 1994). Greater cooperation among the public, youth services, and community-based treatment programs is required to facilitate developing the best program policies and practices (Farnworth, Frazier, and Neuberger, 1988; Kearney, 1989; Krisberg, 1988; McCarthy, 1989). Whenever youths have been taken into custody and have been determined to require special care, to be needy or dependent, or to be otherwise unsupervised by adults or guardians, social welfare agencies or human service organizations may be identified as destinations for their removal from jails. Verification of a youth's identity and contacts with parents may result in verbal warnings by police and return of the youth to the parents. These actions are preliminary dispositions. Status offenders, including truants, runaways, or curfew violators, may be disposed of similarly.

Establishing Jurisdiction and Classifying Youths

Jurisdiction is the power of courts to decide cases. It cuts across geographical boundary lines and territories. Depending on the juvenile court jurisdiction, the majority of alleged or suspected juvenile delinquents will move further into the juvenile justice system. Some status offenders, especially recidivists, will also be funneled further into the system. Some youths are more serious offenders, and therefore authorities may not release these youths to parental custody or to guardians. Realistic classifications of juveniles are crucial at all stages of juvenile justice processing. However, classification is particularly important when youths are first taken into custody. If it is true that the less contact with the juvenile justice system the better for juveniles in terms of lowering their potential of reoffending, then it is logical to conclude that those whose offenses least warrant exposure to the system should be withheld from it. Truants, runaways, curfew violators—status offenders—are particularly vulnerable. However, Baird (1984) observes that often, intuitive systems of classifying youths are used by juvenile professionals at various stages. He says that "juveniles differ considerably in terms of type of offense, likelihood of recommitting crimes, emotional needs, educational levels, vocational skills, honesty, and other factors. To deal effectively with this variety of people and problems requires an understanding of the individual as well as knowledge and flexibility in applying different supervision techniques" (Baird, 1984:32).

But even juvenile courts often fail to train their judges adequately to deal with juveniles or execute the court's philosophy (Mixdorf, 1989:108). Mixdorf (1989:108) says that "the initial contact of children who have gone beyond what schools, families, and communities can handle is the juvenile court and its related functions of probation, detention, and a variety of supervisory and diversionary programs. . . . Practitioners vie for limited resources and often resort to criticism of other services (services they should be supporting), thus undermining general morale within the system. . . . [The] lack of services for seriously troubled juveniles creates community crises."

Responses of police to runaways and others are affected by their perceptions of youths, departmental structure, and policy regarding juvenile operations, statutory constraints, and community characteristics and dispositional alternatives (Maxson, Little, and Klein, 1988). Smaller and more geographically isolated communities may tend to have fewer sophisticated social services available compared with urban areas to accommodate those youths who have been apprehended by police "on suspicion" but who have not otherwise violated the law. For the 10 percent of youths taken into custody by law enforcement officers who are alleged to have committed serious crimes, preventive detention is expected. However, there are potential legal issues and problems arising from detaining youthful offenders in adult jails for any significant time (Dale, 1988:46). Although a direct route to juvenile detention facilities is the desired course of action for apprehended youths if serious offenses are alleged, jurisdiction must first be established.

ARRESTING JUVENILE OFFENDERS

Police Discretion: Use and Abuse

Police officers make up the front line in the prevention and/or control of street crime (Conrad, 1987; Walker, 1984). As has already been discussed, police officers have considerable discretionary powers, depending on the circumstances, ranging from verbal warnings in confrontations with the public to the application of deadly force (Conner, 1986; Scharf and Binder, 1983; *Tennessee v. Garner*, 1985). Police discretion, as we have said, is the range of behavioral choices police officers have within the limits of their power (Davis, 1969). Beyond the formal training police officers receive from law enforcement agency training academies, police discretion is influenced by many other factors, including the "situation" (Brown, 1984; Williams, 1983), as well as the race, ethnicity, gender, socioeconomic status, and age of those confronted (Willis and Wells, 1988). Many of those stopped by police, questioned, and subsequently arrested and detained in jails or other lockup facilities, even for short periods, are juveniles.

The Diversity of Police Officer Roles. Police are expected to cope with a wide variety of neighborhood problems (Whitaker et al., 1985) and ensure that matters do not get worse (Bennett and Baxter, 1985; Bittner, 1985). Depending on community expectations, police training in different jurisdictions reflects this police officer role diversity. For instance, one training manual for police officers includes at least 476 field situations, including how to deal with domestic disturbances, traffic violations, narcotics, civil disorders, vice, drunkenness, federal offenses, and juveniles (Kenney and More, 1986).

Delinquency prevention often involves police officer visits to schools to help youths say "No" to drugs and other temptations. (*Gatewood/The Image Works*)

DELINQUENCY AND JUVENILE VIOLENCE

According to official sources, there were in excess of 1.4 million arrests of youths under age eighteen in the United States in 1988 (U.S. Department of Justice, 1988:172). In 1992, there were 1.3 million arrests involving youths in the same age range (Maguire and Pastore, 1994:455). Self-reports from juveniles in elementary schools and high schools suggest considerably greater delinquent activity as well as contacts with police that do not necessarily result in arrests or being taken into custody for brief periods (Flanagan and Maguire, 1990:322–364). Only a fraction of these youths were maintained in private juvenile facilities. In 1991, for instance, only about 36,000 youths were held in private detention centers and lockups (Moone, 1993:2).

Police officers need little, if any, provocation to bring juveniles into custody, and arrests of juveniles are, by degree, more serious than just bringing them into custody. Since any juvenile may be taken into custody for suspicious behavior or on any other pretext, all types of juveniles may be detained at police headquarters or at a sheriff's station, department, or jail temporarily. Suspected runaways, truants, or curfew violators may be taken into custody for their own welfare or protection, not necessarily for the purpose of facing subsequent offenses. It is standard policy in most jurisdictions, depending on the sophistication of available social services, for police officers and jailers to turn over juveniles to the appropriate agencies as soon as possible after these youths have been apprehended or taken into custody. Many juveniles are caught up in police "sweeps" of certain high-crime areas, particularly where illicit drugs are involved. For instance, in Wilmington, Delaware, in 1993, the Eastside Substance Abuse Awareness Program (ESAAP) involved a police officer-community effort to target and arrest those most deeply involved in illegal drug trafficking. Numerous arrests of drug suspects netted more than a few juveniles, who were detained at local jails prior to making other community arrangements (Mande, 1993). Possession of illegal firearms by youths in various cities has also accounted for large numbers of arrests (Callahan, Rivara and Farrow, 1993; Sheley and Wright, 1993).

Before police officers turn juveniles over to intake officials or juvenile probation officers for further processing, they ordinarily complete an arrest report, noting the youth's name, address, parent's or guardian's name and address, offenses alleged, circumstances, whether other juveniles were involved and apprehended, the juvenile's prior record (if any), height, weight, age, and other classificatory information.

The Jail Removal Initiative. According to the National Advisory Committee on Criminal Justice Standards and Goals (1976), juveniles must be separated from adults and treated as juveniles as soon as possible following their apprehension (unless statutory provisions exist in the jurisdiction for automatic transfers of juveniles to the criminal justice system) (Sweet, 1990:2). This is a part of the general jail removal initiative specifying the removal of juvenile offenders from prisons or jails as soon as their identities as juveniles have been determined. These goals are elaborated in the Juvenile Justice and Delinquency Prevention Act of 1974, with a 1980 amendment requiring all states to remove juveniles from their jails and lockups (Sweet, 1990:1). However, under legislative or automatic waiver action, juveniles who are arrested and charged with offenses that are either felonies or misdemeanors are automatically classified as adults and placed in custody to await further processing.

Problems of classifying youthful offenders haunt police departments. It would be difficult, for instance, to conclude that an eight-, nine-, or ten-year-old could pass for eighteen or older, but many juveniles taken into custody may or may not be under eighteen. Their appearance is deceptive, and if they deliberately wish to conceal information about their identity or age from officers, it is relatively easy for them to do so. This is a common occurrence, since many juveniles are afraid that police will notify their parents. Fear of parental reaction may sometimes be more compelling than the fear youths may have of police officers and possible confinement in a jail.

Because juveniles generally have less understanding of the law than do adults, especially those who make careers out of crime, they may believe that they will fare better if officers believe that they are adults and not juvenile offenders. Perhaps there is a chance they might be released after spending a few hours or even a day or two confined in a jail cell. However, if they are identified positively as juveniles, then parents will invariably be notified of their arrest. But

Easy availability of firearms and escalating gang violence in larger cities has made policing these persons increasingly dangerous. *(Mark Richards/The Stock Market)*

these youths often underestimate the resources police have at their disposal to verify information received from those booked after arrests. With proper identification, adults are ordinarily entitled to make bail and obtain early temporary release from jail. If fake IDs are used by juveniles, however, this phony information is easily detected and arouses police officer suspicions and interest in these youths. They will likely be detained as long as it takes to establish their true identities and ages. Furnishing police officers with false information is a rapid way to be placed in preventive detention for an indefinite period, and police officers can use preventive detention lawfully in such cases (*Schall v. Martin*, 1984).

Juvenile Arrests. Little uniformity exists among jurisdictions about how an arrest is defined. There is even greater ambiguity about what constitutes a juvenile arrest. Technically, an arrest is the legal detainment of a person to answer for criminal charges or (infrequently at present) civil demands (Rush, 1991:16). Early research by Klein, Rosensweig, and Bates (1975) focused on juvenile arrest procedures followed by forty-nine suburban and urban police departments in a large metropolitan county. More than 250 police chiefs and juvenile officers and their supervisors were surveyed, some of whom participated in follow-up, in-depth interviews about juvenile arrests and processing. Among police chiefs, for example, fewer than 50 percent were in agreement that booking juvenile suspects was the equivalent of arresting them. Further, respondents variously believed that arrests involved simple police contact with juveniles and "cautioning" behavior. Others believed that "taking youths into custody" and releasing them to parents constituted an arrest. Fewer than half of those surveyed appeared thoroughly familiar with juvenile rights under the law and the different restrictions applicable to their processing by police officers.

Photographing, Fingerprinting, and Booking Juveniles. The Juvenile Justice and Delinquency Prevention Act of 1974 and its subsequent revisions and recommendations from the National Advisory Committee on Criminal Justice Standards and Goals (1976) place important restrictions on law enforcement agencies about juvenile processing as well as the nature and purpose of records to be maintained relating to such processing. For instance, under the 1974 act, status offenders were separated in treatment from delinquent offenders through deinstitutionalization or DSO. Instead of being taken to jails for temporary detention, status offenders should be taken to juvenile agencies to await less formal dispositions. No doubt one intent of the changes was to minimize the adverse impact and labeling that jail or partial criminal processing might have on status offenders. Many states, however, particularly rural ones, have not made such distinctions between status offenders and delinquents in juvenile processing. In North Dakota, for instance, juvenile courts hear *both* status and delinquent cases, and many status offenders pull hard time along with delinquent offenders in secure juvenile facilities, for periods up to twenty-seven months.

Because most juveniles legally fall within the jurisdiction of juvenile courts and civil authority, police officers and jail officials are prohibited from engaging in certain procedural steps routinely followed when processing adult offenders. For example, whereas it is commonplace for officers to photograph and fingerprint adult offenders as a critical (and normal) part of the booking procedure, ordinarily, officers may not photograph or fingerprint juveniles. Rather, police officers must show that their use of photographs and fingerprints is either (1) for the purpose of establishing a juvenile's identity or (2) for some investigative purpose (e.g., theft of property where fingerprints of the possible youthful thieves have been obtained). Furthermore, once photographs and fingerprints have been taken, they must be destroyed as soon as possible following their use by police. If such records exist in police department files after juveniles have reached the age of their majority, they may have their records expunged or obliterated through **expungement orders.** Usually, judges issue expungement orders to police departments and juvenile agencies to destroy any file material relating to one's juvenile offense history, although policies relating to expungements vary among jurisdictions (Dunn, 1986). Expungement of one's juvenile record, sometimes known as a "sealing" of one's record, is a means of preserving and ensuring confidentiality of information that might otherwise prove harmful to adults if disclosed to others such as employers. Sealing of records is intended as a rehabilitative device, although not all juvenile justice experts believe that sealing records and enforcing confidentiality about a juvenile's past through expungement is always beneficial to the general public (Dunn, 1986).

LEGAL AND EXTRALEGAL FACTORS INFLUENCING POLICE-JUVENILE RELATIONS

Legal Factors

Both legal and extralegal factors play a role in police and intake officer decision making. Legal factors include purely factual information about the offenses alleged, such as age, type of offense committed, offense seriousness, prior juvenile record and adjudications, and the existence of inculpatory (incriminating) or exculpatory (exonerating) evidence. Extralegal factors include, but are not limited to, race and ethnicity, gender, age (which acts as both a legal and extralegal factor), socioeconomic status, attitude, and school grades and standing.

Legal and extralegal factors are important in influencing a probation officer's screening decision during an intake hearing. Although purely legal factors probably should be used exclusively in deciding whether to pursue any case, it is a fact that extralegal factors have an impact on this decision, adversely for some offenders and favorably for others. Thus, it is questionable whether juveniles can receive equitable treatment from those intake officers who stress certain extralegal factors such as gender or race in their decision making. Each of these sets of factors are examined here.

Age. Age is both a legal and an extralegal factor in the juvenile justice system. Age is *legally* relevant in decisions about waivers to criminal court jurisdiction. Waivers of juveniles under the age of sixteen to criminal courts are relatively rare, for example (Nimick, Szymanski, and Snyder, 1986). Older youths perhaps are assumed to be more responsible for their actions compared with younger youths and are often treated accordingly. Also, older youths are more likely to have prior records as juvenile offenders, be more resistant to or unwilling to accept intervention, and manifest greater adultlike self-reliance (Grisso, Tomkins, and Casey, 1988). Further, arrest data show that the peak ages of criminality lie between the sixteenth and twentieth birthdays (Greenwood, 1986).

Snyder (1988:19) suggests that although some research shows that younger youths who have contact with the juvenile justice system are more active and recidivate than youths who have contact with the system in their later teen years, the differences in recidivism rates are not that great. He states that "therefore, early age of onset youth were not more active, they simply had more time to accrue a larger number of court referrals" (1988:19). Interestingly, we can look at the risk instruments for youths devised by most state juvenile justice systems to determine the real predictive power of the age factor. Juvenile risk prediction instruments are intended to indicate a youth's propensity to recidivate or commit new offenses or pose a danger to others. Typically, greater weights are assigned to one's age at the onset of delinquency. If youths commence delinquency at age ten, for instance, they will receive a greater weight compared with youths who commence their delinquency at age twelve. That is, they will be at greater risk. The greater the younger youth's risk score, the greater the likelihood that the younger youth will subsequently be placed in secure confinement for longer periods, compared with youths with lower risk scores (Champion, 1994).

Type of Offense Committed. Another key factor in screening cases for possible processing through the juvenile justice system is the type of crime or delinquent offense committed. Is the offense property-related or violent? Was the act a felony or a misdemeanor? Were there victims with apparent injuries? Did the youth act alone or in concert with others, and what was the nature of the youth's role in the offense? Was the youth the initiator or leader, and did the youth encourage or incite others to commit various offenses? Intake officers are more likely to refer cases to juvenile prosecutors where juveniles are older (i.e., sixteen years of age and over) and where the offenses alleged are especially serious, compared with referring younger, petty offense, first offenders to prosecutors for additional processing.

McCarthy (1989) studied numerous intake decisions and found that at least in some jurisdictions an overwhelming majority of juvenile cases are disposed of informally during intake. McCarthy's data pertained to 76,150 delinquent acts committed by 17,773 juveniles born between 1962 and 1965 in Maricopa County (Phoenix, Arizona). Gathered from juvenile court files, these data showed that the vast majority of first-offenders under age sixteen, 89 percent, were handled informally at the intake level, without the formal filing of delinquency petitions and further juvenile court action. Juveniles committing more violent offenses, such as robbery and aggravated assault and burglary, were more likely to be placed in secure confinement compared with other youthful offenders. Detainees and those who progressed further into the juvenile justice system had much higher recidivism rates compared with nondetainees. However, about half of all offenders became repeat offenders, with approximately 25 percent of these juveniles repeat offending at least three or more times.

Such studies influence juvenile justice policy to the extent that leniency, particularly for first offenders, appears related to less recidivism. This conclusion may be premature and misleading however. McCarthy also noted that greater intrusion into the juvenile justice system characterizes more serious offenders, probably meaning more chronic, persistent, dangerous, or habitual offenders. This is the particular category of youthful offenders who are more likely to reoffend anyway. Strategic leniency might be appropriate here. For instance, Nagoshi (1986) found that among a sample of ninety-three Hawaiian juvenile delinquents, those who received special conditions of probation as punishments, such as restitution and community service, recidivated at a lower rate compared with those youths who were placed on probation without special conditions. One implication is that at least some punishment, properly administered, has therapeutic value for some juvenile offenders compared with no punishment.

For particular juvenile offender categories in selected jurisdictions, intake officers may be obligated to move certain types of offenders deeper into the juvenile justice system. An example of this absence of discretion in the disposition of certain juvenile cases is provided by the policy in the state of Washington. In 1978 the Washington legislature drastically overhauled its juvenile justice system (Schneider and Schram, 1986). One result was to remove completely from intake officers the option of informally adjusting cases at intake. Whereas sentencing guidelines and other criteria had evolved to dictate the direction of intake officers' discretion in many juvenile cases, the legislature's concern was for "just deserts," for fairness, uniformity, and proportionality in the processing of juvenile offenders at all stages in the system. Status offenders were removed from the jurisdiction of juvenile courts, but considerable relabeling of offenders by police officers and others occurred such that the letter of these behavioral guidelines was circumvented at various stages. Changes in system processing of different types of youthful offenders have also made it difficult for Washington officials to measure the impact of their juvenile reforms on recidivism rates among youthful offenders.

Offense Seriousness. Offense or crime seriousness pertains to whether bodily harm was inflicted or death resulted from the youth's act. Those offenses considered as serious include forcible rape, aggravated assault, robbery, and homicide—crimes against persons or violent crimes. By degree, they are more serious than the conglomerate of property offenses, including vehicular theft, larceny, and burglary. In recent years, drug use has escalated among youths and adults in the United States and is considered as one of the most serious of the nation's crime problems. One general deterrent in every jurisdiction has been the imposition of stiff sentences and fines for those who sell drugs to others and lesser punishments imposed on those who possess drugs for personal use. All large cities in the United States today have numerous youth gangs, many of which are involved rather heavily in drug trafficking (Fagan, 1988; Waldorf et al., 1990). One result of such widespread drug trafficking among youths is the provision in most juvenile courts for more stringent penalties to be imposed for drug sales and possession. Thus, crimes don't always have to be violent to be considered serious.

It should be noted that given the vast number of juvenile justice reforms that have occurred in recent years, much ambiguity persists among the various officers of the juvenile justice system as to how best to evaluate crime seriousness (Mahoney, 1989). For example, a survey of thirty-two prosecutors and six law clerks in the Union County, New Jersey, prosecutor's office was conducted to determine how these professionals rated the seriousness of selected crimes when committed by offenders of different ages (Harris, 1988). Five hundred robbery and aggravated assault cases involving male offenders were selected from both juvenile and criminal court records and rated by these prosecutors and clerks according to their seriousness. The study found that, overall, the same robbery and aggravated assault behaviors committed by juveniles were considered as substantially less serious than the same offenses committed by adults. Not only does this finding suggest that more effort should be made to give crime seriousness a more precise definition, it also suggests one important reason why critics of the juvenile justice system contend that juvenile courts are lenient in their treatment of serious juvenile offenders.

Prior Juvenile Record and Adjudications. For intake officers in the state of Washington and other jurisdictions where guidelines are followed relating to intake dispositions, prior records of delinquency adjudications are factored into their decisions. In other jurisdictions, prior records strongly suggest that prior treatments and punishments were apparently ineffective at curbing offender recidivism. It would be logical to suspect that intake probation officers would deal more harshly with those having prior records of delinquency adjudications. In fact, some research has demonstrated that greater numbers of prior offenses tend to result in a youth's further involvement in the juvenile justice process beyond intake (Grisso, Tomkins, and Casey, 1988). One's prior record of juvenile offenses defines persistence and chronicity and perhaps a rejection of attempts at intervention and treatment. In some of these cases, harsher punishments and dispositions have been observed (Greenwood, 1986). However, this is not a blanket generalization designed to cover all offense categories, as some offense categories have priority over others for many intake officers.

In addition, the previous disposition of a particular juvenile's case seems to be a good predictor of subsequent case dispositions for that offender. For example, a study of the influence of prior records and prior adjudications on instant offense dispositions has shown that dispositions for prior offenses have a significant impact on current dispositions for those same offenses, regardless of the type or seriousness of the offense (Thornberry and Christenson, 1984). Thus, if a juvenile has formerly been adjudicated delinquent on a burglary charge and probation for six months was imposed as the punishment, a new burglary charge against that same juvenile will likely result in the same probationary punishment of six months. Only the new offense seriousness has a greater impact on one's current punishment than does the influence of prior dispositions.

It is important to note here that often, repeat offender appearances before the same juvenile judge, regardless of the violent or nonviolent nature of the offending behavior, may result in the repeat offender's transfer of jurisdiction to criminal court. This is the judge's way of getting rid of particularly bothersome juveniles who are neither dangerous nor serious offenders (Champion and Mays, 1991).

Extralegal Factors

A balanced approach has been suggested by Maloney, Romig, and Armstrong (1988). They envision three major goals of probation officers serving in various capacities in relation to their clients. These goals include (1) protecting the community, (2) imposing accountability for offenses, and (3) equipping juvenile offenders with competencies to live productively and responsibly in the community. Ideally, each of these goals is equal. These researchers say that such balanced objectives have been used by probation officers in Deschutes County, Oregon; Austin, Texas; and the Menominee Indian Reservation in Wisconsin, where individuality in decision making—assessing all three goals for each juvenile offender—is sought. These three goals may have variable importance to probation officers performing intake functions in other jurisdictions, however. Depending on their orientation, some intake officers may emphasize their community protection function, whereas others may emphasize juvenile offender accountability and officers with rehabilitative interests may tend to promote educational programs that would enable youths to operate productively in their respective communities.

In the context of attempting to balance these three objectives, several extralegal factors have emerged to influence adversely the equality of treatment these youths may receive from probation officers at intake: age (discussed earlier), gender, and race/ethnicity.

Gender. Generally, traditional patterns of female delinquency have persisted over the years. Because there are so few female juvenile offenders compared with male offenders, the influence of gender on intake decision making and at other stages of the juvenile justice process has not been investigated extensively. Juvenile females make up approximately 10 percent or less of the juvenile detention population in the United States annually (American Correctional Association, 1996). Females are only slightly more represented proportionately among those on probation or involved in assorted public and private aftercare services.

Differential treatment of males and females in both the juvenile and criminal justice systems is well documented. However, some of the traditional reasons given for such differential treatment appear to be largely mythical and misconceived (Curran, 1984; Gelsthorpe, 1987). Contemporary assessments of the impact of gender on intake decision making show that gender is only moderately related to dispositions, consistent with intake guidelines in selected jurisdictions such as Las Vegas, Nevada (Shelden and Horvath, 1987). Investigations of other jurisdictions such as Massachusetts as well as analyses of national figures show generally that female juveniles are detained less often than male juveniles, are returned to the community at a greater rate than males, and are committed to detention at a much lower rate than males (Frazier and Bishop, 1985; Massachusetts Department of Youth Services, 1984; McCarthy, 1985). A strong contributing factor is the paternalistic view of juvenile judges and others in the juvenile justice system that has persisted over time under the influence of *parens patriae*. Differences between the arrest rates of female and male juveniles and the proportion of females to males who are subsequently adjudicated as delinquent suggest that the case attrition rate for females is significantly higher at intake than it is for male juveniles.

Specific studies of intake decision making have disclosed, however, that gender exerts only an indirect impact on such decision making by officers

(McCarthy and Smith, 1986). Paradoxically, female juveniles with prior referrals to juvenile court seem to be treated more harshly than male offenders with prior referrals, especially for committing one of several index violent offenses. Based on his analysis of the juvenile court involvement of 69,504 juvenile offenders in Arizona and Utah, Snyder (1988) calculated probabilities of being referred to juvenile court for an index violent offense, where both male and female juveniles had similar numbers of prior court referrals. He found that males with eight prior referrals were more than three times as likely to be referred to juvenile court for an index violent offense than a male with only one previous referral, and more than twice as likely as a male with two prior referrals. However, females with eight prior referrals were six times as likely to be referred to juvenile court for an index violent offense compared with females who had only one prior referral, and three times as likely to be referred compared with females with two prior referrals (1988:44–45). There were negligible differences between male and female juvenile offenders relating to referrals for property crimes.

Race and Ethnicity. Race and ethnicity are important in differentiating among juvenile arrestees. One investigation of the impact of race on dispositional decision making at intake, conducted by Bell and Lang (1985), found that the relation between race and decision making was apparently indirect. Similarly, Shelden and Horvath (1987) found no direct influence of race on the nature of intake processing in 436 cases they analyzed for a Nevada county. Finally, McCarthy (1985), who studied 649 juvenile delinquents referred to family courts in 1982, said her preliminary impression was that at least at the adjudicatory stage, juvenile judges did not seem to be influenced by racial or gender factors.

A subsequent analysis of the same data by McCarthy and Smith (1986) revealed that some racial discrimination in handling existed, although it was unevenly distributed through various stages of the system. For example, these researchers discovered that at intake hearings, the racial factor did not appear significant in dispositions or adjustments made by intake officers, but juvenile court adjudications and detention decisions seemed influenced by racial factors. Specifically, greater proportions of African Americans than whites were adjudicated delinquent and sentenced to detention. Although this is not absolute proof of discrimination, it nevertheless implies that minority juveniles, particularly African Americans, were disadvantaged by their race in judicial decision making. McCarthy and Smith (1986) suggest that a better idea of the impact of race and other factors on decision making can be obtained by considering several different stages of the juvenile justice process than by focusing on one single stage such as intake or adjudicatory hearings.

A case study of a random sample of 228 cases involving juveniles referred by police officers and others to the juvenile probation intake and detention screening process in Travis County, Texas, determined that most juvenile referrals were between the ages of thirteen and fifteen and were disproportionately African American (Arrigona and Fabelo, 1987). Although fewer than 50 percent of these referrals had subsequent referrals within a six-month period following their initial referrals, about 60 percent of all first referrals were diverted informally by intake officers. Thus, disproportionate racial representations at the front end of intake help to explain subsequent racially disproportionate managements and dispositions of cases through the intake, detention hearing, and adjudicatory stages (Arrigona and Fabelo, 1987).

When the rate of incarcerating African American juveniles compared to whites is considered, there are much sharper distinctions and treatment differentials that suggest that widespread discrimination exists. For instance, the Humphrey Institute for Public Affairs (1986) found that during the period 1979–1982, African Americans and other minorities were incarcerated in secure detention facilities three to four times more than white offenders. More recent research that profiles secure juvenile detention facilities in Wisconsin shows that African American juvenile offenders made up nearly one-half of the incarcerated population, although African Americans comprise only about 12 percent of the entire United States population (Grohmann and Barritt, 1987). However, if McCarthy's and Smith's (1986) observation is accurate, that we can better understand the impact of race by considering all stages of the juvenile justice process, then certainly our attention would be drawn backward in the system to the originating agents, the law enforcement officers who take youths into custody initially.

A majority of police officers patrol the streets and are responsive to street crime. Street crime generally is overrepresented among those in the lower socioeconomic strata, including minority youths. As screening agents, intake probation officers may influence the influx of cases further into the system through informal adjustments, however. These adjustments depend in part on an officer's perception of family stability and the overall environment of the juvenile. The socioeconomically disadvantaged and minority youths are particularly vulnerable here. For instance, Farnworth (1984) argues that the economic dimension of the lives of African American families is more relevant in explaining delinquency among youths than is African American familial instability. However, a similar analysis and conclusion may be made about white youths who are socioeconomically disadvantaged and engage in delinquent conduct. Race and ethnicity appear prominent as predictor variables in arrest and detention discretion, but at present, our accumulated evidence has failed to delineate the precise nature of the race/arrest-detention relation.

Whether juveniles are involved in a gang is another important consideration. Youth gangs often form along racial and ethnic lines. Further, the presence of gangs in neighborhoods makes gang members more visible to police officers (Moore, 1985). In many jurisdictions, such as Milwaukee, Wisconsin, juvenile gang members and their activities have been targeted for special handling and procedures by police department subdivisions (Hagedorn, 1988). Responses to gang members and their activities by police are not always appropriate or productive, however. In some cases, police departments have exaggerated the importance and influence of specific gangs and have equated their organization and operations with organized crime. This approach is destructive and obscures legitimate attempts to reinforce and emphasize conventional behaviors and social linkages available to youths who happen to identify with these gangs (Hagedorn, 1988).

JUVENILE GANGS

Juvenile Units in Police Departments. For many years U.S. police departments, particularly larger municipal departments with 200 or more officers, have operated specialized juvenile units as a part of their organizational structure to deal with different types of offenders (Sanders, 1994). Even relatively small departments in remote areas have at least one juvenile officer who deals exclusively with juvenile affairs. Despite this specialization, however, every police officer who encounters juveniles while policing becomes a juvenile officer temporarily (Rogers and Mays, 1987:314). One example of an intervention strategy involving both citizens and police officers was implemented in Ft. Worth, Texas. Known as Citizens on Patrol, the program involved designated groups patrolling their own neighborhoods (Givens et al., 1993). The St. Louis Police Department established an Assault Crisis Team (ACT) to counteract rising juvenile violence by monitoring youth gangs more effectively. A part of this plan was to work with warring juvenile gangs and create conditions in which neutral parties could initiate selective mediation of disputes (Givens et al., 1993).

The activities of juvenile units, gang units, and "youth squads" are largely directed toward preventing delinquency (Cummings and Monti, 1993). These units tend to be reactive, in that they respond to public requests for intervention and assistance whenever offenses committed by juveniles are reported. That is, these officers react to calls from others about crimes that have already been committed or are in progress. Gang fights or break-ins involving youths would activate these juvenile units, for example. In contrast, police officers who patrol city streets are most often proactively involved in contacts with juveniles who may or may not be offenders or law violators. Almost constantly on the lookout for suspicious activities, they monitor the streets and investigate potentially troublesome situations. In the 1990s the mode of response to gangs in most U.S. jurisdictions has been a proactive one, especially in those areas of the country where there is a significant presence of well-known gangs, such as the Crips and Bloods (Waldorf, 1993). Further, special units within units have been formed to handle female juveniles, who appear to be joining these gangs in greater numbers annually (Chesney-Lind, 1993; Maguire and Pastore, 1994).

Minorities and Youth Gangs. The dramatic increase in the number of delinquent gangs organized along ethnic and racial lines in many cities and the violence such gangs manifest have caused police departments to establish task forces of special police officers who do nothing but monitor and investigate gang activities (Block and Block, 1993; Spergel, 1992). Some professionals have classified these gangs as scavenger gangs and corporate gangs (Taylor, 1986). **Scav-**

enger gangs form primarily as a means of socializing and for mutual protection, whereas **corporate gangs** emulate organized crime (Taylor, 1986). Both types of gangs pose dangers to the public; however, corporate gangs are more profit motivated and rely on illicit activities such as drug trafficking to further their profit interests. Corporate gangs use excessive violence, including murder, to carry out their goals. Often, innocent bystanders are gunned down as victims of gang retaliation against rival gangs and gang members (Taylor, 1986).

Whenever pairs of juveniles are observed on the street, particularly in areas known to be gang dominated, police may assume that these youths are members of gangs. This observation may heighten their interest in these youths and prompt some interaction with them, such as more frequent stopping and questioning of certain juveniles on the basis of their appearance, geographical location, and whether they are minority youths. Although police officers are governed by cases such as *Mapp v. Ohio, Terry v. Ohio,* and *Sibron v. New York,* they often engage in situationally based discretionary actions that might otherwise be considered illegal. The isolated nature of their contacts with juveniles makes legal retaliation against them or the police department extremely unlikely.

CURBSIDE AND STATION HOUSE ADJUSTMENTS

Arresting Juvenile Offenders. Some critics question whether police officers discriminate against certain youths by singling them out and stopping them for questioning on the basis of racial or ethnic factors (Wilbanks, 1987). Other researchers have described patterns of police behavior that appear to be prima facie evidence of discrimination according to racial or ethnic criteria (Huizinga, Esbensen, and Elliott, 1987). At least in some jurisdictions, stops, arrest rates, and detentions of minority youth are at least three times as high as those for white youths (Black and Reiss, 1976; Huizinga and Elliott, 1987).

Much police officer activity is centered in high-crime areas that also tend to be lower socioeconomic areas, and those areas with larger numbers of persons of lower socioeconomic status (SES) are also those that contain larger concentrations of minorities (Sampson, 1986). Thus, there is some selectivity in where police officers concentrate their patrol efforts as well as which youths they target for questioning or choose to ignore. Experts believe that this opens the door to allegations of police officer harassment against certain classes of juvenile offenders on the basis of subjectively determined stereotypical features such as appearance (Yablonsky and Haskell, 1988:38).

How Youths Respond to Police Contacts. How youths behave toward police officers whenever they are stopped and questioned seems to make an important difference as to what the officers will eventually do to these youths. Some studies on the appearance and demeanor of youths stopped by police officers and their subsequent actions indicate that youths who were poorly dressed or behaved defiantly and belligerently toward police were more likely to be harassed and possibly arrested (Tomson and Fielder, 1975). Subsequent research is consistent with these early findings and suggests that cooperative, neatly dressed youths stand a better chance of avoiding being stopped, questioned, or arrested by police (Morash, 1984).

Some police officers claim that a youth's demeanor when answering their questions on the street is the determining factor as to whether the youth will be taken into custody. Therefore, if youths do not exhibit the proper amount of humility toward police officers when they are stopped and questioned, they will stand a good chance of being taken to the police station for further questioning (Smith and Visher, 1981). However, it is also possible for youths to be too polite. Politeness from juveniles arouses police officer suspicions. Thus, an elusive range of politeness exists that minimizes a youth's chances of being taken into custody. Youths can be either too polite or not polite enough so that police officers are sufficiently aggravated and motivated to act. These are occasions when police officer discretionary abuses occur most frequently and when juveniles are detained when there is little or no evidence that detention is necessary or desirable to meet the generally accepted goals of detention (Roberts, 1989:150).

The following are discretionary actions that may be taken by police officers when encountering youths on the street:

1. Police officers may ignore the behaviors of youths they observe in the absence of citizen complaints.
2. Police officers may act passively on someone's complaint about juvenile behaviors.
3. Police officers may take youths into custody and release them to parents or guardians without incident.
4. Police officers may take youths into custody and refer them officially to community service agencies for assistance or treatment.
5. Those juveniles who are deemed dangerous, violent, or persistent-nonviolent are most likely to be subject to detention until adjudication by a juvenile court.
6. Police officers may take youths into custody, file criminal charges against them, and statutorily place them in jails pending their initial appearance, a preliminary hearing, and a subsequent trial.

Thus, police discretion is exercised most during the normal course of police patrols or beats. Youths who have the most chance of being targeted for special police attention include minorities who are acting suspiciously or who live in high-crime neighborhoods known as gang territories. Also increasing the likelihood of being taken into custody is the youth's demeanor or behavior, whether too polite or not polite enough to police officers. In the absence of any actual delinquent conduct observed in the presence of police officers, appearance and behavior are key considerations in whether youths will be harassed and detained temporarily by police. However, comparatively few youths are actually arrested in relation to the actual number of police officer/juvenile encounters on city streets.

There are statutory safeguards about detaining youths in adult jails for long periods. Also, in most jurisdictions, police officers are directed to take juveniles to places other than city or county jails. The division of labor relating to youthful offender processing in any jurisdiction, however, is such that police officers can do whatever they want relative to juveniles they question and who are either acting suspiciously or belligerently. If any pretext exists for assuming that certain youths have been or are engaging in delinquent acts, they are subject to temporary detention by police officers. In many instances, these detention decisions by police are purely arbitrary (Frazier and Bishop, 1985).

It has been suggested that within the framework and spirit of community policing, police officers might consider taking a more proactive role as interventionists in the lives of juvenile offenders encountered on the street. For instance, Trojanowicz and Bucqueroux (1990:238) maintain that "young people do not launch long-term criminal careers with a daring bank robbery, an elaborate kidnapping scheme, or a million-dollar dope deal. Yet the traditional police delivery system does not want officers 'wasting' much time tracking down the kid who may have thrown rocks through a few windows at school. Narcotics officers on their way to bust Mr. Big at the dope house cruise right by those fleet-footed 10-year-old lookouts. And a call about a botched attempt by a youngster to hotwire a car would not be much of a priority, especially where far more serious crimes occur every day." These professionals suggest that officers should be encouraged to take these petty offenses and juvenile infractions seriously and intervene. It is possible for police officers to identify youngsters most at risk in particular neighborhoods and perhaps do something to help them avoid future lives of crime.

The nature of systems is such that the actions of particular parts of the system may not function properly or be permitted to function properly in relation to other parts. It would be difficult, for instance, for Trojanowicz and Bucqueroux to sell their ideas to the police departments in Yakima or Seattle, Washington, or at least to the officers on duty there in the late 1970s and early 1980s. Whether or not these officers were justified in doing so, they took it upon themselves to intervene significantly in the lives of status offenders after divestiture was enacted. But the nature of their intervention was contrary to the spirit of intervention outlined by Trojanowicz and Bucqueroux in their description of police actions under community policing policies. More status offenders and petty offenders on the streets of Yakima and Seattle were herded vigorously into jails and juvenile courtrooms after divestiture than ever before. This is a far cry from officers acting as interventionists and doing something creative for youngsters at risk other than detaining them.

It has been recommended that police departments have separate units to interface with and manage juveniles, but the reality is that many smaller police departments and sheriff's offices do not have the staff or facilities to accommodate such specialties. These luxuries are usually enjoyed only by larger departments. Smaller departments must be content with individual officers who assume responsibilities for managing juvenile offenders and related tasks. The majority of initial contacts with juveniles who engage in unacceptable behaviors continues to be made by uniformed police officers while on patrol (Kratcoski and Kratcoski, 1986:220).

Guarino-Ghezzi (1994) suggests that one effective police officer strategy might be to combine community corrections with community policing. Police officers must learn to differentiate between those hard-core youths who create substantial problems and more vulnerable youths who are, in fact, victims. One important police function is to protect youthful victims by establishing order maintenance and law enforcement practices that do not give youths mixed messages. It is important for police officers to minimize the ambiguity of their relations with youths and to avoid misleading them. Some police officers who police the worst neighborhoods in their communities may form beliefs about the youths in those neighborhoods that are defeatist, that regard these youths as "beyond redemption" (Guarino-Ghezzi, 1994:150–152). It is often easy to include victimized youths together with delinquents when dealing with juveniles on the street. Developing a closer contact with community residents may sensitize police officers to those most in need of their protective services and efforts to maintain order.

DELINQUENCY PREVENTION PROGRAMS AND POLICE INTERVENTIONS

Police officers have done much to create negative images of themselves among youths (Milton S. Eisenhower Foundation, 1993). Juveniles are stopped often, in their opinion, simply because they are teenagers walking the streets. They cannot or do not want to understand the point of view of police officers who may see gang trouble or the potential for violence or crime resulting from youths gathered on corners at night. Police officers acquire a professional defensiveness, assuming that their authority will be challenged. In certain cities, this defensiveness is justified, since police cruisers have sometimes been targets of random shootings from alleyways or rooftops. Community policing is one strategy intended to overcome these negative stereotypes of police officers, because police officers attempt to become acquainted with the neighbors they try to protect.

Many experts believe that effective intervention programs designed to prevent delinquent conduct should be started early in a youth's life. School systems are logical sites for intervention programs because large numbers of youths assemble there regularly (U.S. Senate Majority Staff of the Senate Judiciary Committee, 1994). Moreover, teachers are often aware of illicit activity, including drug use and gang violence, that occurs around schools. In addition, many students walk to school and thus become vulnerable targets for child sexual abusers, youth gangs, and street people (*Corrections Compendium*, 1991; New York Commission for the Study of Youth Crime and Violence and the Reform of the Juvenile Justice System, 1994).

The following are some intervention programs:

1. D.A.R.E. One way of combatting illicit drug use among elementary schoolchildren is a program the Los Angeles Police Department has implemented called Drug Abuse Resistance Education or D.A.R.E. Police officers familiar with drugs and drug laws visit schools in their precincts and speak to youths about how to say no to drugs. Children learn how to recognize illegal drugs and about different types of drugs and their adverse effects.

2. TIPS. TIPS means Teaching Individuals Protective Strategies. It is sponsored by the U.S. Department of Education and is geared to helping youths in schools acquire the reasoning ability for responsible decision making. Especially designed for children in grades K–8, TIPS' two principal objectives are (1) to reduce victimization among youths as well as their vulnerability to become victims, and (2) to identify potential solutions to problems that involve noncriminal activities. Thus, youths in schools are trained to deal with strangers, to become more aware of potentially dangerous social situations, and to channel anger or frustration into productive activities. Part of the TIPS program is incorporated into each youth's educational training. Thus far, the results seem successful at reducing youth victimization by adults or other youths.

3. Project Heavy. Project Heavy is an alternative program located in Los Angeles County. It involves a peer- and group-counseling program for children and youths ages eight to eighteen, and youth leaders are targeted for change so that they can set good examples for others (Keith, 1989:117). The theory underlying Project Heavy is that youth leaders are admired by other youths. If they can set good conduct examples, then more youths will follow these examples rather than those exemplifying delinquent conduct.

4. GREAT (Gang Resistance Education and Training). Because of the powerful influence of youth gangs nationwide, community leaders and educators implemented a program in Phoenix, Arizona, funded by the Bureau of Alcohol, Tobacco, and Firearms, that utilizes police officers who visit schools and interact with students on a regular basis over a specified time period. Classroom sessions consist of eight one-hour periods in which youths can learn to overcome peer pressure involving drug use and joining delinquent gangs. The weekly topics are diverse, including cultural sensitivity and prejudice, crimes, victims and rights, drugs and neighborhoods, diverse responsibilities, goal setting, and conflict resolution and need fulfillment. Parental involvement is encouraged, and police organizations sponsor summer activities to give local youths interesting alternative projects.

5. Alateen. In many instances, youths either have alcohol problems themselves or have parents with alcohol problems. Alateen is the teen counterpart to Alcoholics Anonymous. Police officers function in an instructive capacity to alert children to the signs of alcoholism among themselves and their friends and to help children find additional assistance.

6. Hire a Gang Leader. Hire a Gang Leader originated in El Monte, California, in 1975 as a delinquency prevention program sponsored by members of the local police department. Groups of ten to fifteen gang leaders met with police officers and designed a program to provide job opportunities for gang members who were unemployed. This cooperative effort was successful in several respects. First, it taught gang members that police officers are not always their enemies. Second, it gave them a different view of the police officer role as an enabler and facilitator, since there were numerous successful job placements. Police officers benefited, because delinquency rates in the El Monte area dropped where gangs participated in the program (Amandes, 1979).

7. TOPS. Police officers in Rochester, New York, decided to use teens themselves to "police" other teens in the early 1980s (Lipson, 1982). A privately funded program was implemented known as TOPS (Teens on Patrol). Police officers selected 125 youths to maintain security and patrol city parks and recreational areas. Interestingly, these teens did a reasonably good job at deterring others from committing delinquent acts in the parks and causing trouble for park patrons. Ultimately, some of the TOPS became cops and were hired by the Rochester Police Department.

8. Dickerson's Rangers. Dickerson's Rangers is an antidrug program started in the San Fernando Valley of Southern California. This program, which targets children ages seven through thirteen, operates in various city parks and recreational centers. Children meet weekly and discuss drug abuse in their schools and communities. Police officers advise them how to resist drug dealers or peers who might use drugs. The program also sponsors field trips and speakers on drug abuse and prevention.

9. Campus Pride. Various school districts throughout the United States have instituted Campus Pride, a program that attempts to remove gang graffiti from school grounds. Police officers can assist school leaders in identifying gang slogans and symbols, and often, gang members themselves may be ordered by juvenile courts to remove graffiti. Otherwise, the students work together to keep their schools clean of gang graffiti and possible violence. Gang graffiti is often used to mark off certain areas, including schools, as a gang's turf or territory. Acting together, however, students have been able to force gang members off their turf and other "territories."

10. The Graffiti Removal Community Service Program. One way to combat gang recruitment and involvement in the Southern California area is through the Graffiti Removal Community Service Program (Agopian, 1989). Juveniles who are initially apprehended and determined to be affiliated with gangs are assigned to a community service program as a condition of their probation. They must perform an average of 140 hours of community service, which consists of removing graffiti from buildings and other structures in their communities, together with other probationary conditions. According to Agopian, the removal of gang graffiti benefits the community as well as gang members, who hopefully learn that law-abiding behavior and respect for property are expected. Agopian reports that during the first two years that the program operated, nearly 90 percent of all participating youths completed this requirement of their probation. Further, rearrests of these youths during the two-year interval were minimal. However, these youths, once released from their probation programs, are placed back in their original environments and subject to the same social pressures and economic conditions that brought them to the attention of police officers initially.

11. COPY Kids (Community Opportunities Program for Youth). COPY Kids is a police demonstration project that was undertaken in the summer of 1992 in Spokane, Washington (Thurman, Giacomazzi, and Bogen, 1993:554–555). Officers engaged in weekly interactions with 300 economically disadvantaged youths averaging thirteen years of age. Their program attempted to assist these youths in improving their self-concepts and in following general law-abiding behavior. Parents were involved as well as a large supporting staff. Youths were given an opportunity to participate in various crafts and jobs in which they could acquire skills for subsequent employment. Interviews with parents and workers suggested that these productive activities allowed children to develop a greater sense of responsibility. Particularly encouraging was that these youths developed a more favorable image of police officers and the police department. Although there was limited information to show any effects on curbing delinquency among the participating youths, investigators believed that the plan was a useful deterrent to delinquent conduct.

12. R.O.C.K. (Reaching Out, Convicts and Kids). R.O.C.K., a program established in Visalia, California, by the Tulare County Probation Department in 1992 (*Corrections Compendium*, 1992a), was designed to enable troubled youths to avoid illegal activities. A nontraditional program, R.O.C.K. uses convicted felons as volunteers who give youths first-hand accounts of what led to their crimes and the effects of these crimes on victims. Workshops are used to establish a foundation of honesty among inmates and youths and to help channel the youths' behavior toward law-abiding activities. Education, improving familial relations, and learning ways of coping with peer pressures are emphasized. Those youths who experience R.O.C.K. stand a much better chance of avoiding delinquency than those who do not become involved in the program.

The preceding programs are only a few of the many programs operating throughout the United States involving police in proactive and positive roles. They are taking an active interest in preventing delinquent conduct through interacting closely with youths. These programs will not necessarily turn juvenile offenders around, but they may make many youths aware of a positive side of police officers. Further, the programs may have the positive effect of helping police officers understand juveniles and their motives.

KEY TERMS

Alternative dispute resolution (ADR)
Children in need of supervision (CHINS)
Corporate gangs
Decarceration
Deinstitutionalization of status offenses (DSO)
Divestiture of jurisdiction
Expungement orders
Juvenile delinquents
Juvenile delinquency
Scavenger gangs
Status offenders

QUESTIONS FOR REVIEW

1. Differentiate between proactive and reactive police work. In what sense is every police officer a juvenile officer?
2. Distinguish between corporate and scavenger delinquent gangs. What are their respective objectives and ambitions?
3. Why are police officers interested in gang activities?
4. What are five discretionary options police may exercise in their encounters with juveniles?
5. Under what circumstances are police likely justified in taking youths into custody for further investigation? What factors influence their decision to take youths into custody?
6. What are some general limitations and prohibitions about photographing and fingerprinting juveniles in jails or lockups?
7. What is meant by discretionary power generally? In what way is the police officer role diffuse?
8. How is the "totality of circumstances" relevant to influencing police discretion? What are some of the extralegal or nonlegal factors that cause police officers to take youths into custody who have not otherwise violated the law?
9. What do you think is the nature of the conflict between the *parens patriae* doctrine and due process?
10. What is meant by divestiture as applied to juveniles? In what ways can police officers and judges resist divestiture? Give an example of each type of situation in which police officers and judges might behave in ways that resist divestiture.

11. What is meant by CHINS? Can police officers remove juveniles from their homes and take them into custody? What might be some circumstances that would cause such police officer action?
12. What is the Juvenile Justice and Delinquency Prevention Act of 1974? What did it provide relative to status offenders and juvenile delinquents?

SUGGESTED READINGS

Chiland, Colette, and Gerald J. Young (1993). *Children and Violence.* New York: Jason Aronson.

Collins, James J., et al. (1993). *Law Enforcement Policies and Practices Regarding Missing Children and Homeless Youth: Research Summary.* Washington, DC: U.S. Office of Juvenile Justice and Delinquency Prevention.

Jones, Michael A., and Barry Krisberg (1994). *Images and Reality: Juvenile Crime, Youth Violence, and Public Policy.* San Francisco: National Council on Crime and Delinquency.

Kappeler, Victor E. (ed.) (1995). *The Police and Society: Touchstone Readings.* Prospect Heights, IL: Waveland Press.

U.S. Community Relations Service (1993). *Principles of Good Policing: Avoiding Violence between Police and Citizens.* Washington, DC: U.S. Community Relations Service.

CHAPTER 11

Comparative Community Policing

Introduction

Comparative Community Policing Defined

Police-Community Relations in England
Type of Government
Types of Crimes
Police Supervision and Organization
Community Policing in England

Police-Community Relations in Canada
Type of Government
Types of Crime
Police Supervision and Organization
Community Policing in Canada

Police-Community Relations in Japan
Type of Government
Types of Crime and Crime Rates
Police Supervision and Organization
Community Policing in Japan

International Policing

Are There Any Cultural Universals?

Trends in Comparative Community Policing

Key Terms

Questions for Review

Suggested Readings

INTRODUCTION

During the 1980s and early 1990s public confidence in the police has steadily eroded. Racial and ethnic minorities have been particularly dissatisfied with many police officer behaviors and with how politely they have been treated by police when stopped on the street (Skogan, 1990). Additionally, police officers in certain jurisdictions have been physically attacked by citizens, with substantial peer approval (Noaks and Christopher, 1990). In two jurisdictions, various victims of alleged police misconduct and brutality have come forth with demands for prosecutors to hold the offending police officers accountable for their illegal actions (Miyazawa, 1988; University of Cape Town Institute of Criminology, 1990). Finally, evidence has been disclosed of the existence of a "police culture" designed to disguise and condone police misconduct by an informal officer code of loyalty to other officers. An official government report indicates escalating community distrust of police officers who attempt to hide the misconduct of their fellow officers from public view (Ewin, 1990).

Do these statements and allegations sound familiar? Are these continuing problems stemming from the Rodney King incident in 1990? Is this a current description of the Los Angeles Police Department? Most certainly, all of these statements must pertain to one or more jurisdictions in the United States. Wrong! Respectively, the above paragraph describes criticisms of police officers by concerned citizens of England, South Wales, Japan, South Africa, and Queensland, Australia, and these are not the only countries outside of the United States reporting abuses of police power. Consider the following items:

- Higher standards are now in force for the selection and training of German police officers (Fairchild, 1989).
- The use of deadly force by police officers in Sao Paulo and Rio de Janeiro, Brazil, is disproportionately high, compared with other countries, and officials believe that with proper training and greater selectivity in recruitment, the number of citizen deaths attributable to police use of deadly force can be minimized (Chevigny, 1990).
- Amsterdam officials have implemented new policies to reduce the incidence of police misconduct and theft among Netherlands officers (Van Laere and Geerts, 1984).
- French crime victims report growing alienation between themselves and the police officers who theoretically protect them from criminal victimization. French officials are considering victim-oriented policies to promote better police-community relations in future years (Zauberman, 1991).

These messages convey (1) greater public awareness of police actions, whether favorable or unfavorable; (2) deliberate intent by interested agencies, both public and private, to improve drastically the selection and training methods currently used for guiding police officer socialization and professional conduct; (3) implementation of policies and practices to reduce the incidence of police misconduct and unlawful behaviors; and (4) a recognition of the importance of greater community-police officer contact whereby such interactions will restore and improve public confidence in police agencies as cooperative, helpful, and protective bodies rather than as adversarial ones.

Every civilized country has a law enforcement component. Some nations, such as the United States, have effected major philosophical changes regarding how communities are policed. As we have seen, a growing trend in many American communities is toward community policing, through which both police officers and private citizens work together in creative ways to help solve problems stemming from neighborhood crime, the fear of crime, social and physical disorder, and community decay (Trojanowicz and Bucqueroux, 1990:5). An inspection of the professional literature relating to foreign police structure, operations, and methods suggests a nearly worldwide gradual movement of law enforcement agencies in other nations toward community policing. Thus, it is important to investigate existing law enforcement patterns and functions in other countries in order to understand both the short- and long-term implications of such drastic philosophical changes in these affected nations.

COMPARATIVE COMMUNITY POLICING DEFINED

It is well-known that police agencies in most U.S. jurisdictions exchange information about their structure and operations on a regular basis. New administrative ideas are disseminated in professional journals and at conventions, where panels of scholars and practitioners develop their ideas and make constructive suggestions. Especially during the 1980s and early 1990s, there was a noticeable increase in information sharing at the international level. Such international information sharing continues at an increasing rate. There is considerable interest throughout Europe and other continents in restructuring existing law enforcement agencies according to the principles of community policing (Craen, 1991; Opolot, 1991). Three aspects of police *care* that seem to stress community policing are highlighted: public law and order, public security, and police assistance (Craen, 1991).

It is beyond the scope of this book to examine community policing trends in all countries, but several nations have been selected for close examination because they are undergoing law enforcement transformations similar to those occurring in the United States. Scholars often refer to examinations of foreign systems as crosscultural research or comparative investigations. Applied to this text, **comparative community policing** is the study of community-oriented policing methods and philosophies across two or more countries for the purpose of understanding their similarities and differences and how citizens are affected.

Studying comparative community policing is not particularly easy. Anticipating some of the difficulties, David Bayley (1979:111–112) observes that a major

Fear of crime is an international phenomenon giving rise to similar policing strategies and crime control. *(Nik Kleinberg/Stock, Boston)*

problem is deciding who police are as well as what they do. Bayley defines police as a "group authorized in the name of territorial communities to utilize force within the community to handle whatever needs doing" (1979:113). Bayley also presents us with a "nearly exhaustive" list of crosscultural police functions, including (1) protecting life and property (United States); (2) enforcing the criminal law (Britain); (3) investigating criminal offenses (France); (4) patrolling public places (Germany); (5) advising about crime prevention (Canada); (6) conducting prosecutions (Britain); (7) sentencing for minor offenses (Germany); (8) maintaining order and decorum in public places by directing, interrupting, and warning (United States); (9) guarding persons and facilities (France); (10) regulating traffic

(Norway); (11) controlling crowds (Germany); (12) regulating and suppressing vice (United States); (13) counseling juveniles (Netherlands); (14) gathering information about political and social life (France); (15) monitoring elections (Italy); (16) conducting counterespionage (France); (17) issuing ordinances (Germany); (18) inspecting premises (Germany); (19) issuing permits and licenses (Britain); (20) serving summonses (Norway); (21) supervising jails (Norway); (22) impounding animals and lost property (Britain); (23) advising members of the public and referring them to other agencies (Scotland); (24) caring for the incapacitated (United States); (25) promoting community crime-prevention activities (Scotland); and (26) participating in policy councils of government (France) (1979:111–112).

It is clear that police agencies in most nations require their officers to perform at least five or more of these functions. Yet much diversity exists pertaining to how police officers are defined and what they do. Considering the political and social events that have transformed police agencies and operations in the United States and other countries since 1979, Bayley's early admonition to investigate more thoroughly the functions, structure, and control of police agencies on an international scale is prophetic (Bayley, 1979:135–140).

Three countries have been selected for investigation here: England, Canada, and Japan. These countries were chosen because (1) each country is at a different stage of implementing community policing; (2) the array of offenses that define each country's "crime problem" varies; (3) police officers in each of these countries perform sufficiently different functions that they must relate with the public in diverse ways; and (4) considerable literature has accumulated to permit adequate descriptions of each country's philosophical transformation toward greater community policing. Furthermore, each of these countries, like the United States, has commenced the general shift from incident-driven policing to problem-oriented policing.

Doerner (1992:420) and Goldstein (1990) have described **incident-driven policing** as a technocratic product by which police officers have traditionally responded or reacted to calls for service. At the other end of the role spectrum is problem-oriented policing, which emphasizes why certain community crime problems exist initially and how best to eradicate the conditions that fostered such problems (Doerner, 1992:420). Problem-oriented policing forces police officers to interact with the community and to develop creative and cooperative solutions to community crime problems. This philosophy is quite different from the impersonality and isolation of police officers that is generated by adherence to the rules and procedures of existing bureaucratic law enforcement systems.

The format of our examination of police-community relations in each of these countries is as follows: First, a brief overview of each nation's criminal justice system will be presented. Second, several general crime categories relevant for each country will be defined. Third, police officer roles pertaining to crime detection, criminal apprehension and processing, crime prevention, and assisting/protecting their communities will be described.

POLICE-COMMUNITY RELATIONS IN ENGLAND

Type of Government

England (including Wales) has a parliamentary form of government, in which Parliament consists of the House of Commons, House of Lords, and the monarch. Appointed by the monarch, the twenty-two members of the House of Lords comprise the functional equivalent of the U.S. Supreme Court. The House of Commons is similar to the U.S. Congress, consisting of 635 elected members who pass laws and decide important government issues. Compared with the United States, England relies heavily on **stare decisis,** or the principle of legal precedents established by earlier judicial authority, coupled with numerous civil and criminal statutes.

Types of Crimes

Definitions of crime in England were shaped over several centuries by common law, which divided most misconduct into two broad classes: *mala in se* and *mala prohibita. Mala in se* offenses were "inherently" criminal acts, such as murder or forcible rape. *Mala prohibita* offenses were often considered infractions, codified, and less serious. Currently, almost all conduct considered criminal is codified and reflected in criminal statutes, although common-law infractions may still be alleged where specific statutory authority cannot be cited. Prior to 1967 English law divided crimes similarly to the distinction made between felonies and misdemeanors in the United States. However, the **Criminal Law Act of 1967** created three new major crime categories. These include:

1. **Summary offenses** (e.g., petty theft, disorderly conduct, solicitation, public drunkenness)
2. **Indictable offenses** (e.g., murder, rape, robbery, aggravated assault, arson)
3. **Hybrid offenses** (e.g., embezzlement, white-collar crime)

Summary offenses are least serious and involve petty criminal infractions. Ordinarily, local magistrates (comparable to U.S. justices of the peace or municipal court judges) can hear these cases and process them *summarily* (Stott, 1981:52).

Indictable offenses are the most serious types of crimes and are heard by judges in crown courts. Accused defendants are entitled to an adversarial trial by jury and to publicly appointed counsel (solicitors), if they are indigent.

Hybrid offenses may be heard either by magistrates or by crown courts, depending on prosecutorial discretion. Hybrid offenses may or may not be indictable and are influenced greatly by situational factors, such as a defendant's lack of a prior record, circumstances surrounding the commission of the offense, and harm inflicted on victims. If prosecutors decide certain hybrid offenses merit trial by crown courts in which more serious penalties might be imposed upon conviction, defendants may demand to be tried on indictment. In such instances, a panel of magistrates examines the evidence. This judicial review is comparable to determining whether sufficient evidence exists to establish probable cause to proceed to crown court for formal trial proceedings. Walker (1968:14) indicates that defendants are entitled to be tried on indictment if they face potential imprisonment of three months or more if convicted of the offenses alleged.

Until 1955 the amount of crime in England could be only crudely estimated. However, a systematic criminal records service was begun that year, stemming from specific provisions of the **Criminal Justice Act of 1948.** Under the auspices of the Home Secretary, England now compiles, maintains, and regularly distributes information about crime in England and Wales for both adults and juveniles (Croft, 1983). In 1981, the Home Office established the **British Crime Survey,** an annual compilation of victimization figures for both England and Wales. This annual publication is comparable to the **National Crime Survey** published in the United States.

Property offenses, such as theft, burglary, and vehicular theft, are the most prevalent types of crimes in England and Wales. For instance, of the 3.2 million crimes reported to police in 1985, burglary and theft crimes comprised over 80 percent (International Crime Center, 1986:56). Although both the population and amount of crime in England have increased since 1985, indications are that these figures continue to reflect accurate proportions of property crimes versus violent crimes (Kalish, 1988). Comparatively little violent crime occurs in England, although some experts believe violent crime is increasing (Lea, Matthews, and Young, 1987). There are fewer than two murders and three rapes per 100,000 persons annually, contrasted with the United States, which has more than ten murders and thirty-six rapes per 100,000 persons annually. One plausible explanation for such a low amount of violent crime in England is that the possession of firearms is tightly regulated (Benyon, 1986; Waddington, 1988). Another deterrent to violent crime is that British police officers do not carry firearms, and the penalties imposed on criminals who use deadly weapons are most severe. Table 11.1 shows a general comparison of crime rates for the countries examined in this chapter.

Because of the way that much of the crime in England and Wales is characterized, it would seem that the work of police officers would be comparatively less stressful, particularly contrasted with the work of officers in countries with high rates of violent crime, such as the United States. However, British police officers encounter more than their fair share of terrorism, and they are frequently drawn into large-scale civilian confrontations during riots. Therefore, although they are less at risk from violent criminals than U.S. police officers, there is a substantial amount of work-related stress stemming from their contacts with different types of crime and exposure to more frequent violent civil disorders. Currently, police officer training programs in England include ways of coping with stress on the job and heightening communication with the public sector (Alexander, Innes, and Irving, 1991; Southgate, 1988).

TABLE 11.1 A Comparison of Crime Rates for the United States, England, Canada, and Japan: Selected Offenses, 1984 and 1990. (Rates per 100,000 persons)

Crime	United States 1984	United States 1990	England 1984	England 1990	Canada 1984	Canada 1990	Japan 1984	Japan 1990
Homicide	7.9	9.4	1.1	1.8	2.7	3.5	.8	1.1
Rape	35.7	41.2	2.7	4.2	6.3	9.8	2.8	2.6
Burglary	1263.7	1235.9	1639.7	1841.2	1420.6	1531.9	231.2	224.8
Robbery	205.4	257.0	44.6	54.3	92.8	97.6	1.8	1.9
Auto Theft	437.1	657.8	656.5	689.3	304.9	336.3	29.4	27.9

Source: U.S. Department of Justice, *International Crime Rates.* Washington, DC: Bureau of Justice Statistics, 1992; International Crime Center, *International Crime Statistics, 1991.* Geneva, Switzerland: International Crime Center, 1992.

Police Supervision and Organization

In 1987 there were more than 120,000 police officers and other law enforcement personnel in England (Freeman, 1987:52). The Metropolitan Police of London, known unofficially as the Met, included more than 27,000 police officers (Freeman, 1987:52). Each police force in England has its own promotion policies, although many police officers in higher ranks receive some of their early training at the Police Staff College in Bramshill (Bunyard, 1988:27). The Police Staff College enjoys a prestigious international reputation and trains police officers from many other countries. Currently, there is no national police force in England, such as the Royal Canadian Mounted Police, which has a broad, nationwide jurisdiction. The establishment of a national police force in England has been proposed in past years, although no serious efforts have been made to create one (Bond, 1984).

Supervising the police of England is the secretary of state for the Home Office, often referred to as the Home Secretary, who is appointed by the prime minister. Although each shire or English county has local police officers, political factors have caused police powers at all levels to be increasingly limited during the past century. However, the level of police professionalism and expertise among British law enforcement officers has increased substantially during the same period (Elmsley, 1991).

Several official actions established precedents for local and national law enforcement authority and control. The Metropolitan Police of London was established through the Metropolitan Police Act of 1829. The Municipal Corporation Act of 1835 empowered English boroughs to create their own police forces. The Rural Constabulary Act of 1839 permitted county magistrates to establish county police forces if needed, and the County and Borough Police Act of 1856 consolidated policing functions of counties and boroughs and established the H.M. Inspectorate of Constabulary (Swift, 1988). These police forces were known at the time as "new police," because they were largely products of several large-scale provincial police reforms (Swift, 1988). In 1988 there were forty-three autonomous police forces in England and Wales (Bunyard, 1988:27). (Official statistics collected by the British Crime Survey typically combine Wales with England, although separate figures may be presented for each.)

The organization of most police forces in England is best described as centralized. Thus, the primary responsibility for implementing organizational changes and innovations rests with top-level administrators and police managers. Unfortunately, a survey of 171 British police managers conducted in the mid-1980s found that 87 percent of these lacked interpersonal skills and concerns (Plumridge, 1985). Furthermore, such centralization was perceived by researchers as stifling to innovative thinking in response to external demands for change (Plumridge, 1985). Even the internationally renowned Police College at Bramshill has been criticized for having too few officer-instructors with practical experience and having courses that are too simplistic and brief; students thus have little opportunity to practice their learned skills in live situations (Bourne, 1991).

There is currently a controversy over whose interests are most often served by police agencies. Traditionalism of police organization and operations suggests that the actions of police officers are governed largely by those in political control and that the upper socioeconomic classes are the prime beneficiaries of police activities. In public rioting in Brixton in 1981 and strikes by coal miners in 1984–1985, the nature and severity of police intervention received widespread criticism. In the coal mining strikes, for instance, some citizens regarded police as an occupying army in a class war, tools of a right-wing government intent upon eradicating trade unions from the British economic system (Coulter, Miller, and Walker, 1984; Fine and Millar, 1985). Drastic police reforms were called for, including better mechanisms for establishing police accountability (Benyon, 1984; Reiner, 1984). Although certain reforms were undertaken and will be discussed, Oliver (1987) notes that some experts have recommended that traditional policing methods should be continued. Also, some critics are skeptical about police reforms and believe that their value is at best window dressing rather than an attempt at actual behavioral and procedural change (Reiner, 1984). Despite these disagreements, it is generally conceded that the police of England are currently undergoing a significant transformation in several respects. One such transformation is toward decentralization and widespread community policing.

Community Policing in England

Few scholars would disagree that community policing throughout England is increasing rapidly, but not everyone is certain why this is so. Some experts believe that public confidence in the police has eroded (Kinsey, Lea, and Young,

1986). Others blame technology and claim that obsolete equipment, such as the British Police National Computer (PNC), is outmoded, needs updating and expansion, and causes police ineffectiveness in preventing and solving crimes (Newing, 1987; Pounder, 1983). Other experts believe that the need to increase police accountability to the public has spurred greater police-community contact (Downes and Ward, 1986). Some professionals believe that a recognition of racial insensitivity among police officers has triggered positive actions toward greater interracial awareness and community participation in crime control and prevention (Holdaway, 1991; Willis, 1985).

It is beyond the scope of this chapter to investigate fully all of the causes of societal unrest and factors that have promoted a movement toward greater community policing in England. However, several generalizations, more or less supported by contemporary literature, may be made. When the following generalizations are viewed collectively, it is easier to see why England appears to be adopting community policing as a general law enforcement strategy:

1. The police of England are highly centralized and politicized. A small elite with concentrated power and property insinuates itself into police governance and operations with an interest toward preserving the status quo.

2. Police officers have considerable powers of arrest, search and seizure, and general discretion. Until 1986 police officers both arrested and prosecuted petty offenders in the lower courts. A Crown Prosecution Service (CPS) was instituted at that time, which effectively divided an officer's investigative responsibilities and prosecutorial discretion (Hetherington, 1989).

3. There is little racial or ethnic integration in most English police forces, despite affirmative action programs designed to attract and recruit larger numbers of minorities to officer positions. Thus, policing community enclaves known for their racial or ethnic homogeneity produces interracial relations that are at best strained.

4. Despite the availability of high-quality training programs for police officers, a majority of British police are poorly trained in interpersonal skills and communicative abilities for handling various types of community disputes.

5. Because most crime in England is property related, the public's attention is drawn toward the effectiveness of police officers in solving property crimes. A large percentage of unsolved property crime makes an easy target for police critics and a disgruntled public.

6. A large working class component is frequently drawn into conflicts with police through strikes. The record of British police in responding to strikes is not particularly impressive, and inferences of racial bigotry and upper-class favoritism have been drawn that may be justified.

7. Police managers are often appointed. Likewise, officers are often selected according to nonprofessional criteria, including social connections. Therefore, an inherent class bias may exist that overrides efforts at professionalization of most departments.

8. Despite the feminist movement, few women are employed as police officers in England. The ratio of female to male officers during World War II was 1 to 288. Currently, there is one female officer in the lower ranks for every forty male officers, and one female officer in the upper ranks for every seventy-one male officers (Carrier, 1988).

9. Complaints against British police officers have steadily increased. This may be due, in part, to the establishment of an independent Police Complaints Authority in 1985, which was authorized as one provision of the more comprehensive Police and Criminal Evidence Act of 1984 (Loveday, 1989).

This is by no means a comprehensive list. Some scholars may disagree that some events and factors cited have received more priority or consideration than certain uncited factors. Nevertheless, a portrait of a class-conscious, relatively untrained, and racially, ethnically, and sexually homogeneous aggregate of British officers is sparking public reactions and criticisms. Countering these criticisms and rectifying past mistakes and problems are difficult tasks. Yet England has responded to the challenge, and measurable progress can be charted.

One important way to improve police-community relationships is to change the quality of officer selection methods and restructure officer training in ways that would maximize their effectiveness in public encounters. Since the late 1960s England and Wales have used a **Graduate Entry Scheme** (GES) and a **Special Course,** in which prospective police recruits are selected on the basis of their performance of in-service work and in law enforcement education courses. However, police officers recruited into law enforcement ranks from sources other than the GES appear to be of similar effectiveness compared with those selected through the GES program (Hill and Smithers, 1991). In fact, Hill and Smithers have noted that GES graduates seem to have a high incidence of resignation and that they do not progress upward through the ranks as quickly as they had anticipated. Furthermore, many police officers who entered law enforcement through other channels do not seem to have great regard for GES recruits.

In the wake of various riots and civil demonstrations of the early 1980s, certain members of the House of Lords undertook independent investigations to determine why the riots occurred and what police initiatives could have been taken to minimize resulting social disarray. One set of proposals was advanced by Lord Scarman, who focused heavily on the nature and direction of police recruitment and training (Fielding, 1988). Some of Scarman's proposals included extending the police officer training period and pairing new recruits with more experienced officers while on patrol. These close apprenticeships were viewed as fruitful ways of providing new officers with productive, on-the-job training.

Unfortunately, such apprenticeships involve a considerable investment of time and supervision, and many departments have either been unwilling or unable to do what is necessary to achieve these objectives (Fielding, 1988).

Another effort to improve police-community relations through better selection and training methods has involved an affirmative-action type of recruitment strategy, whereby departments have become more race-sensitive in their recruitment practices. In short, priority has been given certain ethnic and racial minority candidates for police work in many jurisdictions. Although significant increases in minority recruitment have been observed in several jurisdictions, no jurisdiction currently has proportionate racial and ethnic representation in its law enforcement ranks (Holdaway, 1991). Police initiatives to raise the multiracial nature of their forces have been inconsistent. Some forces, such as the Highton Police and the Midshire Constabulary, have done much to promote minority recruitment (Holdaway, 1991), but most departments have demonstrated either inaction or silence regarding the ethnic minority recruitment issue. Further, no clearly positive stance to change recruitment policies among most police departments has been taken thus far by many departments (Holdaway, 1991).

Training programs continue to underemphasize race relations training. Racism awareness programs are not new features of law enforcement training programs in England, however (Oakley, 1990). Southgate (1984) reports that several racism awareness courses were introduced on a pilot basis in 1983, although their impact on officer racial awareness was questionable. The programs and courses, which included role-playing and other sensitivity training experiences, were not well-received by police participants. Officers preferred lectures over group discussion. Some officers blamed trainers, who were perceived as resistant to seasoned officers' opinions and differing beliefs. Furthermore, participants were mixed according to rank, age, and experience, and some junior officers were reluctant to participate more aggressively because of the presence of more senior officers. Despite the program's flaws, Southgate suggests that race relations training should be integrated with other police training and that perhaps the trainers ought to have more direct police experience themselves.

Another facet of law enforcement recruitment that has thus far remained unaddressed is the recruitment of larger numbers of women into police ranks. The entry of women into law enforcement in England has been difficult. Resistance has emanated from various sources, including male officers and citizens who view female police officers as somehow disruptive to family stability (Carrier, 1988). There are currently only a few female police officers in England and Wales—about 5 percent of the total force—although their numbers and proportionate representation are growing annually. From a strategic standpoint, the recruitment of more women into policing is seen as a favorable way of coping with cases involving domestic violence (London Strategic Policy Unit, 1986). No specific evidence exists to suggest that female police officers would handle domestic disputes more effectively than males, although many male police officers express this belief. Regarding views of male officers about whether female officers can do more "macho" types of police work expected of them, samples of police officers interviewed at the Bramshill Police College expressed favorable attitudes toward female officers and their job performance abilities (Pope and Pope, 1986). Those officers with more traditional beliefs about women reported less favorable attitudes toward female police officers, although these views appeared to be in the minority.

Many police departments in England have been restructured to reflect greater accountability among officers, prompted by rising numbers of citizen complaints against alleged officer misconduct. Typical response to such citizen complaints in past years was an internal investigation conducted by other police officers. Thus, these reviews were regarded as both biased and limited (Loveday, 1989). In 1984 England passed a **Police and Criminal Evidence Act,** which was intended to change the nature and scope of police powers. Among its other provisions was the establishment of a **Police Complaints Authority,** an independent investigative body to examine the validity of citizen complaints against police and capable of imposing appropriate administrative sanctions on the offending officers (Loveday, 1987). Some experts, such as Downes and Ward (1986), contend that raising police accountability will not decrease crime, but these authors do not appear to grasp the fact that increased officer accountability is directed at reducing or eliminating police misconduct and not necessarily crime per se.

One issue in accountability is the manner in which police officers have conducted themselves during citizen riots, such as those occurring at Brixton in 1981. Some citizen hostility against police was generated as the result of "aggressive police anti-crime tactics" used by officers to quell civil disturbances at that time (Benyon, 1984). Specifically, some police officers appeared to be particularly abusive toward ethnic and racial minority inhabitants of Brixton. Homes, automobiles, and persons were searched indiscriminately, and property was seized inappropriately. These actions tended to alienate police officers from citizens, especially minorities (Benyon, 1984). Despite racially sensitive courses being included in subsequent police training and greater levels of minority officer recruitment, many police officers continue to be perceived as bullies by large proportions of blacks and as "impartial guardians of order" by fairly large numbers of whites and Asians (Waddington and Braddock, 1991).

The creation of the Police Complaints Authority did not necessarily reduce the annual number of complaints against police officers (Kahn, 1986). However, it did decrease the number of substantiated complaints (Maguire and Corbett, 1991). Currently, complaints against police officers are divided into categories ranging from most serious to least serious, with the most serious investigated by the Police Complaints Authority. Those of moderate seriousness are reviewed internally, and the least serious complaints, which constitute the majority, are handled informally. Informal complaint resolutions (similar to alternative dispute resolution between parties in both civil litigation and criminal proceedings in the United States) have yielded greater citizen satisfaction with police officers (Maguire and Corbett, 1991). Nevertheless, many citizens continue to express opinions that more serious complaints against police are handled secretly and bureaucratically and that this continues to be an unsatisfactory state of affairs.

Another strategic move by police departments to improve police-community relations was to incorporate citizen volunteers in their ranks. Thus, many police departments now have special constabulary known as **specials,** citizen volunteers who are deployed on a part-time basis. They have all powers of a constable, wear police uniforms, and perform many routine police functions (Gill and Mawby, 1990). Interestingly, one outcome of the use of specials is that they tend to identify with the police subculture rather than with the community, and thus they do not necessarily bring the community closer to police. It would appear that the police-community integrative aims of special constabulary are somehow thwarted by elusive variables, such as the influence of the "cop culture" and police socialization, which is strong (Brogden, Jefferson, and Walklate, 1988). Not everyone is enthusiastic about using greater numbers of civilians in police work. Loveday (1989) cautions that although increasing civilianization of police work in England may be cost-effective in the short run, the long-range implications may not be particularly desirable. Loveday says that some departments treat civilian auxiliary personnel as second-class police officers who perform menial duties. Thus, "real" police officers are released from such menial duties to perform "real" police work. These "second-class" police officers may not accept their second-class status on a long-term basis, however, and civilianization of policing may eventually be counterproductive.

John Alderson, a former Chief Constable for Devon and Cornwall, is a leading advocate of community policing (Alderson, 1985). Alderson has proposed a

British "bobbies," named after Sir Robert Peel, use "cautioning" rather than arrest increasingly when minor offenses are observed. *(Homer Sykes/Woodfin Camp and Associates)*

communitarian model of policing and social control that is the functional equivalent of neighborhood policing in the United States. Some critics have suggested that the concept of community policing is flawed by a lack of clarity (Bennett, 1983). The ideal of "greater community involvement" espoused by some may not fit the reality of officers involved in actual back-to-the-community programs. For instance, a survey of 300 constables in five different districts in 1981 showed that less than 14 percent of the constables' time was devoted to the stated purposes of community involvement (Brown and Iles, 1985). Furthermore, "community involvement" generally consisted of formal, superficial visits with public groups and minimal contact with ethnic minorities. The results of greater community involvement as a means of improving police-community relations were considered ineffective in this instance.

On the positive side, a **contact patrol** project that was funded by the Home Office promoted greater police officer contact with community residents through more continuous police presence on beats (Bennett, 1989). This program yielded greater citizen involvement in community crime prevention, somewhat lower crime rates in those affected areas of contact patrols, less fear of crime, and greater satisfaction with police. There is little question that improvements in public relations are obtained through such direct police-community contact. It is also fairly clear that spending more money on policing and security doesn't necessarily result in a commensurate drop in crime rates in the affected communities (Joyce, 1985). There is evidence, however, that conventional deterrent policing (e.g., foot and car patrolling) will reduce crime opportunity. Further, direct public contact through these policing strategies will likely improve relations between the police and the public affected (Clarke and Hough, 1984). England's experience with community policing is still in the experimental stage. Over the next decade, it is likely that pronounced significant improvements in police-community relationships will occur. As police powers are redefined and departments are reshaped in response to cultural needs, greater police effectiveness is expected (McLeay, 1990; Skogan, 1990; Waddington, 1983).

POLICE-COMMUNITY RELATIONS IN CANADA

Type of Government

Canada is made up of two territories (Northwest Territories and Yukon) and ten provinces, including Ontario, Quebec, Manitoba, Saskatchewan, British Columbia, Alberta, New Brunswick, Nova Scotia, Newfoundland, and Prince Edward Island, with a total population reaching nearly 27 million in 1991. Canada is a confederation with a parliament. The head of government is the prime minister. The **Constitution Act of 1867** bestowed the Canadian Parliament with the legislative authority to define all criminal law throughout the provinces, although this act has undergone extensive revision. A Supreme Court was created in 1875, with a chief justice and eight other justices. Like the U.S. Supreme Court, the

Canadian Supreme Court is the "court of last resort" for all civil and criminal appeals. Several courts of appeal are beneath this court. Each province has superior, district, and county courts. Generally, judges for these courts are appointed for specified terms by the federal government or by individual provincial officials.

Types of Crime

In general, crime in Canada is any act done in violation of duties an individual owes to the community, for which act the law has provided that the offender shall be punished. In 1893, various diverse provincial criminal laws were consolidated and codified under the Criminal Code of Canada. This code established a crude set of offenses common to all provinces, including offenses against public order, firearm and other offensive weapon violations, sexual offenses, offenses against public morals, disorderly conduct, invasion of privacy, offenses concerning disorderly houses, gaming and betting, offenses against the person and reputation, offenses against rights of property, fraudulent transactions, willful and forbidden acts in respect to certain property, and offenses relating to currency, including counterfeiting. These laws were refined further in 1971 by the **Law Reform Commission Act,** which was implemented to keep pace with changing Canadian society and to make appropriate reform recommendations to the legislature (Canada Law Reform Commission, 1985).

In several respects, Canadians classify their crimes in ways similar to England. There are three major adult crime categories, which follow:

1. Indictable offenses (violations of the criminal code and offenses against federal statutes)
2. Summary conviction offenses (violations of provincial statutes and municipal bylaws)
3. Dual procedure offenses (similar to British hybrid crimes, in which the prosecutor decides whether prosecution should proceed either by summary conviction or by indictment)

Indictable offenses, such as armed robbery, murder, and rape, are considered most serious. These types of offenses are generally judged by superior courts in the different provinces. Summary offenses are usually disposed of in municipal courts or county courts. **Dual procedure offenses** are tried in higher or lower courts, depending on prosecutorial discretion. The maximum penalties for summary offenses include $500 fines, six months in jail or prison, or both. Jury trials are most frequently held for those charged with indictable offenses. Life terms may be imposed. There is no death penalty in Canada.

Table 11.1 (see p. 327) shows a comparison of selected crime rates for England, Canada, and Japan. Crime is reported annually in Canada by the **Canadian Centre for Justice Statistics,** which is comparable to the Bureau of Justice Statistics in the United States. The centre also operates the Canadian Police Information Center and the Uniform Crime Reporting system (similar to the **Uniform Crime Reports** in the United States). Compared with England, the crime rate in Canada in 1989 was somewhat higher for violent offense categories, such as homicide, robbery, and rape. There are approximately 2 homicides per 100,000 persons in Canada, double the rate of homicide in England. There are about ninety-three robberies per 100,000 persons in Canada, compared with about 45 per 100,000 in England and Wales. The number of rapes in Canada is about triple the rape rate in England, with about 14 rapes per 100,000 persons in Canada and about 4 to 5 rapes per 100,000 persons in England and Wales. Interestingly, the rate of theft in England is about double that of Canada. The rate of auto theft in Canada, for example, is about 305 per 100,000 persons, compared with 660 per 100,000 in England. Geographically, there are higher rates of crime in the Western provinces compared with the Eastern provinces (Hackler and Don, 1990). Thus, there are several dramatic differences in the *nature* of violent and property crime between these two countries. But compared with the United States, and despite these differences, Canada and England have very low rates of crime.

Police Supervision and Organization

Three major police forces exist in Canada. These include the **Royal Canadian Mounted Police** (RCMP) or federal police, the provincial police, and the municipal police. The Canadian RCMP are the equivalent of a national police force, with general jurisdiction in all provinces. With the exception of two provinces, Ontario and Quebec, all other provinces have contracts with the RCMP to enforce all provincial laws, and in fact, the RCMP may extend its jurisdiction into all provinces. The RCMP has a high degree of autonomy and can decide which laws to enforce in which provinces as well as how to process law violators. The RCMP also coordinates its efforts with those of Interpol, especially for offenses such as money laundering, drug trafficking, terrorism, and international fraud (Solicitor General Canada, 1990:32).

The RCMP originated in 1873 and was officially known then as the Northwest Mounted Police. Its name and authority were modified by the Royal Canadian Mounted Police Act of 1970. It is now administered by a commissioner, who appoints officers in all provinces and territories. The RCMP is considered a civil force maintained by the Canadian government, although it enforces all criminal laws as well as civil ones. RCMP officers are also armed officers (Talbot and Jayewardene, 1984). In 1988 there were 20,200 employees of the RCMP; combined with the police forces of the provinces and municipalities, there were about 72,300 employees throughout Canada in 1988 (Solicitor General Canada, 1990:8–9). Ontario has the largest number of officers (excluding the RCMP), with 19,500. The Metropolitan Toronto Police Force consisted of 7,250 officers in 1988, making it the fourth largest police force of any city or provincial force considered as an aggregate.

Most police departments in Canada are centralized, as they are in England. There are several direct and indirect empirical indicators of this centralized organizational structure. First, communication channels are limited, and information is disseminated from the top downward through managers and a managerial core (Adamson, 1987; Adamson and Descza, 1990; Solicitor General Canada, 1990:39). Second, job descriptions are prepared and distributed by the Canadian Public Service Commission, which has succeeded in stamping each police department with a set of common or core characteristics (Slivinski et al., 1990). Third, senior constables in many police departments uniformly report career dissatisfaction, low promotional potential, little input relating to decision making, and a general lack of respect from management (McGinnis, 1991). Fourth, ideological change in police forces is slow, emanating largely from chiefs and superintendents downward. Chiefs of police not only choose their internal and external change agents, but they also handpick their middle-level managerial personnel, largely on the basis of value similarities, which only serves to perpetuate a predetermined set of values and operations (Descza, 1988). Fifth, the role of police unions is growing in strength as a means of facilitating departmental changes that are often blocked by governing authorities (Hann et al., 1985; Jackson, 1986). Sixth, numerous reforms have been proposed in recent years in order to decentralize existing police department structure (Brown, 1986). A prevalent belief is that decentralization would exert largely positive effects on officers at all ranks, despite the possibility that decentralization might pose a set of new, yet minor, problems resulting from participatory management (Brown, 1986; Loree, 1988).

The nature of crime is different in Canada compared with England, and police officers carry firearms. This fact may help explain why Canada has ranked fairly high in the number of police deaths in the line of duty. For instance, during the 1970s, Canada ranked fourth among fourteen nations in the rate of officers murdered in the line of duty (Whittingham, 1984). There is no particular upward or downward trend relating to the rate of Canadian police deaths, however (Janssen and Hackler, 1985). Another factor is the close proximity of Canada to the United States. Various types of smuggling, including drug trafficking, involve violence, and police lives are thus at greater risk because of such border crimes. Access to firearms in Canada is far less restricted than in England; consequently, police work in Canada is more dangerous.

Canadian police departments face some of the same kinds of problems encountered by English police. For instance, Canada is racially and ethnically diverse. Canadian police have their fair share of citizen-initiated complaints, many of which claim police misconduct and the use of excessive force. Often these complaints against police charge abuses based on the citizen's race or ethnicity. The configuration of ethnic and racial minorities is different in Canada from that of England, however. There is considerable cultural pluralism (Loree, 1985): About one-fourth of the Canadian population is French, one-fourth is English, and 30 percent consist of persons of mixed backgrounds, including a sizeable number of North American Indians. Specific complaints alleging police abuse of Indians have been made on a fairly regular basis (Cryderman and

O'Toole, 1986; Normandeau and Leighton, 1991; Rolf, 1991), including allegations by the Blood Tribe of Native Americans that 105 "sudden deaths" of tribe members were attributable to police excessive force. (In these cases, the RCMP as well as the Lethbridge City Police were supposedly involved in the investigation [Rolf, 1991].) Also alleged by members of the Blood Tribe were paternalistic attitudes by police and general insensitivity when handling responses to complaints on reservation areas.

Canadian police departments, regardless of their size, are comprised primarily of male police officers. The first female police officers in Canada were hired in Vancouver in 1912 (Linden, 1983). Their original roles were primarily civilian. Currently, female officers account for about 5 percent of all officers, although since 1975, about 10 percent of all RCMP recruits have been females (Linden, 1983; Linden, 1984). Although recruitment efforts have been aggressive to include more females, they appear to have higher attrition rates than males. Linden (1985a) explains this, in part, by noting that women's departures are often marriage related. He also proposes that changes ought to be made in transfer policies to decrease female officer attrition, if moving might separate female officers from their spouses. Despite these higher attrition rates among female officers, their male colleagues and supervisors tend to give women similar performance marks and evaluations compared with male officers (Linden, 1985b). In some jurisdictions, however, such as the RCMP, traditional views of women among many male officers reflect resentments against female officers assigned to patrol duties, which often involve more physically aggressive activities (Linden, 1983). Despite these unfavorable traditional views, no evidence exists to show that female officers rate lower than men in those jobs requiring greater physical strength or force (Linden, 1983).

Police officers are selected and trained at different sites in each province. The Calgary (Alberta) Police Department uses a Police Applicant Test (PAT), which consists of a written examination derived from the Canadian Multi-Jurisdictional Police Officer Examination (MPOE), as a means of selecting recruits (Gruber, 1986). Comparisons of officers who remain in their jobs with those who resign after one or two years show significant differences on their original PAT scores. Thus, it is believed that the PAT is a valid and useful predictor of officer selection. Police officers in all departments are subject to periodic performance evaluations (Carpenter, 1989). Many training programs, including those in Vancouver and Ottawa, involve race relations courses to promote greater understanding between police officers and the multicultural populace. For example, the Canadian Secretary of State's Multiculturalism Directorate sponsored a Police Intercultural Education Pilot Project, with various workshops dealing with race relations, immigration, presentations about specific ethnocultural groups, and interview/interaction strategies (Ungerleider, 1985). This program and others like it do not especially change officer attitudes toward minority citizens, but they do appear effective in enabling participating officers to develop a better understanding of cultural diversity, and they encourage more positive interactions with various ethnic minorities (McDougall, 1988; Ungerleider, 1985).

Police training also encompasses the proper use of firearms and provides an understanding of when to apply deadly force and engage in deadly pursuits (Canada Solicitor General's Select Committee on Police Pursuits, 1985; Chappell and Graham, 1985; Del Buono, 1986; Sewell, 1985; Solomon, 1985). In the early 1980s the ratio of police killings to murders of police was about 2.5 to 1 (Chappell and Graham, 1985). Over the years, these figures have remained relatively stable (Solicitor General Canada, 1990). Sources of police officer stress are varied, and the likelihood of being killed in the line of duty is only one stressor. Support from fellow officers has been found to reduce job-related stress significantly, however (Graf, 1986). Furthermore, closer working relationships with community residents also promote better officer attitudes toward police work in Canada (Hornick et al., 1990; Loree and Murphy, 1987).

Community Policing in Canada

The Solicitor General's Office of Canada has targeted police-community partnership through community policing as a key goal to be realized by the year 2000 (Solicitor General Canada, 1990:20–21). Canadian officials acknowledge England's influence on their policing methods. They believe that community policing originated with the formation of the Metropolitan Police of London in 1929 and that contemporary community policing in Canada is a reemergence of an "old approach" and the creation of a "new blue line" (Solicitor General Canada, 1990:20–21). The Solicitor General of Canada (1990:20–25) identifies twelve key features of this new role of Canadian police:

1. The role of police officers is one of *peace officers.*
2. Community consultation should be encouraged, so that police officers and the public carry on meaningful and continuing dialogues to share concerns about common crime problems.
3. Policing should be proactive rather than reactive.
4. A problem-oriented policing strategy should be invoked that will address crime and order problems and their causes.
5. There should be broader police response to underlying causes of problems.
6. Greater interagency cooperation is encouraged.
7. Managerial personnel in police departments must learn to be information managers and engage in interactive policing on a reciprocal basis with community leaders through formal contacts and informal networks.
8. The fear of being victimized must be reduced by ensuring the protection of groups prone to victimization, such as the young and the elderly.
9. Police officers must become generalists responsible for broader ranges of activities than is currently required.
10. Front-line officers must be given greater discretion, responsibilities, and autonomy through agency decentralization and widespread resource deployment.

11. Organizational structure of police agencies must be changed from the paramilitary model to a flatter profile, in which a broader array of police services might be provided to the public.
12. There must be better mechanisms in place to promote greater police accountability to the public.

Accomplishing these goals would do much to promote better police-community relations and heighten community awareness of the multifaceted nature of police roles. Evidence indicates that many provinces are responding to the challenge of fostering better police-community relations by establishing community policing programs. For example, twenty-one high-crime areas in Edmonton, Alberta, were selected for a Neighborhood Foot Patrol Program (NFPP) that started in April 1988. Components of the program included foot patrols in high-crime areas, storefront stations in each area, community liaison committees, volunteer activity, and constable problem-solving (Hornick et al., 1990). The direct contact with community residents gave constables a better knowledge of the community and its problems. In turn, this contributed to reductions in numbers of service calls, greater citizen satisfaction with police officers, and higher job satisfaction among constables themselves. Constable visibility seemed to decrease crime in these areas. Recommendations subsequently included extending these foot patrols and storefront stations to other high-crime neighborhoods (Hornick et al., 1990).

Community policing is regarded by some experts as fundamental for crime prevention—that effective crime prevention must involve a true partnership of the police and the citizens they serve (Loree and Walker, 1991). Previous self-imposed professional isolation of police officers must be changed in order to draw closer to special populations affected by high crime rates, such as minorities.

In some localities, however, mere police presence isn't always a solution to citizen complaints against police. The Toronto Police Department, for instance, had a history of citizen complaints alleging police abuse of discretion and unnecessary force. In 1981 an Office of the Public Complaints Commissioner was established by the **Metropolitan Police Force Project Act** (Lewis, Linden, and Keene, 1986), and a **Police Complaints Investigation Bureau** was created, which resulted in satisfactory resolutions of complaints.

In Thunder Bay, Ontario, in 1984, the police department ordered officers to become more visible throughout the community. Further, neighborhood watches were encouraged, involving community resident participation. Survey results indicated that although many respondents were unaware of heightened police presence in their neighborhoods, 91 percent of those requesting police services expressed satisfaction with the police response (Thunder Bay Police Department, 1985). One strong implication of this research was that greater police-public involvement in crime prevention activities should be encouraged.

Crime Stoppers, a Canadian program established in 1976 that uses the mass media to encourage the public to report criminal activity anonymously in exchange for a reward, has also been somewhat helpful in combatting crime

(Carriere, 1987). However, some experts regard Crime Stoppers as more of a symbolic expression of community involvement. This is also believed to be the real power of community policing (Carriere and Ericson, 1989).

In the late 1980s five police **mini-stations** were established in Victoria neighborhoods, where they could function in a semi-autonomous fashion and meet public needs. The structure and management of these stations, emphasizing greater officer community involvement, have been more closely supervised and monitored than any other program of its kind in Canada (Walker and Walker, 1989). One station, for example, created a "Seniors Phoning Seniors" program among its neighborhood elderly residents in the James Bay area (Walker and Walker, 1989). Researchers reported that the presence of these mini-stations in Victoria neighborhoods was viewed by the public as proactive police strategy, and the stations helped decrease public fear of crime. Similar mini-station programs have been implemented in other cities, including Toronto (A.R.A. Consultants, 1985). In the Toronto case, however, the mini-stations were regarded by administrative personnel as "add-ons" and were poorly integrated with other police department functions. Nevertheless, citizen reactions were positive, and greater citizen participation was clearly indicated (A.R.A. Consultants, 1985). One long-term outcome of these community policing strategies has been the general humanization of policing, a favorable, service-oriented objective (Loree and Murphy, 1987).

In 1985 the Halifax Police Department introduced the concept of community-based zone policing, in which the patrol division was reorganized into three districts to promote independent zone integrity and democratic squad leadership styles (Clairmont, 1990). Although this concept did not originate in Halifax, it did result in changing a basically traditional reactive police department into a proactive, full-service one, replete with structural and ideological innovations to benefit community residents. Between 1985 and 1988, these new policies and proactive procedures were evaluated through interviews with community members. Most residents expressed satisfaction with the new program. Officers themselves believed their performance levels were greatly improved because there were more opportunities for innovative, ambitious, and competent officers to combat crime through community crime prevention (Clairmont, 1990). There were also sharp reductions in sick leave among officers.

The Mounted Police have also contributed to community policing. In recent years, the RCMP has established improved community patrols and neighborhood watches, operation identification programs (identifying information is put on property so that owners can be easily identified), youth and public safety programs, seminars on business security, and patrolling geared to improving police-community relations (Canada Royal Canadian Mounted Police, 1987). Compared with England, the Canadian concept of community policing appears to be more clearly defined.

Bayley (1991b) and others are quick to indicate that Canadian law enforcement is in no immediate crisis, but there is a manifest need among many departments to learn more about community policing and how it may be implemented effectively. At least one problem is evident. Many of the community policing projects under way in Canada are in experimental stages. Few of these pilot programs have provisions for longitudinal evaluations. They are often launched in an effort to stem the rising tide of community crime, and as crime prevention measures, they have seemed effective. However, community policing is often "grafted" onto existing police programs and operations, and their influence in promoting better police-community relations and in preventing crime is not evaluated systematically (Kennedy, 1991). Bayley (1991b) observes that "organizational rigidity" may be a temporary impediment to the progress of departmental community policing, although there are indications that many police organizations have changed or are in the process of changing to meet community needs more effectively.

One way of promoting better police-community relations is by recruiting a better-educated police force. Mid-career police officers in various police departments throughout Canada highly value a university education, which they feel is beneficial in the performance of their police functions and interactions with community residents (Buckley, 1991). Experienced Canadian police officers regard community-based policing as the policing style of the future (Braiden, 1986). They view police officers as facilitators for community residents, who are ultimately responsible for maintaining order and preventing crime. The concept of the community in a productive partnership with police officers appears to be evolving among both the management and rank-and-file police officers of most provincial and city departments (Adamson, 1987; Ungerleider, 1985).

Although it may be a premature judgment, the Solicitor General's Office of Canada has declared that "there is . . . no longer any need to look towards examples of community policing outside Canada for lessons and insights" (Solicitor General Canada, 1990:24). Canada does not exist in a cultural vacuum, and it is likely that Canadian police departments will embrace community policing innovations that prove to be of merit in crime prevention or public relations. In the meantime, Canadian policing is definitely set toward creating greater police-public interaction and awareness (Normandeau and Leighton, 1990). The current state of Canadian police education, pressures for legal reforms, and more participative management from an increasingly interested citizenry are strong indicators that this will happen (Del Buono, 1986; Jackson, 1986; Loree and Murphy, 1987; Scanlon, 1991; Sewell, 1985).

POLICE-COMMUNITY RELATIONS IN JAPAN

Type of Government

For practical purposes, the Japanese form of government is best understood in light of political events following World War II. Although pre-World War II Japanese traditions continue to influence Japanese interpersonal relations and the way conflicts are resolved, modern Japanese government is far removed from its pre-World War II configuration. Japan has a parliamentary democracy. The head of state is the emperor, primarily a figurehead position. The head of government is the prime minister. A Diet or bicameral body is the highest authority and consists of a House of Representatives and a House of Councilors, with legislative powers commensurate with those of the U.S. Congress (Nakayama, 1987). In 1990 this Diet administered the affairs of Japan's 124 million people in a territory of 146,000 square miles.

Although the early European principle of common law continues to influence high court decision making in Japan, only statutory law is considered when determining whether certain acts are criminal. The Diet has the legislative authority to define criminal laws and punishments. Japan's highest court is the Supreme Court, with a Chief Justice and fourteen associate justices. These fifteen justices hear all appeals from lower courts. Immediately beneath the Supreme Court are eight high courts, or courts of appeal. These courts are the functional equivalent to U.S. Circuit Courts of Appeal and are presided over by a president and several other judges (a minimum of three judges must convene to hear cases), who hear appeals from lower district courts and family courts. There are 50 district courts distributed throughout various prefectures (the equivalent of Japanese counties) (Terrill, 1984:260–262). District courts are basic Japanese trial courts and hear important criminal and civil cases. The lowest courts, summary courts, of which there are approximately 575, hear minor cases or petty offenses. Punishments imposed by these lower courts are usually fines of varying amounts (Terrill, 1984:262).

Types of Crime and Crime Rates

The **Penal Code of 1907** initially defined a broad range of crimes and punishments (Nakayama, 1987:170). Although there is no formal distinction between felonies and misdemeanors such as is made in the United States, the Japanese penal code defines traditional crimes, including homicide, rape, burglary, robbery, and vehicular theft. The age of criminal responsibility is fourteen, although persons age twenty or over are considered adults. Those between the ages of fourteen and nineteen are usually treated as juveniles in independent juvenile proceedings (Zenon, 1990). Japan imposes the death penalty for particularly serious offenses, including sabotage, insurrection, and homicide. The death penalty is death by hanging, although fewer than five persons per year are executed publicly in this fashion (Zenon, 1990:125). Although the original Japanese penal code has been revised subsequent to the provisions of 1907, it still consists of two books, general provisions and major crimes, which list each of the crime's elements (Terrill, 1984:270–271).

Rather than classifying crimes according to U.S., English, or Canadian methods, Japanese crimes are gradated by specific statutory citations and specific prescribed punishments. Nakayama (1987:175–176) notes that the most common punishment in past years has been imprisonment with labor. The minimum prison term is one month, and the longest is about fifteen years, although sentences of up to twenty years may be imposed, if circumstances are particularly aggravating. Inmates are eligible for parole after serving at least ten years of their sentences. A clearer picture of offender punishment is that about 60 percent of those convicted of crimes are sentenced to community-based probation supervision (Japan Ministry of Justice, 1985). The rate of recidivism among Japan's convicted offenders is about 50 percent (Parker, 1986).

Compared with the United States, England, and Canada, Japan has one of the lowest crime rates in the world. In fact, it is one of the only industrialized nations to report a decrease in its crime rate in recent years (Fishman and Dinitz, 1989; Gomez-Buendia, 1989; Terrill, 1984:252–253). Incredibly, the number of prisoners sentenced and admitted to institutions decreased from about 30,000 in 1926 to 28,000 in 1988 (Shikita and Tsuchiya, 1990). Examining Table 11.1, which illustrates comparative crime rate figures for Japan, England, Canada, and the United States, one sees that for every 100,000 persons Japan in 1990 had fewer than 1 homicide, fewer than 3 rapes, fewer than 2 robberies, and fewer than 30 auto thefts. For the same period, Canada had about 2 homicides per 100,000 persons, 14 rapes, 93 robberies, and 305 auto thefts. By comparison, England had more than 1 homicide per 100,000 persons, 3 rapes, 1,640 burglaries, 45 robberies, and 660 auto thefts. Thus, it is clear that Japan does not have the same degree of a crime problem as England and Canada. There are several important reasons for these differences in crime rates, and most of the reasons relate to the effectiveness of the police and the people of Japan themselves.

Police Supervision and Organization

In the aftermath of World War II, policing in Japan was heavily decentralized, with more than 1,600 different police departments. Each department was an independent agency with different policies, enforcement methods, patrol styles, training methods, and differing degrees of effectiveness at crime prevention. This condition was promoted, in large part, by U.S. occupation officials, who believed that the prior centralization and militarization of policing in Japan were contrary to the democratic form of government being implemented following World War II. By 1954 it was generally acknowledged that such decentralization of the police forces of Japan was an administrative and financial nightmare. The Diet established The Police Law, which effectively reversed the counterproductive decentralized police forces of Japan (Terrill, 1984:249).

In 1954 Japan was divided into forty-seven prefectures, which are the equivalent of U.S. county governments. The Police Law provided for the creation of a **National Police Agency,** which created national police and decentralized police operations throughout the prefectures, including three additional prefecture-equivalent agencies in Tokyo and the island of Hokkaido. These fifty agencies were organized and divided into seven regional bureaus, which have assumed the primary responsibility for officer training and education (Terrill, 1984:

250–251). All police forces are directly accountable to the National Police Agency, which is itself governed by the National Public Safety Commission. The six-member commission consists of prime minister appointees who serve five-year terms (Terrill, 1984:250). The major responsibility for the control and coordination of the prefectural police forces rests with the National Police Agency, however. The agency consists of administration, criminal investigation, traffic, security, and communications (Terrill, 1984:251).

Basic responsibilities of the 260,000 police officers in Japan include the protection of citizen lives and property, crime prevention, investigation and apprehension of suspects, traffic control, and the maintenance of safety and public order. These duties are articulated in greater detail in The Police Law. Most police officers in Japan carry firearms while on duty, although deadly force is used so infrequently that it is not a major civilian complaint issue against police officers. Regarding minority issues, Japanese police officers are in a unique situation compared with the police officers of the United States, England, and Canada. The population is almost completely Japanese (99.4 percent, Koreans 0.4 percent), with other minorities existing in insignificant numbers (World Almanac, 1992:773). Therefore, courses in race relations and ethnic differences would be largely irrelevant in Japanese police training.

Two additional factors are unique to Japanese police organization and operations. First, each prefecture is littered with numerous kobans and chuzaishos. **Kobans** are comparable to police mini-stations or substations in various U.S. neighborhoods (Thornton and Endo, 1992). These police "boxes" are staffed by two or more officers on rotating shifts (Terrill, 1984:252) and are quite visible throughout Japanese communities, helping to minimize citizen fears of criminal victimization. **Chuzaishos** are live-in type units, providing accommodations for an officer's entire family, and are staffed on a twenty-four-hour basis (Terrill, 1984:252). Both kobans and chuzaishos are strategically located to ensure close contacts between police officers and community residents. Police officers meticulously record car license plates, question neighborhood residents of new and unfamiliar faces in their communities, and generally are quite sensitive to the presence of any deviant or foreign elements. Obviously, such close police-public contacts minimize local crime and crime opportunities (Thornton and Endo, 1992).

The second important factor making Japanese policing unique compared with the United States, England, and Canada is the attitude and support of the Japanese people toward police officers in their neighborhoods. Bayley (1976), Schneider (1990), Terrill (1984:253–255), and Vaughn (1990) are only a few of the many experts who highlight the sense of honor and community that characterizes a large proportion of the Japanese people. They view police officers not only as law enforcers but also as symbols of moral authority. Therefore, they are not offended when approached by police officers in their communities and asked about suspicious persons. In fact, the overwhelmingly positive public support of the police has made the incidence of complaints against Japanese police officers almost nonexistent. Thus far, no serious attempt has been made by the public to establish complaint review boards such as those in the United States, Canada, and England.

Community Policing in Japan

It is almost redundant to use the words *community policing* and *Japan* in a single sentence. Japanese policing today *is* community policing. With a ridiculously low rate of crime for a country of its size, Japan has put forth a model of policing to be emulated by other countries (Westermann and Burfeind, 1991:77–79). However, it may be difficult for other countries to establish community policing so easily, as other countries do not have the wealth of community support enjoyed by Japan's national police officers. Kobans and their locations in relatively high-crime community areas have done much for crime prevention (Thornton and Endo, 1992). Besides kobans, there are conventional vehicular police patrols and foot patrols on beats. Community involvement in crime control and the promotion of traffic safety programs has been maximized (Thornton and Endo, 1992).

Attempts by economists and critical criminologists to account for Japanese crime rate fluctuations have failed largely because theoretical models based on Western individualism simply are not applicable to a homogenous, community-solidarity-based society (Schneider, 1990; Vaughan, 1990). Japan's principal crime problem currently is organized crime, such as the Yakuza and Boryokudan, and increasing numbers of drug law violations (Iwai, 1986; Japan Ministry of Justice, 1990; Kakimi, 1988; Kaplan and Dubro, 1986; Yokoyama, 1991). Fishman and Dinitz (1989) attribute much of Japan's low crime rate to a consensual rather than coercive type of policing. They argue that consensual policing, with a high degree of community participation, is culturally suitable for the Japanese as a modern means of crime control. Some experts go so far as to say that the people of Japan, rather than the police themselves, are primarily responsible for their own low level of crime through neighborhood crime control (Parker, 1984).

The picture of Japanese police is not without some flaws, however. Evidence of police misconduct and dishonesty has surfaced in some departments (Miyazawa, 1989). Some corruption through bribery of key police officials has been detected (Lee, 1990), although the National Police Agency has mechanisms to respond quickly to such incidents. Crimes such as bribery, robbery, and even homicide have been reported to police agencies where the alleged perpetrators are police officers, but the offenders have usually been dealt with swiftly and severely (Miyazawa, 1988). In most cases of police misconduct, offenders have been punished if the charges have been substantiated. Departments themselves have tightened controls over individual officers through closer monitoring of each officer's actions.

In a highly publicized incident involving an American entertainer ("the worst case of apparent police brutality against an American"), Tokyo police were accused of having brutally beaten a suspect where drug possession was alleged (Watanabe, 1992:A1). The U.S. entertainer, Donald Wilson, said he was beaten brutally and interrogated for many hours, without access to an attorney's services. He said police officers strip-searched him and beat him repeatedly in order to extract a confession. Japanese police officers have high conviction rates of arrested suspects, largely through confessions extracted from them, and many attorneys from other countries label Japanese interrogation methods among the worst in the world. According to nonofficial figures, about 12,600 complaints of police torture have been filed against Japanese police since 1952 (Watanabe, 1992:A1,A6); however, only 15 of these cases were ever accepted by the courts, and only half resulted in sanctions against the involved police officers. It is not known whether sufficient grounds exist to prove these allegations of brutality against Japanese police officers. One aggravating problem is that suspects may be held by Japanese police for as long as 23 days without being formally charged with a crime. Alleged tortures of Japanese-held foreign suspects have been noted in recent years by the Paris-based International Federation of Human Rights. Japanese officials deny these charges and contend that their system is exceedingly effective at fighting crime. Their low crime figures attest to this effectiveness. The debate continues.

The National Police Agency has attempted to select only the most capable officers for its national police force. High school graduates interested in becoming police officers must undergo one year of agency training, whereas college graduates spend six months in comparable training (Terrill, 1984:255). All new recruits spend an additional year in on-the-job training under the supervision of experienced officers. Following this training, all recruits return to the agency for another four months, during which their educational training is synthesized with their on-the-job experiences (Terrill, 1984:255).

In recent years Japan has drawn more on citizen involvement in law enforcement at all levels, including corrections (Miyazawa, 1990). More citizens work in voluntary capacities in community corrections programs and assist officers in operations near their kobans (Eskridge, 1989; Miyazawa, 1990). Such citizen participation in crime control is consistent with what is known about the general Japanese view toward law enforcement (Parker, 1984). Greater citizen involvement in law enforcement is the ultimate goal and consequence of Japanese community policing. Surveys of private citizens and police officers largely support the aims of community policing and greater police-public interaction for the broad purpose of crime control (Nishimura and Suzuki, 1986). Whatever its relative strengths or limitations, the Japanese system of law enforcement, crime prevention, and crime control inculcates community values so that Japanese police agencies are perceived as maximally effective compared to most law enforcement agencies in other nations (Bayley, 1991a).

INTERNATIONAL POLICING

Although there is currently no international police force with jurisdiction in all major nations, there is a high degree of cooperation among many nations relating to crimes that affect international interests. One of the more powerful organizations with international influence is the United Nations, which originated in 1945 in San Francisco, California, following World War II. Among its objectives are the promotion of world peace and security, observance of international law, and the maintenance of treaty obligations among foreign powers. Not all countries belong to the United Nations, however, and not all of the United Nations membership is necessarily responsive to its sanctions. For instance, the Gulf War of 1991 involved a limited conflict among Iraq and several other nations, including England, the United States, Saudi Arabia, and Kuwait. Numerous resolutions were passed to sanction Iraq, although Iraqi leadership either ignored these resolutions or rejected them outright through Iraq's ambassador. Nevertheless, the United Nations does have some strong sanctioning powers, and economic penalties imposed on countries often seem more effective at resolving differences than does military warfare.

International policing per se is regarded by many police professionals as synonymous with **Interpol,** or the International Criminal Police Organization (Fooner, 1973). The idea of an international police organization such as Interpol is attributed to Baron Pasquier, the prefect of the Paris police in 1809. Supposedly, he employed former criminals to catch other criminals. One example is his use of the ex-criminal Francois Vidocq in his early organization. Using innovative tactics such as sketches of international suspects, he gradually acquired dossiers on numerous criminals (Fooner, 1973:6–13). Interpol did not officially exist until 1945, after a meeting of several European police leaders from Belgium, Brussels, and Paris, when an International Criminal Police Commission was formed, with Paris headquarters. In 1956 this commission changed its name to the International Criminal Police Organization. Interpol cooperates with any foreign police agency to apprehend international criminals. It has made dramatic progress in combating such international crimes as drug trafficking and terrorism (Bossard, 1988; Rowe, 1988).

In recent years an **International Court of Justice** was formed to establish some degree of jurisdiction over international crime (Yarnold, 1991). However, existing extradition practices among countries do not seem to function adequately. The case of the "gunboat extradition" of Panama's General Noriega by the United States in 1989 is cited as an illegal extradition incident and has received criticism from other countries (Yarnold, 1991). Yarnold (1991) observes that the world community of states and political powers should grant jurisdiction to the International Court of Justice over international crimes, because trials of international criminals within a particular nation may be subject to local biases.

In addition, the **Council of Europe** was formed in 1949 (Council of Europe, 1984), and by 1984 there were 21 member nations, representing a total population of 385 million. Its Committee of Ministers and Parliamentary Assembly serves an international secretariat of 850 officials (Schneider, 1984). The council discusses issues such as definitions of crime among different countries and extradition matters. Although council activities have been largely informal, much international cooperation has been achieved to combat certain types of crime effectively (Schneider, 1984). International law and differences in criminal law among countries is a continual topic of concern to both Interpol and the Council of Europe. Frequent colloquiums are held to clarify crime definitions in each system and determine responsibility for administering sanctions, means of appeal, conditions for establishing infractions, and rules of evidence. One such colloquium held in Stockholm in 1987 focused on legal and practical problems associated with criminal and administrative penal law (Association Internationale de Droit Penale, 1988).

ARE THERE ANY CULTURAL UNIVERSALS?

Even the most belligerent nations oppose crime, especially crime affecting cities and neighborhoods. Crime prevention is a dominant theme of most criminal justice research occurring in every industrialized nation. Minimizing crime and lowering crime rates are standard objectives of any police agency, regardless of country. As we have seen, however, different countries usually have different types of crime to contend with, and in varying amounts. Japan's low crime rate and the widespread loyalty of its citizenry to police officers tend to make police officers in departments in other nations somewhat envious, despite some of the criticism Japanese police officials have received about how suspects in custody are treated.

In most countries, police organizations are subject to political influence. Thus, police actions are likely to conform to political interests, whatever they may be. In England the police have been used to quell civil disobedience and rioting. Tactics used by some police officers in their dealings with rioters have been widely criticized, and some changes have been introduced to improve police-public interaction. In the United States there is great discontent concerning the use of deadly force by police officers to apprehend suspects, even dangerous ones. Yet other countries, including Brazil, Argentina, and Jamaica, tend to regard the use of deadly force by police as legitimate. Large numbers of suspects may be executed by police in these countries, and both elite and lower-class opinion is tolerant of such executions. Police officers in these countries have almost always justified the use of deadly force against suspects as acts of self-defense, typically in the context of shootouts (Chevigny, 1990). In Nigeria, police are often used by the government to protect colonialism and upper-class economic and political interests (Ahire, 1991; Alemika, 1988). In South Africa, black-on-black violence between police and citizens is widespread. Police corruption is commonplace, and although efforts have been made to improve recruitment practices and limit police officer tasks, much corruption and abuse of power continues among South African constables (University of Capetown Institute of Criminology, 1990). Ghana has exhibited similar patterns among its police officers and administrators (Arthur, 1989).

Few specific statements about the nature of police organization and operations and police-community relations can apply to all countries. Even among nations that share a common political and social heritage, there are many differences in policing methods and the types of crimes to be prevented.

TRENDS IN COMPARATIVE COMMUNITY POLICING

If we examine the programs of national and international professional organizations such as the American Society of Criminology or the Academy of Criminal Justice Sciences, it is apparent that interest in comparative community policing is increasing among participating professionals. Furthermore, a perusal of the professional literature indicates that increasing numbers of countries are experimenting with community policing as a crime prevention alternative as well as a move toward improved public relations for police.

Besides the countries we have examined here, many additional countries are adopting community policing methods. For example, Australia is implementing improvements in police training and recruitment, as well as extensive measures to further police-community cooperation (Ewin, 1990). Police officers are placed in high-crime areas of communities in order to conduct surveillance and crime control activities. Although the media in Australia have criticized some of this police surveillance, it does appear to be receiving widespread acceptance (Ewin, 1990; Hatty, 1991).

In Germany, major changes have occurred in police organizations, with community-based policing patterns implemented in many communities (Fairchild, 1989). Improvements have been made in the selection, recruitment, and training of new police officers, with more rigorous standards in effect for their deployment during emergencies (Fairchild, 1989).

South Africa, despite its history of apartheid, or racial separation, is doing much to democratize its criminal justice system. This democratization extends to its police force, as South African officials strive to make their officers more accountable to citizens (Steytler, 1991).

Singapore and New Zealand have been making similar progress to professionalize their police forces and bring officers in closer touch with citizens. For instance, Singapore established eight **neighborhood police posts** (NPPs), which are similar to mini-stations or substations (Quah and Quah, 1987). Surveys of citizens in those affected neighborhoods show less fear of crime and less antagonism toward police officers. In fact, Singapore officers in various NPPs make frequent home visits in some neighborhoods to keep pace with changing neighborhood developments. Where NPPs were established in participating neighborhoods, the crime rate dropped by 10 percent in less than four months (Quah and Quah, 1987), and robbery, auto theft, and burglary decreased by 11.4 percent during the same period. These NPPs also resulted in more frequent crime reports by interested citizens. Thus there was a greater feeling among neighborhood residents that their police officers could actually do something to solve crimes in which they had been victimized (Quah and Quah, 1987). In New Zealand, police professionalization has included the recruitment of larger numbers of women into police ranks (Corns, 1988). One hurdle yet to be overcome is the fact that policing in New Zealand is corporation-like, and citizens react to police officers in a bureaucratic or impersonal fashion. Indications are, however, that such police-community exchanges are changing (Corns, 1988).

In Mindanao, the Philippines, numerous vigilante-like organizations of private citizens in communities in recent years have done much to curb crime in their neighborhoods. Cooperation from the government police has been fruitful in promoting greater coordination of their crime prevention and control efforts (Austin, 1988). Governmental police helped to curb some of the self-help abuses that emerged from large-scale vigilantism. (Some citizens began to demand tribute from citizens "protected" by such private crime-fighting groups.)

Finally, in the People's Republic of China, great advancements have been made toward establishing effective community policing. Prior to post-Mao modernization, police reforms were virtually nonexistent (Fu, 1990). Police relations with the public were estranged, particularly because police were used as political instruments to achieve small coalition objectives. Through various police reforms, many urban centers in China have instituted Pi Chu Schuo (PCS), or local police station reforms (Fu, 1990). Under these reforms, more resources are diverted to police stations, and police officers are given broader discretionary powers in investigations and suspect arrests. Additionally, several mechanisms heighten police accountability at all administrative levels (Fu, 1991). The PCS network of neighborhood police stations is a strong move toward community policing (Fu, 1990). Police professionalism is stressed, and the use of extensive neighborhood patrolling by police officers has tended to reduce crime rates in affected communities. However, neighborhood residents do not yet interact closely with these new police patrols. Limited community involvement is seen as a problem for PCS. Greater public support is currently being sought by police administrators as they attempt to emulate the community policing practices of various Western nations (Fu, 1990).

KEY TERMS

British Crime Survey
Canadian Centre for Justice Statistics
Chuzaishos
Communitarian model
Comparative community policing
Constitution Act of 1867
Contact patrols
Council of Europe
Crime Stoppers
Criminal Justice Act of 1948
Criminal Law Act of 1967
Dual procedure offense
Graduate Entry Scheme
Hybrid offense
Incident-driven policing
Indictable offense
International Court of Justice
Interpol
Kobans

Law Reform Commission Act
Mala in se crimes
Mala prohibita crimes
Metropolitan Police Force Project Act (of 1981)
Mini-stations
National Crime Survey
National Police Agency
Neighborhood police posts
Penal Code of 1907
Police and Criminal Evidence Act of 1984
Police Complaints Authority
Police Complaints Investigation Bureau
Royal Canadian Mounted Police
Special course
Specials
Stare decisis
Summary offense
Uniform Crime Reports

QUESTIONS FOR REVIEW

1. Distinguish between incident-driven and problem-oriented policing. What is the significance of this distinction for community policing—its understanding and intent?
2. What is meant by crosscultural community-oriented policing? What are some of its contributions to community policing generally?
3. Differentiate among three types of English crimes. How is each punished? Is there capital punishment in England? Do you think that capital punishment is a crime deterrent? Why or why not?
4. What are three types of offenses in Canada? How does each of these compare with the categories of crime in England?
5. How do England and Canada differ in terms of the types of crimes each has, per 100,000 persons? What explanations might you provide for these differences?
6. Do you think the availability of firearms in Canada and the limited availability of firearms in England has anything at all to do with the violent crime differences between the two countries? Explain.
7. Does England have a national police force? What is the organizational model on which English police agencies are patterned, if any?
8. What evidence indicates that police agencies in Canada and England are doing anything to improve the quality of the police officers they select and train?
9. How are England and Canada coping with complaints by citizens that police officers are prejudiced against minorities and mistreat them?
10. What does Canadian law enforcement hope to achieve by the year 2000?
11. Summarize several key generalizations about the police agencies of England that currently impair the implementation of community-policing on a large scale?
12. Are "specials" in England doing anything constructive to prevent crime, improve community-policing efforts, and further the government interest of bringing police and community residents closer together? What are some criticisms of specials?
13. What is the contact patrol project sponsored by the Home Office in England? What are some of its objectives? Is this project achieving its objectives?
14. Why does Canada seem to have a disproportionate share of money-laundering and drug trafficking problems compared with Japan and England, for example?
15. What is the jurisdiction of the RCMP?
16. What minority complaints seem typical of how the citizenry view some of the police officers of Canada? Do England and Canada have the same types of minority problems? Why or why not?

17. What are some significant elements of the "new mission" of Canadian law enforcement, as envisioned by the Solicitor General of Canada?
18. Why do some persons claim that Canadian community-policing efforts are only cosmetic and not seriously undertaken rather than incorporated as positive program elements?
19. Does Japan have the death penalty, and if so, how frequently is it used?
20. Why does Japan have such a low crime rate?
21. What do you think community policing in Japan has to do with the Japanese crime rate? Explain.
22. How are crimes defined in Japan?
23. What are prefectures in Japan? What are their functions?
24. In Japan, what are kobans and chuzaishos? What are their functions?
25. Why do some people say that community policing and Japanese policing are the same thing?
26. What do the Japanese people themselves have to do with the low Japanese crime rate?
27. Do Japanese police departments have problems of minority relations similar to those of Canada and England? Why or why not?
28. What is Interpol? Briefly discuss its origin and emergence.
29. What world courts exist to try international criminals?
30. What are some major trends in community policing throughout the world? Give some examples of community policing in other countries.

SUGGESTED READINGS

Bierne, Piers, and Joan Hill (eds.) (1991). *Comparative Criminology: An Annotated Bibliography.* Westport, CT: Greenwood Press.
Brogden, Mike, Tony Jefferson, and Sandra Walklate (1988). *Introducing Policework.* London, UK: Unwin Hyman.
Heidensohn, Frances, and Martin Farrell (eds.) (1991). *Crime in Europe.* London and New York: Routledge.
Muncie, John, and Richard Sparks (eds.) (1991). *Imprisonment: European Perspectives.* New York: St. Martin's Press.
Rowe, Dennis (ed.). *International Drug Trafficking (1988).* Chicago: Office of International Criminal Justice, University of Illinois at Chicago.
Yarnold, Barbara M. (1991). *International Fugitives: A New Role for the International Court of Justice.* Westport, CT: Praeger.

CHAPTER 12

Solutions and Recommendations

Introduction

Violence and the American Way of Life

A Summary of Community Problems Involving the Police
Violence in the Schools
Gangs
Victims of Crime

Implementing Reforms
Citizen Involvement and Police Response
Police Retirement
Community and Senior Citizen Involvement
Elderly Citizens: The Graying of America

Explorer Scouts
Cadet Programs
Police Community Awareness Academies
Internships
Risk Management

Police and the Redevelopment of Inner Cities: A Practical Application of Community-Oriented Policing
Columbia, South Carolina
Expanding the New Program
The Roanoke, Virginia, Experience
The Savannah, Georgia, Cop-on-the-Block Program
The Albany, New York, Approach
The Alexandria, Virginia, Residential Police Officers Program

Washington, D.C.
Portland, Oregon
Involvement at the Federal Level

Legal Implications
Hiring Standards
Negligent Training
Weapons Selection
Qualification with Off-Duty
  Weapons
Negligent Retention

Accountability Revisited: Ideal and Real Consequences of Sanctions
Patrol Car Video Cameras
Litigation

Summary

Questions for Review

Suggested Readings

INTRODUCTION

It would require a quantum stretch of an active imagination to believe that the implementation of COP is the answer to American crime problems or that a single incident such as the Rodney King case could alter the delivery style of American policing on a national scale. It appears that COP, as a philosophy, only enhances the *practice* of policing. Perhaps crime in various communities can be reduced to tolerable levels with COP, but even that specific outcome is speculative.

VIOLENCE AND THE AMERICAN WAY OF LIFE

No amount of democratic policing can seemingly abate or divert violence, and to be sure, America is a violent country. For instance, in America firearms kill far more people between the ages of 15 and 24 than do all natural causes combined. (A word of statistical caution: Very few individuals between the ages of 15 and 24 die of natural causes.) However, gun deaths, including suicides of all ages, now total more than 37,000 a year (Morganthau, 1993:33) in a gun-oriented country that has more than 284,000 federally licensed gun dealers (*Los Angeles Times*, 1994:B10). In 1990, 59 percent of the youths killed by guns were victims of homicide; 30 percent were suicides; and 11 percent were as a result of unintentional shootings. Approximately 5,356 people under the age of 19 were killed by guns in 1991; that figure equates to almost 15 youths per day, with thousands more wounded. The medical costs of children wounded by gunfire in the United States averaged $14,434 in 1991, more than a full year's tuition at a private college at that time.

When the polio epidemic killed 3,152 adults and children in 1952, it intensified a global effort to combat the disease that resulted in a vaccine that eradicated polio (Associated Press: 1993b:A32). But it seems similar concerns are not raised regarding the safety of our inner-city residents, who feel they are in a war zone. This perception of a war zone is well justified. In 1992, 39 percent of murders were committed in twenty-five central cities that represent only 12 percent of the population. Detroit and Washington, D.C., had murder rates twelve to sixteen times higher than those of their respective suburbs (Barone, 1994:42).

In the case of firearms, some states have attempted to fight fire with fire: thirteen states have passed laws allowing citizens who have met certain requirements to carry arms. In 1987, for instance, Florida enacted a concealed-carry law guaranteeing a gun permit to any resident who is at least age 21; has no record of crime, mental illness or drug or alcohol abuse; and has completed a firearms safety course. Florida's homicide rate fell following the enactment of this law, as did the rate in Oregon after the enactment of a similar law. Through June 1993, there had been 160,823 permits issued in Florida. Only 530, or 0.33 percent, of the applicants were denied permits, and only 16 permits (less than 1/100 of 1 percent) have been rescinded because of the commission, after issuance, of a crime involving a firearm (Will, 1993:94).

As of January 1, 1994, Florida laws prohibited youths under the age of eighteen from possessing guns unless they are hunting or target shooting. The new laws provide penalties for juveniles, parents, and dealers that range from community service to detention and jail time. The legislation also allows the police to seize guns from minors *whether or not* a crime is being committed. Parents who permit minors to have guns can face up to five years in jail, and dealers who sell weapons to underage customers could serve up to fifteen years in prison (*Los Angeles Times*, 1993:A29).

Urban Carnage. On December 2, 1993, in Oxnard, California, an out-of-work computer engineer killed three people and wounded six others at a state unemployment office, then killed a police officer who pursued him (Morganthau et al., 1993:27). In that same month, an unemployed handyman and Jamaican immigrant, Colin Ferguson, boarded a train carrying commuters from New York City to the Long Island suburb of Hickville, pulled out a semiautomatic pistol, and opened fire (Morganthau et al., 1993:29), shooting twenty-three passengers, five fatally. That same day in Chicago, one teenage girl fired at another in a lunchtime crowd in the Loop. The night before, an Atlanta police officer's son was shot to death in a driveway, and a teacher in Harrisburg, Pennsylvania, was shot in the head as he graded papers in a classroom. Later in that week in December 1993, Polly Klass, age twelve, was buried in Petaluma, California. She had been abducted from her bedroom and slain (Gest, 1993:6). In response to the death toll, a "death clock" in Times Square began operating on New Year's Day 1994, recording nationwide gun fatalities in an attempt to bring attention to and share the horror of victimization (Post et al., 1994:22).

Public response to violence and an apparent loss of confidence in the government's ability to protect people has resulted in record numbers of firearm purchases. Across the United States, sales of weapons, especially in the aftermath of riots and civil disorders, have soared. In 1993, for instance, "laid back" Californians purchased 665,229 firearms (448,246 handguns). Handgun sales have generally been on the rise in California since 1986, and over the eight-year period 1986–1993, more than two and one-half million (2,548,437) revolvers and pistols have been purchased (Ingram, 1994:A31):

1986	254,479
1987	263,223
1988	274,539
1989	308,783
1990	320,657
1991	311,154
1992	367,375
1993	448,247

At the national level it has been estimated that there are 211 million firearms in the United States—nearly one for every man, woman, and child in America (Post et al., 1994:22).

Many critics of COP view it as a potentially dangerous path toward a police state. Central to this position is that the police establishment presents itself as the final authority in the community regarding the handling of crime. Moreover, a substantial portion of the population believes that police *are* the solution to community problems. This idea of allowing the police to "take care of things" is popular and quite strong nowadays, thriving in the absence of other government intervention. The police are applauded for being aggressive in mobilizing the community to promote crime prevention and community safety. Police power rests ultimately on law, but the public may have no other remedy than to rely on the police to prevent chaos and elements leading to chaos (Singer: 1993). Taking this position a bit further, radical criminologists suggest that the police are filling a void left by overwhelmed and undersupported social services. The implementation of COP, according to critics, could render the paucity of services and deterioration of the urban "quality of life" more palatable. To some, COP is merely a contrived placebo that masks the fact that no real cures for crime and misery are on the horizon.

Regardless of the critics and social alarmists, a new policing philosophy is slowly emerging. COP may be piecemeal at present, but the concept is becoming a compelling force. A 1990 National Institute of Justice-sponsored National Assessment Program survey documented a groundswell of interest among law enforcement officials in community-oriented approaches to policing. A full 80 percent of those police departments surveyed ($n = 2,000$) reported a need for research and technical assistance on problem-oriented policing. Seventy-one percent of police cited a need for training in community relations, up from 53 percent in 1986 (National Institute of Justice, 1995:1–2).

BOX 12.1   Gun Exchanges and Buybacks

The gun buyback effort appears to have started in Denver, Colorado, in 1988 when the Reverend Marshall Gourley, a Roman Catholic priest at Our Lady of Guadalupe, asked his parishioners to bring in their guns. He received national attention but only a few guns. The following year the church offered $100 per gun, with money donated anonymously, and the church recovered sixty guns. The idea took root, and a "guns for goods" exchange soon emerged and spread to other cities (Post et al., 1994: 20). Religious institutions and businesspeople, united with local police agencies, have demonstrated that they can make some progress in the area of taking guns out of public circulation. In New York over the 1993 Christmas holiday period, $25,000 was raised by businesses offering a $100 gift certificate to Toys 'R' Us for weapons taken to the 34th Precinct police station in the high-crime rate neighborhood of Washington Heights. The station ran out of certificates after taking in 250 weapons, ranging from broken hunting rifles to a submachine gun, and had to issue IOUs (*Los Angeles Times*, 1993:A23).

The trend to swap weapons for more innocuous items has taken hundreds of guns out of circulation. The city of Dallas, in exchange for guns, gave tickets for a preseason Cowboys game. Denver soon followed by offering tickets to Broncos football games. Los Angeles offered tickets to Lakers basketball games, a Janet Jackson concert, and several other events (*Time*, 1994:14). The exchange in Los Angeles secured 412 weapons (110 rifles, 251 handguns, 2 assault rifles, 49 shotguns) in a five-day period. Oakland, California, offered tickets to a Bette Midler concert, Disney on Ice, or a Sharks hockey game, causing sixty-eight guns to be exchanged in one day (Lacey, 1994:A3, A14). Salt Lake City, Utah, paid $25 cash for each gun in working order, and San Francisco offered tickets to sporting events and concerts (*Time*, 1994:14). Cash bounties brought in almost 8,500 guns in St. Louis, Missouri, during 1991, with most melted down to create a sculpture of a shooting victim. In spite of this effort, St. Louis recorded a new high in gun-related deaths in 1993. The Southern Christian Leadership Conference (SCLC) in Atlanta, Georgia, sponsored four buybacks from April 1993 through January 1994, netting 1,700 weapons. A similar SCLC program in Dayton, Ohio, yielded 1,000 firearms in one day (Post et al., 1994:22).

One of the most recent gun buyback ventures was the joint effort of the Anaheim (California) Police Department and the Mighty Ducks hockey team. The program, the first of its kind in the National Hockey League, awarded two tickets to one of the Ducks's remaining home games to anyone who turned in a firearm. The exchange brought in 104 firearms and sparked program interest in the Angeles Baseball franchise. Other local businesses such as Aamco Transmission and Metro Car Wash also offered services in exchange for guns (Trounson, 1994: A1).

> As attractive as gun exchanges and buybacks seem, the concept is undermined by some police departments that continue to sell or auction confiscated weapons to the public. Although this practice has been discouraged, several cities still allow police departments to raise revenues by returning guns to the public through sales and auctions. Even in financial hard times, the willingness of police departments to put guns back into circulation sends a mixed message.

Although there is mounting interest, COP is not a concept embraced by all urban and rural policing agencies or by certain social critics. For all COP's perceived faults, it is still a cautious step into the future—a future that, if the police and communities can form viable partnerships, holds hope for reasonably safe neighborhoods. The future might also hold community members who trust and esteem their policing partners.

Preventing and controlling neighborhood crime involves citizen participation in the form of radio patrols in agencies such as the Providence (Rhode Island) Police Department. *(Rob Crandall)*

A SUMMARY OF COMMUNITY PROBLEMS INVOLVING THE POLICE

Violence in the Schools

Applying COP strategies, urban and rural police agents can act as community resources by supporting SANE, D.A.R.E., and similar programs. The mere presence of an informed and conscientious uniformed officer on school grounds can defuse negativism and deter some youngsters from bringing weapons to school.

Gangs

Many urban police departments have taken a "search and destroy" approach to combat and suppress gang involvement and gang activity. These tactics in many cases have had a disruptive effect on the entire community. Some cities have changed their tactics to address gang-related problems. Rather than using "hammer" methods, "invading" targeted communities from time to time in somewhat futile attempts to seize weapons and hold gangs in check, cities have explored alternative strategies. COP mandates the police and the community to work together to reduce gang activity. Their strategies might include the issuance of search warrants and subsequent police raids, but these "legal strikes" would be coordinated with a community committee involved with gang suppression. An open communications line could be developed with the community, enabling enforcement officers to receive current information on gang members and their activities. In most communities, gang activity is the scourge of law-abiding residents; the relatively small cohort of gang-bangers should not place an entire community at risk.

Victims of Crime

Developing crime control and crime prevention strategies within the framework of COP includes a commitment to potential victims. There are groups and classes of individuals that require special protective attention from the predators in our society.

The Elderly. The elderly have been regarded as ideal targets for the criminal element. As a group they often must rely on public transportation, and often they shop with local merchants, cashing and paying with their Social Security checks, which arrive on a predictable date. The elderly also make ideal victims because they are often fragile, have failing faculties (hearing, eyesight, and memory), and are highly susceptible to con games and scams.

Juveniles. Because the credibility of their complaints and testimony may be doubted, youngsters often see offenses and crimes committed against them go unresolved. COP programs might include developing youth centers, counseling, and a host of other community outreach activities to assist and protect minors. Such programs include School Resource Officers and special juvenile units.

The Physically and Mentally Challenged. The blind, the deaf, and other physically or mentally impaired individuals have special protective needs. Many of these individuals are preyed upon in the urban streets of America. It is not unusual to read reports of wheelchairs and crutches being stolen *while being used*. Reactive remedies such as sentence enhancements for those convicted of these crimes have not been effective. The private sector should offer incentives to promote the development of antitheft and protective devices to thwart thieves.

The Undocumented. Fear of deportation makes those without legal documentation extremely vulnerable because they have no legal recourse. Only the bravest of the brave will risk deportation to notify the police of crimes committed against them. This fear has allowed unscrupulous individuals to exploit their services and labor and then refuse to pay them.

IMPLEMENTING REFORMS

Citizen Involvement and Police Response

A serious concern for most communities is the staffing of adequate numbers of police officers to patrol and provide services to the community. Although there is no consensus on the precise formula for allotting the optimum number of police per service population, it has been generally accepted that *sufficient* police personnel are required to respond to emergency calls-for-service. Economic constraints have limited the ability of many cities and counties to hire additional officers to keep up with increased populations, density rankings, calls-for-service, and reported crimes. Just keeping pace with normal personnel attrition is expensive because of the costs incurred in recruitment, selection, screening, and training.

Police Retirement

From a police planning standpoint, the implications of a graying America are substantial. Current law enforcement pension plans that cost fifty cents per dollar of wages will be depleted rapidly. Normal retirement benefits, coupled with disability retirements, are slowly pushing some cities toward bankruptcy. To keep pace with the increasing numbers of law enforcement officers who elect to retire, funds set aside by states, counties, or cities for retirements will have to be increased significantly or the retirement scheme altered. There are several distinct possibilities:

> **BOX 12.2   Koreatown**
>
> "Residents, churches, and businesses—nearly all of them Korean-American—have put up $400,000 to turn a boarded-up former bank in the West Adams district into a police station. A grateful Los Angeles Police Department is preparing to house 30 officers there. The station's boosters say they will raise an additional $1.5 million to pay for the station's upkeep when it opens, perhaps in 1996. The substation is such a popular solution to community problems that groups sometimes at odds have rallied collectively behind it."
>
> *Source:* Peter Y. Hong, "L.A.'s Koreatown Funds Own Police Station." *Los Angeles Times,* November 15, 1995:A30.

1. Taxes could be raised to offset the increase in retirement benefits
2. Law enforcement officers could be allowed to retire on or after age sixty (if otherwise qualified)
3. To ease the deficit, police budgets could be cut and equipment might not be replaced or repaired on a timely basis
4. A reliance on retired police officers as unpaid volunteers could ease the financial burden; once an officer elected to retire, he or she could be encouraged to serve in an unpaid police reserve
5. A heavier emphasis on senior citizen volunteers at all levels could be fostered to assist in the administration of police service
6. Police unions could lose influence on the community as a result of sheer economic necessity
7. The tasks, roles, and functions of police officers could be refined to allow for greater utilization of more cost-effective non-sworn personnel
8. Officers could be offered early cash pension settlement bonuses (which is a gamble that the short-term expenditure will be less costly than the long-term retirement payment schedule)
9. Upon initial appointment, officers could be limited to one or two four-year tours with the police department and then told to seek employment elsewhere, with only the exceptional individual allowed to serve until retirement age

Many jurisdictions have asked individuals with law enforcement experience to "return to the fold" in a volunteer capacity, and a number of retired local individuals with law enforcement experience have responded. Many of these people have expertise, training, knowledge of process, and special skills that younger enforcement officers have yet to develop, and many are eager to "get back in harness" and avoid the stagnation that retirement can sometimes bring. One example is the Fort Myers, Florida, G.R.A.M.P.A. Cop Program. Although this particular program was designed to augment their School Resource Officer program, the basic concept could be applied to a myriad of police functions. The initial recruitment drive identified nearly 1,000 senior citizens with varying degrees of law enforcement experience who lived within the Fort Myers area. To qualify, G.R.A.M.P.A. applicants had to meet the following requirements:

- Have a minimum of five years sworn law enforcement experience
- Be at least forty years of age at the date of hire
- Be in good physical condition as determined by the departmental physician
- Meet the basic requirements for admittance to the Florida Criminal Justice Commission

Basic Recruit School for reserve and auxiliary officers

- Have a Florida driver's license and a good driving record
- Submit letters of recommendation from three superior officers from their former departments who have knowledge of their work performance and character
- Successfully pass a thorough background investigation, including a polygraph
- Be screened by a police oral board
- Realize that they are not subject to Civil Service protection
- Understand that the Fort Myers program pays $6 per hour with no benefits

Because many G.R.A.M.P.A. Cops are police retirees, most applicants have years of law enforcement experience, which would make formal training usually unnecessary. However, to ensure the continuity and integrity of the program, accepted applicants attend a two-week training session at the police academy. Aside from the obvious benefit of having experienced and qualified retirees capable of relieving stationbound officers for patrol or special duty, the cost benefits are exceptional. The benefits derived from community members being involved in law enforcement functions also cannot be underestimated. The Fort Myers program promotes citizen involvement, and their combined service efforts contribute to community well-being (Spurlin and Schwein, 1990).

Internal conflicts can harm or impede the use of unpaid volunteers, however. The practice of using retired officers as volunteers may be viewed by the police union as "scab labor": uncompensated labor that would otherwise be performed by regular hires. Unions discourage the use of volunteers because their use simply gives municipalities an excuse not to raise salaries or increase personnel. Some departments refer to this practice of **volunteerism** as "the dinosaur program," a not too subtle expression of in-house dissatisfaction.

Community and Senior Citizen Involvement

There are other highly qualified retired individuals who are part of a large untapped resource pool available to the police as well as other community organizations. A national effort called the **Retired Senior Volunteer Program** places retirees in community volunteer positions and has been seen as another way of addressing police personnel shortages. The Huntington Beach (California) City Council, for example, voted to approve the police department's plan to bring twenty senior citizens into volunteer positions in the department. Although the seniors work without pay, the city purchased their uniforms from asset seizure funds. One of the selling points was the projected increase in revenue through the increased number of parking citations the volunteers were expected to issue (Billiter, 1993b).

However, one or two problems exist with reliance on volunteer services to augment police services. First, there is over time a tendency to rely on volunteer service to perform some services ordinarily taken care of by regular police officers. A distinct problem arises when the volunteer base (for whatever reason) declines. Special programs and the level of service the community has been accustomed to receiving might be severely curtailed or canceled. A point for consideration is the South Plainfield, New Jersey, volunteer firehouse, which had a drop in its active roll from sixty-five to forty-two. South Plainfield is typical of a national problem: The volunteer pool is shrinking. Volunteer ranks nationally have dipped at least 13 percent in the last decade, to about 800,000, while volunteer responsibilities have grown. Paid professionals are not replacing enough of them. A point of interest is that the affluent New York suburb of Dobbs Ferry, to attract volunteer firefighters, opened a low-cost housing development in 1992, so that they could afford to live in town (Krajick, 1993:730). The multiple implications for law enforcement are readily seen. To offer services performed by volunteers is to raise the community's expectation of the availability of police services. When personnel shortages occur and service needs cannot be met, only the police will be blamed.

Elderly Citizens: The Graying of America

Demographics. By the year 2000, the U.S. Census Bureau projects that 76 million Americans will be sixty-five and older, and 13.3 million will be over age eighty-five. These figures assume that the average life expectancy will remain steady, but some forecasters assert that if the dramatic gains in longevity seen in this century continue into the next century, there might be 138 million Americans older than sixty-five by 2040 and as many as 78 million people older than eighty-five by 2080; this is twenty-six times more than there are today (Beck, 1993:65). The potential impact of these demographic projections on public and private service agencies is staggering. The resources required to support quality-of-life services for this aging population will strain our existing revenue base. Law enforcement will share in this social responsibility to provide additional public services. If the projections are remotely accurate, the positive aspect is that there will be an abundant increase in potential public-service volunteers.

Explorer Scouts

Law Enforcement Exploring is a branch of the Boy Scouts of America (BSA), but its members are not Boy Scouts but Explorers: young men and women ranging in age from fourteen to twenty who are interested in law enforcement careers. The Explorer Scout Program brings interested youths into a police department to participate in such activities as traffic and crowd control, crime prevention, security surveys, and patrol ride-along programs. Explorers do not take the place of regular officers but supplement them in nonthreatening activities.

Although the program serves to screen potential police applicants, perhaps more important is the role an Explorer program has in improving the agency's relationship with the community. Explorer advisers are usually assigned to a department's community services section to deal specifically with crime prevention. The Explorers also become involved in the community through senior citizen centers, bicycle rodeos, day schools, and many other programs. In addition, Neighborhood Watch programs enable the Explorers to meet with residents of the community and explain how to mark and safeguard valuables. Within the department Explorers assist in filing, statistical work, and conducting inventories (Farish, 1990).

Cadet Programs

Police **cadet programs** are, on a national scale, designed to bring underage but otherwise qualified individuals into police service. Applicants to the cadet programs undergo preservice screening (oral, physical, and background investigations) and are generally accepted if they have solid recommendations. This particular program is generally seen as a prescreening process to permit the organization as well as the cadet to evaluate a future in law enforcement. The participation of high school or college-level individuals in policing adds another dimension to community involvement. Extreme care must be exercised in the cadet selection process, however, because the reasons older applicants apply may differ greatly from the reasons youngsters seek police service.

Police Community Awareness Academies

The idea of the Citizens Police Academy originated in England, specifically in the Devon and Cornwall Constabulary, Middlemoor Exeter. In 1977 two small British municipal police agencies established a Police Night School, a concept that has come to be known as the Citizens Police Academy in the United States. The idea developed when local citizens asked their constables how the constabulary operated. It was discovered that most townspeople had no idea of the functions of the constabulary. When the night school "graduated" its first class, the constabulary felt those in attendance were highly supportive and realized the program had begun to bridge the gap between the community and law enforcement. It had actually created a closer bond and provided mutual understanding.

Several major cities in the United States, including Austin, Texas, and Phoenix, Arizona, have established Citizen Police Academies, and they have been well-attended since the early 1980s (Burgreen, 1991). The following are sketches of two such academies:

The San Diego Academy. In 1991 the San Diego Police Department embarked on its own *Police Community Awareness Academy.* The academy requires participants to meet one night a week for three hours during the twelve-week course. The goal is to "inform these participants of some of the many services available from the police department, in the hopes that they will take that information and educate the general public by passing on what they have learned."

During this program representatives from units including Vice, Gangs, Drug Enforcement, and Traffic give presentations. Also included is a visit to the Police K–9 Training Facility and the police academy, where participants try out their skills on the F.A.T.S. system (firearms training simulator). Participants also gain ride-along experience with a patrol officer. Because San Diego subscribes to COP, the Police Community Awareness Academy is part of an ongoing effort to promote a cohesive partnership between the San Diego Police Department and the community it serves (Burgreen, 1991).

Course Outline
Session One: Chief's introduction, Office of Professional Responsibility (i.e., internal affairs, inspection, and control), use of force, overview of class, material handouts
Session Two: Vice/prostitution; fugitive detail

Session Three: History and overview of the criminal justice system; SWAT
Session Four: Patrol procedures
Session Five: F.A.T.S. system
Session Six: Ride-along
Session Seven: Discussion of ride-along
Session Eight: Traffic division
Session Nine: Communications
Session Ten: Canine demonstration
Session Eleven: Drugs; gangs
Session Twelve: Graduation

The Westminster, California, Academy. In July 1993 the Westminster (California) Police Department launched a similar nine-week citizen academy, modeled after one in Lincoln, Nebraska (Heiman, 1993: B1). The first class of nineteen residents was designed to give them "a hands-on look at police operations." A spokesman for the department explained, "We're trying to take the time to explain a lot of the things we've been unwilling or unable to explain in the past—why a police officer does this or that. This course is an opportunity for the citizens to interact with employees on a personal basis and give direct feedback." The chief of police said some classes would be selected from people who "aren't the police department's biggest fans, who view us with suspicion," such as residents who have filed complaints. He added, "Hopefully, the program will alleviate their suspicions" (Heiman, 1993:B1).

Internships

Universities and colleges across the United States have well-developed courses in criminal justice, criminology, or justice administration. The majority of these criminal justice programs include an internship program. **Internships** generally are three-unit, upper-division offerings for graduating seniors to allow them practical exposure to the criminal justice system. Several universities make the internship a mandatory subject, requiring up to 160 contact hours per sixteen-week semester. Many graduating criminal justice majors use the intern experience to seek employment with the participating agencies; if not successful, they can at least add another entry to their résumé. The agencies benefit by volunteer assistance that often is in the form of bilingual and bicultural experience or experience in research, statistics, computer literacy, updating or revising of manuals, criminalistics, photography, legal service, or a host of other areas. Universities and colleges are a vast reservoir of generally untested talent and expertise. The communities benefit in that the student interns provide relatively low-cost service and are a positive conduit to the larger community. The downside is that agencies must have a member of their staff assigned to coordinate the program and to ensure a quality experience for the interns. It also requires time to instruct, familiarize, and supervise interns at each job station.

Risk Management

In light of expensive litigation, lawsuits, consent decrees, and summary judgments, many public agencies including the police have entered into a relatively new field, risk management. Risk management has been used in the private sector simply to reduce liability, which can subtract significant amounts from profit margins. Some legal firms specialize in police abuse cases and accept cases on a contingency fee basis. To minimize exposure to civil liability, municipalities have brought in risk managers. These managers are knowledgeable in all protected areas that could result in liability and are charged with taking action to prevent lawsuits. Policing is only one of the agencies under continual review.

POLICE AND THE REDEVELOPMENT OF INNER CITIES: A PRACTICAL APPLICATION OF COMMUNITY-ORIENTED POLICING

In 1937 Congress authorized the establishment of local housing authorities to provide and maintain decent, safe, and sanitary housing for persons who could not afford housing on the private market. When private investors opted out of the affordable housing market, the task of providing affordable housing fell to the public sector. Over the years, for several political reasons, these homes and complexes have been in a general state of decline.

Efforts to combat the decline of many urban areas, especially homes in depressed inner-city areas, have generally proven futile. Innovative approaches to the problems of urban deterioration, neighborhood disorganization, and crime are being initiated in several cities across the nation, however. Some of these programs allow police officers the opportunity to purchase homes in depressed areas. This can be quite an opportunity, as the down payment and monthly installments on a home are often not within the financial grasp of police officers, especially new hires. The majority of such municipal programs are administered by a city unit under such titles as Department of Public Housing, Department of Public Development, Neighborhood Services, or Department of Redevelopment and are coordinated with their respective police departments.

The low-interest loan programs for police officers have helped turn crime-ridden and low-income neighborhoods into desirable places to live, boosting property values and spurring commercial development (Riddle, 1993:32). One of the earlier programs was started in Columbia, South Carolina. The approach

> **BOX 12.3   Attempting to Define Crime**
>
> In attempting to measure the incidence of crime in America, researchers rely heavily on two primary sources, the FBI Index (UCR) and the National Crime Victimization Survey (NCVS). The FBI compiles crime information as reported to the police. The NCVS is a scientifically designed annual survey of a representative sample of some 60,000 households to assess *reported* and *unreported* crime. The 1990 figures indicate that the true level or incidence of crime in the United States is far more serious than the FBI Index indicates:
>
> **UCR and NCVS Crime Rate Figures, 1990**[1]
>
> | Type of Crime | UCR (police) | NCVS (victims) |
> |---|---|---|
> | Rape | 102,555 | 130,260 |
> | Robbery | 639,271 | 1,149,710 |
> | Assault | 1,054,863 | 4,728,810 |
> | Burglary | 3,073,909 | 5,147,740 |
> | Larceny-theft | 7,945,670 | 12,975,320 |
> | Motor vehicle theft | 1,635,907 | 1,967,540 |
> | Totals | 14,452,175 | 26,099,380 |
>
> [1]Federal Bureau of Investigation (1991). *Uniform Crime Reports.* Washington, DC: U.S. Government Printing Office.
>
> Although the implementation of COP will not stop our terrifying urban carnage or cause a dramatic decrease in random lawlessness, neither will solutions to complex social-legal problems come through increased legislation. The Brady Bill will not stop violence, but it and a review of the supply side (licensed dealers) are steps in the right direction. From a practical standpoint, it would be political suicide not to do *something*. Similarly, it could not be expected that the Rodney King incident would reshape American policing, police attitudes, or police training, but the incident did cause many police executives to reflect on their current training and departmental policies, especially in the area of "use of force."

appears to have struck a responsive chord, as other cities are investigating this concept.

Columbia, South Carolina

When rookie Police Officer James Jones helped raid a shabby crack house in 1990 he never dreamed his family would soon be living there. The house, in a middle-class northside community, was an eyesore, a safety hazard, and a drag on a neighborhood that was otherwise trying to lift itself up after a long period of decline. In 1991 Jones, the second officer to take advantage of this novel redevelopment approach, moved into his renovated home after purchasing the property through an innovative city program that provided a 4 percent interest rate on his $53,250 loan. The loan program was originally financed through federal community block grants, but nine local banks signed on to fund 50 percent of the loan program.

In December 1990 officer James Brown knew the house at 911 Sunset Drive was destined to be his. He moved in and became the first officer to participate in the city's program and became one of its best salesmen—holding open houses for other officers and appearing on television to extol the pleasures of home ownership. Resistance within the department at first was high, but on November 18, 1993, a property title was transferred to the eleventh officer homeowner.

The Police Homeowner Loan Program addresses both crime and housing problems of deteriorating low-income neighborhoods by putting police as resident homeowners right in the middle of target neighborhoods. This innovative program offers police 4%, twenty-year financing with no down payment for the purchase and complete rehabilitation of inner-city houses. The loan also includes the closing cost of the loan. It provides an incentive for officers to move from the suburbs into the low-income inner city they serve, with a vested interest as homeowners. (All participating officers acknowledged they would not have purchased in these neighborhoods without this program.)

The program is part of Columbia's effective community-based policing philosophy that resulted in a 15 percent reduction in overall crime. Each house has been rehabilitated exceeding local standards, which has contributed to neighborhood revitalization. Neighborhoods have communicated to the city their pride and satisfaction with police and their families as part of their community, noting the added sense of security and stability. Unexpectedly, community support is so strong that two low-income neighborhoods near the target areas demanded the city also recruit police homeowners for deteriorated houses in their areas. They cited the benefits of police as neighbors and as positive role models for youth (Columbia, 1993).

Ten steps are taken to reach the city's goal of placing police officers in a house:

- The officer contacts the city's loan officer to be prequalified for a loan.
- After preliminary acceptance, the officer searches for the home of choice.
- When a home is found, city staff inspect it to see if it will fit into the program, and estimate repair cost.
- The officer negotiates a purchase price with the seller.
- When a contract is signed, the officer meets with the loan officer to complete an application.
- Specifications are written on the home by a city Community Development staff specification writer.

- The staff assists the officer to get bids for rehabilitation work.
- An acceptable price by a contractor is selected for the rehabilitation work.
- The loan officer presents the loan to the approval committee. The loan is closed when approved.
- Construction begins.

Columbia's police home loan program has the following terms:

- 4 percent rate of interest
- Fixed-rate mortgage
- 20-year term
- No down payment
- $65,000 maximum loan amount (can be waived by loan committee)
- Primarily low- to moderate-income neighborhoods—two-thirds of the city is eligible
- Loans include acquisition, rehabilitation, closing costs
- Homes are selected by officers
- No "sweat equity" (contractors must be hired to rehabilitate the homes)
- Officer must occupy the home as long as the city loan is active
- Program is funded by Community Development Block Grant. However, income will be added along with bank participation

In October 1993 the Columbia loan program was named a winner in the Ford Foundation Innovations in State and Local Government awards program. The selection grew out of two city initiatives: the city's emphasis on community-based policing and the efforts to revitalize housing and promote home ownership. Chief of Police Charles P. Austin, in addition to instituting such measures as decentralized substations, foot beats, and mounted patrols, decided to encourage police officers to live in the city by offering Christmas bonuses to officers who are city residents and requiring city residency for promotion to the rank of captain or higher (Harrison, 1993:A5). Critics claim that such programs could only work in a modest-sized city such as Columbia, where poverty and minority populations are scattered and intermingled in small neighborhoods that lie close to more affluent areas (*Governing*, 1993). Responding to these negative comments, program supporters countered that although Columbia doesn't have vast areas of crime, it does, like many other cities, have isolated high-crime areas (Neff, 1993:5).

Expanding the New Program

At least seven similar programs have taken this novel approach to restore neighborhoods by providing the financial assistance for police officers to purchase homes (Connor, 1993). The program is being replicated in Savannah, Georgia; Rochester,

New York; Albany, New York; St. Petersburg, Florida; Wichita, Kansas; and Roanoke, Virginia. Several other cities, such as Salt Lake City, Utah, and Huntsville, Alabama, have indicated intentions to implement the program. The Columbia program has received national coverage on *ABC World News Tonight with Peter Jennings, NBC Nightly News with Tom Brokaw, CNN Headline News*, and in a May 24, 1992 *Parade Magazine* article. In addition, Dallas, Texas, representatives visited and reviewed the Columbia program with a view toward possible adoption, and Sarasota, Florida, has offered the program to the members of its police department.

The Roanoke, Virginia, Experience

Ordinance No. 31737–101193 approving the loan of Community Development Block Grant funds to qualified police officers in connection with the city's Police Homeowner's Loan Program was adopted by the Council of the City of Roanoke on October 11, 1993. This ordinance is one of a series of programs across the nation specifically intended to bring a police presence into neighborhoods. The Roanoke ordinance reads:

> AN ORDINANCE approving the loan of Community Development Block Grant funds to qualified police officers in connection with the City's Police Homeowner's Loan Program; authorizing the City Manager to execute documents approved as to form by the City Attorney necessary to implement and administer the loans; authorizing the City Attorney and Director of Finance to serve as trustees with regard to the related deeds of trusts securing the notes for the loans; authorizing the City Manager to execute a certificate of satisfaction upon full payment and satisfaction of the loans; authorizing recordation by the City Attorney of the certificate of satisfaction in the Office of the Clerk of the Circuit Court for the City of Roanoke; and providing for an emergency.
>
> WHEREAS, Council has previously approved the concept of the Police Homeowner's Loan Program ("Program") in which the City will provide loans for the purchase or rehabilitation of homes from Community Development Block Grant ("CDBG") funds to qualified police officers agreeing to purchase and occupy homes within certain areas of the City.
>
> THEREFORE, BE IT ORDAINED by the Council of the City of Roanoke that:
>
> 1. This Council approves the establishment of a Police Homeowner's Loan Program to provide interest-free loans from CDBG funds to qualified sworn, non-probationary police officers of the city to purchase and to rehabilitate houses to be occupied as the primary residences of the officers in the Conservation Areas or Rehabilitation Districts of the City.
> 2. Such loans shall be repayable over fifteen (15) years in equal installments to be deducted from the officer's biweekly payroll or by monthly bank debits, as approved by the Director of Finance.
> 3. The criteria for participation in the Program and the terms and conditions of the loans shall be substantially as set forth in the City's Manager's report to Council dated October 11, 1993.

4. The City Manager is hereby authorized for and on behalf of the City, to execute documents approved as to form by the City Attorney necessary to implement and administer the loans made under such Program.
5. To secure payment of the loan of CDBG funds made under the Program and performance by the loan recipients, the recipients shall execute a deed of trust and deed of trust note, which document shall be approved as to form by the City Attorney.
6. The City Attorney, Wilburn C. Divling, Jr., and the Director of Finance, James D. Grisso (hereinafter "Trustees"), are hereby authorized to serve as Trustees for and on behalf of the City as beneficiary.
7. Pursuant to s26–49, Code of Virginia (1950), as amended, City Council reserves the right in its sole discretion for any reason whatsoever to appoint a substitute trustee or trustees.
8. Upon payment or full satisfaction of the debt secured by the deed of trust and delivery of the canceled deed of trust note to the person or persons by whom it was paid, the City Manager shall be authorized to execute a certificate of satisfaction upon formal approval prepared by the City Attorney, and the City Attorney shall be authorized to file such certificate of satisfaction in the Office of the Clerk of Circuit Court of the City of Roanoke.
9. In order to provide for the usual daily operation of the municipal government, an emergency is deemed to exist, and this ordinance shall be in full force and effect upon its passage.

ATTEST
City Clerk

The Savannah, Georgia, Cop-on-the-Block Program

The Columbia venture served as a catalyst for a similar undertaking in Savannah, Georgia. In March 1993, the city initiated a new program to assist Savannah Police Department officers with purchasing and renovating houses in inner-city areas. The program, called Cop-on-the-Block, offers mortgages below market rate to qualified officers who have completed their twelve-month probationary period. The program is designed to renovate houses, promote homeownership, and provide a police presence that can help make a neighborhood safer. Officers can pick their own houses, subject to approval by the housing department, but the houses must be located in one of the city's Showcase Area neighborhoods. The houses should be vacant and in need of significant repairs. The city arranges a first mortgage at favorable rates and may provide down payment assistance. Officers earning under 80 percent of median income may qualify for a 4 percent mortgage. The mortgages could be 95 percent of the property's appraised value (after rehabilitation). Officers have the opportunity to own a $50,000 house for a monthly payment as low as $302.99. The Savannah Housing Department is not actually selling property; they only finance the property. The housing department identifies eligible houses and passes the information along to the police department. All loans under the Cop-on-the-Block program are subject to the following conditions:

1. The recipient must maintain ownership of the property for five years.
2. The recipient must continue to use the property as the primary place of residence for a five-year period.
3. The recipient must continue employment with the Savannah Police Department for a five-year period.
4. Property must be maintained to Housing Quality Standards. This is verified by a yearly inspection conducted by housing department staff.
5. Standard loan underwriting criteria will apply.
6. Past credit difficulties will be reviewed on a case by case basis. All officers are encouraged to apply.

The initial reaction from the police department was very supportive, as eight officers applied to participate in the program, causing the city to search for additional properties. The program started with two abandoned structures donated to the city by the owners. Loans for the renovations were made to the initial two officers by the city through a federal program called Home. Each side of the renovated duplexes has two bedrooms and a bathroom. The officers live in one and rent the other (Beatty, 1993).

The Albany, New York, Approach

The creation of Albany's Community Policing Housing Assistance Program was announced in June 1993. The program, established by three of the city's agencies involved with affordable housing, provides financial assistance to members of the Albany Police Force who choose to live in areas of the city that are both participating in the police department's community policing initiatives and designated as neighborhood strategy areas under the Community Development Block Grant Program.

Mayor Thomas Whalen said, "We believe that by assisting our police officers to rent and buy homes in inner-city neighborhoods with active community policing initiatives we are also helping these neighborhoods. The presence of the police officers as neighbors can only help to enhance the sense of security of these areas and aid in their overall revitalization."

Grants of up to $10,000 are provided to officers who purchase and occupy homes in the designated areas by the Community Development Agency. In addition, the Housing Authority and the Local Development Corporation provide low-cost apartment units for officers who wish to rent.

The Alexandria, Virginia, Residential Police Officers Program

The city of Alexandria, Virginia, has no home loan program but has a "residency cop" program, patterned after an Elgin, Illinois, experiment, that serves similar purposes.

In 1992 a member of city council requested that the police department explore the concept of having a police officer live in a geographically defined area and provide police and other related services to that community. To encourage interest in this concept, the Alexandria Housing and Redevelopment Authority agreed to provide a rent- and utility-free housing unit for the officer. In July 1992 a police officer moved into his public housing unit. That officer has continued to live in the unit and has provided police services using community-oriented policing and problem-solving methodologies. The initial assessment of this pilot program indicated that there was a significant increase in the community's satisfaction with the provision of services and in the identification and reduction of problems.

This program was so well-received by the immediate community that two more officers have since been assigned to other areas as Residential Police Officers. Although these two additional assignments are in the early developmental stages, the community response has been positive. Problems are now being addressed and resolved that had previously been unresponsive to traditional police strategies (George, 1993). The police department developed a mission statement, a goal, and six objectives in creating and achieving the mission of this community policing approach.

Mission Statement

To implement Community Oriented Policing strategies in a geographically defined neighborhood. Strategies will be employed by a sworn officer of the Alexandria Police Department who will live and work in the neighborhood and form cohesive partnerships with its residents for the purposes of solving problems.

Goal One

To coordinate the diverse interests of the community for the purposes of improving the quality of life.

Objective One

To perform a needs assessment of the targeted area for the purposes of identifying problems/conditions/issues of community concern.

Strategies

The officer assigned to the targeted area will make a detailed analysis of the physical problems/conditions/issues, identifying the obvious symptoms or conditions. The officer will then assess the causes for the symptoms or conditions for the purposes of problem solving.

The officer should solicit the expertise of an officer(s) experienced in needs assessment preparation.

The officer will use all available resources within City government for the purposes of validating (or invalidating) his/her conclusions. Available resources include, but are not limited to, crime analysis data, calls for service data, previous Community Oriented Policing programs with similar problems/conditions/issues.

Objective Two

To establish contact with various community business, social and private organizations in the targeted area to determine their needs and concerns. The development of a Civic Problem Solving Committee comprised of diverse representatives from the community provide this group with legitimate social power.

Strategies

The officer will contact Civic Association leaders, business leaders, school representatives, service clubs, religious and social centers and other appropriate institutions with an identifiable membership.

The officer will coordinate a meeting involving persons of influence and community residents for the purpose of soliciting their concern. A written survey will serve as an independent needs assessment for the purpose of validating or invalidating the officer's needs assessment.

Objective Three

To prioritize problems/conditions/issues, and develop solutions/strategies that meet community needs.

Strategies

The officer will consolidate his/her concerns and those of the community and present them to the community for review and further input. Once problems/conditions/issues have been identified, both the officer and members of the community must agree on the general approach and prioritization to the solution of the problem.

Once there is general agreement, the solutions (or objectives and strategies) must be publicly disseminated to all members of the community. This is the responsibility of the officer. Emphasis must be placed on the importance of the police and community working together to solve problems.

Regular meetings, and the officer's availability for citizen contact, will ensure that issues causing concern are addressed or explained.

Objective Four

To coordinate and facilitate the delivery of governmental services to the community; to monitor success; and to modify strategies as needed.

Strategies

The officer must be well-versed in available governmental services.

The officer must have the flexibility to adjust his/her hours to meet the needs of the community.

The officer must have the flexibility to design conventional/unconventional/innovative tactical and strategic solutions to solve problems.

The officer must delegate the coordination of governmental services to members of the community. The officer must exercise general supervisory control and responsibility for accomplishing objectives and strategies.

Objective Five

To encourage development of programs designed to increase citizen satisfaction, reduce crime or the fear of crime, and to reduce calls for service in the targeted area.

Strategies

The officer must mobilize the community as a powerful force of significant influence. The use of Block Watch Captains, citizens trained in crime prevention strategies and follow-up surveys, will keep citizen involvement at a high sustained level.

Objective Six

To regularly assess the success or lack of success of operational strategies with community leaders for the purpose of addressing new or recurring problems/conditions/issues.

Strategies

The officer, with the assistance of his/her supervisor and commander, should monitor the operational strategies of all units of the Police Department (such as Patrol, Vice/Narcotics, Street Crimes Unit, Problem Response Team, Crime Prevention

Unit, Special Operations Section and Criminal Investigations Section) and recommend modifications to their operations if they prove to be ineffective.

Additionally, the regular use of citizen satisfaction surveys will identify new or recurrent problems that demonstrate resistance to currently employed strategies.

Crime Analysis statistics should be distributed to members of the community on a regular basis.

Reporting of community and police efforts will be made to the Uniform Division Commander on a monthly basis by the officer. An in-depth formal analysis of the program must be prepared quarterly, incorporating the results of police and community efforts and modifications/recommendations for refocus of efforts.

Operational strategies available to the officer include, but are not limited to:

Jumpout strategies for street-level drug dealing.

Enforcement of alcohol-related ordinances and/or use of substance abuse diversionary programs.

Development and implementation of a "No Trespassing" authorization program designed to deter loitering and breach of peace violations by transients.

Use of traffic enforcement personnel to deter hazardous traffic violations.

Traditional law enforcement strategies to reinforce respect for the rights of community residents.

Use of Code Enforcement or Zoning Inspectors to address substandard housing issues.

Referrals to appropriate service organizations (e.g., Housing, MHMRSA, Social Services, Domestic Violence).

Use of nuisance abatement strategies to discourage minor breaches of the peace violations.

Although the concept of "pride of ownership"—the actual owning of real property within the targeted communities—is not part of the Alexandria program, officers are physically present in the community to serve as facilitators with express goals to mobilize the community into directed self-help action. Perhaps with "a little help from their friends" local neighborhoods can be reclaimed from gang influences and influence disinterested absentee owners.

Washington, D.C.

The city does not have a residency requirement for its officers, but the police department cooperates with the Department of Public and Assisted Housing. There are currently seven officers living in four separate public housing projects with three assigned patrol cars. According to the Department of Public and Assisted Housing there is a waiting list of officers wanting to participate (Gleaton, 1993).

Portland, Oregon

In November 1993 Charles Moose became chief of police in Portland, Oregon, and purchased a home in the troubled neighborhood of King, located on the northeast side of town. As a prior captain of the precinct, Moose knew the area, and many residents knew him. Moose, a 19-year veteran of the force and an avid supporter of community policing, explained his move thus: "I found myself talking to civic groups and telling them about building up society from the ground up, moving into the community where you work. When it came to buying a house, my wife and I decided to look into a community that was struggling to stabilize itself." The chief, who has a doctorate in urban studies, saw his move as part of "walking the walk and talking the talk." His move into a "troubled" area has led to a call for a community-sponsored program that would offer low-interest loans to encourage police officers to buy homes in similar neighborhoods.

At a Rotary Club meeting, Neil Kelly, a professional home remodeler, offered three rental homes he owns in Portland's Albina district at below-market value to any police officer willing to move in. With the chief making the move and attractive loans being made available to the department, several Portland officers have indicated interest (Wasserman, 1994:A5)

Involvement at the Federal Level

The federal government is also turning over to cities confiscated properties that have been seized in drug raids. For instance, a one-time South-Central Los Angeles PCP laboratory, vacant since 1988, was turned over to the city of Los Angeles for community use. The 10,000-square-foot property was made available under the federal asset forfeiture law that allows seized property to be transferred to cities or nonprofit agencies for positive social uses. The transfer of the property to the city was the first of many anticipated as a component of the federal **Community Projects for Restoration** (CPR) plan, a law enforcement and social welfare program begun under the Bush Administration. In 1992 $18 million in federal funds was targeted for community policing, public housing assistance, and gang prevention efforts under the "weed and seed" program. Since 1985 federal authorities in the Los Angeles area alone have seized $264 million in land, vehicles, and currency under the forfeiture program. Until 1993 the proceeds from the sale of confiscated property had gone to law enforcement agencies exclusively (Feldman, 1993: A36).

Cities across the nation have the opportunity through the federal CPR plan to refurbish property without the cost of initial investment and provide many services that are sorely neglected in many inner cities. These properties could be used as community or day-care centers, recreation halls, police substations or storefront operations, or social services and other special need centers that would improve the quality of life and *raise the sense of community*. Under this plan, it

Some politicians advocate the strict control of handguns to decrease the rising tide of violence among youths. *(AP/Wide World Photo)*

would seem that seized drug houses could be purchased by prequalified police officers in an attempt to revitalize communities, stabilize or increase property values, facilitate community involvement, and encourage public order. To expand the program when community members feel they have reached a reasonable degree of comfort or safety, other qualified government employees could also be encouraged to participate.

LEGAL IMPLICATIONS

Hiring Standards

There are few police agencies that are currently experiencing problems with the number of applicants seeking employment. In times of economic downturns, city or county budgets may allow for the hiring of new officers only through attrition. The large applicant pool should allow police agencies to reexamine their hiring standards. Agencies can be a little more selective and attempt to put the best per-

> **BOX 12.4   COP and Santa Ana, California**
>
> During the first seven months of 1994, the federally funded Community Oriented Policing (COP) task force has used tactics such as foot patrol, school visits, and neighborhood partnerships to tackle the area's entrenched crime. A 1996 report showed a dramatic drop in crime in the area targeted by the federal "Clinton Cops" program.
>
> There has been a 60 percent drop in armed robbery from the same six months in 1994, along with a 42 percent decrease in assaults and a 53 percent decline in burglary and theft. Citizen calls reporting drug dealers have dropped 68 percent, and overall calls for service fell 41 percent.
>
> *Source:* Geoff Boucher, "COP and Santa Ana, California." *Los Angeles Times,* January 27, 1996:A1.

son in a position of public trust. The selection of individuals to enter the process of becoming an enforcement officer could include an in-depth psychological evaluation or battery of examinations to ensure emotional stability, adaptability, trustworthiness, and maturity. The person's motivations for applying for police work could be analyzed.

Some jurisdictions are mandated to hire within certain ethnic guidelines but court mandates do not suggest that hiring standards be lowered, waived, or adjusted to accommodate minority hiring. Members of minority groups and many administrators feel the mere suggestion of a two-tiered hiring process with varying standards based on racial factors is on its face demeaning.

Negligent Training

The term *failure to train* is really an admission of the failure of organizational supervision. It is the responsibility of each supervisor at each level in the organization to function as a trainer. Police officers must be taught how to do their job, receive the proper tools to do it, and learn how to perform specific tasks. Their performance must be evaluated and, if necessary, they must be given remedial training. The old days of having each officer "initial" each page of departmental regulations, general orders, standard operating procedures, and policy statements just won't suffice today. The burden of responsibility is laid directly on supervision. The organization must adequately train personnel in order to satisfy their responsibilities as supervisors, prevent serious incidents from happening, and limit departmental liability. Training encompasses the full range of officers' exposure to *potentially* involved situations that could lead to liability. Liability in this context includes officers, citizens, community, organization, and municipality liability, including physical, emotional, psychological, and fiscal aspects.

Training, therefore, is a holistic approach to the totality of policing, meaning every aspect of the daily enforcement routine, blended with contingency training to deal with events that could easily happen (natural disasters) and response to extraordinary events (human-generated disasters).

A local governmental entity's "failure to train" in the area of firearms can result in liability under 42 U.S.C. 1983. Training in the use of firearms is one of the most traditional training exercises and focuses in American policing. It is also an area of training that proves to be the most exciting to some recruits and a continual source of irritation to others. Historically, police firearm training consisted of a "Camp Perry" style of marksmanship. The trainee would be taught proper sight alignment, breath control, trigger squeeze, stance, and a host of other considerations that would hopefully enable a beginner to qualify. In the 1950s it was recognized that when police officers must use deadly force, the environment is quite different from a National Rifle Association sanctioned match. Night shooting became a requirement along with firing from different positions and from behind barriers and barricades. Today, with the aid of computer-generated visual capabilities and bullet-absorbing walls, practicing shooters and trainers can approximate real-life situations.

Each organization's "use of force" policy clearly delineates the circumstances under which law enforcement officers can use deadly force. The legal aspects of "use of force" are clearly and universally a point of emphasis in firearms training.

Weapon safety involves a knowledge of the safe and prudent use of the weapon and also embraces the mechanical skills necessary to disassemble, clean, and store the firearm properly.

Weapons Selection

The quest for uniformity, prompted in no small part by bulk-buying power, has led many law enforcement executives to mandate the use of one type of sidearm by their officers. The firearm industry and police studies abound pitting the merits of the revolver "wheel gun" against the semiautomatic as well as comparing the quality and impact (stopping power) of the varying calibers. There will be continuing debates regarding the merits of Glock's over the government-issue Colt .45 or a Sig-Sauer 9mm or one of the Smith & Wesson models. Regardless of the pros and cons, most experts in the field of marksmanship agree that the dominating factor is individual preference. NRA-classified Distinguished Master Pistol Shooters do not all use the same type of weapons. The caliber of weapons used in center-fire matches varies greatly. The trend for "single gun and single caliber" weapons for law enforcement is fading.

Some police executives still believe that with the job comes the decision regarding what type of sidearm each officer should carry, but more progressive chief executives as well as the Police Officer Association, after researching and testing several weapons, allow each member of the agency to purchase, qualify, and carry his or her sidearm of choice. Officers can perform best and feel more comfortable with weapons based on individual choice. The basic cost of the regulation weapon could be reimbursed to help defray the cost of the preferred weapon. The only downside is the initial training, which would require range officers, armers, and weapon instructors to possess specific knowledge of additional weaponry. The upside would include participation in the selection of one's own handgun (which equates to an enhancement of the personal safety factor), increased accuracy, and reduced liability. There are different needs for different people regarding the tools or instruments of their trade; all carpenters do not subscribe to a particular hammer, or dentists to the same drill. Weapon competence along with officer safety and legality issues have been an integral part of most police departments' on-going training programs.

Qualification with Off-Duty Weapons

This is a sensitive area that until recently has not received enough attention. In times past, officers were required to qualify with their on-duty weapon but were allowed to carry another weapon of choice while off-duty. Historically, few departments required officers to qualify with their off-duty weapons. With the advent of liability issues, however, most law enforcement agencies, through departmental regulation or policy, provide instruction, qualification, and legal guidelines for the carrying and use of specified off-duty weapons.

Negligent Retention

The thrust of the Christopher Commission report was that the Los Angeles Police Department (and other police agencies) was unable to identify, early on, those officers who might pose disciplinary problems—specifically, liability and disciplinary problems. As a supervisorial activity, agencies must adopt strategies and programs specifically designed to track past performance of officers. Red flags should be raised long before officers cross the line into performance activities that will ultimately result in disciplinary actions. Liability aside, the not-so-hidden cost of late intervention is the negative impact on morale and job satisfaction and the external issue of community condemnation.

ACCOUNTABILITY REVISITED: IDEAL AND REAL CONSEQUENCES OF SANCTIONS

We live in a litigious society. Lawyers across the nation clamor for the opportunity to represent clients on a host of fronts utilizing contingency lawsuits (no up-front fees). The sheer number of lawsuits has exploded, and some suits are simply outrageous. One suit was brought by a Pittsburgh man who sued the Three Rivers Stadium for allowing him to buy too many beers during a 1989 Steelers game. Further, the plaintiff alleges, stadium authorities failed to warn him adequately of the dangers of riding on escalator handrails. Obviously, if a twenty-seven-year-old man gets intoxicated and falls off an escalator, it's the stadium authorities' fault. Or in Tacoma, Washington, we find a lawsuit filed by Mrs. Christine Lauritzen against her husband, Bret. It seems that while they were on vacation in Miami, Bret ignored her driving instructions and got them lost in "a bad part of town." As a result of Bret's negligence in failing to act on her navigational guidance, they were robbed, and she suffered an arm injury (*PORAC News*, 1993, 33).

Patrol Car Video Cameras

There is a movement in law enforcement, because of camera-recorded incidents, to mount cameras in patrol cars to videotape activities outside the vehicle. Crimtech, a company in Livonia, Michigan, is one company that supplies the equipment. In the wake of litigation and conflicting accounts of incidents, the Orange County (California) Sheriff's Department equipped more than 100 patrol cars with these devices, and other cities are following suit.

Litigation

In October 1992 a special Police Litigation Unit was established in the Los Angeles City Attorney's Office to handle lawsuits. The number of officers assigned was increased from 39 to 46, reducing the average caseload of the lawyers from 130 to approximately 50. A program was also launched to fully computerize the division. The unit handled cases against individual police officers and the LAPD that resulted in $10.7 million in judgments and awards in calendar year 1993, much less than the $19.7 million awarded in judgments during 1992 and $14.7 million in 1991. City attorneys in the unit went to trial in police cases 36 times during 1993, winning 27 cases. One was a high-profile lawsuit filed by the manager of a McDonalds restaurant who accused the department's controversial Special Investigation Section (SIS) of watching as robbers broke into her restaurant at closing time and terrorized her. In a surprise move, even though the SIS officers acknowledged they allowed the robbery to take place, the judge took the case away from a jury and ruled that the police should not be held liable for damages sought by the manager.

Claims against the police are still on the rise in Los Angeles. In 1992, 585 claims were filed resulting in 226 lawsuits, and in 1993, 726 claims were filed, with 246 going to trial (Meyer, 1994:A32).

Although it is easy to cite frivolous lawsuits and cast doubts regarding their legitimacy, those suits filed against law enforcement officers accused of brutality, insensitivity, or rude behavior register on the community at large and on citizens' pocketbooks. In Los Angeles alone during the three-year period 1991–1993, $45.1 million was paid in awards and judgments. Litigation is a very costly affair. The community is severely affected, and the police must be held accountable to their occupation, the department, and the community. The adoption of COP will certainly move police toward accountability, professionalism, and a vision of public trust. The ideals of fiduciary trust, altruism, and commonweal cannot be neglected or violated without serious ramifications.

SUMMARY

One of the earlier attempts to change organizational philosophy and develop a true community-oriented policing style was undertaken in Menlo Park, California, in 1968 under the late Chief Victor I. Cizanckas (Cizanckas, 1971). In the fall of 1969 the department published and posted this "Theory Y" policy statement (McGregor, 1960):

1. The expenditure of physical and mental effort in work is as natural as play or rest.
2. External control and the threat of punishment are not the only means for bringing about effort toward organizational objectives. Man will exercise self-direction and self-control in the service of objectives to which he is committed.
3. Commitment to objectives is a function of the rewards associated with their achievement.
4. The average human being learns under proper conditions not only to accept but to seek responsibility.
5. The capacity to exercise a relatively high degree of imagination, ingenuity and creativity in the solution of organizational problems is widely, not narrowly, distributed in the population.
6. Under the conditions of modern industrial life, the human intellectual potentialities of the average human being are only partially utilized.

The Menlo Park philosophy succinctly stated their new commitment:

> The Menlo Park Police Department is a municipal multiservice designed to provide better living and safety for citizens.
>
> Recognizing it must relate and respond to community needs that are dynamic and constantly changing, the department is pledged to recruiting talented personnel who are committed to their fellow man and are free from color and economic bias.
>
> While rejecting an authoritarian approach to problem solving, the department is continually involved in enforcement, prevention and education programs designed to control and reduce crime and traffic accidents.
>
> The department commits itself to its employees and will make every effort to provide a work atmosphere conducive to personal and career development.
>
> Ultimately we hope to provide quality police service at minimum cost to the citizens we serve. (Cizanckas, 1971)

These objectives and policy statements are still being given lip service and being studied by many urban enforcement agencies. Organizational change is impossible without dedicated leadership having the patience and managerial expertise to slowly initiate change. Large ships can be turned; they may have to make very wide turns, but without power they will drift. Smaller ships, like organizations, can change directions rather quickly, but they still have to possess the knowledge and power of direction combined with commitment.

The implementation of community policing in the United States, because of local autonomy and lack of common purpose, will be piecemeal at best, and in some jurisdictions the police as well as the community will see COP as another liberal gimmick. In an article entitled "Implementing Community Policing: The Administrative Problem (Kelling and Bratton, 1993), the authors suggest that police executives visualize three separate forces that seem foremost in their minds: unions, detectives, and mid-management. The impact of police associations and unions has been discussed as a formidable foe or ally. Within police organizations certain positions have perks and status. For instance, the function of a detective is highly desirable and sought after. This particular assignment bears with it a certain elite status and is a informal power source in the department. When changes are in the planning stages, all power sources, formal and informal, must be coordinated and utilized. The problem regarding middle-management (lieutenants and captains) is generally one of noninvolvement in the upper-level decision making process. As previously discussed, total involvement and dedication to the principles of COP at each stratum of the organization will facilitate the implementation of COP; to prevent any element or individual from participating in the achievement of organizational goals would be counterproductive.

For community oriented policing to exist, the following guidelines need to be addressed.

Law Enforcement Organization. To create a climate of personal and professional commitment by every individual at every level within the department, agencies must undergo an examination and possible redefinition of goals and objectives by creating a

mission statement

value statement

shift toward a consultative participatory management style and a shift away from a reliance on the military model, the legalistic model, and the order maintenance model of policing

Time. Radical change does not occur overnight. Community policing is a revolutionary concept to many officers and not readily embraced. Executives must allow for long implementation periods and not expect immediate results.

Training and Retraining. It is imperative that police supervisors first discover inappropriate actions and then cause change in behavior patterns that will eventually cause attitudinal changes. It is not suggested that police supervisors be Renaissance people capable of any task. It is suggested that law enforcement organizations have a variety of resources available to supervisors and that supervisors be not only cognizant of their choices but be empowered to make them. Agencies should establish ties with community-based support groups that provide nonthreatening encouragement and commitment to group and personal goals.

A review of the California Peace Officer Association (CPOA) Training calendar for 1993–1994 provides an example of the varied types of courses offered to law enforcement personnel. The topics include canine liability; role of the police chief; police pursuits; 1994 legislative update; the Americans with Disabilities Act; use of force; officer-involved shootings; preventing sexual harassment; police discipline; legal update regarding discovery, personnel, and civil liability; and the Public Records Act (*Network*, 1993).

Training workshops offered at the 1993 CPOA's All-Committee Training Conference in San Diego offered such special contemporary topics as "The Rodney King Incident—The Gap between Use of Force Policy and Training"; "Field Crisis Intervention"; "Guns and Violence in the 90s—NRA vs. Handgun Control"; "Violence in the Workplace"; "Accountability in Management"; "Gaming Issues in California"; "Grassroots Lobbying and You"; and "POST Command College Papers" (CPOA flier).

Political Support. A system of community policing cannot exist or be expected to prosper without the complete support of elected officials and those who serve at their behest. This category also includes appropriate funding to sustain a commitment to COP.

Community Involvement. Cooperation and true participation in policy are generally the hallmarks of an informed community. Involvement, albeit not a crime-suppression function, will go far to alleviate misunderstandings regarding policy and practice. Citizen involvement in policy and disciplinary review as well as Citizen Police Academies are a step in the right direction.

Communication. Open and honest communication with the community and media regarding police actions is imperative. If wrong, admit it. No one is perfect, nor should anyone be held to unrealistic expectations of perfection. Use outside enforcement agencies to investigate allegations of internal wrongdoings. Open agencies will provide the media with information and allow (encourage) the publication of findings of investigative boards and disciplinary actions. The shroud of secrecy that surrounds internal disciplinary mechanisms is not conducive to community trust. Eliminate the overpowering tendency toward negative reinforcements (punishment) and provide a positive organizational and supervisorial environment.

TQM and COP. The continuous commitment to client satisfaction is a primary focus of both total quality management (TQM) and community-oriented policing (COP). It would be extremely difficult to practice one without the other. For those police executives encountering pressure to avoid COP and other liberal "gimmicks," another approach might be a slow transition into the practice and application of TQM. But the implementation of TQM has its own problems. TQM (and also COP) will not work if the organization is not willing to commit to a total quality effort. An organizational climate of cohesive cooperation must replace competition, distrust, and arbitrariness. Employees at all levels (including executives) must have job security in the transition process, for mistakes will be made. Without the realities of trial and error, progress will be an illusive ideal. There must be quid pro quo arrangements. Adequate and appropriate employees' incentives must accompany organizational requests for redirected commitments.

Community. The law enforcement community is not alone in the quest for a safe environment and freedom from unwanted and often illegal intrusions. Community members must take an active part in the various *processes* of government to ensure adequate protection and service. This means the majority of the community, not just a few selected or self-appointed leaders. The majority of homeowners or renters must be willing to cooperate in joint crime prevention and crime reduction efforts and participate in a cooperative venture.

In the strictest sense, COP is not a goal or an end result. It is a journey instead of a destination. The primary purpose of COP is to maintain community standards, enforce laws abetting a safe environment, and provide proactive crime preventive strategies. With COP, like TQM, the clients not only pay the bills and support quality enforcement but can also become disenchanted, dissatisfied consumers and shop elsewhere (i.e., adopt contract law enforcement).

Other Recommendations and Observations: Internal

1. Law enforcement organizations must create individual charts to show the past performance of officers visually. The past is an excellent barometer of the future. Early intervention, additional training, and other remedial strategies can only be predicated on accurate data. These charts would reveal early-warning indicators and, in a positive mode, would provide indicators of officer potential. The monitoring of officers' activities can result in reduced liability, which can also mean reduced costs and improved community attitudes toward the police. In terms of COP, the monitoring could ferret out those officers whose emerging patterns could spell disaster in terms of citizen complaints and subsequent disciplinary actions.

The monitoring of radio transmissions has also been recommended to discover "unauthorized" or "inappropriate" language, terms or inferences that could be considered racially or gender biased. It is recommended that departments with computer capability have all radio transmissions routed through a software program such as Word Check. This program would eliminate labor-intensive monitoring of radio calls and would, on a continuing basis, discourage the use of derogatory and offensive terms.

2. Teachers are given sabbatical leaves every seven years in some jurisdictions. This is ostensibly for scholarly research or other preapproved projects, but these hiatuses are also a welcome relief and are considered prized entitlements.

It is suggested that police officers below the rank of lieutenant be given (or collectively bargain for) a six-month paid leave of absence during every five years of employment, the stipulations being that they may not enter a police station unless reporting a crime and may not perform *any sort of police work.* Upon being selected for "vacation" they must turn in their badge and weapon(s). There would be no restrictions regarding their activities except they may not be paid or reimbursed for any type of outside employment. They would be encouraged to pursue their hobbies, take up new interests, become involved in community projects and affairs, or attend college. Should they opt to attend college, all tuition and textbook fees would be reimbursable. The express purpose of this program would be to return these individuals to the community as community members, provide a stress-free six-month rest period, encourage new interests, and continue college aspirations. Allowing officers the opportunity to take a break could well be the key to emotional, psychological, and physical wellness. A program of this nature, in the short term, might stem officer turnover rates, reduce stress-related injuries, revitalize organization members, and provide an incentive for continued performance. The long-term results could be improved officer morale, a reduction of organizational stress, and a favorable impact on community-oriented policing.

3. The educational entry standard for most (95 percent) national police agencies is either a high school diploma or GED. Independent surveys indicate that most academy class graduates have at least sixty units of college credit. As many agencies impose advanced educational requirements for promotion, it places those without at least an Associate of Arts/Science degree at a distinct disadvantage. If, for instance, the department requires an associate's degree for promotion to sergeant, new hires with only a high school diploma must attend night school to obtain the requisite education. This means four years or more of night classes (depending on shift changes and availability of classes).

We recommend that the first educational requirement for promotion (2 years of college) be set as the entry-level requirement. This simply reduces the stress placed on new hires to spend off-duty hours away from their families in the pursuit of a promotability factor. It does provide an occupational window to learn the job without the added concern of promotion. The first year is generally a probationary period with little thought of educational pursuits. The long-term results might well be a department with individuals with higher educational levels. The old argument that "I would rather have a person with common sense than a person with a degree" does not hold water. We can have new hires with two years of college *and* common sense. Police associations will soon realize that in order to continue their quest for more pay and benefits, they must be able to offer more in service, community responsibility, and caliber of employee. The Dallas Police Department has a forty-five-unit requirement that has, to date, withstood legal challenges and is supported by employee associations.

4. Probably one of the more controversial recommendations is to promote officers through the rank of lieutenant based on peer evaluation. Promotions to senior officer or corporal, sergeant, and so forth are based largely on the perceptions of supervisors, and quite frankly, supervisors can be fooled. You cannot, however, fool the people you work with on a day-to-day basis. They know the workers, and they definitely know the shirkers. When a righteous apple-polisher is promoted, the damage to morale and belief in the system is incalculable. Some managers and supervisors suggest that peer review would result in politics, favoritism, and gamesmanship. That argument presupposes that these elements are not currently considerations for promotion. But peer review might be better than the current promotional practices; at least it would add legitimate and sensible standards to the process, and any blame for the decision would not be directed at a deceived supervisor. Moreover, long-term benefits might be the promotion of qualified supervisors supported by their peers. Morale and productivity might improve, supervisors might lead by example, organizational disharmony might be reduced, and a more satisfying organizational environment might easily lead to improved attitudes and service toward the community.

5. Traditionally, police unions or associations and police management have been cast in adversarial roles. Unions are a fact of life and will continue to be a recognized power source within the organization. The president of local police unions and associations should be a voting or consulting member of the chief of police or sheriff's executive board, and in this role he or she should be actively involved in all matters regarding policy. This executive-level involvement might not prevent job actions and demonstrations, but it might serve as a legitimate outlet for grievances, and the practice would certainly provide another dimension to organizational decision making and reduce costly litigation.

6. Psychological testing should be mandated as an integral part of the promotional process *at all levels.* The testing process is not necessarily a disqualifying factor but it might serve as an early psychological detection method to discover and remedy symptoms before they become problems. Methods to detect substance abuse should also be put into place (e.g., testing, observation), and outreach programs should be established to assist in combating the problem. The goal is to assist members at risk.

7. The training aspects of policing should be divorced from the military model. Close order drill, Marine Corps type drill instructors, and undue regimentation only serve to structure individuals, instill a lockstep mentality, and foster blind obedience. The training of law enforcement officers might be redirected and revamped to reflect the actual tasks to be performed under COP. In very few preservice police training facilities is COP taught as an *operational* philosophy. Many local and regional training academies only offer COP as a one- or two-hour topic of discussion.

A modified version of the British model of personnel selection and training might also serve the purpose of bringing into the occupation a higher quality of police aspirant. Although initially somewhat expensive, the more extended training would result in better service, increased productivity, and less litigation.

8. Police management and supervision practices should mirror contemporary management approaches. Those managers and supervisors who resist the COP philosophy or who cannot make the change should be strongly encouraged to seek employment elsewhere.

Each agency should have a liaison with the city attorney's office to receive the latest court decisions and legislative mandates that affect policing, that is, the Americans with Disabilities Act (ADA) and Title VII, Civil Liability (U.S. Code, 1996). Some agencies have established a legal section in the agency's training unit to facilitate the communication of current legal issues. To promote information sharing, those executives with vested interests in any municipal activity should be involved at all stages of development.

9. To ensure proper conduct and maintain discipline many departments still rely on such vague enforcement descriptors as "conduct unbecoming." In some agencies, to be thought of as being a "soft" supervisor is tantamount to being called a liberal. This lack of clarity leaves far too much room for supervisors who wish to build a reputation as being tough taskmasters to root around for nitpicking activities that might or might not result in some form of supervisorial action. For many supervisors the search for misconduct is a prime factor in their self-styled job descriptions. Of primary importance are thorough and detailed "officer rights" articulated and understood by supervisors at all levels. Agencies should reevaluate their disciplinary processes to eliminate those problems that should be dealt with on lower levels, as the internal system is often clogged with minor infractions. To observe due process, disciplinary and review actions should be as swift as possible. Agencies should also evaluate supervisors on their ability to influence the actions of others by "leadership through example." If supervisors have a difficult time supervising and rely heavily on disciplinary actions, that should be indicated in their evaluations and periodic reviews.

10. Initial applicant screening should emphasize psychological screening to cull those who fall into a borderline category. To reverse trends of the not too distant past, psychological factors that suggest a propensity for aggressive behavior (above an established norm) and authoritarianism should serve to disqualify candidates. In the same vein, background investigations need to be thorough to fully examine the applicant's past. This is particularly true for out-of-state applicants and lateral transfers.

11. Police involvement in community activities should also encompass involvement in the educational process. As criminal justice is a subject not specifically taught at the secondary or high school levels, many police agencies have assigned school resource officers to either hold workshops or teach law enforcement sections at the elementary, secondary, and senior levels. These officers additionally serve to resolve school-related problems. Those departments with school resource officers provide an invaluable service to the school, the student population, and the community. Within the classroom setting many myths are exposed, stereotypes squashed, and questions answered. For the police to be part of the community, they should assist in augmenting the education of students.

12. Each position in the police department should be evaluated and reexamined to determine which tasks could be performed by civilian (non-sworn) personnel. The benefits include releasing sworn officers to perform actual law enforcement-related functions; a subsequent increase in the availability of sworn enforcement personnel; a reduction in personnel costs (training, fringe benefits, and the like) as opposed to hiring new officers; and community participation and involvement. In assessing national averages, most police and sheriff departments utilizing civilian employees have 30 percent to 40 percent of their total strength in non-sworn positions. One situation that must be addressed is the bifurcation of the department. When two separate entities are performing related functions in two separate employment classes within the same agency, there can be problems. To promote a joint venture, executives must provide civilian employees with training, incentives, empowerment, and an equal share in the department's vision, mission, and goals.

13. Police departments should not take credit whenever crime declines. They must realize that forces well removed from their realm of influence are major causal factors. They certainly do not admit liability when crime rates rise. Additional police personnel will not necessarily reduce crime. In actuality, more police on the street should result in more arrests, which would drive the index upward. Honesty and straightforward reporting are the prerequisites for community respect.

14. The concept of decentralization of police functions appears to serve the best interests of diverse communities. Mini-stations are expensive but they allow personal and immediate access to service. Mini- or substations also serve to unify communities by providing a focal point to address community problems.

Other Recommendations and Observations: External

1. The creation of a truly independent and impartial ombudsman or review board to which citizens can take their complaints concerning government actions or inactions is a major step toward establishing common trust. The investigative agency should be a separate public entity external to all other government operations. This agency would review public complaints concerning any segment of publicly provided municipal service. The perennial problem of politics must be addressed and eliminated: Should the board be politicized, its value is worthless. Such an agency with the *power* to address, investigate, subpoena, and pass judgment on complaints would serve to resolve the issues of mistrust brought about by agencies policing themselves. Police advisory councils generally lack formal power to resolve complaints, are time-consuming, and serve primarily political ends.

2. Municipalities should implement a short-term rotational system in which police managers and officers could exchange positions periodically with their colleagues in other governmental agencies such as courts, probation, parole, city planning, parks and recreation, and welfare. It is felt that the experience of all involved parties would be one of increased understanding of and commitment to the singular purpose of community service.

3. Cities with decaying urban centers might consider offering a few of the more dilapidated dwellings to police officers with attractive prices, mortgage rates, tax incentives, and home improvement loans. Many officers, especially new hires, simply cannot afford to purchase housing. This would be an opportunity for the city to restore certain homes in depressed areas, which, in turn, might serve as the motivation to turn some communities around. The additional factor of having a police presence in the neighborhood is not without merit. Bringing the police into the community is basic to COP, and programs of this nature might prove beneficial to all concerned.

4. Communities and the politicians who represent them must make a lifetime commitment to COP and provide the necessary equipment and funds to support the philosophy. Communities cannot expect quality police service when their law enforcement officers are experiencing equipment failure or a shortage of resources and authorized personnel. Police equipment must be serviced, maintained, and replaced according to accepted industry practices. Many law enforcement agencies need updated or improved computer systems to support information management, crime analysis, and investigations. The physical appearance of station houses should mirror the pride the community has in its service functions. Police precincts or station houses should be at least on par (in appearance and maintenance) with city halls. Providing beat foot patrols is expensive, with high community visibility but with little impact on crime. A realistic reassessment of police personnel resources and allocations, with a view toward civilianization, could release sworn officers to the activity of field patrol.

5. Municipal administrators must immediately begin short- and long-term planning with police officials regarding projected juvenile population cohorts. By the year 2005, the number of fifteen- to nineteen-year-olds, who are the most violence-prone age group, will increase by 23 percent over 1993 figures. This single factor, if not addressed, will strain criminal justice resources and cause crime rates to soar.

6. Each major urban center in the United States should have a language-specific phone number. This phone number could be printed in the foreign-language newspapers that serve various ethnic populations. Bilingual operators would be able to answer questions and relay information to the appropriate service entity (public service or emergency, medical, fire, police). In Switzerland, for example, the four major spoken languages are German, French, Italian, and Romansch. English-speaking tourists may use "Anglo-Phone" (156–6531) from anywhere in the country to reach English-speaking operators. If similar language-specific phone assistance were available in the United States, many of our community members would not feel alienated from public services, including police protection.

7. To encourage law enforcement participation in revitalizing neighborhoods and improving the quality of life in urban cities, local governments could add "enrichment" or "enhancement" pay provisions or bonuses for law enforcement officers who are bilingual in a language common to the city and officers who are residents of the city or municipality. A program of this nature (separate from home ownership programs) might encourage officers to live in the city and compensate those officers already in residence. In the long term the city could benefit from decreased crime, fewer calls-for-service, increased neighborhood stability, and higher property values, which could increase the tax base and additionally serve to attract new businesses and other employment-generating centers.

8. Community associations and organizations should be included in the formation of policy. Traditional municipalities rely on groups that are already highly supportive of police practices. In addition to parent-teacher associations, Elks, Lions, VFW, YMCA, Knights of Columbus, and similar organizations, the inclusion of civil and criminal rights activists, environmentalists, the American Civil Liberties Union, and similar organizations can provide a rich and valuable mix. Notably, and on a slightly different scale, representation of diverse groups outside the mainstream should be sought, such as the homeless, gangs, and taggers.

QUESTIONS FOR REVIEW

1. Explain the necessity for developing crime prevention strategies.
2. Discuss the elderly as a victimized group.
3. How can community involvement abate gang violence?
4. What are the goals of Police Cadet programs?
5. What were the origins of Police Community Awareness Academies?
6. Explain the dynamics of Police Community Awareness Academies.
7. In what way can colleges and universities cooperate in the law enforcement field?
8. Discuss police involvement in the redevelopment of inner cities.
9. How can the federal government, through the Community Projects for Restoration, affect urban development?
10. What is the future of community-oriented policing?

SUGGESTED READINGS

Kappeler, Victor E. (1993) *Critical Issues in Police Civil Liability.* Chicago: Waveland Press.

Simmons, J.L. (1993) *67 Ways to Protect Seniors From Crime.* New York: Henry Holt & Company, Inc.

APPENDIX

Christopher Commission Report

SUMMARY[1]

The videotaped beating of Rodney G. King by three uniformed officers of the Los Angeles Police Department, in the presence of a sergeant and with a large group of other officers standing by, galvanized public demand for evaluation and reform of police procedure involving the use of force. In the wake of the incident and the resulting widespread outcry, the Independent Commission on the Los Angeles Police Department was created. The Commission sought to examine all aspects of the law enforcement structure in Los Angeles that might cause or contribute to the problem of excessive force. The Report is unanimous.

The King beating raised fundamental questions about the LAPD, including:

- the apparent failure to control or discipline officers with repeated complaints of excessive force
- concerns about the LAPD's "culture" and officers' attitudes towards racial and other minorities
- the difficulties the public encounters in attempting to make complaints against LAPD officers
- the role of the LAPD leadership and civilian oversight authorities in addressing or contributing to these problems

[1]Reprinted with permission.

These and related questions and concerns form the basis for the Commission's work.

LOS ANGELES AND ITS POLICE FORCES

The LAPD is headed by Police Chief Daryl Gates with an executive staff currently consisting of two assistant chiefs, five deputy chiefs, and 17 commanders. The City Charter provides that the Department is ultimately under the control and oversight of the five-member civilian Board of Police Commissioners. The Office of Operations, headed by Assistant Chief Robert Vernon, accounts for approximately 84% of the Department's personnel, including most patrol officers and detectives. The Office of Operations has 18 separate geographic areas within the City, divided among four bureaus (Central, South, West, and Valley). There are currently about 8,450 sworn police officers, augmented by more than 2,000 civilian employees.

While the overall rate of violent crime in the United States increased three and one-half times between 1960 and 1989, the rate in Los Angeles during the same period was more than twice the national average. According to 1986 data recently published by the Police Foundation, the Los Angeles police were the busiest among the officers in the nation's largest six cities. As crime rates soar, police officers must contend with more and more potential and actual violence each day. One moment officers must confront a life-threatening situation; the next they must deal with citizen problems requiring understanding and kindness. The difficulties of policing in Los Angeles are compounded by its vast geographic area and the ethnic diversity of its population. The 1990 census data reflect how enormous that diversity is: Latinos constitute 40% of the total population; Whites 37%; African-Americans 13%; and Asian/Pacific Islanders and others 10%. Of the police departments of the six largest United States cities, the LAPD has the fewest officers per resident and the fewest officers per square mile. Yet the LAPD boasts more arrests per officer than other forces. Moreover, by all accounts, the LAPD is generally efficient, sophisticated, and free of corruption.

THE PROBLEM OF EXCESSIVE FORCE

LAPD officers exercising physical force must comply with the Department's Use of Force Policy and Guidelines, as well as California law. Both the LAPD Policy and the Penal Code require that force be reasonable; the Policy also requires that force be necessary. An officer may resort to force only where he or she faces a credible threat, and then may use only the minimum amount necessary to control the suspect.

The Commission has found that there is a significant number of LAPD officers who repetitively misuse force and persistently ignore the written policies and guidelines of the Department regarding force. The evidence obtained by the

Commission shows that this group has received inadequate supervisory and management attention.

Former Assistant Chief Jesse Brewer testified that this lack of management attention and accountability is the "essence of the excessive force problem. . . . We know who the bad guys are. Reputations become well known, especially to the sergeants and then of course to lieutenants and the captains in the areas. . . . But I don't see anyone bring these people up." Assistant Chief David Dotson testified that "we have failed miserably" to hold supervisors accountable for excessive force by officers under their command. Interviews with a large number of present and former LAPD officers yield similar conclusions. Senior and rank-and-file officers generally stated that a significant number of officers tended to use force excessively, that these problem officers were well known in their divisions, that the Department's efforts to control or discipline those officers were inadequate, and that their supervisors were not held accountable for excessive use of force by officers in their command.

The Commission's extensive computerized analysis of the data provided by the Department (personnel complaints, use of force reports, and reports of officer-involved shootings) shows that a significant group of problem officers poses a much higher risk of excessive force than other officers:

- Of approximately 1,800 officers against whom an allegation of excessive force or improper tactics was made from 1986 to 1990, more than 1,400 had only one or two allegations. But 183 officers had four or more allegations, 44 had six or more, 16 had eight or more, and one had 16 such allegations.
- Of nearly 6,000 officers identified as involved in use of force reports from January 1987 to March 1991, more than 4,000 had fewer than five reports each. But 63 officers had 20 or more reports each. The top 5% of the officers (ranked by number of reports) accounted for more than 20% of all reports.

Blending the data disclosed even more troubling patterns. For example, in the years covered, one officer had 13 allegations of excessive force and improper tactics, 5 other complaint allegations, 28 use of force reports, and 1 shooting. Another had 6 excessive force/improper tactics allegations, 19 other complaint allegations, 10 use of force reports, and 3 shootings. A third officer had 7 excessive force/improper tactic allegations, 7 other complaint allegations, 27 use of force reports, and 1 shooting.

A review of personnel files of the 44 officers identified from the LAPD database who had six or more allegations of excessive force or improper tactics for the period 1986 through 1990 disclosed that the picture conveyed was often incomplete and at odds with contemporaneous comments appearing in complaint files. As a general matter, the performance evaluation reports for those problem officers were very positive, documenting every complimentary comment received and expressing optimism about the officer's progress in the Department. The performance evaluations generally did not give an accurate picture of the officers' disciplinary history, failing to record "sustained" complaints or to discuss their significance, and failing to assess the officer's judgment and contacts with the public in light of disturbing patterns of complaints.

The existence of a significant number of officers with an unacceptable and improper attitude regarding the use of force is supported by the Commission's extensive review of computer messages sent to and from patrol cars throughout the City over the units' Mobile Digital Terminals ("MDTs"). The Commission's staff examined 182 days of MDT transmissions selected from the period from November 1989 to March 1991. Although the vast majority of messages reviewed consisted of routine police communications, there were hundreds of improper messages, including scores in which officers talked about beating suspects: "Capture him, beat him and treat him like dirt." Officers also used the communications system to express their eagerness to be involved in shooting incidents. The transmissions also make clear that some officers enjoy the excitement of a pursuit and view it as an opportunity for violence against a fleeing suspect.

The patrol car transmissions can be monitored by a field supervisor and are stored in a database where they could be (but were not) audited. That many officers would feel free to type messages about force under such circumstances suggests a serious problem with respect to excessive force. That supervisors made no effort to monitor or control those messages evidences a significant breakdown in the Department's management responsibility.

The Commission also reviewed the LAPD's investigation and discipline of the officers involved in all 83 civil lawsuits alleging excessive or improper force by LAPD officers for the period 1986 through 1990 that resulted in a settlement or judgment of more than $15,000. A majority of cases involved clear and often egregious officer misconduct resulting in serious injury or death to the victim. The LAPD's investigation of these 83 cases was deficient in many respects, and discipline against the officers involved was frequently light and often nonexistent.

While the precise size and identity of the problem group of officers cannot be specified without significant further investigation, its existence must be recognized and addressed. The LAPD has a number of tools to promote and enforce its policy that only reasonable and necessary force be used by officers. There are rewards and incentives such as promotions and pay upgrades. The discipline system exists to impose sanctions for misconduct. Officers can be reassigned. Supervisors can monitor and counsel officers under their command. Officers can be trained at the Police Academy and, more importantly, in the field, in the proper use of force.

The Commission believes that the Department has not made sufficient efforts to use those tools effectively to address the significant number of officers who appear to be using force excessively and improperly. The leadership of the LAPD must send a much clearer and more effective message that excessive force will not be tolerated and that officers and their supervisors will be evaluated to an important extent by how well they abide by and advance the Department's policy regarding use of force.

RACISM AND BIAS

The problem of excessive force is aggravated by racism and bias within the LAPD. That nexus is sharply illustrated by the results of a survey recently taken by the LAPD of the attitudes of its sworn officers. The survey of 960 officers found that approximately one-quarter (24.5%) of 650 officers responding agreed that "racial bias (prejudice) on the part of officers toward minority citizens currently exists and contributes to a negative interaction between police and community." More than one-quarter (27.6%) agreed that "an officer's prejudice towards the suspect's race may lead to the use of excessive force."

The Commission's review of MDT transmissions revealed an appreciable number of disturbing and recurrent racial remarks. Some of the remarks describe minorities through animal analogies ("sounds like monkey slapping time"). Often made in the context of discussing pursuits or beating suspects, the offensive remarks cover the spectrum of racial and ethnic minorities in the City ("I would love to drive down Slauson with a flame thrower . . . we would have a barbecue"; "I almost got me a Mexican last night but he dropped the damn gun too quick, lots of wit"). The officers typing the MDT messages apparently had little concern that they would be disciplined for making such remarks. Supervisors failed to monitor the messages or to impose discipline for improper remarks and were themselves frequently the source of offensive comments when in the field.

These attitudes of prejudice and intolerance are translated into unacceptable behavior in the field. Testimony from a variety of witnesses depicts the LAPD as an organization with practices and procedures that are conducive to discriminatory treatment and officer misconduct directed to members of minority groups. Witnesses repeatedly told of LAPD officers verbally harassing minorities, detaining African-American and Latino men who fit certain generalized descriptions of suspects, employing unnecessarily invasive or humiliating tactics in minority neighborhoods and using excessive force. While the Commission does not purport to adjudicate the validity of any one of these numerous complaints, the intensity and frequency of them reveal a serious problem.

Bias within the LAPD is not confined to officers' treatment of the public, but is also reflected in conduct directed to fellow officers who are members of racial or ethnic minority groups. The MDT messages and other evidence suggest that minority officers are still too frequently subjected to racist slurs and comments and to discriminatory treatment within the Department. While the relative number of officers who openly make racially derogatory comments or treat minority officers in a demeaning manner is small, their attitudes and behavior have a large impact because of the failure of supervisors to enforce vigorously and consistently the Department's policies against racism. That failure conveys to minority and non-minority officers alike the message that such conduct is in practice condoned by the Department.

The LAPD has made substantial progress in hiring minorities and women since the 1981 consent decree settling discrimination lawsuits against the Department. That effort should continue, including efforts to recruit Asians and other minorities who are not covered by the consent decree. The Department's statistics show, however, that the vast majority of minority officers are concentrated in the entry level police officer ranks in the Department. More than 80% of African-American, Latino and Asian officers hold the rank of Police Officer I-III. Many minority officers cite white dominance of managerial positions within the LAPD as one reason for the Department's continued tolerance of racially motivated language and behavior.

Bias within the LAPD is not limited to racial and ethnic prejudices but includes strongly felt bias based on gender and sexual orientation. Current LAPD policy prohibits all discrimination, including that based on sexual orientation. A tension remains, however, between the LAPD's official policy and actual practice. The Commission believes that the LAPD must act to implement fully its formal policy of nondiscrimination in the recruitment and promotion of gay and lesbian officers.

A 1987 LAPD study concluded that female officers were subjected to a double standard and subtle harassment and were not accepted as part of the working culture. As revealed in interviews of many of the officers charged with training new recruits, the problem has not abated in the last four years. Although female LAPD officers are in fact performing effectively, they are having a difficult time being accepted on a full and equal basis.

The Commission heard substantial evidence that female officers utilize a style of policing that minimizes the use of excessive force. Data examined by the Commission indicate that LAPD female officers are involved in use of excessive force at rates substantially below those of male officers. Those statistics, as confirmed by both academic studies and anecdotal evidence, also indicate that women officers perform at least as well as their male counterparts when measured by traditional standards.

The Commission believes that the Chief of Police must seek tangible ways, for example, through the use of the discipline system, to establish the principle that racism and bias based on ethnicity, gender, or sexual orientation will not be tolerated within the Department. Racism and bias cannot be eliminated without active leadership from the top. Minority and female officers must be given full and equal opportunity to assume leadership positions in the LAPD. They must be assigned on a fully nondiscriminatory basis to the more desirable "coveted" positions and promoted on the same nondiscriminatory basis to supervisory and managerial positions.

COMMUNITY POLICING

The LAPD has an organizational culture that emphasizes crime control over crime prevention and that isolates the police from the communities and the people they serve. With the full support of many, the LAPD insists on aggressive detection of major crimes and a rapid, seven-minute response time to calls for service. Patrol officers are evaluated by statistical measures (for example, the number of calls handled and arrests made) and are rewarded for being "hard-nosed." This style of policing produces results, but it does so at the risk of creating a siege mentality that alienates the officer from the community.

Witness after witness testified to unnecessarily aggressive confrontations between LAPD officers and citizens, particularly members of minority communities. From the statements of these citizens, as well as many present and former senior LAPD officers, it is apparent that too many LAPD patrol officers view citizens with resentment and hostility: too many treat the public with rudeness and disrespect. LAPD officers themselves seem to recognize the extent of the problem: nearly two-thirds (62.9%) of the 650 officers who responded to the recent LAPD survey expressed the opinion that "increased interaction with the community would improve the Department's relations with citizens."

A model of community policing has gained increased acceptance in other parts of the country during the past 10 years. The community policing model places service to the public and prevention of crime as the primary role of police in society and emphasizes problem solving, with active citizen involvement in defining those matters that are important to the community, rather than arrest statistics. Officers at the patrol level are required to spend less time in their cars communicating with other officers and more time on the street communicating with citizens. Proponents of this style of policing insist that addressing the causes of crime makes police officers more effective crime-fighters, and at the same time enhances the quality of life in the neighborhood.

The LAPD made early efforts to incorporate community policing principles and has continued to experiment with those concepts. For example, the LAPD's nationally recognized DARE program has been viewed by officers and the public alike as a major achievement. The LAPD remains committed, however, to its traditional style of law enforcement with an emphasis on crime control and arrests. LAPD officers are encouraged to command and to confront, not to communicate. Community policing concepts, if successfully implemented, offer the prospect of effective crime prevention and substantially improved community relations. Although community-based policing is not a panacea for the problem of crime in society, the LAPD should carefully implement this model on a City-wide basis. This will require a fundamental change in values. The Department must recognize the merits of community involvement in matters that affect local neighborhoods, develop programs to gain an adequate understanding of what is important to particular communities, and learn to manage departmental affairs in ways that are consistent with the community views expressed. Above all, the Department must understand that it is accountable to all segments of the community.

RECRUITMENT

Although 40% of the candidates for admission to the Police Academy are disqualified as a result of psychological testing and background investigation, the Commission's review indicated that the initial psychological evaluation is an ineffective predictor of an applicant's tendencies toward violent behavior and that the background investigation pays too little attention to a candidate's history of violence. Experts agree that the best predictor of future behavior is previous behavior. Thus, the background investigation offers the best hope of screening out violence-prone applicants. Unfortunately, the background investigators are overworked and inadequately trained.

Improved screening of applicants is not enough. Police work modifies behavior. Many emotional and psychological problems may develop during an officer's tenure on the force. Officers may enter the force well suited psychologically for the job, but may suffer from burnout, alcohol-related problems, cynicism, or disenchantment, all of which can result in poor control over their behavior. A person's susceptibility to the behavior-modifying experiences of police work may not be revealed during even the most skilled and sophisticated psychological evaluation process. Accordingly, officers should be retested periodically to determine both psychological and physical problems. In addition, supervisors must understand their role to include training and counseling officers to cope with the problems policing can often entail, so that they may be dealt with before an officer loses control or requires disciplinary action.

TRAINING

LAPD officer training has three phases. Each recruit spends approximately six months at the Police Academy. The new officer then spends one year on probation working with more experienced patrol officers who serve as field training officers (FTOs). Thereafter, all officers receive continuing training, which includes mandatory field training and daily training at roll call. The Commission believes that in each phase of the training additional emphasis is needed on the use of verbal skills rather than physical force to control potentially volatile situations and on the development of human relationship skills.

The quality of instruction at the Police Academy is generally impressive. However, at present the curriculum provides only 8 hours in cultural awareness training. No more than 1½ hours is devoted to any ethnic group. Substantially more training on this important topic is essential. In addition, the Academy's current Spanish language program needs to be reviewed and current deficiencies corrected. Officers with an interest in developing broader language skills should be encouraged to do so.

Upon graduation the new officer works as a "probationary officer" assigned to various field training officers. The FTOs guide new officers' first contacts with citizens and have primary responsibility for introducing the probationers to the culture and traditions of the Department. The Commission's interviews of FTOs in four representative divisions revealed that many FTOs openly perpetuate the siege mentality that alienates patrol officers from the community and pass on to their trainees confrontational attitudes of hostility and disrespect for the public. This problem is in part the result of flaws in the way FTOs are selected and trained. The hiring of a very large number of new officers in 1989, which required the use of less experienced FTOs, greatly exacerbated the problem.

Any officer promoted to Police Officer III by passing a written examination covering Department policies and procedures is eligible to serve as an FTO. At present there are no formal eligibility or disqualification criteria for the FTO position based on an applicant's disciplinary records. Fourteen of the FTOs in the four divisions the Commission studied had been promoted to FTO despite having been disciplined for use of excessive force or use of improper tactics. There also appears to be little emphasis on selecting FTOs who have an interest in training junior officers, and an FTO's training ability is given little weight in his or her evaluation.

The most influential training received by a probationer comes from the example set by his or her FTO. Virtually all of the FTOs interviewed stated that their primary objective in training probationers is to instill good "officer safety skills." While the Commission recognizes the importance of such skills in police work, the probationers' world is quickly divided into "we/they" categories, which is exacerbated by the failure to integrate any cultural awareness or sensitivity training into field training.

The Commission believes that, to become FTOs, officers should be required to pass written and oral tests designed to measure communications skills, teaching aptitude, and knowledge of Departmental policies regarding appropriate use of force, cultural sensitivity, community relations, and nondiscrimination. Officers with an aptitude for and interest in training junior officers should be encouraged by effective incentives to apply for FTO positions. In addition, the training program for FTOs should be modified to place greater emphasis on communication skills and the appropriate use of force. Successful completion of FTO School should be required before an FTO begins teaching probationers.

PROMOTION, ASSIGNMENT, AND OTHER PERSONNEL ISSUES

In the civil service process for promotion of officers in the LAPD, the information considered includes performance evaluations, educational and training background, and all sustained complaints. The number and nature of any not sustained complaints, however, are not considered. The Commission recommends that a summary of not sustained complaints be considered in promotion decisions, as well as in paygrade advancements and assignments to desirable positions that are discretionary with the LAPD and outside the civil service system.

This is not to say that a past complaint history, even including a sustained complaint for excessive force, should automatically bar an officer from promotion. But there should be a careful consideration of the officer's complaint history including a summary of not sustained complaints, and particularly multiple complaints with similar fact patterns.

Complaint histories should also be considered in assignment of problem officers who may be using force improperly. For example, a problem officer can be paired with an officer with excellent communications skills that may lessen the need for use of force, as opposed to a partner involved in prior incidents of force. Another example is assignments to the jail facilities where potential for abuse by officers with a propensity to use excessive force is high. As several incidents examined by the Commission made clear, transfer of an officer to another geographical area is not likely to address a problem of excessive force without other remedial measures such as increased supervising, training and counseling.

Since 1980 the Department has permitted police officers working in patrol to select the geographic area of division for their patrol assignment subsequent to their initial assignment after completion of probation. As a result, sergeants and patrol officers tend to remain in one division for extended periods. The Commission believes that assignment procedures should be modified to require rotation through various divisions to ensure that officers work in a wide range of police functions and varied patrol locations during their careers. Such a rotation program will increase officers' experience and also will enable the Department to deploy police patrols with greater diversity throughout the City.

Under the current promotion system officers generally must leave patrol to advance within the Department. Notwithstanding the importance of the patrol function, therefore, the better officers are encouraged to abandon patrol. To give patrol increased emphasis and to retain good, experienced officers, the LAPD should increase rewards and incentives for patrol officers.

PERSONNEL COMPLAINTS AND OFFICER DISCIPLINE

No area of police operations received more adverse comment during the Commission's public hearings than the Department's handling of complaints against LAPD officers, particularly allegations involving the use of excessive force. Statistics make the public's frustration understandable. Of the 2,152 citizen allegations of excessive force from 1986 through 1990, only 42 were sustained.

All personnel complaints are reviewed by a captain in the LAPD's Internal Affairs Division ("IAD") to determine whether the complaint will be investigated by IAD or the charged officer's division. Generally IAD investigates only a few cases because of limited resources. Wherever investigated, the matter is initially adjudicated by the charged officer's division commanding officer, with a review by the area and bureau commanders.

The Commission has found that the complaint system is skewed against complainants. People who wish to file complaints face significant hurdles. Some intake officers actively discourage filing by being uncooperative or requiring long waits before completing a complaint form. In many heavily Latino divisions, there is often no Spanish speaking officer available to take complaints.

Division investigations are frequently inadequate. Based on a review of more than 700 complaint investigation files, the Commission found many deficiencies. For example, in a number of complaint files the Commission reviewed, there was no indication that the investigators had attempted to identify or locate independent witnesses or if identified, to interview them. IAD investigations, on the whole, were of a higher quality than the division investigations. Although the LAPD has a special "officer involved shooting team," the Commission also found serious flaws in the investigation of shooting cases. Officers are frequently interviewed as a group, and statements are often not recorded until the completion of a "pre-interview."

The process of complaint adjudication is also flawed. First, there is no uniform basis for categorizing witnesses as "independent" or "non-involved" as opposed to "involved," although that distinction can determine whether a complaint is "not sustained" or "sustained." Some commanding officers also evaluate witnesses' credibility in inconsistent and biased ways that improperly favor the officer. Moreover, even when excessive force complaints are sustained, the punishment is more lenient than it should be. As explained by one deputy chief, there is greater punishment for conduct that embarrasses the Department (such as theft or drug use) than for conduct that reflects improper treatment of citizens. Statistical data also support the inference that the Department treats excessive force violations more leniently than it treats other types of officer misconduct.

Perhaps the greatest single barrier to the effective investigation and adjudication of complaints is the officers' unwritten code of silence: an officer does not provide adverse information against a fellow officer. While loyalty and support are necessary qualities, they cannot justify the violation of an officer's public responsibilities to ensure compliance with the law, including LAPD regulations.

A major overhaul of the disciplinary system is necessary to correct these problems. The Commission recommends creation of the Office of the Inspector General within the Police Commission with responsibility to oversee the disciplinary process and to participate in the adjudication and punishment of the most serious cases. The Police Commission should be responsible for overseeing the complaint intake process. Citizens must believe they can lodge complaints that will be investigated and determined fairly. All complaints relating to excessive force (including improper tactics) should be investigated by IAD, rather than at the involved officer's division, and should be subject to periodic audits by the Inspector General. While the Chief of Police should remain the one primarily responsible for imposing discipline in individual cases, the Police Commission should set guidelines as a matter of policy and hold the Chief accountable for following them.

STRUCTURAL ISSUES

Although the City Charter assigned the Police Commission ultimate control over Department policies, its authority over the Department and the Chief of Police is illusory. Structural and operational constraints greatly weaken the Police Commission's power to hold the Chief accountable and therefore its ability to perform its management responsibilities, including effective oversight. Real power and authority reside in the Chief.

The Chief of Police is the general manager and chief administrative officer of the Police Department. The Police Commission selects the Chief from among top competitors in a civil service examination administered by the Personnel Department. Candidates from outside the Department are disadvantaged by City Charter provisions and seniority rules.

The Chief's civil service status largely protects him or her from disciplinary action or discharge by giving him a "substantial property right" in his job and declaring that he cannot be suspended or removed except for "good and sufficient cause" based upon an act or omission occurring within the prior year. In addition, recently enacted Charter Amendment 5 empowers the City Council to review and override the actions of the City's commissions, including the Police Commission.

The Police Commission's staff is headed by the Commanding Officer, Commission Operations, a sworn LAPD officer chosen by the Police Commissioners, who normally serves in that post for two to three years. Because the Police Commission depends heavily on the Commanding Officer to review information received from the Department and to identify issues, it must also rely on his willingness to criticize his superior officers. However, he lacks the requisite independence because his future transfer and promotion are at the discretion of the Chief of Police, and he is part of the Chief's command structure as well as being answerable to the Police Commission.

The Police Commission receives summaries, prepared by the Department, of disciplinary actions against sworn officers, but cannot itself impose discipline. The summaries are brief and often late, making it impossible for the Police Commission to monitor systematically the discipline imposed by the Chief in use of force and other cases.

The Commission believes that the Department should continue to be under the general oversight and control of a five-member, part-time citizen Police Commission. Commissioners' compensation should be increased substantially. They should serve a maximum of five years with staggered terms. The Police Commission's independent staff should be increased by adding civilian employees, including management auditors, computer systems data analysts, and investigators with law enforcement experience. It is vital that the Police Commission's staff be placed under the control of an independent civilian Chief of Staff, a general manager level employee.

The Chief of Police must be more responsive to the Police Commission and the City's elected leadership, but also must be protected against improper political influences. To achieve this balance, the Chief should serve a five-year term, renewable at the discretion of the Police Commission for one additional five-year term. The selection, tenure, discipline, and removal of the Chief should be exempted from existing civil service provisions. The Chief should be appointed by the Mayor, with advice from the Police Commission and the consent of the City Council after an open competition. The Police Commission should have the authority to terminate the Chief prior to the expiration of the first or second five-year term, but the final decision to terminate should require the concurrence of the Mayor and be subject to a reversal by a vote of two-thirds of the City Council.

IMPLEMENTATION

Full implementation of this Report will require action by the Mayor, the City Council, the Police Commission, the Police Department, and ultimately the voters. To monitor the progress of reform, the City Council should require reports on implementation at six month intervals from the Mayor, the Council's own Human Resources and Labor Relations Committee, the Police Commission, and the Police Department. The Commission should reconvene in six months to assess the implementation of its recommendations and to report to the public.

Chief Gates has served the LAPD and the City 42 years, the past 13 years as Chief of Police. He has achieved a noteworthy record of public service in a stressful and demanding profession. For the reasons set forth in support of the recommendation that the Chief of Police be limited to two five-year terms, the Commission believes that commencement of a transition in that office is now appropriate. The Commission also believes that the interests of harmony and healing would be served if the Police Commission is now reconstituted with members not identified with the recent controversy involving the Chief.

More than any other factor, the attitude and actions of the leaders of the Police Department and other City agencies will determine whether the recommendations of this Report are adopted. To make genuine progress on issues relating to excessive force, racism and bias, leadership must avoid sending mixed signals. We urge those leaders to give priority to stopping the use of excessive force and curbing racism and bias and thereby to bring the LAPD to a new level of excellence and esteem throughout Los Angeles.

Glossary

Accountability and control Organizational subunits and work environments that greatly inhibit personal discretion and lower-echelon decision making; a disciplinary structure within which ordinary people can be hired for an exacting job and in which they can be trained, equipped, and motivated to function effectively.

ACT-UP An acronym for Aids Coalition to Unleash Power, an aggressive organization expressly formed to protest the lack of governmental funding for AIDS research; has used disruptive tactics and occasionally has resorted to civil disobedience as a means of promoting its cause.

Alternative Dispute Resolution A civil means of resolving a criminal or delinquent charge through a civil process whereby a third party, ordinarily a judge or attorney, decides how the controversy or dispute ought to be resolved to the satisfaction of both parties.

Americans with Disabilities Act (ADA) Act making it illegal to discriminate against persons with disabilities; these individuals are entitled to equal access to employment, including the processes of recruitment, hiring, promotion, and any other benefits and privileges of employment.

Back-to-the-community movement Community-oriented policing; focus on foot patrols and neighborhood beats; proactive policing stressing community wellness.

Basic car plan Method to prevent and control crime; car teams consisted of nine officers: a lead officer, five senior officers with two to three years experience, and three probationary officers; operated on workload analysis factors that provided a minimum radio car plan (basic car plan) for all watches.

Beat patrolling Police patrol style originating in early 1900s designed to bring officers into closer physical contact with area residents; beats arranged for small geographical areas of neighborhoods or cities that are patrolled by individual officers, usually on foot.

Blue curtain   When police agencies investigate their own, the very language used in such investigations is telling; reluctance among police officials to punish "one of their own" when a citizen complains; a barrier of silence to protect the police force.

Bow Street Runners   A small organization of paid police officers who attempted to apprehend criminals in England beginning in 1754.

British Crime Survey   Annual compilation of victimization figures for both England and Wales; comparable to the National Crime Survey published in the United States.

Budget   Plan for the accomplishment of programs relating to objectives and goals within a definite time period including an estimate of resources required together with an estimate of resources available, usually compared with past periods and showing future requirements.

Bureaucracy   Organizational model that vests individuals with authority and spheres of competence in a predetermined hierarchy with abstract rules and selection by test.

Cadet program   Program designed to bring underage but otherwise qualified individuals into police service; applicants undergo preservice screening such as oral, physical, and background investigations and are generally accepted upon solid recommendations.

Canadian Centre for Justice Statistics   Reports annually the amount of crime in Canada; comparable to the Bureau of Justice Statistics in the United States.

Career integrity workshops   Los Angeles County Sheriff's Department initiated an in-service training program; in-house instructors were trained in methods of leading small groups of deputies into "questionable conduct" scenarios and facilitating group discussions that delved into possible causes of actions or inactions and possible results; students are made to see behaviors more clearly and are brought more closely in tune with reality than if exposed to "canned" situations in the training environment.

Cause célèbre   Major publicized incident (in this context, involving police officers) that receives widespread attention by media; Rodney King beating was a cause célèbre.

Centurions   In early Roman times, from about 100 B.C. to A.D. 200, centurions were used as either military or paramilitary units for policing purposes; usually commanded units of 100 men and were used for both policing and combat.

Chancellors   King's agents used to settle disputes in his behalf among neighbors, such as property boundary issues, trespass allegations, and child misconduct; early equivalent of the chancellor with similar duties and responsibilities was the justice of the peace, dating back to about 1200 A.D.

Children in need of supervision (CHINS)   Typically, unruly or incorrigible children who cannot be supervised effectively by their parents; also includes children from homes in which parents are seldom present; state agencies exist to find housing for such children.

Chinese Exclusion Act   Congress passed the Chinese Exclusion Act in 1882, imposing a head tax and excluding whole categories of people—convicts and the mentally ill; for the first time there were real limits on European immigration.

Chuzaishos   Live-in-type units providing accommodations for an officer's entire family; these are staffed on a twenty-four-hour basis; both kobans and chuzaishos are strategically located to ensure close contacts between police officers and community residents.

Civilian complaint review boards   Panels of citizens that judge acts of misconduct committed by police officers and recommend appropriate sanctions.

Civil Rights Institute   Established in Birmingham, Alabama, November 15, 1992; tells its story of those events that helped change the nation and the world. Situated at the corner of 16th Street and Sixth Avenue North (520 Sixteenth Street North), the Birmingham Civil Rights Institute is the centerpiece in the city's historic Civil Rights District.

Civil Rights Movement   Multiracial movement commenced in 1960s to combat racial injustice and inequality.

Code of silence   Informal arrangement among police officers that discourages "whistleblowing" regarding misconduct of fellow officers; negative and potentially self-destructive.

Patrick Colquhoun   An influential London magistrate in 1792; promoted and endorsed some rather novel ideas at the time concerning the functions of police; believed that police should be used to establish and maintain order, control and prevent crime, and set an example of good conduct and moral sense for the citizenry; believed that existing enforcement methods, at least in London, were decidedly antiquated and improper; believed that some degree of professionalism among officers was necessary and should be independently funded by the particular jurisdiction.

Community   The idea of police officers and community residents as a partnership devoted to combat crime and promote public safety is not a particularly novel one; however, changing ethnic and racial composition of most U.S. communities has slowed efforts by police agencies to pull citizens together for the common purposes of preventing crime and fostering public safety.

Community-based policing   An umbrella term encompassing any law enforcement agency- or community-initiated plan or program to enable police officers and community residents to work cooperatively in creative ways that will (1) reduce or control crime, fear of crime, and the incidence of victimizations; (2) promote mutual understanding for the purpose of enhancing police officer/citizen promotion of community safety and security; and (3) establish a police-citizen communications network through which mutual problems may be discussed and resolved.

Community Patrol Officer Program (CPOP)   A problem-oriented community policing effort commenced as a pilot project in 1984 in New York City; officers were assigned to foot patrols for 16- to 60-block beats; seventy-five precincts used the CPOP by 1989; most important function of CPOP was the prevention of street-level drug problems.

Community Patrol Officers   Program to determine the feasibility of permanently assigning police officers to foot patrol in fairly large neighborhood beat areas; officers required to perform a variety of nontraditional tasks besides their normal law enforcement duties, to be full-service police officers, and to serve as community resource; additional tasks included helping residents to organize community groups, attending community meetings, making service referrals, and helping to devise strategies to deal not only with local crime and order-maintenance problems, but also with social needs.

Community-Police Educational Program   Program implemented by the Philadelphia Police Department in 1980; designed to educate citizens by explaining the necessity for certain police actions and to reduce their criticism of police performance.

Community policing   A philosophy rather than a specific tactic; a proactive, decentralized approach designed to reduce crime, disorder, and fear of crime by intensely involving the same officer in a community for a long term so that personal links are formed with residents.

Community Projects for Restoration Federal law enforcement and social welfare program begun under the Bush Administration; in 1992, $18 million in federal funds was targeted for community policing, public housing assistance, and gang prevention efforts under the "weed and seed" program.

Community wellness A proactive collaborative effort between police departments and community residents to initiate watch and alert programs to inform police about possible criminal activities; as neighborhood residents take a more active role in preventing crime, there are substantial decreases in crime observed in those neighborhoods over time.

Comparative community policing Examination of community-oriented policing programs in other countries.

Constables Favored noblemen of the king who commanded neighborhood groups; were the forerunners of modern-day police officers.

Constitution Act of 1867 Bestowed on the Canadian Parliament the legislative authority to define all criminal law throughout the provinces, although this act has undergone extensive revision.

Contact patrols A project funded by the British Home Office; promoted greater police officer contact with community residents through more continuous police presence in "beat" areas.

Corporate gangs Juveniles who form coalitions to emulate organized crime.

Council of Europe Formed in 1949; discusses issues, including definitions of crime among different countries and extradition matters; although council activities have been largely informal, much international cooperation has been achieved to combat certain types of crime effectively.

Crime Stoppers A Canadian program established in 1976 that uses the mass media to encourage the public to report criminal activity anonymously in exchange for a reward; has been somewhat helpful in combatting crime.

Crime Watch A crime reduction and control program; facilitated through greater police presence in neighborhoods and use of neighborhood observers.

Criminal Justice Act of 1948 Act that authorizes the compilation, maintenance, and distribution of information about crime in England and Wales for both adults and juveniles.

Criminal Law Act of 1967 Created three new major crime categories: *summary offenses* (e.g., petty theft, disorderly conduct, solicitation, and public drunkenness); *indictable offenses* (e.g., murder, rape, robbery, aggravated assault, arson); and *hybrid offenses* (e.g., embezzlement, white-collar crime).

Day watch Citizens were obligated to perform day or night watch duties on a rotating basis; comparable to modern-day shift work; watchmen would be expected to create a hue and a cry in the event they detected crimes in progress or any other community disturbance, such as a fire or other emergency situation.

Deadly force Use of force resulting in death of suspects.

Decarceration Removal of juveniles or adults from institutionalization or confinement.

"Defense-of-life" standard Standard set by *Tennessee v. Garner* (1985) whereby police officers may shoot fleeing felons only if their own lives or the lives of others are directly threatened by suspects who are attempting to avoid apprehension or are resisting arrest.

Deinstitutionalization of status offenses (DSO) Movement to remove nondelinquent juveniles from secure facilities; specific status offenses include, but are not limited to, truancy, curfew violation, and runaway behavior.

Density Number of persons per square mile in given geographical areas; more people per square mile signifies greater density.

Divestiture of jurisdiction Judicial relinquishing of control or power over cases involving certain types of juvenile offenders, such as runaways, truants, and curfew violators.

"Dropsy" testimony Perjured testimony by police officers in an attempt to solidify a weak case; defendants are often alleged to have "dropped" drugs on ground during automobile stops for traffic violations, for example; hence, "dropsy" testimony; more prevalent after exclusionary rule became search and seizure standard following *Mapp v. Ohio* (1961).

Dual procedure offense Similar to British hybrid crimes, in which the prosecutor decides whether prosecution should proceed either by summary conviction or by indictment.

Emotional numbing Condition in which officers distance themselves from a stressful incident and make an effort not to feel anything; a denial of having an emotional component and the appearance of being in a state of shock; officers usually say, however, that they are in control and are having no problems dealing with the situation.

Empowerment The essence of both organizational mission and values statements; gives employees the latitude to perform at their highest levels.

Ethics A body of moral values; codes of honor tacitly or overtly observed by law enforcement officers; upholding both the spirit and letter of the law and fulfilling the mission statement of police agencies.

Ethnocentricity The general feeling that one's cultural group is the best group.

Excessive force Any exceptional force extending beyond that necessary to disable suspects or to take them into custody through arrest.

Exigent circumstances Circumstances in which quick action is necessitated, such as searches for drugs and other contraband that might be destroyed easily; exception to exclusionary rule.

Expungement orders Juvenile court orders to seal juvenile records.

Sir John Fielding Organized Bow Street Runners in 1748; utilized semi-formal policing methods to detect and arrest criminals.

FLETC model Graduated or escalating amounts of force, applied in accordance with the degree of suspect cooperation or resistance; suspects who are cooperative are given verbal orders by officers, whereas other suspects may require varying degrees of force to subdue them.

Foot patrols Originating in Flint, Michigan; have been moderately successful in bringing community residents into closer touch with patrolling officers; officers patrol on foot, presumably to bring them in closer touch with citizens.

Force Continuum Graduated or escalating amounts of force, applied in accordance with the nature of arrested suspect cooperation or resistance.

Frankpledge System requiring loyalty to the King of England and shared law and order responsibilities among the public; system directed that neighbors should form into small groups to assist and protect one another if they were threatened by criminals.

Frumentarii First professional criminal investigative units in Western history; had three principal duties: (1) to supervise grain distribution to Rome's needy; (2) to oversee the personal delivery of messages among government officials; and (3) to detect crime and prosecute offenders.

Gaols Fifteenth-century English jails.

Golf cart patrolling Combined with sector patrolling, has been instrumental in bringing police officers closer to community residents; use of golf carts to patrol neighborhoods.

"Good faith" exception Exception to exclusionary rule whereby police officers wish to conduct search and seizure on basis of faulty warrant; acting in "good faith" presumably excuses conduct.

Graduate Entry Scheme In England and Wales, special course in which prospective police recruits are selected on the basis of their performance of in-service work and their law enforcement education.

Graft Gratuities accepted in the course of one's police role in exchange for favors or concessions usually involving violations of the law.

Hate crimes Crimes committed against victims of specific ethnic or racial categories.

Hue and cry Warning shouted by early day and night watchmen if they observed a crime.

Human relations Organizational behavior stressing personal qualities of those in roles, such as police officers; stresses persons as personality systems with emotional components.

Hybrid offense May be heard either by magistrates or by crown courts, depending on prosecutorial discretion; may or may not be indictable; influenced greatly by situational factors, such as a defendant's lack of a prior record, circumstances surrounding the commission of the offense, and harm inflicted on victims.

Incident-driven policing A technocratic approach whereby police officers respond or react to calls-for-service, that is, incidents.

Indentured servant system System in which persons paid for their passage to the American Colonies from England by selling their services for a period of seven years; also considered a "voluntary slave" migration pattern.

Indictable offense A serious crime; the equivalent of a felony.

Internal affairs Department in police agencies charged with the responsibility to investigate misconduct and possible criminal behavior on the part of police officers; comprised of other police officers.

International Court of Justice Formed to establish some degree of jurisdiction over international crime.

Internships These programs generally are three-unit, upper-division offerings for graduating seniors to allow them practical exposure to the criminal justice system. Several universities make the internship a mandatory subject requiring up to 160 contact hours per sixteen-week semester.

Interpol International Criminal Police Organization; the idea is attributed to Baron Pasquier, the prefect of the Paris police in 1809; cooperates with police agencies to apprehend international criminals.

Job satisfaction Degree of contentment with work performed.

Justice of the peace Minor judicial official overseeing trivial offenses.

Juvenile delinquency Offenses committed by minors that would be crimes if committed by adults.

Juvenile delinquents Any minor who commits an offense that would be a crime if committed by an adult.

Kobans Japanese mini-stations comparable to police substations in U.S. communities; these Japanese police "boxes" are staffed by two or more officers on rotating shifts.

Law Enforcement Assistance Administration (LEAA) An outgrowth of the President's Crime Commission during the period 1965–1967, a time of great social unrest and civil disobedience. Racial and political tensions were exceptionally high; allocated millions of dollars to researchers and police departments over the next decade for various purposes; many experiments conducted with these monies led to innovative patrolling strategies in communities.

Law Reform Commission Act Implemented by Canadian legislature to keep pace with changing Canadian society and to make appropriate reform recommendations to the legislature.

Legalistic model Emphasized the importance of written procedure and limited individual officer discretion; promoted a "Joe Friday" strictly-by-the-book mentality among law enforcement officers.

Letter of the law Strictly legalistic approach to law enforcement; zero-tolerance interpretation of the law.

Liberal policing ideals Liberalism is an ideology, a political philosophy, and related policies aimed at social reform designed to increase equality and democratic participation in governance; liberals advocate the use of state power to aid disadvantaged individuals and groups; they support a position that much criminal activity has roots in the social fabric.

Mala in se **crimes** Illegal acts that are inherently wrong.

Mala prohibita **crimes** Illegal acts that have been codified or reduced to writing.

Mentally ill Persons who cannot conform their conduct to normal behavior (e.g., to the law); who don't know the difference between right and wrong; who possibly have a mental disease or defect.

Metropolitan Police Act of 1829 Act that empowered Sir Robert Peel to select and organize the Metropolitan Police of London.

Metropolitan Police Force Project Act of 1981 Toronto complaint review authorized by act to investigate citizen complaints against police.

Metropolitan Police of London Organized in 1829 by Sir Robert Peel, a prominent British government official; included duties that emphasized close interaction with the public and maintenance of proper attitudes and temperament.

Military syndrome Propensity of police organizations to organize and operate police departments according to military organization and protocol, including use of ranks and similar hierarchies of authority.

Mini-stations Small police stations strategically located in high-crime neighborhoods; staffed by one or more police officers.

Mission statements Goals and orientation statements of organizations designed to disclose their purposes and responsibilities; used to vest employees with direction and motivation.

National Advisory Commission on Criminal Justice Standards and Goals Promulgated several important goals for police departments in order to clarify their policing functions, including maintenance of order; enforcement of the law; prevention of criminal activity; detection of criminal activity; apprehension of criminals; participation in court proceedings; protection of constitutional guarantees; assistance to those who cannot care for themselves or who are in danger of physical harm; control of traffic; resolution of day-to-day conflicts among family, friends, and neighbors; creation and maintenance of a feeling of security in the community; promotion and preservation of civil order.

National Commission on Law Observance and Enforcement Commission created by Herbert Hoover in 1929; designed to investigate law enforcement practices and standards.

National Crime Survey Annual survey of crime victims.

National Police Agency Japanese national police and decentralized police operations throughout the forty-seven prefectures, plus three additional prefecture-equivalent agencies in Tokyo and the island of Hokkaido.

Negative reinforcements Punishments administered to subordinate police officers by higher-ups to discourage particular kinds of undesirable conduct.

Negligent hiring and selection Basis for civil lawsuit in showing that incompetent persons have been selected to perform important tasks, such as police work, and where injuries to victims are caused by such incompetent persons.

Negligent retention Basis for civil lawsuit against public officials in showing that ineffective or poorly trained personnel are retained despite their poor work record.

Negligent training Basis for civil lawsuit in showing that clear duty to train employees (e.g., to use firearms) is lacking.

Neighborhood police posts Police posts in Singapore similar to U.S. mini-stations or substations.

Neighborhood team policing Cooperative enterprise among neighborhood citizens and police officers to maintain continuous vigil in communities and to report suspicious behavior or criminal activity.

Neighborhood Watch Program using neighborhood residents, particularly during evening hours, to watch for criminal conduct.

Night watch Early English watchman program designed to report crime if observed.

Operation Blockade An INS experiment launched with $250,000 in extra overtime funds; agents shifted from inland posts in El Paso, Texas, to prevent the influx of illegal aliens into the United States.

Operation CLEAN In Dallas, Texas, a seven-phase program known as Operation CLEAN was implemented in March 1989. Specific areas of the city were targeted for Operation CLEAN, and concerted action between several municipal departments (police, fire, streets and sanitation, housing and neighborhood services departments, and the city attorney's office) resulted in a major cleanup effort leading to a 71 percent reduction in street crime. Citizens established Crime Watch Programs and increased their cooperativeness with police officers.

Organizational values Standards imparted by organizations to membership designed to instill in them work motivation and goals.

Participative management Theory of organizations in which employees have some input regarding departmental operations.

Patrol car video cameras Videotape units in police vehicles used for various purposes (e.g., to tape arrests of suspected drunk drivers, to illustrate causes for stops and arrests of motorists for various charges).

Peace Officer Standards and Training (POST) Generally recognized criteria used to select and train persons for police work.

Sir Robert Peel British official who established Metropolitan Police of London in 1829 and set early standards for police officer selection and training.

Penal Code of 1907 Initially defined a broad range of crimes and punishments in Japan; although there is no formal distinction between felonies and misdemeanors such as the distinction made in the United States, the Japanese Penal Code defines traditional crimes, including homicide, rape, burglary, robbery, and vehicular theft; the age of criminal responsibility has been set at fourteen, although persons age twenty or over are considered adults. Those between the ages of fourteen and nineteen are usually treated as juveniles in independent juvenile proceedings.

Perjury Lying under oath in court.

Plain view rule Exception to exclusionary rule; illegal contraband may be seized because it is in plain view; in order to use this rule, officers who seize contraband must be in places where they are permitted to be.

Police and Criminal Evidence Act of 1984 British act authorizing the establishment of an independent Police Complaints Authority in 1985.

Police brutality Any unnecessary physical force used by police officers against arrested citizens in which injuries to citizens are sustained.

Police Community Awareness Academies The formation of a Citizens Police Academy occurred in England, specifically from the Devon and Cornwall Constabulary, Middlemoor Exeter; in 1977, two small British municipal police agencies established Police Night School, a concept that was transplanted to the United States; the idea was formulated when local English citizens asked their constables how the agency operated.

Police-community relations A generic concept including any program designed to promote or make more visible law enforcement strategies that are aimed at crime prevention and control; varying degrees of proactive citizen involvement are solicited.

Police Complaints Authority An independent English investigative body established to examine the validity of citizen complaints against police; capable of imposing appropriate administrative sanctions against the offending officers.

Police discretion Choices by police officers to act in given ways in citizen-police encounters; selection of behaviors among alternatives.

Police misconduct Any one of several different types of illegal and/or improper behavior of police officers, including graft, falsifying police reports, and perjury.

Police mission Either implicit or explicit statements about general goals and objectives of police departments and officers.

Planning Short- or long-term calculations and strategies for implementation of goals.

Positive reinforcements Rewards given by administrators to lower-level police officers for good conduct or for otherwise conforming to the requirements set forth in the police mission.

Posttrauma strategies Officer help programs designed to provide individual or group counseling to officers involved in stressful events such as shootings.

Precinct Community Councils (PCCs) Established as liaisons between police officers and local residents; these face-to-face councils have done much to foster better police-community cooperation and create better conditions of community crime control.

Problem-oriented policing Citizen involvement in defining community crime problems and suggesting solutions for them.

Productivity Either measured or unmeasured output by officers, including numbers of arrests, time on duty, tickets issued, and participation in public events.

Professionalization movement Efforts by various interests to encourage higher standards of selection for police officers, including more formal education and training.

Psychiatric Emergency Coordinating Committee Formulated a comprehensive Memorandum of Agreement that took effect on April 1, 1985; the administrator of each participating agency agreed in writing to a list of specific actions; these steps were designed to divert mentally ill persons involved in minor criminal behavior from the criminal justice system into the health care system, where they can receive more appropriate care.

Psychological screening Administration of tests or assessment devices designed to exclude police officer applicants whose personal behavior and personality might be unsuitable for police work.

Public disclosure Information about police agencies and officers disseminated to the public by a public relations officer.

Public relations Persons or bureaus involved in creating more effective communication and pleasant interactions and working associations between citizens and police officers.

Quality circles An application of TQM; approach encourages workers classified similarly (e.g., dispatchers, detectives, or patrol) to interact in group settings to resolve problems common to their particular work specialties; acting as a team, personnel can often offer recommendations that lead to savings in labor and time, enhanced service, and/or improved working conditions.

Queer Nation Organization formed in May 1990 in New York City after M–80 bombs were exploded in trash cans adjacent to a gay nightclub; a group of individuals marched down the street to protest the incident and subsequently formed a looseknit organization called the Queer Nation to advocate rights for gays.

Reeves Chief law enforcement officers of English shires or counties; forerunners of county sheriffs.

Refugee Act of 1980 Radically expanded the definition of those eligible for political asylum; but because it has been poorly enforced and easily abused, it helped bring on today's growing demand for new limits on aliens.

Retired Senior Volunteer Program A national effort that places retirees in community volunteer positions; seen in many quarters as one approach to augment police personnel.

Royal Canadian Mounted Police Federal police of Canada; the Canadian RCMP are the equivalent of a national police force, with general jurisdiction in all provinces.

Scavenger gangs Juvenile coalitions formed primarily as a means of socializing and for mutual protection.

Section 1983 actions Title 42, Section 1983 of the U.S. Code, setting forth grounds for legal actions involving civil rights violations by police officers against citizens.

Selective enforcement Prioritizing by police officers particular offenses; enforcing some laws and not enforcing others.

Sense of community Psychological milieu established between police officers and citizens whereby citizens acquire feeling of security and safety in their neighborhoods.

Sentencing Project A 1990 project by a Washington-based nonprofit group to study comparative sentencing of minorities and whites; reported that 23 percent of young African American men were in jail, on probation, or on parole on any given day; for whites, the figure was 6.2 percent; for Hispanics, 10.4 percent; those figures reflected, in part, the effects of newly toughened drug laws that caused a fivefold increase in state and federal prison populations since 1973.

Service model Approach designed to meet community needs and expectations.

Sexual harassment Disturbing behavior toward member of the opposite sex based on gender; unwelcome treatment in the workplace based on gender; perceived disrespect based on gender.

Sheriff Chief county law enforcement officer.

Shires Early English counties.

Shouts and rattles Early New York persons who were equipped with noise-making rattles and who were expected to shout and shake their rattles in the event they observed crimes in progress or fleeing suspects.

Situationally based discretion Options exercised by police officers during police-citizen encounters based on the particular situation; may or may not include letter-of-the-law interpretations of events.

Socioeconomic status Level of income and general social standing or prominence of neighborhood residents.

Spirit of the law Efforts by police officers to exhibit leniency where law violations are observed; usually first offenders may receive leniency because of extenuating circumstances.

Stare decisis Legal precedent; lower courts must follow precedents established in higher courts when facts are substantially the same.

Station house adjustments Decisions by police officers to deal informally with arrestees, often at the police station; actions often do not involve arrests, but warnings.

Status offenses Any misdeed committed by a juvenile that would not be a crime if committed by an adult (e.g., runaway behavior, truancy, and curfew violation).

Stonewall riots New York Police Department raid of a gay bar in Greenwich Village using a warrant stating that liquor was being sold in violation of the existing premises permit; the patrons of the bar resisted, and in the ensuing melee that became the Stonewall riots, four police officers were seriously injured and thirteen patrons were arrested.

Stress training Police officer training in which officers are subjected to situations involving role strain and conflict, generating stress; process involves how to cope with stress and reduce its adverse effects.

Subculture Social cliques and behavior patterns of selected groups, such as gangs.

Summary offenses Least serious British law violations, involving petty criminal infractions.

Team policing Investigative teams of police officers, detectives, and other personnel assigned to a particular community area to work in a coordinated way in solving crimes.

Tennessee v. Garner **(1985)** Case involving the shooting and death of a teenager by police; landmark decision governing the use of deadly force against fleeing felons; standard is not to use deadly force unless officer's life is threatened or someone else's life is threatened by a fleeing felon.

Thief-takers Persons who were "fleet of foot" in early England; selected to pursue and apprehend fleeing criminals for a fee.

Total quality management (TQM) Similar to participative management and quality control, "management by objectives," and several other civilian industry managerial concepts; objective is to involve as many subordinates in decision making as possible to improve the meaningfulness of their work roles.

Totality of circumstances Exception to exclusionary rule, in which officers may make warrantless searches of property and seizures of illegal contraband on the basis of the entire set of suspicious circumstances, known as the "totality of circumstances."

Traffic Enforcement and Management System (TEAMS) Principles include (1) continuous training; (2) genuine employee participation throughout the organization; (3) changing the role of the manager or sergeant from "cop" to "facilitator"; and (4) the encouragement of risk taking. An evaluation of this program suggests favorable results in improving staff morale, work satisfaction, and job effectiveness.

Uniform Crime Reports Document published annually by the FBI detailing reported crimes in the United States by state, county, and other variables.

United Kingdom Model A rigorous recruitment and training program used in England and Wales for the purpose of police officer selection and training.

Urbanization Increasing population density in urban centers; the spread of industry and business in small geographical areas.

Urban renewal Destruction of older buildings and run-down properties and the construction of modern buildings, businesses, and residences to replace them.

August Vollmer Chief of Police of Berkeley, California, who professionalized policing by recommending educational training for police officers; relied heavily on academic specialists in various forensics areas; pioneered informal academic regimen of police training, including investigative techniques, photography, fingerprinting, and anatomy, among other academic subject areas.

Volunteerism Performing tasks willingly, without payment; propensity of citizens to become actively involved in various auxiliary police functions, such as Neighborhood Watch.

Warrantless searches and seizures Any search of a person or a person's car and/or premises that is not preceded by the issuing of a valid search warrant by a judge based on probable cause and obtained under oath.

Watchmen Citizens in early England who were paid to observe in their neighborhoods for possible criminal activity.

Wickersham Commission Commission established in 1929 to investigate police agencies and the state of training and education among police officers; generally critical of contemporary methods of police organization and operation.

O.W. Wilson A former police chief in Wichita, Kansas, and Chicago, Illinois; became first dean of the School of Criminology at the University of California-Berkeley, in 1950; was successful in centralizing police administration and creating command decision making not only in Berkeley, but in many other cities during the 1950s and 1960s.

References

Adamson, Patrick B.
    1991   "Some Comments on the Origin of the Police." *Police Studies* **14**:1–2.

Adamson, Raymond S.
    1987   "Police Force Communication: Member Perceptions." *Canadian Police College Journal* **11**:233–272.

Adamson, Raymond S., and Gene Descza
    1990   "Police Force Communications: Managing Meaning on the Firing Line." *Canadian Police College Journal* **14**:155–171.

The Advocate
    1991   "How Bad Are Relations between Gays and the LAPD?" May 7, p. 106.

Agopian, Michael W.
    1989   "Targeting Juvenile Gang Offenders for Community Service." *Community Alternatives: International Journal of Family Care* **1**:9–108.

Agyapong, Owusu-Ansah
    1987   "Professionalism and the Police: A Critical Look." Unpublished paper presented at the annual meeting of the Academy of Criminal Justice Sciences, St. Louis, MO.

Ahire, Philip Terdoo
    1991   *Imperial Policing: The Emergence and Role of the Police in Colonial Nigeria 1860–1960.* Milton Keynes, UK: Open University Press.

Alderson, John
    1985   *Law and Disorder.* London, UK: Hamish Hamilton.

Alemika, Etannibi E.O.
    1988   "Policing and Perceptions of Police in Nigeria." *Police Studies* **11**:161–176.

Alexander, David A., George Innes, and Barrie L. Irving
    1991   *Health, Stress, and Policing: A Study in Grampian Police.* London: The Police Foundation.

Allen, N.H.
　1980　*Homicide: Perspective on Prevention.* New York: Human Sciences Press.

Allen, Ronald J.
　1991　"Supreme Court Review." *Journal of Criminal Law and Criminology* **81**:727–1001.

Alpert, Geoffrey P., and Roger G. Dunham
　1986　"Community Policing." *Journal of Police Science and Administration* **14**:212–222.

Alter, Jonathan
　1993　"There's a War on at Home." *Newsweek,* September 27, p. 42.

Amandes, Richard B.
　1979　"Hire a Gang Leader: A Delinquency Prevention Program That Works." *Juvenile and Family Court Journal* **30**:37–40.

American Bar Foundation
　1957　*American Bar Foundation Survey of Criminal Justice: Pilot Project Reports, 7 vols.* Madison, WI: The University of Wisconsin, Madison Law School. Mimeographed.

American Civil Liberties Union of Southern California
　1992　*The Call for Change Goes Unanswered.* Los Angeles: American Civil Liberties Union of Southern California.

American Correctional Association
　1996　*ACA Directory.* Laurel, MD: American Correctional Association.

Anderson, Dennis R., and Donald F. Schoen
　1985　"Diversion Programs: Effect of Stigmatization on Juvenile Status Offenders." *Juvenile and Family Court Journal* **36**:13–25.

Anechiarico, Frank
　1984　"Suing the Philadelphia Police: The Case for an Institutional Approach." *Law and Policy* **6**:231–250.

Applegate, Jane
　1993　"Employer Helps Homeless Conquer Their Despair." *Los Angeles Times,* February 19, p. D3.

A.R.A. Consultants
　1985　*Final Report on the Evaluation of the Toronto Mini-Station Pilot Project.* Ottawa, CAN: Ministry of the Solicitor General of Canada.

Aromaa, Kauko
　1989　"Violent Encounters in Police Work." Unpublished paper presented at the annual meeting of the American Society of Criminology, November, Reno, NV.

Arrigona, Nancy, and Tony Fabelo
　1987　*A Case Study of Juvenile Probation in Texas.* Austin, TX: Criminal Justice Policy Council.

Arthur, John, and Charles E. Case
　1994　"Race, Class and Support for Police Use of Force." *Crime, Law and Social Change* **2**:167–182.

Assefa, H., and P. Wahrhaftig
　1988　*Extremist Groups and Conflict Resolution: The MOVE (The Movement) Crisis in Philadelphia.* New York: Praeger.

Associated Press
　1993b　"New Survey Charts High Cost of Treating Young Gunfire Victims." *Los Angeles Times,* November 26, p. A32.

Associated Press
　1993a　"U.S. War on Drugs Cost $23.7 Billion in '91." *The San Diego Union-Tribune,* December 2, p. A11.

Associated Press
　　1994　"Japanese Student Shot in Denver by Carjacker." *Los Angeles Times,* April 16, p. A31.
Association Internationale de Droit Penale
　　1988　"The Legal and Practical Problems Posed by the Difference between Criminal Law and Administrative Penal Law." *Revue Internationale de Droit Penale* **59**:1–539.
Austin, David, and Marshall, James
　　1992　"Community Policing: The Critical Partnership." *Sourcebook Community Oriented Policing: An Alternative Strategy.* New York: International City Managers Association.
Austin, W. Timothy
　　1988　"Fieldnotes on the Vigilante Movement in Mindanao: A Mix of Self-Help and Formal Policing Networks." *International Journal of Comparative and Applied Criminal Justice* **12**:205–217.
Avins, Alfred
　　1970　"Equal Protection against Unnecessary Police Violence and the Original Understanding of the Fourteenth Amendment: A Comment." *Buffalo Law Review* **19**:599–608.
Bailey, Frankie
　　1987　"Managing Conflict: Law Enforcement and Social Control in Danville, Virginia, 1900–1930." Unpublished paper presented at the annual meeting of the Academy of Criminal Justice Sciences, April, St. Louis, MO.
Bailey, William G.
　　1986　*Police Science, 1964–1984: A Selected, Annotated Bibliography.* New York: Garland.
Baird, S. Christopher
　　1984　*Classification of Juveniles in Corrections: A Model Systems Approach.* Washington, DC: Arthur D. Little.
Baker, James N. et al.
　　1991　"Battling the Bias." *Newsweek,* November 25, p. 25.
Balistreri, Ted
　　1990　"Implementing Community Policing in Madison." Unpublished paper presented at the annual meeting of the American Society of Criminology, November, Baltimore, MD.
Barker, Thomas
　　1986　"Peer Group Support." In *Police Deviance,* edited by Thomas Barker and David L. Carter. Cincinnati, OH: Pilgrimage Press.
Barnett, Camille Cates, and Bowers, Robert A.
　　1992　"Community Policing." *Sourcebook on Community-Oriented Policing: An Alternative Strategy.* Washington, DC: International City Management Association.
Barone, Michael
　　1994　"Time to Shatter the Crime Culture." *U.S. News & World Report,* January 17, p. 42.
Bayley, David H.
　　1976　"Learning about Crime—The Japanese Experience." *Public Interest* **44**:55–68.
Bayley, David H.
　　1979　"Police Function, Structure, and Control in Western Europe and North America: Comparative and Historical Studies." In *Crime and Justice: An Annual Review of Research,* edited by Norval Morris and Michael Tonry. Chicago: University of Chicago Press.
Bayley, David H.
　　1986　"The Tactical Choices of Police Patrol Officers." *Journal of Criminal Justice* **14**:329–348.

Bayley, David H.
  1991a *Forces of Order: Policing Modern Japan.* Berkeley: University of California Press.
Bayley, David H.
  1991b *Managing the Future: Prospective Issues in Canadian Policing.* Ottawa, CAN: Solicitor General of Canada.
Beattie, Cheryl-Ann
  1992 "Conflicts between Democratic Accountability, Law and Bureaucracy: Consequences for Civilian Review." Unpublished paper presented at the annual meeting of the American Society of Criminology, November, New Orleans, LA.
Beatty, Brian P.
  1993 Personal correspondence with Project Coordinator, City of Savannah, Georgia.
Beck, Melinda
  1993 "The Gray Nineties." *Newsweek,* October 4, p. 65.
Beck, Melinda, Peter Katel, Vern E. Smith, and Ginny Carroll
  1993 "In a State of Terror." *Newsweek,* September 27, pp. 40–41.
Bell, D., and K. Lang
  1985 "The Intake Dispositions of Juvenile Offenders." *Journal of Research on Crime and Delinquency* **22**:309–328.
Benda, Brent B.
  1987 "Comparison of Rates of Recidivism among Status Offenders and Delinquents." *Adolescence* **22**:445–458.
Bennett, Richard R., and Sandra Baxter
  1985 "Police and Community Participation in Anti-Crime Programs." In *Police Management Today: Issues and Case Studies,* edited by James J. Fyfe. Washington, DC: International City Management Association.
Bennett, Richard R., and R. Bruce Wiegand
  1990 "Victimization and the Police: Exploring the Determinants of Crime Reporting in a Developing Nation." Unpublished paper presented at the annual meeting of the American Society of Criminology, March, Baltimore, MD.
Bennett, Trevor, ed.
  1983 *The Future of Policing: Papers Presented to the 15th Cropwood Round-Table Conference, December, 1982,* Cropwood Conference Series, no. 15. Cambridge, UK: University of Cambridge, Institute of Criminology.
Bennett, Trevor
  1989 *Contact Patrols in Birmingham and London: An Evaluation of a Fear Reducing Strategy.* Cambridge, UK: University of Cambridge, Institute of Criminology.
Bennett, Trevor
  1990 "Getting Back in Touch." *Policing* **6**:510–522.
Bennett, Trevor
  1991 "The Effectiveness of a Police-initiated Fear-reducing Strategy." *British Journal of Criminology* **31**:1–14.
Bennett, Wayne W., and Karen M. Hess
  1992 *Management and Supervision in Law Enforcement.* St. Paul, MN: West Publishing Company.
Benyon, Helen
  1986 "The Ideal Civic Condition, Part 2." *Criminal Law Review,* October, pp. 647–659.
Benyon, John
  1984 *Scarman and After: Essays Reflecting on Lord Scarman's Report, the Riots and Their Aftermath.* Oxford, UK: Pergamon.
Berkley, George E.
  1969 *The Democratic Policeman.* Boston: Beacon Press.

Bernsen, Rod
    1988   "Meeting the Press." *American Journal of Police* **7**.

Betsalel, Kenneth Aaron
    1990   "Police Leadership and the Reconciliation of Police-Minority Relations." *American Journal of Police* **9**:63–77.

Billiter, Bill
    1993a   "Asian-Americans Organize AWARE." *Los Angeles Times,* September 29, p. B4.

Billiter, Bill
    1993b   "Retired Seniors Sought for Unpaid Police Positions." *Los Angeles Times,* May 4, p. B12.

Binder, Arnold, and Gilbert Geis
    1984   "Ad Populum Argumentation in Criminology: Juvenile Diversion as Rhetoric." *Crime and Delinquency* **30**:309–333.

Birmingham Civil Rights Institute
    1990   Brochure. Birmingham, AL: Birmingham Civil Rights Institute.

Bittner, Egon
    1985   "The Capacity to Use Force as the Core of the Police Role." In *Moral Issues in Police Work,* edited by Frederick A. Elliston and Michael Feldberg. Totowa, NJ: Rowman and Allanheld.

Black, Henry Campbell
    1990   *Black's Law Dictionary.* St. Paul, MN: West Publishing Company.

Blackmore, John, Marci Brown, and Barry Krisberg
    1988   *Juvenile Justice Reform: The Bellwether States.* Ann Arbor: University of Michigan Press.

Block, Carolyn R.
    1985   "Race/Ethnicity and Patterns of Chicago Homicide 1965 to 1981." *Crime and Delinquency* **31**:104–116.

Block, Carole R., and Richard Block
    1993   *Street Gang Crime in Chicago.* Washington, DC: U.S. National Institute of Justice.

Bond, Kevin
    1984   "The Case for a National Force." *Policing* 4:293–308.

Blustein, Jeffrey
    1983   "On the Doctrine of *Parens Patriae:* Fiduciary Obligations and State Power." *Criminal Justice Ethics* **2**:39–47.

Bossard, Andre
    1988   "Interpol and Law Enforcement: Response to Transnational Crime." *Police Studies* **11**:177–182.

Boucher, Geoff
    1993   "Covered by Blanket Policy." *Los Angeles Times,* July 14, pp. B1, B7.

Bourne, Dennis
    1991   "Do We Need Bramshill?" *Policing* **7**:258–270.

Bouza, Anthony V.
    1990   *The Police Mystique: An Insider's Look at Cops, Crime, and the Criminal Justice System.* New York. Plenum Press.

Bouza, Anthony V.
    1993   *How to Stop Crime.* New York: Plenum.

Boxall, Bettina
    1993   "Lesbians Shed 'Invisible Gays' Label." *Los Angeles Times,* December 27, pp. A3, A26.

Boxall, Bettina, and Torres, Vicki
　1993　"LAPD Settles Suit Claiming Anti-Gay Bias." *Los Angeles Times,* February 11, pp. A1, A32.
Bradel, Don and Rodney Witt
　1993　*Evaluation of a Community Outreach Program (ACOP) Phase II: Final Report.* St. Paul, MN: St. Paul Police Department and St. Paul Public Housing Agency.
Braiden, Chris
　1986　*Bank Robberies and Stolen Bikes: Thoughts of a Street Cop.* Ottawa, CAN: Ministry of the Solicitor General of Canada.
Brewer, John D.
　1991　"Policing in Divided Societies: Theorising a Type of Policing." *Policing and Society* **1**:179–191.
Britz, Marjie T., and Dennis M. Payne
　1994　"Policy Implications for Law Enforcement Pursuit Driving." *American Journal of Police* **13**:113–142.
Brogden, Mike, Tony Jefferson, and Sandra Walklate
　1988　*Introducing Policework.* London, UK: Unwin Hyman.
Brookhiser, Richard
　1993　"The Melting Pot Is Still Simmering." *Time,* March 1, p. 72.
Brown, B.J.
　1986　"Structural Reform in Municipal Policing." *Canadian Police College Journal* **10**:75–85.
Brown, David, and Susan Iles
　1985　*Community Constables: A Study of Policing Initiative.* Research and Planning Unit Paper 30. London, UK: Home Office.
Brown, Gary, and Peart E. Leo
　1981　"Police Chiefs: An Endangered Species." *Western Cities Magazine,* pp. 32–35.
Brown, Lee P.
　1971　"Evaluation of Police-Community Relations Programs." Unpublished doctoral dissertation, University of Michigan. Ann Arbor: University Microfilms International.
Brown, Lee P.
　1984　"A Police Department and Its Values." *Police Chief* **51**:24–25.
Brown, Lee P.
　1989a　"Community Policing: A Practical Guide for Police Officials." *NIJ Reports.*
Brown, Lee P.
　1989b　*Community Policing: A Practical Guide for Police Officials.* Washington, DC: U.S. Department of Justice, Office of Justice Programs.
Brown, Lee P.
　1991a　"'P-CR-Typology' Orientation of Police-Community Relations Programs." *The Police Chief* **28**.
Brown, Lee P.
　1991b　"Special Focus: Policing in the '90s." *Police Chief* **58**:20–47.
Brown, Lee P.
　1992　"Community Policing: A Partnership With Promise." *The Police Chief* **59**:45–48.
Brown, Lee P., and Mary Ann Wycoff
　1987　"Policing Houston: Reducing Fear and Improving Service." *Crime and Delinquency* **33**:71–89.
Brown, M. Craig, and Barbara D. Warner
　1992　"Immigrants, Urban Politics, and Policing in 1900." *American Sociological Review* **57**:293–305.

Brownstein, Ronald
    1993   "GOP Wins Governorship in N.J., Virginia, Plus N.Y. Mayoral Race." *Los Angeles Times*, November 3, p. A18.

Buckley, Leslie Brian
    1991   "Attitudes toward Higher Education among Mid-Career Police Officers." *Canadian Police College Journal* **15**:257–273.

Bunyard, Robert S.
    1988   "On British Police Higher Training." *C.J. International* **4**:27–28.

Bureau of Justice Statistics
    1992   *State and Local Police Departments, 1990.* Washington, DC: U.S. Department of Justice.

Bureau of Justice Statistics
    1993   *Using NICBRS Data to Analyze Violent Crime.* Washington, DC: U.S. Department of Justice.

Burgreen, Bob
    1991   Letter and handout material, February 26. San Diego: San Diego Police Department.

Burton, Velmer S., Jr., James Frank, Robert H. Langworthy, and Troy A. Barker
    1993   "The Prescribed Roles of Police in a Free Society: Analyzing State Legal Codes." *Justice Quarterly* **10**:683–695.

Business Week
    1988   "Homelessness: The Policy Failure Haunting America," **123**:132–136.

Butler, T.
    1985   "Objectives and Accountability in Policing." *Policing* **1**:174–186.

Cairns, Kathleen
    1993   "L.B. Panelists Seek Answers to Homeless Economics." *Long Beach Press-Telegram*, June 24, p. A6.

Callahan, Charles M., Frederick P. Rivara and James A. Farrow
    1993   "Youth in Detention and Handguns." *Journal of Adolescent Health* **14**:350–355.

Cameron, Neil
    1990   "The Police and Crime Control: Effectiveness, Community Policing, and Legal Change." *Criminal Law Forum: An International Journal* **1**:477–512.

Canada Law Reform Commission
    1985   *Post-Seizure Procedures.* Ottawa, CAN: Canada Law Reform Commission.

Canada Solicitor General's Select Committee on Police Pursuits
    1985 *Report.* Toronto, CAN: Solicitor General for Ontario.

Caplan, Gerald M, ed.
    1983   *Abscam Ethics: Moral Issues and Deception in Law Enforcement.* Washington, DC: Police Foundation.

Carpenter, G.J.
    1989   *Police Officer Performance Evaluation Systems.* Ottawa, CAN: Canadian Police College.

Carrier, John
    1988   *The Campaign for the Employment of Women as Police Officers.* Aldershot, UK: Avebury.

Carriere, Kevin D.
    1987   "Crime Stoppers Critically Considered." *Canadian Criminology Forum* **8**:104–115.

Carriere, Kevin D., and Richard V. Ericson
    1989   *Crime Stoppers: A Study in the Organization of Community Policing.* Toronto, CAN: Centre of Criminology, University of Toronto.

Carter, David L.
　1986　"A Taxonomy of Prejudice and Discrimination by Police Officers." In *Police Deviance*, edited by Thomas Barker and David L. Carter. Cincinnati, OH: Pilgrimage Press.

Cashmore, Ellis, and Eugene McLaughlin, eds.
　1991　*Out of Order? Policing Black People.* New York: Routledge.

Champion, Dean J.
　1994　*Measuring Offender Risk.* Westport, CT: Greenwood Press.

Champion, Dean J., and G. Larry Mays
　1991　*Juvenile Transfer Hearings: Some Trends and Implications for Criminal Justice.* New York: Praeger Publishers.

Chappell, Duncan, and Linda P. Graham
　1985　*Police Use of Deadly Force: Canadian Perspectives.* Toronto, CAN: Center of Criminology, University of Toronto.

Chen, Mark M.C.
　1990　"Scientific Approach to Managing Policing: Systematic Public Needs Oriented Planning." Unpublished paper presented at the annual meeting of the American Society of Criminology, November, Baltimore, MD.

Chesney-Lind, Meda
　1993　"Girls, Gangs and Violence: Anatomy of a Backlash." *Humanity and Society* **17**:321–344.

Chevigny, Paul G.
　1990　"Police Deadly Force as Social Control: Jamaica, Argentina, and Brazil." *Criminal Law Forum: An International Journal* **1**:389–426.

Cizanckas, Victor I.
　1971　"Uniform Experiment and Organization Development." *Police* **16**:45–49.

Clairmont, Donald
　1990　*To the Forefront: Community-Based Zone Policing in Halifax.* Ottawa, CAN: Canadian Police College.

Clarke, Ronald V., and Mike Hough
　1984　*Crime and Police Effectiveness.* Home Office Research Study No. 79. London, UK: Her Majesty's Stationery Office.

Cockburn, Alexander
　1993　"The Rambos Still Run Drug Policy." *Los Angeles Times,* October 27, p. B7.

Cohen, Fred
　1972　"Police Perjury: An Interview with Martin Garbess." *Criminal Law Bulletin* **8**:365–375.

Cohen, Howard
　1985　"A Dilemma for Discretion." In *Police Ethics: Hard Choices for Law Enforcement*, edited by William C. Heffernan and Timothy Stroup. New York: John Jay Press.

Cohen, Howard S., and Michael Feldberg
　1991　*Power and Restraint: The Moral Dimension of Police Work.* New York: Praeger.

Cole, Don, ed.
　1991　*The Encyclopedic Dictionary of Economics,* 4th ed. Los Angeles: The Dushkin Publishing Group.

Colley, Lori L., and Robert G. Culbertson
　1988　"Status Offender Legislation and the Courts." *Journal of Offender Counseling, Services and Rehabilitation* **12**:41–56.

Collins, James J. et al.
　1993　*Law Enforcement Policies and Practices Regarding Missing Children and Homeless Youth.* Washington, DC: U.S. Office of Juvenile Justice and Delinquency Prevention.

Columbia (SC), City
   n.d. *Police Homeowner Loan Program.* Undated publication.

Commentary
   1968 "Effect of *Mapp v. Ohio* on Police Search and Seizure Practices in Narcotics Cases." *Columbia Journal of Law and Social Problems* **4**:94.

Connor, Christina
   1993 "Loan Program a Finalist for National Award." *The Charlotte Observer,* July 20, p. A4.

Conner, G.
   1986 "Use of Force Continuum." *Law and Order* **34**:18–19, 60.

Conrad, John P.
   1987 "Dealing with Crime on the Streets." In *Handbook on Crime and Delinquency Prevention,* edited by Elmer H. Johnson. Westport, CT: Greenwood Press.

Copeland, Arthur R.
   1986 "Police Shootings: The Metropolitan Dade County Experience from 1956 to 1982." *American Journal of Forensic Medicine and Pathology* **7**:39–45.

Cordner, Gary W., and Donna C. Hale, eds.
   1992 *What Works in Policing? Operations and Administration Examined.* Cincinnati, OH: Anderson Publishing Company.

Corns, Christopher
   1988 "Policing and Social Change." *Australian and New Zealand Journal of Sociology* **24**:32–46.

Correction News
   1993 "All Staff to Get TB Tests: Hepatitis B Vaccine Available to At-Risk Employees." September–December, p. 1.

Corrections Compendium
   1991 "Teenagers Victims of Violent Crime More Often than Adults," **16**.

Corrections Compendium
   1992a "R.O.C.K.: Reaching Out, Convicts and Kids," **17**.

Corrections Compendium
   1992b "Runaways Flee Severe Problems," **17**.

Corwin, Miles
   1993a "Guns for Hire." *Los Angeles Times Magazine,* November 28, pp. 24, 26, 28, 58, 59.

Corwin, Miles
   1993b "LAPD Graduates Schooled by Case." *Los Angeles Times,* April 17, pp. A32–33.

Cory, Bruce
   1979 "Minority Police: Tramping through a Racial Minefield." *Police Magazine,* March.

Cose, Ellis
   1993 "Larger than Life." *Newsweek,* April 26, pp. 30–31.

Coulter, Jim, Susan Miller, and Martin Walker
   1984 *State of Siege: Politics and Policing the Coalfields: Miner's Strike 1984.* London, UK: Canary Press.

Council of Europe
   1984 *The Criminal Record and Rehabilitation of Convicted Persons.* Strasbourg, FR: Council of Europe.

Couper, David C., and Sabine H. Lobitz
   1991 *Quality Policing: The Madison Experience.* Washington, DC: Police Executive Research Forum.

Cox, Stephen M., and James Frank
   1992 "The Influence of Neighborhood Context and Method of Entry on Individual Styles of Policing." *American Journal of Police* **11**:1–11.

Craen, Andre
    1991   "Law Enforcement in Europe after 1992." *Police Studies* **14**:72–75.

Crank, John P.
    1990   "The Influence of Environmental and Organizational Factors on Police Style in Urban Environments." *Journal of Research in Crime and Delinquency* **27**:166–189.

Crime Control Digest
    1989   "Honolulu Pays $100,000 to Settle Police Brutality 'Toad Bobbing' Urination Suit." January, pp. 9–10.

Criminal Justice Newsletter
    1988   "Juvenile Justice." *Criminal Justice Newsletter* **19**:1–8.

Crocker, Brenda D.
    1981   "When Cops are Robbers: Municipal Liability for Police Misconduct under Section 1983 and Bivens." *University of Richmond Law Review* **15**:295–317.

Croft, John
    1983   "Criminological Research in Great Britain, with a Note on the Council in Europe." In *Crime and Justice: An Annual Review of Research,* edited by Michael Tonry and Norval Morris. Chicago: University of Chicago Press.

Cryderman, Brian K., and Chris N. O'Toole
    1986   *Police, Race, and Ethnicity: A Guide for Law Enforcement Officers.* Toronto, CAN: Center of Criminology, University of Toronto.

Cummings, Scott, and Daniel J. Monti
    1993   *Gangs: The Origins and Impact of Contemporary Youth Gangs in the United States.* Series on Urban Public Policy. Albany: State University of New York Press.

Curran, Daniel J.
    1984   "The Myth of a 'New' Female Delinquent." *Crime and Delinquency* **30**:386–399.

Dahl, Jonathan
    1991   "Up to 20% of Homeless People Carry AIDS Virus, Says New Report by CDC." *The Wall Street Journal,* November 12, p. B4.

Dale, Michael J.
    1988   "Detaining Juveniles in Adult Jails and Lockups: An Analysis of Rights and Liabilities." *American Jails* (Spring), pp. 46–50.

Dallas Times-Herald
    1990   "Trial Is Test of Santa Monica's Empathy towards Homeless," June 20, p. A8.

Dane, N.N., Jr.
    1989   *Police and Fire Consolidation: What Is Concept Viability in Urban California by 1999?* Sacramento, CA: Commission on Peace Officer Standards and Training.

Dantzker, Mark
    1987   "Police Education—Perceptions: Pro and Con." St. Louis, MO. Unpublished paper presented at the annual meeting of the Academy of Criminal Justice Sciences, March, St. Louis, MO.

Dantzker, Mark
    1995   *Understanding Today's Police.* Englewood Cliffs, NJ: Prentice Hall.

Das, Dilip K.
    1986   "Police and Community in America: Influences from Across the Atlantic." *Police Studies* **9**:138–147.

Database
    1993   *U.S. News & World Report,* November 22, p. 11.

Datesman, Susan K., and Mikel Aickin
    1985   "Offense Specialization and Escalation among Status Offenders." *Journal of Criminal Law and Criminology* **75**:1246–1275.

Davidson, William S., et al.
   1987   "Diversion of Juvenile Offenders: An Experimental Comparison." *Journal of Consulting and Clinical Psychology* **55**:68–75.

Davis, Kenneth C.
   1969   *Discretionary Justice: A Preliminary Inquiry.* Baton Rouge: Louisiana State University Press.

Dawidoff, Robert
   1993   "Gays and Lesbians Need a Real Movement." *Los Angeles Times,* October 12, p. B9.

DeAngelo, Andrew J.
   1988   "Diversion Programs in the Juvenile Justice System: An Alternative Method of Treatment for Juvenile Offenders." *Juvenile and Family Court Journal* **39**:21–28.

Del Buono, Vincent M.
   1986   "Toward a New Criminal Code for Canada." *Criminal Law Quarterly* **28**:370–389.

Deming, Romaine, and Galan Janeksela
   1976   *The Theory of Conflict Management for Criminal Justice.* Boston, MA: Northeastern University Press.

Deszca, Gene
   1988   "The Communication of Ideology in Police Forces." *Canadian Police College Journal* **12**:240–268.

DeWitt, Charles B.
   1992   *Community Policing in Seattle: A Model Partnership Between Citizens and Police.* Washington, DC: U.S. Department of Justice.

Dilworth, D., ed.
   1976   *The Blue and the Brass: American Policing 1890–1910.* Gaithersburg, MD: International Association of Chiefs of Police.

Ditton, J.
   1977   "Alibis and Aliases: Some Notes on the 'Motives' of Fiddling Bread Salesmen." *Sociology* **4**:233–255.

Dombrink, John
   1991   "The Touchables: Vice and Police Corruption in the 1980s." In *Police Deviance 2nd ed.,* edited by Thomas Barker and David L. Carter. Cincinnati, OH: Anderson Publishing.

Dotson, L.L.
   1993   "LAPD Training Costs Up in Response to Call for New Officers." *Los Angeles Times,* December 26, p. M6.

Downes, David, and Tony Ward
   1986   *Democratic Policing: Towards a Labour Party Policy on Police Accountability.* London, UK: Labour Campaign for Criminal Justice.

Doyle, James F.
   1985   "Police Discretion: Legality and Morality." In *Police Ethics: Hard Choices in Law Enforcement,* edited by William C. Heffernan and Timothy Stroup. New York: John Jay Press.

Duffy, Brian
   1993   "The State of Rage." *U.S. News & World Report,* October 11.

Dunn, Allyson
   1986   "Juvenile Court Records: Confidentiality vs. the Public's Right to Know." *American Criminal Law Review* **23**:379–398.

Dunham, Roger C., and Geoffrey P. Alpert
   1988   "Neighborhood Differences in Attitudes toward Policing: Evidence for a Mixed-Strategy Model of Policing in a Multi-Ethnic Setting." *Journal of Criminal Law and Criminology* **79**:504–523.

Dwyer, Sandy
   1991   "Current LAPD Officer Comes Out." *Vanguard,* June 14, p. 1.

Earnest, Leslie
   1993   "Gay Ban Stands or No Explorers, Laguna Warned." *Los Angeles Times,* September 29, pp. A1, A6.

Eaton, William J.
   1993a   "Senate Supports Life Terms for '3-Time Losers.'" *Los Angeles Times,* November 9, p. A3.

Eaton, William J.
   1993b   "U.S. Files First Suit under Disabilities Act in Illinois." *Los Angeles Times,* December 29, p. A16.

Eaton, William J.
   1993c   "Virtual Ban on Handguns for Juveniles OKd." *Los Angeles Times,* November 10, p. A3.

Eaton, William J.
   1993d   "U.S. Poverty Total Rises to 3-Decade High." *Los Angeles Times,* March 23, p. A19.

Eck, John E., and William Spelman
   1987   "Who Ya Gonna Call? The Police as Problem-Busters." *Crime and Delinquency* **33**:31–52.

Edwards, Don
   1993   "Federal Courts Are Casualties in War on Drugs." *Los Angeles Times,* October 25, p. F13.

Eisenberg, Justin
   1993   "Burnout: The Patrol Officer's Perspective." *The Journal of California Law Enforcement* **27**.

Einstadter, W.J.
   1984   "Citizen Patrols: Prevention or Control?" *Crime and Social Justice* **21**:200–221.

Elmsley, Clive
   1991   *The English Police: A Political and Social History.* New York: St. Martin's Press.

Elson, John
   1993   "The Great Migration." *Time,* June 6, p. 41.

Encyclopedic Dictionary of Sociology
   1991   Guilford, CT: Dushkin Publishing Company.

Enter, Jack E.
   1991   "Police Administration in the Future: Demographic Influences as They Relate to Management of the Internal and External Environment." *American Journal of Police* **10**:65–81.

Eskridge, Chris
   1989   "Correctional Practices in Japan." *Journal of Offender Counseling, Services, and Rehabilitation* **14**:5–23.

Ewin, R.E.
   1990   "Loyalty: The Police." *Criminal Justice Ethics* **9**:3–15.

Fagan, Jeffrey A.
   1988   *The Social Organization of Drug Use and Drug Dealing Among Urban Gangs.* New York: John Jay College of Criminal Justice.

Fagan, Michael M.
   1985   "How Police Officers Perceive Their Field Training Officer." *Journal of Police Science and Administration* **13**:138–151.

Fair, Frank, and Wayland D. Pilcher
　1991　"Morality on the Line: The Role of Ethics in Police Decision Making." *American Journal of Police* **10**:23–38.

Fairchild, Erika S.
　1989　"National Culture and Police Organization in Germany and the United States." *Public Administration Review,* October, pp. 454–462.

Falcone, David L.
　1994　"Police Pursuits and Officer Attitudes: Myths and Realities." *American Journal of Police* **13**:143–155.

Farish, Steve
　1990　"Law Enforcement Exploring." *FBI Law Enforcement Bulletin,* May, pp. 20–23.

Farnworth, Margaret
　1984　"Male-Female Differences in Delinquency in a Minority-Group Sample." *Journal of Research in Crime and Delinquency* **21**:191–212.

Farnworth, Margaret, Charles E. Frazier, and Anita R. Neuberger
　1988　"Orientations to Juvenile Justice: Exploratory Notes from a Statewide Survey of Juvenile Justice Decisionmakers." *Journal of Criminal Justice* **16**:477–491.

Farrell, Michael J.
　1986　*C.P.O.P. Community Patrol Officer Program.* New York: Vera Institute of Justice.

Feldman, Paul
　1993　"U.S. Giving Seized Drug Houses to L.A." *Los Angeles Times,* December 22, p. A36.

Feldman, Paul, and Leslie Berger
　1993　"Drug Czar Sells New Strategy to L.A. Audiences." *Los Angeles Times,* October 24, p. A38.

Felkenes, George T., and Paul M. Whisenand
　1972　*Police Patrol Operations: Basic Car Plan.* New York: McCutchan Publishing Corporation.

Ferrell, Jeff
　1995　"Urban Graffiti: Crime, Control and Resistance." *Youth and Society* **27**:73–92.

Fielding, Nigel G.
　1988　*Joining Forces: Police Training, Socialization, and Occupational Experience.* London and New York: Routledge.

Findley, Kenneth W., and Robert W. Taylor
　1990　"Re-Thinking Neighborhood Policing." *Journal of Contemporary Criminal Justice* **6**:70–78.

Fine, Bob and Robert Millar, eds.
　1985　*Policing the Miner's Strike.* London, UK: Lawrence & Wishart.

Fine, Kerry Kinney
　1984　*Alternative Dispute Resolution Programs for Juveniles.* St. Paul: Minnesota House Research Department.

Finn, Peter E.
　1988　*Street People.* Washington, DC: U.S. Department of Justice.

Finn, Peter E., and Walter J. De Cujir
　1988　"Law Enforcement and the Social Service System." *FBI Law Enforcement Bulletin,* July.

Finn, Peter, and Daniel McGillis
　1990　"Public Safety at the State Level: A Survey of Major Services." *Journal of Police Science and Administration* **17**:133–146.

Finn, Peter E., and Monique Sullivan
　1988　"Police Respond to Special Populations." *NIJ Reports,* May/June.

Fishkin, Gerald L.
    1987   *Police Burnout: Signs, Symptoms, and Solutions.* Gardena, CA: Harcourt Publications.
Fishman, Gideon, and Simon Dinitz
    1989   "Japan: A Country with Safe Streets." In *Advances in Criminological Theory* (Vol. I), edited by William S. Laufer and Freda Adler. New Brunswick, NJ: Transaction Books.
Fitch, Bob
    1992   *The Assassination of New York.* New York: Routledge.
Flanagan, Timothy J., and Kathleen Maguire
    1990   *Sourcebook of Criminal Justice Statistics, 1990.* Albany: Hindelang Criminal Justice Research Center.
Fleissner, Dan et al.
    1991   *Community Policing in Seattle: A Descriptive Study of the South Seattle Crime Reduction Project.* Seattle, WA: Prepared for the National Institute of Justice.
Fooner, Michael
    1973   *Interpol: The Inside Story of the International Crime-Fighting Organization.* Chicago: Henry Regnery.
Foscarinis, Maria, and Jim Scheibel
    1993   "Homelessness Is the Foe, Not the Homeless." *Los Angeles Times,* December 16, p. B7.
Fosdick, Raymond B.
    1920   *American Police Systems.* New York: Macmillan.
Fraser, Craig B.
    1989   "The Police, Values, and Ethics." Unpublished paper presented at the annual meeting of the American Society of Criminology, November, Reno, NV.
Frazier, Charles E., and Donna M. Bishop
    1985   "The Pretrial Detention of Juveniles and Its Impact on Case Dispositions." *Journal of Criminal Law and Criminology* **76**:1132–1152.
Freeman, John C.
    1987   "England." In *Major Criminal Justice Systems: A Contemporary Survey* (2nd ed.), edited by George F. Cole, Stanislaw J. Frankowski, and Marc G. Gertz. Beverly Hills, CA: Sage.
Friedman, Ruth
    1988   "Municipal Liability for Police Misconduct: Must Victims Now Prove Intent?" *Yale Law Journal* **97**:448–465.
Friedmann, Robert R.
    1992   "Community Policing: From Officer Smiley to Interagency Cooperation." Unpublished paper presented at the annual meeting of the American Society of Criminology, November, New Orleans, LA.
Fritz, Noah
    1990   "Community-Oriented Policing and Beat Integrity." Unpublished paper presented at the annual meeting of the Academy of Criminal Justice Sciences, March, Denver.
Fu, Hualing
    1990   "Patrol Police: A Recent Development in the People's Republic of China." *Police Studies* **13**:111–117.
Fuller, John R., and William M. Norton
    1993   "Juvenile Diversion: The Impact of Program Philosophy on Net Widening." *Journal of Crime and Justice* **16**:29–45.
Fyfe, James J.
    1985   "Reviewing Citizens' Complaints against the Police." In *Police Management Today: Issues and Case Studies,* edited by James J. Fyfe. Washington, DC: International City Management Association.

Gage, Richard
　1993　"The Supreme Court's Quick Turn." *U.S. News & World Report,* November 22, p. 11.

Galvin, G.T.
　1987　*Community Based Policing.* Sacramento, CA: California Commission on Peace Officer Standards.

Garborino, James, Janis Wilson, and A.C. Garbarino
　1986　"The Adolescent Runaway." In *Troubled Youths, Troubled Families,* edited by James Garbarino et al. Hawthorne, NY: Aldine.

Garner, Gerald
　1988　"Police News Conference." *Law and Order,* February.

Gates, Daryl L., and Diane K. Shah
　1992　*Chief: My Life in the LAPD.* New York: Bantam.

Gebbie, Amalia
　1993　*Editor and Publisher, All-in-One.* New York: Gebbie Press.

Gelsthorpe, Loraine R.
　1987　"The Differential Treatment of Males and Females in the Criminal Justice System." In *Sex, Gender and Care Work,* edited by Gordon Horobin. Aberdeen, UK: Department of Social Work, University of Aberdeen.

Geis, Gilbert, and Arnold Binder
　1990　"Non-Lethal Weapons: The Potential and the Pitfalls." *Journal of Contemporary Criminal Justice* **6**:1–43.

Geller, William A., ed.
　1991　*Local Government Police Management.* New York: International City Management Association.

George, Lenny
　1993　Interview by correspondence with Lenny George, assistant chief, uniform division, Alexandria, VA, Police Department, November 24.

Georgetown Law Journal
　1971　"Police Perjury in Narcotics 'Dropsy' Cases: A New Credibility Gap." **60**:507–523.

Gerstenzang, James, and Ronald J. Ostrow
　1993　"NAFTA Seen as Aid to Cutting Drug Flow." *Los Angeles Times,* October 26, p. A10.

Gest, Ted
　1993　"Violence and Its Terrifying Randomness." *U.S. News & World Report,* December 20, p. 14.

Gianakis, Gerasimos A.
　1992　"Appraising the Performance of Police Patrol Officers: The Florida Experience." *Journal of Criminal Justice* **20**:413–428.

Gill, M.L., and R.L. Mawby
　1990　*Special Constable: A Study of the Police Reserve.* Aldershot, UK: Gower.

Gilsinan, James F.
　1990　*Criminology and Public Policy: An Introduction.* Englewood Cliffs, NJ: Prentice Hall.

Gilsinan, James F., and James R. Valentine
　1987　"Bending Granite: Attempts to Change the Management Perspective of American Criminologists and Police Reformers." *Journal of Police Science and Administration* **15**:196–203.

Givens, Greg et al.
　1993　"A Concept to Involve Citizens in the Provision of Police Services." *American Journal of Police* **12**:1–88.

Glastris, Kukula
  1993 "The Brave New World of the Hmong." *U.S. News & World Report,* October 4, p. 49.
Gleaton, Janice
  1993 Interview, Department of Public and Assisted Housing. Washington, DC.
Goldman, John J.
  1993 "Giuliani Beats Dinkins To Be GOP N.Y. Mayor." *Los Angeles Times,* November 3, p. A18.
Goldman, Roger, and Steven Puro
  1987 "Decertification of Police: An Alternative to Traditional Remedies for Police Misconduct." *Hastings Constitutional Law Quarterly* **15**:45–80.
Goldstein, Herman
  1967 "Administrative Problems in Controlling the Exercise of Police Authority." *Journal of Criminal Law, Criminology, and Police Science* **58**:160–172.
Goldstein, Herman
  1977 *Policing a Free Society.* Cambridge, MA: Ballinger Publishing Company.
Goldstein, Herman
  1987 "Toward Community-Oriented Policing: Potential, Basic Requirements, and Threshold Questions." *Crime and Delinquency* **33**:6–30.
Goldstein, Herman
  1990 *Problem-Oriented Policing.* New York: McGraw-Hill.
Goldstein, Herman
  1993 "Confronting the Complexity of the Policing Function." In *Discretion in Criminal Justice: The Tension between Individualization and Uniformity,* edited by Lloyd E. Ohlin and Frank J. Remington. Albany, NY: SUNY Press.
Gomez-Buendia, Hernando, ed.
  1989 *Urban Crime: Global Trends and Policies.* Tokyo, Japan: United Nations University.
Gordon, Larry
  1993 "Bring Restrooms to the Street." *Los Angeles Times,* September 29, pp. A1, A16–A17.
Governing
  1993 "3BR, 2BR, and A Cop Next Door," November, pp. 42–45.
Grabosky, P.N.
  1992 "Law Enforcement and the Citizen: Non-Governmental Participants in Crime Prevention and Control." *Policing and Society* **2**:249–271.
Graf, Francis A.
  1986 "The Relationship between Social Support and Occupational Stress among Police Officers." *Journal of Police Science and Administration* **14**:178–186.
Gray, Kelsey, Mary K. Stohr-Gillmore, and Nicholas P. Lovrich
  1991 "Adapting Participatory Management for a Paramilitary Organization: The Implementation of Teams in the Washington State Patrol." *American Journal of Police* **10**:27–47.
Greenberg, Martin A.
  1990 "The Control of Police Conduct: A Key Issue for Security Executives." *Journal of Security Administration* **13**:63–72.
Greene, Jack
  1987a "Police Officer Job Satisfaction and Its Effects on Police and Community Relations." Unpublished paper presented at the annual meeting of the Academy of Criminal Justice Sciences, March, St. Louis, MO.
Greene, Jack R., ed.
  1987b Special Issue on Foot Patrol and Community Policing. *American Journal of Police* **6**:1–119.

Greene, Jack R.
   1988 "Police Perceptions of Community Policing in Philadelphia." Unpublished paper presented at the annual meeting of the American Society of Criminology, November, Chicago, IL.

Greene, Jack R., and Scott H. Decker
   1989 "Police and Community Perceptions of the Community Role in Policing: The Philadelphia Experience." *Howard Journal of Criminal Justice* **28**:105–123.

Greene, Jack R., and Stephen D. Mastrofski, eds.
   1988 *Community Policing: Rhetoric or Reality?* New York: Praeger.

Grennan, Sean A.
   1987 "Police Use of Deadly Force." Unpublished paper presented at the annual meeting of the Academy of Criminal Justice Sciences, March, St. Louis, MO.

Greenwood, Peter W., ed.
   1986 "Predictors of Chronic Behavior." In *Intervention Strategies for Chronic Juvenile Offenders: Some New Perspectives.* New York: Greenwood Press.

Greiner, John M.
   1986 *Multi-Criterion Decision Procedures and the Assessment of Police Department Performance.* Washington, DC: Urban Institute.

Grieco, Eileen Spillane
   1984 "Characteristics of a Helpful Relationship: A Study of Empathic Understanding and Positive Regard Between Runaways and Their Parents." *Adolescence* **19**:63–76.

Grisso, Thomas, Alan Tomkins, and Pamela Casey
   1988 "Psychosocial Concepts in Juvenile Law." *Law and Human Behavior* **12**:403–438.

Griswold, David
   1990 "Small Town Police: Some Unanswered Questions." Unpublished paper presented at the annual meeting of the American Society of Criminology, November, Baltimore, MD.

Griswold, David B.
   1994 "Complaints against the Police: Predicting Dispositions." *Journal of Criminal Justice* **22**:215–221.

Grohmann, Stephen W., and Melissa Barritt
   1987 *Secure Detentions of Juveniles in Wisconsin, 1985.* Madison: Wisconsin Statistical Analysis Center, Wisconsin Council on Criminal Justice.

Gruber, Gerald
   1986 "The Police Applicant Test: A Predictive Validity Study." *Journal of Police Science and Administration* **14**:121–129.

Guarino-Ghezzi, Susan
   1994 "Reintegrative Police Surveillance of Juvenile Offenders: Forging an Urban Model." *Crime and Delinquency* **40**:131–153.

Guggenheim, Martin
   1985 *The Rights of Young People.* New York: Bantam Books.

Guttman, Monika
   1993 "In Hollywood, To Have and Have Not." *U.S. News & World Report,* October 4, p. 52.

Guyot, Dorothy
   1991 *Policing as though People Matter.* Philadelphia, PA: Temple University Press.

Hacker, Andrew
   1992 *Two Nations Black and White, Separate, Hostile, Unequal.* New York: Ballantine Books.

Hackler, Jim, and Kim Don
   1990 "Estimating System Biases: Crime Indices that Permit Comparison across Provinces." *Canadian Journal of Criminology* **32**:243–264.

Hageman, Mary Jeanette
    1985   *Police-Community Relations*. Beverly Hills, CA: Sage.
Hann, Robert G. et al.
    1985   "Municipal Police Governance and Accountability in Canada: An Empirical Study." *Canadian Police College Journal* **9**:1-35.
Harris, Patricia M.
    1988   "Juvenile Sentence Reform and Its Evaluation: A Demonstration of the Need for More Precise Measures of Offense Seriousness in Juvenile Justice Research." *Evaluation Review* **12**:655–666.
Harrison, Eric
    1993   "Community-Based Policing Takes On New Meaning." *Los Angeles Times*, November 17, p. A5.
Harvard Law Review
    1991   Comment, March-April, pp. 70–74.
Hatler, Richard W.
    1990   "Operation CLEAN: Reclaiming City Neighborhoods." *FBI Law Enforcement Bulletin* **59**:22–25.
Hatry, H.P., and J.M. Greiner
    1984   *How Can Police Departments Better Apply Management by Objectives (MBO) and Quality Circle Programs?* Washington, DC: Urban Institute.
Hatty, Suzanne
    1991   "Police, Crime, and the Media: An Australian Tale." *International Journal of the Sociology of Law* **19**:171–191.
Hawkins, D.F.
    1985   "Black Homicide: The Inadequacy of Existing Research for Devising Prevention Strategies." *Crime & Delinquency* **31**:83–103.
Hayeslip, David W., and Preszler, Alan
    1993   *NIJ Initiative on Less-Than-Lethal Weapons*. Washington, DC: U.S. Department of Justice.
Heck, William P.
    1992   "Police Who Snitch: Deviant Actors in a Secret Society." *Deviant Behavior* **13**:253–270.
Heiman, Andrea
    1993   "Busting Vietnamese Language Barrier." *Los Angeles Times*, April 4, p. B3.
Heiman, Andrea
    1993   "Public Gets Cop's View." *Los Angeles Times*, July 30, p. B1.
Hernandez, Greg
    1993   "Spreading Seeds of Hope." *Los Angeles Times*, December 13, pp. B1, B7.
Hesketh, Brian
    1992   "The Police Use of Surveys: 'Valuable Tools or Misused Distractions?'" *Police Studies* **15**:55–61.
Hetherington, Sir Thomas
    1989   *Prosecution and the Public Interest*. London, UK: Waterlow.
Hickman, Kenneth G., ed.
    1990   "Urban Police Management." *Journal of Contemporary Criminal Justice* **6**:49–105.
Hill, Elaine et al.
    1988   "Types of Police/Citizen Co-Production." Unpublished paper presented at the annual meeting of the American Society of Criminology, November, Chicago, IL.
Hill, Susan, and Alan Smithers
    1991   "Enough of a Good Thing: Is There Still a Real Need for the Graduate Entry Scheme?" *Policing* **7**:297–323.

Hillbery, Rhonda
   1993 "Mayoral Contest Paints a Darker Twin Cities." *Los Angeles Times,* November 2, p. A5.

Holdaway, Simon
   1991 "Race Relations and Police Recruitment." *British Journal of Criminology* **31**:365–382.

Holden, Richard
   1990 "Who Was Truly the Father of Modern Policing?" Unpublished paper presented at the Academy of Criminal Justice Sciences, April, Denver, CO.

Holland, Gale
   1988 "Ex Sergeant Files Gay Bias Suit." *The Outlook,* September 28, p. A11.

Holzworth, R. James, and Catherine Woods Brown
   1990 "Follow-Up Analyses of Police Judgments." *Journal of Police Science and Administration* **17**:95–104.

Homant, Robert J., and Daniel B. Kennedy
   1994 "The Effect of High Speed Pursuit Policies on Officers' Tendency to Pursue." *American Journal of Police* **13**:91–111.

Hoover, Larry
   1990 "Extent and Nature of Citizen Contact with Police." Unpublished paper presented at the annual meetings of the Academy of Criminal Justice Sciences, March, Denver.

Hoover, Larry T., and Edward T. Mader
   1990 "Attitudes of Police Chiefs Toward Private Sector Management Principles." *American Journal of Police* **9**:25–37.

Horne, Paul
   1975 *Women in Law Enforcement.* Springfield, IL: Charles C. Thomas Publisher.

Hornick, Joseph P. et al.
   1990 *An Evaluation of the Neighborhood Foot Patrol Program of Edmonton Police Service.* Ottawa, CAN: Solicitor General Canada.

Horovitz, Bruce
   1993 "Alternative Approach: Finding New Ways to Appeal to Gays, Lesbians." *Los Angeles Times,* February 23, pp. D1, D12.

Hubler, Shawn
   1994 "2 Arrested in Carjack Deaths of 2 Students." *Los Angeles Times,* March 31, p. A1.

Hughes, Stella P., and Anne L. Schneider
   1989 "Victim-Offender Mediation: A Survey of Program Characteristics and Perceptions of Effectiveness." *Crime and Delinquency* **35**:217–233.

Huizinga, David, Finn-Aage Esbensen, and Delbert S. Elliott
   1987 "Development of Delinquency in High Risk Neighborhoods: The Denter Study." Unpublished paper presented at the American Society of Criminology meetings, November, Montreal, CAN.

Humphrey Institute of Public Affairs
   1986 *The Incarceration of Minority Youth.* Minneapolis, MN: Author.

Hunt, Raymond G., and John M. Magenau
   1993 *Power and the Police Chief: An Institutional and Organizational Analysis.* Newbury Park, CA: Sage.

Hymas, Michael
   1989 "Enhancing the Selection and Role of the Field Training Officer." *The Journal of California Law Enforcement* **23**:1–5.

Ingram, Carl
   1994 "State Gun Sales Set Record, Lungren Says." *Los Angeles Times,* January 7, p. A31.

Inkster, Norman D.
  1992 "The Essence of Community Policing." *The Police Chief* **59**:28–31.
International Association of Chiefs of Police
  1985 *Police Supervision: A Manual for Police Supervisors.* Gaithersburg, MD: Author.
International Association of Chiefs of Police
  1988 *Developing Neighborhood Oriented Policing in the Houston Police Department.* Gaithersburg, MD: Author.
International Crime Center
  1986 *International Crime Statistics.* Geneva, SWITZ: International Crime Center.
Iwai, H.
  1986 "Organized Crime in Japan." In *Organized Crime: A Global Perspective,* edited by R.J. Kelly. Totowa, NJ: Rowman and Littlefield.
Iwata, Edward
  1990 "Homeless Delivery." *Los Angeles Times,* February 19, pp. E1, E3.
Jackson, R.L.
  1986 "Canadian Police Labour Relations in the '80s: New Environmental Concerns." *Canadian Police College Journal* **10**:86–138.
Janssen, Christian T.L., and James C. Hackler
  1985 "Police Killings in Perspective." *Canadian Journal of Criminology* **27**:227–232.
Janus, Mark-David et al.
  1987 *Adolescent Runaways: Causes and Consequences.* Lexington, MA: Lexington Books.
Japan Ministry of Justice
  1985 *Community-based Treatment of Offenders in Japan.* Tokyo, JAPAN: Ministry of Justice, Rehabilitation Bureau.
Japan Ministry of Justice
  1990 *Summary of the White Paper on Crime—1990.* Tokyo, JAPAN: Ministry of Justice, Research and Training Institute.
Jeffers, H.P.
  1991 *Who Killed Precious?* New York: Pharos Books.
Johnson, John Mark
  1992 *The Georgia State Patrol's In-Car Video System.* Lexington, KY: Council of State Governments.
Johnson, Rodney
  1994 "Japanese Students Killed in Northern California." *Los Angeles Times,* January 12, p. B11.
Joyce, M.A.S.
  1985 *Spending on Law and Order: The Police Service in England and Wales.* London, UK: National Institute of Economic and Social Research.
Justice Research and Statistics Association
  1992 *Report from the States on What Works at the State and Local Levels: A Compendium of Assessment and Evaluation Results.* Washington, DC: Author.
Kahn, Andy N.
  1986 "The Police and Criminal Evidence Act of 1984: Part II: New Police Complaints Procedures." *Police Journal* **59**:134–142.
Kakimi, Takashi
  1988 "Organized Crime in Japan: The Boryokudan Groups." *Police Chief* **55**:161–162.
Kalinich, David B., and Jeffrey D. Senese
  1987 "Police Discretion and the Mentally Disordered in Chicago: A Reconsideration." *Police Studies* **10**:185–191.
Kalish, Carol B.
  1988 *International Crime Rates.* Washington, DC: Bureau of Justice Statistics.

Kang, K. Connie
   1993 "First National Civil Rights Group Organized for Asian-Americans." *Los Angeles Times*, May 13, p. A34.

Kaplan, David E., and Alec Dubro
   1986 *Yakuza: The Explosive Account of Japan's Criminal Underworld*. Reading, MA: Addison-Wesley.

Kaplan, Lisa et al.
   1989 "Runaway, Homeless and Shut-Out Children and Youth in Canada, Europe, and the United States." *Children and Youth Services Review* **11**:1–108.

Kappeler, Victor E., Richard D. Sluder, and Geoffrey P. Alpert
   1994 *Forces of Deviance: Understanding the Dark Side of Policing*. Prospect Heights, IL: Waveland Press.

Kaune, Michael M.
   1990 "Liability and Police Use of Force: The Continued Expansion of a Fourth Amendment Standard." Unpublished paper presented at the annual meeting of the Academy of Criminal Justice Sciences, March, Denver.

Kavanagh, John
   1994 "The Occurrence of Violence in Police-Citizen Arrest Encounters." *Criminal Justice Abstracts* **26**:319–330.

Kearney, William J.
   1989 "Form Follows Function—And Function Follows Philosophy: An Architectural Response." *Juvenile and Family Court Journal* **40**:27–34.

Keith, Richard G.
   1989 *Children and Drugs: The Next Generation*. Los Angeles: Los Angeles Unified School District Police Officers Association.

Kelling, George L.
   1987 "Acquiring a Taste for Order: The Community and Police." *Crime and Delinquency* **33**:90–102.

Kelling, George L., and James K. Stewart
   1989 *Neighborhoods and Police: The Maintenance of Civil Authority*. Washington, DC: U.S. Department of Justice, Office of Justice Programs.

Kelling, George L., and James K. Stewart
   1990 "Neighborhoods and Police: The Maintenance of Civil Authority." *Criminal Law Forum: An International Journal* **1**:459–476.

Kelly, Patricia A., ed.
   1987 *Police and the Media: Bridging Troubled Waters*. Springfield, IL: Thomas.

Kennedy, D.M.
   1993 "Strategic Management of Police Resources." *NIJ Bulletin*, p. 3.

Kennedy, Leslie W.
   1991 "The Evaluation of Community-Based Policing in Canada." *Canadian Police College Journal* **15**:275–289.

Kenney, John P., and Harry W. More
   1986 *Patrol Field Problems and Solutions: 476 Field Situations*. Springfield, IL: Thomas.

Kinsey, Richard, John Lea, and Jock Young
   1986 *Losing the Fight against Crime*. Oxford, UK: Basil Blackwell.

Kirk, A.R.
   1982 "Black Homicide." In *The Human Side of Homicide*, edited by B.L. Danto, J. Bruhns, and A. H. Kutscher. New York: Columbia University Press.

Kleinig, John, and Albert J. Gorman
   1992 "Professional Courtesies: To Ticket or Not to Ticket." *American Journal of Police* **11**:97–113.

Klockars, Carl B.
    1985   "The Dirty Harry Problem." In *Moral Issues in Police Work,* edited by Frederick A. Elliston and Michael Feldberg. Totowa, NJ: Rowman and Allanheld.
Klockars, Carl B.
    1989   "Transforming a Police Agency: The Role of the Researcher in Changing Police Practice in Hartford County." Unpublished paper presented at the annual meeting of the American Society of Criminology, November, Reno, NV.
Knoxville Police Department
    1991   *Systems Approach to Community Crime Prevention: Implementation Guide.* Knoxville, TN: Knoxville Police Department.
Krajick, Kevin
    1993   "Fighting Fire With . . . What?" *Newsweek,* December 13, p. 730.
Kraska, Peter B., and Victor E. Kappeler
    1995   "To Serve and Pursue: Exploring Police Sexual Violence against Women." *Justice Quarterly* **12**:85–111.
Kratcoski, Peter C., and Lucille Dunn Kratcoski
    1986   *Juvenile Delinquency,* 2nd ed. Englewood Cliffs, NJ: Prentice Hall.
Krause, Wesley, and Marilyn D. McShane
    1994   "A Deinstitutionalization Retrospective: Relabeling the Status Offender." *Journal of Crime and Justice* **17**:45–67.
Krisberg, Barry
    1988   *The Juvenile Court: Reclaiming the Vision.* San Francisco: National Council on Crime and Delinquency.
Kufeldt, Kathleen, and Philip E. Perry
    1989   "Running Around with Runaways." *Community Alternatives: International Journal of Family Care* **1**:85–97.
Lacey, Marc
    1994   "Gun Exchanges Catch On—But Are They Effective?" *Los Angeles Times,* January 4, pp. A3, A14.
Lane, Virginia K.
    1990   "The Implementation of Minnesota Legislation on Bias-Motivated Crime." Unpublished paper presented at the annual meeting of the American Society of Criminology, November, Baltimore, MD.
Larsen, Peter
    1991   "Gay Officers Recruit for Department." *Daily News,* June 23, p. 13.
Larson, Jan.
    1993   "Density is Density." *American Demographics,* February.
Layne, Karen
    1990   "Unanticipated Consequences of the Provision of Information: The Experience of the LVMPD." *Journal of Police Science and Administration* **17**:20–31.
Le, Thuan
    1993   "Crackdown on Graffiti Yields 240 Arrests" *Los Angeles Times,* April 3, p. B5.
Lea, John, Roger Matthews, and Jock Young
    1987   *Law and Order: Five Years On.* Enfield, UK: Centre for Criminology, Middlesex Polytechnic.
Leddy, Daniel D.
    1985   "Families in Need of Supervision." *Criminal Justice Ethics* **4**:19–38.
Lee, M.
    1901   *A History of Police in England.* London, UK: Methuen and Company.
Lee, Patrick
    1994   "Business Is a Victim, Too." *Los Angeles Times,* April 3, p. D3.

Lee, Soon Young
    1990 "Morning Calm, Rising Sun: National Character and Policing in South Korea and in Japan." *Police College Journal* **7**:217–229.

Leighton, Barry
    1990 "Community Policing in a Multicultural Society." Unpublished paper presented at the annual meeting of the American Society of Criminology, November, Baltimore, MD.

Leo, John
    1993 "The New Highwaymen." *U.S. News & World Report,* September 27, p. 18.

Levine, Charles H.
    1986 "Police Management in the 1980s: From Decrementalism to Strategic Thinking." *Public Administration Review* **45**:691–700.

Lewis, Clare E., Sidney B. Linden, and Judith Keene
    1986 "Public Complaints against Police in Metropolitan Toronto—the History and Operation of the Office of the Public Complaints Commissioner." *Criminal Law Quarterly* **29**:115–144.

Liberman, H., Richard Lamb, and William Davis
    1993 "A Plan for Rescuing the Mentally Ill." *Los Angeles Times,* September 6, p. B11.

Linden, Rick
    1983 *Women in Policing: A Study of Lower Mainland R.C.M.P. Detachments.* Ottawa, CAN: Ministry of the Solicitor General of Canada.

Linden, Rick
    1985a "Attrition among Male and Female Members of the RCMP." *Canadian Police College Journal* **9**:86–97.

Linden, Rick
    1985b *Women in Policing: A Study of the Vancouver Police Department.* Ottawa, CAN: Ministry of the Solicitor General of Canada.

Lindsay, Betsy
    1988 "Community-Based vs. Police-Based Models of Problem Definition and Organizing." Unpublished paper presented at the annual meeting of the American Society of Criminology, November, Chicago, IL.

Lipson, Karin
    1982 "Cops and TOPS: A Program for Police and Teens That Works." *Police Chief* **49**:45–46.

Littlejohn, Edward J.
    1981 "The Civilian Police Commission: A Deterrent to Police Misconduct." *University of Detroit Journal of Urban Law* **59**:6–62.

Loeb, Penny, Dorian Freedman, Mary C. Lord, Dan McGraw, and Kukula Gastris
    1993 "To Make a Nation." *U.S. News & World Report,* October 4, pp. 47–54.

Loeb, Roger C., Theresa A. Burke, and Cheryl A. Boglarsky
    1986 "A Large-Scale Comparison of Perspectives on Parenting Between Teenage Runaways and Nonrunaways." *Adolescence* **21**:921–930.

Logan, Charles H., and Sharla P. Rausch
    1985 "Why Deinstitutionalizing Status Offenders is Pointless." *Crime and Delinquency* **31**:501–517.

London Strategic Policy Unit
    1986 *Police Response to Domestic Violence.* London, UK: London Strategic Policy Unit, Police Monitoring and Research Group.

Loree, Donald J.
    1985 "Police in a Plural Society." *Canadian Police College Journal* **12**:205–239.

Loree, Donald J.
  1988 "Innovation and Change in a Regional Police Force." *Canadian Police College Journal* **12**:205–239.
Loree, Donald J., and Chris Murphy, eds.
  1987 *Community Policing in the 1980s: Recent Advances in Police Programs.* Ottawa, CAN: Ministry of Supply and Services Canada.
Loree, Donald J., and Robert W. Walker, eds.
  1991 *Community Crime Prevention: Shaping the Future.* Ottawa, CAN: Royal Canadian Mounted Police and the Canadian Police College.
"Los Angeles Hires Williams as Chief."
  1992 *Long Beach Press Telegram,* August 15, p. A9.
Los Angeles Times
  1988. October 14, p. B1.
Los Angeles Times
  1989 October 6, pp. I, 36.
Los Angeles Times
  1990a July 13, pp. A1, A23.
Los Angeles Times
  1990b "Orange County Focus." August 15, p. B2.
Los Angeles Times
  1993a "Three Strike Law Passed in Washington." July 29, p. A24.
Los Angeles Times
  1993b "Reno Orders FBI to Discard Anti-Homosexual Hiring Policy." December 4, p. A28.
Los Angeles Times
  1993c "Half of the Female Lawyers Report Sex Harassment." December 13, p. D2.
Los Angeles Times
  1993d "Immigration: Washington Fiddles, California Hurts." December 20, p. B12.
Los Angeles Times
  1993e "New Law Puts Limits on Minors, Guns." November 26, p. A29.
Los Angeles Times
  1993f "Police Issue IOUs as Toys for Guns Scores Sellout in High-Crime Area." December 26, p. A23.
Los Angeles Times
  1994 "Tough on Guns, Tough on Crime." January 5, p. B10.
Loveday, Barry
  1989 "Poor Prospects for Police Civilians." *Policing* **5**:86–95.
Lyman, J.L.
  1964 "The Metropolitan Police Act of 1829." *Journal of Criminal Law, Criminology and Police Science* **55**:141–154.
Maggs, Christopher
  1986 "Police and Community Liaison in New York." *Policing* **2**:4–16.
Maguire, Brendan
  1990 "The Police in the 1800s: A Three-City Analysis." *Journal of Crime and Justice* **13**:103–132.
Maguire, Kathleen, and Ann L. Pastore
  1994 *Bureau of Justice Statistics Sourcebook of Criminal Justice Statistics, 1993.* Albany: The Hindelang Criminal Justice Research Center.
Maguire, M., and C. Corbett
  1991 *A Study of the Police Complaints System.* London, UK: Her Majesty's Stationery Office.

Maharaj, Davan
   1993 "Police Show Video on Gay Sensitivity for Officer Training." *Los Angeles Times,* October 6, pp. B1, B5.

Mahoney, Anne Rankin
   1989 "Nonresident Delinquents: Whose Problem Are They?" *Journal of Juvenile Law* **10**:179–192.

Maloney, Dennis M., Dennis Romig, and Troy Armstrong
   1988 "Juvenile Probation: The Balanced Approach." *Juvenile and Family Court Journal* **39**:1–63.

Mande, Mary J.
   1993 *A Qualitative Assessment of the Implementation of Community Policing on the Eastside.* Dover, DE: Delaware Statistical Analysis Center.

Manning, Peter K.
   1977 *Police Work: The Social Organization of Policing.* Cambridge: MIT Press.

Manning, Peter K.
   1984 "Community Policing." *American Journal of Police* **3**:205–227.

Manning, Peter K
   1992 "Technological Dramas and the Police: Statement and Counterstatement in Organizational Analysis." *Criminology* **30**:327–346.

Mapstone, Richard
   1992 "The Attitudes of Police in a Divided Society: The Police of Northern Ireland." *British Journal of Criminology* **32**:183–192.

Marenin, Otwin
   1989 "The Utility of Community Needs Surveys in Community Policing." *Police Studies* **12**:73–81.

Marenin, Otwin
   1990 "The Village Public Safety Officer Program in Alaska: A Mechanism for Integrating Traditional and U.S. Law." Unpublished paper presented at the annual meeting of the American Society of Criminology, November, Baltimore, MD.

Marenin, Otwin, and Gary Copus
   1991 "Policing Rural Alaska: The Village Public Safety Officer (VPSO) Program." *American Journal of Police* **10**:1–26.

Marsolais, John
   1993 News release. Albany: City of Albany, Office of the Mayor, June 8.

Martin, Lynn
   1992 "Community Policing: Its Past and Its Future." Unpublished paper presented at the annual meeting of the American Society of Criminology, November, New Orleans, LA.

Martinez, Gebe
   1994 "Wilson Swings Through O.C. to Push Anti-Crime Ideas." *Los Angeles Times,* March 29, p. A25.

Maslach, C.
   1979 "Burned-Out Cops and Their Families." *Psychology Today,* May.

Maslow, Abraham
   1954 *Motivation and Personality.* New York: Harper.

Massachusetts Department of Youth Services
   1984 *Pre-Trial Detention of Juveniles in Massachusetts: A Profile of Children Detained During a Six-Month Period.* Boston: Author.

Mastrofski, Stephen D. et al.
   1990 "The Future of Policing." *American Journal of Police* **9**:1–207.

Matarese, Leonard A., and Kenneth R. Chelst
  1991   "Forecasting the Outcome of Police/Fire Consolidations." *MIS Report* **23**:1–22.
Maxson, Cheryl L., Margaret A. Little, and Malcolm W. Klein
  1988   "Police Response to Runaway and Missing Children: A Conceptual Framework for Research and Policy." *Crime and Delinquency* **34**:84–102.
Mayer, Martin J.
  1993   "AIDS and Other Communicable Diseases." *California Police Officer,* **13**.
Mayhall, Pamela D.
  1985   *Police-Community Relations and the Administration of Justice.* Englewood Cliffs, NJ: Prentice Hall.
Mayhall, Pamela D., Thomas Barker, and Ronald D. Hunter
  1995   *Police-Community Relations and the Administration of Justice.* Upper Saddle River, NJ: Prentice Hall.
McCarthy, Belinda R.
  1985   "An Analysis of Detention." *Juvenile and Family Court Journal* **36**:49–50.
McCarthy, Belinda R.
  1987   "Case Attrition in the Juvenile Court: An Application of the Crime Control Model." *Justice Quarterly* **4**:237–255.
McCarthy, Belinda R.
  1989   "A Preliminary Research Model for the Juvenile and Family Court." *Juvenile and Family Court Journal* **40**:43–48.
McCarthy, Belinda R., and B. L. Smith
  1986   "The Conceptualization of Discrimination in the Juvenile Justice Process: The Impact of Administrative Factors and Screening Decisions on Juvenile Court Dispositions." *Criminology* **24**:41–64.
McCormack, Arlene, Mark-David Janus, and Ann Wolbert Burgess
  1986   "Runaway Youths and Sexual Victimization: Gender Differences in an Adolescent Runaway Population." *Child Abuse and Neglect* **10**:387–395.
McCoy, Candace
  1984   "Lawsuits against Police: What Impact Do They Have?" *Criminal Law Bulletin* **20**:49–56.
McDougall, Allan K.
  1988   "The Police Mandate: The Modern Era." *Canadian Police College Journal* **12**:14–174.
McDowell, Jeanne
  1992   "Are Women Better Cops?" *Time,* February 17, p. 67.
McElroy, Jerome E., Colleen A. Cosgrove, and Susan Sadd
  1990   *CPOP: The Research—An Evaluative Study of the New York City Community Patrol Officer Program.* New York: Vera Institute of Justice.
McEvoy, Glenn M.
  1987   "Using Subordinate Appraisals of Managers to Predict Performance and Promotions: One Agency's Experience." *Journal of Police Science and Administration* **15**:118–124.
McEwen, J. Thomas
  1984   *Evaluation of the Differential Police Response Field Test: Final Report.* Alexandria, VA: Research Management Associates, Inc.
McGinnis, James H.
  1991   "Adaptation to Career Constable Status." *Canadian Police College Journal* **15**:26–71.
McGregor, Douglas
  1960   *The Human Side of Enterprise.* New York: McGraw-Hill.

McKenzie, Ian
   1990   "Discretion in Danger." *Policing* **6**:422–439.

McLeay, E.M.
   1990   "Defining Police Policies and the Political Agenda." *Political Studies* **38**:620–637.

Meeks, Daryl H.
   1993   "Dispute Resolution and Law Enforcement in the 1990s: A System Design." *Journal of California Law Enforcement* **27**.

Meese, Edwin III
   1993   *Community Policing and the Police Officer.* Washington, DC: National Institute of Justice.

Melekian, Barney
   1990   "Police and the Homeless." *FBI Law Enforcement Bulletin*, November, pp. 1–7.

Mendoza, N.F.
   1993   "Crossing the Thin Blue Line." *Los Angeles Times*, May 11, pp. F1, F7.

Meyer, Josh
   1994   "Payouts Drop in Litigation against LAPD." *Los Angeles Times*, February 21, p. A32.

Michaud, Anne
   1993   "Cultural Differences Creating Confusion in Sex-Bias Litigation." *Los Angeles Times*, March 21, p. D9.

Miller, Larry S., and Michael C. Braswell
   1986   "The Utility of Experiential Case Studies in Police Education: A Comparative Analysis." *Criminal Justice Review* **11**:9–14.

Miller, Larry S., and Michael C. Braswell
   1992   "Police Perceptions of Ethical Decision Making: The Ideal vs. the Real." *American Journal of Police* **11**:27–45.

Miller, Linda S., and Karen M. Hess
   1994   *Community Policing: Theory and Practice.* Minneapolis/St. Paul: West Publishing Company.

Millon, T., and G. Everly Jr.
   1985   *Personality and Its Disorders: A Biosocial Learning Approach.* New York: John Wiley & Sons.

Milton S. Eisenhower Foundation
   1993   *Investing in Children and Youth, Reconstructing Our Cities: Doing What Works to Reverse the Betrayal of American Democracy.* Washington, DC: Author.

Mitchell, Jeff
   1988   "Gay Ex-Officer Files $5 Million Suit against LAPD." *Los Angeles Herald-Examiner*, September 29, p. A9.

Mixdorf, Lloyd
   1989   "Pay Me Now or Pay Me Later." *Corrections Today* **51**:106–110.

Miyazawa, Setsuo
   1988   "Scandal and No Reform: Organizational Police Crime in Japan." Unpublished paper presented at the annual meeting of the American Society of Criminology, November, Chicago, IL.

Miyazawa, Setsuo
   1989   "Scandal and Hard Reform: Implications of a Wiretapping Case to the Control of Organizational Police Crimes in Japan." *Kobe University Law Review* **23**:13–27.

Miyazawa, Setsuo
   1990   "Privatization of Law Enforcement in Japan: A Critical Appraisal." Unpublished paper presented at the annual meeting of the American Society of Criminology, November, Baltimore, MD.

Moffat, Susan, and Anna Cekola
 1994 "U.S. Rushes to Reassure Japan after Carjacking." *Los Angeles Times*, March 29, pp. A1, A26.

Moone, Joseph
 1993 *Children in Custody 1991: Private Facilities.* Washington, DC: U.S. Department of Justice, Office of Juvenile Justice and Delinquency Prevention.

Moore, Joan W.
 1985 "Isolation and Stigmatization in the Development of an Underclass: The Case of Chicano Gangs in Los Angeles." *Social Problems* **33**:1–12.

Moore, Mark H.
 1992 "Problem-Solving and Community Policing." In *Modern Policing*, edited by Michael Tonry and Norval Morris. Chicago: University of Chicago Press.

Moore, Mark H., and Darrel W. Stephens
 1991 *Beyond Command and Control: The Strategic Command of Police Departments.* Washington, DC: Police Executive Research Forum.

Morash, Merry
 1986 "Gender, Peer Group Experiences, and Seriousness of Delinquency." *Journal of Research on Crime and Delinquency* **22**:43–67.

More, Harry W.
 1992 *Special Topics in Policing.* Cincinnati, OH: Anderson.

Morgan, Anthony D.
 1990 "Uniformed Bicycle Proposal." Oakland Police Department, November 21.

Morganthau, Tom, Miller, Susan, O'Donnell, Paul, Clift, Eleanor, and Milinda Liu
 1993 "Death Ride." *Newsweek*, December 20, pp. 27–31.

Morganthau, Tom
 1993 "Why Not Real Gun Control?" *Newsweek*, October 11, p. 33.

Morrill, S.
 1984 "Tampa Likes Sector Patrolling." *Law and Order* **32**:37–40.

Murphy, Patrick V.
 1994 "The Invisible Minority: Irish Offenders and Criminal Justice." *Probation Journal* **4**:2–7.

Murray, Tonita
 1992 "Community-Based Policing Inside Out." Unpublished paper presented at the annual meeting of the American Society of Criminology, November, New Orleans, LA.

Nagoshi, Jack T.
 1986 *Juvenile Recidivism: Third Circuit Court.* Honolulu: Youth Development and Research Center, University of Hawaii-Manoa.

Nakayama, Kenichi
 1987 "Japan." In *Major Criminal Justice Systems: A Comparative Survey (2nd ed.)*, edited by George F. Cole, Stanislaw J. Frankowski, and Marc G. Gertz. Beverly Hills, CA: Sage.

National Advisory Commission on Criminal Justice Standards and Goals
 1973 *Report of the National Advisory Commission on Criminal Justice Standards and Goals.* Washington, DC: U.S. Government Printing Office.

National Advisory Commission on Criminal Justice Standards and Goals
 1976 *Task Force Report on Juvenile Justice and Delinquency Prevention.* Washington, DC: Law Enforcement Assistance Administration.

National College of Juvenile and Family Law
    1989   "Court-Approved Alternative Dispute Resolution: A Better Way to Resolve Minor Delinquency, Status Offense, and Abuse/Neglect Cases." *Juvenile and Family Court Journal* **40**:51–98.

National Institute of Justice
    1985   *Topical Bibliography: Police Brutality and Use of Deadly Force.* Washington, DC: National Institute of Justice, U.S. Department of Justice.

National Institute of Justice
    1995   *Community Policing Strategies.* Washington, DC: U.S. Department of Justice.

Nazario, Sonia
    1993   "A Force To Be Reckoned with." *Los Angeles Times,* June 5, pp. A1, A18.

Neely, Richard
    1990   *Take Back Your Neighborhood: A Case for Modern-Day 'Vigilantism.'* New York: Donald I. Fine.

Neff, Andy
    1993   "Columbia Police Move in To Keep Neighborhoods Safe." *Nation's Cities Weekly,* July 26, p. 39.

Nehrbass, Arthur F.
    1988   "Promoting Effective Media Relations." *The Police Chief,* January.

Neiderhoffer, Arthur, and Blumberg, Abraham S.
    1976   *The Ambivalent Force: Perspectives on the Police,* 2nd ed. Hinsdale, IL: The Dryden Press

Network
    1993   Newsletter of the California Peace Officers' Association **8**:5–6.

Newell, Charldean, Janay Pollock, and Jerry Tweedy
    1992   *Financial Aspects of Police Liability.* Washington, DC: International City/County Management Association, Baseline Date Report, Vol. 24, No. 2.

Newing, John
    1987   "The Future PNC." *Policing* **3**:287–301.

Newton, Jim
    1993   "Antiquated Equipment Hinders LAPD." *Los Angeles Times,* November 14, pp. A3, A38.

New York Commission for the Study of Youth Crime and Violence and the Reform of the Juvenile Justice System
    1994   *Preliminary Report to the Governor.* New York: New York Commission for the Study of Youth Crime and Violence and the Reform of the Juvenile Justice System.

New York Commission to Investigate Allegations of Police Corruption
    1994   *Commission Report.* New York: New York Commission to Investigate Allegations of Police Corruption.

New York Times
    1988   "Homelessness: Crack Use Pervades Life in a Shelter." February 18, p. I:1.

Nila, Michael J.
    1990   "Community Policing." *Police Chief* **57**:43–104.

Nimick, Ellen H., Linda Szymanski, and Howard Snyder
    1986   *Juvenile Court Waiver: A Study of Juvenile Court Cases Transferred to Criminal Court.* Pittsburgh: National Center for Juvenile Justice.

Nimocks, Rudolph
    1988   "Implementing the Co-Production of Public Safety in Chicago: The Police Administrative Perspective." Unpublished paper presented at the annual meeting of the American Society of Criminology, November, Chicago, IL.

Nishimura, Haruro, and Shingo Suzuki
　1986　"Citizen-Helping Role of the Police and Inhabitants in the Community: Residents' Perceptions of Criminal Law, Law Enforcement and Police Services, and Police Officers' Understanding of Them." *Reports of the National Research Institute of Police Science* **27**:127–140.

Noaks, Lesley, and Steven Christopher
　1990　"Why Police are Assaulted." *Policing* **6**:625–638.

Normandeau, Andre, and Barry Leighton, eds.
　1990　*A Vision of the Future of Policing in Canada: Police-Challenge 2000: Background Document.* Ottawa, CAN: Solicitor General Canada.

Normandeau, Andre, and Barry Leighton
　1991　"Police and Society in Canada." *Canadian Journal of Criminology* **33**:241–585.

Oakley, Robin
　1990　"Police Training in Ethnic Relations in Britain." *Police Studies* **13**:47–56.

Oliver, Ian
　1987　*Police, Government, and Accountability.* Houndmills, UK: Macmillan.

Olivero, J. Michael, Russell Hansen, and Amelia M. Clark
　1993　"An Assessment of Police Implementation of the Texas Public Intoxication Law in Small Texas Cities: What is Dangerous to Self or Others?" *American Journal of Police* **12**:127–148.

Ohlin, Lloyd E., and Frank J. Remington, eds.
　1993　*Discretion in Criminal Justice: The Tension between Individualization and Uniformity.* Albany, NY: SUNY Press.

Opolot, James S.E.
　1991　"Police Training in the New States of Africa." *Police Studies* **14**:62–71.

Orange County Register
　1994　"Business Breaks Top Aid to Poor, Nader Says." January 6, p. 5.

Orlov, Rick, and Lisa Pope
　1991　"Gates Says Decision Will Stand." *Daily News,* June 21, p. 1.

Ortega, Ruben B. et al.
　1989　"Special Focus: Police Budgeting." *Police Chief* **56**:50–59.

Osgood, D. Wayne
　1983　"Offense History and Juvenile Diversion." *Evaluation Review* **7**:793–806.

Ottemeier, Timothy
　1990　"Researching Community Policing in Houston." Unpublished paper presented at the annual meeting of the American Society of Criminology, November, Baltimore, MD.

Parker, Craig
　1984　*The Japanese Police System Today: An American Perspective.* Tokyo, JAPAN: Kodansha International.

Parker, L. Craig, Jr.
　1986　*Parole and the Community Based Treatment of Offenders in Japan and the United States.* New Haven, CT: University of New Haven Press.

Parker, Mary F.
　1993　Personal correspondence, October 15, Roanoke, VA.

Payne, D.M., and Robert C. Trojanowicz
　1985　*Performance Profiles of Foot versus Motor Officers.* Community Policing Series No. 6. East Lansing, MI: National Neighborhood Foot Patrol Center, Michigan State University.

Peak, Kenneth J.
    1990 "The Quest for Alternatives to Lethal Force: A Heuristic View." *Journal of Contemporary Criminal Justice* **6**:8–22.
Peak, Kenneth J.
    1993 *Policing America: Methods, Issues, and Challenges.* Englewood Cliffs, NJ: Regents/Prentice Hall.
Peak, Kenneth J., Robert V. Bradshaw, and Ronald W. Glensor
    1992 "Improving Citizen Perceptions of the Police: 'Back to the Basics' with a Community Policing Strategy." *Journal of Criminal Justice* **20**:25–40.
Pennisi, Joseph F.
    1993 Personal correspondence with Commissioner Pennisi, City of Albany, New York, December 6.
Peoples, Edward E.
    1993 "Police Selection and Training: A Comparison between California and United Kingdom Models." *The Journal of California Law Enforcement* **27**.
Perez, Douglas W.
    1994 *Common Sense about Police Review.* Philadelphia, PA: Temple University Press.
Petersilia, Joan, Allan Abrahamse, and James Q. Wilson
    1987 *Police Performance and Case Attrition.* Santa Monica, CA: Rand.
Pettijohn, Terry F.
    1991 *The Encyclopedic Dictionary of Psychology (4th ed.).* New York: Dushkin Publishing Group.
Phelps, Lourn, and Murphy Robert B.
    1969 "The Team Patrol System in Richmond, California." *The Police Chief* **26**:48–51.
Philadelphia Police Study Task Force
    1987 *Philadelphia and Its Police: Toward a New Partnership.* Philadelphia, PA: Philadelphia Police Study Task Force.
Pine, Art
    1993 "Building Not-So-Lethal Weapons." *Los Angeles Times,* December 19, pp. A1, A27.
Plumridge, M.D.
    1985 "Dilemmas of Police Management and Organisation." In *Contemporary Policing: An Examination of Society in the 1980s,* edited by J.R. Thackrah. London, UK: Sphere.
Police Foundation Reports
    1992 "Reconciling Higher Educational Standards and Minority Recruitment: The New York City Model." Washington, DC: The Police Foundation, September, pp. 1–8.
Polk, Kenneth
    1984 "Juvenile Diversion: A Look at the Record." *Crime and Delinquency* **30**:648–659.
Pollock-Byrne, Joycelyn M.
    1989 *Ethics in Crime and Justice: Dilemmas and Decisions.* Pacific Grove, CA: Brooks/Cole Publishing.
Pope, Karen E., and David W. Pope
    1986 "Attitudes of Male Police Officers towards Their Female Counterparts." *Police Journal* **59**:242–250.
Pope, Lisa
    1991a "Gay Officers to Recruit for LAPD." *Daily News,* June 19, p. 1.
Pope, Lisa
    1991b "Gay Officer Ready to Face the Public." *Daily News,* June 20, p. 20.
PORAC News
    1993a "Off the Cuff." May 6, p. 26.

PORAC News
 1993b "Off the Record." September, p. 33.
Post, Tom et al.
 1994 "Farewell to Arms." *Newsweek,* January 10, pp. 20–22.
Pounder, Chris
 1983 "Data Protection and the Police." *Journal of Law and Society* **10**:109–118.
Powell, Dennis D.
 1990 "A Study of Police Discretion in Six Southern Cities." *Journal of Police Science and Administration* **17**:1–7.
Price, Kendall O., and Lloyd, Kent
 1967 *Improving Police-Community Relations through Leadership Training.* Inglewood, CA: Creative Management Research and Development.
Quah, Stella R., and Jon S. Quah
 1987 *Friends in Blue: The Police in Singapore.* Oxford, UK: Oxford University Press.
Radelet, Louis A., and David L. Carter
 1994 *The Police and the Community, Fifth Ed.* New York: Macmillan.
Rankin, Blair
 1990 "A New Approach to FTO Training." *FBI Law Enforcement Bulletin* **19**:19–21.
Rankin, J.H., and L.E. Wells
 1985 "From Status to Delinquent Offenses: Escalation?" *Journal of Criminal Justice* **13**:171–180.
The Rap Sheet
 1993 "Chief Potter will Retire June 30" **24**:1.
Regalado, Jeannette
 1993 "On Skid Row, a Cardboard Castle." *Los Angeles Times,* December 23, p. A26.
Regoli, Robert M., et al.
 1987 "Police Professionalism and Cynicism Reconsidered: An Assessment of Measurement Issues." *Justice Quarterly* **4**:257–286.
Reiner, R.
 1984 "Is Britain Turning into a Police State?" *New Society* **69**:51–56.
Reiss, Albert J.
 1967 *Occupation and Social Status.* New York: The Free Press.
Reiss, Albert J., Jr.
 1992 "Police Organization in the Twentieth Century." In *Modern Policing,* edited by Michael Tonry and Norval Morris. Chicago: University of Chicago Press.
Reith, C.
 1952 *The Blind Eye of History.* London, UK: Faber and Faber.
Ressler, R., & Shachtman, T.
 1992 *Whoever Fights Monsters.* New York: St. Martin's Press.
Reyes, David
 1993 "Language a Barrier to Rescuers." *Los Angeles Times,* January 17, p. B16.
Rhoades, Philip W.
 1991 "Political Obligation: Connecting Police Ethics and Democratic Values." *American Journal of Police* **10**:1–22.
Rich, T.F., and M.F. Cahn
 1984 *Revealed Preferences of the Criminal Justice System During a Period of Workload Shedding, Report 2: National Survey of Police Departments.* Washington, DC: Police Executive Research Forum.

Richardson, James F.
   1970 *The New York Police: Colonial Times to 1901.* New York: Oxford University Press.

Riddle, Lyn
   1993 "With a Mortgage Program Peace of Mind." *New York Times,* November 14, p. B12.

Ritter, Bruce
   1987 *Covenant House: Lifeline to the Street.* New York: Doubleday.

Roan, Shari
   1994 "Street Fighter." *Los Angeles Times,* January 3, p. E2.

Roberts, Albert R.
   1989 *Juvenile Justice: Politics, Programs, and Services.* Chicago: Dorsey Press.

Robinson, Cyril D., and Richard Scaglion
   1987 "The Origin and Evolution of the Police Function in Society: Notes toward a Theory." *Law & Society* **21**:109–153.

Robison, Clay
   1988 "Survey Shows Some Mental Patients Not Receiving Follow-up Services." *Houston Chronicle,* March 8, p. 9.

Rogers, Joseph W., and G. Larry Mays
   1987 *Juvenile Delinquency and Juvenile Justice.* New York: Wiley.

Rolf, C.H.
   1991 *Policing in Relation to the Blood Tribe: Report of a Public Inquiry.* Edmonton, CAN: Alberta Solicitor General.

Rotella, Sebastian
   1993 "Border Crackdown Stems Tide, Heightens Tensions." *Los Angeles Times,* October 2, pp. A25–A26.

Rowe, Dennis, ed.
   1988 *International Drug Trafficking.* Chicago: Office of International Criminal Justice.

Royal Canadian Mounted Police
   1987 *Crime Prevention and Community Relations.* Ottawa, CAN: Royal Canadian Mounted Police.

Roybal, Frances
   1993 Interview. Richmond, CA: Richmond Police Department, Office of the Chief of Police, October 4.

Rubenstein, Jonathan
   1973 *City Police.* New York: Ballantine Books.

Rubin, Paula N.
   1993 *The Americans with Disabilities Act and Criminal Justice: An Overview.* Research in Action, September. Washington, DC: Department of Justice, National Institute of Justice.

Rush, George E.
   1991 *The Dictionary of Criminal Justice,* 3rd ed. Los Angeles: Dushkin Publications.

Rush, George E.
   1994 *Dictionary of Criminal Justice.* Westport, CT: Guilford Press.

Sametz, Lynn
   1984 "Revamping the Adolescent's Justice System to Serve the Needs of the Very Young Offender." *Juvenile and Family Court Journal* **34**:21–30.

Sampson, Robert J.
   1986 "Effects of Socioeconomic Context on Official Reaction to Delinquency." *American Sociological Review* **51**:876–885.

Sanders, William B.
   1994 *Gangbangs and Drive-Bys: Grounded Culture and Juvenile Gang Violence.* Hawthorne, NY: Aldine de Gruyter.

Savage, David G.
   1993a "Court Clarified Sex Harassment." *Los Angeles Times,* November 10, pp. A1, A28.

Savage, David G.
   1993b "Fight to Ease Drug Terms Unlikely to Gain Ground." *Los Angeles Times,* October 12, p. A5.

Scanlon, Joseph
   1991 "Reaching Out: Getting the Community Involved in Preparedness." *Canadian Police College Journal* **15**:1–25.

Scharf, P. and Arnold Binder
   1983 *The Badge and the Bullet: Police Use of Deadly Force.* New York: Praeger.

Schmidt, Wayne W.
   1985 "Section 1983 and the Changing Face of Police Management." In *Police Leadership in America,* edited by William A. Geller. New York: Praeger.

Schneid, T., and Gaines, L.
   1991 "The Americans with Disabilities Act: Implications for Police Administrators." *Police Liability Review* Winter, p. 4.

Schneider, Anne L.
   1984 "Deinstitutionalization of Status Offenders: The Impact of Recidivism and Secure Confinement." *Criminal Justice Abstracts* September, pp. 410–432.

Schneider, Anne Larson, and Donna D. Schram
   1986 "The Washington State Juvenile Justice System Reform: A Review of Findings." *Criminal Justice Policy Review* **1**:211–235.

Schneider, Hans Joachim
   1990 "Crime and Its Control in Japan and in the Federal Republic of Germany: A Study in Comparative Criminology." In *Euro-Criminology (Volume III),* edited by Brunon Holyst. Warsaw, POL: Polish Scientific Publishers. Distributed by Criminal Justice Press, Monsey, NY.

Schneider, W.
   1984 "Development of International Cooperation involving the Federal Republic of Germany in the Area of the System of Justice Concerning Prevention of Crime and Treatment of Offenders with Particular Regard to the Conditions in the Member States of the Council of Europe." In *Resource Material No. 26.* Tokyo, JAPAN: United Nations Asia and Far East Institute for the Prevention of Crime and the Treatment of Offenders.

Schulman, Rena, and Beryl Kende
   1988 "A Study of Runaways from a Short-Term Diagnostic Center." *Residential Treatment for Children and Youth* **5**:11–31.

Schwartz, Ira M.
   1989 *(In)Justice for Juveniles: Rethinking the Best Interests of the Child.* Lexington, MA: Lexington Books.

Scrivner, Ellen M.
   1994 *The Role of Police Psychology in Controlling Excessive Force.* Washington, DC: National Institute of Justice.

Seiffert, J.M.
   1984 "Alexandria's Citizen Awareness Program." *FBI Law Enforcement Bulletin* **53**:16–20.

Sewell, John
   1985 *Police: Urban Policing in Canada.* Toronto, CAN: James Lorimer.

Seyfrit, Carole L., Philip L. Reichel, and Brian L. Stutts
   1987 "Peer Juries as a Juvenile Justice Diversion Technique." *Youth and Society* **18**:302–316.

Shadmi, Erella.
   1994   "Controlling the Police: A Public and Integrative Approach." *Policing and Society* **4**:119–129.

Shaffer, David, and Carol L.M. Caton
   1984   *Runaway and Homeless Youth in New York City.* New York: Division of Child Psychiatry, New York State Psychiatric Institute and Columbia University College of Physicians and Surgeons.

Shane, Paul G.
   1989   "Changing Patterns Among Homeless and Runaway Youth." *American Journal of Orthopsychiatry* **59**:208–214.

Shelden, Randall G., and John A. Horvath
   1987   "Intake Processing in a Juvenile Court: A Comparison of Legal and Nonlegal Variables." *Juvenile and Family Court Journal* **38**:13–19.

Shelden, Randall G., John A. Horvath, and Sharon Tracy
   1989   "Do Status Offenders Get Worse? Some Clarifications on the Question of Escalation." *Crime and Delinquency* **35**:202–216.

Sheley, Joseph F., Zina T. McGee, and James D. Wright
   1992   "Gun-Related Violence in and around Inner-City Schools." *American Journal of Diseases of Children* **146**:677–682.

Sheley, Joseph F., and James D. Wright
   1993   *Gun Acquisition and Possession in Selected Juvenile Samples.* Washington, DC: U.S. Office of Juvenile Justice and Delinquency Prevention.

Sheppard, David L., and Mary Ann Wycoff
   1992   "Community-Oriented Policing: A National Survey." Unpublished paper presented at the annual meetings of the American Society of Criminology, November, New Orleans, LA.

Sherman, Lawrence K.
   1992   "Attacking Crime: Policing and Crime Control." In *Modern Policing,* edited by Michael Tonry and Norval Morris. Chicago: University of Chicago Press.

Sherman, Lawrence W.
   1980   "Execution without Trial: Police Homicide and the Constitution." *Vanderbilt Law Review* **33**:71–100.

Sherman, Lawrence W.
   1986   "Policing Communities: What Works?" In *Communities and Crime,* edited by Albert J. Reiss and Michael Tonry. Chicago: University of Chicago Press.

Sherman, Lawrence W., Michael Buerger, and Patrick Gartin
   1989   "Beyond Dial-A-Cop: The Minneapolis Repeat Call Address Policing (RECAP) Experiment." Unpublished paper presented at the annual meeting of the American Society of Criminology, November, Reno, NV.

Shikita, Minora, and Shinichi Tsuchiya, eds.
   1990   *Crime and Criminal Policy in Japan from 1926 to 1988: Analysis and Evaluation of the Showa Era.* Tokyo, JAPAN: Japan Criminal Policy Society.

Shogren, Elizabeth
   1993   "Families Total 43% of Homeless, Survey Reports." *Los Angeles Times,* December 22, pp. A1, A16.

Singh, Mahendra
   1987   "'New Police' of 1829: Myths and Realities." Unpublished paper presented at the annual meeting of the Academy of Criminal Justice Sciences, April, St. Louis, MO.

Sipchen, Bob
   1989   "A Gay Officer's Lonely Patrol." *Los Angeles Times,* April 24, Part V, pp. 1, 10.

Skogan, Wesley G.
   1990   *The Police and the Public in England and Wales: A British Crime Survey Report.* London, UK: Her Majesty's Stationery Office.
Skolnick, Jerome H.
   1986   *Police Innovation in Six American Cities: The New Blue Line.* New York: The Free Press.
Skolnick, Jerome H.
   1994. *Justice Without Trial: Law Enforcement in Democratic Society,* 3rd ed. New York: Macmillan.
Skolnick, Jerome H., and David H. Bayley
   1988a *Community Policing: Issues and Practices around the World.* Washington, DC: U.S. National Institute of Justice.
Skolnick, Jerome H., and David H. Bayley
   1988b "Theme and Variation in Community Policing." *Issues in Crime and Justice,* edited by Norval Morris and Michael Tonry. Chicago: University of Chicago Press.
Slivinski, L.W. et al.
   1990   "A Profile of Leaders and Managers in the Public Service." *Canadian Police College Journal* **14**:172–183.
Smegal, Thomas
   1994   Special Operation Division correspondence. January 12. LAPD—Los Angeles, CA.
Smith, Douglas, and Christy Visher
   1981   "Street-Level Justice: Situational Determinants of Police Arrest Decisions." *Social Problems* **29**:167–177.
Smith, R.L., and R.W. Taylor
   1985   "A Return to Neighborhood Policing: The Tampa, Florida Experience." *Police Chief* **52**:39–44.
Snyder, Howard N.
   1988   *Court Careers of Juvenile Offenders.* Pittsburgh: National Center for Juvenile Justice.
Solicitor General Canada
   1990   *A Vision of the Future of Policing in Canada: Police-Challenge 2000.* Ottawa, CAN: Ministry of the Solicitor General of Canada.
Solomon, Peter H.
   1985   "The Law Reform Commission of Canada's Proposals for Reforms of Police Powers: An Assessment." *Criminal Law Quarterly* **27**:321–351.
Southgate, F. Peter E., ed.
   1988   *New Directions in Police Training.* London, UK: Her Majesty's Stationery Office.
Southgate, F. Peter E.
   1989   "Traffic Policing: The Challenge to Managers and Evaluators." Unpublished paper presented at the annual meeting of the American Society of Criminology, November, Reno, NV.
Sparrow, Malcolm K.
   1993   *Information Systems and the Development of Policing.* Perspectives on Policing, no. 16. Washington, DC: U.S. Department of Justice, National Institute of Justice.
Spelman, William, and John E. Eck
   1987   *Problem-Oriented Policing.* Research in Brief. Washington, DC: National Institute of Justice.
Spergel, Irving A.
   1992   "Youth Gangs: An Essay Review." *Social Service Review* **66**:121–140.
Springer, Merle E.
   1988   "Youth Service Privatization: The Experience of a Provider." *Corrections Today* **50**:88–93.

Spurlin, Jere L., and Steve Schwein
   1990   "G.R.A.M.P.A. Cops." *FBI Law Enforcement Bulletin* May, pp. 2–4.

Star & Shield
   1993   "136 Police Deaths Reported in 1992 Lowest Number in Nearly 30 Years" **20**.

Staub, E.
   1989   *The Roots of Evil: The Origins of Genocide and Other Group Violence.* Cambridge, MA: Cambridge University Press.

St. Clair, James D. et al.
   1992   *Report to the Boston Police Department Management Review Committee.* Boston, MA: Boston Police Department Management Review Committee.

Steinman, Michael
   1986   "Managing and Evaluating Police Behavior." *Journal of Police Science and Administration* **14**:285–292.

Stenning, Philip C., and Clifford D. Shearing
   1991   "Policing." In *Criminology: A Reader's Guide,* edited by Jane Gladstone, Richard Ericson, and Clifford Shearing. Toronto, CAN: Centre of Criminology, University of Toronto.

Stephens, Darrel
   1990   "Prolem-Oriented Policing as a Means of Addressing Drug Problems in the Community." Unpublished paper presented at the annual meeting of the Academy of Criminal Justice Sciences, March, Denver.

Stephens, Darrel
   1987   "Research Results from the Problem-Oriented Policing Experiment in Newport News, Virginia." Unpublished paper presented at the annual meeting of the Academy of Criminal Justice Sciences, March.

Stewart, Robert W.
   1988   "Forced To Quit, Gay Ex-Officer Charges in Suit." *Los Angeles Times,* September 29, p. 8.

Steytler, Nico
   1991   "Democratizing the Criminal Justice System in South Africa." *Social Justice* **18**:141–153.

Stott, Vanessa
   1981   *English Legal System.* London, UK: Anderson Keenan.

Stromberg, C. et al.
   1988   *The Psychologist's Legal Handbook.* Washington, DC: The Council for the National Register of Health Service Providers in Psychology.

Sweet, Robert W., Jr.
   1990   *OJJDP Helps States Remove Juveniles from Adult Jails and Lockups.* Washington, DC: U.S. Department of Justice, Office of Justice Programs.

Swift, Roger
   1988   *Police Reform in Early Victorian York, 1835–1856.* York, UK: University of York.

Sykes, Gresham, and David Matza
   1957   "Techniques of Neutralization." *American Sociological Review* **22**:664–670.

Tafoya, William L. et al.
   1992   "Futuristic Views on Policing." *Journal of Contemporary Criminal Justice* **8**:183–264.

Taft, Phillip B., Jr.
   1986   *Fighting Fear: The Baltimore County COPE Project.* Washington, DC: Police Executive Research Forum.

Talbot, C.K.
   1984   "Policing in Canada: A Development Perspective." *Canadian Police College Journal* **8**:218–288.

Talbot, C.K., and C.H.S. Jayewardene
    1984   "Policing in Canada: A Development Perspective." *Canadian Police College Journal* **8**:218–288.
Tassy, Elaine
    1993   "Lucky Stores Agrees to Settle Sex Bias Suit." *Los Angeles Times,* December 17, p. D1.
Taylor, Carl S.
    1986   *Black Urban Youth Gangs: Analysis of Contemporary Issues.* Unpublished paper presented at the American Society of Criminology meetings. San Francisco. (November)
Taylor, R.W.
    1984   "Historical Developments and Contemporary Concepts in Police-Community Relations." *American Journal of Police* **3**:145–167.
Teplin, Linda A.
    1986   *Keeping the Peace: The Parameters of Police Discretion in Relation to the Mentally Disordered.* Washington, DC: U.S. National Institute of Justice.
The Thin Blue Line
    1991   Los Angeles: Los Angeles Protective League.
Thompson, George J.
    1993   *Verbal Judo.* New York: William Morrow and Company.
Thornberry, Terence, and R.L. Christenson
    1984   "Juvenile Justice Decision-Making as a Longitudinal Process." *Social Forces* **63**:433–444.
Thornton, Robert Y., and Katsuya Endo
    1992   *Preventing Crime in America and Japan: A Comparative Study.* Armonk, NY: M.E. Sharpe.
Thunder Bay Police Force
    1985   *Public's Perception of the Provision of Police Services in the City of Thunder Bay, 1984.* Thunder Bay, CAN: Author.
Thurman, Quint C., Andrew Giacomazzi, and Phil Bogen
    1993   "Research Note: Cops, Kids, and Community Policing—An Assessment of a Community Policing Demonstration Project." *Crime and Delinquency* **39**:554–564.
Time
    1993   "Hatred Turns Out Not To Be Color-Blind." *Time,* January 18, p. 22.
Time
    1994   "The Most Unusual Crowd Ever at a Bette Midler Concert." *Time,* January 10, p. 14.
Toch, Hans
    1992   *Violent Men: An Inquiry into the Psychology of Violence.* Washington, DC: American Psychological Association.
Toch, Hans, and J. Douglas Grant
    1991   *Police as Problem Solvers.* New York: Plenum.
Tomson, Barbara, and Edna R. Fielder
    1975   "Gangs: A Response to the Urban World." In *Gang Delinquency,* edited by Desmond S. Cartwright, Barbara Tomson, and Hershey Schwartz. Monterey, CA: Brooks/Cole.
Tonry, Michael, and Norval Morris, eds.
    1986   *Crime and Justice: An Annual Review of Research,* Vol. 7. Chicago: University of Chicago Press.
Tonry, Michael, and Norval Morris
    1992   *Modern Policing.* Chicago: University of Chicago Press.
Tremblay, Pierre, and Claude Rochon
    1991   "Police Organizations and Their Use of Knowledge: A Grounded Research Agenda." *Policing and Society* **1**:269–283.

Trojanowicz, Robert C.
   1988 "Community Policing: Implications for Police Selection." Unpublished paper presented at the annual meeting of the American Society of Criminology, November, Chicago, IL.

Trojanowicz, Robert, and Joanne Belknap
   1986 *Community Policing: Training Issues.* East Lansing: National Neighborhood Foot Patrol Center, School of Criminal Justice, Michigan State University.

Trojanowicz, Robert, and Bonnie Bucqueroux
   1990 *Community Policing: A Contemporary Perspective.* Cincinnati, OH: Anderson.

Trojanowicz, Robert, and Bonnie Bucqueroux
   1991 *Community Policing and the Challenge of Diversity.* East Lansing, MI: National Center for Community Policing Series No. 21.

Trojanowicz, Robert C., and David L. Carter
   1988 *The Philosophy and Role of Community Policing.* Community Policing Series No. 13. Flint, MI: National Neighborhood Foot Patrol Center.

Trojanowicz, Robert C., and H.A. Harden
   1985 *The Status of Contemporary Community Policing Programs.* Community Policing Series No. 3. East Lansing: National Neighborhood Foot Patrol Center, School of Criminal Justice, Michigan State University.

Trojanowicz, Robert C., and Mark H. Moore
   1988 *The Meaning of Community in Community Policing.* East Lansing, MI: National Neighborhood Foot Patrol Center.

Trompetter, Philip S.
   1993 "Pre-employment Psychological Screening of Violence-Prone Peace Officer Applicants." *The Journal of California Law Enforcement* **27**:36–45.

Trounson, Rebecca
   1994 "Police Net 104 Guns in Ducks Ticket Swap." *Los Angeles Times,* February 20, p. A1.

Tunnell, Kenneth D., and Larry K. Gaines
   1992 "Political Pressures and Influences on Police Executives: A Descriptive Analysis." *American Journal of Police* **11**:1–16.

Ungerleider, Charles S.
   1985 "Police Intercultural Education: Promoting Understanding and Empathy between Police and Ethnic Communities." *Canadian Ethnic Studies Association Bulletin* **17**:51–66.

University of Cape Town Institute of Criminology
   1990 *Kitskonstabels in Crisis: A Closer Look at Black on Black Policing.* Cape Town, SA.

USA Today
   1988 November 4, p. 3A.

U.S. Bureau of the Census
   1990 *Population of the United States, 1990.* Washington, DC: U.S. Government Printing Office.

U.S. Code
   1996 Washington, DC: U.S. Government Printing Office.

U.S. Department of Justice
   1987 *Principles of Good Policing: Avoiding Violence between Police and Citizens.* Washington, DC: U.S. Government Printing Office, Community Relations Service.

U.S. Department of Justice
   1988 *Report to the Nation on Crime and Justice.* Washington, DC: U.S. Department of Justice, Bureau of Justice Statistics.

U.S. National Advisory Commission on Law Enforcement
   1990 *Report, April 1990.* Washington, DC: Comptroller General of the United States.

U.S. Senate Judiciary Committee
  1984a *Catalogue of Hope: Crime Prevention Programs for At-Risk Children.* Washington, DC: U.S. Senate Majority Staff of the Senate Judiciary Committee.

U.S. Senate Judiciary Committee
  1984b *Deinstitutionalization of Juvenile Nonoffenders: Hearing.* Washington, DC: U.S. Government Printing Office.

U.S. News & World Report
  1991 September 30, p. 26.

U.S. News & World Report
  1993 "Joe Morgan." November 29, p. 18.

Van Laere, E.M.P., and R.W.M. Geerts
  1984 "Law Enforcers or Law Evaders: Deviant Behavior in the Amsterdam Police." *Police Studies* **7**:200–208.

Vaughn, Michael S.
  1990 "A Legal Analysis of Sobriety Checkpoints." *American Journal of Criminal Justice* **15**:24–52.

Vera Institute of Justice
  1968 *CPOP Community Policing in Practice.* New York: The Vera Institute.

Vera Institute of Justice
  1984 *The Community Police Officer Program: A Pilot Program in Community Oriented Policing in the 72nd Precinct, Interim Progress Report.* New York: Vera Institute of Justice.

Virginia State Crime Commission
  1994 *Police Accountability.* House Document No. 51. Richmond, VA: Virginia State Crime Commission.

Virginia State Legislature
  1950 *Code of Virginia.* Roanoke, VA: Author.

von Hoffman, Alexander
  1992 "An Officer in the Neighborhood: A Boston Patrolman on the Beat in 1895." *Journal of Social History* **26**:309–330.

Vrij, Albert
  1989 "Perceptions of Police Misconduct: Social-Psychological Analyses of Reporting Intentions among Police Officers in the Netherlands." *Police Studies* **12**:104–114.

Waddington, P.A.J.
  1983 *Are the Police Fair?* London, UK: Social Affairs Unit.

Waddington, P.A.J.
  1988 *Arming an Unarmed Police: Policy and Practice in the Metropolitan Police.* London, UK: Police Foundation.

Waddington, P.A.J., and Quentin Braddock
  1991 "'Guardians' or 'Bullies'? Perceptions of the Police amongst Adolescent Black, White, and Asian Boys." *Policing and Society* **2**:31–45.

Waddington, P.J.
  1984 "Community Policing: A Sceptical Appraisal." In *Law and Order and British Policies,* edited by Philip Norton. Brookfield, VT: Gower.

Wadman, Robert C., and Robert K. Olson
  1990 *Community Wellness: A New Theory of Policing.* Washington, DC: Police Executive Research Forum.

Waldorf, Dan
  1993 "When the Crips Invaded San Francisco: Gang Migration." *Gang Journal* **1**:11–16.

Waldorf, Dan et al.
　1990　"Needle Sharing Among Male Prostitutes: Preliminary Findings of the Prospero Project." *Journal of Drug Issues* **20**:309–334.

Walker, Christopher, and S. Gail Walker
　1989　*The Victoria Community Police Stations: An Exercise in Innovation.* Ottawa, CAN: Canadian Police College.

Walker, Nigel
　1968　*Crime and Punishment in Britain.* Chicago: Aldine.

Walker, Samuel
　1984　"'Broken Windows' and Fractured History: The Use and Misuse of History in Recent Police Patrol Analysis." *Justice Quarterly* **1**:75–90.

Walker, Samuel
　1992　*The Police in America: An Introduction,* 2nd ed. New York: McGraw-Hill.

Walker, Samuel
　1993　*Taming the System: The Control of Discretion in Criminal Justice.* New York: Oxford University Press.

Walker, Samuel, and Victor W. Bumphus
　1992　"Civilian Review of the Police: Recent Trends, New Issues." Unpublished paper presented at the annual meeting of the American Society of Criminology, November, New Orleans, LA.

Walker, Sandra Gail, Christopher R. Walker, and James C. McDavid
　1992　*The Victoria Police Stations: A Three-Year Evaluation.* Ottawa, CAN: Canadian Police College.

Wallace, Charles P.
　1994　"In Singapore, What Price Justice?" *Los Angeles Times,* April 2, p. A8.

Walsh, James
　1993　"The Perils of Success." *Time,* September 14, p. 29.

Warren, Jenifer
　1993　"FBI Settles Gay Agent's Suit, Vows Reforms." *Los Angeles Times,* December 11, p. A1.

Wasserman, Stuart
　1994　"Chief Walks the Walk, Talks the Talk on Portland Streets." *Los Angeles Times,* March 23, p. A5.

Watanabe, Teresa
　1992　"Victims of Japan's Safe Society." *Los Angeles Times,* February 27, pp. A1, A6–A7.

Wax, Jack
　1987　"Criminal Treatment." *The Progressive,* October, p. 26.

Weber, Alan M.
　1992　"Crime and Management: An Interview with New York City Police Commissioner Lee P. Brown." *Sourcebook Community-Oriented Policing: An Alternative Strategy.* New York: International City Management Association.

Websdale, Neil
　1991　"Disciplining the Non-Disciplinary Spaces: The Rise of Policing as an Aspect of Governmentality in 19th Century Eugene, Oregon." *Policing and Society* **2**:89–115.

Webster's New Riverside Dictionary
　1984　New York: World Publishing Company.

Weisburd, David, Jerome McElroy, and Patricia Hardyman
　1988　"Challenges to Supervision in Community Policing: Observations on a Pilot Project." *American Journal of Police* **7**:29–50.

Weitzer, Ronald
　1992　"Northern Ireland's Police Liaison Committees." *Policing and Society* **2**:233–243.

Weitzer, Ronald
 1995 *Policing under Fire: Ethnic Conflict and Police-Community Relations in Northern Ireland.* Albany, NY: State University of New York Press.

Westermann, Ted D., and James W. Burfeind
 1991 *Crime and Justice in Two Societies: Japan and the United States.* Pacific Grove, CA: Brooks/Cole.

Westley, William
 1970 *Violence and the Police: A Sociological Study of Law, Custom, and Morality.* Cambridge, MA: MIT Press.

Whisenand, Paul M., and Fred R. Ferguson
 1973 *The Managing of Police Organizations.* Englewood Cliffs, NJ: Prentice Hall.

Whisenand, Paul M., and Fred R. Ferguson
 1978 *The Managing of Police Organizations,* 2nd ed. Englewood Cliffs: Prentice Hall.

Whisenand, Paul M., and James L. Cline
 1979 *Patrol Operations.* Englewood Cliffs, NJ: Prentice Hall.

Whitman, David
 1987 "Down and Out in the 'Path Hotel'." *U.S. News & World Report,* March 23, pp. 69–70.

Wilbanks, William
 1987 *The Myth of a Racist Criminal Justice System.* Monterey, CA: Brooks/Cole.

Wilderman, Elizabeth
 1984 "Juvenile Diversion: From Politics to Policy." *New England Journal of Human Services* 3:19–23.

Will, George F.
 1993 "Are We a Nation of Cowards?" *Newsweek,* November 15, p. 94.

Williams, Frank P., III, and Carl P. Wagoner
 1992 "Making the Police Proactive: An Impossible Task for Improbable Reasons." *Police Forum* **2**:1–5.

Williams, Gerald
 1990 "Holistic Community Policing: The Aurora, Colorado Experience." Unpublished paper presented at the annual meeting of the Academy of Criminal Justice Sciences, March, Denver.

Williams, Hubert
 1992 *Introduction: Police Foundation Reports: Reconciling Higher Educational Standards and Minority Recruitment: The New York City Model.* Washington, DC: The Police Foundation.

Williams, J. Sherwood et al.
 1983 "Situational Use of Police Force: Public Reactions." *American Journal of Police* 3:37–50.

Williams, Jerry, and Ron Sloan
 1990 *Turning Concept into Practice: The Aurora, Colorado Story.* Community Policing Series No. 19. East Lansing: National Center for Community Policing, Michigan State University.

Willis, Carole F.
 1985 "The Police and Race Relations in England." *Police Studies* **8**:227–230.

Willis, Cecil L., and Richard H. Wells
 1988 "The Police and Child Abuse: An Analysis of Police Decisions to Report Illegal Behavior." *Criminology* **26**:695–716.

Wilson, O.W., and Roy C. McLaren
 1977 *Police Administration,* 4th ed. New York: McGraw-Hill.

Wilson, James Q.
 1968 *Varieties of Police Behavior.* Cambridge, MA: Harvard University Press.

Witkin, Gordon, and Tharp, Mike
    1992 "What the LAPD Ought to Try." *Sourcebook Community-Oriented Policing: An Alternative Strategy.* New York: International City Management Association.

Witte, Jeffrey H., Lawrence F. Travis III, and Robert H. Langworthy
    1990 "Participatory Management in Law Enforcement: Police Officer, Supervisor, and Administrator Perceptions." *American Journal of Police* **9**:1–23.

Witter, Jere
    1993 "No Place in Their Hearts for the Homeless." *Los Angeles Times,* April 22, p. B11.

Womack, Morris M., and Hayden H. Finley
    1986 *Communication: A Unique Significance for Law Enforcement.* Springfield, IL: Thomas.

The World Almanac and Book of Facts
    1992 New York: Scripps Howard Company.

Yablonsky, Lewis, and Martin R. Haskell
    1988 *Juvenile Delinquency,* 4th ed. New York: Harper & Row.

Yarnold, Barbara M.
    1991 *International Fugitives: A New Role for the International Court of Justice.* Westport, CT: Praeger.

Yokoyama, Minora
    1991 "Development of Japanese Drug Control Laws toward Criminalization." *Kokugakuin Journal of Law and Politics* **28**:1–21.

Young, Eric
    1993 "Experiment in Policing Beats Back Crime on Garden Grove Street." *Los Angeles Times,* August 19, pp. B1, B12.

Zauberman, R.
    1991 "Victimes en France: Des Positions, Interets, et Strategies Diverses." *Deviance et Societé* **15**:27–49.

Ziegenhagen, Eduard A., and Dolores Brosnan
    1991 "Citizen Orientations toward State and Non-State Policing." *Law and Society* **13**:245–257.

Zenon, Carl
    1990 "Journey to Japan." *Corrections Today* **52**:118–127.

Zevitz, Richard, and James S. Albritton
    1992 "Variation in Residents' Experiences Related to Problem-Oriented Policing: The Metcalf Park Experience in Milwaukee." Unpublished paper presented at the annual meeting of the American Society of Criminology, November, New Orleans, LA.

Zevitz, Richard G., and Robert J. Rettammel
    1990 "Elderly Attitudes about Police Service." *American Journal of Police* **9**:25–39.

Zunno, Frank A.
    1969 "A Changing Concept." *The Police Chief* **26**:44–46.

Zureik, Elia
    1990 "Control of the Palestinians in the Jewish State: A Review Essay." *Social Justice* **17**:55–69.

List of Cases Cited

Baker v. Glover, 646 F. Supp. 1511 (1991)
Bemis v. Kelley, 857 F. 2d 14 (1987)
Brewer v. Williams, 430 U.S. 387 (1977)
Cody v. United States, 460 F. 2d 34 (1972)
Commonwealth v. Bosurgi, 375 U.S. 910 (1963)
Graham v. Connor, 109 Sup. Ct. 1865 (1989)
Garrett v. Fleetwood, 644 So.2d 664 (1994)
Jonelis v. Russo, 863 F. Supp. 84 (1994)
Kreimer v. Bureau of Police for Town of Morristown, 958 F. 2d 1242 (1992)
Mapp v. Ohio, 367 U.S. 643 (1961)
Miranda v. Arizona, 384 U.S. 436 (1966)
Parrish v. Lukie, 963 F. 2d. 8th Cir. (1992)
Pestrak v. Ohio Elections Commission, 926 F. 2d 573 (1987)
Peterson v. State, 857 S.W.2d 927 (1993)
Rodriguez v. Fuetado, 575 F. Supp. 1439 Mass. (1991)
Rowland v. Perry, 41 F. 3d 167 (1994)
Sibron v. New York, 392 U.S. 40 (1968)
Sloman v. Tadlock, 21 F. 3rd 1462 (1994)
State v. Jones, 865 P. 2d 138 (1993)
State v. Jones, 649 A. 2d 89 (1994)
State v. Spencer, 876 P. 2d 939 (1994)
Stone v. Agnos, 960 F. 2d 893 (1992)
Tennessee v. Garner, 471 U.S. 1 (1985)

Terry v. Ohio, 392 U.S. 88 (1968)
Tilson v. Forrest City Police Department, 28 F. 3rd 802 (1994)
Timberlake v. Benton, 786 F. Supp. 676, M.D. Tenn. (1992)
United States v. Clark, 24 F. 3rd 299 (1994)
United States v. Leal, 409 U.S. 889 (1972)
United States v. Romero, 484 F. 2d 1324 (1973)
Weaver v. Williams, 509 F. 2d 884 (1975)

Name Index

A

Adamson, Patrick B. 21
Adamson, Raymond S. 337, 342
Advocate 150
Agopian, Michael W. 316
Agyapong, Owusu-Ansah 5
Ahire, Philip Terdoo 349
Aickin, Mikel 296
Albritton, James S. 7, 15-16
Alderson, John 333
Alemika, Etannibi E.O. 349
Alexander, David A. 326
Allen, Ronald J. 179
Alpert, Geoffrey P. 5, 13, 225
Alter, Jonathan 246
Amandes, Richard B. 316
American Bar Foundation 181
American Civil Liberties Union of Southern California 220
American Correctional Association 307
Anderson, Dennis R. 294
Anechiarico, Frank 195
Applegate, Jane 270
A.R.A. Consultants 341
Armstrong, Troy 306-307
Arrigona, Nancy 308-309
Arthur, John 219, 349
Associated Press 245, 279, 356
Association Internationale de Droit Penale 349
Austin, David 101
Austin, W. Timothy 350
Avins, Alfred 195

B

Bailey, William G. 21
Baird, S. Christopher 297
Baker, James N. 147
Barker, Thomas 196-197, 216
Barker, Troy A. 177
Barnett, Camille Cates 72
Barone, Michael 356
Barritt, Melissa 309
Baxter, Sandra 9, 298
Bayley, David H. 6, 322-323, 341, 345, 347
Beatty, Brian P. 374
Beck, Melinda 365
Belknap, Joanne 4
Bell, D. 308
Benda, Brent B. 294
Bennett, Richard R. 9, 298
Bennett, Trevor 7, 334
Bennett, Wayne W. 16
Benyon, Helen 326, 328
Berger, Leslie 280
Berkley, George E. 71
Berman, J. Stuart 21
Bernsen, Rod 83
Betsalel, Kenneth Aaron 3
Billiter, Bill 249, 364

Name Index

Binder, Arnold 137, 139, 294, 298
Bishop, Donna M. 307, 313
Bittner, Egon 298
Black, Donald 311
Black, Henry Campbell 289-290
Blackmore, John 295-296
Block, Carolyn R. 310
Block, Richard 310
Blumberg, Abraham S. 70
Blustein, Jeffrey 291
Bogan, Phil 317
Boglarsky, Cheryl A. 292
Bond, Kevin 327
Bossard, Andre 348
Boucher, Geoff 270
Bourne, Dennis 328
Bouza, Anthony 70
Bowers, Robert A. 72
Boxall, Bettina 151, 258
Braddock, Quentin 332
Bradel, Don 9
Bradshaw, Robert V. 5
Braiden, Chris 342
Braswell, Michael C. 177
Bratton, William J. 386
Brewer, John D. 94
Britz, Marjie T. 221
Brogden, Mike 333
Brookhiser, Richard 233
Brosnan, Dolores 13
Brown, B.J. 337
Brown, David 334
Brown, Gary 61
Brown, Lee P. 2, 6-7, 9, 72, 87, 298
Brown, Marci 295-296
Brown, M. Craig 4, 11
Brownstein, Ronald 110-111
Buckley, Lesley Brian 342
Bucqueroux, Bonnie 5, 23-24, 313, 322
Bumphus, Victor W. 227
Bunyard, Robert S. 327-328
Bureau of Justice Statistics 88
Burfeind, James W. 346
Burgess, Ann Wolbert 292
Burgreen, Bob 366
Burke, Theresa A. 292
Burton, Velmer S. Jr. 177
Business Week 267
Butler, T. 197

C

Cahn, M.F. 58
Cairns, Kathleen 267
Callahan, Charles M. 300
Cameron, Neil 6
Canada Law Reform Commission 335
Canada Royal Canadian Mounted Police 341
Canada Solicitor General's Select Committee on Police Pursuits 339

Carpenter, G.J. 338
Carrier, John 330-331
Carriere, Kevin D. 341
Carter, David L. 2, 9-10, 16, 209, 211
Case, Charles E. 219
Casey, Pamela 303, 306
Cashmore, Ellis 193
Caton, David 292
Cekola, Anna 244
Champion, Dean J. 292, 304, 306
Chappell, Duncan 339
Chen, Edwin 51
Chesney-Lind, Meda 310
Chevigny, Paul L. 321, 349
Christenson, R.L. 306
Christopher, Steven 321
Cizanckas, Victor I. 385
Clairmont, Donald 341
Clark, Amelia M. 184
Clarke, Ronald V. 334
Cockburn, Alexander 280
Cohen, Fred 219
Cohen, Howard S. 177, 195
Cole, Don 255
Colley, Lori L. 296
Collins, James J. 293
Connor, Christina 371
Connor, G. 221, 298
Conrad, John P. 298
Copus, Gary 4, 92-93
Corbett, C. 332
Cordner, Gary W. 40, 179
Corns, Christopher 350
Correction News 265
Corrections Compendium 296, 314, 317
Corwin, Miles 114, 128
Cory, Bruce 247-248
Cose, Ellis 242
Cosgrove, Colleen A. 12
Coulter, Jim 328
Council of Europe 348
Couper, David C. 7
CPOA flier 387
Craen, Andre 322
Crank, John P. 54, 59
Crime Control Digest 213
Criminal Justice Newsletter 198
Crocker, Brenda D. 195
Croft, John 326
Cryderman, Brian K. 337-338
Culbertson, Robert G. 296
Cummings, Scott 310
Curran, Daniel J. 307

D

Dahl, Jonathan 265
Dale, Michael J. 298
Dane, N.N., Jr. 54
Dantzker, Mark 5, 187-189

Das, Dilip K. 2-3
Database 114
Datesman, Susan K. 296
Davidson, William S. 294
Davis, Kenneth C. 298
Davis, Wally 170
Davis, William 275
Dawidoff, Robert 261
DeAngelo, Andrew J. 294
Decker, Scott H. 5
DeCujir, Walter J. 276-278
Del Buono, Vincent M. 339, 342
Descza, Gene 337
DeWitt, Charles B. 2
Dilworth, D. 261
Dinitz, Simon 344, 346
DiRado, Alicia 269
Doerner, William G. 324
Dombrink, John 216
Don, Kim 336
Dotson, L.L. 56
Downes, David 329, 332
Doyle, James F. 177
Dubro, Alec 346
Duffy, Brian 244, 246
Dunham, Roger G. 5, 13
Dunn, Allyson 302-303

E

Earnest, Leslie 260
Eaton, William J. 111, 160, 256
Eck, John E. 9, 11-12, 18, 52, 97-99
Edwards, Don 279-280
Einstadter, W.J. 9
Eisenberg, Justin 167
Milton S. Eisenhower Foundation 314
Elliott, Delbert S. 311
Elmsley, Clive 327
Elson, John 233
Encyclopedic Dictionary of Sociology 67
Endo, Katsuya 345-346
Enter, Jack E. 52
Erikson, Richard V. 341
Esbensen, Finn-Aage 311
Eskridge, Chris 347
Ewin, R.E. 321, 350

F

Fabelo, Tony 308-309
Fagan, Jeffrey A. 305
Fagan, Michael M. 133
Fair, Frank 196, 219
Fairchild, Erika S. 321, 350
Falcone, David L. 221
Farish, Steve 365
Farnworth, Margaret 297, 309
Farrell, Jeff 109
Farrell, Michael J. 12, 95

Farrow, James A. 300
Feldberg, Michael 195
Feldman, Paul 280, 379
Felkenes, George T. 97
Ferguson, Fred R. 74-77
Fielder, Edna R. 312
Fielding, Nigel G. 330-331
Findley, Kenneth W. 2
Fine, Bob 328
Fine, Kerry Kinney 294
Finley, Hayden H. 4
Finn, Peter E. 47, 263-264, 268, 271-274, 276-278
Fishkin, Gerald L. 167
Fishman, Gideon 344, 346
Fitch, Bob 262
Flanagan, Timothy J. 299
Fleissner, Dan 13, 103-104
Fooner, Michael 348
Foscarinis, Maria 264, 270
Fosdick, Raymond B. 25
Frank, James 177
Frazier, Charles E. 296, 307, 313
Freeman, John C. 327
Friedman, Ruth 210
Friedmann, Robert R. 16, 106
Fritz, Noah 7
Fu, Hualing 351
Fuller, John R. 297
Fyfe, James J. 202

G

Gage, Richard 151-153
Gaines, L. 158
Gaines, Larry K. 51, 59
Galvin, G.T. 13
Garborino, A.C. 292
Garborino, James 292
Garner, Gerald 83
Gates, Daryl L. 45
Geerts, R.W.M. 321
Geis, Gilbert 137, 139, 294
Geller, William A. 58, 105, 276
Gelsthrope, Loraine R. 307
George, Lenny 375
Georgetown Law Journal 219
Gerstenzang, James 280
Gest, Ted 356
Giakomazzi, Andy 317
Gianakis, Gerasimos A. 5
Gill, M.L. 333
Gilsinan, James F. 51
Givens, Greg 310
Glastris, Kukula 237
Gleaton, Janice 378
Glensor, Ronald W. 5
Goldman, John 111
Goldstein, Herman 6, 18, 51, 70, 99, 134, 181-182, 208, 324

Name Index

Gomez-Buendia, Hernando 344
Gordon, Larry 266
Gorman, Albert J. 216
Governing 371
Grabosky, P.N. 13
Graf, Francis A. 339
Graham, Linda P. 339
Grant, J. Douglas 12
Graves, F.R. 221
Gray, Kelsey 17, 40, 51
Greenberg, Martin A. 217
Greene, Jack R. 5, 9-11, 13, 106
Greenwood, Peter W. 294, 303, 306
Greiner, John M. 46, 51-52, 61
Grieco, Eileen Spillane 293
Grisso, Thomas 303, 306
Griswold, David B. 220
Grohmann, Stephen W. 309
Gruber, Gerald 338
Guarino-Ghezzi, Susan 314
Guggenheim, Martin 289-290
Guttman, Monika 237
Guyot, Dorothy 5, 16, 18

H

Hacker, Andrew 241
Hackler, James C. 337
Hackler, Jim 336
Hagedorn, John 309-310
Hageman, Mary Jeanette 23, 27
Hale, Donna C. 40, 179
Hann, Robert G. 337
Hansen, Russell 184
Harden, H.A. 9
Harris, Patricia M. 305
Harrison, Eric 371
Harvard Law Review 91
Haskell, Martin R. 311
Hatler, Richard W. 7
Hatry, H.P. 52
Hatty, Suzanne 350
Hayeslip, David W. 108
Heck, William P. 226
Heiman, Andrea 249, 367
Hernandez, Greg 284
Hesketh, Brian 52
Hess, Karen M. 16, 24, 178
Hetherington, Sir Thomas 329
Hickman, Kenneth G. 51, 55
Hill, Elaine 12, 18
Hill, Susan 330
Hillbery, Rhonda 110
Holdaway, Simon 329, 331
Holden, Richard 21
Holland, Gale 148
Homant, Robert J. 221
Hoover, Larry T, 5, 59, 177
Horne, Paul 142
Hornick, Joseph P. 339-340

Horovitz, Bruce 258
Horvath, John A. 293, 307-308
Hough, Mike 334
Hubler, Shawn 245
Hughes, Stella P. 294
Huizinga, David 311
Humphrey Institute for Public Affairs 309
Hunt, Raymond G. 55
Hunter, Ronald D. 196-197
Hymas, Michael 134

I

Iles, Susan 334
Ingram, Carl 357
Inkster, Norman D. 20
Innes, George 326
International Association of Chiefs of Police 5, 58-59
International City Management Association 44
International Crime Center 326
Irving, Barrie L. 326
Iwai, H. 346
Iwata, Edward 270

J

Jackson, R.L. 337, 342
Janssen, Christian T.L. 337
Janus, Mark-David 292-293
Japan Ministry of Justice 344, 346
Jaywardene, C.H.S. 336
Jefferson, Tony 333
Johnson, Rodney 245
Joyce, M.A.S. 334

K

Kahn, Andy N. 332
Kakimi, Takashi 346
Kalinich, David B. 185
Kalish, Carol B. 326
Kang, K. Connie 249
Kaplan, David E. 346
Kaplan, Lisa 293
Kappeler, Victor E. 210, 212, 215, 225
Kavanagh, John 220
Kearney, William J. 297
Keene, Judith 340
Keith, Richard G. 315
Kelling, George L. 11, 386
Kelly, Patricia A. 21
Kende, Beryl 293
Kennedy, D.M. 46
Kennedy, Daniel B. 221
Kennedy, Leslie W. 342
Kennedy, Will 5

Kenney, John P. 298
Kinsey, Richard 328-329
Kirk, A.R. 244
Klein, Malcolm W. 298
Kleinig, John 216
Kline, James L. 101
Klockars, Carl B. 55, 197
Knoxville Police Department 5
Krajick, Kevin 364
Kraska, Peter B. 215
Kratcoski, Lucille Dunn 314
Kratcoski, Peter C. 314
Krause, Wesley 297
Krisberg, Barry 295-297
Kufeldt, Kathleen 293

L

Lacey, Marc 358
Lamb, Richard 275
Lang, K. 308
Langworthy, Robert H. 51, 177
Larsen, Peter 150
Larson, Jan 88
Layne, Karen 47
Lea, John 326, 328-329
Leddy, Daniel D. 290
Lee, M. 21, 24
Lee, Patrick 245
Lee, Soon Young 346
Leighton, Barry 338, 342
Leo, John 244
Levine, Charles H. 51, 61-62
Lewis, Clare E. 340
Liberman, H. 275
Linden, Rick 338
Linden, Sidney B. 340
Lindsay, Betsy 12
Lipson, Karin 316
Little, Margaret A. 298
Littlejohn, Edward J. 227
Lloyd, Kent 74
Lobitz, Sabine H. 7
Loeb, Penny 235, 237
Loeb, Roger C. 292
Logan, Charles H. 296
London Strategic Policy Unit 331
Long Beach Press Telegram 52
Loree, Donald J. 337, 339-342
Los Angeles Times 111, 152, 256-257, 266, 268, 271-275, 355-356, 358
Loveday, Barry 330, 332-333
Lovrich, Nicholas P. 17, 40, 51
Lyman, J.L. 24

M

Mader, Edward T. 59
Magenau, John M. 55

Maggs, Christopher 7, 15
Maguire, Brendan 21
Maguire, Kathleen 299, 310
Maguire, M. 332
Maharaj, Davan 260
Mahoney, Anne Rankin 305
Maloney, Dennis M. 306-307
Mande, Mary J. 300
Manning, Peter K. 3, 54-55, 182
Mapstone, Richard 94
Marenin, Otwin 4, 92-93, 182
Marshall, James 101
Martin, Lynn 2
Martinez, Gebe 245
Maslach, C. 167
Maslow, Abraham 45
Massachusetts Department of Youth Services 307
Mastrofski, Stephen D. 18
Matthews, Roger 326
Matza, David 225
Mawby, R.L. 333
Maxson, Cheryl L. 298
Mayer, Martin J. 265
Mayhall, Pamela D. 19, 21, 24, 196-197
Mays, G. Larry 292, 306, 310
McCarthy, Belinda R. 294, 297, 304, 307-309
McCormack, Arlene 292
McCoy, Candace 214
McDavid, James C. 9
McDougall, Allan K. 338
McDowell, Jeanne 144
McElroy, Jerome E. 12
McEvoy, Glenn M. 51
McEwen, J. Thomas 46
McGee, Zina T. 289
McGillis, Daniel 47
McGinnis, James H. 337
McGregor, Douglas 44, 385
McKenzie, Ian 196
McLaren, Roy C. 26
McLaughlin, Eugene 193
McLeay, E.M. 334
McLeod, Ramon G. 257
McNamara, Chief Joseph D. 3
McShane, Marilyn D. 297
Meeks, Daryl H. 167
Meese, Edwin, III 38, 40, 47, 51, 134
Melekian, Barney 272-273
Mendoza, N.F. 153
Meyer, Josh 384
Michaud, Anne 151
Millar, Robert 328
Miller, Larry S. 177
Miller, Linda S. 24, 178
Miller, Susan 328
Mitchell, Jeff 148
Mixdorf, Lloyd 198, 297
Miyazawa, Setsuo 321, 346-347
Moffat, Susan 245
Monti, Daniel J. 310

Moone, Joseph 299
Moore, Joan 309
Moore, Mark Harrison 2, 9, 12, 18, 42, 54
Morash, Merry 312
More, Harry W. 55, 298
Morgan, Anthony D. Sergeant 104
Morganthau, Tom 355
Morrill, S. 10
Morris, Norval 20, 294
Murphy, Chris 339, 341-342
Murphy, Patrick V. 94
Murphy, Robert B. 101

N

Nagoshi, Jack T. 304
Nakayama, Kenichi 343
National Advisory Commission on Criminal Justice Standards and Goals 27, 300, 302
National College of Juvenile and Family Law 294
National Institute of Justice 95, 357
Nazario, Sonia 143
Neeley, Richard 13
Neff, Andy 371
Nehrbass, Arthur F. 83
Neiderhoffer, Arthur 70
Network 387
Neuberger, Anita R. 297
Newell, Charldean 209
Newing, John 329
Newton, Jim 55-56, 166
New York Commission for the Study of Youth Crime and Violence and the Reform of the Juvenile Justice System 314
New York Commission to Investigate Allegations of Police Corruption 216
New York Times 268
Nila, Michael J. 12, 18
Nimick, Ellen H 303
Nimocks, Rudolph 12
Nishimura, Haruro 347
Noaks, Lesley 321
Normandeau, Andre 338, 342
Norton, William M. 297

O

Oakley, Robin 331
Ohlin, Lloyd E. 181
Oliver, Jan 328
Olivero, J. Michael 184
Olson, Robert K. 7
Opolot, James S.E. 322
Orange County Register 270
Orlov, Rick 150
Ortega, Ruben B. 58
Osgood, D. Wayne 294
Ostrow, Ronald J. 280

O'Toole, Chris N. 337-338
Ottemeier, Timothy 11

P

Packer, Herbert 32
Parker, Craig 346-347
Pastore, Ann L. 299, 310
Pate, A.M. 5
Payne, D.M. 9-10
Payne, Dennis M. 221
Peak, Ken 5, 20, 23, 70, 138, 142
Peart, Leo E. 61
Peoples, Edward E. 83, 123
Perez, Douglas W. 225
Perry, Philip E. 293
Pettijohn, Terry F. 169
Phelps, Lourn 101
Philadelphia Police Study Task Force 12
Pilcher, Wayland D. 196, 219
Pine, Art 137, 139-140
Plumridge, M.D. 328
Police Foundation Reports 146
Polk, Kenneth 294
Pollock, Janay 209
Pollock-Byrne, Joycelyn M. 201
Pope, David W. 332
Pope, Karen E. 332
Pope, Lisa 148, 150
PORAC News 170, 384
Post, Tom 356, 358
Pounder, Chris 329
Powell, Dennis D. 184-185
Preszler, Alan 108
Price, Kendall O. 74

Q

Quah, Jon S. 350
Quah, Stella R. 350

R

Radelet, Louis A. 209
Rankin, Blair 79-80
Rankin, J.H. 293, 296
Rap Sheet 62, 259-260
Rausch, Sharla P. 296
Regalado, Jeannette 271
Reichel, Philip L. 294-295
Reiner, R. 328
Reiss, Albert J., Jr. 56, 120, 311
Reith, C. 21
Remington, Frank J. 181
Reyes, David 240
Rhoades, Philip W. 195-196, 219
Rich, T.F. 58
Richardson, James F. 23

Riddle, Lyn 368
Riordan, Mayor Richard 55-56
Ritter, Bruce 293
Rivara, Frederick P. 300
Roan, Shari 267
Roberts, Albert R. 312
Robinson, Cyril D. 21
Robison, Clay 276
Rochon, Claude 54
Rogers, Joseph W. 310
Rolf, C.H. 338
Romig, Dennis 306-307
Rotella, Sebastian 282
Rowan, Colonel Charles 27
Rowe, Dennis 348
Roybal, Francis 101
Rubin, Paula 158-160
Rubinstein, Jonathan 19
Rush, George E. 88, 114, 147, 259, 301

S

Sadd, Susan 12
Sametz, Lynn 294
Sampson, Robert J. 311
Sanders, William B. 310
Savage, David G. 279
Scaglion, Richard 21
Scanlon, Joseph 342
Scharf, P. 298
Scheibel, Jim 264, 270
Schmidt, Wayne W. 212
Schneid, T. 158
Schneider, Anne L. 294-295, 305
Schneider, Hans Joachim 345-346, 348
Schoen, Donald F. 294
Schram, Donna D. 305
Schulman, Rena 293
Schwartz, Ira M. 294
Schwein, Steve 363
Scrivner, Ellen M. 220
Senese, Jeffrey D. 185
Serpico, Frank 216-217
Sewell, John 339, 342
Seyfrit, Carole L. 294-295
Shadmi, Erella 225
Shaffer, David 292
Shah, Diane K. 45
Shane, Paul G. 293
Shearing, Clifford D. 177
Shelden, Randall G. 293, 307-308
Sheley, Joseph F. 289, 300
Sheppard, David L. 17
Sherman, Lawrence W. 18, 195-196
Shewhart, W.A. 48
Shikita, Minora 344
Shogren, Elizabeth 268
Sieffert, J.M. 10
Singh, Mahendra 20
Sipchen, Bob 148-149

Skogan, Wesley G. 5, 321, 334
Skolnick, Jerome H. 6, 70, 92, 106, 177
Slivinski, L.W. 337
Sloan, Ron 13, 66
Sluder, Richard D. 225
Smegal, Thomas Sergeant 103
Smith, Brent L. 308-309
Smith, Douglas 311
Smith, R.L. 10
Smithers, Alan 330
Snyder, Howard 303, 308
Solicitor General of Canada 336-337, 339, 342
Solomon, Peter H. 339
Southgate, F. Peter E. 326, 331
Sparrow, Malcolm K. 99-100, 105
Spelman, William 9, 11-12, 18, 52, 97-99
Spergel, Irving A. 310
Springer, Merle E. 292
Spurlin, Jere L. 363
Star and Shield 165
St. Clair, James D. 1, 18
Steinman, Michael 47, 51
Stenning, Philip C. 177
Stephens, Darrel 13, 18, 42, 54
Stewart, James K. 11
Stewart, Robert W. 148
Steytler, Nico 350
Stohr-Gillmore, Mary K. 17, 40, 51
Stutts, Brian L. 294-295
Sullivan, Monique 278
Suzuki, Shingo 347
Sweet, Robert W., Jr. 300
Swift, Roger 328
Sykes, Gresham 225
Szymanski, Linda 303

T

Tafoya, William L. 4, 37
Taft, Phillip B., Jr. 20
Talbot, C.K. 336
Tassy, Elaine 153
Taylor, Carl S. 310-311
Taylor, R.W. 10
Taylor, Robert W. 2
Teplin, Linda A. 185
Terrill, Richard J. 343-347
Tharp, Mike 70
Thin Blue Line, The 170
Thompson, George J. 73-74, 140
Thornberry, Terence 306
Thornton, Robert Y. 345-346
Thunder Bay Police Department 340
Thurman, Quint 317
Time 246, 358
Toch, Hans 12
Tomkins, Alan 303, 306
Tomson, Barbara 312
Tonry, Michael 20, 294
Torres, Vicki 151

Name Index

Tracy, Sharon 293
Travis, Lawrence F., III 51
Tremblay, Pikerre 54
Trojanowicz, Robert C. 2-5, 9-10, 16, 23-24, 313, 322
Trompetter, Philip S. 124
Trounson, Rebecca 358
Tsuchiya, Shinichi 344
Tunnell, Kenneth D. 51, 59
TV Times 69
Tweedy, Jerry 209

U

Ungerleider, Charles S. 338, 342
USA Today 269
U.S. Department of Justice 299
U.S. Department of Justice, Community Relations Service 4-5, 16-17
U.S. National Advisory Commission on Law Enforcement 48
U.S. News & World Report 144, 247, 259
U.S. Senate Judiciary Committee 296
U.S. Senate Majority Staff of the Senate Judiciary Committee 314
University of Cape Town Institute of Criminology 321, 349

V

Valentine, James R. 51
Van Laere, E.M.P. 321
Vargas, Officer Jose Diaz 283-284
Vaughn, Michael S. 179, 345-346
Violante, William C. 56
Virginia State Crime Commission 202
Visher, Christy 311
von Hoffman, Alexander 21
Vollmer, August 25-26
Vrij, Albert 210

W

Waddington, P.A.J. 10, 326, 332, 334
Wadman, Robert C. 7
Wagoner, Carl P. 7
Waldorf, Dan 305, 310
Walker, Christopher R. 9, 341
Walker, Martin 328
Walker, Nigel 326
Walker, Robert W. 340
Walker, Samuel 19, 25-26, 185, 227, 298
Walker, Sandra Gail 9, 341
Walklate, Sandra 333
Wallace, Charles P. 245
Walsh, James 111, 235

Ward, Tony 329, 332
Warner, Barbara D. 4, 11
Warren, Jenifer 257
Wasserman, Stuart 379
Watanabe, Teresa 346-347
Wax, Jack 275-276
Weber, Alan M. 71
Websdale, Neil 62
Weitzer, Ronald 94
Wells, Alice 142
Wells, L.E. 293, 296
Wells, Richard H. 298
Westermann, Ted D. 346
Westley, William 70
Whisenand, Paul M. 74-77, 97, 101
Whitaker, Gordon 298
Whitman, David 274
Whittingham, Michael D. 337
Wilbanks, William 311
Will, George F. 111-112, 356
Williams, Frank P., III 7
Williams, Hubert 145-146
Williams, J. Sherwood 298
Williams, Jack 13
Williams, Jerry 13, 66
Williams, Chief Willie 56
Willis, Carol F. 329
Willis, Cecil L. 298
Wilson, James Q. 32, 70
Wilson, Janis 292
Wilson, O.W. 26
Witkin, Gordon 70
Witt, Rodney 9
Witte, Jeffrey H. 51
Witter, W.D. 269
Womack, Morris M. 4
World Almanac 345
Wright, James D. 289, 300
Wycoff, Mary Ann 6, 17

Y

Yablonsky, Lewis 311
Yarnold, Barbara M. 348
Yokoyama, Minora 346
Young, Eric 96
Young, Jock 326, 328-329

Z

Zauberman, R. 321
Zenon, Carl 343
Ziegenhagen, Eduard A. 13
Zevitz, Richard G. 7, 15-16
Zunno, Frank A. 100
Zureik, Elia 94

Subject Index

A

Aberdeen Plan 100
Abuses of discretion 195-196
Academy training 127-133
A Community Outreach Program (ACOP) 7
Accountability 383-384
Act Up (Aids Coalition to Unleash Power) 258-259
Affirmative action 144-145, 157
Affirmative Action Unit 157
Affordable housing 261-262
   homelessness 261-262
AIDS 113-114, 147, 151, 258-259
   homeless 265-266
AIDS Foundation 147
Air Carrier Access Act of 1986 158
Alaska Village Public Safety Officer (VPSO) Program 92-93
   components 93
Alateen 315
Albany, New York, Approach 374
Alcoholics Anonymous 171
Alcoholism and substance abuse 171
Alexandria, Virginia, Residential Police Officers Program 375-378
Alienation, police-citizen 26
Alternative dispute resolution 294
American Bar Foundation Survey 181-182
Americans with Disabilities Act (ADA) 158-160, 391
   reasonable accommodations 158-159
Antitraction technology 139
Arrest rates by race 243
Asian American Legal Defense and Education Fund 249
Asian-American Legal Law Caucus 249
Asian Pacific American Legal Center 249
Assaults on police officers 136
"Atta Boys" 42-45
Autonomy 179-180
"Aw Shits" 42-45

B

Background checks and interviews 124-125
Back-to-the-community movement 88-89
Baker v. Glover (1991) 191
Balanced approach 306-307
Basic Car Plan 97
Beat patrolling 9, 26
Bemis v. Kelly (1987) 193
Bicycle patrols 103-104
Black crime 243
Black law enforcement officers 142-144
Black police officer associations 247-248
Blue curtain 227
"Blue Humor" 169-171
Boston Police Department 18
Bow Street Runners 23
Boy Scouts 87, 96

Branch Dividian cult 137
British Crime Survey 326
British Police National Computer (PNC) 329
Brixton riots 332-333
Brown v. Board of Education (1954) 158
Budget 58-59
   defined 58
Budget Review Committee 107
Bureaucracy 38-39
Burnout 80, 164-169
   defined 165-166
   effects on organizations 168-169
Burnout Syndrome 167-169
Burntout Policeman's Association and Friends (BPA) 169

C

Cadet programs 365-366
Calgary, Alberta, Police Department 338
California Commission on Peace Officers Standards and Training (POST) 140-142
California League of Cities 141
Calls-for-service 45-47
Calmative agents 140
Campus Pride 316
Canada 334-342
   community policing 339-342
   police supervision and organization 336-339
   type of crime 335-335
   type of government 334-335
Canadian Center for Justice Statistics 335-336
Canadian Multi-Jurisdictional Police Officer Examination (MPOE) 338
Canadian Secretary of State's Multiculturalism Directorate 338
Career Integrity Workshops 160-162
   defined 161
Cargo cats 245
Casablanca 76-77
Catholics in Northern Ireland 94
Census tracts and crime reporting 54
Centurions 21
Certification letters 126-127
Chain of custody 188
Chancellors 22
Chicago Afro-American Patrolmen's League (AAPL) 247
Chicago, Illinois, mentally ill offenders 185
Children in need of supervision (CHINS) 295
Christian burial case 186-187
Chuzaishos 345
Citizen involvement 361
City budgets and crime control 58
City planning and crime 54
Civil Communications Section, U.S. Army 48
Civil disobedience 27
Civilian complaint review boards 227-228
   defined 227

Civil Rights Act of 1964 153, 156, 158
Civil rights violations 212-213
Civil service examinations 123-134
Clearance rates 45
Code of silence 70-72, 78-79, 149, 215, 217
   academy training and 78-79
   corruption 79, 215, 217
   defined 70
   misconduct 215, 217
Codes of ethics 34-37
Cody v. United States (1972) 1972
Colquhoun, Patrick 24
Columbia, South Carolina, program 369-372
Columbus, Ohio, Training Program 132-133
Combustion alteration technology 139
Command decision making 26
Commonwealth v. Bosurgi (1963) 192
Community, concept of 3, 11-13
Community-based policing 17-18
Community crime control 27-28
Community Officer COPE Program 2
Community-oriented policing 87
Community Patrol Officer Program (CPOP) 2, 12, 95-96
Community-police educational program (COPE) 5
Community policing 2-12, 20-28, 89-90
   components 89-90
   defined 3, 14
   evolution of 20-28
   homeless and 263-264
   latent functions 105-106
   manifest functions 105
   reasons for studying 19-20
Community Projects for Restoration (CPR) Plan 379-380
Community wellness 7
Comparative community policing 321-351
   defined 322
   trends 349-351
Conservative law enforcement views 249-250
Constables 22-23
Constitution Act of 1867
Contact patrols 334
Contempt-of-cop 73, 75
Contract law enforcement 56-58
Contracting 56-57
Controlling police discretion 201-203
COPY Kids 317
Core values 50
Council of Europe 348
County and Borough Police Act of 1856 327
Cover Your Ass Syndrome (CYA syndrome) 32, 51
Coyotes 281
Criminal Code of Canada 335
Criminal Justice Act of 1948 326
Criminal Law Act of 1967 325
Crime 369
   defining 369

SUBJECT INDEX

Crime control 66, 74
Crime rates 45, 88-89
   measures of police effectiveness 45-46
   population density 88-89
Crime Stoppers 340-341
Crime Watch programs 7
Criminal Investigation Division 100
Crown Prosecution Service 329
Cultural universals 349
Culture 67-68
Curfew violators 293

D

D.A.R.E. 315
Day watch 22
Deadly force 107-109, 211, 223-225
Deaths of police officers, line of duty 165
Decarceration 295-296
Decertification 228
Decision making 50-51
"Defanging" courses 136-137
"Defense-of-life" standard 195, 220, 223-224
   provisions outlined 223-224
Deinstitutionalization of status offenses (DSO) 289, 295-297, 302
   criticisms 296-297
   decarceration 295-296
Delinquency prevention programs 314-318
   Alateen 315-316
   Campus Pride 316
   COPY Kids 317
   D.A.R.E. 315
   Dickerson's Rangers 316
   Graffiti Removal Community Service Program 316
   GREAT 315
   Hire a Gang Leader 316
   Project Heavy 315
   R.O.C.K. (Reaching Out, Convicts and Kids) 317
   TIPS 315
Deming, Dr. Romaine 48
Demographics 87-88
Density 87-88
Detroit, Michigan Police Department 91-92
   community-oriented policing 91-92
Deviance, socially approved 256-257
Dickerson's Rangers 316
Differential Police Response (DPR) 46
Directed Area Responsibility Team (DART) 2
"Dirty Harry" phenomenon 160-161
Discrimination by police 246-247, 260-261
   mechanisms for controlling 247
Divestiture of jurisdiction 296-297
Dropsy testimony 217-219
Drug users and police 278-280
Drummond, Oliver "Lee" 49
Dual procedure offenses 335-336

Due process model 32
DWI drivers 184, 216

E

Eastside Substance Abuse Awareness Program (ESAAP) 300
Elderly citizens 364-365
Electromagnetic pulse 139
Emotional numbing 169-170
Empathy training 73-77
Empowerment 50-51
   defined 50-51
England 325-334
   community policing 328-334
   police supervision and organization 327-328
   types of crimes 325-327
English system 23
Equal protection clause 190
Ethical conduct 34-37
Ethnic enclaves 255-256
Ethnocentricity 241
Evidence falsification 79
Excessive force 211, 220-221
Exclusionary rule 194, 218
Executive selection 59
"Exigent circumstances" exception 194
Explorer Scouts 87, 260, 365

F

Failure to train 381-382
Fair Housing Amendments Act of 1988 158
Failure to train 210
False arrest 212
False imprisonment 212
Family Crisis Intervention 278
Fear of crime 115-116
Federal Law Enforcement Training Center (FLETC) 221
Field Training Officers (FTOs) 79-80, 134-135
   functions 134
   training programs and 79-80
Fielding, Henry 23
Fielding, Sir John 23
First Amendment 190-191
   cases 191
Fleeing felon rule 108-109, 211-212, 220, 223-224
   invalidated 223-224
Fluid patrol 100
Foot patrols 2, 10, 12
Force continuum 221-223
Fourteenth Amendment 192-195
   cases 192-195
Fourth Amendment 108-109, 192, 224
   cases 192
   deadly force 108-109

Fourth Amendment *(cont.)*
   "good faith" exception 192
   "objective reasonableness" 224
   warrantless searches 192
Frankpledge system 22
"Front-end" solutions 228
Frugal Flush 270
Frumentarii 21

G

Gangs 360-361
Gaols 22
Garden Grove, California, Police Department 96-97
Garrett v. Fleetwood (1994) 212-213
Gay and Lesbian Chapter 147
Gay and Lesbian Police Advisory Task Force 150
Gay-bashing 256
Gay Officers Action League 147
Gay police officers 144-151
Gay Pride Day 258-260
Geneva Convention 137
Georgia Highway Patrol 183
Girl Scouts 96
Golden parachutes 59
Golden State Peace Officers Association 147
Herman Goldstein Excellence in Problem-Solving Award 269
Golf cart patrolling 2, 10, 104-105
"Good faith" exception 192
Graduate Entry Scheme (GES) Program 330
Graffiti 96, 109-110
Graffiti Removal Community Service Program 316-317
Graft 216-217
Graham v. Connor (1989) 224
G.R.A.M.P.A. Cop Program 363
"Grass-eaters" 217
GREAT (Gang Resistance Education and Training) 315
Grobeson, Sergeant Mitchell 147-151
Guardian Angels 2, 13
Gun control 115-116, 357-358
   Florida licensees 115-116
Gun Society 245

H

Harris v. Forklift Systems, Inc. (1993) 155
Hawthorne, California, Police Department 48-49
   mission statement 49
Hell's Angels 76
Hierarchies of authority 38-39, 51
High-crime areas 6, 15
High Point (NC) Police Department 79-80
High-powered microwave 139

Hippie "love-ins" and the police 76
Hire a Gang Leader 316
Hiring and retention of minorities 248-249
Hiring standards 380-381
HIV 151, 265-267
Homelessness and the police 261-268
   affordable housing 261-262
   composition 267-268
Homophobia 259-260
Homosexual police officers 144-151
Hoover, President Herbert 26
"Hot pursuit" exception 213, 220-221
Houstonians on Watch 106
Houston, Texas, Police Department 106
Hue and cry 22
Human relations 4-5, 16-17
   courses 4
   defined 16
Humor, police 169-171
Hybrid offenses 324

I

Ideal-real dilemma 80-81
Illegal immigrants 236-237, 281-284
Illinois Act of 1899 289
Immigrants 237-240
Immigration and Naturalization Service (INS) 281-283
In-Car Video System 183
Incentive programs 52
Incident-driven policing (*see also* Problem-oriented policing) 97, 324
Indentured servant system 22
Indictable offenses 325
Infrasound 139
Inner-city programs 368-371
Internal affairs divisions 202, 225-226
Internal police discipline 83-84
Internalization 225
International Association of Chiefs of Police (IACP) 34
International Court of Justice 348
International policing 347-349
Internships 367-368
Interpol 348
Irish Republican Army (IRA) 93-94
Isotrophic radiators 139
Israel 94

J

"Jail experience" 136-137
Jail Removal Initiative 300-301
Jails 275-276
   mentally ill and 275-276
Japan 342-348
   community policing 346-348
   police supervision and organization 344-346

type of crime and crime rates 343-344
type of government 342-343
Job satisfaction 59
John Wayne Syndrome 72-73
Jonelis v. Russo (1994) 222-223
Justices of the peace 22
Juvenile delinquents 290, 299-303
   arrests 301-302
   extralegal factors 306-310
   jail removal initiative 300-301
   legal factors 303-306
   photographing and fingerprinting 302-303
Juvenile gangs 310-311
   defined 311
Juvenile Justice and Delinquency Prevention Act of 1974 300, 302
Juvenile offenders 289-290, 360-361
   age jurisdiction 289
   classification 296-297
Juvenile units in police departments 310-311
Juvenile violence 299-303

K

K-9 units 153
King, Rodney 6, 43, 183-184, 213
   compared with other cases 213
Knapp Commission 216-217
Knapp Report 216-217
Kobans 345
Kreimer v. Bureau of Police for Town of Morristown (1992) 191

L

La Migra 281
Lateral transfers 3
Law-and-order political platforms 110-111
Law enforcement 144-145
   census of occupations 144
Law Enforcement Assistance Administration (LEAA) 9, 27, 248
   origin 9
Law Enforcement Code of Ethics 35-37
Law enforcement organization 386-388
Law Reform Commission Act 335
Legal abuse/violations of civil rights 212-213
Legalistic approach 32-33
Legalistic model 32-33
Lesbian Avengers 258
Lesbian Nation 258
Less-than-lethal devices 108-109, 137-138
   use of 137-138
Letter of the law 112-113
Letters of interest 122
Liabilities of police officers 79-80
Liberal law enforcement views 249-250
Lie detectors 126-127
Litigation 384-385

Los Angeles County Sheriff's Department 50
Los Angeles Police Department (LAPD) 56
Low-energy lasers 139

M

Madison, Wisconsin, Police Department 90-91
Mafia 241
Male prostitution 113-114
Management by objectives 40
Mandated participation 141
Mandatory arrest policies 179-180
Mapp v. Ohio (1961) 198-199, 218, 311
Maryland Citizen Oriented Police Enforcement Program (COPE) 5
Maslow's hierarchy of needs 168
Matrix Quality of Life program 264
"Meat-eaters" 217
Media 45, 65-70, 83
   influence on police performance 45, 65-70
   public disclosure 83-84
Medical Operations Committee 108
Mental Evaluation Unit 276-277
Mentally ill and police 275-276
   jails 275-276
   public policy 276-277
Metal-embrittling liquids 139
Metropolitan areas 88
Metropolitan Police Act of 1829 24, 327-328
Metropolitan Police Force Project Act 340
Metropolitan Police of London 21, 24-25, 27, 327-328
   general principles of 24-25
Military style of policing 26-27, 37-38, 45
   hindrance to employee effectiveness 40, 45
   use of regalia 40
Military syndrome 40-42
Ministations 2, 17
Minnesota Multiphasic Personality Inventory (MMPI) 124-125
Minorities 310-311
Miranda v. Arizona (1966) 186
Misconduct 208-222, 224-225
   nonviolent 215-219
   rationalizing 224-225
   violent 219-224
Mission statements of police departments 48-49
Motorized police force 26, 89-90
Mounted patrol 101-102
Multilingual society 4
Municipal Corporation Act of 1835 327

N

National Advisory Commission on Criminal Justice Standards and Goals 27-28
   community policing and 27-28
   functions 27

SUBJECT INDEX

National Assessment Program 95
National Black Police Officer's Association 247-248
National Commission on Law Observance and Enforcement 26
National Crime Survey 326
National Gay Rights Activists 148
National Law Enforcement Officers Memorial Fund 165
National Organization of Black Law Enforcement Executives (NOBLE) 247
National Police Agency 344, 347
National Study of Law Enforcement Policies and Practices Regarding Missing Children and Homeless Youth 293
Negative reinforcements 42
Negligent retention 383
Negligent training 381-382
Neighborhood Foot Patrol Program (NFPP) 340
Neighborhood police posts (NPP) 350
Neighborhood Sector Patrol System (Tampa, FL) 10
Neighborhood team policing 19
Neighborhood Watch 2, 7, 13
Net-widening 184
Neutralization techniques 224-225
Newington, Connecticut, Police Department 14
New Orleans Mounted Patrol 102-103
Newport News, Virginia, Police Department 51-52
New York City Foot Beat 95-96
New York City Police Department 25, 39, 60, 95-96
  history 25
  size 39
New York Police Department Police Cadet Corps 145-146
New York Transit Police 13
Night watch 22
Night watchmen 22
NIMBY Syndrome 263
Nonlethal weapons 136-138
Nonstress training 134-137
  defined 135
Nonverbal communication 4
Nonviolent police misconduct 215-219
  graft 216-217
  perjury and dropsy testimony 217-218
  unofficial "perks" 216
Norman Conquest 21-22
North American Free Trade Agreement (NAFTA) 280
Northern Ireland 93-94

O

Oakland, California, Police Department 103-104

Objective reasonableness 224
Office of Public Complaints Commissioner 340
Officer-offender relations 183-184
"Open-door" policy 3
One Institute of Homophile Studies 149
Operation Blockade 281-283
Operation CLEAN 2, 7
Operation Empathy 74-76
Operation Empathy-Skid Row 75-76
Operation Identification 2
Orange County Sheriff's Academy 140
Order maintenance model 32
Organizational goals and values 48-50
Organizational models 47-48
Organizational problems 38
Organizational structure 37-38
Organizational values 49-50
Organization of police systems 32-62
  hierarchies of authority 34
Oxnard, California, Police Department 99

P

Palestinians 94
Parens patriae 290-292, 307
Parrish v. Lukie (1992) 215
Participatory (participative) management 17, 40, 51-52
Pasquier, Baron 348
"Pat-downs and frisks" 194, 198-199, 201
Patrol car video cameras 384
Peace Officer Standards and Training (POST) 26, 140-141
Peel, Sir Robert 21, 24
Peer juries 294
Peer pressure 80
Penal Code of 1907 (Japan) 343
Penalty assessments 141
Perjury by police officers 217-219
  defined 217
"Perks" as a form of misconduct 216
Pestrack v. Ohio Elections Committee (1987) 191
Peterson v. State (1993) 194
Physical abuse 211-212
Physical agility medical evaluations 123
Physically and mentally challenged 360-362
"Plain view" doctrine 189, 194
Planning 52-53
Plessy v. Ferguson (1896) 158
Police administration 26, 34-62
Police and Criminal Evidence Act 332
Police Applicant Test (Canada) 338
Police Athletic League 87
Police brutality 212-213, 220-221
Police Cadet Corps 145-146
Police chiefs 40
Police-citizen alienation 9, 26
Police-community awareness academies 364-367
Police-community relations 3, 16

defined 16
Police Complaints Authority 332
Police Complaints Investigation Bureau 340
Police department productivity 38-39
Police discretion 175-203, 298, 311-314
   abuses 195-196
   control of 201-203
   customized interpretations of law 196-197
   defined 177
   juveniles 298
   mandatory arrest policies 179-181
   police mission 177-178
   rationale for 175
   station house adjustments 311-314
   traditional 179
Police ethics 34-37
Police Executive Research Forum 18
Police-juvenile relations 303-310
Police Intercultural Education Pilot Project 338
Police lawlessness 26
Police liaison committees (PLC) 94
Police management 42
Police misconduct 18, 34, 38, 208-228
   code of silence 215
   defined 208-209
   examples 209
   forms 211-217
   importance for studying 209-210
Police mission 41, 177-178
Police officer assaults 136
Police officer-corrections relation 189-190
Police officer deaths 165
Police officer education 5
Police organizations 32-62
   job performance 45-46
   operations 38-40
   similarity to military units 40
Police personality 121
Police professionalization 26-27, 34-37, 121-122, 151-153
Police Protective League of Los Angeles 55-56, 170
Police recruitment process 121-128
   advertising 122
   letters of interest 122
   written and oral examinations 122-123
Police reform 24-27
Police sexual violence (PSV) 214-215
Police Staff College 327-328
Police stress and burnout 164-169
Police subcultures 66-72
   defined 70
   media effect upon 69-70
Police training 26-27, 34-37, 56, 79-80
   code of silence 79-80, 215
   costs 56
   ethics 34-37
   evaluation 79-80
   field training officers 79-80
   formal schools 26-27
   ideal-real dilemma 80-81

peer pressure 80
selection methods 26-27, 34
Policing 21-27
   functions 66
   history 21-27
Policy formulation 34
Politics and crime reduction 55-56
Polygraph tests and recruitment 126-127
Portland, Oregon, Program 379
Positive reinforcements 42
Posttrauma information and strategies 162-164
Poverty and crime 255-256
Precinct Community Councils (PCCs) 7
President's Crime Commission 27
Private policing 13, 114-115
Private security 114-115
Problem-oriented policing 12, 18, 46, 52, 87, 97-100
   defined 18
   parts 98-99
   themes of 97-98
Productivity 45-46
   defined 46
Professionalization movement 26
Project Heavy 315
Prostitution 113-114
   selective law enforcement 113-114
Protestants in Northern Ireland 94
Protests 266-267
Psychiatric Emergency Coordinating Committee (PECC) 277
Psychological screenings 124-125
Psychologists for officer selection 26
Public disclosure 83-84
Public Information Office (PIO) 83-84
Public Intoxication Law (PIL) 184
Public relations 15

Q

Quality circles (QC) 52
Quality control 40
Quality Control Section, U.S. Army 48
Queer Nation 258
Questionable-conduct scenarios 161

R

Racism in policing 237-238
Rallies 266-267
Real police work 77-79, 87-88
Recruitment incentive plan 122
Recruitment process 121-123, 142-151
   gay officers 144-151
   minorities and women 142-144
Recruits 26
Reeves 21-22
Reforms 361-363
Refugee Act of 1980 233

Rehabilitation Act of 1973 158
Reno, Nevada, Police Department 46-47
Report Incidents Directly Program (RID) 2
Reporting Districts 54
Resistance to change 40, 66
Retirement 361-362
Revenue sharing 54
Revolutionary War 23
Risk management 368
Riverside County (CA) Jail 74
Roanoke, Virginia, experience 372-373
Rochester, New York, Police Department 19
R.O.C.K. (Reaching Out, Convicts and Kids) 317
Rodriguez v. Fuetado (1991) 215
Role-playing 75
Romans and policing 21
Rowland v. Perry (1994) 222-223
Royal Canadian Mounted Police 327-328, 336-337, 341
    defined 336
Runaways 293
Rural Constabulary Act of 1839 327

S

Salford Plan 100
San Diego Police Academy 366-367
Santa Ana, California, Police Department 98, 109-110, 268-269
    graffiti removal programs 109-110
    homeless and 268-269
Savannah, Georgia, Cop-on-the-Block Program 373-374
Scab labor 363-364
Scanning 98-99
Schall v. Martin (1984) 301
Seattle Police Department 104-105
Second Amendment 191-192
    cases 192
Section 1983 Civil Rights actions 212-213
Sector patrolling 10, 95
Security 114-115
Selection and training methods 26-27
Selective enforcement of laws 112-113
Senior citizen involvement 364
Seniors Phoning Seniors Program 341
Service delivery 46
Service model 32
Service orientation 33
Service-oriented policing 50
Sexual harassment 151-162
    cases filed 151-152
    defined 154-155
    guidelines and policies 154-158
    judgments awarded 153
    strategies to eliminate 155-156
Sexual violence by officers toward women 214-215

Sheriffs 22-23
    tasks 23
Shift work 22
    origins 22
Shires 21-22
Shouts and rattles 23
Sibron v. New York (1968) 194, 198, 200-201, 311
Simpson, O.J., trial 188
Situationally based discretion 179-180, 183-185
Situational training 80-81
Sloman v. Tadlock (1994) 191
Socioeconomic status and crime 254-255
Sodomy laws 147
South Seattle Crime Prevention Council (SSCPC) 8-9
Special Course 330
Special Investigation Section (SIS) 384
Specials 333
Spirit of the law 112-113
Stare decisis 22
State v. Jones (1993) 191
State v. Jones (1994) 212
State v. Spencer (1994) 192
Station house adjustments 311-314
Status offenders 289-290, 292-293
    compared with delinquents 292-293
    defined 290
Sting nets 139
Sting operations 6
Stone v. Agnos (1990) 191
Stonewall riots 259
Street News 269
Stress 45, 164-169
    sources 164-165
Stress training 134
Subcultures 66
Substance abuse 171
Summary offenses 324
SWAT units 139

T

Tagging Enforcement Program 109
Take Care of Our Own (TCOO) 70
Team building 40
Team Patrol System (TPS) 101
Team policing 18-19, 100-101
    defined 18-19, 100
    philosophy 100-101
Tenderloin Times 269-270
Tennessee v. Garner (1985) 107-108, 195, 208, 211, 223-224, 298
Terry v. Ohio (1968) 194, 198-200, 311
Tension 107
Theory X 44
Theory Y 44
Thief-takers 23
Thin blue line 66
"Three strikes, you're out" legislation 111-112

SUBJECT INDEX 483

Tilson v. Forest City Police Department (1994) 213-214
Timberlake v. Benton (1992) 215
TIPS (Teaching Individuals Protective Strategies) 315
Topeka, Kansas, Training Program 128-132
TOPS 316
Total quality management (TQM) 40, 48, 52, 388-389
  defined 48
  elements 48
"Totality of circumstances" exception 192, 194
Tourism and crime 244-245
Traditional police discretion 179
Traditional police organization 38-39
Traffic Enforcement and Management System (TEAMS) 17
Transportation 22
Truants 293
Two-way radios 26

U

Uniform Bicycle Proposal 103-104
Uniform Crime Reports 336
United Kingdom Model 80-83
United States v. Clark (1994) 194
United States v. Leal (1972) 194
United States v. Romero (1973) 193
Unwritten codes of conduct 210-211
Urban renewal 261-262
Use of force 107-108

V

Verbal/psychological abuse 212-213
Verbal judo 140
Victimization 6
Victimization rates 88
Victims of crime 360-261
Videotaped police incidents 183-184
Vietnamese police officers 248-249

Village Public Safety Officer Program (VPSO) 2
Violence 355-360
Violent Crime Control and Law Enforcement Act of 1994 53
Violent crime rates 110
Violent police misconduct 219-224
  deadly force 223-224
  excessive force 220
  hot pursuit 220-221
  police brutality 220
Visual stimulus and illusion 140
Volunteer police 13, 363-364

W

Walnut Creek, California 107
War on Drugs 280
Warrantless searches 192, 198-201
Washington, DC, program 378
Watchman model 32
Watchman style 33-34
Watchmen 22
Watch-your-back syndrome 39
Weapons selection 382-383
Weapons qualification 383
Weaver v. Williams (1975) 192
"Weed-and-seed" program 379
White-collar crime 243
Wickersham Commission 26
Wickersham Report 181
Women in policing 142-144
  history 142-143
Working personality 72-73

X

Xenophobia 237

Y

Youth gangs 310-311

Cases Cited

Baker v. Glover (1991) 191
Bemis v. Kelly (1987) 193
Brewer v. Williams (1977) 186
Brown v. Board of Education (1954) 158
Cody v. United States (1972) 192
Commonwealth v. Bosurgi (1963) 192
Garrett v. Fleetwood (1994) 212-213
Graham v. Connor (1989) 224
Harris v. Forklift Systems, Inc. (1993) 155
Jonelis v. Russo (1994) 222-223
Kreimer v. Bureau of Police for Town of Morristown (1992) 191
Mapp v. Ohio (1961) 198-199, 218, 311
Miranda v. Arizona (1966) 186
Parrish v. Lukie (1992) 215
Pestrack v. Ohio Elections Commission (1987) 191
Peterson v. State (1993) 194
Rodriguez v. Fuetado (1991) 215
Rowland v. Perry (1994) 222-223
Schall v. Martin (1984) 301
Sibron v. New York (1968) 194, 198, 200-201, 311
Sloman v. Tadlock (1994) 191

State v. Jones (1993) 191
State v. Jones (1994) 212
State v. Spencer (1994) 192
Stone v. Agnos (1992) 191
Tennessee v. Garner (1985) 107, 195, 208, 211, 223-224, 298
Terry v. Ohio (1968) 194, 198-200, 311
Tilson v. Forest City Police Department (1994) 213
Timberlake v. Benton (1992) 215
United States v. Clark (1994) 194
United States v. Leal (1972) 194
United States v. Romero (1973) 193
Weaver v. Williams (1975) 192